ISBN 978-1-5281-9963-6
PIBN 10965166

English
Français
Deutsche
Italiano
Español
Português

www.forgottenbooks.com

Mythology Photography **Fiction**
Fishing Christianity **Art** Cooking
Essays Buddhism Freemasonry
Medicine **Biology** Music **Ancient
Egypt** Evolution Carpentry Physics
Dance Geology **Mathematics** Fitness
Shakespeare **Folklore** Yoga Marketing
Confidence Immortality Biographies
Poetry **Psychology** Witchcraft
Electronics Chemistry History **Law**
Accounting **Philosophy** Anthropology
Alchemy Drama Quantum Mechanics
Atheism Sexual Health **Ancient History**
Entrepreneurship Languages Sport
Paleontology Needlework Islam
Metaphysics Investment Archaeology
Parenting Statistics Criminology
Motivational

Bradshaw, Charles, LL. B., '73·
Bradshaw, Leonard, LL. B., '94, LL. M. , '95.
Bradshaw, Moses, LL. B., '7ι.
Brady, Edmund, LL. B., '04 (Att'y at
    Law) ....412 5th St. N.W., Wash., D. C.
Brady, Edward J., A. B., '98·
Brady, Eugene D. F., A. B., '70, A. M.,
    '72, LL. B., '72 (Lawyer).............. 1110 F St. N.W., Wash., D. C.
Brady, George Moore, A. M , '01, Ph.
    L., '02, Ph. D , '03, LL. B., '03.........1009 Calvert Bldg., Baltimore, Md.;
                                   410 5th St. N.W., Wash., D. C.
Brady, James T., LL. B., '92, LL. M.,
    '93 (Lawyer).......................515 Ashland Block, Chicago, Ill.
Brady, Joon Stanley, A. B., '01 (Physi-
    cian) ....St. Vincent's Hospital, New York.
Brady, Joseph P., LL. B., '96 (Lawyer)...Clerk's Office, U. S. Courts, Rich-
                                   mond, Va.
Branagan, Francis A., LL. B., '89·
Brand, Carl Martin, LL. B., '03·
Brantley, A. Augustus, LL. B., '96........Orangeburg, S. C.
Brantley, Thomas F., LL. B., '94, LL. M., '95·
Brashears, John W., jr., LL. B., '03, LL. M., '04·
Brashears, Shipley, jr., LL. B., '99, LL. M., 1900.
    (Ins. Broker and Notary Public).....1319 F St N. W., Wash , D. C.
Braud, Peter S., A. B., '59·
Brawley, Wm. C., LL. B., '96·
Brearton, John L., LL. B., '02 (Att'y
    at Law) ....Savanna, Ill.
Brech, Gen. Samuel, U. S. A., M. D., '67.
Breckous, Robert W., LL. B., '90·
Breen, James, M. D., '71·
Breitenbucher, Ed. E., LL. B., '03.
Bremner, Vincent Aloysius, A. M., '03
    (Planter) ....5001 Greenwood Ave., Chicago, Ill.
Brennan, Charles, LL. B., '99·
Brennan, George R., LL. B., '94, LL. M., '95·
Brennan, James Joseph, A. B., '05·
Brennan, James Smith, A. B , '83
    (Banking) ....1010 Del. Ave., Wilmington, Del.
Brennan. John E.. M. D., '05·
Brennan, John P., LL. B., '04·
Brennan, Michael F., LL. B., '99, LL. M., '00·
Brennan, Patrick H. C., LL. B., '93, LL. M., '94, deceased.
Brennan, Patrick H., LL. B., '91 (Con-
    tractor and Builder)................31st and K Sts., Washington, D. C.
Brennan, Patrick H., M. D., '67 (Jesuit
    Priest) ....17th and Stiles Sts., Phila., Pa.

Brent, Hon. Judge George, A. B., '33,
    A. M., '37, LL. D., '68; deceased
    Jan. 6, 1881.........................Charles Co., Md.
Brent, George, LL. B., '90, LL. M., '92·
Brent, Henry M., A. B., '63, A. M., '67; deceased Oct. 16, 1892, Bay City, N. Y.
Brent, Henry W., A. B., '52·
Brent, John Carroll, A. B., '33, A. M., '49; deceased Feb. 10, 1876.
Brent, Robert J., LL. B., '54·
Brent, Wm. M., A. B., '74; deceased.
Bresnahan, Francis J., LL. B., '03, LL. M., '04·
Briant, Lassaline P., A. B., '61 (Lawyer)..138 S. White St., New Orleans, La
Brice, Charles H., LL. B., '87.
Brickenstein, John H., LL. B., '91·
Brickley, Bartholomew A., LL. B., '04·
Bride, William W., LL. B., '04·
Bridges, Walter S., LL. B., '87·
Brien, L. Tiernan, A. B., '46·
Briggs, Edmund B., LL. B , '75 (Lawyer)..Hurley, S. D.
Brisbane, Howard P., M. D., '82·
Briscoe, Arthur, LL. B., '91, LL. M., '92
    (Clerk, P. O. Dept.)..................601 Spruce St., Washington, D. C.
Briscoe, Walter C., M. D., '69; deceased May 16, 1896.
Brock, Fenelon B., LL. B., '96, LL. M., '97·
Brockbank, Senes T., LL. M., '88·
Broderick, Dr. John Kern, A. M., '97......809 N. Main St., St. Louis, Mo.
Broe, William B., LL. B., '84·
Brogan, Francis Albert, A. B., '83
    (Lawyer) ....412 N. Y. Life Bldg., Omaha, Neb.
Bronson, Charles E., M. D., '83.
Brooke, Albert G., LL. B., '90·
Brooke, John Cooke, LL. B., '05 (Clerk
    P. O. Dept.)........................Washington, D. C.
Brookes, William P., A. B., '44; deceased June 15, 1885.
Brooks, J. Henry, M. D., '65·
Brooks, John Dosher, M. D., '95·
Brosnan, Eugene, jr., LL. B., '97, LL. M., '98; deceased, 1901.
Brosnan, John J., LL. B., '01 (Lawyer)....482 La. Ave. N.W., Wash., D. C.
Brower, Daniel Roberts, M. D., '64, LL. D., '99·
Brown, Andrew Rothwell, M. D., '68·
Brown, C. F., M. D., '65·
Brown, Charles J., LL. B., '90, LL. M., '92..Room 319, Bond Bldg., Wash., D. C.
Brown, Charles Orton, LL. B., '94·
Brown, Charles O., LL. B., '73·
Brown, Everard C., LL. B., '88, LL. M., '89·
Brown, Dr. Francis E., A. B., '87·
Brown, Harry S., LL. B., '99·

....409 Commercial B'k., Wash., D. C.

sed Feb. 16, 1895.

....Juneau, Alaska.

er).Care C. H. Brown & Co., Fitchburg, Mass.

, '91·

....416 5th St. N. W., Wash., D. C.

....243 E. Larned St., Detroit, Mich.

St. Paul, Minn.

....905 Mass. Ave N. W., Wash., D. C.
3.
'89 (Lawyer).

3s.), deceased at Halifax, N. S.

LL. M., '04.

eceased June 1, 1899, Montville, Conn.

'96·

....Washington, D. C.

Burg, Joseph P., LL. B., '94·
Burger, John C. S., LL. B., '73·
Burger, Leopold C. E., LL. B., '99
    (Legal Reviewer)....................Pension Bureau, Wash., D. C.
Burk, James W., A. B., '95, LL. B., '97·
Burke, Francis Hunter, LL. B., '03........Louisville Trust Co. Bldg., Louis-
                                   ville, Ky.
Burke, John C., LL. B., '96, LL. M., '97·
Burke, Thomas W., M. D., '84·
Burnam, Harry E., LL. B., '87, LL. M., '88·
Burnett, Swan M., Ph. D., '90 (Physi-
    cian); deceased Jan. 18, 1906, Washington, D. C.
Burns, James Philip, A. B., '05·
Burns, R. P. Miles, A. B., '73; deceased Feb. 28, 1875, Nashville, Tenn.
Burroughs, Dent, M. D., '59·
Burton, Linnoir, LL. B., '83·
Busey, Samuel Clagett, LL. D., '99; deceased Feb. 12, 1901.
Butcher, C. Tyson, LL. M., '86·
Bute, James H., M. D., '99·
Butler, A. Jeter, LL. B., '01 (Attorney
    at Law) ....Union, S. C.
Butler, Henry, A. B., '87·
Butler, John A., LL. B., '88, LL. M., '89·
Butler, John H., LL. B., '02·
Butler, Patrick J., LL. B., '88, LL. M., '89·
Butler, Ulysses, LL. B., '01·
Butts, Elias M., LL. M., '95·
Byington, Francis, M. D., '58·
Byrne, Edward Louis, A. B., '01·
Byrne, Francis Joseph, A. B., '99·
Byrne, John F., LL. B., '04·
Byrne, Walter C., M. D., '92·
Byrne, Very Rev. William, V. G.,
    D. D., '81..........................St. Cecilia St., Boston, Mass.
Byrne, William M., A. B., '87·
Byrnes, Dr. James C., M. D., '70·
Byrnes, Thomas, M. D., '65·
Byrnes, William F., M. D., '73 (Physi-
    cian) ....1509 U St. N.W., Washington, D. C.
Byrnes, William Henry, jr., A. B., '03·

Cabaniss, E. Gerry, LL. B., '95, LL. M., '96·
Cahill, Jos. Henry, A. B., '98.............57 Colony St., Meriden, Conn.
Cahill, William Ambrose, B. S., '82
    (Physician) ....1310 N. Salina St., Syracuse, N. Y.
Cain, Wm. S., M. D., '02·
Caine, David M., LL. B., '87; deceased 1888.

Caldwell, George H., M. D., '65.

Caldwell, Samuel W., M. D., '67·

Calhoun, Charles A., LL. B., '96, LL. M., '97·

Calkins, Thomas Joseph, A. M., '99, M. D., '00·

Callaghan, D. O'C., LL. B., '73, A. M., '89·

Callaghan, James Edward, A. B., '80

    (Publisher Banking Law).............114 Monroe St., Chicago, Ill.

Callaghan, William John, M. D., '01·

Callan, Cornelius Van Ness, M. D., '68

    (Physician) ....721 19th St. N. W., Wash., D. C.

Callan, Guida C., LL. B., '94, LL. M.,

    '96 (Clerk, Patent Office).............Washington, D. C.

Callan, John F., A. B., '56; deceased.

Callanen, Joseph P., A. B., '53, A. M., '55·

Camalier, Benj. Harris, A. M., '84· ·

    Lawyer) ....Leonardtown, Md.

Camalier, Franklin A., A. B., '04.

Campbell, Charles B., M. D., '94

    (Pharmacist) ....17th and Park Sts. N. W, Wash-
                                  ington, D. C.

Campbell, Daniel G., LL. B., '89, LL. M., '90·

Campbell, Joseph Henry, LL. B., '03; deceased Feb. 24, 1905.

Campbell, Richard, LL. B., '99·

Camper, Capt. Charles, LL. B., '73; deceased Dec. 2, 1885, in Washington.

Canario, Lawrence Virgil, A. B., '05

    (Law Student)......................Georgetown Law Sc., Wash., D. C.

Canfield, Andrew N., LL. B., '84, LL. M., '85; deceased July 10, 1905.

Cannon, Walter D., M. D., '90·

Cantwell, Edward J., LL. B., '04 (Sec-

    retary National Association of

    Letter Carriers)....................945 Pa. Ave. N. W., Wash., D. C.

Capehart, Poindexter W., M. D., '98·

Caperton, Hugh, A. B., '41; deceased Sept. 14, 1877.

Carabedian, Aram L., D. D. S., '03·

Carleton, Robert P., LL. B., '95, LL.

    M., '96 (Lawyer)...................Fernandina, Fla.

Carlin, Frederick Theo., A. B., '05·

Carlin, Harry Vincent, A. B., '04·

Carlon, Frederick A., A. B., '02·

Carlon, Patrick Joseph, A. B., '93

    (Lawyer) ....27 Williams St., New York City.

Carman, Louis D., M. D., '89·

Carmody, Francis Joseph, LL. B., '04·

Carmody, Robert Francis, A. M., '93, M. D., '95 (deceased).

Carne, Rev. Richard L., A. M., '68

    (Priest) ....Fortress Monroe, Va.

Carney, Patrick Joseph, M. D., '04·
Carney, Thomas Francis, A. B., '91; deceased Feb. 8, 1897.
Carpenter, Matthew Hale, A. M., '04
(Law Student) ....325 35th St., Milwaukee, Wis.
Carr, John McAuliffe, A. B., '97, A. M.,
'98, LL. B., '99, LL. M., '00 (Attor-
ney at Law).........................548-50 Spitzer Bldg , Toledo, Ohio.
Carr, W. Saunders, A. M , '88·
Carr, Wilbur John, LL. B., '94 (Chief,
Consular Bureau)....................Dept of State, Washington, D. C.
Carr, Wm. Beresford, A B., '61, A. M., '72; deceased Nov., 1881.
Carraher, J. B., M. D., '86
Carriel, Lafayette J., A. B., '51·
Carroll, Augustine Livius, A. B., '98·
Carroll, Hon. John Lee, LL. D., '89
(Ex-Governor of Maryland)...........Doughregan Manor, Ellicott City,
Md.
Carroll, Lafayette J., A. M., '82·
Carroll, Philip, M. D., '79·
Carroll, Timothy A., LL. B., '93, LL.
M , '94 (Special Agent)..............Bureau of Corporations, Wash.,
D. C.
Carroll, Vincent Levins, A. B., '01·
Carson, Frederick D., LL. B , '82·
Carter, Charles T., LL B , '95·
Carter, J Barrett, LL. B., '05 (Lawyer) ....Colorado Bldg., Wash., D. C.
Carusi, Charles Francis, A. B., '94
(Lawyer) ....1331 F St. N. W., Wash., D. C.
Carusi, Thornton A., LL. B., '74·
Carvill, William B , A. B , '79; deceased Dec. 9, 1890
Cary, Joseph M , LL. B., '91, LL. M., '92·
Casey, Rev. John T., A. B , '99 (Priest)....Lenox, Mass.
Casey, Stephen J., LL. B., '96, LL. M., '97·
Cashell, Joseph, LL. B., '77·
Cashman, Joseph T , LL. B., '02·
Cashman, Thomas F., M. D , '02·
Cass, Philip H., LL. B., '95, LL. M., '96.
Casserly, Daniel A , A. B., '62, A. M., '68 (Lawyer and Journalist); deceased
July 4, 1887, in New York City.
Casserly, Hon Eugene, A. M., '56, LL. D , '72·
Cassidy, John Hughes, A. B., '97
(Lawyer) ....95 Bank St., Waterbury, Conn.
Cassidy, Louis T., A. B., '04 (Medical
Student) ....Norwich, Conn.
Cassin, John Leo, LL. B., '01 (Lawyer)....1331 F St. N. W., Wash., D. C.
Catlin, Benjamin Rush, LL. B., '73
(Patent Lawyer)....................622 F St. N. W., Washington, D. C.

Caulfield, Bernard G., A. B., '48, A. M., '50 (deceased Dec. 19, 1887, at Deadwood, Dak.).

Caulfield, John, Mus. Doc., '65·

Cauthorn, Robt. Gabriel, A. B., '99
(Attorney at Law)................Bishop Block, Vincennes, Ind.

Cavanaugh, Richard B., LL. B., '01·

Cavanaugh, Thomas Ed., M. D., '00
(Physician) ....245 Maple St., Holyoke, Mass.

Cecil, Henry A., A. M., '66·

Chamberlin, Frank T., M. D., '85 (Physician) ·····························1323 M St. N. W., Wash., D. C.

Chamberlin, J. A., M. D., '63·

Chamberlin, Justin Morrill, LL. B., '97,
LL. M., '98 (Attorney at Law)........482 La. Ave., Washington, D. C.

Chamberlin, William L., M. D., '91·

Chambers, J. Paul, M. D., '84.

Charles, Garfield, LL. B., '04, LL. M., '05....U. S. Senate, Washington, D. C.

Chauveau, Judge Alexander T., A. B., '95·

Chauveau, Chas. Auguste, A. B., '96,
A. M., '96 (Advocate, Quebec Bar).....75 Peter St., Quebec, Canada.

Cheney, Jasper Edwin, A. M., '68, M. D, '68·

Chew, John Paul, A. B., '82, LL. B., '84,
LL. M., '85 (Editor "The Church
Progress") ....520 Fullerton Bldg., St. Louis, Mo.

Chew, Philemon W., LL. B., '93, LL. M., '94·

Chez, Joseph, LL. B., '97 (Lawyer)......Ogden, Utah.

Chism, Warren P., A. B., '72; deceased.

Choate, Rufus, M. D., '67·

Choice, William, A. B., '57, A. M., '60·

Choppin, Julius A., A. B., '52, A. M., '53·

Christiancy, George A. C., LL. B., '92·

Christie, F. C., M. D., '59·

Church, J B., LL. B., '75 (Lawyer)......McGill Building, Wash., D. C.

Clabaugh, Hon. Harry M., LL. D., '03
(Chief Justice Supreme Court of
District of Columbia) ....City Hall, Washington, D. C.

Clagett, Henry William, A. B., '60·
(Farmer) ....Rosaryville, Prince George Co.,
Md.

Clagett, Howard C., LL. B., '79; deceased May 9, 1893.

Clancy, John F., A. B., '63, (H. C. Mass).

Clapp, Harry M., LL. B., '93, LL. M., '94·

Clark, Elroy Newton, LL. B., '92
(Lawyer) ....420 Equitable Bldg., Denver, Colo.

Clark, Eugene B., M. D., '72·

Clark, John Alexander, M. D., '98 (First Lieut. and Ass't Surgeon, U. S. A.)

Clark, John Francis, A. B., '93·
Clark, J. Nelson, M. D., '67·
Clark, Julius S., M. D., '69·
Clark, Leon A., LL. B., '03·
Clark, Ronald Eugene, LL. B., '04
   (Lawyer) ....Houlton, Me.
Clarke, Daniel Boone, M. D., '57
   (Pharmacy, Banking, and Ins.).......1422 Mass. Ave. N.W., Wash., D. C.
Clarke, George B., A. B., '41·
Clarke, James H., A. M., '31·
Clarke, Joseph B. C., M. D., '55·
Clarke, Richard H., A. B., '46, A. M.,
   '49, LL. D., '72 (Lawyer).............60 W. 76th St., New York City.
Clarke, Walter S., A. B., '80..............Australia.
Clarke, Rev. William F., S. J. (Priest), A. B., '33; deceased Oct. 17, 1890.
Clarke, William H., A. B., '75·
Clary, William G., LL. B., '90·
Clay, William Rogers, LL. B., '88,
   LL. M., '89 (Lawyer)................Lexington, Ky.
Clayson, Frederick H., LL. M., '00·
Clayson, H., LL. B., '00·
Cleary, James T., LL. B., '05 (Lawyer)....Grand Island, Nebr.
Cleary, Reuben, M. D., '59, A. M., '60·
Cleary, Reuben, A. B., '34·
Clements, James E., LL. B , '81·
Cleveland, Jeremiah, A. B., '54, A. M., '60·
Cleveland, Jesse F., A. B., '53, A. M., '55.
Claverdon, J. S., M. D., '72·
Coad, Wm. James, A. M., '00 (Lawyer)....407 1st Nat. Bank Bldg., Omaha
                                    Nebr.
Cobb, James S., M. D., '93·
Cockran, Hon. W. Bourke, LL. D., '99....House of Rep., Washington, D. C
Corcoran, Richard P., LL. B., '94,
   LL. M., '95 (Mining).................Tonopah, Butler P. O., Nev.
Cody, John K. I., LL. B., '98·
Coffron, W. H., M. D., '88·
Cogswell, Julius E., LL. B., '88 (Lawyer)..Charleston, S. C.
Colbert, Michael J., A. B., '83, LL. B.,
   '85, LL. M., '86, and A. M., '89
   (Lawyer) ....Century Law Bldg., Wash., D. C
Cole, Hon. Charles C., LL. D., '02 (deceased).
Cole, Halbert Benton, LL. B., '04
   (Lawyer) ....Newkirk, Okla.
Cole, John T., M. D., '91 (Physician).....820 H St. N.E., Wash., D. C.
Cole, Peter L., LL. B., '92, LL. M., '93·....New Bridge, N. J.
Coleman, David Charles, M. D., '04·

Coleman, James Valentine, A. B., '69,
  A. M., '71, LL. B., '73·
Coleman, Watson E., LL. B., '94 (L'y'r)....626 F St. N.W., Washington, D. C.
Colesberry, William H., M. D., '80·
Colgin, Edward Broadnax, A. M., '00,
  LL. B., '01 (Lawyer).................65-66 Theater Bldg., Houston, Tex.
Collier, Judge C. Needham, A. B., '68, A. M , '95, LL. D., '98 (Associate Jus-
  tice of the Supreme Court of the Territory of New Mexico).
Colliere, George Riggs, A. B., '04 (Law
  Student) ....:..1410 G St. N.W., Wash., D. C.
Collier, Robert Joseph, A. B., '94·
  ˙ (Publisher) .:......................413-24 W. 13th St., New York City.
Colliflower, Charles Ernest, jr., LL. B., '05·
Collins, James Marshall, LL. B., '96,
  LL. M., '97 (Lawyer)................216 Court St., Marysville, Ky.
Collins, Joseph Francis, A. B., '97,
  A. M,. '98, LL. B., '99, LL. M., '00·
Collins, Robert L., LL. B , '91·
Collins, Walter Homer, LL. B., '01
  (Clk. Eng Dept., War Dept.).........P. O. Box 455, Wash. Barracks,
                                      Washington, D. C.
Collins, William Granville, LL. B., '05
  (Proofreader) ....Vienna, Fairfax Co., Va.
Collins, William Joseph, A. B., '93; deceased Feb., 1902, at Dedham, Mass.
Collins, William T., M. D., '65·
Combs, Robert Cornelius, A. B., '55,
  A. M., '59 (Lawyer)............... ...Leonardtown, Md.
Comerford, Peter Patrick, Ph. B., '93·
Compton, Edmund, LL. B., '92·
Compton, William P., M. D., '89·
Conant, Thomas, M. D., '67·
Conaty, Rt. Rev. Thomas, D. D., '89
  (Bishop) ....114 E. 2d St., Los Angeles, Cal.
Conboy, Martin, LL. B., '98, LL. M., '99
  (Lawyer) ....27 Pine St., New York City.
Concilio, Rt Rev. Mons. J. de, D. D., '89; deceased March 22, 1898, at Jersey
  City, N. J.
Condon, William F., A. M., '03 (Law
  Student and Clerk)................Library, Navy Dept., Wash., D. C.
Coneby, William H., LL. B.,' 04.
Coniff, John J., LL. B., '89·
Conigisky, Joseph Perl, D. D. S., '04·
Conlin, Charles Francis, M. D., '04
Conlin, Charles F., LL. B., '98 (Law-
  yer) ....New Britain, Conn.

Conlin, Rev. John A., A. B., '58 (H. C.
    Mass); deceased June 23, 1888,
    (Clergyman).
Conly, Francis, A. B., '53·
Connellan, James A., LL. B., '96·
Connelly, Benjamın M, LL. B., '97ͺ
    LL M , '98.........................Govt. Printing Office, Wash., D. C.
Connelly, Dennis J., LL. B., '98·
Conner, William Wallace, LL. B., ·02
    Sec'y. of the Board of Education
    of the District of Columbia).........Franklin Sch. Bldg, Wash., D. C.
Connolly, Anthony, A , LL. M., '90·
Connolly, Ed. D , A M., '75 (Clergyman)..Hotel Bristol, Boston, Mass.
Connolly, Jeremiah Ed., A. B , '04·
Connolly, John E., LL. B., '01·
Connolly, John W., A. B , '04 (Broker)....174 Liberty St., Lynn, Mass.
Connolly, Joseph B , LL. M., '90·
Connolly, Timothy Stanislaus, A. B., '97
Connor, George A , LL. B , '02·
Connor, John Edward, M. D., '04·
Connors, George Robert, D. D. S., '04·
Conover, J. C., M. D., '71·
Conradis, Charles, LL. B , 'ɔ0, LL. M , '91
Constas, John N., M. D., '04.
Contee, John B., LL. B., '87; deceased, May 30, 1904.
Conway, John Joseph, M. D., '01·
Conway, William O., LL. B., '76·
Cook, Ansel B , A. B., '75ͺ LL. B., '77·
Cook, James C , LL. B., '97ͺ LL. M., '98 (Clerk).
Cook, Robert M., LL. B., '95ͺ LL. M.,
    '96 (Lawyer).......................416 5th St. N. W., Wash., D. C.
Cook, Wilson E., LL. B , '95·
Cooney, James Joseph, LL. B., '98ͺ LL. M , '99·
Cooper, John S , M. D., '69·
Cooper, Moses, M. D., '74·
Cooper, Sam Bronson, jr., LL. B., '99ͺ
    LL. M , '00 (Lawyer)............... .Beaumont, Tex.
Copeman, William H , LL. M , '87·
Corbett, John Walter Healy, A. M , '99·
Corbin, E Lyon, M. D., '59·
Corbin, William E., M. D , '91·
Corcoran, Hon. John W , LL D., '95
    (deceased, 1905, at Clinton, Mass).
Corcoran, Richard P., LL. B., '94ͺ
    LL. M., '95 (Mining)................Tonopah, Butler P. O., Nev.
Corcoran, William J., A. B., '63 (H. C. Mass.); deceased, Feb. 21, 1897.
Corey, Charles A , LL. B , '95ͺ LL. M. '96·

Cortelyou, George Bruce, LL. B., '95,
   LL. D., '03 (Postmaster General of
   t'.e United States)...................Washington, D. C.
Costello, James E. T., LL. B., '03 (Artist).
Costigan, Ignatius J. J., A. B., '02,
   LL. B., '04 (Lawyer)................77 Fendall Bldg., Wash., D. C.
Cottrell, Samuel, jr., LL. B., '96 (Clerk)....War Department, Wash., D. C.
Coughlan, J. Vincent, LL. B., '01·
Coughlin, John T., LL. B., '81, LL. M., '82·
Coulthurst, John ·A., A. M., '93 (Law-
   yer) ....1 Beacon St., Boston, Mass.
Coumbe, J. T., M. D., 72.
Cowan, Francis, M. D., '69·
Cowardin, Charles O'B., A. B., '74, A. M., '85; deceased, 1900.
Cowles, A. E., D. D. S., '02·
Cowling, William W., M. D., '72·
Cox, Charles Robert, LL. B., '04 (Sec-
   retary) ....Volta Bureau, Washington, D. C.
Cox, Francis Marcellus, LL. B., '74
   (Lawyer) ....2029 4th St. N. E., Wash., D. C.
Cox, Frank B , LL. B., '96, LL. M., '97·
Cox, Walter S., A. B., '43, A. M., '47; deceased, 1903, at Washington, D. C.
Cramer, Dick, LL. B., 90, LL. M., '91
   (Clerk) ....Pension Office, Washington, D. C.
Cramer, Herman W., LL. B., '97..........La Crosse, Kans.
Crauch, Edw., M. D., '73·
Craven, Charles A., LL. B., '93 (Corre-
   spondent) ....The Buchs Stove and Range Co.,
                                       St. Louis, Mo.
Craven, Thomas J., A. B., '87·
Crawford, Charles A., LL. B., '05 (Law-
   yer) ....U. S. Trust Co. Bldg., Terre Haute,
                                       Ind.
Crawford, James C., LL. B., '98, LL.
   M., '99 (Accountant)................Treasury Dept., Wash., D. C.
Crawford, William Gordon, LL. B., '98
   (Lawyer) ....1407 F St. N. W., Wash., D. C.
Crittenden, Thomas B., M. D., '95·
Croggon, Richard C., M. D., '60·
Cronin, Patrick W., A. B., '64 (H. C. Mass.); (Physician).
Cronin, William Joseph, LL. B., '94, LL. M , '95, A. M., '95; deceased, Nov.
   30, 1899. .
Crook, Harrison, M. D., '78 (Physician)....The Sherman, 15th and L Sts.,
                                       Washington, D. C.
Crosby, Charles F., LL. B., '97, LL. M., '98·
Crossfield, Amasa S., LL. B., '83, LL. M., '84·

Crosson, Henry J., M. D., '90 (Phy-
    sician) ....1746 M St. N. W., Wash., D. C.
Crow, Philip M., LL. B., '88, LL. M., '89·
Crowe, John W., M. D., '97 (Physician)....704 T St. N. W., Wash., D. C.
Crowley, Jeremiah J., A. B., '64 (H. C. Mass.); deceased, Jan. 16, 1906.
Crozier, St. George B., Mus. Doc., '70·
Cruickshank, Thomas Antisell, LL. B.,
    '96, LL. M., '97 (Clerk, City P. O.)....1312 Irving St., Wash., D. C.
Cruse, George E., LL. B., '96·
Cuddy, Stephen A., LL. B., '95·
Cudlipp, Malcolm A., M. D., '90·
Cuenco, Jose Maria, A. M., '05 (Law
    Student) ....301 C St. N. W., Wash., D. C.
Cull, Abner H., M. D., '68.
Cullen, Livingston James, A. B., '99·
Cullen, Rev. Thomas Francis, A B , '99
    (Priest) ....St. Patrick's, Providence, R. I.
Cullinane, James A., LL. B., '87, LL. M., '88·
Cullinen, Alexander A., A. B., '86·
Culver, Ira J., M. D., '68·
Cummings, Francis J., A. M , '89; deceased, August, 1890.
Cummings, George W., M. D., '65·
Cummiskey, Edward Francis, M. D., '96·
Cummiskey, Eugene, A. B., '44, A. M., '49.
Cunniff, Patrick S., LL. B., '99, LL. M.,
    '00 (Lawyer).........................12 Pemberton Sq., Boston, Mass.
Cunningham, Francis Aloysius, A. B.,
    '72, A. M., '74 (Publisher and
    Bookseller, Att'y-at-Law, Manu-
    facturer of Chemicals)...............825 Arch St., Philadelphia, Pa.
Curley, Charles Fallon, A. B., '97
    (Lawyer) ....Church Bldg., Wilmington, Del.
Curran, John D. J., M. D., '03·
Curran, Joseph J., LL. B., '05·
Curriden, Samuel W., LL. B., '77·
Curry, Daniel, LL. B , '01·
Curtin, Richard A., LL. B., '04 (Lawyer)...707 G St. N. W., Wash., D. C.
Curtis, George F., LL. B., '89, LL. M., '90..Shanghai, China.
Cutts, Richard D., A. B., '35, A. M., '42; deceased, Dec. 14, 1883.
Cuyler, George A., A. B., '38, A. M., '42·

Dahlgren, John Vinton, A B., '89,
    A. M., '91, LL. B., 91, LL. M., '92;
    deceased Aug. 11, 1899
Dailey, O. A., M. D., '55.
Daily, B. E , M. D., '74·

Daish, John Broughton, LL. B., '99,
    LL. M., '00 (Lawyer)................1416 F St. N.W., Wash., D. C.
Dallas, Everett Jerome, LL. B., '73·
Dalton, Alfred S., LL. B., '97 (Clerk)......War Department, Wash., D. C.
Daly, Francis J. M., A. M., '75, LL. B., '75; deceased, Feb. 19, 1892, at Macon,
                                 Ga.
Daly, J. Harry, LL. B., '92, LL. M., '93·
Daly, Joseph T., LL. B., '95, LL. M., '97
   ' (Stenographer) ....Navy Dept., Washington, D. C.
Daly, Walter F., LL. B., '91, LL. M., '92·
Damman, Milton, LL. B., '99·
Danforth, R. Foster, M. D., '86.
Daniels, John W., LL. B., '01.
Daniels, Rees P., LL. M., '86·
Darby, John J., M. D., '83·
Darby, Samuel E., LL. B , '90, LL M , '91·
Darlington, Joseph James, LL. D., '86
    (Lawyer) ....410 5th St. N. W., Wash., D. C.
Darr, Charles W., LL. B., '94, LL. M.,
    '95 (Lawyer).......................707 G St. N. W., Wash., D. C.
Darrah, John R., LL. M , '94·
Dartt, James F., LL. B , '77·
Davenport, Benjamin, LL. B., '74·
Davenport, Henry B., LL. B., '05 (Ste-
    nographer) ....Office Compt. Cur'c'y, Wash , D. C.
David, Edward, LL. B , '91, LL. M., '92
David, Frederick E., LL. B., '87, LL. M , '88·
David, Levi, LL. B., '98, LL. M., '99·
Davidson, Edwin R., LL. B., '05·
Davidson, Falconer, M. D., '93·
Davies, Gomer, M. D., '88·
Davis, Beverly A., LL. B., '91·
Davis, Bliss N., LL. B., '97·
Davis, Charles S , LL. B., '96, LL. M.,
    '97 (Clerk)........................Pension Office, Wash., D. C.
Davis, Daniel Grant, M. D., 97 (Clerk)....Com'tee of Private Land Claims,
                        House of Reps., Wash., D. C.
Davis, Eugene A., LL. B., '93, LL. M., '94·
Davis, George M., M. D., '71·
Davis, John G., M. D., '68·
Davis, John H., LL. B., '93, LL. M., '94·
Davis, John M., A. B., '62·
Davis, John N., M. D., '60·
Davison, John W., LL. B., '93·
Dawley, William Joseph, LL. B., '03
    (Lawyer) ....7 Wall St., New York City.

Dinnies, Charles, A. B., '17·
Dinnies, George, A. B., '17·
Dixon, William S., M. D., '68 (Surgeon)....Care U. S. N. Dept., Wash., D. C.
Dixon, William Wirt, Jr., LL. B., '99; deceased.
Dodge, Clarence, LL. B., '05 (Real Es-
tate) ....1416 F St. N. W., Wash., D. C.
Dodge, Robert H., M. D., '93·
Dohan, Joseph M., A. B., '86, A. M., '89
(Att'y at Law).....................1012' Stephen Girard Bldg., Phila-
delphia, Pa.
Doherty, Michael L., A. B., '63 (H. C.
Mass); deceased, Aug. 28, 1886 (C'ergyman).
Dolan, John J., LL B , '93, LL. M., '94; deceased, Aug , 1900.
Dolan, P. V., LL. B., '85, M. D., '90·'
Dolloway, Louis Marsh, M. D., '00·
Dolmage, Mihran M., D. D. S., '03·
Dominguez, Virgil F., A. B., '63·
Donahoe, Alphonsus Richara, A. M.,
'05 ....27 S Park St , Halifax, N. S.
Donahue, Charles Louis, A B., '00 (At-
torney at Law)....................390 Congress St , Portland, Me.
Donahue, Francis William, A. B., '97
(Physician and Surgeon).............Greenfield, Mass.
Donaldson, R. Newton, LL. B., '90, LL. M , '91·
Donaldson, Robert Golden, LL. B., '95
(Lawyer) ....Century Bldg., Washington, D. C.
Donaldson, Walter A., A. B., '75, A. M.,
'91 (Gov. Officer and Lawyer)........20 Exch'ge Place, New York City.
Donaldson, Walter Franklin, LL. B.,
'05 (Lawyer).......................Century Bldg , Washington, D. C.
Donch, William A , LL. B., '91, LL. M , '92
Donegan, James H., A. B., '47.
Donegan, Maurice Francis, A. M., '98, Ph D , '99
Donegan, Patrick J., LL. B., '97, LL. M , '98
Donlon, Alphonsus J., S. J. (Jesuit
Priest, A. B , '88.................. ...Georgetown Univ'ty, Wash , D. C.
Donnelly, Charles, LL. B., '96·
Donnelly, Edward C , A. B., '44; deceased, Jan. 4, 1891.
Donnelly, James P., A. B., '53.
Donnelly, Joseph Patrick, A. M , '98·
Donnelly, Richard J., LL. B., '89, LL. M., '90·
Donnelly, William J., A. B., '91 (Real
Estate and Notary Public)...........1008 F St., Washington, D. C.
Donohoe, Clarence F., LL. B., '97, LL.
M , '98 (Real Estate Broker).........308 E. Cap. St., Wash., D. C.

Donohue, Florence, M. D., '72 (Physi-
cian and Surgeon)....................1134 8th St. N. W., Wash., D. C.
Donovan, Jennis D., LL. B., '95 (Lawyer)..Napoleon, Ohio.
Donovan, George Timothy, A. B., '05
(Shoe Manufacturing)...............Liberty Sq., Lynn, Mass.
Donovan, Joseph M., LL. B., '89·
Donovan, Michael R., A. B., '80·
Donovan, Thomas J., LL. B., '95·
Donworth, George, A. B., '81 (Lawyer)....Burke Bldg., Seattle, Wash.
Dooley, Francis X., M. D., '65 (Physi-
cian) ....1346 I St., Washington, D. C.
Dooley, James H., A. B., '60, A. M., '65
(Lawyer) ....1103 E. Main St., Richmond, Va.
Doran, Charles M. Cantwell, LL. B.,
'98, LL. M., '99 (Lawyer)............Norfolk, Va.
Dorman, Joseph Edward, D. D. S., '04·
Dorsey, Roscoe J. C., LL. B., '02, LL.
M., '03 (Lawyer)...................12th and G Sts., Wash., D. C.
Doufour, J. F. R., M. D., '73.
Dougherty, Francis P., LL. B., '05
(Lawyer) ....Pittsfield, Mass.
Dougherty, James D., A. B., '57, A. M.,
'60; deceased, April 2, 1878.
Dougherty, Very Rev. James J., D. D.,
'89, LL. D., '97; deceased.
Dougherty, John Francis, A. B., '04
(Law Student)....................Park River, N. Dak.
Dougherty, Philip Joseph, A. M., '98, Ph. D., '99, LL. B., '99, LL. M., '00.
Douglas, John J., LL. B., '96.
Douglas, R. V., A. B., '96·
Douglas, Hon. Robert M., A. B., '67, A M., '70, LL. D., '97·
Douglas, Stephen Arnold, A. B., '01
(Lawyer) ....Las Vegas, N. Mex.
Douglas, George, A. B., '73, A. M., '77;
deceased, March 8, 1888, at Washington, D. C.
Douglass, Henry J., M. D., '73·
Douglass, Will W., LL. B., '87·
Douglass, Wm. B., LL. M., '88·
Dowd, Ed. F., A. B., '94·
Dowd, Patrick, A. B., '53·
Dowling, Patrick V., LL. B., '04 (L'y'r)....Fendall Bldg., Washington, D. C.
Downing, Augustine H., LL. B., '05·
Downing, George E., LL. B., '01·
Downing, Mortimer A., LL. B., '88·
Downing, Rossa F., LL. B., '89, LL. M.,
'90 (Lawyer).......................6th and D Sts. N. W., Wash., D. C.
Downing, Thomas R., Phar. B., '73.

Downs, N. Carroll, LL. B , '99 (Lawyer)...713 14th St. N.W., Wash , D. C.

Downs, Thomas Charles, LL. B., '99,
LL. M., '00, A. M., '00 (Lawyer).......556 Main St., Fond du Lac, Wis.

Doyle, Edward F., A. B , '35, A. M., '39.

Doyle, Francis Joseph, M. D., '01.

Doyle, John T., A. B , '38, A. M., '42,
LL D , '89........................ ...Menlo Park, California.

Doyle, Robert Emmet, A. B., '46; deceased, 1899.

Doyle, W. T. Sherman, A. B., '97, LL. B., '99.

Dragicsevics, Alex. O , M. D., '90.

Drake, Otis Branch, LL. B., '03.

Dreaper, Edward Bernard, A. B., '03.

Dresbach, H. V., M. D., '94.

Drill, Lewis L , LL. B., '03 (Lawyer)......611 New York Life Bldg., St. Paul, Minn.

Driscoll, Thomas A., A. B., '96, LL. B., '97.

Drown, J. H., M. D., 94.

Drum, John William, LL. B , '95.

Drum, Joseph C., LL. B., '99.

DuCharme, Alfred Joseph, A. B., '91
(Lawyer) ....34 Buhl Block, Detroit, Mich.

Dudley, John Gurney, LL. M., '02.

Duff, Edwin H., LL B., '97.

Duffey, Arthur Francis, LL. B., '03
(Editor) ....807 Flatiron Bldg, New York City.

Duffey, H. C., M. D., '91 (Physician).......1248 11th St. N. W., Wash., D. C.

Duffy, Bernard F., A. B., '01.

Duffy, C. Hugh, LL B., '98, LL. M., '99
(Lawyer) ....612 F St. N. W., Washington, D. C.

Duffy, Francis, A. B., '79, A. M., '89; deceased.

Duffy, James Patrick Bernard, A. B.,
'01 ....12 Rochester Savings Bank Bldg., Rochester, N. Y.

Duffy, T. Joseph, LL. B., '93, LL. M., '94.

Dufour, Rev. Alphonse, S. J., A. M., '96 (Jesuit Priest).

Dufour, Clarence R , M. D., '90.

Dufour, Everett, LL. B., '02, LL. M., '03
(Lawyer) ....53 and 54 Le Droit Bldg., Wash., D. C.

Dugan, James Henry, 'A. B., '96; deceased, March 2, 1903, at La Salle, Ill.

Duggan, Jeremiah, A. B , '02.

Duke, Douglas William, M. D., '90.

Duke, Thomas, LL. B , '76; deceased Feb. 3, 1888

Dulin, Edgar A., M. D., '65.

Dumont, Very Rev. Francis, SS., D. D., '89.

Duncan, Joseph M., M. D., '69.

Duncan, Rev. William H., S. J., A. B.,
   '53, A. M, '60; deceased, Dec. 20,
   1894, at Georgetown College, D C.

Dunn, Charles Aloysius, LL. B., '91,
   LL. M, '92 (Clerk)..................Secretary's Office, Navy Depart-
                                    ment, Wash., D. C.

Dunn, John Thomas Francis, M. D., '01·

Dunn, L. B., M. D., '58·

Dunn, William Gilmer, LL. B., '99
   (Lawyer) ....Charlottesville, Va.

Dunne, James P., LL. M., '04.

Dunne, William G., jr., LL. B., '91, LL. M, '92·

Dunnigan, John Patrick, M. D, '01·

Dunphy, John F., M. D, ¡3.

Dunton, John F., LL. B., '94, LL. M., '95·

Durant, Horace B, LL. B., '97 (Lawyer)...Quapaw Agency, Wyandottes, I. T.

Durfee, Raphael Burke, M. D., '00·

Durkee, Robert A., A. M., '31·

Durnin, James A., A. B., '51 (H. C.
   Mass.); deceased, April 15, 1873 (Clergyman).

Duross, Charles E., A. B., '9ɔ (Real
   Estate) ....155 W. 14th St., New York City.

Duross, James Edward, A. B., '91
   (Lawyer) ....220 Broadway, New York City.

Duvall, Charles, A. B., '30·

Duvall, Edward S, Jr., LL. B, '93, LL.
   M, '94 (Lawyer)....................Washington Loan and Trust Bldg.,
                                     Washington, D. C.

Duvall, William H., LL B., '91.

Duvall, William S., LL. B, '93 (Lawyer
   and Patent Expert)..................914 Loan and Trust Bldg., Wash-
                                      ington, D. C.

Duvall, William T. S., M. D., '65·

Dwight, Thomas, LL D., '89·

Dwyer, William A., B S., '88 (vice-
   President and General Manager)......The Art Stove Co, Detroit, Mich.

Dyer, Rev. David Marcus, A. B., '92, A.
   M., '93 (Priest)......................Sacred Heart Church, High Bridge,
                                      New York.

Dyer, Dr. George H., A. M., '56; deceased, Jan 12, 1879.

Dyer, Joseph T., Jr., LL. B, '04·

Dyer, Philip Eugene, A. B., '96·

Dyer, Richard Nott, LL. B., '78, LL. M. '79·

Dykers, Francis H., A. B., '44, A. M., '45·

Eagan, Sylvester Broezel, A. D., '03
   (Automobile Business)...............437 Pearl St., Buffalo, N. Y.

Earl, Charles, LL. B., '95, LL. M., '96·

Earle, Henry Montague, LL. B., '93
   (Lawyer) ....1 Nassau St., New York City, N. Y.

Earls, Michael, S. J., A. M., '97 (Jesuit
   Scholastic) ....Boston College, Boston, Mass.

Easby-Smith, James Stanislaus, A. B.,
   '91, A. M., '92, LL. B., '93, LL. M.,
   '94 (Lawyer; Sec'y Alumni Ass'n,
   Ass't Dist. Att'y).....................Century Bldg., Wash., D. C.

Easterday, George J., LL. B., '86 (Real
   Estate Dealer and Stock Broker).....1410 G St. N.W., Wash., D. C.

Easterling, Horace V., LL. B., '94, LL. M., '95·

Easterling, J. Morgan, LL. M., '85·

Eastman, Joseph A., M. D., '65·

Easton, Edward D., LL. B., '88, LL. M., '89·

Eccleston, Charles A., LL. B., '92, LL.
   M., '93; deceased, Jan. 24, 1901, at Wash., D. C.

Eccleston, G. Malcolm, LL. B., '99, LL. M., '00·

Eckfeldt, Frederick, M. D., '82·

Eckhardt, Charles H., M. D., '71·

Eckstein, Otto G., LL. M , '87·

Edelen, E. Gardiner, LL. B., '90; deceased, March 18, 1891, at Baltimore, Md.

Edmonds, Dean Stockett, LL. B., '99, LL. M., '00·

Edmondston, Preston Paul, A. B., '02......New York City, N. Y.

Edmondston, Raphael Augustine, M. D
   '97 (Ass't Surgeon of the 34th
   Vol. Inf.); deceased, 1900, in the
   Philippine Islands.

Edmundson, James P., A. B., '35·

Edwards, Joseph F., A. M., '82; deceased.

Edwards, Richard Lee, LL. B., '02, LL.
   M., '03 (Clerk).......................Treasury Dept., Wash., D. C.

Edwards, Robert H , M. D., '68·

Edwards, William A., LL. B., '92, LL. M , '93·

Edwards, W. Walton, LL. B., '91, LL.
   M., '92 (Lawyer).....................9 Equity Bldg., Wash., D. C.

Egan, Dr. Maurice Francis, LL. D., '89·...212 N. Capitol St., Wash., D. C.

Eggleston, James Denslow, M. D., '95.

Elbridge, William A., LL. B., '76·

Eldridge, Stuart, M. D., '68·

Elia, Ezechiel de, A. B., '74·

Eline, Francis M., LL. B., '94, LL. M., 95, A. B., '95·

Eliot, Thomas Johnson, M. D., '90
   (Physician) ....718 H St. N. E., Wash., D. C.

Eliot, J. Llewellyn, M. D., '74·

Eliot, Johnson, A. M , '69, Phar. B., '71,
    Phar. D., '72; deceased, Dec. 30, 1883.
Elliot, John J., A. B., '61·
Elliott, Charles A., A. B., '72, LL. B.,
    '74, A. M., '89, deceased, Aug. 1, 1894.
Elliott, Jerre B., M. D., '93·
Ellis, Don Carlos, A. B , '04 (Semi-
   narian) .... .St. Mary's Seminary, Balto., Md.
Ellsworth, Goodwin D., LL. B., '97, LL. M., '99·
Emery, William H., LL. B., '96·
Emmons, Charles M., M. D., '93 (Phys-
   ician) ....1100 Pa. Ave. S. E., Wash., D. C.
English, Charles Henry, LL. B., '05
   (Lawyer) ....Erie, Pa.
English, John J., A. B., '00 (Trader)......4114 Michigan Ave , Chicago, Ill..
Ennis, Charles H., LL. B., '94, LL. M.,
   '95 (Lawyer) ....1405 F St. N. W., Wash., D. C.
Ergood, Clarence Elmo, LL. B., '96,
   LL. M , '97 (Wholesale Grocer).......416 9th St. N. W., Wash., D. C.
Eriksson, Leonard, LL. B , '04 (Lawyer)..Fergus Falls, Minn.
Errazurez, Senor Don Ysidoro, A. B.,
   '52; deceased, March 12, 1898.
Erskine, Harlow L., LL. M., '86·
Ervin, Artemus J , Jr , LL. B., '96, LL. M , '97·
Escobar, J., A. B., '60, A. M., '62.
Esling, Charles H., A. M., '89·
Eslin, James T., M. D., '91·
Estabrook, Leon M., LL. B., '97·
Etchison, Howard M., LL. B., '04·
Ethridge, Bell W., A. B., '76; de-
   ceased, March 26, 1901, at Dresden, Tenn.
Etty, Robert A., LL. B., '91, LL. M., '92·
Evans, John M., M. D., '61·
Evans, Paul Warrington, A. B., '94,
   LL. B., '98 (Dentist)................Bond Bldg., Washington, D. C.
Evans, W. Warrington, A. B., '91
   (Honorary) (Dentist) ....Bond Bldg., Washington, D. C.
Evans, Warwick, M. D., '52..
Eve, Oswell R., LL. B., '99 (Lawyer)......Augusta, Ga.
Evert, Henry C., LL. B., '91, LL. M.,
   '92 (Patent Lawyer).................305 Smithfield St., Pittsburg, Pa.
Ewing, Thomas, Jr., LL. B., '99 (Lawyer)..67 Wall St., New York City, N. Y.
Ewing, Thomas, Jr., LL. D., '70·

Fague, Joseph R., LL. B., '97, LL. M., '98·
Fairclough, Rev. John, A. M., '21·

Fairfax, John Wheeler, Jr , A. B., '04
   (Stocks and Bonds).................218 Hennen Bldg , New Orleans,
                                          La.
Falconer, Balivar Lang, M. D., '95·
Fallon, Frederick B , LL B , '?
   (Lawyer) ....39 Sanford Bldg , Bridgeport,
                                          Conn.
Fallon, James, LL. B., '96 (Lawyer)......24 North St., Pittsfield, Mass.
Fallon, John T., LL. B , '78· LL. M., '79·
Fallon, Joseph D , A. B , '58· (H. C.,
   Mass.), A M., '64 (Lawyer and
   Justice of the Municipal Court of
   the South Boston District)......... ..56 Pemberton Sq , Boston, Mass
Fallon, Joseph P , LL. B., '81·
Falls, Alexander J., LL B., '73·
Farish, John Hamilton, A. B , '79
   (Real Estate and Loans)...........112 N. 8th St., St. Louis, Mo.
Farrell, Edward G , LL. B , '97· LL. M.,
   '98 (Copy Editor)..................Gov. Printing Office, Wash., D. C.
Farrell, Ed. P., A. B , '83·
Farrell, Emmet Lee, A M , '93· LL. B.,
   '94: deceased, Feb. 23, 1895.
Farrow, Patillo, LL. B., '97·
Faulkner, James Burton, LL. B., '05
   (Lawyer) .. ..McClelland Bldg , Lexington, Ky.
Faulkner, James F , A. B , '22
Fay, Andrew Edwin, LL. B , '98·
Fay, John Baptist, jr , A. B., '02· A. M.,
   '03 (Ass't Editor)..................Grafton, W. Va.
Fegan, Edward John, A. M , '03· LL.
   B , '05 (Lawyer)...................1048 Hancock St , Quincy, Mass.
Fegan, Hugh J , jr , A. B., '01· A. M.,
   '02 (Law Clerk)................... .. Office of the Solicitor, Agricultural
                                          Dept., Wash , D. C.
Fellows, Harry A , LL B , '8·, LL. M., '92
Fenton, David H , LL. B., '96· LL M.,
   '97 (Lawyer)......................812 Colorado Bldg , Wash., D. C.
Fenwick; George, A. B., '32·
Fergell, J A , D D S , '02·
Ferguson, John H , LL B , '04 (Clerk)....Library of Congress, Wash , D. C.
Ferguson, Daniel John, A. B., '98
   (Lawyer) ....New O'Hara Theater Bldg., Shen-
                                          andoah, Pa.
Ferguson, S Colfax, LL M , '02 (Law-
   yer) ....Prestonsburg, Ky.
Ferguson, Arthur W , LL. B , '85· LL. M , '86

1810041

Ferneding, Thomas A., A. B., '01 (Sup-
  erintendent) The Dayton & Xenia
  Transit Co. ....Dayton, Ohio.
Ferry, Joseph T., LL. B., '91, LL. M,
  '92 (Clerk) ....1944 Calvert St., Wash., D. C.
Ferry, Lemuel A., M. D., '79-
Fetterman, Wilfrid B , A. B., '52 (deceased).
Ficklin, Col. Theodore Hamilton, A.
  M.' '69 (Principal, George Wash-
  ington High School)..................714 Duke St., Alexandria, Va.
Fields, Frank h., LL. B., '92-
Fillette, St Julian, LL. B., '86, LL. M., '87 (deceased).
Fink, Rev. Edward X , S. J., A. B., '73
  (Jesuit Priest)........................Gonzaga' College, Wash., D. C.
Finke, Alvin J., A. B., '96.
Finn, William T., LL. B., '01, LL. M.,
  '02 (Lawyer) ....Fendall Bldg, Washington, D. C.
Finnegan, John J., LL. B , '01.
Finney, Francis, M. D., '82-
Finney, Robert Gordon, LL. B., '98,
  LL. M., 99 (Lawyer)...............Fairfax, Va.
Finney, William Brantner, A. M., '98-
Finning, Rev. Thomas James., A. B.,
  '95 (Priest)........................79 Whitney St., Nashua, N. H.
Fisher, C. Henry, M. D., '91-
Fisher, Charles, LL. B., '99, LL. M.,
  '00 (Clerk) Chief Clerk's Office,
  Treasury Department ....Washington, D. C.
Fisher, George P., jr., A. B., '74, LL. B. '76-
Fisher, George W., M. D., '70-
Fisher, Samuel P., LL. B., '95, LL. M., '96-
Fitch, George A , M. D., '68, A. M , '69-
Fitch, William S., LL. B., '95, LL. M ,
  '97 (U. S. Special Pension Examiner)....Pueblo, Col.
Fitnam, Thomas H., LL. B., '84, LL. M., '85.
Fitzgerald, Edward, A B., '32-
Fitzgerald, Edward H., A. M., '50
  (U. S. A.) Cap't. 22d Inf.............Manila, P. I.
Fitzgerald, George W., LL. B., '88-
Fitzgerald, John J., LL. B., '95, LL M.,
  '96 ....255 Main St., Pawtucket, R. I.
Fitzgerald, Joseph S., M. D., '70-
Fitzgerald, Thomas J., LL. B , '96, LL M , '97-
Fitzgerald, William Joseph, A. B., '98
  (Lawyer) ....Mears Bldg., Scranton, Pa.

Fulton, Creed M., LL. B , '90, LL. M , '91.
Furlong, Francis Mohur, M. D , '95

Gaddis, Edgar T., LL. B., '92, LL. M.,
    '93 (Lawyer) ....1017 E. Capitol St., Wash., D. C.
Galiher, Samuel S , LL. B., '91·
Gall, John Camden, LL. B., '99 (Ass't.
    Cashier) ....201 New High St., Los Angeles,
                                            Cal.
Gallagher, Anthony J., LL. M , '87·
Gallagher, John Martin, B. S , '96 (In-
    structor) English High School......Worcester, Mass.
Gallagher, Joseph Aloysius, A. M , '97·
Gallagher, M. F., M D , '89·
Gallagher, P. J., M. D., '91·
Gallagher, Thomas D. J., A. B , '84·
Gallatin, Daniel B., LL B., '76
Gallen, William J A., LL. B , '03, (Law-
    yer) ....4823 Lancaster Ave. Phila., Pa.
Galligan, John H., A. B., '72 (deceased, Sept. 8, 1893).
Gallinger, William Henry Augustine,
    LL. B., '93 (Lawyer) (Clerk) G. F.
    & O. D. Ry. Co......................3609 M St. N.W., Wash , D. C.
Gazdarillas, Rev. Joaquin Larrain Y., D. D., '52·
Gantt, Daniel J., LL. B., '95, LL. M., '95
Gantt, Robert Joseph, LL. B., '96
    (Lawyer) ....Spartanburg, S. C
Gapen, Nelson, M. D., '00
Gardiner, George, A. B , '24·
Gardiner, John B., A. B , '59·
Gardiner, Richard A., A. B., '55, A. M., '56.
Gandiner, W. Gwynn, LL. B , '99, LL. M., '00
Gardner, W. H , M. D , '61 .
Gardner, R. Bennett, LL. B., '96·
Garesche, Lieutenant Julius P., U. S.
    A., A. M., '42 (deceased, Dec. 13,
    1862. Was appointed chief of staff
    to General Rosecrans, command-
    ing the Department of Cumber-
    land, and served in that capacity
    from Nov. 9, 1862, until his death.
    He fell in the battle of Stone
    River).
Garesche, William A , A. B., '71·
Garland, Hon. Augustus H , LL. D., '89 (deceased).

Garland, Rufus Cummings, Ph. B., '87·
    LL B., '91 (deceased March 11,
    1901, at Fort Worth, Tex)
Garnett, Dr. Algernon S , A. M., '75·
Garnett, Leslie C., LL. B., '99, LL. M.,
    1900 (Lawyer) ....Mathews, Va.
Garnett, Robert Stanislaus, M. D., '03· •
Garrison, F. H., M. D., '93·
Garvey, Thomas Q , M. D., '94·
Garvy, William J., LL. D , '94, A. M.,
    '94 (President & Treasurer, The
    Garvy Co. ....80-86 Norton St., Chicago, Ill.
Gaston, Hugh J., A. B., '55·
Gately, M. J., M. D., '72·
Gates, Charles J., LL. B., '04 (Lawyer)
    Treasury Department ....Washington, D. C.
Gavan, Joseph W., LL. B., '04·
Gaynor, Hugh Augustine, S. J., A. B.,
    '95, A. M., '96 (Jesuit Scholastic)
    Georgetown University ....Washington, D. C.
Geary, Daniel J., A. B., '89 (Manufac-
    turer & Street Railroads) ....Oil City, Pa.
Gelpi, Maurice Joseph, A. B., '05,.........1333 Esplanade Ave., New Orleans,
                                             La.
Gentsch, Charles, M. D., '73·
Gentsch, Daniel C., M. D., '89.
George, Isaac Stewart, A. M., '04..........864 W. North Ave., Baltimore, Md.
George, John M., LL. B., '92, LL. M., '93.
Gering, Matthew, LL. B., '83, LL. M., '84·
Geringer, Emil J., LL. B., '03·
Gery, Raymond E., LL. B., '93, LL. M., '94·
Gibbon, D. J., M. D., '69·
Gibbs, Thomas F., M. D., '70.
Gibson, Frederick P., LL. B., '98·
Gibson, T. Catlett, M. D., '93·
Gieseking, Henry N , M. D , '76·
Gilchrist, Walter Schell, A. B., '02
    (Clk) Post-office Department.........Washington, D. C.
Gill, James Edward, M. D., '01·
Gillan, Edward Francis, LL. B., '01,
    LL. M., '02 (Clerk)..................Bureau of Census, Wash., D. C.
Gillespie, John B., LL. B , '89, LL. M.,
    '90 (Alderman and Police Magis-
    trate) ....103 W. Market St., Scranton, Pa.
Gillespie, Robert K., LL. B., '94·
Gillis, Lieut. J. Merville, U. S. N., M. A., '43 (deceased, Feb. 9, 1865.)

Griffith, James E , LL. B , '77·

Griffith, M. J., M. D., '69

Griffiss, Edward J., A. B., '74.

Griffiss, John I , A. B., '76 (deceased,
   Feb. 19, 1904, at Washington, D. C.).

Grima, Alfred, A. B , '04 (Law Studen) .. .1604 4th St., New Orleans, La.

Grimes, Junius D., LL. B., '02 (Lawye_)

Grimes, William H., LL B , '92' LL. M , '93·

Grogay, Patrick J , LL. B., '96' LL. M., '97·

Grogan, Stephen Syivester, A. M., '03
   (Student) .... .Milwaukee, Wis.

Grogan, Thomas J , LL. B , '96' LL. M., '97·

Gross, Alfred Gregory, M. D., 1900.

Grymes, James W., M. D , '53·

Guidry, Onesimus, A. B., '36·

Gulentz, Cnarles, LL. B., '90' LL. M.,
   '92 (Lawyer)........................Bakewell Bldg., Pittsburg, Pa.

Gunnell, Francis M , A. B., '44' A. M.,
   '46 (Medical Direccor) ....U. S. N., Washington, D. C.

Gwynn, Raphael N , LL. B., '98' LL. M., '99·

Gwynn, William Clarance, M. D., '98
   (Physican) ....3336 O St. N. W., Wash , D. C.

Gwynn, William, LL. D., 31.

Gwynn; Dr. William H , A. B., '55' A. M., '57·

Haag, Harry O., LL. B., '97 (Lawyer).....Pottsville, Pa.

Haag, Jackson D., LL. B , '90' LL. M., '91·

Haas, Carlton Daniels, M. D , '97·

Hagan, Christopher J., A. B., 1900
   (General Insurance Agent)..........Room 44, Donovan Bldg., Lowell,
                                       Mass.

Hahn, Harry William, LL. B , '03
   (Shoe Dealer) ....7th & K Sts., Washington, D. C.

Haines, Walter S , M D., '91·

Hale, William, M. D., '67·

Hall, Arthur A , LL. B , '93' LL. M , '95·

Hall, Henry S , M. D., '71.

Hall, Harry Thomas, A. B., '05.

Hall, John Dillan, LL. B , '99, LL. M.,
   '01 ....Tensaw, Baldwin County, Ala.

Hall, John H , A. B , '53·

Hall, Joseph Edward, LL. B., '98·

Hall, Ross C , LL B , '88·

Hallahan, John William, A. B , '99' A. M., 1900.

Halstead, Thomas, LL. B., '89' LL. M.,
   '90 ....2047 Ontario St , Philadelphia, Pa.

Haltigan, Patrick J., LL. B., '97·

Ham, Henry H., LL. B., '05·

Hamersly, Lewis Randolph, LL. B.,

'92 (Publisher) ....49 Wall St , New York City, N. Y.

Hamilton, Edward J., M. D., '95·

Hamilton, Charles William, B. S., '81

(Banker) ....1112 Park Ave., Omaha, Nebr.

Hamilton, George E., A. B., '72· LL. B.,

'74· A. M., '82· LL. D., '89.............Century Bldg,. Washington, D. C.

Hamilton, Harper, LL. B., '83·

Hamilton, John B , LL. B., '89 (deceased).

Hamilton, John C. C , A B., '51·

Hamilton, John J., LL. B., '91· LL. M., '92

Hamilton, Patrick H., A. B., '35 (deceased).

Hamilton, Ralph Alexander, M. D., '04·

Hamlet, William, M. D., '69·

Hammett, C M., M. D , '56 (deceased, Nov. 22, 1898, at Washington, D. C.).

Hammett, Charles Maddox, M. D., '92

(Physician) ....The Brunswick, Washington, D. C.

Hammond, William A., A. B , '68· A. M., '71 (deceased, Sept. 1892, near Ellicott

City, Md.)

Hamner, Edward D., LL. B., '88· LL.

M., '89 (Lawyer)...................Attalla, Etowah County, Ala.

Hamner, George W., LL. M , '87

(Clerk) Auditor for Post-office........Treasury Dept., Washington, D. C.

Hampson, Thomas, LL. B., '82 (deceased, 1888).

Hampton, J. Rodolph, LL. B., '89· LL. M., '90·

Hanawalt, George P., M. D , '64·

Hanger, Hugh H., LL. B., '03 (Sales

Agent) ....National Bank Cash Register, St.
Paul, Minn.

Hanley, Bernard T., LL. B , '73 (deceased, 1882).

Hanna, John F., A. M., '70 (deceased, Oct 31, 1885, at Washington, D. C.).

Hannegan, Edward A , LL. B., '90·

Hanrahan, James Vincent, A M., '96·

Hanretty, Lawrence Michael, jr., A. B., '04

Harbin, George Francis, jr., A. B., '02· . ..11 7th St. N. W., Washington, D. C.

Hardie, Joseph Cuyler, LL. B , '92· LL

M , '93 (Clerk)......................War Dept , Washington, D. C.

Hardin, Palmer, LL. B , '92·

Hardin, Thomas B., jr., LL. B , '84· LL M., '85·

Harding, W. R , A. B , '36·

Hardisty, John T., LL. B., '04·

Hardy, Calvin S., LL. B., '96· LL M..

'97 (Clerk) ....Pension Bureau, Washington, D. C.

Hare, William C , LL. B., '95·

Harker, Charles O., LL. B., '99·

Harley, Richard Joseph. A. B., '96
   (Hotel Business) ....1842 Market St., Philadelphia, Pa.
Harlow, Leo P., LL. B., '98, LL. M.,
   '99 (Lawyer).................................412 5th St., Washington, D. C.
Harmon, John Oregon, LL. B , '99·
Harper, B. E., D. D. S., '02·
Harper, James E., LL. B., '97·
Harper, Robert W., A. B., '52·
Harr, William R., LL. B., '95, LL. M.,
   '96 (Lawyer)......................... ...Dept. of Justice, Washington, D. C.
Harrington, Edward ι·., LL. B., '86,
   LL. M., '87 (Clerk)..................Treasury Dept., Washington, D. C.
Harris, Charles N., A. B., '71, A. M.,
   ·'89 (Lawyer) ....2 Tryon Row, New York City.
Harris, Edward F., LL. M., '88·
Harrison, John C., M. D., '60.
Harrison, Walton, LL. B., '97·
Harrison, William Barnett, M. D., '05·
Harrison, William Clinton, LL. B., '99·
Harrison, William H., LL. B., '81·
Harrown, William S , M. D., '65·
Hart, Harry L., LL. B., '03
Hart, James H., D. D. S., '05.
Hart, John T., LL. B., '95, LL. M., '96
  . (Clerk) ....:...Pension Office, Washington, D. C
Hartigan, James F., M D., '68 (deceased).
Hartnett, Daniel J., LL B., '03·
Hartsfield, Augustus M., LL B., '95
   (Clerk) ....Interstate Commerce Commission,
                                   Washington, D. C.
Harvey, A. Thomas, A. B., '76 (deceased, Oct 6, 1882, at Washington, D. C.).
Harvey, George E , M. D., '84·
Harvey, Levin Allen, M. D., '75·
Harvey, Richard E., LL. B , '05 (Law-
   yer) . ...Portland, Me.
Harvey, Thomas M , A. B., '89 (Jour-
   nalist) ....U. S. Court House, City Hall,
                                     Washington, D. C.
Harvey, William F., M. D., '68·
Harveycutter, Austin, LL. B., '05 (Spe-
   cial Agent),.........................Dept. of Justice, Washington, D. C.
Hasbrouck, Edwin Marble, M. D., '95
   (Physician) ....1819 Adams Mill Road, Wash., D. C.
Haskell, Lewis W., LL. B., '94·
Hassan, Dudley T., LL. B , '96, LL. M., '97· ·
Hassler, Alpha M., LL. B., '95·

Hastings, Edward, A. B., '36·
Haswell, John H., LL. B., '73·
Hatch, William B., LL. B., '94 (Lawyer)...11 Huron St., Ypsilanti, Mich.
Haven, Charles L., M. D., '65·
Hawes, John B., M. D., '86·
Hawken, Samuel McComas, LL. B., '05·
Hawkes, Dr. William H., A. M., '90·
Hawley, Cornell S., LL. B., '97 (General Sales Agent, Consolidated Car Heating Company) ....42 Broadway, New York City.
Hayden, Daniel B., M. D., '04·
Hayden, Joseph E., LL. B., '76·
Hayden, Reynolds, M. D., '05·
Haydon, William Thomas, A. B., '94 (Lawyer) ....209 St. Paul St., Baltimore, Md.
Hayes, Edward, LL. B., '72·
Hayes, Henry L., M. D., '90·
Hayes, Noah, M. D., '76·
Hayes, Stephen H., LL. B., '89, LL. M., '90·
Hayes, Stephen Quentin, A. B., '92·
Hays, Melville Ambrose, M. D., 1900.
Hays, W. W., M. D., '61.
Hayward, William H., M. D., '69·
Hazard, Daniel C., M. D., '71·
Hazen, David W., M. D., '73.
Hazen, William P. C., M. D., '77 (Physician) ....511 E. Capitol St., Wash., D. C.
Head, Paul Jones, A. B., 1900 (Lawyer)...Greensburg, Pa.
Head, Morris William, A. B., '98·
Healy, Hugh C., A. B., '49 (H. C. Mass.) (Merchant); deceased Sept 23, 1852.
Healy, Rt. Rev. James Augustine, A. B., '49 (H. C. Mass), A. M., '51 (deceased, Aug. 5, 1900)................Bishop of Portland, Me.
Healy, James M., A. B., '72, A. M., '89·
Healy, Patrick F., A. B., '50 (H. C. Mass.) (Jesuit Priest) ....980 Park Ave., New York City.
Healy, Thomas F., LL. B., '99, LL. M., 1900 (Imposer) ....Gov. Printing Office, Wash., D. C.
Heard, John M., A. B., '42, A. M., '47·
Hearst, William T., LL. B., '92, LL. M., '95·
Heaton, Harry, LL. B., '03 (Lawyer)......Century Building, Wash., D. C.
Hechtman, Henry J., LL. B., '73·
Hedrick, Charles Joseph, LL. B., '84 (Lawyer) ....606 F St. N.W., Washington, D. C.
Hedrick. John T., S. J., A. B., '71, A M., '74 (Jesuit Priest)..............Georgetown U., Washington, D. C.

Heffernan, John Francis, LL. B., '04,
  LL. M., '05 (Legal Ass't)............213 Treasury Dept., Wash., D. C.
Hegarty, Harry A , LL. B , '01 (Lawyer)..512 F St. N.W., Wash , D. C.
Heideman, Ivan, LL. B., '01 (Lawyer)....Stewart Bldg., 412 6th St. N.W.,
                                        Washington, D. C.
Heimler, Rev. Alphonsus, O. S. B., A.
  M , '60...............................St. Boniface, Cambria Co., Pa.
Heintzelman, Joseph A , jr., M. D., '02·
Heiskell, Raymond Angelo, A. B., '91,
  LL. B., '93, LL. M , '94·............Century Bldg., Washington, D. C.
Heitmuller, H Anton, LL. B., '97, LL.
  M , '98 (Lawyer) .'...................458 La. Ave. N.W., Wash., D. C.
Heizman, Col. Charles L., A B., '64
  (Ass't Surg) ....Surg. Gen. Office, Wash., D. C.
Heller, Joseph Milton. M. D., '96·
Heller, P. F., Phar. B , '11, M. D., '74·
  (Physician) ....Pueblo, Colo.
Helm, Dr. Charles J., A. B., '83·
Helm, Gratz W., LL. B , '01·
Helmer, William Francis, M. D , '04·
Helmer, Burton K J J B , '91
Helmick, William J., A. B., 1900.
Helton, A. S , M. D., '90·
Henderson, James Aboy, LL. B., '93
  (Lawyer) ....Rockville, Md.
Henderson, John M., LL. B., '90 (Real
  Estate) ....1418 F St. N.W., Washington, D. C.
Hendler, Charles F , LL. B., '96, LL.
  M., '97 (Lawyer) ....Fendall Bldg., Wash., D. C.
Henning, R. E., M. D., '85·
Hennon, John Francis, A. B , '93, A. M. '94·
Henry, Charles T , LL B , '92, LL M , '93·
Henry, Thomas Stanhope, LL. B., '99
  (Lawyer) ....Dept. of Justice, Washington, D. C.
Henry, William J., M. D., '66·
Herbert, J Wells, M. D., '59·
Hernitz, Stanislaus, M. D., '53·
Heron, Alexander P , LL. B., '99·
Herran, Hon. Thomas, A. B , '63, A. M.,
  '68, LL D., '99 (deceased, 1904)....Late Minister of U. S. of Colom-
                                        bia to U. S. of America.
Herring, Carl E., LL. M , '89·
Herring, James L., LL. B., '98·
Herron, W. Francis D., LL. B., '99, LL. M., 1900.
Hickcox, John Howard, jr., LL. B., '79.

Hickling, Daniel Percy, Phar. B., '71,
Phar. D., '72, M. D., '84, (Physi-
cian) ....1304 R. I. Ave., Washington, D. C.
Hickman, G. W. Vintow, M. D , '72·
Hicks, Frederick Charles, LL. B., '01
(Librarian) ....U. S. Naval War College, Newport,
R. I.
Hicks, Jesse Addison, LL. B., '99
(Lawyer) ....306 Bond Bldg , Washington, D. C.
Hicks, Leo Richard, A. B., '05 (Law
Student at Harvard Law School).....Cambridge, Mass.
Higgins, James H., LL. B., '99, LL. M.,
1900 (Lawyer and Mayor) ....Pawtucket, R. I.
Higgins, Reginald H., LL. B., '90, LL. M., '91·
Higgins, William Lawrence Denis, A. B., '97·
Hill, Eugene F', A. B. 70.
Hill, F. Snowden, A. B., '73·
Hill, G. W., M. D., '59·
Hill, J. Chambers, M. D., '91·
Hill, Josua, LL. B., '93·
Hill, Major Nicholas S., A. B., '58, A. M , '60·
Hill, Raymond J , A B , '60 (H. C
Mass) (Lawyer); deceased, in California.
Hill, Richard S., M. D., '86·
Hill, William Costilo, M. D., '97·
Hill, William J., A. B., '57, A. M., '60 (deceased).
Hillen, Solomon, A. B., '27·
Hilliard, Patrick R., LL. B., '93, LL.
M., '94 (Lawyer) ....Century Bldg., Washington, D. C.
Hillyer, Clair Richards, LL. B., '99,
LL. M , 1900 (Special Attorney)......Bureau of Corporations, Dept of
Commerce and Labor, Wash-
ington, D. C.
Hilton, James Franklin, M. D., '04
(Physician) ....924 23d St. N.W., Wash., D. C.
Hindmarsh, Walter B., LL. B., '96, LL.
M , '97 (Clk.) Light House Board....719-721 13th St. N. W., Wash., D. C.
Hine, Oliver C., LL. B., '92, LL. M., '93·
Hines, J. Arthur, M. D., '69·
Hipkins, William A., LL. B., '89, LL. M., '90·
Hird, John Denby, LL B., '01·
Hirschman, Morris, LL. B., '05 (L'y'r)....416-417 Law Bldg., Baltimore, Md.
Hirst, Anthony A., M. A., '71, LL. D.,
'01 (Lawyer) ....211 S. 6th St., Philadelphia, Pa.
Hirst, William L., A. B., '63·
Hitchcock, Thomas D., LL. B., '90, LL. M., '91.

Hitz, William Henry, LL. B., '98, LL. M., '99·
Hoard, Francis De V., ... D., '79·
Hoban, James F., A. B., '60·
Hodge, Edwin R., M. D., '92·
Hodge, Howard B., LL. B , '96, LL. M., '97·
Hodges, Benjamin F., M. D., '58·
Hodges, E. F., A. M., '83·
Hodges, E. F , M. D., '74·
Hodges, Henry W., LL B , '92, LL. M.,
    '93 (Clerk, Court of Appeals).........City Hall, Washington, D. C.
Hodges, William S., LL. B., '93, LL. M.,
    '94 (Patent Lawyer).................930 F St. N.W., Wash., D. C.
Hodgkins, Chester Lyman, M. D., 1900.
Hodgson, Telfair, LL. B., '89.
Hof, Charles R., LL. B , '93, LL. M., '94
    (Clerk) ....General Land Office, Wash., D.
Hoffar, Noble S., A. B., '66, A. M., '67·
    (Architect) ....419 Hastings St., Vancouver, B.
Hogan, Frank J., LL. B., '02 (Lawyer)....Colorado Bldg., Washington, D.
Holcombe, E. Prosser, LL. B., '95·
Holden, Raymond T., M. D., '81 (Phy-
    sician) ....802 6th St. S.W., Wash., D. C.
Holder, Willis B., LL. B., '90, LL. M., '91·
Holland, William Joseph, M. D., '03·
Hollander, Harry H., LL. B., '99, LL. M., 1900.
Hollinger, Frank S., LL. M., '98·
Hollingsworth, John S., A. B., '73; deceased Jan. 14, 1895.
Holt, George A., M. D., '80·
Holt, John Henry, LL. B., '97 (Patent
    Lawyer) ....McGill Bldg., Washington, D. C.
Holt, John Herrimon, LL. B., '81 (Lawyer).
Holt, Robert Oscar, LL. B., '91, LL. M.,
    '92 ....1200 E. Cap. St., Wash., D. C.
Holtzman, Ernest, LL. B., '93, LL. M., '94·
Homer, Charles C., A. B., '67, A. M., '96
    (President) ....Second National Bank, Balto., M
Hood, Col. Arthur, A. B., '77; deceased Feb. 24, 1901, Cuthbert, Ga.
Hootec, Louis C., M. D., '61·
Hoover, George Rendelton, LL. B., '97
    (Lawyer) ....Century Bldg., Washington, D.
Hoover, William D., LL. B., '88, LL. M.,
    '89 (Second Vice President, Attor-
    ney, and Trust Official of the Na-
    tional Life Deposit & Trust Co. of
    the District of Columbia)............15th St. and N. Y. Ave., Wash.,
                                   D. C.

Hopkins, Alfred Francis, D. D. S., '03.....1730 I St., Washington, D. C.
Hopkins, Francis A., LL. B., '90·
Hopkins, Louis M., LL. B., '87.
Hopkins, Ralph, A. B., '95·
Hopkins, William A., LL. B., '05·
Horah, James H., LL. B., '89, LL. M., '93·
Horgan, John C., LL. B., '84·
Horgan, John J., LL. B., '88, LL. M., '89
Horigan, James Bernard, A. B., '01,
    A. M., '02, LL. B., '04................3601 O St. N.W., Wash., D. C.
Horigan, Dr. William D., LL. B., '99
    (Librarian) ....Naval Observatory, Wash., D. C.
Horkan, George Augustus, LL. B., '02
    (Lawyer) ....Forsyth, Mont.
Horrigan, James J., LL. B., '92, LL. M.,
    '93 (Pension Examiner)............Charrton, Iowa.
Horsey, Charles C. L., A. B., '01, LL. B.,
    '04 (Lawyer) ....207 N. Calvert St., Balto., Md.
Horsey, Outerbridge, jr., A. B., '96·
Horton, William Ed., LL. B., '92, LL. M., '93·
Hough, J. Spencer, M. D., '93·
Hough, William Hite, M. D., '04·
Houghton, Percy Francis, M. D., '01·
Houston, Charles James, LL. B., '05
    (Lawyer) ....669 Schrader St., San Francisco,
        Cal.
Houston, Samuel, M. D., '68·
Howard, A. Clinton, LL. B., '95·
Howard, Arcturus L., M. D., '93·
Howard, Flodoardo, Phar. B., '71,
    Phar. D., '72; deceased Feb., 1888,
    at Washington, D. C.
Howard, John Chalmers, LL. B., '01·
Howard, Joseph T., M. D., '59 (Phy-
    sician) ....1126 9th St. N.W., Wash., D. C.
Howard, Joseph T. D., M. D., '89
    (Physician) ....U. S. Bureau of Pensions, Wash.,
        D. C.
Howard, Leland O., Ph. D., '96·
Howard, Robinson, M. D., '67, A. M., '70, LL. B., '74·
Howard, Stanton Wren, M. D., '03·
Howe, Franklin Theodore, M. D., '67, A. M., '89·
Howe, Theodore Gilman, M. D., '03·
Howell, Rev. R., LL. B., '75·
Howle, Peter C., A. B., '45; deceased Nov. 24, 1865.
Hoyt, Allen G., LL. B., '02 (Banker)......52 Wall St., New York City.

Hoyt, Charles A., A. B., '57, A. M., '60;
    deceased Aprıl 18, 1903, at Pasadena, Cal.
Hubachek, Francis R., LL. M., '87·
Hubbard, Oliver P., LL. B., '91
Hubbell, Santiago F., LL. B., '74·
Hughes, Arthur L., LL. B., '88' LL. M., '89.
Hughes, Charles L., LL. B., '73·
Hughes, Ellis, LL. B., '99·
Hughes, Harry Canby, LL. B., '99·
Hughes, William J., LL. B., '91' LL. M.,
    '92 (Lawyer) ....·...........Dept. of Justice, Wash., D. C.
Hull, Marion McHenry, M. D., '95·
Hullihen, Alfred F., A. B., '55·
hullihen, Manfreu F., A B , '55' A. M., '70·
Hummer, Harry R., M D., '99·
Hunt, Granville M., LL. B., '89' LL. M., '90·
Hunt, Presley C., M. D , '91·
Hunter, Edwin Clarence, M. D., '03·
Huntoon, Andrew J., M. D., '6(·
Husselton, William S., M. D., '65·
Hussey, John Patrick, M. D., '03·
Hutchins, Frank W., LL. B., '99' LL. M , '00·
Hutchinson, Claudius P., M. D., '99·
Hutchinson, Edmund Archus, LL. B., '03.
Huyck, Thomas B., LL. B , '92' LL. M., 93.   ·
Hyams, William Washington, LL. B.,
    '03 (Lawyer) ....Muskogee, I. T.
Hyatt, P. F , M. D., '65·
Hyatt, William A., LL. M., '88.

Iglehart, James Alexis, A. B., '45
    (Agriculturist) ....,....Davisonville P. O., Md.
Illman, Harold, LL B., '75·
Ingalls, Ellsworth, LL B , '88·
Ingalls, Ralph, LL. B., '91·
Ironside, Charles Norton, LL. B., '82·
Ironside, George E., LL. D., '22·
Irwin, John, jr., LL. M., '94·
Irwin, John W., LL B , '82
Isbell, John B., LL. B , '01 (Lawyer)......Fort Payne, Ala.
Israeli, Baruch, M. D., '97·
Ittig, Henry, LL. B , '03' LL. M., '04·
Ives, Eugene S., A. B., '78' A. M., '88'
    Ph. D., '89 (Lawyer).................Tucson, Ariz.

Jackson, Albert L., M. D., '89·   . . . .

Jackson, John Joseph, A. M., '97·
Jackson, William A., LL. B., '94, LL. M , '96·
Jackson, William C., LL. B., '98·
Jackson, William S., LL. B., '80, LL. M , '81·
Jaffe, Saul Sydney, D. D. S., '05·
James, C. Clinton, LL. B , '97, LL. M., '98·
James, Judge Charles P., LL. D., '70; deceased.
James, Howard, M. D., '93·
Jamison, Albion B , M. D., '67·
Jenkins, Charles, LL. B., '03·
Jenkins, Lewis W., A. B., '22, A. M., '31·
Jenkins, T. Robert, A. B., '40·
Jenkins, Theodore, A. B., '26·
Jenner, Norman R., M. D., '91·
Jennings, David E., LL. B., '91, LL. M., '92·
Jennings, Edward James, LL. B., '80, LL. M., '80·
Jennings, John W., LL. B., '03, LL. M., '04·
Jennings, Robert W., LL. B., '87, LL. M., '88·
Jerrell, Herbert P., LL. B., '90·
Jessup, Wilfred, LL. M., '01 (Lawyer).....Richmond, Ind.
Jewell, J. Gray, M. D., '55·
Jewell, William R., jr., LL. B., '92........209 Daniel Bldg., Danville, Ill.
Jirdinston, William C., LL. B., '80·
Johnson, Benjamin R., LL. B., '01
    (Patent Lawyer) ....605 7th St. N.W., Wash., D. C.
Johnson, Dallas, M. D., '68·
Johnson, Frank G., M. D., '91·
Johnson, Hayden, LL. B., '95, LL. M.,
    '96 (Lawyer).........................416 5th St. N.W., Wash., D. C.
Johnson, Jeremiah, LL. B., '85, LL. M., '86·
Johnson, John Althens, LL. B., '82,
    LL. M., '87 (Lawyer)................408 5th St. N.W., Wash., D. C.
Johnson, John Lewis, LL. B., '04 (Law-
    yer) ....500 5th St. N.W., Washington, D. C.
Johnson, Joseph, A. B., '42, A. M., '46·
Johnson, Joseph Tabor, M. D., '65,
    Ph D., '89.........................926 17th St., Washington, D. C.
Johnson, Loren Bascom Taber, M. D.,
    '00 (Physician) ....1211 Conn. Ave. N.W., Washing-
                                              ton, D. C.
Johnson, Louis Alward, M. D., '92·
Johnson, Paul Bowen Alden, M. D., '05·
Johnson, Paul E., LL. B., '90, LL. M.,
    '91 (Lawyer) ....512 F St. N.W., Washington, D. C.
Johnson, Richard W., LL. B., '89·
Johnson, Robert, LL. B., '80·

Johnson, Stuart Clarke, M. D., '97·
Johnson, Titian W., LL. B., '94·
Johnson, Walter A., A. B., '91; deceased Dec. 16, 1899.
Johnson, William A., LL. M., '87·
Johnson, William Carey, LL. B., '99, LL. M., '00·
Johnson, William H., LL. M., '86·
Johnston, James A., LL. B., '92.
Johnston, James M., LL. B., '95·
Johnston, Robert D., jr., LL. B., '01
　　(Lawyer) ....503 Title Guarantee Bldg., Bir-
　　　　　　　　　　　　　　　　　　mingham, Ala.
Jones, Alvah W., M. D., '91·
Jones, Benjamin C., M. D., '68·
Jones, Bennett S., LL. B., '89, LL. M., '90; deceased.
Jones, Charles M., LL. B., '97.
Jones, Charles S., LL. B., '91, LL. M., '92·
Jones, Senator Charles W., LL. D., '82; deceased.
Jones, E. S., M. D., '72·
Jones, Edward, M. D., '70·
Jones, Edwin C., LL. B., '95, LL. M., '96·
Jones, Elcon, A. M., '32·
Jones, Elwyn Thornton, LL. B., '03·
Jones, Frank A., LL. B., '96, LL. M., '97·
Jones, George Wilson, M. D., '05·
Jones, Jacobus S., LL. M., '98·
Jones, James K., LL. B., '89 (Lawyer).....621 Colorado Bldg., Wash., D. C.
Jones, John B., LL. B., '88·
Jones, Richard Henry, LL. B., '98·
Jones, Richard J., LL. B., '03·
Jones, Thomas, LL. B., '05·
Jones, William E., LL. B., '77·
Jones, William J., LL. B., '02·
Jones, Winfield, A. B., '01 (Lawyer).......Fourth National Bank Bldg., At-
　　　　　　　　　　　　　　　　　　　lanta, Ga.
Jordan, Edward L., LL. B., '96 (Editor)....515 9th St. N.W., Wash., D. C.
Jordan, James Hammer, M. D., '56·
Jordan, Llewellyn, LL. B., '89, LL. M., '90·
Jorrin, Leonardo Sorzaro, A. B., '99·
Jourdan, Arthur J., A. B., '52 (H. C. Mass); deceased 1853.
Jourdan, Charles A., Ph. D., '81·
Jouy, Joseph, M. D., '69; deceased Jan. 5, 1901.
Joyce, J. Williamson, M. D., '73·
Joyce, Joseph I., LL. B., '81·
Judd, Sylvester D., M. S., '97, Ph. D., '98; deceased 1905.
Judd, Theodore Mann, LL. B., '05
　　(Real Estate) ....602 F. St. N.W., Washington, D. C.

Julihn, Magnus L., M. D., '66·
Jullien, Cyrus, LL. B., '04, LL. M., '05
    (Lawyer) ....146 Broadway, New York City.
Junghans, John Henry, A. B., '88, A. M., '91·

Kalbfus, Samuel T., LL. B., '01·
Kalussowski, H. Corwin, M. D., '52·
Kanaley, Francis Thomas, A. B., '02.......Weedsport, N. Y.
Kane, Denis D., LL. B., '75·
Kane, Frank Anthony, A. B., '03·
Kane, Henry Victor, A. M., '00, Ph. D.,
    '01, LL. B., '02 (Atty. & Counsellor)...47 Loan and Trust Bldg., Milwau-
                                    kee, Wis.
Kappler, Charles J., LL. B., '96,
    LL. M., '97 (Lawyer)................Bond Bldg., Washington, D. C.
Karch, Charles M., LL. B., '01·
Karicofe, W. H. A., LL. B., '87·
Kathman, James A., A. M., '00, LL. B., '02·
Kauffman, Harry B., A. B., '91, M. D., '94·
Kaveney, Joseph James, M. D., '04·
Keables, Dr. T. A., M. D., '72; deceased March 2, 1902.
Kean, Thomas J., M. D., '93.
Keane, Michael Aloysius, LL. B., '01·
Keane, Michael J., LL. B., '97, LL. M.,
    '98 (Lawyer) ....412 5th St. N.W., Wash., D. C.
Kearney, George, A. B., '88, LL. B., '90,
    LL. M., '91, A. M., '91 (Librarian).....Dept. of Justice, Wash., D. C.
Kearney, Richard F., M. D., '66·
Keating, J. Percy, A. B., '75, A. M., '91
    (Lawyer) ....701 Arcade Bldg., Philadelphia, Pa.
Keating, John Joseph, LL. B., '03·
Keaton, James R., LL. B., '90·
Keegin, William C., LL. B., '91, LL. M.,
    '92 (Lawyer) ....McGill Bldg., Washington, D. C.
Keene, P. T., M. D., '70·
Keene, Walter Prince, M. D., '00·
Keith, Robert Lee, A. M., '97 (Phy-
    sician and Surgeon)................Seattle, Wash.
Keleher, Michael Joseph, A. B., '04·
Kelley, Daniel J., A. M., '73, M. D., '75·
Kelley, John J., LL. B., '97 (Lawyer).....40 W. Broad St., Tamaqua, Pa.
Kellogg, Daniel M., LL. B., '93, LL. M., '94·
Kelly, Charles B., LL. B , '96·
Kelly, Rev. Charles F., S. J., D. D., '89
    (Jesuit Priest) ....321 Willing's Alley, Phila., Pa.
Kelly, Charles M., LL. B., '97 (Lawyer)....Baltimore, Md.

Kelly, Howard Ignatius, A. B., '96
   (Theatrical) ....:............National Theater, Philà., Pa.
Kelly, James Vincent, LL. b., '99, LL. M., '00·
Kelly, Peter A., A. B., '70 (Traveling
   Salesman) ....102-104 W. Lombard St., Balti-
                                        more, Md.
Kelly, William E., LL. B., '97·
Kelso, Felix A., A. B., '89·
Kelso, Paul, LL. B., '97·
Kemp, James Finley, M. D., '98·
Kendall, William Converse, M. D., '96·
Kengla, Bernard A., LL. B., '87; de-
   ceased Feb. 18, 1891, at Washington, D. C.
Kengla, Louis A., B. S., '82, A. B., '83,
   M. D., '86; deceased 1904.
Kennedy, Beverly C., A. B., '58·
Kennedy, Charles T., M. D., '92·
Kennedy, Daniel B., A. B., '62, (H. C. Mass); Mt. Hope Retreat, Mt. Hope
                                        P. O., Md.
Kennedy, Duncan A., A. B., '34·
Kennedy, Frank P., LL. B., '97 (Presi-
   dent Newark Trust Co.)..............Newark, Ohio.
Kennedy, George S., A. B., '34·
Kennedy, John A., A. B., '40·
Kennedy, Judge Thomas H., A. B., 32.
Kennedy, William E., A. M., '32·
Kennelly, James, LL. B., '88, LL. M., '90·
Kenney, Alfred E., LL. B., '94, LL. M.,
   '95 (Lawyer).........................Parkersburg, W. Va.
Kennon, J. C. W., M. D., '57·
Kenny, Charles Borromeo, A. B., '58
   (Lawyer) ....
Kenny, Lawrence, A. B , '60; (H. C.
   Mass); deceased about 1886.
Kernan, Senator Francis, LL D., '80;
   deceased Sept. 8, 1892.
Kernan, Leslie Warnick, A. B., '86; de-
   ceased, 1903, at Utica, N. Y.
Kernan, Nicholas Edward, A. B., '03
   (Law Student) ....3 Rutger Place, Utica, N. Y.
Kernan, Thomas P., A. B., '78·
Kernan, Walter N., A. B., '85 (Lawyer)....Utica, N. Y.
Kernan, Warnick Joseph, A. B., '01
   (Lawyer) ....Utica, N. Y.
Kernan, William J., A. B., '80; deceas-
   ed Dec. 8, 1900, at Utica, N. Y.

Kerns, Francis Joseph, M. D., '03·

Kerr, Denis, LL. B., '81, LL. M., '82·

Kerrigan, George Edward, A. M., '96,
LL. B., '97, LL. M., '98·

Ketcham, Orlando E., M. D., '71·

Kett, Michael C., M. D., '04·

Kettler, Milton A., LL. B., '04·

Keyes, Dr. Edward L., jr., A. B., '92,
Ph. D., '01 (Physician)..............,109 E. 34th St., New York City.

Keyes, Francis Corey, A. B., '93·

Keys, Frank R, LL. B, '90, LL. M., '91·

Kidwell, Edgar, A. B., '86, A. M., '89,
Ph. D., '97 (Mechanical Engineer)....Dooley Bldg., Salt Lake City, Utah.

Kidwell, John W., A. B., '60, A. M., '66·

Kieckhoefer, Frank J., A. B., '68,
LL. B., '87, LL. M., '88, A. M., '89·.....148 W. 65th St., New York City.

Kiernan, Cortland A, A. B., '01 (Law-
yer) ....27 William St., New York City.

Kiggins, F. M., LL. B., '85, LL. M., '86·

Kilcullen, P. E., LL. B., '99 (Lawyer).....612 Mears Bldg., Scranton, Pa.

Kilkenny, Francis J., LL. B., '02·

Killeen, Thomas, A. B., '58 (St. Francis Xavier College, N. Y.).

Kilroy, Dr. James Joseph, M. D., '98
(Physician) ....16 I St. N.E., Washington, D. C.

Kimball, Charles O., LL. B., '92, LL. M., '93·

Kimball, E. S., M. D., '66·

Kincaid, Douglas F, M. D., '91·

King, Alexius S, LL. B., '78·

King, Claude F., LL. B., '89, LL. M., '90·

King, Edwin F., A. B., '51, A. M., '55·

King, George Sherman, LL. B., '99, LL. M., '00.

King, J. T., M. D., '94·

King, John F., A. B., '52·

King, Michael H., LL. B., '97·

King, Thomas B., A. B., '52, A. M., '60.

Kingsbury, Albert D., M. D., '69·

Kingsley, Hiram A., LL. B., '93 (U. S.
Special Pension Examiner)..........P. O. Box 353, Topeka, Kans.

Kingston, A. T. Y., M. D., '02·

Kinsell, Tyson, LL. B., '05·

Kinyoun, Joseph J., Ph. D., '96.

Kirby, John Joseph, A. M., '98, LL. B.,
'99, LL. M., '00 (Lawyer)..............32 Nassau St., New York City.

Kirby, Maurice Brown, A. B., '98
(Journalist) ....New York Theater Bldg., New
York City.

Kirby, Thomas, jr., LL. B., '05 (Jour-
    nalist) ....The Post, Washington, D. C.
Kirkpatrick, John L., A. B., '43.
Kirtland, Michael, LL. B., '92.
Kitch, James Barbour, LL. B., '05....1827 18th St. N.W., Washington, D. C.
Kitchin, Edgar M., LL. B., '99 (Lawyer)...602 F St. N.W., Washington, D. C.
Klein, Anthony Eller, M. D., '00 (Phy-
    sician and Surgeon)..................168 National Ave., Corona, N. Y.
Kleinschmidt, Charles H. A., M. D., '62,
    Ph. D., '89; deceased 1905.
Kleinschmidt, Harry C., LL. B., '02
    (Clerk) ....3066 M St. N.W., Wasn., D. C.
Klinger, David B., LL. B., '93, LL. M., '94.
Klopfer, Walter H., LL. B., '91, LL. M.,'92.
Knight, Henry E., LL. B., '84, LL. M., '85.
Knight, Hervey S., LL. B., '88.........McGill Bldg., Washington, D. C.
Knight, Joseph Sheridan, LL. B., '03
    (Seminarian) ....St. Charles College, Ellicott City,
                                        Md.
Knight, William E., LL. B., '91.
Knighton, Nicholas S., A. B., '45; deceased.
Knowlan, Dominic F., A. B., '90; de-
    ceased July, 1899.
Kober, George Martin, M. D., '73 (Dean
    Georgetown University Medical
    Department) ....920 H St. N.W,. Washington, D. C.
Koch, Adolph A., LL. B., '02.
Kolipinski, Louis, M. D., '83 (Physi-
    cian) ....631 I St. N.W., Wash., D. C.
Koonce, Claude J., M. D., '96.
Koentz, Clarke, A. B., '51.
Kopmeier, Norman J., LL. B., '05 (Ice
    Merchant) ....234 Wells Bldg., Milwaukee, Wis.
Kram, Charles A., LL. B., '92, LL. M.,
    '93 (Law Clerk)....................Auditor of Post-office, Post-office
                                        Department, Wash., D. C.
Krantz, John A., jr., LL. B., '04.
Krebs, Conrad, LL. B., '92 (Merchant)....Salem, Oreg.
Krichelt, Frederick W., LL. B., '99,
    LL. M., '00 (Clerk)................War Dept., Washington, D. C.
Kuehn, Otto Frederick, D. D. S., '05.
Kuhn, James O'Reilly, A. B., '99, LL. B., '02.
Kuhn, John Frederick, M. D., '01.
Kuhn, Joseph Aloysius, A. B., '02.

Laboule, John F., LL. B., '85·

Lacey, Anderson B., LL. B., '89 (L'y'r)....Pacific Bldg., Washington, D. C.

Lacson, Roman J., Ph. L., '02, Ph. D.,
    '03, LL. B., '04 (Lawyer)..............88 Santo Thomas, Manila, P. I.

Lacy, Eugene B., LL. B., '93, LL. M., '9).

Lafferty, Daniel L., A. B., '64·

Lafferty, Francis P. S., A. B., '65·

Lagarde, Ernest, A. M., '69·

LaGrange, Ernest H., LL. B., '88, LL. M., '89·

Lamar, George H., LL. B., '89, LL. M.,
    '90 (Lawyer)........................Fendall Bldg., Wash., D. C.

Lamar, Lucius Q. C., LL. B., '95·

Lamar, William H., Jr., LL. B., '84,
    LL. M., '85 (Lawyer)................Rockville, Md.

Lamb, Daniel S., M. D., '67 (Physician)....Army Med. Museum, Wash., D. C.

Lamb, William James, M. D., '03·

Lambert, Wilton J., LL. B., '93, LL. M.,
    '94 (Lawyer) ....410 5th St. N.W., Wash., D. C.

Lambert, Tallmadge A., A. B., '62, A.
    M., '71, LL. D., '94.................410 5th St. N.W., Wash., D. C.

Lamkin, Griffin, LL. M., '01 (Lawyer).....411-412 Title Guarantee Bldg.,
                                    Birmingham, Ala.

Lancaster, C. C., A. B., '74, LL. B., '76·

Lancaster, Rev. Clement S., S. J., A. B.,
    '59 (Jesuit Priest)....................Leonardtown, Md.

Lancaster, Dr. F. M., A. B., '51, A. M.,
    '57, M. D., '57; deceased.

Lancaster, Francis A., A. B., '57·

Lancaster, George D., LL. B., '86, LL. M., '87·

Landa, Gabriel M., A. B., '77·

Landry, Anatole, A. B., '60·

Landry, L. Valery, A. B., '48·

Landry, Prosper R., A. B., '46·

Lang, Charles J., M. D., '87·

Lang, Henry J., A. B., '40; deceased.

Langan, Raymond Charles, LL. B., '95
    (Lawyer) ....Clinton, Iowa.

Langley, John W., LL. M., '94 (L'y'r).....Census Office, Wash., D. C.

Lannon, John David, A. B., '94..........32 Nassau St., New York City.

Lanston, Aubrey, LL. B., '99 (Novelist
    and Playwright......................Care Tolbert Lanston, 1101 O St.
                                      N.W., Washington, D. C.

Lantry, Thomas B., A. B., '89 (L'y'r).....537-539 The Rookery, Chicago, Ill.

Laphen, James S., A. B., '37·

Laplace, Albert J., A. B., '79·

Laplace, Dr. Ernest, A. B., '80, A. M.,
    '87, LL. D., '95 (Surgeon)............1828 S. Rittenhouse Sq., Phila., Pa.

Lapretre, J. B. Adrien, A. B., '49·
Larcombe, James A., LL. B., '88, LL. M., '89·
LaRoche, Dr. C. Percy de, A. B., '53, A. M., '61·
Lastrappes, Ludger, A. B., '51 (H. C.,
    Mass.) (Merchant)...................Louisiana.
Latham, Benjamin F., M. D., '76·
Latham, Charles L, LL. B., '04·
Latham, Samuel B., LL. B., '85' LL. M., '37·
Lathrop, John P., LL. B., '74·
Latimer, E. F., D. D. S., '02·
Latshaw, Henry J., Ph. B., '85 (Lawyer)...838 N. Y. Life Bldg., Kansas City
                                            Mo.
Latshaw, Ralph S., A. B., '85·
Laughborough, L. H., Ph. B., '87 (Ag-
    riculturalist) ....Bethesda, Md.
Laughlin, John Edward, A. B., '00
    (Lawyer) ....Fidelity Bldg., Pittsburg, Pa.
Laumont, Henry B., A. B., '48·
Lauve, Louis L., A. B., '01 (Employer,
    Old Dominion Copper Mining and
    Smelting Co.).....................Globe, Ariz.
Lavalle, Don Jose Antonio de, A. M., '69·
Lavin, James P., LL. B., '94' LL. M.,
    '96 (U. S. Immigrant Inspector)..
Lawler, Hon. Dan. W., A. B, '81' A. M.,....Seattle, Wash.
    '89' LL. D., '97·
Lawler, Francis J., A. B, '85; deceased
    1890, at Prairie du Chien, Wis.
Lawler, Joseph C., A. B., '85·
Lawler, Thomas C., A. B., '79·
Lawrence, James B., M. D., '73·
Lawton, John M., LL. B., '86' LL. M., '87·
Leach, Hamilton E., M. D., '72·
Leahy, John Stephen, A. M., '95' LL.
    B., '96 (Lawyer).....................Carleton Bldg., St. Louis, Mo.
Leahy, Rev. Michael David, A. B., '92
    (Priest) ....35 Raymond Ave., Shelby, Ohio.
Leary, Francis Paul, LL. B., '04 (L'y'r)....610 13th St. N.W., Wash., D. C.
Leary, Robert J., LL. B., '99·
LeBoeuf, Peter George, A. B., '96·
Leckie, A. E. Lloyd, LL. B., '94' LL.
    M., '95 (Lawyer).....................Fendall Bldg., Wash., D. C.
Leckie, Richard, LL. B., '92·
LeComte, S. B., M. D., '68·
LeCouteulx, Louis, A. B, '49·
Lee, Albert James, LL. B., '03·

Lee, Arthur, A. B., '67; deceased, April
    12, 1899, at St. Louis, Mo.
Lee, Chapman, M. D., '66·
Lee, F. D., M. D., '94·
Lee, Orr W., LL. B., '89, LL. M., '90·
Legare, George S , LL. B., '92·
Legendre, Adolphus, A. B., '25·
Lehmann, Frederick A., LL. B., '75.
Lennon, Joseph Arthur, A. M., '03........86 South St., Jamaica Plain, Bos-
                                      ton, Mass.
Lennon, Leo Camillo, A. M., '00, Ph.
    D., '01 (Lawyer)....................4 Sutter St., San Francisco, Cal.
Lennon, Milton Byrne, A. M., '98
    (Physician) ....918 Eddy St., San Francisco, Cal.
Leonard, John D., LL. B., '92, LL. M., '93·
Leonard, Richard B , D. D. S., '03·
Lett, Frederick R., A. B.,, '86; deceased
    Sept. 14, 1900.
Lever, Asbury Frank, LL. B., '99·
Levey, A. L., M. D., '94·
Lewis, Fielding, LL. B., '89, LL. M., '90·
Lewis, J. Edward, LL. B., '97, LL. M.,
    '98 (Lawyer).........................617 E St. N.W., Washington, D. C.
Lewis, James P., M. D., '78·
Lewis, William H., LL B., '87, LL. M.,
    '88 (Principal Examiner).............General Land Office, Wash., D. C.
Lewis, William H., A. B., '40·
Liebermann, Charles D., LL. B., '77·
Lieuallen, William Grant, LL. B., '99·
Lilly, Samuel M., A. B., '42.
Lincoln, John Ledyard, A. B., '81, A.
    M., '89...............................First National Bank Building,
                                      Cincinnati, Ohio.
Lindsay, Davi? R., M. D., '60·
Linn, Samuel F., M. D., '76·
Linnehan, George Albert, M. D., '04
    (Physician) ....352 Fulton St., Jamaica, N. Y.
Linney, Romulus Zachariah, M. D., '01·
Little, John J., M. D , '71·
Littlewood, James B., M. D., '68·
Litzinger, Lewis P., LL. B., '02, LL. M., '03.
Lloyd, George H., A. B., '50 (H. C.,
    Mass.) (Merchant)...................74 W. Cottage St., Boston, Mass.
Lobit, Joseph, jr., A. B., '99·
Lochboehler, George J , M. D , '89
Locke, Herbert M., LL. B., '94, LL. M., '95.

Logan, Alonzo T., LL. B., '88, LL. M.,
Logan, Eugene Adolphus, LL. B., '98,
   LL. M., '99 (Clerk)...............

Long, Charles A., LL. B., '01.
Long, Elia A. C., LL. B., '01, LL. M., '0
Long, William, M. D., '87.
Longshaw, Luther M., LL. M., '87.
Longstreth, John Cook, A. B., '47, A.
Longuemare, Eugene, A. B., '54.
Looby, Patrick W., LL. B., '03.
Loomes, Lalas L., M. D., '57.
Loomis, L. C., M. D., '63.
Lordan, John J., LL. B., '95, LL. M., '9
Loughborough, Alexander H., A. B., '5
   28, 1897.
Loughran, John M., LL. B., '05 (Com-
   positor) ....
Loughran, Joseph E., LL. B., '01 (Lawy
Loughran, Patrick H., LL. B., '96 (Spe-
   cial Agent) ....
Lovelace, Robert, A. B., '59.
Lovett, John W., LL. B., '72.
Lowe, E. Louis, LL. D., '53 (ex-Gover
Lowe, Enoch M., A. B., '52; deceased,
Lowe, Francis M., LL. B., '93, LL. M.,
Lowe, Louis, LL. B., '05...............
Lowe, Thomas F., M. D., '02 (Physician
Lowrie, H. H., M. D., '63.
Lozano, Charles I., LL. B., '99, LL. M.,
Luby, Emanuel S., LL. B., '98, LL. M.,
   '99 (Bookbinder).................

Lucas, Charles, M. D., '93.
Luce, Dr. Charles Roscoe, M. D., '85
   (Physician) ....
Luckett, Oliver A., A. B., '39; deceased,
Luckey, Nelson E., LL. B., '94, LL. M.,
Lusk, Hall Stoner, A. B., '04.
Luthy, John H., LL. B., '97 (Clerk)...
Luttrell, Walter M., M. D., '93.
Lyden, Michael J., LL. B., '95, LL. M.,
Lyles, D. C., A. B., '68, A. M., '71.
Lynch, Edward A., A. B., '22, A. M., '3
Lynch, Rev. James, A. M., '28.
Lynch, James D., A. M., '93.
Lynch, John G., A. B., '24

ynch, Rt. Rev. Mgr. James S. M., D.
   D., '89.............................St. John's Church, Utica, Oneida
                                       County, N. Y.
ynch, Rev. Joseph Thomas, A. B., '02
   (Priest) ....South Hadley Falls, Mass.
ynch, Patrick H., A. B., '77·
ynch, Patrick Michael, M. D., '01.
ynch, William D., A. B., '86; deceased, 1888.
ynch, Captain W. F., U. S. N., A. M., '44; deceased, Oct. 17, 1865.
ynch, William Francis, A. B., '04
   (Medical Student)...................29 Lake St., E. Weymouth, Mass.
yon, Francis, LL. B., '89, LL. M., '90·
yon, Rutherford B. H., LL. B., '99,
   LL. M., 1900 (Lawyer)...............1416 F St. N.W., Washington, D. C.
yon, Simon, LL. B., '90, LL. M., '91
   (Lawyer) ....1416 F St. N.W., Washington, D. C.
yon, William B., M. D., '67·
yons, Hilary Herbert, A. M., 1900.
yons, Thomas H., A. B., '85·

abrey, Richard L., LL. B., '96·
acdonald, Alexander A., M. D., '95·
Macdonald, Clarence J., A. M., '97·
Macdonald, Martin A., LL. B., '93, LL. M., '94·
MacDonald, Michael R., M. D., '95.
MacDonald, Thomas H., A. M., '97
   (Physician) ....Port Hawkesburg, Nova Scotia.
Machen, Francis Stanislaus, M. D., '01·
Mackall, Bruce McVean, M. D., '03·
Mackall, James McV., A. B., '70, A. M.,
   '73, M. D., '73 (Physician)...........1203 31st St. N.W., Wash., D. C.
MacKaye, Harold Steele, LL. B., '91,
   LL. M., '91 (Patent Lawyer)........119 Nassau St., New York City.
Mackey, Beekford, LL. B., '83·
Mackey, Crandal, LL. B., '89 (Lawyer)....416 5th St. N.W., Wash., D. C.
Mackin, Very Rev. Dean Thomas, V. G., A. B., '71, A. M., '89; deceased, Feb.
   15, 1905.
Mackley, Arthur R., LL. B., '04, LL. M., '05·
MacMahon, Paul William Arthur, A.
   B., '98·............................Room 1012, 8 Bridge St., New York
                                       City.
MacMahon, Thomas, jr., A. B., 1900.
Macnamee, Arthur Munson, M. D., '98·
MacShane, Col. James, A. M., '58.
Mandan, Philip A., A. B., '58.

Maddox, George Edmonson, LL. B,
   '99 (Lawyer)..................... ...Rome, Ga.
Madeira, Francis P., LL. B , '96·
Madigan, Albert W., A. B., '72· A. M.,'89·.Houlton, Me.
Madigan, James C., A M., '50·
Madigan, Hon. John B , A. B., '83· A.
   M , '89 (Lawyer)..................... Houlton, Me.
Madison, B. F , M. D , '84·
Magale, Joseph F., A. B , '91; deceased.
Magee, M. D'Arcey, M. D., '96......... ...1355 Corcoran St., Wash., D. C.
Magie, Edward R., LL. M , '99·
Maginnis, Charles B., A. B., '62 (H. C., Mass.); deceased, July 6, 1867.
Maginnis, Charles H., LL. B., '92·
Magruder, Caleb C , jr., LL. B , '97
   (Teller) ....U S Treasury Dept , Wash., D.
Magruder, Caleb C., A. M , '34·
Magruder, Caleb Clarke, A. B , '58· A.
   M., '61 (Lawyer)................... Upper Marlboro, Md.
Magruder, George Lloyd, M. D , '70· A.
   M , '71 (Physician)...................4 Jackson Place, Lafayette Squar
                                   Washington, D. C.
Magruder, Mercer Hampton, LL. B , '98
   (Lawyer) ....Upper Marlboro, Md.
Maguire, Charles F., jr., LL. B., '05
   (Law Student)................... ...Hornellsville, N. Y.
Maguire, Dominic, A. B., '52 (H. C., Mass).
Maguire, Dominic, A. M., '58·
Maguire, Francis S., LL. B , '04· LL.
   M., '05 (Lawyer) ....908 G St N.W , Washington, D.
Maguire, Joseph I , LL B., '05·
Mahoney, Ed. Joseph, A. M., '93· M. D.,'95.
Mahoney, John J., LL B., '03
Mahoney, Daniel W., LL. B., '02 (Law-
   yer) ....412 Bay State Building, Lawrenc
                 •   Mass.
Mahoney, William F., LL. B., '96 (Clerk)..Gov. Printing Office, Wash., D.
Major, Daniel G., A. M., '59; deceased.
Major, Henry, A. B., '64· A. M., '66.......45 Broadway, New York City.
Major, John J., A. B., '64· A. M., '72; deceased, 1889.
Malcolm, Dr. Granville, M. D., '67
   (Real Estate and Loans)............Denver, Colo.
Mallan, Thomas F., M. D., '80·
Mallory, Hon. Stephen R , A. B., '69·
   A. M., '71· LL. D., '04 (Lawyer
   and U. S. Senator from Florida)......Pensacola, Fla.
Malone, Henry D , A. B., '85· LL. B., '87· LL. M., '88· A. M., '88·

Malone, John, M. D., '56·

Malony, John M., M. D., '70·   .

Malony, William Reufield Proctor, LL.

    B , '03, LL. M., '04 (Lawyer).........47 Cedar St., New York City.

Mangan, Michael F , LL. B., '03, LL.

    M., '05 (Lawyer);.....................Century Bldg., Washington, D. C.

Mangan, William J , LL. B., '97·

Manly, Clement, A. B., '76·

Mann, Harry E., A. M., '89............ ...100 E. Lexington St., Balto., Md.

Manning, John N., LL. M., '86·

Manogue, William H., LL. B., '86

    (Lawyer) ....·.......402 6th St. N.W., Wash., D. C.

Mansell, Edward R, M. D., '88·

Marble, John O., M D., '68·

Marbury, Charles C , M. D., '93·

Marbury, William, A. B., '43; deceased, Dec. 18, 1879.

Marcy, William L., LL B., '85, LL. M., '86·

Markey, James F., LL. B., '01·

Markriter, John J., M. D., '82·

Marmion, William Vincent, A. M., '83

    (Physician) ....·...................1110 8th St. N.W., Wash., D. C.

Maroney, Edward B., LL. M., '92·

Marple, Raleigh W.. LL. B , '95·

Marr, Samuel S., M. D., '76·

Marshall, George, A. B., '44·

Marshall, John F., A. B., '59·

Marshall, P. J., D. D. S., '02·

Marshall, Percival H., LL. B., '95, LL. M., '96·

Marshall, T. W. M , LL. D., ,2; deceased, Dec. 14, 1877, at Surrey, England.

Marstelleo, Massillon H , LL. B., '74·

Martell, Charles J , LL B., '99, LL. M.,

    1900 ....1119 Barrister's Hall, Boston,

                                       Mass.

Martin, F P , jr , LL. B., '83 (Lawyer)....128 Walnut St., Johnstown, Pa.

Martin, James J , A. B., '01·

Martin, James O , A. B., '59·

Martin, John H., LL. B., '90, LL. M., '91·

Martin, Hon. John M , A. M., '91, LL. D., '94; deceased.

Martin, John T., LL. B., '82·

Martin, Robert H., LL. B., '94, LL. M.,

    '95 (Clerk).........................U. S Treasury Dept., Wash., D. C.

Martin, Walter Stanislaus, A. B., '96......916 Market St., San Francisco, Cal.

Martinson, Joseph E , LL. B., '96, LL. M., '97·

Martyn, Francis G , LL. B., '90· LL. M., '91·

Mason, E., A B., '23·

Mason, Hugh L., LL. B., '73·

Mason, John E., M. D., '68·

Masterson, Daniel Stephen, LL. B., '02, LL. M., '03,

Matthews, William, LL. B., '05·

Mattingly, Francis Carroll, LL. B., '97, LL. M., '98·

Mattingly, Joseph Carbery, A. B., '93,
LL. B, '95, LL. M., '96 (Lawyer)........Fendall Bldg., Washington, D. C.

Mattingly, Leonard H., LL. B., '98, LL.
M., 1900 (Expert Accountant).........Office of the Comptroller of the
Treasury, Washington, D. C.

Mattingly, Robert E., LL. B., '91, LL.
M., '92 (Lawyer)....................472 La. Ave. N.W., Wash., D. C.

Maury, Matthew F., U. S. N., A. M., '45; deceased, Feb. 1, 1873, at Lexington,
Va.

Mauss, Richard G., M. D., '72·

Maxey, James H., LL. M., '02 (Lawyer)....Shawnee, Okla. Ter.

Mayer, Robert Daniel, M. D., '95·

Mayo, George Upshur, A. M., '89; deceased, Feb. 3, 1896.

McAleer, John Hugh, A. B., '98·

McAleer, Joseph Leo, A. B., 1900, A.
M., '01, Ph. D., '05 (Lawyer).........710 North American Building,
Philadelphia, Pa.

McAleer, William, jr., A. B., '98·

McAllister, Richard, jr., LL. B., '73; deceased.

McAnerney, Frank Bernard, A. B., '98
(Real Estate)......................500 5th Ave., New York City.

McArdle, Thomas E., M. D., '79 (Phy-
sician) ....1604 19th St. N.W., Wash., D. C.

McAuley, John, A. B., '55 (St. F. X., N. Y.).

McBlair, J. Hollins, jr., M. D., '69·

McBride Charles R., LL. B., '92, LL. M., '93·

McBride, Parks R., LL. B., '94, LL. M., '95·

McCabe, John, A. B., '49 (H. C., Mass.) (Merchant); deceased, in Providence,
R. I.

McCahill, Edwin, A. B., '65, A. M., '67; deceased, Oct. 23, 1878, at New Brunswick, N. J.

McCall, Robert S., LL. B., '89, LL. M.,
'90 (Special Examiner)...............United States Pension Bureau,
Newark, N. J.

McCardle, Battle, LL. B., '94, LL. M., '96.

McCarthy, Charles C., A. B., '05 (Law
Student) ....Harvard Univ., Cambridge, Mass.

McCarthy, Daniel Joseph, A. B, '95·
A. M., '99, M. D., '99 (Physician).....Davenport, Iowa.

McCarthy, James C., A. B., '52·

McCarthy, John J., LL. B., '99, LL. M., 1900.

McCarthy, John Linus, D. D. S., '03.

McCarthy, William T., LL. B., '93.

McCauley, Francis Harney, A. M., '99·

McCauley, Joseph A., M. D., '72·

McChesney, Charles E., M. D., '67·

McClellan, Frederick F., LL. B., '04
(Lawyer) ....123 1-2 W. Main St., Muncie, Ind.

McCloskey, Felix R., LL. B., '92·

McCloskey, Very Rev. George, D. D., '89; deceased, Aug. 3, 1890.

McCloskey, Very Rev. John, D. D., '75; deceased, Dec. 24, 1880.

McCloskey, Joseph J., LL. B., '85·

McCloskey, William C., LL. B., '93, LL. M., '94·

McCloskey, William J., A. B., '89·

McClure, James, A. B., '85, M. D., '99·

McCole, Thomas A., LL. B., '02 (Law-
yer) ....170 Broadway, New York City.

McComas, Hon. Louis E., LL. D., '02......1628 K St. N.W., Wash., D. C.

McConnell, Frank Stevenson, D. D. S., '04·

McConnell, James C., M. D., '68·

McCormick, Charles, M. D., '61·

McCormick, John Joseph, M. D., '04·

McCoy, Edward A., A. B., 1900.

McCoy, George, M. D., '57·

McCoy, Joseph S., LL. B., '93, LL. M., '94.

McCoy, Washington J., M. D., '80·

McCreedy, Dr. Jeremiah, A. B., '24, A. M., '32·

McCullough, Frisby H., LL. B., '89·

McCullough, Henry L., A. B., '63·

McDermott, Francis Borgia, A. B., '96·

McDermott, John A., A. B., '84·

McDermott, Thomas Joseph, A. M., '96
(Priest) ....618 Main St., Paterson, N. J.

McDevitt, William M., LL. B., '94, LL. M., '95·

McDonald, Allen C., LL. B., '96, LL.
M., '97 (Lawyer)....................Kuhn's Building, Dayton, Ohio.

McDonald, James C., LL. M., '92·

McDonald, Richard Francis, D. D. S., '05.

McDonald, Thomas Benton, M. D., '95·

McDonnell, Rev. Eugene de L., S. J.,
A. B., '85 (Jesuit Priest).............Gonzaga College, Wash., D. C.

McDonogh, James S., LL. B., '01 (Law-
yer) ....44 Broadway, New York City.

McDonough, Francis Patrick, A. B., '93·

McDonough, Francis Xavier, LL. B.,
'05 (Lawyer).......................512 F St. N.W., Washington, D. C.

McDonough, James A., A. B., '63 (H. C., Mass.) (Physician).

Madison, B. F..............M. D., '84
Physician,
417 B St S. E, Washington, D. C.

Magale, Joseph F..........A. B, '91
Deceased.

Magee, M. D'Arcey.........M. D., '96
1355 Corcoran St., Wash, D. C.

Magie, Edward R..........LL. M.,'99
Law Clerk,
Dept. of Com. and Labor, Wash, D. C.

Maginnis, Charles B........A B., '62
H. C, Mass., Deceased, July 6, 1867.

Maginnis, Charles H.........LL. B, '92

Magruder, Caleb C, Jr......LL. B, '97
Clerk,
U. S. Treasury Dept., Wash, D. C.

Magruder, Caleb C..........A. M., '34
Deceased.

Magruder, Caleb Clarke......A. B, '58
Lawyer,   A. M, '61
Clerk of Maryland Court of Appeals,
Com. Nat. Bank Bldg, Wash, D C.

Magruder, George Lloyd.....M. D, '70
Physician, G. U. Med. Fac, A M., '71
Stoneleigh Court, Washington, D. C.

Magruder, Mercer Hampton, LL. B, '98
Lawyer,
Upper Marlboro, Md.

Maguire, Charles F., Jr......LL. B., '05
Lawyer,   LL. M,'06
Hornell, N. Y.

Maguire, Dominic...........A. B, '52
H. C., Mass., Deceased.   A. M, '58

Maguire, Dominic...........A. M., 58

Maguire, Francis S.........LL. B., '04
Lawyer,   LL. M.,'05
908 G St. N. W., Washington, D C.

Maguire, Joseph I..........LL. B., '05
1376 V St, Washington, D. C.

Maguire, Robert F..........LL B, '09
, Toled, Ohio.

Maher, Benedict F..........A. B, '97
Augusta, Me.

Mahoney, Ed. Joseph........A. M, '93
Physician,   M. D., '95
250 Maple St, Holyoke, Mass.

Mahoney, John J............LL B, '03

Mahoney, Matthew P.......A. B., '06
Medical Student.
46 Butterfield St, Lowell, Mass.

Mahony, Daniel W..........LL B, '02
Lawyer,
505 Bay State Bldg, Lawrence, Mass

Mahony, William F.........LL. B., '96
Patent Lawyer,
1203 Girard St. N. W., Wash, D. C.

Major, Daniel G............A. M., '59
Deceased.

Major, Henry..............A. B, '64
Lawyer,   A. M., '66
45 Broadway, New York City.

Major, John J..............A. B, '64
Deceased, 1889   A M, '72

Malabre, Alfred L..........M. D., '08
Physician,
603 West 184th St, New York City.

Malcom, Dr. Granville ......M. D, '67
Real Estate and Loans,
700 Ernest-Cranner Bldg., Denver, Col.

Mallan, Thomas F..........M. D., '80
Physician,
820 Conn. Ave. N. W., Wash., D. C.

Mallory, Hon. Stephen R....A. B, '69
                        A. M, '71, LL. D., '04
Deceased, Dec 23, 1907, while U. S.
Senator from Fla.....Pensacola, Fla.

Malone, E. Halsey..........LL. B., '08
Lawyer,
24 Broad St, New York City.

Malone, Henry D., A. B., '85, LL. B., '87
Lawyer,   LL. M., '88, A. M., '88
336 Adams St. N. E., Wash., D. C.

Malone, James B............LL. B., '06
Lawyer,
Fairbanks Bldg, Springfield, Ohio.

Malone, John...............M. D., '56
Physician,
Dundee, N. Y.

Maloney, John M...........M. D., '07
Physician and Surgeon,
559 Liberty St., Springfield, Mass.

Malony, John M............M. D., '70

Malony, William Redfield Proctor,
Lawyer,   LL. B, '03, LL. M., '04
47 Cedar St, New York City.

Mandan, Philip A..........A. B., '58

Mangan, Michael F.........LL. B, '03
Lawyer,   LL. M., '05
412 5th St N. W., Washington, D. C.

Mangan, William J.........LL. B., '97

Manly, Clement............A. B, '76
Lawyer,
Winston, N. C.

Mann, George M............LL. B., '07
Lawyer,
612 F St. N W.; Wash., D. C.

Mann, Harry E.............A. M , '89
Lawyer,
100 E. Lexington St., Baltimore, Md

Manning, John N..........LL M ,'86
Clerk,
War Dept., Washington, D. C.

Manogue, William H.......LL B , '86
Lawyer,
509 E. Capitol St , Washington, D. C.

Mansell, Edward R , Hon...M. D , '88
England.

Manson, C. Farraud.........LL. B , '09
Canton, So. Dak.

Marble, John O.............M. D , '68
Physician,
16 Murray Ave , Worcester, Mass

Marbury, Charles C.........M D , '93
Physician, G. U. Med. Fac,
1015 16th St. N. W., Wash, D. C

Marbury, William............A. B , '43
Deceased, Dec. 18, 1879.

Marcy, William L...........LL. B , '85
LL. M., '86

Markey, James F...........LL. B , '01
Clerk,
1413 5th St. N. W., Wash, D. C.

Markriter, John J...........M. D , '82
Deceased, July 13, 1891, Wash , D. C.

Marmion, William Vincent..A. M., '83
Physician,
1211 13th St. N. W., Wash, D C

Maroney, Edward B.........LL. M ,'92

Marple, Raleigh W..........LL. B , '95

Marr, Samuel S.............M D , '76
1318 Corcoran St , Wash, D. C.

Marsden, Francis Thomas....A. B , '09
472 E St. S. W., Washington, D. C.

Marshall, Cary A.......... LL. B., '07
Lawyer,
Markham, Va.

Marshall, George...........A. B., '44

Marshall, John P..........A B , '59
Deceased.

Marshall, P. J.............D D. S ,'02

Marshall, Percival H.......LL. B , '95
Lawyer, LL M., '96
Columbian Bldg , Wash., D. C.

Marshall, T. W. M.........LL. D , '72
Deceased, Dec. 14, 1877, Surrey, Eng.

Marshell, Cloud ....LL. B , '08
Special Agent,
Interstate Commerce Commission,
Wash, D. C.

Marstelleo, Massillon H.....LL B , '74

Martell, Charles J..........LL. B , '99
Lawyer, LL. M.,'00
1101-2 Barrister's Hall, Boston, Mass.

Martell, Leon Alphonse.....M. D., '08
Physician,
389 Front St , Weymouth, Mass.

Martin, F. P., Jr...........LL. B., '83
Lawyer,
Johnstown, Pa.

Martin, Frederick R........LL. B., '09
Anniston, Ala.

Martin, James J.............A. B., '01

Martin, James O............A. B., '59
Deceased.

Martin, John H............LL. B, '90
Lawyer, LL. M.,'91
Fendall Bldg., Washington, D. C.

Martin, Hon. John M.......A. M., '91
Deceased. LL. D., '94

Martin, John T.............LL. B., '82
Lawyer,
Williams Bldg., Scranton, Pa.

Martin, Robert H..........LL. B., '94
Clerk, LL. M.,'95
U. S. Treasury Dept., Wash., D. C.

Martin, Villard.............LL. B., '08
Lawyer,
Muskogee, Okla.

Martin, Walter Stanislaus...A. B., '96
Claus Spreckels Bldg.,
San Francisco, Cal.

Martinson, Joseph E........LL. B , '96
LL. M.,'97

Martyn, Francis G..........LL. B, '90
LL. M.,'91

Mason, E...................A. B., '23
Deceased.

Mason, Hugh L.............LL. B., '73

Mason, John E.............M. D., '68

Masterson, Daniel Stephen...LL. B., '02
Private Secretary, LL. M.,'03
The Rochambeau, Wash., D. C.

Matthews, William.........LL. B., '05
Law Clerk, LL. M ,'07
Treasury Dept., Wash., D. C.

Mattingly, Charles M.......LL. B., '07
Lawyer,
Columbian Bldg , Wash., D. C.

Mattingly, Francis Carroll...LL. B., '97
Deceased, Mch. 5, 1908, LL. M ,'98
Washington, D. C.

Mattingly, Joseph Carbery...A. B., '93
Lawyer, LL. B., '95, LL. M.,'96
Fendall Bldg , Washington, D. C.

McRae, Irwin C., LL. B., '96 (Timber-
man) ....Calvert, Ala.
McSheehy, Thomas, LL. B., '84·
McSherry, James, A. B., '33.
McSherry, William D., A. B., '42·
McSorley, Charles D., LL. B., '92, LL. M., '93.
McVary, Stephen A., M. D., '80·
Mead, F. W., M. D., '58·
Mead, Theodore, M. D., '69·
Mellen, Edward L., B. S., '81·
Melville, George Wallace, LL. D., '99
(Rear Admiral).....................615 Walnut St., Philadelphia, P.
Mercer, Claude, LL. B., '96 (Lawyer).....Hardinsburg, Ky.
Mercier, Hon. Honore, LL. D., '89·
Meredith, Edward C., jr., LL. B., '99.
Menke, John B., M. D., '80; deceased, Sept. 30, 1882.
Merrick, Richard T., LL. B., '96, LL. M., '97·
Merrick, Richard T., LL. D., '73; deceased, June 23, 1885.
Merrick, Col. William D., A. M., '31·
Merrick, Hon. William M., LL. D., '75; deceased, Feb. 4, 1889.
Merrill, H. Clay, LL. B., '91, LL. M., '92.
Merritt, Addis D., LL. B., '87, LL. M., '88·
Merritt, Edgar Bryant, LL. B., '98·
Merrow, David W., LL. B., '87, LL. M.,
'90 (Lawyer).........................Omaha, Nebr.
Meyer, Robert, LL. B., '01·
Meyerhardt, Louis, LL. B., '86·
Metzger, Percy, LL. B., '88, LL. M., '89
(Lawyer) ....472 La. Ave. N. W., Wash., D.
Meyers, William F., LL. B., '91, LL.
M., '92 (Assistant Secretary).........District Commissioner, Washing-
ton, D. C.
Michener, Algernon S., LL. B., '93, LL. M., '94·
Middleton, Johnson V. D., M. D., '55·
Miles, Matthew James, A. M., '98
(Lawyer) ....305 1st Ave., Cedar Rapids, Iow
Millard, Edward M., A. B., '32; deceased, 1882, at Grand Coteau, La.
Miller, Charles A., LL. B., '96.
Miller, Charles Colden, A. B., '04·
Miller, Charles H., M. D., '72·
Miller, James, M. D., '99 (Physician)......Congo, Perry County, Ohio.
Miller, James E., LL. B., '75·
Miller, James H., LL. B., '97, LL. M., '98·
Miller, John S., M. D., '65·
Miller, Joseph Zachary, III, A. B., '04.....Belton, Tex.
Miller, Samuel F., LL. D., '72.

iller, W. W., M. D., '69·
iller, Wilbur G., LL. B., '04·
illrick, Daniel A., LL. B., '04, LL. M.,
'05 ....617 F St. N. W., Washington, D. C.
ills, Charles A., LL. B., '89, LL. M.,'90.
ills, Ellis, LL. B., '87, LL. M., '88.
Miner, Francis Hannibal, M. D., '95·
Minnick, W. H. H., M. D., '73·
Minor, Louis J., LL. B., '99·
Mitchell, Charles Piquette, A. B., '93,
LL. B., '96 (Lawyer).................War Dept., Washington, D. C.
Mitchell, George D., LL. B., '89, LL. M., '90·
Mitchell, Herbert Francis, LL. B., '04
(Clerk) ....Civil Service Commission, 8th and
E Sts. N. W., Wash., D. C.
Mitchell, Richard Clarke, A. M., '97.......Care Robert Mitchell Furniture
Company, Cincinnati, Ohio.
Mitchell, William Ansel, LL. B., '94
(Editor and Publisher)..............Columbus, Kans.
Mitchell, William M., M. D., '70·
Mock, James K., LL. B., '97 (Clerk).......General Land Office, Wash., D. C.
Mohrman, Henry Joseph, A. M., '02
(Real Estate).......................216 Wainwright Building, St.
Louis, Mo.
Mohun, Barry, LL. B., '96, LL. M., '97
(Lawyer) ....1414 F St. N.W., Wash., D. C.
Mohun, Philip V., LL. B., '93.
Monaghan, Hugh I., LL. B., '05·
Monaghan, Joseph Patrick, A. B., '96
(Lawyer) ....Wilkinson Bldg, Shenandoah, Pa.
Monaghan, Martin M., LL. B., '98·
Monohan, Edward Sheehan, Jr., A. B.,
'05 (Student)......................St. Matthews, Ky.
Montgomery, Charles P., LL. B., '97·
Montgomery, Denny, LL. B., '96, LL. M , '98·
Montgomery, Francis Stanton, A. M.,'05 (Law Student).
Montgomery, George C., LL. B., '94·
Montgomery, James P., B. S., '88, LL. B., '89·
Montgomery, Hon. Zachariah, LL. D.,'89·
Moon, John B., LL. B., '96, LL. M., '97
(Clerk) ....U. S. Gov. Board, Treasury De-
partment, Washington, D. C.
Mooney, Henry F., LL. B., '95, LL. M., '96·
Mooney, Paul, A. B., '21.
Moore, Charles T., LL. B., '83 (Inventor)..31 E. 17th St., New York City.
Moore, J. B., M. D., '71·

Moore, J. Hall, M. D., '54·
Moore, John Edward, A. B., 1900.
Moore, Samuel Broder, M. D., '97·
Morales, Aug. Jose, LL. D., '59·
Moran, Charles Vincent, A. B,, '02·
Moran, Dennis C., A. B., '62 (H. C., Mass) (Clergyman); deceased July 23, 1889.
Moran, John•F., M. D., '87, A. B., '94
   (Physician) ....2426 Pa. Ave., Washington, D. C.
Moran, Timothy J., A. B., '01 (Assistant)..Will's Eye Hospital, Phila., Pa.
Morgan, Cecil, LL. B., '87, LL. M., '88·
Morgan, D. Oswald, LL. B., '96, LL. M., '97·
Morgan, Daniel H., LL. B., '95 (Lawyer)...Cookeville, Tenn.
Morgan, Daniel P., LL. B., '93, LL. M., '94·
Morgan, Ethelbert C., Ph. D., '89; deceased, May 5, 1891, at Wash., D. C.
Morgan, Haze, LL. B., '99 (Lawyer).. ...Clarksburg, W. Va.
Morgan, J. Dudley, A. B., '81, M. D., '85
   (Physician) ....919 15th St. N.W., Wash., D. C.
Morgan, J. Felix, M. D., '58·
Morgan, James LaMotte, A. B., '78; deceased, Jan 30, 1904, at New York.
Morgan, William M., LL. M , '99 (Law-
   yer; Mayor of Moscow).............Commercial Block, Moscow, Idaho.
Morgan, Zachariah R., M. D., '80·
Moroney, Edward B., LL. B., '91·
Moróss, W. Paul Dwight, A. B., '88
   (Manager Cement Mfg. Co.)..........Chattanooga, Tenn.
Morrill, Charles P., M. D., '66·
Morris, Ballard, LL. M., '87·
Morris, James L., A. B , '82 (Lawyer)....36 Hollenback Coal Exchange
                                    Bldg., Wilkesbarre, Pa.
Morris, John Penn, A. B., '82·
Morris, Hon. Martin F., LL D., '77
   (Associate Justice of the Court of
   Appeals) ....Washington, D. C.
Morris, P. Pemberton, A. B., '36, A. M,
   '40; deceased, 1888, at Phila , Pa.
Morse, Alexander Porter, LL. B., '72
   (Lawyer ana Author)..............1505 Pa. Ave. N.W., Wash., D. C.
Morthrop, George, LL. B., '87·
Mortimer, Charles G., LL. B., '95, LL. M , '96·
Moulton, Charles L., M. D., '87·
Moulton, Clarence E., LL. B., '88·
Moulton, Irwin B., LL. B., '91 (Assist-
   ant Chief).........................Bureau of Engraving and Print-
                                      ing, Wash., D. C.

Moynihan, Dennis L., LL. B., '02
(Clerk) ....Post-office Dept., Wash., D. C.
Mudd, Jeremiah, A. M., '24·
Mueller, J. Max, Mus. Doc., '82·
Mulcahy, Daniel D., M. D., '99·
Mulhall, Francis J., LL. B., '99› LL. M.,
1900 (Assistant to Finance Clerk)....Bureau of Medicine and Surgery,
Navy Dept., Washington, D. C.
Mulhearn, Charles E., LL. B., '02 (Law-
yer) ....402 Banigan Building, Providence,
R. I.
Mulhearn, Francis Richard, D. D. S., '04· ·
Mullaly, James F., LL. B., '93› LL. M.,
'94 (Lawyer)........................National Union Bldg., Wash., D. C.
Mullaly, James P., A. B., '73; deceased,
at Spokane Falls, Wash.
Mullally, George LeGuere, A. B., '03› A. M., '04 (Actor).
Mullan, Frank Drexel, A. B., '93 (Jour-
nalist) ....Colorado Bldg., Washington, D. C.
Mullan, Horace E., LL. B., '86·
Mullen, Clarence Vincent, A. M., '05.....1007 10th St., Denver, Colo.
Mulligan, Rev. John, A. B., '50 (H. C., Mass.), A. M., '52; deceased, Dec. 16,
1861.
Mulvihill, John Aloysius, A. B., '96› LL. B., '98·
Muncaster, Alexander, LL. B., '91› LL.
M., '92 (Lawyer).................·......482 La. Ave., Washington, D. C.
Muncaster, Stewart B , M. D., '85 (Phy-
sician) ....907 16th St. N.W., Wash., D. C.
Mundell, John Joseph, M. D., '03.........Jackson, Anacostia, D. C.
Munger, M. J., M. D.,'65.
Munson, Leonard Walter, M. D., '96.
Murchison, Kenneth S., LL. B., '86, LL. M., '99·
Murdock, Edwin F., LL. B., '89·
Murphey, John J., LL. B., '92 (Super-
intendent) ....Station D, Washington, D. C.
Murphey, Charles J., LL. B., '92› LL.
M., '93 (Lawyer)....................Century Bldg., Washington, D. C.
Murphy, Charles J., LL. B., '99› LL. M., 1900.
Murphy, Cornelius A., A. B., '04·
Murphy, Daniel, LL. B., '96› LL. M., '97·
Murphy, Daniel C., LL. B., '90 LL. M.,'91.
Murphy, Edward F., jr., A. B., '90·
Murphy, Edward V., jr., LL. B., '05·
Murphy, James A., A. B., '72 (B. C. Mass.).
Murphy, James A., A. B., '63› A. M., '66·
Murphy, James Wilmot, LL. B., '99·
LL. M., 1900 (Official Reporter)......U. S. Senate, Wash., D. C.

Murphy, John F., LL. B., '04.............1116 Alaska Bldg., Seattle, Wash.
Murphy, John J., LL. B., '94, LL. M., '95·
Murphy, John Maxwell, A. B., '02·
Murphy, Martin, A. B., '95·
Murphy, Patrick J., M. D., '73, A. M., '73; deceased Oct. 3, 1891, at Wash., D. C.
Murphy, Richard, LL. B., '91·
Murphy, Thomas J., LL. B., '74·
Murphy, William A., A. M., '92·
Murphy, William Joseph, LL. B., '97·
Murray, George E., A. B., '61·
Murray, Lawrence O., LL. M., '95·
Murray, Neal T., A. B., '73, LL. B., '76 (deceased, 1898).
Murray. Thomas, LL. B., '76·
Murray, Thomas J., LL. B., '94·
Muruaga, Hon. Emiliode, LL. D., '89·

Nadeau, Arthur J., LL. B., '04 (Lawyer)...Fort Kent, Me.
Nally, Charles F., M. D., '68·
Nally, Denis, A. B., '27·
Nast, Conde Montrose, A. B., '94, A. M.,
    '95 (Business Manager of Collier's
    Weekly) ....416 W. 13th St., New York City.
Naylor, Levi W., LL. M., '87·
Naylor, Van Denson, M. D., '60·
Neale, Augustine W., A. B., '60 (Agri-
    culturalist) ....Bel Alton, Charles Co., Md.
Neale, Francis, A. M., '69·
Neale, James Pye, A. M., '59·
Neale, R. A., M. D., '70·
Neas, William H., LL. B., '88, LL. M., '89·
Neel, William J., LL. B., '87, LL. M., '88·
Neely, Edgar A., LL. B., '05·
Neely, John R., M. D., '91·
Neill, Charles P., A. B., '91 (U. S. Com-
    missioner of Labor) ....1429 N. Y. Ave., Wash., D. C.
Neis, Claudius J., LL. B., '99, (Asso-
    ciate Editor) ....Southern Ry. Co., Wash., D. C.
Nelligan, John J., LL. B., '94·
Nelms, William H., LL. M., '98 (Spe-
    cial Examiner) ....Bureau of Pensions, Montpelier,
                                      Vt.
Nelson, James Edward, M. D., '95·
Nelson, Thomas Clement, A. B., '96
    (Bank Auditor) ....419 N. Y. Life Bldg, Larkin, K.
                                      Co., Kans.

Nemmers, Edwin Plein, A. M., '99, Ph-
D., 1900, LL. B., '01, LL. M., '02
,Lawyer) (President Wisconsin
Alumni Association) ....506 Germania Bldg., Milwaukee,
Wis.

Netherland, Thomas H., LL. B., '95
(Gov. Clerk) ....The White House, Wash., D. C.

Neubeck, Francis L., LL. B., '03 (Law-
yer and Notary) ....510 Bond Bldg., Wash., D. C.

Neuhaus, Paul Immanuel, LL. B., '83,
LL. M., '84 (Librarian & Superin-
tendent) ....Masonic Temple, 9th and F Sts.,
Washington, D. C.

Nevins, John C., A. B., '46.

Nevins, Joseph D., LL. B., '92, LL. M., '93.

Newbern, John Melvin, M. D., '98.

Newberne, R. L. E., M. D., '93.

Newman, Charles R., A. B., '77, LL. B., '80, LL. M., '81.

Newman, Enos S., LL. B., '92.

Newman, Henry M., M. D., '76.

Newton, James Thornwell, LL. B., '95
(Principal Examiner) ....Patent Office, Wash., D. C.

Newton, Louis E., M. D., '68.

Niblack, W. Caldwell, A. B., '74 (Lawyer) (Vice President Chicago Title
& Trust Co. ....100 Washington St., Chicago, Ill.

Nichols, Edmund L., LL. B., '87.

Nichols, Henry J., A. B., '89.

Nichols, John L., LL. B., '96.

Nichols, Joshua, A. B., '3b.

Nicholson, John T., LL. B., '78.

Nicodemus, Bvt. Maj. William Joseph
Leonard U. S. A., A. M., '65, M. D.,
'67 (deceased, Jan. 1879.)

Nishio, Shohaku, M. D., '94.

Noeker, Joseph John, jr., A. M., '98, M.D , '02.

Nolan, John M., LL. B., '01 (Lawyer)....20 Broad St., New York City, N. Y.

Nolan, Joseph A., A. M , '66.

Nolan, Thomas J., A. B., '02.

Noonan, Louis T., A. B., '95, LL. B., '97, LL. M., '98.

Norcross, Frank H., LL. B., '94 (Jus-
tice of Supreme Court) ....Carson City, Neva.

Norcross, George J., M. D., '65.

Nordlinger, Isaac W., A. B., '83, LL. B.,
'85, LL. M., '86 (Lawyer)...........Stewart Bldg., Wash., D. C.

Normile, Judge James C., A. M., '67 (deceased 1892).

Normoyle, John D., LL. B., 98, LL. M.,
'99 (Lawyer & Real Estate Agent)....Alexandria Nat. Bk. Bldg., Alexandria, Va.

Norton, Frank P., LL. B., '98, LL. M., '99.

Norton, John M., LL. B., '94·

Nourse, C. H , jr., M. D., '69·

Nourse, Upton Darby, M. D., 1900.

Nowlin, Homer Edgar, M. D., '96·

Noyes, George F., LL. B., '86, LL. M.,
'86 (Lawyer) .... .98 Exchange St., Portland, Me.

Nunez, Manuel I., M. D., '05·

Obenchain, Charles Austin, LL. B., '99,
LL. M., 1900 (Clerk)...............:..Gen. Land Office, Wasn., D. C.

Ober, George C., M. D., '82·

Oblinger, Edward Vincent, A. B., '05·

O'Brien, Hon. Denis, LL. D . '93.

O'Brien, Dennis F , LL B , '01 (Lawyer)..402 Banigan Bldg , Providence,
R. I.

O'Brien, Gen. Edward C., LL. D., '97·

O'Brien, Edward D., A. B , '90 (Lawyer)...120 Broadway, New York City.

O'Brien, John Lawrence, LL B., 99,
LL. M., 1900 (Lawyer)..............Tennallytown, Washington, D. C.

O'Brien, John, A. B., '55 (St. F. X. New York).

O'Brien, John F., A. B., '96·

O'Brien, John Henry, A. B., '04 (Law
Student) ....Clinton, Mass.

O'Brien, John P ,. A. M , '95, LL B ,
'97 (Lawyer) ....44 E. 23d St., New York City.

O'Brien, Joseph P., A. B., '80, LL. B., '82, A. M , '89 (deceased, 1904).

O'Brien, Miles M , Jr., LL. B., '99, LL
M., '00 (Lawyer)................... 206 Broadway, New York, N. Y.

O'Bryan, John Duross, A B., '62, A. M , 64 (deceased, March 1, 1904, at Paris,
France).

O'Byrne, Dominic A , A. B:, '51 (deceased, Feb. 17, 1896).

O'Connell, Daniel, LL. B., '86 (L'y'r)..515-517 James Flood Bldg , San Fr. Cal.

O'Connell, Jeremiah D , LL. B., '80, LL.M., '81

O'Connell, John J., LL. M., '87·

O'Connell, Richard F , M. D., '94·

O'Connor, F. J., M. D., '77·

O'Connor, Charles E., A. B., '78 (deceased, 1899).

O'Connor, Charles Emmet, M. D., '95
(Physician) ....1429 U. St. N.W., Wash , D. C.

O'Connor, Jeremiah I., A. B., '92, LL.
B , '94, LL. M., '95 (Dramatist)........101 2d St. N.E., Wash., D. C.

O'Connor, Joseph T., M. D., '67..........Garden City, N. Y.
O'Connor, Michael F., A. B., '98, LL. B., '01·
O'Connor, Patrick J., LL. B., '80·
O'Day, Charles F., Ph. B., '89.
O'Day, Daniel E., A. B., '89·
O'Dea, Patrick H., LL. B., '94, LL. M.,
    '95 (Clerk) ....Navy Dept., Wash., D. C.
Odell, Willmot Mitchell, LL. M., 1900
    (Lawyer) ....Cleburne, Tex.
O'Doherty, George, LL. B., '84, LL. M., '95·
O'Doherty, John D., M. D., '88 (Phy-
    sician) ....Dover, N. H.
O'Donnell, Daniel J., A. B., '89, LL. B., '92 (deceased, March 3, 1893).
O'Donnell, Edward Pius, A. B., '02
    (Med. Student) ....Heckschersville, Penn.
O'Donnell, Patrick Henry, A. B., '92,
    A. M., '93, LL. B., '94...............1218 Ashland Block, Chicago, Ill.
O'Donnell, Rev. William Aloysius, A.
    B., '94 (Priest) ....48th St. and Lancaster Ave., Phila-
        delphia, Pa.
O'Donoghue, Daniel William, A. B.,
    '97, A. M , '98, Ph D., '99, LL. B.,
    '99, LL. M , '00 (Lawyer)... ....412 5th St. N.W., Wash., D. C.
O'Donoghue, John Alphonso, A. M., '97,
    M. D., 1900 ....3311 N St. N.W., Wash., D. C.
O'Donovan, Charles, A. B , '78, A. M ,
    '88 (Physician) ....10 E. Read St., Baltimore, Md.
Offutt, George W., M. D., '74 (deceased, Sept. 13, 1878, at Washington, D. C.)
O'Flynn, Cornelius John, A. B., '58
    (Lawyer) ....Bahl Block, Detroit, Mich.
Ogden, Herbert Gouverneur, LL. M.,
    1900 (Patent Lawyer) ....141 Broadway, New York, N. Y.
Ogden, Warren Greene, LL. B., '05,
    (Patent Lawyer) ....205 Lincoln Ave., Boston, Mass.
O'Gorman, Maurice J. C , A. B., 1900
    (Real Estate & Builder)............208 Willis Ave , and 681 East 140th
        · St., New York City, N. Y.
O'Halloran, Thomas M., LL. B., '92·
O'Hanlon, Michael, LL. B., '99, LL. M.,
    1900 (Liquor Dealer) ....1325 7th St., N.W., Wash., D. C.
O'Hara, Francis James, A. M., '01, M. D., '04·
O'Hara, John J , LL. B., '04 (Lawyer).....11 Hancock Bldg., Quincy, Mass.
O'Hara, The Very Rev. William Louis, LL. D., '01·
O'Keefe, Rev. Charles M., D. D , '89 (deceased, Sept., 28, 1892).
O'Keeffe, Lawrence E. A., LL. B., '05
    (Stenographer) ....War Dept., Washington, D. C.

O'Laughlin, James P., LL. B., '95, LL.
    M., '96 (Lawyer) ....Clearfield, Clearfield Co., Pa.
O'Leary, Charles R., LL. B., '98 (Pay-
    master) ....care U. S. N. Dept., Wash., D. C.
O'Leary, Charles W., M. D., '74.
O'Leary, John G., A. B., '95 (Broker)......17 Battery Pl.,New York City, N. Y.
O'Leary, Timothy S., LL. B., '93, LL. M., '94.
O'Leary, William Joseph, A. M., '94.
Olesen, Robert, M. D., '05.
Oller, George E., LL. B., '05.
Olmstead, Edwin B., M. D., '87 (Spe-
    cial Pension Examiner) ....Pension Office, Washington, D. C.
O'Malley, Austin, A. M., '88, Ph. D., '89,
    M. D., '93 (Physician) ....2228 S. Broad St., Philadelphia, Pa.
O'Malley, Joseph M., M. D., '93.
O'Neil, Albert Murray, A. B., '04, A. M.,
    '05 (Law Student)..................Binghamton, New York.
O'Neill, Eugene J. B., LL. B., '88, LL. M., '89.
O'Neill, Francis J., LL. B., '88, LL. M., '89.
O'Neill, Ignatius P., A. B., '80, A. M., '89 (deceased, Aug. 8, 1898).
O'Neill, Hon. James F., A. B., '83, A. M., '89.
O'Neill, John B., LL. B., '87, LL. M., '88.
O'Neill, John H., A. B., '41 (deceased, Dec. 1890, at Chicago, Ill.).
O'Neill, John H, A. M., '55.
O'Neill, John Joseph, A. B., '94 (Lawyer)..77 Bank St., Waterbury, Conn.
O'Neill, Thomas Jeremiah, A. B., '99.
O'Neill, William A., LL. B., '99.
O'Neill, William E., LL. B., '88, LL. M., '89.
Ongley, A. Hugh, LL. B , '97 (deceased, 1898).
Opisso, Antonio M., LL. B., '03, LL. M.,
    '04 (Lawyer) ....31 Plaza Moraga, Manila, P. I.
Oppenheimer, Bernard, A. B., '72 (deceased, Feb. 26, 1882).
O'Reilly, J., A. B., '36.
O'Reilly, John Boyle, LL. B., '89 (deceased, Aug. 10, 1890).
O'Reilly, Thomas, M. D., '89.
Orleman, Carl S., LL. B., '91, LL. M.,
    '95 (Secretary) Chapin Jacks Mfg.
    Co. ....Washington, D. C.
Orleman, Louis H., jr., LL. B., '94.
Osborn, Harry S., LL. B., '03.
Osborne, Henry G., LL. B., '88.
Osburn, Alexander, M. D., '68.
Osenton, Charles W., LL. B., '95, LL. M , '96.
O'Shea, James Aloysius, A. B., '99, A.
    M., 1900, Ph. D., '01, LL. B., '02
    (Lawyer) ....Century Bldg., Wash., D. C.

O'Sullivan, Florence T., A. B., '43·
O'Toole, Lawrence J., A. B., '72 (B. C. Mass).
Ourdan, Vincent L., LL. B., '95·
Owen, Frederick Wooster, M. D., '67.
Owens, Samuel Logan, M. D., '03
   (Physician) ....2418 Pennsylvania Ave., N.W.,
                                      Washington, D. C.
Owens, William Dunlop, M. D., '01·
Owens, Winter, LL. B., '98.
Owings, William Randall, A. B., '01, A.
   M., '02· LL. B., '04· Ph. L., '04, LL.
   M., '05· Ph., D., '05·
Oxnard, George C., B. S., '79.

Pace, Charles F., LL. B., '94·
Pace, Lewis D., LL. B., '90· LL. M., '91
   (Clerk) ....Gen. Land Office, Wash., D. C.
Packard, Harry M., LL. B., '97· LL. M., '98·
Page, R. A., M. D., '71·
Paine, A. Elliot, M. D., '65·
Painter, John Isaac, LL. B., '98· LL. M., '99·
Pallen, Conde Benoist, A. B., '80· A.
   M., '83· LL. D., '96 (Author and
   Editor) President of the New
   York Branch of the Georgetown
   University Alumni Society............1 Union Square, New York City,
                                 N. Y. Home: 197 Weyman
                                 Ave., New Rochelle, N. Y.
Palmer, Dennis, LL. B., '98· LL. M., '99·
Palmer, Oscar, M. D., '64·
Palmer, Theodore Sherman, M. D., '95.
Palms, Charles Louis, Ph. B., '89.
Palms, Francis A., A. B., '04.............Michigan Stove Co., Detroit, Mich.
Pardee, Munson D., LL. B., '98· LL. M., '99·
Pargon, Augustine Joseph A., M. D., '05·
Parkhurst, Lincoln A., LL. B., '91·
Parkinson, Clinton, M. D., '69·
Parks, Charles J., LL. B., '04·
Parrott, John, jr., A. B., '05 (Student)....The Bungalow, San Mateo, Cal.
Parrott, P. Bishop, LL. B., '96·
Parsons, Isaac, A. B., '61·
Parsons, John D., M. D., '70·
Paschal, George, LL. B., '76·
Paschal, Hon. George W., LL. D., '75 (deceased, Feb. 16, 1878, in Texas).
Patterson, Herbert Stewart, A. B., '98·
Patterson, John C. C., LL. B., '94· LL. M., '95·

Patterson, John Scott, M. D., '70.
Patterson, Richard, J. A. B., '63 (H. C.
   Mass.) (Clergyman) deceased, Dec.
   31, 1900.
Pattirson, Allen S., LL. B., '89, LL. M.,
   '90 (Patent Lawyer) ....629 F St. N.W., Wash., D. C.
Payn, Abbott Smith, M. D., '95 (Physi-
   cian) ....545 W. 148th St., New York City.
Payne, Howard T., M. D., '70.
Payne, Col. James G., LL. D., '85.
Payne, John Carroll, A. B., '76 (Lawyer)..Atlanta, Ga.
Payne, Rev. W. Gaston, A. B., '79
   (Priest) ....Clifton Forge, Va.
Peabody, James H., M. D., '60.
Pearson, Joseph W., LL. B., '97, LL. M '98.
Peck, C. W., M. D., '63.
Peck, Herbert E., LL. B , '90, LL. M.,
   '91 (Patent Lawyer)................629 F St. N.W , Wash., D. C.
Peck, William D., LL. B., '95.
Pell, George Pierce, LL. B , '96 (Lawyer)..Winston-Salem, N. C.
Pendergast, Robert Joseph, A. B., '05
   (Law Student) ....841 O. C. S. Bank Bldg., Syracuse,
                                       N. Y.
Pennington, Polk K., LL. B., '95, LL. M., '96.
Pennybacker, Isaac S., LL. B., '97
   (Clerk) ....Dept. of Agriculture, Wash., D. C.
Pennybacker, James Edmund, LL. B.,
   '99 (Chief Clerk of U. S. Office of
   Public Roads.......................Dept., of Agriculture, Wash., D. C.
Pentecost, William Chester, LL. B., '02
   (Lawyer) ....Knox, Ind.
Perkins, Edward Dyer, M. D., '95.
Perkins, Louis L., LL. B., '90, LL. M.,
   '91 (Lawyer) ....606 F St. N.W., Wash., D. C.
Perry, David B., LL. B., '98, LL. M.,
   '99 (Clerk) ....Pension Office, Wash., D. C.
Perry, Frank Sprigg, LL. B , '02
   (Lawyer) ....Bond Bldg., Washington, D. C.
Perry, Frederick Charles, D. D. S., '05.
Perry, R. Ross, jr., LL. B., '94, LL. M.,'95.
Perry, Richard Ross, A. B , 04, A. M.,
   '65, LL. D., '92 (Lawyer) ....Fendall Bldg., Washington, D. C.
Perry, Walter S., A. B., '74.
Petteys, C. V , M. D., '73.
Pettijohn, J. W., M. D., '64.
Peyser, Julius I., LL. B., '99 (Lawyer).....Century Bldg., Washington, D. C.

Pfirman, Franklin, LL. M., '04 (Lawyer)..Wardner, Idaho.

Phelan, Francis M., A. M., '95 (Lawyer)...73 Tremont St., Boston, Mass.

Phillips, Bennett, LL. B., '89·

Phillips, Edmund Lawrence, A. B., '97
  (Med. Student) ....102 E. Madison St., Baltimore, Md.

Phillips, Frederick E., LL. D., '98, LL. M., '99·

Phillips, Lewis H., LL. M., '94·

Phillips, Robert L., LL. M., '95·

Pickens, Alvin H., LL. B., '87·

Pickett, Thomas J., LL. B., '87, LL. M., '88·

Pierce, Albert S., M. D., '67·

Pierce, Henry Fletcher, LL. B., '04·

Pierce, Thomas Murray, Jr., A. B., '98
  (Lawyer) ....502 Laclede Bldg., St. Louis, Mo.

Pierce, William P., LL. B., '73·

Pierce, William Percy, LL. M., '80·

Pierson, Henry C., M. D., '68·

Pirtle, William J., LL. B., '99, LL. M.,1900.

Pise, Rev. Charles Constantine, A. M.,
  '30 (deceased, May 26, 1866, at
  Brooklyn, N. Y.)

Pitts, George B., LL. B., '04 (Patent
  Attorney) ....507 E. St. N.W., Wash., D. C.

Pitts, W. Stanley, M. D., '92·

Pizzini, Juan A., A. B., '65, A. M., '82 (deceased, Nov. 1891).

Pless, William A., LL. M., '95·

Poland, John A., A. M., '92, LL. B., '92
  (Lawyer) ....Chillicothe, Ohio.

Poland, Nicholas Albert, LL. B., '98, LL. M., '99·

Polk, James K., LL. B., '90, LL. M., '91
  (Lawyer) ....1407 F St. N.W., Wash., D. C.

Pollock, George F, LL. M., '87 (Clerk)....Gen. Land Office, Wash., D. C.

Pool, Solomon C., LL. B., 9ı, LL. M., '98·

Pope, Francis, LL. B., '90, LL. M., '91·

Porter, Henry C., M. D, 69.

Porter, Henry R., M· D., '12·

Porter, Horace T., M. D., '70·

Porter, J. H., M. D., '61·

Porter, John Waterman, ... D., '68

Posey, Fabien, LL. B., '01, (Lawyer &
  Editor of the Examiner) ....Frederick, Md.

Posey, G. Gordon, A. B., '71 (deceased,
  May 29, 1891, at Silver City, New
  Mexico.)

Posey, Richard B., LL. B., '95.

Pospispel, Joseph, M. D., '94.

Postley, Charles E., M. D., '91.

Potbury, Edwin, jr., M. D., 1900 (deceased Feb. 18, 1901, at Washington, D. C.).

Potbury, Jesse E., LL. B., '96, LL. M., '97.

Potts, Louis Joseph, A. M., '98, Ph. D.,
'99, LL. B., '99, LL. M., 1900.

Poulton, William E., M. D., '64.

Poulton, William F., LL. B., '92, LL. M., '93.

Powell, Benjamin F., LL. B., '97.

Power, Charles Benton, A. B., '88
(Rancher) ....Helena, Mont.

Power, Edwin Murray, M. D., 1900.

Power, James D'Alton, LL. B., '80, LL.M., '81.

Power, James Henry, A. M., '93.

Power, J. Neal, A. B., '95, LL. B., '97
(Lawyer) (Secretary of the Pacific Coast Branch of the Georgetown University Alumni Associa-
tion ....Mills Bldg., San Francisco, Cal.

Power, Very Rev. John, D. D., '33 (deceased, April 14, 1849).

Power, John J., A. B., '51 (H. C. Mass.) (Clergyman) (deceased, Jan. 27, 1902).

Power, Dr. Maurice A., A. M., '31.

Powers, Edward Parnell, M. D., '05.

Powers, William, LL. D., '22.

Pratz, Frederick C., LL. B., '91, LL. M., '92.

Prendergast, Very Rev. P. J., D. D., '89 (deceased, Oct. 1, 1899).

Prendergast, Rev. Jere M., S. J., A. B.,
'89, A. M., '92 (Jesuit Priest).........Jersey City, N. J.

Prentiss, Charles E., M. D., '68.

Prescott, Charles C., LL. B., '91, LL. M., '92.

Preston, Thomas, A. B., '37.

Preston, Rt. Rev. Mgr. Thomas S.,
D. D., '89 (deceased, Nov. 4, 1891).

Price, John G., LL. B., '05.

Prince, Sydney R., LL. B., '98.

Pritchard, Henry T., LL. B., '99.

Pritchard, Howard Dallas, LL. B., '02
(Lawyer) ....Garfield Bldg., Cleveland, Ohio.

Pryal, Andrew D., jr., LL. B., '88 (deceased, June 2, 1892, at Wash., D. C.).

Puebla, Luis de, A. B., '68, A. M., '69 (deceased, July 24, 1893).

Pugh, Henry L., LL. B., '90.

Pugh, James L., jr., LL. B., '84, LL. M.,
'85 (Treas.) ....4000 Laclede Ave., St. Louis, Mo.

Pugh, John C., LL. B., '88 (Lawyer)......Steiner Bldg., Birmingham, Ala.

Pulskamp, Bernard, M. D., '90.

Purcell, John B., A. B., '64 (H. C. Mass.) (Clergyman) (deceased, March 24,
1873).

Purman, Louis C., M. D.,91.
Putman, William D., M. D., '68·
Pye, James B., A. M., '67·

Quay, John B., M. D., '93·
Queen, Charles R., M. D., '55.
Quicksall, William F., A. B., '61, LL. B., '72, A. M., '72·
Quigley, Edward T., LL. B., '05·
Quigley, Francis Leo, M. D., '04·
Quinlan, George Austin, A. B., '02·
Quinlan, Richard J., A. B., '63 (H. C.
    Mass.) (Clergyman) ....St. Mary's Church, Holliston,
                                                    Mass.
Quinn, Edwin L., LL. B., '02·
Quinn, Harry I., LL. B., '04, LL. M.,
    '05 (Lawyer).....................Century Bldg., Washington, D. C.
Quinn, John, LL. B., 93.
Quinn, Joseph Gray, A. B., '04.

Rabbett, James Aloysius, M. D., 1900.
Radcliffe, Samuel J., M. D., '52, A. M., 66.
Ragan, Gillum T., M. D., '66·
Rague, Charles W. S., LL. B., '03 (Law-
    yer) ....188 Montague St., Brooklyn, N. Y.
Raines, Benjamin R., M. D., '67·
Rainey, Francis H., A. B., '63, LL. B.,
    '74 (Chief Clerk, M. O. Division)....Post-office Dept., Wasn., D. C.
Ralston, Jackson Harvey, LL. B., '76
    (Lawyer) ....Bond Bldg., Washington, D. C.
Ramage, Joseph C., LL. B., '99, LL. M., 1900.
Ramsdell, George P., M. D., '69·
Rand, Charles F., M. D., '73·
Randall, Thomas G., LL. B., '89·
Randle, Edward Thomas, LL. B., '03
    (Lawyer) ....Reinhardt Bldg., Dallas, Tex.
Raney, Roscoe J., LL. B., '04 (Clerk)......Census Office, Washington, D. C.
Rankin, John M., LL. B., '85, LL. M., '87·
Ransom, Stacy A., M. D., '93·
Ransom, Thomas R., A. B., '85 (deceased November 14, 1896).
Rask, Harry George, LL. B., '96.........Frewsburg, New York.
Rauterberg, Louis E., M. D., '67 (Phy-
    sician) ....The Farragut, Wash., D. C.
Rawlings, Carroll M., M. D., '84·
Ray, Charles B., A. B., '74·
Ray, J. Enos, jr., LL. B., '96, LL. M., '97.

Ray, Hon. Robert, A. B., '54, A. M., '59 (deceased, Oct. 25, 1899).

Rea, George W., LL. B., '90, LL. M., '91.

Read, William G., LL. D., '42.

Ready, Michael J., A. B., '01, M. D., '05
(Physician) ....Conduit Road, Wash., D. C.

Reagan, Francis Charles, A. M., '01,
LL. B., '03 (Lawyer).................602 N. Y. Blk., Seattle, Wash.

Reavis, Wade, LL. B., '02 (Lawyer)......Pittsboro, N. C.

Reddy, Anthony Cosgrove, A. M., '94
(Lawyer) ....100 Pleasant St., Malden, Mass.

Redmond, Edward J., LL. B , '90, LL. M., '91.

Redrow, Walter L., LL. B., '04(Ass't.
Examiner) ....Patent Office, Washington, D. C.

Reese, Henry F., LL. B., '85, LL. M , '88.

Reeside, Frank Palton, LL. B., '94
(Secretary Co-operative Building
Association) ....1003 F St. N. W., Wash., D. C.

Reeve, Jesse N., M. D., '93 (Physician) ..916 17th St. N. W., Wash., D. C.

Reeves, Isaac Stockton K., M. D., '03
(Ass't. Surgeon U. S. Navy)...........U. S F. S., Minneapolis, care
                                       Postmaster, New York City.

Reeves, John R. .T., LL. B., '05 (L'y'r)....617 La. Ave. N. W, Wash., D. C.

Reeves, William P., M. D., '99 (Physi-
cian) ....206 Delaware Ave., Wash., D. C.

Regan, Ralston Byrnes, D. D. S., '04.

Regli, J. A. S., M. D., '02.

Reid, George Conrad, A. B., '02, LL. B.,
'05 (Lawyer) ....Century Bldg., Wash., D. C.

Reid, John, A. B., '49, A. M., '51.

Reid, Louis Henry, M. D., '70.

Reilly, Harold Aloysius, A. B., '03
(Jesuit Novice) ....St Andrew-on-Hudson, Pough-
                                       keepsie, N. Y.

Reilly, Henry Francis, A. M., '96, Ph.
D., '97, LL. B., '97, LL. M., '98
(Lawyer) ....389 Broadway, Milwaukee, Wis.

Reilly, Joseph A , D. D. S., '05, (Den-
tist) ....2418 Pennsylvania Ave. N. W.,
                                       Washington, D. C.

Reilly, William B., LL. B , '92, LL. M.,
'93 (Lawyer) ....486 Louisiana Ave. N. W., Wash.,
                                       D. C.

Reisinger, Emory William, M. D., '93......1209 13th St. N. W., Wash., D. C.

Remus, Ramon Eduardo, A. M., '98.

Repetti, Frederick Francis, M. D., '95.

Repetti, John Joseph, M. D., '97 (Phy-
sician) ....404 Seward Square, Wash., D. C.
Rex, Thomas A., M. D., '65·
Reynolds, Edward C., LL. M., '86
(Lawyer) ....31 1-2 Exchange St., Portland, Me.
Reynolds, Walter B., M. D., '74·
Reynolds, William C., LL. B., '88, LL.
M., '89 (Merchant) ....Mesilla, N. Mex.
Reynolds, William E., LL. B., '92, LL. M., '93·
Rhodes, Eugene, LL. M., '94·
Rice, Charles Edward, LL. B., '80·
Rice, James Willie, A. M., '53·
Rice, Joseph A., A. B., '63, A. M., '64; deceased, Oct., 1901, at Alexandria, Va.
Rice, Nathan E., M. D., '80·
Rice, William J., A. B., '50·
Rice, Thomas C., M. D., '69·
Rice, William James, LL. B., '98,
LL. M., '99 (Principal Examiner).....Patent Office, Washington, D. C.
Rich, John S., LL. M., '87·
Richards, Alfred, M. D., '97 (Physician)....314 S. Cap. St., Washington, D. C.
Richards, F. P., M. D., '63·
Richardson, John Robert, LL. B., '96·
Richardson, Hon. William A., LL. D., '81; deceased.
Richmond, Charles Wallace, M. D., '97·
Richmond, Elbert E., LL. B., '96,
LL. M., '97· (Clerk)..................Treasury Dept., Washington, D. C.
Richmond, James A., LL. B., '03 (L'y'r)...605 7th St. N. W., Wash., D. C.
Richmond, John Albert, A. M., '05
(Law Student) ....3 Hasting Hall, Cambridge, Mass.
Richmond, Paul, M. D., '92·
Riddelle, Philip S., M. D., '79·
Ridgely, Harry S., LL. B., '96, LL. M.,
'97 (Private Secretary)..............Dept. of Justice, Washington, D. C.
Ridgway, Frank H., LL. B., '01·
Rieckelmann, John, A. B., '56, A. M., '59·
Riehle, Charles F., LL. B., '93; deceased 1894.
Riley, Ambrose Joseph, A. M., '98·
Riley, Benjamin C., M. D., '52·
Riley, John C., A. B., '48, A. M., '51;
(deceased Feb. 22, 1879, at Wash., D. C.).
Riley, John F., LL. B., '73·
Riley, Edward S., A. B., '64, LL. B., '72,
A. M., '76; deceased 1882 at Cone-
wago, Pa.
Rindge, Joseph B., A. B., '40·
Ring, John, LL. B., '01·

Riordan, J. Allen, LL. B., '04·

Risque, F. W., A. B., '71·

Ritche, Abner Cloud, A. B., '98 (Lawyer)..400 5tn St. N.W., Wash., D. C.

Ritchie, Joshua A., A. B., '35, A. M., '40·

Ritchie, Louis W., M. D., '63·

Rivera-Pagan, Pedro M., M. D., '04·

Rix, Carl B., LL. B., '03, LL. M., '04
 (Lawyer) ....8th Floor, Wells Bldg., Milwaukee, Wis.

Roach, Charles Edward, A B, '95
 LL. B., '97, LL. M., '98 (Lawyer)......Century Bldg., Washington, D. C.

Roach, William Nathaniel, jr., A. B.,
 '96, LL. B., '98 (Lawyer)..............412 5th St. N. W., Wash., D. C.

Roane, James, M. D, '82·

Roane, Samuel B., LL. M., '86·

Robbins, A. J., M. D., '91·

Robbins, Thomas A, LL. M., '87·

Roberts, Charles Francis, LL. B., '94,
 LL. M., '95 (Notary and Insurance)...700 14th St. N. W., Wash., D. C.

Roberts, E. E., M. D., '94·

Roberts, Thomas W., LL. B., '91, LL. M., '92·

Roberts, William, M. D., '94·

Robertson, Frederick C., LL. B., '89·

Robertson, J. Caldwell, A B., '75,
 A. M., '77 (Capitalist)................Loan and Exchange Bank, Columbia, S. C.

Robertson, Samuel A., A. M., '70·

Robinson, Samuel A., A. B., '58; deceased Dec., 1894.

Robinson, Thomas, M. D., '76·

Robinson, Thomas Somerset, M. D., '58·

Roche, Charles H., A. B., '86·

Roche, Peter A., A. M., '91·

Rochford, Richard, A. B., '47·

Rodrique, A., M. D., '71·

Roebuck, Jarvis H., A. B., '20·

Rogers, Frank Leo, A. B., '03 (Law
 Student) ....97 Acushnet Ave., New Bedford, Mass.

Rogers, Hamilton, LL. B., '04 (Lawyer)...1014 E. Main St., Richmond, Va.

Rogers, James Charles, LL. B., '86
 (Lawyer) ....344 D St. N. W., Wash., D. C.

Rogers, Joseph Sebastian, Ph. B., '92,
 LL. B., '94; deceased Aug. 20, 1898.

Rogers, Thomas Mitchell, LL. B., '98·

Rogers, William Elwin, M. D., '04·

Romadka, Charles Aloysius, A. B., '95,
    A. M., '96.........................Care Globe Mine, Nacozari, Sono-
                                            ra, Mexico.
Romadka, Francis Joseph, A. M., '01
    (Trunk Manufacturer) ....222-225 3d St., Milwaukee, Wis.
Romaine, Frank William, M. D., '05.
Roman, Richard, LL. B., '77.
Ronning, Henry T., LL. M., '02 (Lawyer)..Glenwood, Minn.
Rooney, Charles Daniels, A. B., '87,
    A. M., '89, LL. B., '95, LL. M., '96
    (Lawyer and Reporter)..............Care Boston Globe, Boston, Mass.
Rorke, Alexander I , LL. B , '04
    (Lawyer) ....:...Rooms 1 and 2, Fendall Bldg.,
                                         Washington, D. C.
Rosecrans, Gen. William S., U. S. A.,
    LL. D., '89; deceased March 11, 1898.
Rosell, Claude A., LL. B., '86.
Rosenberg, Maurice D., LL. B., '96,
    LL. M., '97 (Lawyer)...............Jenifer Bldg., Washington, D. C.
Ross, John R., A. B., '72, A. M., '89.
    (Lawyer) ....Belcamp, Md.
Ross, John R., A. B., '72, A. M., '89
Ross, Ralph H., M. D., '91.
Ross, Tenney, LL. B., '95.
Ross, William H., M. D., '69.
Rosse, Irving C., A. M., '89; deceased May 3, 1901.
Rost, Alphonse, A. B., '60.
Rost, Hon. Emile, A. B., '57, A. M., '60,
    LL. D., '89 (Planter)...............521 Godehaux Bldg., New Orleans,
                                         La.
Roth, Joseph A., LL. B., '04 (Lawyer)....412 5th St. N. W., Wash., D. C.
Rothchild, David, LL. B., '02.
Rowland, Hugh B., LL. B., '97, LL. M.,
    '98 (Lawyer) ....705 Colorado Bldg., Wash., D. C.
Roys, Chase, M. D., '67.
Roysten, J. Perry, LL. B., '99.
Rudd, Frank, A. B., '61, A. M., '68........26 Liberty St., New York City.
Rudd, John S., A. M., '58.
Rudd, Thomas S., A. B., '64, A. M., '66.
Rudge, William H., A. B., '93 (Presi-
    dent and Manager of the Forsyth
    Pattern Co.) ....Youngstown, Ohio.
Ruff, John A., M. D., '64.
Ruffin, Thomas, LL. B., '96, LL. M., '97.
Rupli, J. Theodore, LL. B., '94, LL. M., '95.
Russell, Charles W., LL. B., '83, LL. M., '84.

Russell, Edward O., A. B., '79, LL. B.,
   '81, LL. M., '82, A. M., '89 (Lawyer)...244 Equitable Bldg., Denver, Colo.
Russell, George M., LL. B., '87·
Russell, Henry M., A. B., '69, A. M., '71
   (Lawyer) ....Wheeling, W. Va.
Russell, Murray Alfred, A. B., '03·
Ruth, Charles H., LL. B., '95.·
Rutherford, Robert Gedney, jr., LL. B.,
   '99 (1st Lieut. 24th U. S. Infantry)....Manila, P. I.
Ryan, James A., LL. B., ∪6, LL. M., '97
   (Lawyer) ....Nashville, Tenn.
Ryan, James H., LL. B., '04·
Ryan, John McNulty, A. B., '93·
Ryan, Patrick J·, LL. B., '94·
Ryan, Thomas J., LL. B., '85, LL. M., '86·

St. Clair, Francis A., M. D., '90 (Phy-
   sician) ....1319 T St. N. W., Wash., D. C.
St. Clair, F. O., M. D., '69, A. M., '89·
Salomon, Joseph, LL. B., '97, LL. M.,
   '98 (Lawyer) ....416 5th St., N. W., Wash., D. C.
Salten, George W., LL. B., '72·
Salter, George W., LL. B., '79·
Sanders, William, A. B., '57·
Sands, Francis P. B., A. B , '61, A. M., '68·.1333 F St. N. W., Wash., D. C.
Sands, William Franklin, A. B., '96, LL. B., '96·
Sanford, Joseph L., M. D., '92·
Saul, John Aloysius, LL. B., '91,
   LL. M , '92 (Lawyer)...............Fendall Bldg., Washington, D. C.
Saunders, Joseph N., LL. B., '91,
   LL. M., '92 (Lawyer)...............412 5th St. N. W., Wash., D. C.
Sawtelle, Henry W., M. D., '68 (Sur-
   geon, Marine Hospital Service); in
   command U. S. Marine Hospital......San Francisco, Cal.
Sawyer, Glen R., LL. B., '03 (Lawyer).....222-224 S. Main St., Elkhart, Ind.
Saxton, Francis G., LL. B., '73
Scaggs, James F., LL. B., '84, LL. M.,
   '85 (Lawyer) ....:...Century Bldg., Washington, D. C.
Scanlan, Andre Christie, A. M., '95
   (Agriculturalist) ....Richmond, Ky.
Scanlan, Rev. Michael James, A. M., '96
   (Priest) ....Concord, Mass.
Scanlon, Edward, LL. B., '98, LL. M.,
   '99 (Journalist) ....408 9th St. N. W., Wash., D. C.
Schade, Frederick, LL. B , '95, LL. M., '99.
Schade, Herman R., LL. B , '99·

Scharf, J. Thomas, A. M., '81, LL. B., '85·
Schaus, James Peter, A. M., '93, LL. B., '94·
Scheib, Prof. Edward E., A. B., '71·
Schildroth, Henry T., M. D., '93·
Schleimer, David, M. D., '73·
Schley, Winfield Scott (Rear Admiral,
 U. S. N.), LL. D., '99.
Schmidt, Oscar P., LL. B., '90, LL. M., '91·
Schneider, Elwin Carl, M. D., '05·
Schneider, Ferdinand Turton, LL. B.,
 '99 (Architect) ....1110 F St. N. W.; Wash., D. C.
Schoolfield, Charles S., A. B., '78 (deceased).
Schott, G. J. VanVerbeek, M. D., '89·
Schreiner, Edmund, LL. B., '0x.
Schubert, Bernhard F., LL. B., '99,
 LL. M., '00 (Clerk) ....Pension Office, Washington, D. C.
Schuler, Harry R., LL. B., '02, LL. M.,
 '03 (Lawyer) ....Galion, Ohio.
Schulteis, Herman J., LL. M., '02·
Scott, Thomas Edward, A. B., '97·
Scott, Thomas W., LL. B., '96·
Searcy, Reuben Martin, M. D , '92·
Sears, Fulton H., LL. B., '96 (Lawyer)....500 Journal Bldg., Chicago, Ill.·
Seaton, Charles H., LL. B., 91, LL. M., '92·
Seawell, Charles W., A. B., '85, LL. B., '86, LL. M., '87·
Seay, Harry L., LL. B., '94 (Lawyer)......Trust Bldg., Dallas, Tex.
Sibiakin, Ross W., M. D., '81·
Sefton, Edwin, LL. B., '96 (Lawyer)......68 William St., New York City.
Seger, William Thomas, A. B., '94
 (Pianos and Sheet Music)............50 W. 125th St., New York City.
Seitz, Charles J., LL. B , '05...............1609 35th St. N.W., Wash., D. C.
Seitz, Joseph William, A. B., '03, A. M.,
 '04 ....San Francisco, Cal.
Semmes, Alexander Harry, A. B., 81
 (Lawyer) ....Dept. of Justice, Wash., D. C.
Semmes, Rev. Alexander J., A. B., '50,
 A. M., '52; deceased Sept., 1898.
Semmes, Alphonso T., A. B., '50, A. M., '53·
Semmes, Benedict I., A. B., '53, A. M., '55·
Semmes, Francis Joseph, A. B., '90·
Semmes, P. Warfield, A. B., '60·
Semmes, Thomas J., A. B., '42, A. M.,
 '45, LL. D., '80; deceased June 23, 1899.
Senn, Charles A , LL. B., '83·
Sessford, Charles E., LL. B., '95·
Sessford, Joseph S., M. D., '85·

Settle, Tecumseh Gore, LL. B., '97;
 LL. M., '98 (Proofreader, American)...520 Church St., Nashville, Tenn.
Sewall, Eugene D., LL. B., '89, LL. M.,
 '90 ....Patent Office, Washington, D. C.
Shannon, Andrew C., LL. B., '95 (General Manager) ....616 E St. N. W., Wash., D. C.
Sharbaugh, Frank C., LL. B., '95.
Sharp, DeHaven, M. D., '04.
Sharp, Edwin H., LL. B., '98.
Shaw, Clarence, LL. B., '99, LL. M., '00.
Shaw, Clarence Edward, M. D., '01.
Shea, Charles Augustus, A. B., '97
 (Lawyer) ....4 and 5 People's Bldg., Wilkesbarre, Pa.
Shea, E. M., A. B., '98.
Shea, John Gilmary, LL. D., '89; deceased Feb. 23, 1892.
Shea, Michael Ignatius, M. D., '04.
Shea, Thomas J., A. B., '86.
Shealey, Robert Preston, LL. B., '97,
 LL. M., '98 (Lawyer) ....Equity Bldg., Washington, D. C.
Sheean, John A. Rawlins, LL. B., '99
 (Lawyer) ....Lexington, Nebr.
Sheehan, Dennis John, M. D., '04.
Sheehan, John D., LL. B., '95.
Sheehy, Francis Patrick, A. B., '93, LL. B., '95, LL. M., '96.
Sheehy, Joseph C., LL. B., '02 (Lawyer)...Colorado Bldg., Washington, D. C.
Sheehy, Vincent Alphonsus, A. B., '93, LL. B , '95, LL. M., '96.
Sheibley, Sinclair B., LL. B., '86, LL. M., '87.
Shekell, Abraham B., M. D., '63 (Physician) ....1529 Wisconsin Ave., Wash., D. C.
Shekell, Ben R., A. B., '59.
Shenners, Martin Joseph, LL. B., '03
 (Lawyer) ....378 National Ave., Milwaukee, Wis.
Shepard, Hon. Seth, LL. D., '95 (Associate Justice, Court of Appeals).......1447 Mass. Ave. N.W., Washington, D. C.
Shepard, Seth, jr., A. B., '04 (Student,
 Law) ....1447 Mass Ave. N.W., Washington, D. C.
Sheppard, Walter W., LL. M., '94
 (Lawyer) ....Savannah, Ga.
Sheridan, Denis, A. B., '71.
Sheridan, Denis R., A. M., '66, (A. B., '64, H. C. Mass.).
Sheriff, A. Rothwell, LL. B., '92.
Sherman, Henry C., Mus. Doc., '89.

Sherman, Rev. Thomas Ewing, S. J.,
 A. B., '74 (Jesuit Priest) (Mission-
 ary Apostolic) ....413 W. 12th St., Chicago, Ill.
Sherrett, William L., LL. B.,'88, LL. M., '89·
Sherrill, Edgar Beverly, LL. B., '98, LL. M., '00·
Shinn, George Curtis, LL. B., '03·
Shipley, Charles E., LL. B., '04; deceased June 14, 1904.
Shipman, Andrew J., A. B., '78, A. M.,
 '87 (Lawyer) ....7 Wall St., New York City.
Shipman, J. Bennett Carroll, A. B., '92·
Shipp, E. Richard, LL. B., '95, LL. M.,
 '96 (Lawyer) ....Casper, Natrona Co., Wyo.
Shoemaker, Albert Edwin, B. S., '88,
 LL. B , '92, LL. M., '93 (Lawyer)......Columbian Bldg., Wash., D. C.
Shoemaker, F., M. D., '9⊾
Shoemaker, Louis P., LL. ß., '80, LL. M., '81·
Sholes, William H., LL. B., '87, LL. M., '88·
Shomo, Harvey L., LL. B., 'ö6, LL. M., '87·
Short, Francis Jerome, M. D., '04·
Short, William Henry, M. D., '04·
Short, William O., LL. B., '03 (General
 Office, Southern Railroad, Audit-
 ing Department) ....1300 Pa. Ave. N. W., Wash., D. C.
Shoulters, George H., M. D., '83·
Shyne, Michael R., M. D., '55·
Sigur, Lawrence S., A. B., '37·
Sillers, Albert, LL. B., '88 (Lawyer).......472 La. Ave. N. W., Wash., D. C.
Sillers, Robert Fry, M. D., '90·
Simmons, Leo, LL. B., '90, Lᴌ. M., '91·
Simons, H. N., LL. B., '85·
Simenton, John P., LL. B., '78·
Simonton, Vincent DePaul, LL. B., '01
 (Lawyer) ....Pocahontas, Tazewell Co., Va.
Sims, Charles, LL. B., '83, LL. M., '84·
Sims, Grant, LL. M., '91·
Sinclair, A. Leftwich, LL. ß., '93, LL. M., '94·
Sinclair, J. McDonald, ᴌL. ß., '02·
Singleton, Joseph Nilson, LL. B., '88,
 Ph. B., '88..........................16-17 Ingram Block, Eau Claire,
                                      Wis.
Sizer, Adrian, LL. B., '01, LL. M., '02·
Skerrett, Robert Gregg, ᴌL. B., '91,
 LL. M., '92 (Submarine Specialist)....Universitat Strassez, Berlin, Ger-
                                      many.
Skinner, George, M. D., 'ö8.
Slattery, Daniel J., LL. B., '02.

Slattery, Francis Edward, A. B., '96·
Slattery, John R., A. B., '85 (Physician)...520 Broadway, So. Boston, Mass.
Slaughter, William D., LL. B., '93, LL. M., '94·
Sloan, J. G., M. D., '69·
Sloan, Robert Neale, A. B., '85 (Capi-
    talist) ....Stevenson, Md.
Sloane, James H., A. B., '81; deceased
    Oct. 23, 1884, at Baltimore, Md.
Slough, Martin, LL. B., '84·
Smart, Robert, M. D., '96·
Smart, William M., M. D., '02·
Smith, Antonio Justinian, A. B., '96,
    A. M., '97, LL. B., '98, LL. M., '99
    (Lawyer) ....234 Main St., Norfolk, Va.
Smith, Augustine P., LL. B., '88·
Smith, Benjamin, M. D., '73.
Smith, Charles P., LL. B., 82.
Smith, Dexter A., M. D., '84.
Smith, E. Vincent, A. B., 95 (Dry
    Goods) ....298 Main St, Norfolk, Va.
Smith, Edward D., LL. B., '98 (Lawyer)...Birmingham, Ala.
Smith, Edward J., A. B., '01 (Lawyer).....Frederick, Md.
Smith, Edward Joseph, A. B., '01·
Smith, Edmund L., A. B, '49·
Smith, Edmund R., A. B., '48·
Smith, Ernest Renard, A. B., '91·
Smith, Francis T., A. M., '89·
Smith, Frank E., LL. B., '98, LL. M., '99·
Smith, Fred L., A. B., '54, A. M., '58; deceased 1898.
Smith, Giles W. L., LL. B., '93 (Lawyer)..Brewton, Ala.
Smith, Harlan S., M. D., '67·
Smith, Hugh M., M. D., 68.
Smith, James Alexander, LL. B., '99
    (Deputy Tax Collector, 2d District,
    Parish of Orleans) ....St. Anthony Alley, Chartres St.,
                                    New Orleans, La.
Smith, James F., LL. B., '89, LL. M., '90·
Smith, John E., M. D., '67·
Smith, John Francis, A. B., '94 (Lawyer)..Frederick, Md.
Smith, Joseph A., M. D., '55·
Smith, Joseph Edward, M. D., '00·
Smith, Joseph Ernest, D. D. S., '03
    (Dentist) ....631 Pa. Ave. N. W., Wash., D. C.
Smith, Joseph S., M. D., '57·
Smith, L. A., LL. B., '82, LL. M., '84·
Smith, Lloyd, M. D., '70·

Smith, Lucius, M. D., '59·

Smith, P. M., M. D., '94·

Smith, P. W., LL. B., '87·

Smith, Peter D., A. B., '84 (Attorney
    and Counselor at Law...............222 1-2 4th St., Logansport, Ind.

Smith, Peter Xavier, A. B., '82, A. M.,
    '84, LL. B., '84; deceased Feb. 3, 1896.

Smith, Philip, A. B., '18.

Smith, Robert E. L., LL. B., '95,
    LL. M., '96 (Lawyer)..................Columbian Bldg., Wash., D. C.

Smith, Thomas C., M. D., '64·

Smith, Thomas W., A. B., '01·

Smith, Walter, A. B., '43·

Smith, William F., A. B., '78, LL. B., '80.

Smith, William M., A. B., 53, A. M., '57;
    deceased May 4, 1892.

Smith, William Meredith, A. B., '00,
    M. D., '04 (Physician)................Frederick, Md.

Smyth, James J., LL. B., '92, LL. M., '93·

Snow, William S., A. B., '61·

Snyder, Harold C., LL. B., '96

Sohon, Frederick, M. D., '88 (Physician)...512 I St. N. W., Washington, D. C.

Sohon, Henry W., LL. B., '84, LL. M.,
    '85, A. M., '89 (Lawyer)..............Fendall Bldg , Washington, D. C.

Solignac, Gustave L., LL. B., '92·

Solis, Frederico, A. M., '01 (Manager·
    Foreign Department) ....Care Messrs. Bolin & Co., Málaga,
                                        Spain.

Somers, Paul Joseph, A. M., '99, LL. B.,
    '01 (Lawyer) ....27 Cawker Bldg , Milwaukee, Wis.

Sonnenschmidt, C. W., M. D., '67 (Phy-
    sician) ....The Thomas, Thomas Circle,
                                        Wash., D. C.

Soper, Julius S., A. B., '66, A. M., '67·

Sothoron, James J., M. D., '65; deceased Sept. 27, 1897.

Sothoron, Levin Johnson, M. D., '96·

Sour, Louis, M. D., '55·

Spalding, Samuel E., M. D., '58·

Spangler, William A., LL. B., '88, LL. M., '90.

Sparks, Augustus R., M. D., '59·

Spear, J. M., LL. B., '91·

Spier, Alexander M , LL. B., '91, LL. M , '92·

Spellacy, Thomas J., LL. B , '01 (Law-
    yer) ....26 State St , Hartford, Conn.

Spellissy, James M., A. B., '55, A. M.,
    '56; deceased June, 1875, at New York City.

Spellissy, Joseph H., A. B., '85, A. M., '90·
Spratt, Maurice Charles, A. B., '88
    (Lawyer) ....736 Ellicott Square, Buffalo, N. Y.
Springer, Ruher W., LL. B., '89, LL. M., '90·
Sprinkle, Thomas H., LL. M., '93·
Sproules, Joseph Aloysius, A. B., '95·
    (Physician) ....Boston, Mass.
Squier, Algernon Marble, M. D., '67·
Stack, John B., LL. B., '87·
Stack, Joseph C., LL. B., '04 (Patent
    Lawyer) ....Pacific Bldg., Washington, D. C.
Stack, Maurice J., M D., 76.
Stackhouse, George M., LL. B., '98·
Stead, Mark Aloysius, A. M., '98 (Law-
    yer) ....108 1-2 N. 8th St., St. Louis, Mo.
Stafford, Rev. Denis J., D. J., '90·.........St. Patrick's Rectory, 619 10th St.
                                           N. W., Washington, D. C.
Stafford, James Raymond, LL. B., '98·
Stafford, John J., M. D., 65, A. M., '86·
Stagg, John Alfred, LL. B., '97, LL. M., '98·
Staley, Charles Melrose, LL. B., '87
    (Clerk) ....War Dept., Washington, D. C.
Staley, William 'F., LL. B., '92, LL. M.,
    '93 (Examiner).....................General Land Office, Wash., D. C.
Stallings, Thomas B., LL. B., '05 (Law-
    yer) ....1828 Lincoln Ave., Denver, Colo.
Stang, Rt. Rev. William, D. D., '89........163 Winter St., Fall River, Mass.
Stanion, Ralph P., LL. B., '05 (Super-
    intendent Indian School).............Darlington, Okla.
Stansell, Wallace K., LL. B., '90, LL. M., '91·
Stanton, Lemuel J., LL. M., '87·
Starek, Emil, LL. B., '89, LL. M., '90·
Starkweather, Carlton Lee, M. D., '98.
Starr, Joseph A., M. D., '02·
Stearns, Joseph Sargent, M. D., '94
    (Physician) ....1425 R. I. Ave. N. W., Wash., D. C.
Stearns, Dr. S. S., M. D., '66 (Physician)...1425 R. I. Ave. N. W., Wash., D._C.
Stein, Robert, M. D, '86 (U. S. Geolog-
    ical Survey) ....306 L St. S.E., Washington, D. C.
Steinmertz, William R., M. D., '65·
Stephan, Anton, LL. B., '91, LL. M., '92·...Care Messrs. Wm. H. McKnew Co.,
                                           Washington, D. C.
Stephens, F. Wilson, LL. B., '01·
Stephens, John J., M. D., '68·
Stephens, Thomas A., A. B., '74 (Mer-
    chant) ....709 12th St., Washington, D. C.

Stephenson, Joseph Gwynn, M. D., '75·
Sterling, Hugh M., LL. B., '91, LL. M., '92.
Stetson, Charles W., LL. B., '90,
    LL. M., '92 (Lawyer)................482 La. Ave. N. W., Wash., D. C.
Stevens, Eugene E., LL. B., '88, LL. M.,
    '89 (Lawyer)..........................817 14th St. N. W., Wash., D. C.
Stevens, Frank L., LL. B., '92, LL. M., '93·
Stewart, Fenwick Joseph, A. B., '91·
Stewart, John Frew, LL. M., '96 (L'y'r)....Pension Office, Washington, D. C.
Stewart, William Walter, LL. B., '97, LL. M., '98·
Stier, Henry Clay, Jr., LL. B., '98, LL. M., '00·
Stitt, Frederick S., LL. B., '98·
Stockbridge, Virgil D., LL. B., '75 (As-
    sistant Examiner) ....Patent Office, Washington, D. C.
Stockly, Charles Daniel, LL. B., '04
    (Lawyer) ....715 Market St., Wilmington, Del.
Stockman, Charles W., M. D., '65·
Stockstill, Francis W., LL. B., '83·
Stone, Addison G., LL. B., '75·
Stone, Charles, A. B., '59 (H. C. Mass.)
    (Journalist); deceased 1867.
Stone, George H., M. D., '68; deceased
    Feb. 19, 1899, at Savannah, Ga.
Stone, Ralph W., A. B., '95, LL. B., '95, LL. M., '96·
Stone, Warren C., LL. B., 73.
Stonebraker, Samuel E., LL. B., '04·
Stonestreet, Rev., Charles H., S. J.,
    A. B., '33 (Jesuit Priest and Presi-
    dent of Georgetown University);
    deceased July 3, 1885.
Stonestreet, Nicholas, A. B., '36, A. M., '40; deceased 1889.
Storer, Hon. Bellamy, LL. D., '02·
Story, Leon Ellery, M. D., '01·
Stout, Alexander M., M. D., '80·
Stout, Stanley S., LL. B., '74.
Stoutenberg, J. A., M. D., '91·
Strasburger, Milton, LL. B., '96,
    LL. M., '98 (Lawyer)................Columbian Bldg., Wash., D. C.
Strass, Henry, A. B., '26·
Stratton, John T., M. D., '73·
Strawbridge, Henry, A. B., '37·
Streater, Wallace, LL. B., '93, LL. M.,
    '94 (Lawyer) ....Interior Dept., Washington, D. C.
Street, Daniel B., M. D., '74·
Street, Garfield A., LL. B., '04·
Street, H. R., M. D., '91.

Strickland, Reeves T., LL. B., '97, LL. M., '98·
Stringfield, Francis M , M. D , '70·
Strittmatter, Thomas P., LL. B., '95
    (Manufacturer) ....3115 N. 5th St., Phila., Pa.
Strong, Michael R., A. B., '60, A. M.,'62·
Stuart, Benjamin R., LL. B., '96·
Sudbrink, John T., LL. B., '99·
Sudler, Oden Rochester, M. D., '03.
    (Physician and Surgeon) ....462 H St. N. W., Washington, D. C.
Sullivan, Francis Paul, A. B., '04.........1823 Vernon Place, Wash., D. C.
Sullivan, Francis W., A. B., '87............512 1st Nat. Bank, Duluth, Minn.
Sullivan, George E , LL. B., '02·
Sullivan, George M., LL. B., '74 (Clerk)....Bureau of Engraving and Print-
                                            ing, Wash., D. C.
Sullivan, James F., A. B., '52 (H. C.
    Mass.); (Clergyman); deceased July 26, 1905.
Sullivan, Jere A., LL. B., '05 (Law
    Student) ....15 3d St., Newport, R. I.
Sullivan, J. H., A. B., '93 (Stockman)......Temple, Tex.
Sullivan, John Joseph, A. B., '98·
Sullivan, John K., LL. B., '76.
Sullivan, Joseph Daniel, A. B., '97,
    LL. B., '99, LL. M., '00 (Lawyer)......Columbian Bldg , Wash., D. C.
Sullivan, Joseph David, D. D. S., '03·
Sullivan, Michael William, LL. B., '03,
    LL M., '05 (Lawyer).·...............Elmira, N. Y.
Sullivan, Patrick Thomas, M. D , '95
Sullivan, Simon E., LL B., '96, LL. M.,'97·
Sullivan, Thomas J., LL. B., '85, LL. M., '86·
Sullivan, Thomas V., A. B., '00·
Sullivan, Timothy Joseph, M. D., '04·
Sullivan, W. L., M. D., '94·
Sullivan, William Cleary, LL. B., '01
    (Lawyer) ....·.....410 5th St. N. W., Wash., D. C.
Sullivan, William D., LL B.,.'01 (Real
    Estate, Loans, and Insurance)........707 13th St. N. W., Wash., D. C.
Summy, B. W., M D., '86·
Swayne, Noah H., jr., LL. B., '73·
Swayze, S Courtland, A. B., '53·
Sweeney, Harry J , LL. B., '04·
Sweeney, John E., LL. B., '89, LL. M.,'90.
Sweetman, James T., M. D., '72.
Swetman, Charles R. Keith, M. D., '04·
Sylvester, George, M. D., '64. .
Sylvester, J. Henry, M. D., '71·

Taggart, Hugh Fairgreave, LL. B., '92,
    LL. M., '93 (Lawyer)................400 5th St. N. W., Wash., D. C.
Talbot, J. Theodore •(U. S. A.), A. M.,
    '47; deceased, April 22, 1862.
Talbott, Edward Melville, M. D., '01·
Talmadge, Theodore, LL. M., '89·
Tarkington, J. A., M. D., '70·
Tastet, Joseph M., M. D , '53·
Tatum, Thomas H., LL. B., '02 (Law-
    yer) ....Bishopville, S. C.
Tauzin, Emile M., A. B., '55·
Taylor, A. S., LL. B , '81, LL. M,, '82.
Taylor, Charles B., LL. B., '99·
Taylor, Charles Benjamin, M. D., '05·
Taylor, George W , LL. B , '90, LL. M., '91·
Taylor, James A., Ph. B., '88·
Taylor, Judge John Lewis, LL. D., '28 (Supreme Court); deceased, Jan. 29,
    1829, at Raleigh, N. C.
Taylor, John Louis, LL. D., '22·
Taylor, Leroy M., M. D., '60; deceased.
Taylor, Dr. J. Archibald, M. D , '85; deceased.
Taylor, Thomas, M. D.; 82.
Taylor, Walter I., LL. M., '91.
Taylor, William C., LL. B , '91, LL. M., '93·
Teeling, Very Rev. John, D. D., '54·
Teicher, John G., LL. B., '88, LL. M.,
    '89 (U. S. Special Examiner of
    Pensions) ....Dept. of Interior, Wash., D. C.
Telford, Erastus Dalson, LL. B., '99,
    LL. M , '00 (Lawyer) ....Salem, Ill.
Tepper, Joseph L , LL. B., '04 (Lawyer)...Columbian Bldg., Wash , D. C.
Test, Frederick Cleveland, M. D., '95·
Tete, Leo Frederick, B. S., '83·
Thatcher, John, M. D., '68·
Thian, Louis R., A. B , '75 (Lawyer)......Minneapolis, Minn.
Thian, Prosper E., A. B., '81·
Thomaides, George Th., LL. B., '05·
Thomas, Charles Theodore, LL. B., '94, LL. M., '95.
Thomas, Edward H., LL. B., '77 (Law-
    yer) ....916 F St. N. W., Washington, D. C.
Thomas, Edward J., LL. B., '76·
Thomas, Roy, LL. B., '97 (Electrotyper)...Navy Dept., Washington, D. C.
Thompson, Charles F., LL. B , '02·
Thompson, Edwin S., LL. B., '91, LL. M., '92·
Thompson, Frederick M., LL. B., '91·
Thompson, Granville S , M. D., '67·

Thompson, John C., A. B., '42; deceased, May, 1895.

Thompson, Dr. John H., A. M , '65·

Thompson, John H., jr., M. D., '75·

Thompson, John S., M. D., '95·

Thompson, Michael Joseph, A. M., '01·

Thompson, Smith, jr., LL. B., '96, LL. M., '97·

Thorn, Charles Edwin, LL. M., '94·

Thornton, Richard H., LL. B., '78·

Thurn, George A., M. D., '70·

Tibbals, W. F., M. D., '65·

Tibbitts, Orlando O., LL. B., '05 (Law-
yer) ....Oklahoma City, Okla. Ter.

Tierney, Rev. John J., D. D., '93 (Pro-
fessor) ....Mt. St. Mary's College Emmitsburg, Md.

Tierney, Matthew D., LL. B., '88, LL. M., '89·

Tierney, Michael V., LL. B., '86, LL. M , '87.

Tierney, Myles Joseph, A. B., '95 (Phy-
sician) ....143 W. 74th St., New York City.

Tilden, William C., M. D., '67·

Tillman, Lloyd Montgomery, LL. B.,
'99, LL. M., 1900 (Clerk).............Treasury Dept., Washington, D. C.

Timmes, John W., A. B., '01 (Lawyer)....Shamokin, Pa.

Timmins, Dr. P. J., M. D., '78·

Timmins, Thomas J., A. B., '78·

Tindall, William, M. D., '69, LL. B., '82.

Tinley, John A., LL. B., '97·

Tobin, Clement P., LL. B., '93·

Tobin, Edward James, A. B., '95, A. M., '96, Ph. D., '97, LL. B., '97.

Tobin, James H., LL. B., '93, LL. M.,
'94 (Clerk)...........................U. S. Pension Agency, Milwaukee,
Wis.

Tobin, Joseph E., jr., LL. B., '90.

Tobin, Richard Francis, M. D., '05
(Physician) ....·....Washington Asylum Hospital,
Washington, D. C.

Toner, John E., M. D., '91 (Physician)....214 14th St. N. E., Wash., D. C.

Toner, Joseph M., A. M., '67, Ph. D., '89; deceased July 30, 1896.

Tonry, Prof. William P., Ph. D., '75; deceased.

Toomey, James A., A. B., '96, A. M., '97, LL. B., '01·

Torrey, Earl G., LL. B., '92, LL. M., '93·

Torrey, Turner, M. D., '73·

Totten, Howe, LL. B., '95, LL. M., '96
(Lawyer) ....Room 306, Pope Bldg., Wash., D. C.

Touart, Tisdale Joseph, A. M., '02
(Lawyer) ....Mobile, Ala.

Toumay, Francis, LL. B., '82.

Tower, Frederick W., LL. B., '90' LL. M., '91·

Towsend, Charles G., LL. B., '92' LL. M., '93·

Townsend, Samuel D., LL. B., '05.

Tracy, James, A. B., '59 (H. C., Mass.) (Clergyman); deceased, July, 1866.

Tracy, James F., A. B., '74 (Justice of
the Supreme Court of the Philip-
pine Islands)........................Manila, Philippine Islands.

Tracey, Luke Louis, A. M., '96' Ph. D.,
'97 (Lawyer).......................Union Trust Bldg., Detroit, Mich.

Tralles, George Edward, LL. B., '97'
LL. M., '98 (Lawyer)................Berry & Whitmore Building,
                                    Washington, D. C.

Trautman, B., M. D., '74·

Tree, Charles M., M. D., '67; deceased, Dec. 3, 1881.

Trembly, Royal H., LL. B., '99' LL. M., 1900.

Tremoulet, Joseph Sydney, A. B., '97
(New Orleans Manager, The Gras-
selli Chemical Co.)...................P. O. Box 1108, Cleveland, Ohio.

Trenholm, Frank, LL. B., '92' LL. M.,
'93 (Lawyer)........................141 Broadway, New York City.

Trenholm, W. de Saussure, LL. B., '90·

Triplet, Caius E., LL. B., '88, LL. M., '89·

Trott, Thomas H., M. D., '67·

Troy, Robert P., LL. B., '99 (Lawyer).....Call Building, San Francisco, Cal.

Tschiffely, Stuart Aloysius, A. B., '02
(Pharmacist) ....924 F St. N. W., Washington, D. C.

Tucker, Maurice, M. D., '62·

Tuomy, Rev. John, LL. D., '21·

Tureaud, Benjamin, A. B., '88·

Turner, Emmett, LL. B., '90' LL. M., '91.

Turner, Henry V., A. B., '80·

Turner, John F., LL. B., '05 (Lawyer).....Grafton, W. Va.

Turner, Lawrence J., M. D., '64·

Turner, O. C., M. D., '64·

Turner, S. S., M. D., '63·

Turpin, Henry W., M. D., '64.

Twibill, Aloysius Holland, A. M., '01......Philadelphia, Pa.

Tyler, Frederick S., LL. B., '05 (Law-
yer) ....Colorado Bldg., Washington, D. C.

Ucker, Clement S., LL. B., '98' LL. M.,
'99 (Law Service, General Land
Office) ....Washington, D. C.

Underwood, Fred Rutan, M. D., '97·

Underwood, Robert L., LL. B., '99
(Clerk) ....Pension Bureau, Wash., D. C.

Vale, Frank P., M.'D., '92 (Physician).....1616 I St. N. W., Washington, D. C.
Valentine, Charles Francis, A. B., '96·
Van Arnum, John W., M. D., '67; deceased, 1884.
Van Bibber, Claude, A. B., '74 (Physi-
cian and Surgeon)....................9 E. Read St., Baltimore, Md.
Van Casteel, Gerald, LL. B., '99, LL.
M., 1900 (Lawyer)....................Bond Building, Washington, D. C.
Vander Chatten, Baron, A. M., '45·
Vanderhoff, George, A. M., '58·
Vandeventer, Braden, LL. B., '99·
Van Duzer, Clarence, LL. B., '93, LL. M., '94·
Van Dyne, Frederick, LL. B., '90, LL.
M., '91 (Assistant Solicitor).........Dept. of State, Washington, D. C.
Vanel, Andrew V., A. B., '39·
Van Gieson, Henry C., M. D., '64·
Van Vranken, Frederick, LL. B., '92,
LL. M., '93 (Clerk)...................War Dept., Washington, D. C.
Vaughan, Daniel C., LL. B., '95, LL.
M., '96 (Clerk).......................Department of Commerce and La-
bor, Washington, D. C.
Vaughan, Walter J., LL. B., '96, LL.
M., '97 (Journalist and Publisher).....Millidgeville, Ga.
Verrill, Charles H., LL. B., '90, LL. M.,
'91 (Statistician)....................1429 N. Y. Ave., Wash., D. C.
Vest, Hon. George Graham, LL. D., '00; deceased.
Via, Lemuel R., LL. B., '98·
Vierbuchen, Julius, LL. B., '05·
Vincent, Thomas N., A. B., '85, A. M., '91·
Von Rosen, Ferdinand G., LL. B., '87, LL. M., '93.
Von Rosenberg, Fred C., LL. B., '89·
Voorhees, Charles S., A. B., '73·

Wadden, John Joseph, A. B., '04 (Im-
plement and Gasoline Engine
Business) ....Madison, S. Dak.
Wade, Edward Julius, A. B., '04 (Stu-
dent) ....1410 N. Broad St., Phila., Pa.
Waggaman, Samuel John, jr., A. B., '98·
Wagner, G. Henry, M. D., '85.
Wagner, R. B., M. D., '70·
Waguespeck, William J., A. B., '82
(Lawyer) ....219 Carondelet St., New Orleans,
La.

Wahly, William H., LL. B., '96' LL. M., '97.

Wainscott, George, LL. B., '74·

Waite, George W. C., LL. B., '74·

Waldo, G. S., D. D. S., '02·

Wales, Orlando G., LL. B., '87·

Walker, Charles M., LL. B., '93 (Secretary, Monroe Cotton Mills).........Monroe, Ga.

Walker, Francis B., LL. B., '89' LL. M., '90·

Walker, James S., LL. B., '83·

Walker, John Brisben, Ph. D., '89 (Writer and Business Manager).......Irvington-on-Hudson, N. Y.

Walker, John B. Fuller, LL. B., '98·

Walker, Lewis Albert, jr., M. D., '98·

Walker, Ralph E., LL. B., '01·

Walker, Reginald Redford, M. D., 1900 (Physician) ....1710 H St. N. W., Wash., D. C.

Walker, W. Henry, LL. B., '88' LL. M., '89·

Walker, William A., A. B., '60'(H. C., Mass.) (Teacher); deceased, at New Orleans, La.

Walker, William Gillespie, LL. B., '97 (Clerk) ....Treasury Dept., Washington, D. C.

Walker, William H., M. D., '02 (Physician) ....Franklyn Ave., New Brighton, Staten Island, New York.

Walker, Gen. William Stephen, A. B., '41·

Wall, Joseph Stiles, M. D., '97·

Wall, Maurice J., LL. B., '05 (Examiner) ....U. S. Patent Office, Wash., D. C.

Wall, Michael, A. M., '66·

Wall, Very Rev. Stephen, V. G., D. D., '89; deceased, Aug. 21, 1894.

Walace, Hamilton S., LL. B., '84·

Wallace, Joseph F., M. D., '99 (Physician and Surgeon)...................Leavenworth, Kans.

Wallace, M. T., M. D., '73·

Wallis, Samuel B., A. B., '84·

Wallis, Samuel T., A. M., '87·

Walsh, Edward F., LL. B., '02·

Walsh, Ed. J., LL. B., '93' LL. M., '94 (Manager Northwestern National Insurance Company).................1302 F St. N. W., Wash., D. C.

Walsh, Francis, M. D., '66·

Walsh, Henry Collins, A. M., '88 (Editor) ....452 5th Ave., New York City.

Walsh, John H., A. B., '73' A. M., '89·

Walsh, John K., M. D., '65·

Walsh, Julius Sylvester, jr., A. B., '98·
Walsh, Michael James, A. B., '01 (Law-
    yer) ....Mayfield, Pa.
Walsh, R. S. L., M. D., '63·
Walsh, Redmond D., A. B., '78·
Walsh, Thomas, Ph. B., '92, Ph. D., '99
    (Author) ....227 Clinton St., Brooklyn, N. Y.
Walsh, Thomas J., A. B., '94, A. M., '96·
Walsh, William A., LL. B., '97 (Lawyer)....2-8 Hudson St., Yonkers, N. Y.
Walsh, William S., A. M., '89·
Walshe, Patrick J., LL. B., '98, LL. M.,99.
Walter, Dr. John, jr., M. D., '68.
Walter, William Francis, M. D., '92
    (Physician) ....487 H St. S. W., Wash., D. C.
Walters, Harris A., LL. B., '99 (Gen-
    eral Manager, Washington Hy-
    draulic Press Brick Company)........Colorado Bldg., Washington, D. C.
Walters, Henry, A. B., '69, A. M., '71
    (Chairman, Atlantic Coast Line).....5 South St., Baltimore, Md.
Walthall, Wilson J., A. B., '54·
Wanamaker, William H., LL. B., '99·
Wand, Arthur J., LL. B., '05·
Ward, Elijah J., M. D., '80·
Ward, Francis M., M. D., '81.
Ward, Francis X., A. B., '59, A. M., '67·
Ward, George A., LL. B., '98, LL. M.,
    '99 (Assistant Chief, Land Di-
    vision) ....Indian Office, Washington, D. C.
Ward, Samuel B., M. D., '64·
Ward, Samuel R., M. D., '68·
Ward, William, M. D., '71·
Wardwell, Eugene McC., LL. B., '93, LL. M., '94·
Ware, Edward H., M. D., '65·
Warfield, Ralph Sturtevant, LL. B.,
    '98, LL. M., '99 (Patent Lawyer)......407 Eddy Bldg., Saginaw, Mich.
Warman, Philip C., LL. B., '80 (Editor)...Geological Survey, Wash., D. C.
Warner, Richard Ambrose, M. D., '01
    (Assistant Surgeon).................U. S. Navy, Washington, D. C.
Warren, Bates, LL. B., '92, LL. M., '93·
Warren, Charles, M. D., '68·
Warren, John L., LL. B., '99, LL. M., 1900.
Warriner, William F., LL. M., '87·
Washburn, Albert H., LL. B., '95·
Washington, Joseph E., A. B., '73, A.
    M., '89 (Planter).....................Wessyngton, Tenn.
Wasson, Robert Bingham, LL. B., '99·

Waters, Bowie F., LL. B., '93 (Lawyer)...Rockville, Md.

Waters, David C., M. D., '67·

Waters, Elkhanah N., LL. B., '76·

Waters, Francis, A. B., '55, A. M., '56·

Waters, Thomas B., LL. B., '91·

Watkins, John C., M. D., '65·

Watkins, Richard James, A. B., '97,
LL. B., '99, LL. M., 1900 (Lawyer;
Secretary Georgetown University
Law School)........................Century Bldg., Washington, D. C.

Watkins, Samuel Evans, M. D., '92
(Physician) ....1246 10th St., Washington, D. C.

Watkins, Victor E., M. D., '94·

Watson, James A., M. D., '90 (Physi-
cian) ....201 Monroe St., Anacostia, D. C.

Watson, James M., LL. B., '02·

Watson, Joseph Twichell, LL. M., '03
(Lawyer) ....Alaska Bldg., Seattle, Wash.

Watson, Martin M., LL. B., '05 (Fancy
Grocer) ....Center Market, Washington, D. C.

Watson, Richard F., LL. B., '05 (At-
torney at Law).....................Greenville, S. C.

Watson, Robert, LL. B., '95 (Patent
Lawyer) ....McGill Bldg., Washington, D. C.

Watterson, George W., A. B., '32, A. M., '43, LL. D., '59·

Watterson, Rt. Rev. John Ambrose, D. D., '78; deceased, April 7, 1899. ·

Watts, Reuben Benjamin, LL. B., '98
(Lawyer) ....Birmingham, Ala.

Wayland, Confucius L., LL. M., '89·

Weaver, Alfred S., D. D. S., '02 (Dentist)..729 15th St. N. W., Wash., D. C.

Webb, Daniel Aloysius, A. M., '95, M.
D., '96 (Surgeon) ....310 Wyoming Ave., Scranton, Pa.

Weber, Casper C., LL. B., '90, LL. M., '91·

Weber, Julius Henry, LL. B., '99 (U. S. A., Retired).

Webster, Ben, M. D., 1900.

Webster, Ben Temple, LL. B., '98.

Webster, Charles S., LL. B., '89.

Wedderburn, George C., LL. B., '92, LL. M., '96·

Weed, Chester A., LL. M., '92·

Welch, Benjamin T., LL. B., '90·

Welch, Thomas Francis, M. D., '04·

Welch, Timothy J., A. B., '97·

Wellenreiter, Otto Francis, M. D., '01·

Weller, James Ignatius, A. B., '93, LL.
B., '95 (Real Estate Broker).........602 F St. N. W, Washington, D. C.

Wellman, George M., M. D., '68·

Wellman, George T., LL. B., '91, LL.
   M., '92 (Lawyer)....................930 3d Ave., Sheldon, Iowa.
Wells, George M., Phar. B., '72.
Wells, John Bernard, A. M., '05 (Jour-
   nalist) ....326 N. Howard St., Baltimore, Md.
Wells, Walter A., M. D., '91 (Physician)...The Rochambeau, Wash., D. C.
Wells, Walter H., M. D., '68.
Welsh, John Joseph, LL. B., '03.
Wendel, Robert Paine, M. D., '92.
Werle, Charles M., LL. B., '96.
Wertenbacker, C. I., M. D., '94.
Wessel, John Frederick, A. B., '96
   (Electrical Engineer)................Gen. Electric Co., Baltimore, Md.
West, Bertram H., LL. B., '75.
Westfall, Harry M., LL. B., '90.
Westenhaver, David C., LL. M., '84
   (Lawyer) ....929 Garfield Bldg., Cleveland, Ohio.
Westmore, James A., LL. B., '96 (Chief
   of Law and Records Division, Su-
   pervising Architect's Office)...........Treasury Dept., Washington, D. C.
Weyrich, John Raymond, LL. B., '04,
   LL. M., '05 (U. S. Attorney's Office)...City Hall, Washington, D. C.
Wheatly, J. Walter, LL. B., '89, LL.
   M., '90 (Clerk)......................Treasury Dept., Washington, D. C.
Wheaton, Henry, M. D., '66.
Wheaton, Isaac S., LL. B., '85.
Wheeler, Arthur M., jr., LL. B., '94
   (Stenographer) ....3 B St. S. E., Washington, D. C.
Wheeler, General Joseph, U. S. A., LL.
   D., '99; deceased, Jan., 1906.
Wheeler, Laban Homer, LL. M., '87
   (Lawyer) ....546 N. Y. Block, Seattle, Wash.
Wheeler, William D., LL. B., '04 (Clerk)...Patent Office Dept., Wash., D. C.
Wheelock, George L., LL. B., '89, LL. M., '90.
Whelan, Benjamin L., A. M., '57.
Whelan, John A., LL. B., '03, LL. M., '04.
Whilley, William H., A. M., '85.
Whipple, Ulysses V., LL. B., '89, LL. M., '90.
White, Charles Albert, A. B., '90, LL.
   B., '92, LL. M., '93 (Lawyer).........Bond Bldg., Washington, D. C.
White, Columbus J., M. D., '66.
White, Hon. Edward Douglass, LL. D.,
   '92 (Associate Justice U. S. Su-
   preme Court; President Alumni
   Association of Washington, D. C.)......Washington, D. C.
White, Edward H., A. B., '68.

White, Francis P., LL. B., '87, LL. M.,
  '88 (Clerk).........................Bureau of Pensions, Wash., D. C.
White, Guy Harris, D. D. S., '02 (Den-
  tist) ....825 Vermont Ave., Wash., D. C.
White, James R., LL. B., '89, LL. M., '90.
White, John W., M. D., '70.
White, Louis C., B. S., '87, LL. B., '89,
  LL. M., '90 (Lawyer)................170 Broadway, New York City.
White, Robert R., LL. B., '99, LL. M., 1900.
White, Thomas J., LL. B., '82, LL. M.,
  '83 (Lawyer) ....Commercial National Bank, Kan-
                                         sas City, Kans.
White, William Henry, LL. B., '97
  (Lawyer) ....715 Columbian Bldg., Wash., D. C.
Whitefoot, R. M., M. D., '66.
Whitehouse, Joseph S., LL. M., '87
  (Lawyer) ....Tacoma, Wash.
Whiteley, Richard Peyton, A. B., '01,
  LL. B., '04 (Lawyer)................1419 G St. N. W., Wash., D. C.
Whiting, William H. C., U. S. A., A. B.,
  '40, A. M., '50 (Confederate Gen-
  eral); deceased, March 10, 1865.
Whitley, W. H., M. D., '66.
Whitney, C. F., M. D., '90.
Whitten, John L., LL. M., '91 (Lawyer)...Point Pleasant, W. Va.
Whitthorne, Washington C., jr., LL.
  B., '88 (Lawyer).....................Columbia, Tenn.
Wibirt, William C., LL. B., '89.
Wiecker, Otho, LL. B., '86.
Wiggenhorn, Edwin C., LL. B., '89, LL. M., '90.
Wiggin, Augustus W., M. D., '65.
Wikle, Douglas, LL. B., '80.
Wikoff, William, A. B., '27.
Wilcox, Adolphus D., LL. B., '94 (Chief
  Clerk) ....Bureau of Insular Affairs, War
                                         Department, Wash., D. C.
Wilcox, John A., M. D., '57.
Wilcox, John H., Mus. Doc., '64.
Wilder, A. M., M. D., '63.
Wildman, Joseph C., LL. B., '73.
Wilkerson, Oliver D., LL. B., '95, LL. M., '96.
Wilkinson, A. D., M. D., '93.
Willcox, James M., jr., A. B., '81, A.
  M., '89 (Vice President of the
  Philadelphia Saving Fund Society)...700 Walnut St., Philadelphia, Pa.
Willcox, William J., A. B., '76, A. M., '89, deceased, 1895.

Willett, Archibald M., LL. B., '95; deceased, Oct. 19, 1905.

Willett, J. Edward, M. D., '55·

Willey, Harry P., LL. B., '92, LL. M.,
'93 (Clerk)...........................Law Division, Bureau of Pensions,
Washington, D. C.

Williams, A. Roy, LL. B., '04·

Williams, Charles Fuller, LL. B., '05
(Lawyer) ....10 W. 33d St., New York City.

Williams, George Francis, LL. M., '89
(Lawyer) ....606 F St. N. W., Washington, D. C.

Williams, Hugh H., LL. B., '96, LL. M., '97·

Williams, John G., LL. B., '97 (Auditor
Norfolk and Washington Steam-
boat Company).......................7th Street Wharf, Wash., D. C.

Williams, Dr. R. E., M. D., '70·

Williams, Sherman, M. D., '98·

Williams, W. Mosby, LL. B., '90, LL.
M., '91 (Lawyer)....................Columbian Bldg., Wash., D. C.

Williams, William F., A. B., '63; deceased, Sept. 9, 1892.

Williamson, Frank E., LL. B., '03, LL. M., '04·

Williamson, George M., LL. M., '93·

Williamson, Hugh C., A. B., '66, A. M., '72·

Williamson, Joseph A., LL. B., '05·

Willige, Louis C., LL. B., '90·

Wills, Joseph W., LL. B., '93, LL. M., '94·

Wills, William Xavier, A. B., '51, A. M.
'59; deceased, June, 1865, in Charles
County, Md.

Willson, Prentiss, M. D., '05·

Willson, S. C., M. D., '88·

Wilson, Andrew, LL. B., '90, LL. M.,
'91 (Lawyer).......................504 E St. N. W., Wash., D. C.

Wilson, Augustus, A. B., '60; deceased, Sept., 1903.

Wilson, Calvert, A. B., '86, A. M., '90
(Lawyer) ....Los Angeles, Cal.

Wilson, Clarence R., LL. M., '99.

Wilson, Edwin L., LL. B., '95·

Wilson, Eliel Soper, A. B., '46, A. M.,
'48; deceased, Sept. 1860, in Anne
Arundel County, Md.

Wilson, Henry O., LL. B., '89, LL. M., '90·

Wilson, Henry Peter, A. B., '91; deceased.

Wilson, Hon. Jeremiah M., LL. D., '83·

Wilson, John Chamberlin, A. B., '65
(by profession, Lawyer; not prac-
ticing) ....Cosmos Club, Washington, D. C.

Wilson, John E., A. B., '45, A. M., '47·

Wilson, Lawrence, M. D., '70·

Wilson, Nelson, LL. B., '04, LL. M., '05
(Lawyer) ....408 5th St. N. W., Wash., D. C.

Wilson, Thomas J., LL. B., '92·

Wimberly, Warren W., M. D., '92·

Wing, George C., LL. B., '73·

Wingard, Edward V., M. D., '80·

Wimsatt, William Kurtz, A. B., '00·
(Wholesale Lumber, Johnson &
Wimsatt Company)..................1212 Water St. S. W., Wash., D. C.

Winkle, Douglas, LL. B., '80·

Winter, John T., M. D., '70.

Winthrop, William, LL. D., '96·

Wise, James A., A. B., '58; deceased, Feb. 23, 1875, at Austin, Tex.

Wise, Thomas W., M. D., '66; deceased, Feb. 17, 1892.

Wissner, Frank J., LL. B., '01·

Woerner, Otto E., LL. B., '04·

Wolf, Alexander, LL. B., '92, LL. M.,
'93 (Lawyer).........................Jenifer Bldg., Washington, D. C.

Wolf, Dr. J. S., M. D., '67; deceased, Dec. 7, 1898.

Wolfe, John Loyola, A. M., '02, LL. B.,
'04 (Lawyer).........................302-4-6 Weston Building, Clinton,
Iowa.

Wolfe, John Magruder, A. B., '01 (Key-
stone Coal and Coke Company)......New Alexandria, Pa.

Wolfe, William Lloyd, A. B., '92·

Wolhanpter, William E., M. D., '90; deceased, Jan. 21, 1896.

Wollenberg, Robert A. C., M. D., '05·

Wood, George F., M. D., '65·

Wood, George William, M. D., '94
(Physician) ....2906 P St. N. W., Wash., D. C.

Wood, Leonard C., LL. B., '85, LL. M., '86·

Wood, William C., LL. B., '89, LL. M., '90·

Woodburn, William, jr., LL. B., '03·

Woodbury, Edward C., M. D., '63·

Woodbury, H. E., M. D., '63·

Woodley, Robert D., A. B., '25·

Woodley, Thomas A., M. D., '57·

Woods, Joseph, A. B., '55 (St. F. X., New York).

Woodson, L. C., M. D., '91·

Woodward, Herbert E., LL. B., '85, LL.
M., '87 (Clerk)......................Assessor's Office, District Building,
Washington, D. C.

Woodward, Rigual Duckett, A. B., '85
(Lawyer) ....17 Battery Place, New York City.

Woodward, Roland E., M. D., '64·
Woodward, Thomas Purcell, LL. B., '89
    (Lawyer) ....610 13th St. N. W., Wash., D. C.
Woodward, William Creighton, M. D.,
    '89, LL. B., '99, LL. M., 1900 (Phy-
    sician) ....Health Department, Wash., D. C.
Woolf, Oliver P., LL. B., '89, LL. M.,
    '90 (Clerk)..........................Office Auditor for Post-office De-
                  partment, Washington, D. C.
Wootton, Edward, A. B., '58·
Worthington, A. Saunders, LL. B., '97,
    LL. M., 1900 (Lawyer)...............306-9 Bond Bldg., Wash., D. C.
Wright, A. Claude, A. B., '82, A. M., '84, LL. B., '84·
Wright, Arthur W., LL. B., '92·
Wright, J. Henry, M. D., '67·
Wright, Joseph D., LL. B., '97, LL. M.,
    '98 (Lawyer)........................Fendall Bldg., Washington, D. C.
Wright, Wilbur L., M. D., '94.............1439 Fairmont St., N. W., Wash-
                  ington, D. C.
Wrightman, Charles J., LL. B., '90·
Wynne, Robert F., LL. B., '97·

Yancey, G. Earle, LL. B., '99 (Clerk)......Navy Department., Wash., D. C.
Ycaza, Ignatio de, A. M., '03, Ph. L., '05.
Yeatman, Charles R., LL. B., '98, LL.
    M., '99 (Metropolitan Life Insur-
    ance Company).....................Santa Barbara, Cal.
Yeatman, Samuel M., LL. B., '83, A. M., '89; deceased, Dec., 1905, at Washing-
                  ton, D. C.
Yoder, Frank W., LL. B., '05·
Yoshida, C., D. D. S., '02·
Young, Noble, A. M., '76; deceased, about 1883, at Sacketts Harbor, N. Y.
Young, Parks G., M. D., '72.
Youngblood, Robert K., LL. B., '87·
Yount, Clarence Edgar, M. D., '96.
Yount, Marshall H., LL. B., '97 (Law-
    yer) ....Hickory, N. C.
Yrarrazabal, Manuel, A. B., '52·
Yturbide, Augustine de, Ph. B., '84·

Zane, Edmund P., A. B., '55, A. M., '60·
Zappone, A., M. D., '60.
Zegarra, Felix Cypriano, A. B., '64·
    A. M., '65, LL. D., '77 (deceased, April, 1897).
Zepp, Jesse, M. D., '70·
Zimmerman, Harvey J., LL. B., '05·
Zuniga, Manuel G. de, A. B., '55, A. M., '56·

LIST OF GRADUATES

1909

GEORGETOWN UNIVERSITY

WASHINGTON, D. C.

PUBLISHED BY

GEORGETOWN UNIVERSITY

QUARTERLY

(JULY TO SEPTEMBER, 1909)

Contents .

Directory

GEORGETOWN UNIVERSITY
Washington, D. C.

Rev. Joseph Himmel, S. J., President:
> Georgetown University.

The Secretary:
> North Building, Georgetown University.

The Treasurer and Bursar:
> Healy Building, Georgetown University.

The College (Graduate and Undergraduate Schools):
> The Registrar, 37th and O Sts. N. W.

The School of Medicine:
> The Dean, 920 H St. N. W.

The Training School for Nurses:
> Georgetown University Hospital.

The School of Dentistry:
> The Dean, 920 H St. N. W.

The School of Law:
> The Dean, 506 E St. N. W.

The Astronomical Observatory:
> The Director, Georgetown University.

The Riggs Library:
> The Librarian, Georgetown University.

The Seismograph Observatory:
> The Director, Georgetown University.

Foreword

After a lapse of three years the list of Graduates from all departments of Georgetown University has again been prepared and is herewith presented to all the Alumni of the University. The Secretary regrets that there are many graduates whose addresses and occupations he could not ascertain and that the financial limits imposed on him prohibited the publication of brief biographical notes on others which would have been of deep interest to the living Alumni. It is his desire that some generous, loyal alumnus would set aside a fund the interest from which would enable the University to publish every three years a bound volume containing short biographical sketches of all the living and the dead students who had completed at least two years in course in any department of the University. Such a publication would be of untold interest to the living Alumni, of profit and incentive to the undergraduate body and worthy of the glorious history and noble traditions of Georgetown and of the great achievements and triumphant failures of her host of loyal sons.

The Secretary takes this opportunity of extending his gratitude to the secretary of the Washington, of the Boston, and of the New York Alumni Society and to all the others who in devotion to Alma Mater rendered him the most cordial and thorough assistance in preparing the Graduate list, and he urges on every alumnus the necessity of forwarding to him information about any of the graduates whose names or addresses have been omitted from this list.

JOHN B. CREEDEN, S. J., Secretary,.
Georgetown University,
Washington, D. C

The Presidents of Georgetown University

. The list of the Presidents of Georgetown University is worthily headed by the illustrious Founder of the University:

The Most Rev. John Carroll, (S. J.),
Prefect Apostolic of the Catholic Church in the U. S.,
First Archbishop of Baltimore.

The Presidents

Rev. Robert Plunkett. 1791–1793
    Deceased, January 15, 1815, Prince George's Co., Md.

Rev. Robert Molyneux, S. J. 1793–1796
    Deceased, February 9, 1809, Georgetown, D. C.   1806–1808

Most Rev. William L. Dubourg, (S. S.) 1796–1799
    Bishop of New Orleans, Bishop of Montauban in France, and
    Archbishop of Besancon, France.
    Deceased, December 12, 1833, Besancon, France.

Most Rev. Leonard Neale, (S. J.) 1799–1806
    Second Archbishop of Baltimore.
    Deceased, June 15, 1817, Georgetown.

Rev. William Matthews. 1808–1810
    Vicar Apostolic and Administrator of Philadelphia. Pastor of
    St. Patrick's Church, Washington, D. C.
    Deceased, April 30, 1854, Washington, D. C.

Rev. Francis Neale, S. J. 1810–1812
    Deceased, December 20, 1837, St. Thomas's Manor, Md.

Rev. John A. Grassi, S. J. 1812–1817
    Deceased, December 12, 1849, Rome.

Rt. Rev. Benedict J. Fenwick, (S. J.) 1817–1818
    Bishop of Boston 1825.   1822–1825
    Deceased, August 11, 1846, Boston, Mass.

Rev. Anthony Kohlmann, S. J. 1818–1820
    Deceased, April 10, 1836, Rome.

Rev. Enoch Fenwick, S. J. 1820–1822
    Deceased, November 25, 1827, Georgetown, D. C.

Rev. Stephen L. Dubuisson, S. J. 1825–1826
    Deceased, August 14, 1864, Pau, France.

Rev. William Feiner, S. J. 1826–1829
    Deceased, June 9, 1829, Georgetown, D. C.

Rev. John William Beschter, S. J. 1829
    Deceased, January 4, 1842, Paradise, Pa.

Rev. Thomas F. Mulledy, S. J..1829–1837
    Deceased, July 20, 1860, Georgetown, D. C.   1845–1848

Rev. William McSherry, S. J..1837–1840
    Deceased, December 18, 1839, Georgetown, D. C.

Rev. Joseph A. Lopez, S. J. 1840
    Deceased, October 5, 1841, St. Inigoes, Md.

Rev. James Ryder, S. J...1840–1845
    Deceased, January 12, 1860, Philadelphia, Pa.   1848–1851

Rev. Samuel A. Mulledy, S. J. 1845
    Deceased, January 8, 1866, New York.

Rev. Charles H. Stonestreet, S. J..1851–1852
    Deceased, July 3, 1885, Holy Cross College, Worcester, Mass.

Rev. Bernard A. Maguire, S J 1852–1858
    Deceased, April 26, 1886, Philadelphia, Pa.   1866–1870

Rev. John Early, S. J. 1858–1866
    Deceased, May 24, 1873, Georgetown, D. C.   1870–1873

Rev. Patrick F. Healy, S. J. 1873–1882
    Georgetown University, Washington, D. C.

Rev. James A. Doonan, S. J..1882–1888
    Georgetown University, Washington, D. C.

Rev. J. Havens Richards, S. J. 1888–1898
    Church of St. Ignatius, 84th St., New York City.

Rev. John D. Whitney, S. J..1898–1901
    Loyola College, Baltimore, Md.

Rev. Jerome Daugherty, S. J 1901–1905
    Woodstock College, Woodstock, Md.

Rev. David H. Buel, S. J..1905–1908
    Holy Cross College, Worcester, Mass.

Rev. Joseph J. Himmel, S. J..1908–

Prefects of Studies, College Department

Rev. Daniel Lynch, S. J..1850–1855
   Deceased, April 1, 1884, Washington, D. C.
Rev. George Fenwick, S. J...1855–1857
   Deceased, November 27, 1857, Georgetown, D. C.
Rev. Joseph O'Callaghan, S. J..1857–1858
   Deceased, January 21, 1869, at sea   1867–1868
Rev. J. Robert Fulton, S. J..1858–1860
   Deceased, September 4, 1895, San Francisco, Cal.
Rev. Charles H. Stonestreet, S. J.......................................1860–1862
   Deceased, July 3, 1885, Holy Cross College,   1863–1864
     Worcester, Mass.
Rev. Edward McNerhany, S. J..1862–1863
   Deceased.
Rev. James A. Ward, S. J...1864–1867
   Deceased May 29, 1895, Georgetown, D. C.
Rev. Patrick F. Healy, S. J..1868–1879
   Georgetown University, Washington, D. C.
Rev. William T. Whiteford, S. J...1879–1881
   Deceased April 16, 1883, Georgetown, D. C.
Rev. James A. Doonan, S. J...1881–1882
   Georgetown University, Washington, D. C.
Rev. James B. Becker, S. J...1882–1883
   Georgetown University, Washington, D. C.
Rev. Edward I. Devitt, S. J..1884–1886
   Georgetown University, Washington, D. C.
Rev. Edward H. Welch, S. J..1888–1890
   Deceased December 2, 1904, Georgetown, D. C.
Rev. Edward Connolly, S. J...1890–1891
   Boston, Mass.
Rev. Thomas E. Murphy, S. J..1891–1893
   President of Holy Cross College, Worcester, Mass.
Rev. Jerome Daugherty, S. J..1893–1894
   Woodstock College, Woodstock, Md.
Rev. Francis P. Powers, S. J..1894–1895
   Boston College, Boston, Mass.
Rev. William J. Ennis, S. J..1895–1897
   St. Joseph's College, Philadelphia, Pa.
Rev. John A. Conway, S. J...1897–1899
   Georgetown University, Washington, D. C.   1901–1903
Rev. James B. Fagan, S. J..1899–1901
   Deceased, April 28, 1906, New York City.
Rev. W. G. Read Mullan, S. J..1903–1905
   Baltimore, Md.
Rev. Charles Macksey, S. J..1905–1909
   St. Francis Xavier's College, New York City, N. Y.
Rev. John B. Creeden, S. J...1909–

Founders of the School of Medicine

Joshua A. Ritchie, A. M. '40' M. D , Noble Young, M. D., Flodoardo Howard, M. D., Charles H. Lieberman, M. D., and Johnson Eliot, M. D

Deans of the School of Medicine

Flodoardo Howard, M. D...1851–1855
    Deceased, January 1888, Rockville, Md.
Johnson Eliot, M. D...1855–1876
    Deceased, December 30, 1883, Washington, D. C.
Robert Reyburn, M. D..1876–1878
    Deceased, March 25, 1909, Washington, D. C.
Francis A. Ashford, M D...1878–1883
    Deceased, May 18, 1883, Washington D. C.
J. W. H. Lovejoy, M. D...1883–1888
    Deceased, March 18, 1901, Washington, D. C.
G. L. Magruder, M D., A. M...1888–1900
    Stoneleigh Court, Washington, D C.
George M. Kober, M. D., LL. D..1900–
    1600 T Street, Washington, D. C.

Dean of the Dental School

William N. Cogan, D. D. S. 1901–
    920 H Street N. W , Washington, D. C.

Founders of the School of Law

Hon. Martin F. Morris, Hon. Charles W. Hoffman and Dr. Joseph M. Toner.

Deans of the School of Law

Hon. Charles P. James, LL. D...1870–1875
    Deceased.
Hon. George W. Paschal, LL. D...1875–1876
    Deceased, February 16, 1878.
Hon. Charles W. Hoffman, LL. D..1876–1890
    Deceased.
Hon. Martin F. Morris, LL. D..1890–1895
    1314 Massachusetts Avenue, Washington, D. C.
Hon. Jeremiah M. Wilson, LL. D..1895–1900
    Deceased, October, 1901, Washington, D. C.
Hon. George E. Hamilton, LL. D..1900–1903
    Lawyer and President of the Capital Traction Co., Union Trust Co., Washington, D. C.
Hon. Harry M. Clabaugh, LL. D...1903–
    Chief Justice of the Supreme Court of the District of Columbia.

Alumni Societies of Georgetown University

National Society

OFFICERS.

President .... George E. Hamilton . ... Washington, D. C.
First Vice-President .... William F. Quicksall .... Washington, D. C.
Second Vice-President.....Dr. S. S. Adams .... Washington, D. C.
Third Vice-President...... Charles A. Decourcy.........Lawrence, Mass.
Fourth Vice-President.... Robert J. Collier............ .... New York City.
Fifth Vice-President.......J. Percy Keating .... Philadelphia, Pa.
Treasurer.............................. Charles Harper Walsh.......Washington, D. C.
Secretary .. .. Henry R. Gower,
Union Trust Building, Washington, D. C.

EXECUTIVE COMMITTEE—Rev. Joseph J. Himmel, S J., ex officio; George E. Hamilton, ex officio; Charles Harper Walsh, ex officio; Henry R. Gower, ex officio; Raymond A. Heiskell, Washington, D. C.; Joseph I. Weller, Washington, D. C.; Dr. Roy D. Adams, Washington, D. C.; Dr. C. P. Neil, Washington, D. C.; Clarence E. Fitzpatrick, Boston, Mass.; Grafton L. McGill, New York City; William V. McGrath, Philadelphia, Pa.; C. Moran Barry, Norfolk, Va.

New York Society

President, Joseph Healy, 57 Fulton St., New York City, N. Y.; Secretary and Treasurer, James S. McDonogh, 80 Wall St., New York City, N. Y.

Philadelphia Society

President, 'Anthony A. Hirst; Vice-President, William V. Mc-Grath, Jr.; Secretary and Treasurer, Joseph M. Dohan; Executive Committee, John H. McAleer, Dr. Joseph M. Spellissy, J. Ashton Devereux.

Northeastern Pennsylvania Society

President, John O'D. Mangan, Pittston, Pa.; Vice-President, James L. Morris, Wilkesbarre; Secretary and Treasurer, Francis M. Foy, Pittston, Pa.

Pacific Coast Society

President, James V. Coleman; Vice-President, Walter S. Martin; Secretary-Treasurer, J. Neal Power; Directors, Dr. J. Dennis Arnold, Joseph S. Tobin, Thomas N. Driscoll.

Wisconsin Society

President, Erwin Plein Nemmers, Milwaukee; Vice-President, Thomas C. Downs, Fond du Lac; Secretary, Harry V. Kane, Milwaukee; Treasurer, James T. Fitzsimmons, Milwaukee; Executive Committee, Henry F. Reilly, Chairman, Milwaukee; Joseph W. Singleton, Eau Claire, ; Otto Bosshard, La Crosse; Wisconsin Correspondent of Georgetown College Journal, Francis X. Boden, Milwaukee.

Georgetown University Club of New England

President, Hon. John D. McLaughlin; Vice-Presidents Dr. John R. Slattery, Hon. Benedict F. Maher; Secretary, Clarence E. Fitzpatrick; Treasurer, Charles J. Martell; Executive Committee, B. A. Brickley, C. Woodbury Gorman, Dr. M. F. Donovan.

Georgetown University
List of Alumni

Abbaticchio, Raymond J. A..LL. B, '05
Lawyer,
Trust Bldg, Fairmount, W. Va.

Abel, Joseph...............LL. B., '96
Stenog. & Typewriter,   LL. M.,'97
Dept. of Agriculture, Wash., D. C.

Abell, Charles S...........A. B.,   '68
Deceased.   A. M.,   '71

Abell, Enoch B............A. B.,   '77
Lawyer,   A. M,   '89
Editor, Court Clk., Leonardtown, Md.

Abell, Walter R..........:..A. B,   '69
Deceased,   A. M.,   '89

Abrahams, Horatio Ely.....M. D.,   '03
Physician,
Trinidad, Colo.

Acker, Albert E...........M. D.,   '07
Physician,
Jacksonville, Fla.

Adair, George Fitzpatrick....M. D,   '00
Physician,
Fort Wood, N. Y.

Adams, Alfred A...........LL. B.,   '89
Lebanon, Tenn.   LL. M.,   '90

Adams, Allen R............LL. B.,   '01
Deceased, Philadelphia, Pa.

Adams, Arthur W..........M. D.   '78
Deceased, 1898, at St. Louis, Mo.

Adams, Benjamin B.......M. D.,   '76
Deceased, Jan. 25, 1897, at Wash., D. C.

Adams, C. B. S............M. D.,   '86
Deceased, May, 1896, at Wash., D. C.

Adams, E. A..............M. D.,   '65

Adams, Edward H.........M. D.,   '76
Physician,
McLean Hospital, Waverly, Mass.

Adams, Francis J..........M. D.,   '81
Physician,
1008 3d Ave., Great Falls, Mont.

Adams, J. Lee.............M. D.,   68
Deceased, April 16, 1905, Wash., D. C.

*Adams, Jesse Lee, Jr......:..M. D.,   '98
Tacoma Park, D. C.

Adams, J. Ray.............LL. B.,   '97
Clerk, Capitol,   LL. M.,   '98
Washington, D. C.

Adams, John Warren.......LL. B.,   '02
Lawyer,
Alturas, Modoc County., Cal.

Adams, Roy Delaplaine......M. D,   '04
Physician,
926 17th St. N. W., Washington, D. C.

Adams, Samuel Shugart.....M. D.,   '79
Physician, and G. U. Med. Fac.,
1 Dupont Circle, Washington, D. C.

Addison, Joseph............LL. B., '08
Lawyer,   LL. M., '09
Mitchellville, Md., R. F. D. No. 1.

Adkins, Jesse Corcoran......LL. B.,   '99
Lawyer,   LL. M.,'00
Columbian Bldg., Washington, D. C.

Adler, Leon................LL. B.,   '91
Lawyer,   LL. M.,'92
U. S. Pension Office, Wash., D. C.

Agar, John G......A. B., '76, A. M.,'88
Lawyer,   Ph. D., '89
31 Nassau St., New York City.

Aiken, William E. A........LL. D., '45

Akin, William E. .LL. B.,.'96, LL. M., 97

Albertsen, Walter F....:.....LL. B., '03
Cashier,
Natl. Copper Bank, N. Y. City, N. Y.

Albrecht, Joseph A..........LL. B., 09
Clerk,
Navy Dept., Washington, D. C.

Alexander, Arthur A........A. B.,   '97
Lawyer,   LL. B., '02
412 5th St. N. W., Washington, D. C.

Alexander, Chas. W........LL. B., '89
                         LL. M.,'90

Alexander, George W......M. D., '08
Physician,
Orono, Me.

Alexander, Walter O.......M. D.,   '67
'Deceased, May 23, 1904, at Wash., D.C.

Alford, James R...........LL. B., '99

Algue, Rev Jose, S J......Ph D., '04
Director U. S. Weather Bureau,
Manila Observatory, Manila, P. I.

Allain, Louis Bush.........A B, '87
Manufacturer,
Seattle, Wash

Allee, John G ....LL B., '05
Lawyer,
Miles City, Mont

Alleger, Walter W...... ...M D, '90
Medical Examiner,
U S Pension Bureau, Wash, D C

Allemong, Alex A.........A. B, '48

Allen, Albert R ....LL B., '88
326 Chester St, Anacostia, D C

Allen, Charles.............M. D, '61
Deceased, Dec 24, 1898, at Wash, D C.

Allen, Edward.. ....LL B, '90
Clerk,
Dept of Agriculture, Wash, D. C.

Allen, Rt Rev Edw. P....D. D., '89
R C Bishop,
Cathedral, Mobile Ala.

Allen, Harlan C ....LL M., '94
Clerk, Coast and Geodetic Survey,
1216 N C Ave N E, Wash, D C

Allen, John ....M D, '08
Resident Physician,
Wash Asylum Hospital, Wash, D C.

Allen, Joseph B LL B, '94, LL M, '95

Allen, Thomas B..........LL B, '91
Lawyer,   LL M., '92
St Joseph, Mo

Allen William. ....A. B., '75
Lawyer,
67 Wall St, New York City, N. Y.

Allison, Geo Wm..LL B, 98, LL M., '99

Aplin, Alfred.............M. D., '88
England

Altman, John W..........LL B, '01
Register in Chancery,
Court House, Birmingham, Ala.

Amery, Samuel A.........M D, '66
Deceased, Aug, 1881, at Cincinnati, O.

Anderson, Geo M.........LL B., '99
Lawyer,
705 G St N W, Washington, D. C.

Anderson, James W........LL B, '04
Principal Examiner,
Patent Office, Washington, D C.

Anderson, Jos. W..M. D.,'94, LL. B., '89
Bureau of Lands,   LL M., '90
Manila, P I

Anderson, Lindley S.......LL. B., '87
Asst. Examiner,   LL. M.,'88
Patent Office, Washington, D. C.

Anderson, Richard T.......LL. B., '05
Special Agent, General Land Office,
Denver, Colo.

Anderson, Dr. Sam. H......A. B, '67
Physician,
Woodwardville, Md

Andrade-Penny, Ed........M. D., '94
Deceased, Sept. 20, 1896, N. Y. City.

Andrews, Burt W.........LL. M,'99
Clerk,
Treasury Dept., Washington, D. C.

Andrews, Marshall V . .....LL. M.,'93
Clerk,
Pension Office, Washington, D. C.

Andrews, Olivera... .. ....A. B., '47
621 St. Paul St,   A M., '70
Baltimore, Md.

Andrews, Wm. A.........LL B, '94
Fendall Building,   LL. M.,'95
Washington, D C

Andrews, Wm. Robert......LL. B., '97
Lawyer,   LL. M.,'98
344 D St. N. W., Washington, D. C.

Andrews, Wm. T..........LL B, '88
Clerk,   LL. M.,'89
P O. Dept, Washington, D. C.

Ansell, Aaron...... ....M. D, '62
Deceased.

Antisell, Thomas...........Ph D, '81
Deceased, June 14, 1893.

Antisell, Thomas, Jr......M. D., '81
Deceased, Nov. 26, 1896,
Warm Springs, Mont

Appleby, J. F. R...........M. D, '68
Deceased, Sept. 27, 1907, at Wash., D.C.

Applegarth, Wm F., Jr......A B, '99
Lawyer,
Golden Hill, Md.

Appleman, Frank S ....LL B, '92
Patent Lawyer,
16 Warder Bldg., Washington, D. C.

Archer, James B, Jr........LL. B., '97
Lawyer,
458 La Ave. N W, Wash., D. C.

Archer, John W., A B, '45, A M, '51

Arment, Leopold L.,........A. B., '55
Colonel, C. S A,
Killed at Battle of Mansfield, La.

Armstrong, John D.........LL. B, '02,
Inventor,
311 Gay St., Phoenixville, Pa.

Armstrong, Wm. J..........M. D., '70
1629 Connecticut Ave. N. W.,
Wash, D. C

Armstrong, Wm. P.........LL. B., '88·
U. S Envelope Agent,
Hartford, Conn

Arnold, Eugene F..........LL. M., '79
Lawyer,   A. M., '90
1633 31st St. N. W., Wash., D. C.

Arnold, Francis S., LL. B., '91, LL. M., '92

Arnold, Dr. J. Dennis.......A. B., '73
Physician,   A. M., '77
2201 Cal. St., San Francisco, Cal.

Arnold, J. De Witt, LL. B , '93, LL..M.. '94

Arnold, Paul...............LL. B., '83

Arnold, T. J..............M. D, '69

Arth, Chas. Woodbury......LL. B., '03
Lawyer,   LL M., '04
Corcoran Bldg., Washington, D. C.

Ashfield, John M...........M. D., '73

Ashford, Bailey Kelly.......M. D, '96
U S A Medical Corps,
War Department, Washington, D. C.

Ashford, Francis Asbury....M. D., '01
Asst. U. S. M. H. S,
Public Health Hospital, Wash., D. C.

Ashford, Mahlon... .. ..M D, '04
1st Leut. Medical Corps, U. S. A.,
1763 P St. N. W., Washington, D. C.

Ashley, Wm. F., Jr........LL B, '99
Lawyer,   LL. M., '00
40 Exchange Place, New York City.

Ashmore-Noakes, S. S......M. D, '88
England.

Ashton, Hon. J Hubley.....LL. D, '72
Deceased, March 14, 1907, Wash , D. C.

Aspern, Henry T ....LL. B, '86
Lawyer,   LL. M., '87
822 1st Nat. Bk. Bldg., Chicago, Ill.

Athey, Thomas Franklin.....LL. B, '01
Lawyer,
Larned, Kansas.

Atkins, John W. G.........LL. B., '87

Atkinson, Charles D........LL M, '04
Lawye',
Pocahontas, Iowa

Atkinson, Lawrence C.......A. B., '04
1329 St. Mary St., New Orleans, La.

Atkinson, Wade H.........M. D., '89
Physician,
1402 M St. N. W., Washington, D. C.

Atkisson, Horace L. B......LL. B., '94
- Lawyer,   LL. M., '95
612 F St N. W., Washington, D. C.

Austin, Walter F..........LL M., '00·

Ayer, David E..............LL. B , '95,

Ayer, F. Carleton..........M. S , '05,
Teacher,
Tempe, Ariz.

Ayer, Richard B........ ..LL M., '92·
President, Piedmont Paving Co,
Oakland, Cal.

Babcock, Benjamin B.... ..M. D , '67·
Deceased, January 21, 1868

Babcock, Henry J., Jr......LL. B , '06·
Electrotyper,
Gov't Printing Office, Wash., D. C.

Baby, Francis W....... ...A B , '53

Baby, Michael W...... . ..A M, '60·

Baby, Raymond Francis.....A. B , '95·
803 Land Title Bldg , Phila., Pa

Bach, Edmund J., A. M , '97, LL. B , '98·
Manufacturer,   LL M., 99
2500 Grand Ave., Milwaukee, Wis.

Backes, Edward H..........LL. B , '06,
Lawyer,
135 William St , New York City.

Bacon, William J., Jr........LL B , '09·
Boston, Mass.

Badeaux, Thomas A... . . A B , '71
Lawyer,   A M, '73,
Thibodaux, La.

Baden, James H...... .....LL B , '02·
Bk. Clerk,
U. S. Trust Co , Washington, D. C.

Baden, William H....... ...LL B , '91·
Lawyer,   LL M , '92·
Colorado, Bldg , Washington, D. C.

Bailey, George A.......... .M. D., '94

Bailey, Lorenzo Alton......LL B , '76
Lawyer,
Columbian Bldg., Washington, D. C.

Baily, Thomas B...... .....M. D , '86
Deceased,   A. M., '88

Baker, Hon. Daniel W......LL. B , '
U. S. District Atty,   LL M., '93
Colorado, Bldg., Washington, D. C.

Baker, Francis B...........LL. B., '85
Asst. Chief, Pen. Office,   LL. M., '86
1619 17th St. N. W , Wash , D. C.

Baker, Frank, Dr........ ..A M, '88·
Superintendent,   Ph D., '90
Nat. Zoological Park, Wash , D. C.

Baker, Frank C ....M D , '99·
Physician,
1728 Columbia Road, Wash , D. C.

Baker, Gibbs Latimer........LL. B., '99
Lawyer,
Colorado, Bldg., Washington, D. C.

Baker, J. Newton...........LL. B., '04
Lawyer,   LL. M.,'05
Interstate Com. Com., Wash., D. C.

Baker, Jason E.............LL. B., '94

Baker, John G.............LL. B., '93
Lawyer,
Eshcol, Pa.

Baker, Ril T...............LL. B , '97
General Agent,   LL. M.,'98
Un. Cen. Life Ins. Co., Greenville, O.

Baker, Samuel S...........LL. B., '94
Lawyer,
Shelton, Neb.

Baker, William W.........M. D., '91
P. O. Dept., Washington, D. C.

Ball, Walter J..............A. B., '74
Sec. Lafayette Loan and Trust Co.,
Lafayette, Ind.

Ballard, Thomas V........LL. B., '96
Navy Yard, Portsmouth, Va.

Ballentine, John G., Jr......A. B., '87
Pulaski, Tenn.

Bandel, George E..........LL. B., '04
Clerk,   LL. M , '05
P. O. Dept., Washington, D. C.

Banfield, Charles P........M. D., '09
Intern,
G. U. Hospital, Washington, D. C.

Bangs, Roscoe E..:........LL. B., '09
1768 Willard St., Washington, D. C.

Bankhead, John H., Jr......LL. B., '93
Lawyer,
Jasper, Ala.

Bankhead, William B.......LL. B., '95
Lawyer,
Jasper, Ala.

Barbee, Robert A..........LL. B., '08
Lawyer,
Prospect Hill, Va.

Barber, Horace W.........LL. B., '08
Clerk,
Dept. of Agriculture, Wash., D. C.

Barber, James H. Morgan...M. D., '88
918 E St. N. W., Washington, D. C.

Barber, Samuel J..........A. B., '30
Priest, S. J.,
Deceased, Feb. 23, 1864, St. Thos., Md.

Barbarin, Francis S........M. D., '56
Deceased, March 29, 1900.

Barbour, Clement C........M. D., '64

Bargy, Ludin Albert........A. B., '54
Killed in Mexico by Indians, 1860.

Barker, Howard H.........M. D., '70
Physician,
1116 H St. N. W., Washington, D. C.

Barksdale, Noel W.........LL. B., '90
Lawyer,   LL. M., '91
504 E St. N. W., Washington, D. C.

Barnard, Clarence..........LL. B., '99
Automobile Sales Manager,
17th and U Sts., Washington, D. C.

Barnard, Ralph P..........LL. B., '92
Lawyer,   LL. M., '93
416 5th St. N. W., Washington, D. C.

Barnard, T. W.............M. D., '70
Deceased.

Barnes, Benjamin F........LL. B., '95
Postmaster,
Washington, D. C.

Barney, J. W..............M. D., '71

Barnhart, Wm. P..........LL. B., '03

Barnitz, Harry D..........M. D., '80
Physician, E. Houston & Losoya Sts.,
San Antonio, Tex.

Barr, A. Jefferson..........LL. B , '90

Barrett, Geo. T............M. D., '08
Physician,
Franklin, Pa.

Barrett, John Michael......A. B., '99
Asst. Corp. Counsel,
10 W. 90th St., N. Y. City, N. Y.

Barrett, Wm. H............A. B., '61

Barrie, George.............M. D., '92
Surgeon,
2131 Mass Ave. N. W., Wash., D. C.

Barrington, Richard L......M. D., '89
Physician,
5658 Cates Ave., St. Louis, Mo.

Barron, Clement Laird......M. D., '98
Physician,
St. Mary's, W. Va.

Barrow, Wylie M..........LL. B., '97
Sec'y of Railroad Commission,
Baton Rouge, La.

Barrows, Frederick I.......LL. B., '01
Cashier Cent. State Bank,
Connersville, Ind.

Barry, A. R...............M. D., '61
Deceased, Aug. 4, 1903,
Weatherford, Tex.

Barry, Cheevers Moran......A. B., '01
Real Estate and Ins.,   LL. B., '04
Norfolk, Va.

Barry, Cornelius Neal........M. D., '95
Deceased, April 30, 1897.

Barry, John A.............M. D., '91
Physician,
45 Monument Sq., Charlestown, Mass.

Barry, William E...........LL. B., '96

Barry, Wm. Foley.........'...LL. B., '95
Lawyer,
Cranston, R. I.

Bartlett, George A.........LL. B., '94
Lawyer,
Eureka, Nev.

Barton, Frederick Rae......M. D., '04

Barton, McKinney, Jr.......LL. B., '07
Lawyer,
600 Memphis Trust Bldg., Mem, Tenn.

Barton, Wilfred M.........M. D., '92
G. U. Medical Faculty,
1338 H St. N. W., Washington, D. C.

Bastion, Joseph Edward.....M. D., '06
Physician,
43 Lincoln St , Pittsfield, Mass.

Bates, John Savage.........A. B., '98
Captain U. S. Marine Corps,
Navy Dept., Washington, D. C.

Baukhages, Frederick E., Jr..LL. B., '97
Lawyer,
700 Law Bldg., Baltimore, Md.

Baumgardner, Ray.:........LL. B.. '07
Lawyer,
Muncie, Ind.

Bawtree, Harvey............A. B., '54
Deceased, Aug. 13, 1889. A. M., '56

Baxter, George T.........LL. M., '87
Deceased.

Bayard, Hon. Thomas F....LL. D., '89
Ex-Secretary of State.

Bayly, Chas. B............LL. B., '92
Mgr. John F. Ellis Co.,
937 Penn. Ave. N. W., Wash., D. C.

Bayne, Jos. Breckenridge....M. D., '03
1141 Conn. Ave. N. W., Wash., D. C.

Beahn, Edward F..........A. B., '58
Fi. C., Mass.,
Deceased, in California.

Beale, J. F................LL. B., '72
Patent Lawyer;
Com. Nat. Bank Bldg., Wash., D. C.

Beale, James S............M. D., '69
Deceased, Feb. 12, 1884, Wash., D. C.

Beall, Benjamin M.........M. D., '73
Physician,
417 H St. N. E., Washington, D. C.

Beall, John J..............A. B., '54

Beary, John Van Hall.......A. B., '04
Thibodaux, La.

Beaven, Rt. Rev. Thomas D.D. D., '89
R. C. Bishop,
260 State St., Springfield, Mass.

Beck, Henry K...LL. B., 95, LL. M.,'96

Becker, Jos................LL. B., '88
Patent Attorney, LL. M., '89
1315 Fairmont St. N. W., Wash., D.C.

Becket, John J. A...........Ph. D., '87
Writer,
44 E. 21st St., N. Y. City, N. Y.

Becnel, Alphonse............A. B.,· '55

Beegan, Joseph Francis......LL. B., '80

Beers, J....................M. D., '64
Deceased, Dec. 5, 1901.

Behrend, Adajah............M. D., '66
Physician,
1214 K St. N. W., Washington, D. C.

Behrend, Ed. B.............M. D., '94
1214 K St. N. W., Washington, D. C.

Behrend, Rudolph B.......LL. B., '97
Lawyer, LL. M.,'98
416 5th St. N. W., Washington, D. C.

Belew, Russell P..........LL. B., '07
Clerk's office, City Hall, Wash., D. C.

Belisle, George E..........LL. B., '97
Lawyer, LL. M.,'98
340 Main St., Worcester, Mass.

Bell, Charles...............M. D., '02

Bell, David Wilkinson.......LL. M.,'05
Newburne, N. C.

Bell, Henry................M. D., '74

Bell, James Fisher.........A. B., '99
Lawyer,
506 Dime Bank Bldg., Scranton, Pa.

Bell, Ralph.................M. D., '69

Benet, Stephen V..........LL. D., '84
U. S. A. Brigadier General,
War Dept., Washington, D. C.

Benfer, Jas. P.............LL. B., '99
Lawyer,
Dundee, Ohio.

Benham, Wm. R............LL. B., '97
Lawyer,
319 John Marshall Place, Wash., D. C.

Benjamin, Chas. F..........LL. B., '76
Lawyer,
506 11th St. N. W., Wash., D. C.

Bennett, Hilary F..........LL. B., '95

Bennett, Wm. Aloysius.....M. D., '95
Physician,
2810 Wentworth Ave., Chicago, Ill.

Bennewitz, John A.........LL. B., '04
Lawyer,
1st Nat Bk. Bldg , Omaha, Nebr.

Benson, Charles J..........LL. B., '91
Lawyer,
Shawnee, Oklahoma.

Bergen, James C............A. B , '52
H. C , Mass ,
Deceased at sea.

Bergh, Edwin...... ...... A B , '19
Deceased

Bernhard, Eugene J........LL B., '92
LL. M , '93

Bernstein, Hyman.. ....M. D., '04
Physician,
1008 Wylie Ave , Pittsburg, Pa.

Bernstein, J. Gadore,.........LL B , '09
New York City.

Berry, Albert E , LL. B ,'03, LL. M.,'04
Manager, Bell Telephone Co ,
17th and Filbert Sts , Phila., Pa.

Berry, Andrew ... .A. B , '96
Deceased.

Berry, Washington R.. .....LL. B , '93
LL. M , '94

Betts, Albert P . ... M. D , '94
Physician,
Woodburn, Ind

Bevans, James H ... . ..A B , '42

Bevington, Morris R . .. .LL. M , 09
Indianapolis, Ind.

Bierer, A. G Curtin ... . LL M ,'86
Lawyer, Former Asso Jus. S. Court,
Guthrie, Okla.

Binckley, J M.... ... .M D , '61

Bingham, Goundry W .....LL B , '98

Binley, Walter S . ...LL. B , '06
Lawyer,
Newburyport, Mass

Binns, Douglass .... M D , '76
Physician,
New Holland, Ohio

Birckhead, Edward. . .. .LL B. '01
Lawyer,
906 5th St. N W , Washington, D. C.

Birckhead, Oliver W.......LL. B., '08
Clerk Treasury Dept., Wash , D. C.

Bird, William E .. .. A. B , '44

Birge, Harry C, LL B ,'91' LL M ,'92

Birgfeld, Frank A . . ..LL. B., '01

Birgfeld, Wm. Ed ... ..LL B , '03
Clerk, Isthmian Canal Commission,
Washington, D. C

Birney, Theodore Weld......LL. B., '87
Deceased, July 24, 1897.

Biscoe, Frank Lee..........M. D., '01
Physician,
The Farragut, Washington, D. C.

Bishop, Arthur Garnett......LL. B., '98
Lawyer,   LL. M., '99
412 5th St. N W , Washington, D. C.

Bitting, Louis C...........M. D , '65

Bittinger, Charles..........M. D., '73
Deceased, Aug 31, 1879, Wash , D. C.

Bivins, James Daniel........LL. B , '98
Lawyer & Editor.
Albemarle, N. C. '

Black, Paul S ...LL B , '94, LL. M.,'95
Law Examiner,
The Loretto, Washington, D C.

Black, Richard R ....LL B , '96
129 C St S. E , Washington, D. C.

Blackburn, James W., Jr....LL. B , '86
Lawyer, Gunton Bldg ,
472 La. Ave. N. W , Wash, D. C.

Blackburn, Samuel E........LL. B., '91
Lawyer,
Frankfort, Ky.

Blackistone, Frank D........LL. B , '94
Lawyer,
Colorado, Bldg., Washington, D. C.

Blackistone, Julien C........M D , '06
Physician,
Wash. Asylum Hospital, Wash , D. C.

Blackmon, Henry C ....LL. B , '97
Lawyer,
Vaiden, Miss.

Blackmon, John Powell. ..LL B , '95
Deceased, Oct 10, 1907,   LL. M.,'96
El Reno, Okla.

Blackwell, Samuel...........LL. B , '95
Lawyer,   LL. M ,'96
New Decatur, Ala.

Blaine, Robert G............M D., '07
Physician,
133 C St. S. E , Washington, D. C.

Blake, George W............M. D., '67
Deceased, June, 1885,
Lower Salem, Ohio.

Blake, Thomas C....:......A. B , '79
Lawyer, Asst Corp Coun , A. M , '89
90 W. Broadway, New York City.

Blakely, William J ....A M , '76
Deceased, Jan 7, 1877, Erie, Pa.

Blanc, Charles de..........A. B., '47
Deceased,   A M , '50
March, 1891, Curacoa, W. I.

Blanchard, Edwin C.........LL. B , '08
Clerk,
Interstate Com. Com., Wash , D C.

Blandford, J. Walter.......LL. B , '88
Deceased, LL M ,'89
March 12, 1898.

Blandeford, Joseph H.......A. B , '54
Agric. & Physician, A M , '56
T. B., Prince George Co., Md.

Blease, Cole L ....LL. B , '89

Blease, Henry H...........LL. B., '87

Blewett, Robert L..........LL B , '02
Lawyer,
426 Coleman Bldg , Seattle, Wash.

Bliss, Geo. R..............LL. B , '09
1923 15th St , Washington, D. C.

Block, Emil H.............LL. B., '93
Clerk, War Dept., LL. M.,'94
1917 I St. N. W., Washington, D. C.

Boardman, Herbert.........M. D , '72
Deceased.

Boardman, Myron...........M. D., '75

Boarman, Charles V.......M. D , '71
Deceased, Nov. 2, 1901.

Boarman, Wm. T..........A. B., '52

Bocock, Jas. B.............LL. B., '06
District of Columbia.

Boden, Francis X..A. M.,'98, LL. B , '99
Attorney, LL. M.,'00, Ph. D., '00
162 Wisconsin St., Milwaukee, Wis.

Bodisco, Waldemar de......A. B., '45
Deceased, July 31, 1878, A. M., '48
Russian Consul General at New York.
Died at Jordan Alum Spgs. Remains
brought to Georgetown and interred,
August 4, at Oak Hill Cemetery.

Boehs, Charles J..?........M. D , '09
Intern,
Children's Hospital, Wash., D. C.

Boeinstein, Augustus S.....M. D , '73
Deceased, June 21, 1901.

Bogan, Joseph A...........LL. B., '05
Clerk,
P. O. Dept., Washington, D. C.

Boggs, Walter J...........A. B., '98
Lawyer,
215 St. Paul St., Baltimore, Md.

Bogue, A. P.............M. D., '72
Bureau of Education, Wash , D. C.

Boiseau, Louis T..........LL. B., '90
1st Lieut. Art , U. S. A., LL. M., '91
War Dept., Washington, D. C.

Bolan, Herbert A..........A. B , '92
Physician,
518 N. 40th St , Philadelphia, Pa

Bolan, T. V...............A. B , '88
Deceased, Feb , 1908, A. M , '92
Philadelphia, Pa.

Boland, J. Bernard.........LL. B., '08
Broker,
Tremont Bldg., Boston, Mass

Boland, Joseph Emmet......A B , '09
Carbondale, Pa.

Boldrick, Samuel J.........LL. B , '92
Lawyer,
408-409 Walker Bldg , Louisville, Ky.

Bolen, Hubert L...........LL. B., '05
Lawyer,
Am. Nat. Bk. Bldg., Okla. City, Okla.

Bolway, Wm. J..LL. B., '93, LL. M.,'94

Bomberger, Lincoln.........LL. B , '99
Prin. Ex. Pen. Bureau, LL. M.,'00
1607 7th St. N W., Washington, D. C.

Bond, George J............LL. B., '72
Lawyer,
623 F St. N. W., Washington, D. C.

Bond, Samuel S...........M. D., '65
Deceased, July 4, 1899, Wash , D. C.

Bonford, P. E.............A. B., '36

Bonic, Wm. Garner........LL B , '97
Lawyer,
Hot Springs, Garland Co., Ark.

Boone, Edward D.........A. B , '51
H. C., Mass., Jesuit Priest,
Loyola Col., Baltimore, Md.

Boone, John F............A B , '55

Boone, Nathan F...........LL. B , '96
Lawyer, LL M ,'97
R. D. R , No. I Mulberry, Tenn.

Boone, Thomas B..........A. B , '53

Booth, Clarence M.........LL. B , '06
Special Agent G. L. O.,
Boise, Idaho.

Booth, Edward H..........LL. B , '93
Clerk, War Department,
717 21st St. N. W., Washington, D. C.

Booth, John F...LL. B., '92, LL. M ,'93

Boothby, A................M. D , '63
Deceased, Feb. 8, 1902, Boston, Mass.

Borden, Frank Wheeler.....M. D., '95
Physician,
904 E. Capitol St., Wash., D. C.

Borden, Joseph A..........LL. B., '88
LL. M ,'89

Borroughs, Dent...........M. D , '59

Bosshard, Otto B L........LL. B, 'oo
Lawyer, President, Bank of Holmen,
Batavian National Bank Building,
La Crosse, Wis.

Bossidy, John C............M. D, '85
Physician,
419 Boylston St, Boston, Mass

Bossier, Paul.............-.......A. B, '60

Bossier, Placide............A B, '60
Killed at battle of Shiloh

Boswell, E V. B............M. D., '65
Deceased, Dec. 9, 1878, Wash., D. C.

Boughter, John Frazer......M. D, '67

Bounds, Edgar W.........,LL. B, '93
Lawyer,
Marlin, Tex.

Bourne, Caleb P............LL. M.,'87
Chief of Division Stamps & Supplies,
Manila, P. I.

Bowen, H. Morton.........M. D, '93
Physician,
Aquasce, Md.

Bowen, Thomas............M. D, '63

Bower, S. W..............M. D, '86

Bowles, Benjamin A........LL. B, '08
Cashier,
Potomac Savings Bank, Wash., D. C.

Bowles, Norman S.........LL. B, '09
1814 G St. N. W., Wash, D. C.

Bowling, Henry A.........A. B., '57

Boyd, Carl Bainbridge,......M. D., '98
Physician,
San Carlos, Ariz.

Boyd, Howard.............LL. B., '95
Lawyer,   LL. M.,'96
Columbian Bldg., Washington, D. C.

Boyd, John Aloysius........A. M., '97
.   LL. B, '99
713 N. Calvert St., Baltimore, Md.

Boyd, Wm. H.............LL. B., '08
Clerk,
Army War College, Wash., D. C.

Boykin, Lester E...........LL. B, '08
Expert, Public Roads,
Dept. of Agriculture, Wash., D. C.

Boyle, Frank A.............LL. B., 09
Lawyer,
Ivers, Idaho.

Boyle, Thomas Maurice.....A. B., '09
Shenango House, Sharon, Pa.

Braden, Frank Wheeler.....M D, '95
Physician,
904 E. Capitol St, Washington, D. C.

Bradenbaugh, Claude C......A. B, '89

Bradfield, Jefferson Davis...M. D., '91
Physician,
1506 N. Capitol St., Wash., D. C.

Bradford, John K, A. B, '78, A. M., '89
Deceased, July 6, 1901,
Wilmington, Del.

Bradford, William M........A. B., '42

Bradley, Howard Alnsen....D. D. S.,'04

Bradley, Thomas Henry.....LL. B, '74

Bradley, W. D..............A. B., '95
Deceased, Nov., 16, 1906, Montana. -

Bradshaw, Aaron............LL. B, '77

Bradshaw, Charles..........LL. B., '73

Bradshaw, Leonard.........LL. B, '94
                          LL. M., '95

Bradshaw, Moses...........LL. B., '77

Brady, Edmund.............LL. B., '04
Lawyer,
412 5th St. N. W., Washington, D. C.

Brady, Edward J..........A. B., '98
621 13th St. N. W., Washington, D. C. .

Brady, Eugene D. F.........A. B., '70
Lawyer,   A. M., '72, LL. B., '72
621 13th St. N. W., Washington, D. C.

Brady, George M..A. M., 'oi, Ph. L., '02
Lawyer,   Ph. D., '03, LL. B., '03
838 Equitable Bldg., Baltimore, Md.

Brady, James T...........LL. B., '92
Lawyer,   LL. M.,'93
515 Ashland Block, Chicago, Ill.

Brady, John Stanley........A. B., 'oi
Physician,
60 W. 76th St, New York City.

Brady, Joseph P...........LL. B., '96
Clerk, U. S. Circuit Court,
Richmond, Va.

Branagan, Francis A........LL. B., '89

Brand, Carl Martin.........LL. B., '03

Brand, Edward A...........LL. B., '09
Roanoke, Va.

Brantley, A. Augustus.......LL. B., '96
U. S Commissioner of Dist. Court.
Orangeburg, S. C.

Brantley, Thomas F.........LL. B., '94
Lawyer,   LL. M., '95
Orangeburg, S. C.

Brashears, John W., Jr......LL. B., '03
Clerk,   LL M.,'04
Winthrop Heights, Washington, D. C.

Brashears, Shipley, Jr.......LL. B., '99
Insurance,   LL. M.,'oo
1319 F St. N. W., Washington, D. C.

Braud, Peter S..............A B , '59
Brawley, Wm. C............LL B., 96
Lawyer,
Wausau, Wis.

Brearton, John L...........LL. B., '02
Lawyer,
Savanna, Ill.

Breck, Gen. Samuel........M. D., '67
U. S. A , Retired,
1651 Beacon St., Boston, Mass.

Breckenridge, Scott Dudley...M. D , '07
Physician,
Columbia Hospital, Wash , D C.

Breckous, Robert W........LL. B., '90
Lawyer,
Honolulu, Hawaii.

Breen, James..............M. D , '71

Breitenbucher, Ed. E......".. LL. B., '03
Lawyer,
Stockton, Cal.

Bremner, Vincent Aloysius..A. M., '03
Biscuit Manufacturer,
270 Forquer St , Chicago, Ill.

Brennan, Charles...........LL. B., '99

Brennan, Frederick J.......LL. B., '09
Bridgeport, Conn.

Brennan, Geo. R..LL. B.,'94, LL. M.,'95

Brennan, James Joseph......A. B., '05
70 Orford St., Somerville, Mass.

Brennan, James Smith......A. B., '83
Banking,
1011 Del. Ave , Wilmington, Del.

Brennan, John E...........M D , '05
Physician,
321 Banigan Bldg., Providence, R. I.

Brennan, John..............LL. B , '04
Mining Engineer,
Mexico City, Mex.

Brennan, Leslie W..........A. B., '06
Cotton Business,
117 Columbia St , Utica, N. Y.

Brennan, Michael F........LL. B., '99
2715 14th St. N. W.,   LL. M.,'09
Washington, D. C.

Brennan, Patrick H. C......LL. B., '93
Deceased,   / LL. M.,'94

Brennan, Patrick J.........LL. B , '91
Deceased August 10, 1909.
Washington, D. C.

Brennan, Rev. Patrick H....M. D., '67
Jesuit Priest,
Trinity Church, Washington, D. C.

Brent, Hon. Judge George...A. B , '33
Deceased,   A. M , '37, LL D., '68
Jan. 6, 1881, Charles Co, Md

Brent, George...............LL. B , '90
Lawyer,   LL. M ,'92
118 Van Buren St , Brooklyn, N. Y

Brent, Henry M., A. B , '63, A. M , '67
Deceased, Oct. 16, 1892,
Bay City, N. Y.

Brent, Henry W.............A. B , '52

Brent, John Carroll........A. B , '33
Deceased,   A. M., '49
Feb. 10, 1876.

Brent, Robert J.............LL. B , '54

Brent, Wm. M..............A. B., '54
Deceased.

Bresnahan, Francis J.......LL. B , '03
Real Estate,   LL. M ,'04
424 M St. N. W , Wash., D. C.

Briant, Lassaline P.........A. B , '61
Lawyer,
137 S. Gayoso St., New Orleans, La.

Brice, Charles H............LL. B , '87

Brickenstein, John H.......LL. B., '91

Brickley, Bartholomew A....LL. B., '04
Lawyer,
18 Tremont St , Boston Mass.

Bride, William W...........LL. B., '04
Lawyer,
Westory Bldg., Washington, D. C.

Bridges, Walter S...........LL. B , '87
U. S. Special Examiner,
U. S. Crt. & P. O. Bldg., Chicago, Ill.

Brien, L. Tiernan...........A. B., '46

Briggs, Edmund B..........LL. B., '75

Brisbane, Howard P........M. D., '82
Physician,
745 Camp St., New Orleans, La.

Briscoe, Arthur.............LL. B , '91
Clerk, P. O. Dept.,   LL. M ,'92
143 T St. N. W , Washington, D. C.

Briscoe, Walter C...........M. D., '69
Deceased, May 16, 1896.

Brock, Fenelon B...........LL. B , '96
Lawyer,   LL. M.,'97
902 F St. N. W., Washington, D. C.

Brockbank, Senes T........LL. M.,'88

Broderick, Dr. John K......A. M., '97
Manager, Broderick Rope Co.,
809 N. Main St., St. Louis, Mo.

Broe, William B............LL. B., '84

Brogan, Francis Albert......A. B , '83
Lawyer,
548 Bee Bldg , Omaha, Neb.

Pronson, Charles E.... ....M D, '83
Clerk. Treas. Dept,
936 T St N. W, Washington, D. C.

Brooke, Albert.......... .. LL. B, 'oo
Deceased, Jan , 18, 1908,
Benning D C.

Brooke, John Cooke........LL B, '05
Lawyer,
1424 New York Ave., Wash, D'C.

Brookes, William P.. ......A B, '44
Deceased, June 15, 1885

Brooks, J Henry,...........M D, '65
Physician,
3737 Mich. Ave. N. E, Wash, D. C.

Brooks, John Dosher...... .M D, '95
Surgeon, U. S. A.
, Fort Snelling, Minn.

Brosnan, Eugene, Jr........LL. B, '97
Deceased, 1901.   LL. M., '98

Brosnan, John J............LL B, '01
Lawyer
482 La Ave. N. W., Wash, D. C.

Brower, Daniel Roberts.....M. D, '64
Deceased, Mar. 1, 1909   LL D., '99
Chicago. Ill.

Brown, Andrew Rothwell...M. D, '68
Deceased. Dec. 16, 1900.

Brown, C. T................M. D, '65

Brown, Charles J...........LL. B, '90
Lawyer,   LL. M, '92
Bond Bldg., Washington, D C.

Brown, Charles Orton.......LL. B, '94

Brown, Charles O..........LL. B, '73

Brown, Everard C.......·...LL. B, '88
                          LL. M, '89

Brown, Dr Francis E.......A. B, '87
Physician,
917 St. Paul St, Baltimore Md.

Brown, Harry S ....LL B, '99
Clerk,
1502 Meridian St. N. W, Wash, D C

Brown, James C........ ...LL B, '76

Brown, Oliver P. M ....LL B, '95
Lawyer,
409 Com Bank Bldg, Wash, D C

Brown, Orlando,...... .....A B, '52

Brown, Paul J.............A. B, '02
45 E Willis Ave, Detroit, Mich.

Brown, Robert Y.... ....A. B, '60
Deceased:

Brown, Sevellon A.. ....LL B, '73
,Deceased, Feb 16, 1895

Brown, Thomas H........ . LL B, '92

Brown, Rev. V Howard....A. B, '79
Jesuit Priest,
Juneau, Alaska.

Brown, Walter E...........LL B., '98

Brown, Walter N...........LL. B., 08
Lawyer,
Interstate Com Com, Wash, D. C.

Brown, Walter S...........LL. B., '09
Laurel, Md.

Brown, Wm Arthur ....A. M, '00
Care C. H. Brown & Co,
Fichburg, Mass.

Brown, Wm. H. J..........LL. B, '98

Brown, Wm. J.............LL. B, '08
Lawyer,
1413 H St. N. W., Washington, D. C.

Brownell, Henry B.........LL. B., '90
Lawyer,   LL. M, '91
41 Park Row, N. Y. City.

Browning, A. G............M. D., '60
Physician,
305 Market St., Maysville, Ky.

Browning, George L........LL. B., '95
Lawyer,
Rediviva, Va.

Browning, Wm. Livingston..LL. M, '01
Lawyer,·
416 5th St. N. W., Washington, D. C

Brownlow, J H............M D, '65
Deceased, Oct 10, 1899, N Y. City.

Brownson, Henry Francis...A B, '52
H. C, Mass, Lawyer,   A M, '55
243 E. Larned St., Detroit, Mich

Brownson, John H.........A. B., '49
H. C., Mass.,   A. M, '51
Deceased, 1857, at St. Paul, Minn

Brownson, Orestes A., Jr . A B, '55
Deceased, April, 1892.

Bruhl, Charles Emile........M. D, '00
Physician,
Scanlan Bldg., Houston, Tex

Brumbaugh, Dr. Gains... ..M D, '88
Physician,
905 Mass. Ave. N. W., Wash, D C.

Brummett, Randolph Breese. M D., '93
Navy Dept., Washington, D. C.

Bryan, Henry L..LL. B, '88, LL M, '89
Editor U S Statutes at Large,
Dept. of State, Washington, D. C.

Bryan, Paul S.............LL. B., '92

Bryan, Richard H.... .....A. B, '50

Bryant, Frank W...... .....LL B, '04

Brylawski, Fulton.... .. ..LL B., '08
Lawyer, LL M, '09
Fendall Bldg, Washington, D. C.

Buard, Louis A... .. ..A .B, '60

Buckley, Patrick.. ....A B, '63
H. C, Mass
Deceased, at Halifax, N. S.

Buchanan, Edwin...........M D., '85
Deceased, Oct, 1895, Seattle, Wash.

Buck, Alonzo M...........M D, '66
Deceased, Feb 29, 1905.

Buck, Llewellyn A......... M D., '65
Deceased, Dec 13, 1906, El Reno, Okla

Buckley, John J ....LL B, '09
1719 S St N W, Wash, D. C

Buckley, John T............LL. B., '08
Lawyer,
69 Arcade Bldg, Utica, N. Y.

Budlong, Orsemus W.......M. D., '80
Physician,
Belford, N. J.

Buie, Walter A.............LL. B, '92
Lawyer,
Kimball Bldg, Boston, Mass.

Bullock, Edmund Cooper....LL. B., '03
Lawyer, LL M, '04
Lewisburg, Tenn.

Burbank, Caryl............M D, '03
Physician,
2147 F St. N. W, Washington, D C

Burchard, William M., Jr....M. D., '65
Deceased, June 1, '89, Montville, Conn.

Burche, John A. W..... ..LL B, '87

Burchmore, John S.. ....LL B, '09
Evanston, Ill

Burdine, Elbert F........ ..LL. B, '95
LL. M, '96

Burg, John B.............LL. B., '97
Lawyer, LL M, '98
Albuquerque, N. M.

Burg, Joseph P.............LL. B., '94
Lawyer,
3701 13th St N. E, Washington, D C

Burger, John C. S.........LL B, '73
Clerk, War Dept,
1412 Delafield Place, Wash, D C.

Burger, Leopold C E.......LL B, '99
Legal Reviewer,
Room 44 P O,
Newark, N. J.

Burk, James W... ....A. B, '95
Lawyer, LL B, '97
Canton, Pa.

Burke, Francis Hunter......LL B, '03
Lawyer,
Louisv Tr. Co Bldg., Louisville, Ky.

Burke, Frederick B ..... .M D, '06
Physician,
2384 Woodward Ave, Detroit, Mich

Burke, John C , .LL B., '95, LL M., '97

Burke, Thomas W........ M D, '84
Medical Examiner,
Pension Office, Washington, D C

Burnam, Harry E ....LL. B, '87
City Attorney, LL M, '88
Omaha, Neb

Burnett, Swan M... ....Ph D, '90
Physician,
Deceased, Jan 18, 1906, Wash, D. C

Burns, James Philip .. ....A B, '05
Hyde Park, Mass.

Burns, James W ....LL B, '08
Gov. Print. Office, Wash, D. C

Burns, R P Miles..........A. B, '73
Deceased, Feb. 28, 1875, Nashv, Tenn.

Burton, Clarence F..........LL. B, '07
Mgr. for John S. Cook & Co, Bankers, care H R. Burton, Union Trust
Bldg, Washington, D C

Burton, Hiram Ralph........LL B, '08
Lawyer,
Union Trust Bldg, Wash, D C.

Burton, Linnoir.............LL. B, '83

Busey, Samuel Clagett......LL. D, '99
Deceased, Feb 12, 1901

Butcher, C Tyson..........LL. M., '86

Bute, James H...... ....M D, '99
Physician,
P. O Box 163, Houston, Tex

Butler, A. Jeter.............LL B, '01

Butler, Bartholomew W ....LL B. '07
Worcester, Mass.

Butler, Francis J,..........M D, '08
Physician,
10 Britton St, Worcester, Mass.

Butler, Henry...............A B, '87

Butler, John A ....LL. B, '88
520 R I Ave. N E, LL M, '89
Washington, D C

Butler, John H.............LL B, '02

Butler, Patrick J..LL. B, '88, LL M, '89

Butler, Ulysses..............LL. B, '01
Interstate Com. Com, Wash, D. C.

Butts, Elias M.............LL. M., '95

Byington, Francis..........M. D., '58
Deceased, Jan. 14, 1905,
Charlestown, W. Va.

Byrne, Edward Louis........A. B, 'o1
Supt Brooklyn Union Gas Co.,
Brooklyn, N. Y.

Byrne, Francis Joseph........A B., '99
The Evening Times, Phila., Pa

Byrne, John F..............LL. B., '04
Auburn, N. Y.

Byrne, John J...............LL. B., '09
Boston, Mass.

Byrne, Walter C...........M. D., '92
Elmira, N. Y.

Byrne, Rt. Rev. William....D. D, '81
Proth Apost,
St. Cecelia St, Boston, Mass

Byrne, Hon William M.....A. B., '87
Lawyer,
220 Broadway, N. Y. City.

Byrnes, Charles W..........A. B, '07
Law Student,
743 5th Ave, San Rafael, Cal.

Byrnes, Dr. James C........M. D, '70
Medical Corps U S. Navy,
Washington, D. C.

Byrnes, Thomas.............M. D, '65
Deceased, Wolcott, Iowa.

Byrnes, William Henry, Jr..A B, '03
Lawyer,
305 Camp St., New Orleans, La.

Byrns, William F..........M. D., '73
Physician,
1923 Calvert St. N. W, Wash., D. C

Cabaniss, E. Gerry.........LL B, '95
                           LL M., '96

Cahill, Jos. Henry..........A. B., '98
57 Colony St, Meriden, Conn.

Cahill, William Ambrose... .B. S, '82
Physician,
1310 N. Salina St, Syracuse, N Y.

Cain, James P..............LL. B, '08
Lawyer,
Natl Ger. Am. Bank Bldg, St. Paul,
Minn.

Cain, Wm S...............M. D., '02
Physician,
Cor Main and 2d Sts., Elmira, N. Y.

Caine, David M............LL B., '87
Deceased, 1888

Caldwell, George H........M. D, '65

Caldwell, Samuel W........M D, '67

Calhoun, Charles A.........LL. B., '96
Lawyer,   LL. M, '97
1st Nat. Bk. Bldg, Birmingham, Ala.

Calkins, Thomas Joseph.....A M, '99
Physician,   M. D, '00
8912 Superior Ave, Cleveland, Ohio.

Callaghan, D. O'C..........LL. B., '73
Lawyer,   A. M, '89
616 18th St. N. W., Wash., D. C.

Callaghan, James Edward...A. B, '80
Law Book Publisher,
114 Monroe St, Chicago, Ill.

Callaghan. William John....M. D., '01
Physician,
Chevy Chase, Md.

Callan, Cornelius Van Ness, M. D, '68
Physician,
1816 M St. N. W, Wash, D C.

Callan, Guida C.............LL. B, '94
Clerk,   LL M, '96
Patent Office, Washington, D. C.

Callan, John F..............A. B, '56
Deceased.

Callanen, Joseph P..........A. B, '53
                           A. M., '55

Calvert, Clarence W.........LL. B. '09
Lancaster, Wis.

Camalier, Benj. Harris......A. M., '84
Lawyer,
Leonardtown, Md.

Camalier, Franklin A ....A. B, '04
Physician,   M. D, '08
Providence Hospital, Wash, D C.

Campbell, Charles B.........M. D., '94
Pharmacist,
17th and Park Sts. N. W., Wash, D. C.

Campbell Daniel G.........LL B, '89
                          LL. M., '99

Campbell, Joseph Henry.....LL B., '03
Deceased, Feb. 24, 1905.

Campbell, Hon. Richard.....LL. B, '99
Judge, Supreme Court,
Manila, P. I.

Camper, Capt Charles... ...LL B, '73
Deceased, Dec. 2, 1885, Wash., D. C.

Canario, Lawrence Virgil....A. B, '05
Clerk. Olaa Sugar Co,
Mountainview, Hawaii

Canfield, Andrew N........LL. B, '84
Deceased, July 10, 1905. LL M., '85

Cannon, Walter D..........M. D, '90
Physician,
The Alabama, Washington, D C

Cantwell, Edward J.........LL. B., '04
Sec. Nat. Asso. of Letter Carriers.
945 Pa Ave. N. W., Wash., D. C.

Cantwell, Thomas...........A. B. '08
Law Student,
471 I St. S. W., Wash., D. C.

Capehart, Poindexter W.....M. D., '98
Deceased, June 29, 1907.

Caperton, Hugh.............A. B, '41
Deceased, Sept. 14, 1877,
Georgetown, D. C.

Carabedian, Robert P........LL. B., '95
LL. M., '96

Carleton, Hon. Robert P.....LL. B., '95
County Judge, LL. M., '96
Fernandina, Fla.

Carlin, Frederick Theo......A. B., '05
Metropolitan Life Bldg, N. Y. City.

Carlin, Harry Vincent.......A. B, '04
Metropolitan Life Bldg, N. Y. City.

Carlon, Frederick A.........A. B, '02
Metropolitan Life Bldg, N. Y. City.

Carlon, Patrick Joseph......A. B., '93
Lawyer,
Saranac Lake, N. Y.

Carman, Louis D............M. D., '89
Pension Office,
1351 I St. N. W., Washington, D. C.

Carmody, Francis Joseph....LL. B., '04
Deceased, Feb. 16, 1907, Wash., D. C.

Carmody, Robert Francis....A. M, '93
Deceased, . M. D., '95

Carnahan, Joseph H..........LL. B., '09
Little Rock, Ark.

Carne, Rev. Richard L......A. M., '68
Priest,
Duke & Columbia Sts., Alexandria, Va.

Carney, Patrick Joseph......M. D., '04
Physician,
626 Southbridge St., Worcester, Mass.

Carney, Thomas Francis......A. B., '91
Deceased, Feb. 8, '96, Lawrence, Mass.

Carpenter, Matthew Hale....A. M., '04
Law Student,
325 35th St., Milwaukee, Wis.

Carr, John McAuliffe........A. B., '97
A. M., '98, LL. B., '99, LL. M., '00
Lawyer,
548-50 Spitzer Bldg., Toledo, Ohio.

Carr, W. Saunders..........A. M., '88
9 E. Lexington St., Baltimore, Md.

Carr, Wilbur John..........LL. B., '94
Chief Clerk,
Dept. of State, Washington, D. C.

Carr, Wm Beresford.......A. B., '61
Deceased, Nov., 1881. A. M., '72

Carraher, J. V.............M. D., '86
Deceased, May 1, 1908.

Carriel, Lafayette J.........A. B., '51

Carroll, Augustine Levins....A B., '98
Asst. Mgr. Colorado Golf Club,
Denver, Colo.

Carroll, J. Camillus.........LL. B., '07
Lawyer,
716-718 Calhoun St., Fort Wayne. Ind.

Carroll, John Lee...........LL. D., '89
Agriculturer,
Doughregan Manor, Ellicott City, Md.

Carroll, Lafayette J.........A. M., '82

Carroll, Philip.............M. D., '79
Deceased, Manzanilla, Dec. 15, 1906.

Carroll, Timothy A.........LL. B., '93
Special Agent, LL. M., '94
Bureau of Corporations, Wash., D. C.

Carroll, Vincent Levins......A. B., '01
Wall Paint Co.,
Cor. Mark. & 29th Sts., Paterson, N. J.

Carson, Frederick D.......LL. B., '82

Carter, Charles T...........LL. B., '95

Carter, G. William Jr........LL B, '09
Markham, Va.

Carter, J. Barrett...........LL. B., '05
Lawyer, LL. M., '06
Evans Bldg, Washington, D. C.

Carter, Paul................LL. B, '06
Lawyer,
Marianna, Fla.

Carter, Hon. Thomas H. ....LL. D, '08
U. S. Senator from Montana,
1528 16th St. N. W.. Wash, D. C

Carusi, Charles Francis.....A. B., '94
Lawyer,
Nat. Met. Bank Bldg., Wash., D. C.

Carusi, Thornton A.........LL. B., '74

Carvill, William B..........A. B., '79
Deceased, Dec. 9, 1890, St. Johns, N. B.

Cary, Joseph M..LL. B., '91, LL. M., '92

Casey, Daniel E.............LL. B., '09

Casey, Rev. John T........A. B., '99
Priest,
Athol, Mass.

Casey, Stephen J............LL. B, '96
Lawyer, LL. M., '97
Banigan Bldg., Providence, R. I.

Cashell, Joseph.............LL. B., '77

Cashman, Joseph T.........LL. B., '02
Lawyer,
Singer Bldg, 149 B'way, N Y. City.

Cashman, Thomas F........M. D, '02
Physician,
Washington, Pa

Cass, Philip H.............LL. B, '95
LL M,'96

Casserly, Daniel A.........A. B, '62
Deceased,   A. M, '68
July 4, 1887, New York City.

Casserly, Hon. Eugene......A. M., '56
LL. D, '72

Cassidy, John Hughes.......A. B, '97
Lawyer,
95 Bank St., Waterbury, Conn.

Cassidy, Louis T...........A. B, '04
104 Washington St,   M. D, '08
Norwich, Conn.

Cassin, John Leo ....LL B, '01
Lawyer,
Nat Met. Bank Bldg., Wash, D. C.

Casteel, Frank A..........D D. S,'08
Dentist,
Philippi, W. Va.

Catlin, Benjamin Rush......LL. B, '73
Patent Lawyer,
622 F St. N. W., Washington, D. C.

Caulfield, Bernard G........A. B., '48
Deceased   A M., '50
Dec 19, 1887, Deadwood, Dak.

Caulfield, John..........Mus. Doc., '65

Cauthorn, Hon Robt. Gabriel, A B, '99
Lawyer, Police Commissioner,
Bishop Block, Vincennes, Ind.

Cavanagh, Richard B.......LL. B, '01
Lawyer,
50 Church St, New York City.

Cavanaugh Thomas Ed.....M. D, '00
Physician,
245 Maple St., Holyoke, Mass.

Cecil, Henry A.....~.......A M, '66

Chalmars, Nils..............LL. B., '09
Alexandria, Va.

Chamberlin, Frank T........M. D, '85
Physician,
1323 M St. N. W., Washington, D. C.

Chamberlin, J. A.............M. D, '63
Deceased, Sept. 27, 1868.

Chamberlin Justin Morrill, LL. B., '97
Lawyer,   LL. M.,'98
482 La. Ave., Washington. D. C.

Chamberlin, William L......M. D, '91

Chambers, J. Paul..........M. D, '84
530 Media St, Philadelphia, Pa.

Chapin, Harry B............M. D, '08
Physician and Surgeon,
Garfield Hospital, Wash, D. C

Charles, Garfield ....LL B, '04
Clerk,   LL. M., '05
U. S. Senate, Washington, D. C

Chauveau, Chas. Auguste....A. B, '95
Advocate,   A M, '96
75 Peter St, Quebec, Canada

Cheney, Archie W. .. ..LL B, '09
Fairview, Utah.

Cheney, Jasper Edwin ......A. M, '68
M. D, '68

Chew, John Paul, A. B., '82, LL B, '84
Ed in Chf., Church Prog, LL. M.,'85
520 Fullerton Bldg, St Louis, Mo.

Chew, Philemon W.........LL. B, '93
Lawyer,   LL. M,'94
512 F St. N. W., Washington, D. C.

Chewning, Alexander C.....LL. B., '09
Old Point, Va.

Chez, Joseph................LL. B., '97
Lawyer,
First Nat. Bk Bldg., Ogden, Utah

Chism, Warren P...........A. B, '72
Deceased.

Choate, Rufus. ....M D, '67
Physician,
The Farragut, Washington, D C.

Choice, William, A. B, '57, A. M, '69

Choppin, Julius A, A. B., '52, A. M, '53

Christiancy, George A. C....LL B., '92
Lawyer,
141 Broadway, New York City.

Christie, F. C...............M. D., '59
Deceased, England.

Church, J. B...............LL. B, '75
Patent Lawyer,
McGill Bldg, Washington, D. C.

Clabaugh, Hon. Harry M....LL D, '03
Chief Jus Sup. Court, Dis. Columbia,
Dean of G. U. Law School.
U. S. Court House, Wash., D. C.

Clagett, Henry William .....A. B., '66
Agriculturer,
Rosaryville, Prince George Co., Md.

Clagett, Howard C.........LL. B, '79
Deceased May 9, 1893.

Clancy, John F............:...A. B, '63
H. C, Mass.

Clapp, Harry M, LL. B, '93, LL. M., '94
U. S Special Deputy Appraiser,
641 Washington St., New York City.

Clapp, Woodbridge ....LL. B, '01
Boston, Mass.

Clark, Elroy Newton.......LL. B, '92
Lawyer,
Genl. Atty, Denver & Rio Grande Ry,
405-09 Equitable Bldg, Denver, Colo.

Clark, Eugene B...........M D, '72

Clark, John Alexander.....M. D, '98
1st Lieut. and Ass't Surgeon, U. S A
War Dept, Washington, D. C.

Clark, John Francis.....\...A. B, '93
122 W. 10th St, N. Y. City.

Clark, J. Nelson...........M. D, '67
Physician,
306 Broad St, Harrisburg, Pa.

Clark, Julius S.............M. D, '69
Physician,
109 Myrtle St, Melrose, Mass

Clark, Leon A.............LL. B, '03
Deputy District Attorney,
Oakland, Cal.

Clark, Manley T.. ....LL B., '09
Buffalo, N. Y.

Clark, Roland Eugene.......LL. B., '04
Lawyer,
Houlton, Me.

Clarke, Daniel Boone.......M. D., '57
Deceased, Aug. 4, 1906, Wash, D. C.

Clarke, George B..........A. B, '41
Deceased, Baltimore.

Clarke, Harold H...........LL. B. '09
627 E St. N. W., Wash., D. C.

Clarke, Joseph H..........A. M., '31
Deceased, 1885, Washington, D. C.

Clarke, Joseph B. C.......M. D, '55

Clarke, Richard H..A. B, '46, A. M., '49
Lawyer,   LL. D, '72
340 W. 71st St., N. Y. City.

Clarke, Walter S..........A. B., '80
Australia.

Clarke, Rev William F......A B., '33
Jesuit Priest,
Deceased, Oct. 17, 1890.

Clarke, William H.........A. B., '75
Deceased, July, 1876.

Clary, Wilham G..........LL. B., '90
Clerk,
513 L St. N. W., Washington, D. C.

Clay, William Rogers.......LL. B, '88
Com Court of Appeals,   LL. M, '89
Frankfort, Ky.

Clayson, Frederick H.......LL. M., '00
Deceased, 1902.

Clayson, H.................LL B, '09

Cleary, Francis J..........:.LL B, '06
Asst in Document Section,
Dept of Agriculture, Wash, D C.

Cleary, James T...........LL B, '05
Lawyer,
Merchants' Tr. Bldg, Los Angeles, Cal.

Cleary, Reuben...... -.......M. D., '59
Deceased,   A. M., '60
Feb. 12, 1898, Rio Janiero.

Cleary, Reuben.............A. B, '34
Novice, S. J,
Deceased, July 5, 1835, Frederick, Md.

Cleary, Thomas J..........M. D, '08
House Surgeon, L. I. City Hospital,
688 10th St, Brooklyn, N. Y.

Clements, James E.........LL. B, '81
Lawyer,
1406 G St. N. W., Washington, D C.

Cleveland, Jeremiah........A. B, '54
                          A. M., 60

Cleveland, Jesse F.........A. B, '53
                         ' A. M, '55

Cleverdon, J S............M D, '72

Coad, Wm. James.........A M, '00
Lawyer,
407 1st Nat. Bank Bldg, Omaha, Neb.

Cobb, James S.............M. D, '93
Physician,
Clayton, Del

Cobb, Norvell H...........LL B, '07
Merchant,
1107 G St. N. W., Wash, D. C.

Cockran, Hon W. Bourke...LL D, '99
Lawyer,
31 Nassau St., N. Y. City.

Cockrell, Alston.............A. B, '06
Lawyer,
703 Laura St, Jacksonville, Fla

Cody, John K. I...........LL. B, '98
Manager Ogden-Howard Co,
5th and King Sts, Wilmington, Del.

Coffron, W. H............M. D, '88
Deceased, April 7, 1905,
Grindstone City, Mich.

Coflin, Charles B..........LL M., '09
Lawyer,
1116 15th St. N. W., Wash, D. C.

Cogswell, Julius E.........LL. B, '88
Lawyer,
Charleston, S. C.

Cohnan, Edward J.........LL. B, '07
Clerk Treasury Dept.,
730 5th St. N. E., Washington, D. C.

Colbert, Michael J..A. B., '83, LL. B., '85
Lawyer,   LL. M., '86, A. M., '89
Century Bldg., Washington, D. C.

Cole, Hon. Charles C.......LL. D., '02
Deceased, Mar. 17, 1905, Wash., D. C.

Cole, Halbert Benton.......LL. B., '04
Lawyer,
Newkirk, Okla.

Cole, John T.................M. D., '91
Physician,
820 H St N. E., Washington, D. C.

Cole, Peter L....LL. B., '92, LL. M, '93
Coleman, David Charles.....M. D., '04
Physician,
377 Cabot St., Beverly, Mass.

Coleman, James Valentine...A. B, '69
     A. M, '71, LL. B, '73
1718 Laguna St, San Francisco, Cal.

Coleman, Watson E........LL. B., '94
Lawyer,
612 F St N. W, Washington, D. C.

Colesberry, William H......M D, '80

Colgin, Edward Broadnax...A M, '00
Lawyer,   LL B, '01
65-66 Theater Bldg., Houston, Tex.

Collier, Judge C. Needham..A. B, '68
     A. M, '95, LL. D, '98
Associate Justice of the Supreme Court
of the Territory of New Mexico.

Collier, Robert Joseph.......A. B, '94
Publisher and Editor,
413-24 W. 13th St., New York City.

Colliere, George Riggs.......A. B, '04
Real Estate and Insurance, LL. B, '07
1410 G St. N. W., Washington, D. C.

Colliflower, Charles E., Jr...LL. B, '05
Stenographer,
156 Tenn. Ave. N. E., Wash., D. C.

Colliflower, James E........A. B, '06
Law Student,
408 A St. S. E, Washington, D. C.

Collins, J. Harry...........M. D, '06
Physician,
6304 Frankstown Ave., Pittsburg, Pa.

Collins, James Marshall......LL. B, '96
Lawyer,   LL. M., 97
216 Court St, Marysville, Ky.

Collins, Joseph Francis .....A. B, '97
A. M, '98, LL. B, '99, LL. M, '00
Lawyer,
43 Cedar St, New York City.

Collins, Robert L............LL. B, '91
Wellington, Kansas.

Collins, Walter Homer......LL. B, '01
Clerk, U. S. Soldiers Home,
Soldiers Home, D. C.

Collins, William Granville...LL. B., '05
Lawyer,
Clarendon, Alex. Co., Va.

Collins, William Joseph.....A. B, '93
Deceased, Feb, 1902, Dedham, Mass.

Collins, William T.........M. D, '65
Deceased, Nov., 1906,
Santa Monica, Cal.

Columbus, Wm. F...........LL. B., '07
Lawyer,   LL. M., '08
Columbian Bldg., Washington, D. C.

Combs, Robert Cornelius....A. B., '55
. Lawyer,   A. M. '59
Leonardtown, Md.

Comerford, Peter Patrick...Ph. B., '93
480 8th Ave, New York City.

Compton, Edmund...........LL. B., '92
Lawyer,
Aquasco, Ind.

Compton, William P........M. D, '89
Physician,
1709 H St. N. W., Washington, D. C.

Conant, Thomas.............M. D, '67

Conaty, Rt Rev Thomas....D. D., '89
R. C. Bishop, Monterey & Los Angeles,
114 E. 2d St, Los Angeles, Cal.

Conboy, Martin..............LL. B., '98
Lawyer,   LL. M., '99
27 Pine St., New York City.

C ncilio, Rt Rev. Mons. J. de, D. D., '89
dDeceased, March 22, 1898,
Jersey City, N. J.

Condon, Francis W.........LL. B., '06
Lawyer,   LL. M., '07
Fort Dodge, Iowa.

Condon, William F., A. M., '03, LL. B., '06
Lawyer,   LL. M., '07
Fort Dodge, Iowa.

Coneby, William H.........LL. B., '04

Coniff, John J..............LL. B, '89

Conigisky, Joseph Perl......D. D. S,'04

Conley, Martin S..........A. B., '08
Law Student,
40 Brackett St., Portland, Me.

Conlin, Charles Francis......M D, '04
Deceased, Dec. 24, 1907,
Worcester, Mass.

Conlin, Rev. John A........A. B., '58
H. C, Mass.
Deceased, June 23, 1888.

Conlon, Charles F. ....LL. B., '98
Lawyer,
New Britain, Conn.

Conly, Francis..............A. B., '53

Connellan, James A.........LL. B., '96

Connelly, Benjamin M......LL. B., '97
Govt. Print. Office,   LL. M.,'98
Washington, D. C.

Connelly, Dennis J.........LL. B., '98
Lawyer,
Elmira, N. Y.

Connelly, Martin F.........LL. B., '09
Amesbury, Mass.

Conner, William Wallace....LL. B., '02
Sec. and Counsel Con. Sales Co.,
814 14th St., Washington, D. C.

Connolly, Anthony A.......LL. M.,'90

Connolly, Arthur L.........LL. M ,'06
Boston, Mass

Connolly, Rev. Ed D........A. M., '75

Connolly, J. Edward........A. B, '04
Special Agt, G. L. O.,   LL. B, '07
Fargo, N. D.

Connolly, John E...........LL B, '01
Lawyer,
Banigan Bldg., Providence, R. I.

Connolly, John W..........A. B., '04
Broker,
Nahant, Mass.

Connolly, Joseph B.........LL M.,'90

Connolly, Timothy Stanislaus.A. B., '97
Care Chas. Libby, Portland, Me.

Connor, George A...........LL. B., '02
Clerk to Member of Congress,
604 21st N. W, Washington, D. C

Connor, John Edward .....M. D , '04
Physician,
Holmesdale, Pittsfield, Mass.

Connor, Wm. P.............M. D., '08
Physician,
740 Crossman Av., Youngstown, Ohio

Connors, George Robert.....D. D S ,'04

Conover, J. C..............M. D , '71

Conrad, Thomas K.........M. D , '08
House Physician,
Garfield Hospital, Washington, D. C.

Conradis, Charles.LL. B.,'90, LL. M.,'91

Constas, John N............M. D., '04
Physician, G. U. Med. Fac,
925 N. Y. Ave. N. W., Wash., D. C.

Contee, John B.............LL. B., '87
Deceased, May 30, 1904.

Conway, John Joseph........M. D., '01
Physician,
Warren, R. I.

Conway, William O........LL. B., '76

Cook, Ansel B....A.B., '75, LL. B., '77

Cook, James C.............LL. B., '97
Clerk,   LL. M.,'98
Anacostia, D. C.

Cook, Robert M............LL. B., '95

Cook, Wilson E............LL. B., '95
Vice-Pres. Corydon, Nat. Bank,
Corydon, Ind.

Cooney, James J..LL. B., '98, LL. M.,'99

Cooper, John S.............M. D., '69
Physician,
1353 S. Second St., Louisville, Ky.

Cooper, Moses..............M. D., '74

Cooper, Sam Bronson, Jr....LL. B., '99
Lawyer,   LL. M.,'00
Beaumont, Tex.

Copeman, William H........LL. M.,'87

Copp, Zed H...............LL. B, '09
1675 Wisconsin Ave., Wash., D. C.

Corbett, Rev. John Walter Healy,
Priest,   A. M , '99
177 Ashland St., W. Roxbury, Mass.

Corbin, E. Lyon............M. D., '59

Corbin, William E.........M D., '91

Corcoran, Hon. John W.....LL. D., '95
Deceased, 1905, Clinton, Mass.

Corcoran, Richard P.......LL B , '94
Mining,   LL. M.,'95
Tonopah, Butler P. O., Nev.

Corcoran, Vincent A........A. B., '09
6554 Stewart Ave , Chicago, Ill.

Corcoran, William J........A. B , '63
H. C , Mass
Deceased, Feb. 21, 1897, Boston, Mass.

Corey, Chas. A..LL. B., '95, LL. M.,'96

Corgan, Charles E.........LL. B., '07
Lawyer,
Nanticoke, Pa.

Cortelyou, George Bruce....LL. B., '95
                          LL. D., '03
Pres. Con. Gas. Co, of New York,
New York City.

Costello, James F..........LL. B , '03
Artist,
504 Talbot Ave , Dorchester, Mass.

Costello, John, F............LL B , '08
Hutchins Bldg , Washington, D. C.

Costello, Michael F . ...   LL B , '08
Lawyer,
376 Weeden St , Pawtucket, R I

Costigan, Ignatius J. J......A B , '02
Lawyer,   LL B , '04
Fendall Bldg , Washington, D C.

Cottrell, Samuel, Jr.... ...LL B , '96
Clerk,
War Dept , Washington, D C

Coughlan, J Vincent.......LL B., '01
Special Agent, Gen Land Office,
Salt Lake City, Utah.

Coughlin, John T...........LL B , '81
Clerk,   LL M , '82
State Department, Washington, D. C.

Coulthurst, John A... ......A M , '93
Lawyer,
1 Beacon St , Boston, Mass

Coumbe, J T.............M D , '72
Deceased Mar. 7, 1895, Wash , D. C.

Cowan, Francis............M D , '69
Deceased, Feb. 12, 1905, Pennsylvania

Cowardin, Charles O'B......A. B., '74
Deceased, 1900.   A. M., '85

Cowhig, John J...........LL B , '09
Casanova, Va.

C les, A E... ....D. D. S ,'02

Cowling, William W.......M D , '72

Coyle, Dennis J............D D S., 08
Dentist,
4th & New Sts , So. Bethlehem, Pa.

Coyle, William E..........M D , '08
Physician,
45 Hawkins St , Waterbury, Conn.

Cox, Charles Robert.......LL B , '04
3422 O St. N. W., Washington, D. C.

Cox, Francis Marcellus......LL B , '74
Lawyer,
1324 4th St. N. E , Wash , D. C

Cox, Frank B...... ......LL. B , '96
Lawyer,   LL. M , '97
Ellenville, N. Y.

Cox, Walter S.............A. B , '43
Deceased, 1903,   A. M , '47
Washington, D. C.

Craig, Albert E...........M. D , '06
Physician,
3125 O St , Washington, D. C.

Craighill, G. Bowdoin.......LL. B., '06
Lawyer,
Care McKinney & Flannery, Hibbs
Bldg , Washington, D C.

Cramer, Dick...............LL. B , '90
Clerk,   LL M , '91
Pension Office, Washington, D C

Cramer, Herman W........LL. B , '97
Lawyer,
Junction City, Kans

Cranch, Edw..............M D , '73
Physician,
109 W. 9th St , Erie, Pa.

Crandall, Samuel B........LL. B , '06
Asst U S Attorney,
Independence, N. Y

Crane, G William...........LL B , '09
McGraw, Kan

Crane, Wm. L.............LL B , '09
Albuquerque, N. Mex.

Craven, Charles A........ .LL B , '93
Correspondent,
The Buck Stove & Range Co ,
St. Louis. Mo.

Craven, Thomas J.........A. B , '87
958 26th St. N. W , Washington, D. C.

Crawford, Charles A.......LL B , '05
Lawyer,
U. S Tr. Co. Bldg , Terre Haute, Ind.

Crawford, James C ....LL. B , '98
Accountant,   LL M , '99
Treasury Dept., Washington, D C

Crawford, Wm. A..........LL B , '07
Clerk G. L. O ,
128 C St. N. E., Washington, D. C.

Crawford, William Gordon. .LL B , '98
Lawyer,
1407 F St. N. W , Washington, D C.

Crittenden, Thomas B.. ...M. D., '95
Physician,
Horton, W. Va.

Croggon, Richard C..... ..M D , '60

Croghan, Francis E.. ..... M D , '08
Physician,
1924 Westminster St , Providence, R I.

Cronin, Patrick W........ .A. B , '64
H. C. Mass.
Deceased, Lawrence, Mass.

Cronin, William Joseph. ....LL B , '94
Deceased,   LL. M.,'95, A M , '95
Nov. 30, 1899, Pawtucket, R I.

Crook, Harrison ....M. D , '78
Physician, G. U. Med. Fac.,
The Sherman, 15th & L Sts.,Wash ,D.C.

Crosby, Chas. F..LL. B , '97, LL. M., '98

Crossfield, Hon. Amasa S....LL B., '83
Judge,   LL M , '84
Army and Navy Club, Manila, P I

Crosson, Henry J.......... M. D , '90
Physician,
1746 M St. N. W , Washington, D. C.
Crow, Philip M., LL B , '88, LL. M., '89
Crowe, John W.............M. D, '97
Physician,
704 T St. N. W , Washington, D. C.
Crowley, Jeremiah J........A B , '64
H. C., Mass.,
Deceased, Jan 16, 1906, Chicago, Ill.
Crowley, Leo Francis.......M. D., '09
Intern,
Providence Hospital, Wash., D. C.
Crowley, Robert E.........LL. B , '06
Special Agent G L. O., LL M., '07
Portland, Oregon.
Crozier, St. George B....Mus., Doc , '70
Cruickshank, Thomas Antisell, LL. B., 96
Clerk, City P. O., LL. M, '97
3125 11th St. N. W., Wash, D. C.
Crummey, Edw. J...........A. B., '08
Law Student,
7 Madison Place, Albany, N. Y.
Cruse, George E............LL. B., '96
Cuddy, Stephen A...........LL. B , '95
Cudlipp, Malcolm A........M. D , '90
Physician,
Baltimore, Md.
Cuenco, Jose Maria........A. M, '05
Ph. D., '07, LL. B., '07
Teacher,
Calle Colon, No. 26, Cebu, P. I.
Culkin, William Purcell.....A B , '09
Carthage, Ill.
Cull, Abner H.............M. D, '68
Cullen. Livingston James....A B , '99
Lawyer,
181 La Salle St, Chicago, Ill.
Cullen, Rev. Thomas Francis, A. B., '99
Priest,.
St. Patrick's, Providence, R. I
Cullinane, James A..... ....LL B , '87
LL. M., '88
Cullinen, Alexander A .....A. B , '86
Culver, Ira J...............M. D., '68
Physician,
Knox City, Texas
Cummins, J. Wm............LL. B , '07
Lawyer,
1425 Chapline St., Wheeling, W. Va.
Cummings, Francis J........A. M., '89
Deceased, August, 1890.
Cummings, George W.......M. D., '65

Cummiskey, Edward Francis, M D , '96
Physician.
1342 U St. N. W , Washington, D. C..
Cummiskey, Eugene........A B , '44
A. M , '49
Cunniff, Patrick S..........LL. B , '99
Lawyer, LL. M, '00
12 Pemberton Sq , Boston, Mass.
Cunningham, F. A , A B , '72, A. M., '74
Civ Eng, Lawyer, Manf of Chem
508 W. Maple Ave., Merchantville, N.·J.
Curley, Charles Fallon ......A. B , '97
Lawyer,
Ford Bldg., Wilmington, Del.
Curran, John D. J..........M. D , '03
Curran, Joseph J............LL. B , '05
Lawyer,
38 Auburndale Ave., W. Newton, Mass.
Curriden, Samuel W........LL B., '77
Lawyer,
Centre Market, Washington, D. C.
Curry, Daniel..............LL. B , '01
Ins. Dept District Government,
Washington, D. C.
Curry, Frank L.............D. D. S.,'07
Dentist,
29 Clinton St., Waltham, Mass.
Curtin, Richard A.....,......LL B , '04
Lawyer,
705 G St. N. W., Washington, D. C.
Curtis, George F............LL. B., '89
LL. M.,'90
Cuttle, Ignatius X...........LL. B., '07
Lawyer, .. LL. M., '08
Fall River, Mass.
Cutts, Richard D............A. B , '35
Deceased, ·A. M, '42
Dec. 14, 1883, Washington, D. C.
Cuyler, George A., A. B , '38, A, M., '42
Dahlgren, John Vinton.......A. B., '89
A. M., '91, LL. B , 91, LL. M , 92
Deceased, Aug 11, 1899,
Colorado Springs, Colorado.
Daiker, Frederick H........LL. B , '07
Clerk, LL. M, '08
Pension Office, Washington, D C
Dailey, Oliver A.............M. D.,'55
Deceased, Jan. 5, 1896,
Kansas City, Mo
Daily, B E................M. D , '74
Daish, John Broughton......LL .B , '99
Lawyer, LL. M ,'00
723 15th St. N W , Washington, D. C.
Dallas, Everett Jerome .....LL. B , '73

Dalton, Alfred S...........LL B , '97
Clerk,
War Dept., Washington, D. C.

Daly, Francis J. M.........A. M., '75
Deceased, LL. B., '75
Feb, 19, 1892, Macon, Ga.

Daly, J. Harry..LL. B., '92' LL M.,'93

Daly, Joseph Russel.........A. B , '09
198 Palisade Ave., Yonkers, N. Y.

Daly, Joseph T..............LL B , '95
Stenographer, LL. M.,'97
Navy Dept., Washington, D C.

Daly, Walter F..LL. B , '91' LL M.,'92

Damman, Milton............LL B, '99
Lawyer,
141 Broadway, N. Y. City.

Danforth, R. Foster.........M. D., '86
Physician,
919 12th St, Washington, D C.

Daniels, John W............LL. B., '01
Lawyer,
Pawtucket, R. I.

Daniels, Rees P............LL. M., '86

Darby, John J..............M. D., '83
Physician,
311 A St. N. E., Washington, D. C.

Darby, Samuel E..........LL. B , '90
Patent Lawyer, LL. M., '91
220 Broadway, N. Y. City.

Darlington, Joseph James....LL. D., '86
Lawyer,
410 5th St. N. W., Washington, 'D. C.

Darr, Charles W............LL. B , '94
Lawyer, LL M.,'95
705 G St. N. W., Washington, D. C.

Darrah, John R.............LL. M., '94

Dartt, James F.............LL. B., '77

Davenport, Benjamin........LL. B., '74

Davenport, Henry B.......LL. B , '05
Stenographer, LL M.,'06
Office Compt. Currency, Wash , D. C.

David, Edward..LL. B., '91' LL. M.,'92

David, Frederick E.........LL. B., '87
LL. M.,'88

David, Levi...............LL. B., '98
Lawyer, LL. M., '99
Fendall Bldg., Washington, D. C.

Davidson, Edwin R........LL B , '05
LL M.,'07

Davidson, Falconer.........M. D , '93
Deceased.

Davies, Hon. Gomer........M. D., '88
Physician,
England.

Davis, Beverly A.... ... ...LL B., '91

Davis, Bliss N.............LL B , '97

Davis, Charles S...........LL B ,'96
Special Examiner, LL M ,'97
Bureau of Pensions, Wichita, Kas.

Davis, Daniel Grant........M. D., '97
Secretary,
1979 Biltmore St. N. W., Wash , D. C.

Davis, Eugene A...........LL. B., '93
LL. M ,'94

Davis, George M...........M. D, '71

Davis, John G.............M. D., '68

Davis, John H...LL. B , '93' LL. M ,'94

Davis, John M.............A. B., '62

Davis, John N.............M. D , '60

Davison, John W...........LL. B., '93

Dawley, William Joseph.....LL .B., '03
Lawyer,
25 Broad St., N. Y. City.

Dawson, Andrew D........LL. B , '09
Waterbury, Conn.

Day, Ewing W.............M. D, '89
1005 Westingh. Bldg., Pittsburg, Pa.

Deane, Julian W...........M. D , '68
Deceased, May 6, 1905, Wash , D. C.

DeCourcy, Hon. Charles A...A B , '78
Justice, A. M., '89' LL. D , '04
Mass. Superior C'rt, Lawrence, Mass.

Deery, James P.............A. B., '27
Priest, S. J,
Deceased, June 21, 1833, Wash., D. C.

Deery, James P.............A. B., '95
P. O. Box 605, Ware, Mass.

Degges, Addison B.........LL. B., '95
LL. M., '96

DeKnight, Edward W.......LL. B , '92
LL. M ,'93

DeLacy, William Henry.....LL. B , '83
Justice Juvenile Court, LL. M., '84
Washington, D. C.

Delacroix, Jules D..........A. B., 54

Delacroix, Peter D.........A. B ; '49

Delaney, Martin Donohue...M. D., '98
Physician,
911 Prince St., Alexandria, Va.

Delany, Francis Xavier, S. J..A. B., '97
Jesuit,
Woodstock, Md.

Delaplaine, Patrick H.......LL. B., '07
Train Director,
1010 6th St. N. E., Washington, D. C.

Deloughery, Edward........A. B , '26
Deceased, Nov. 18, 1885,
Baltimore, Md.

Demeritt, J. Henry..........M. D , '68
Clerk Navy Department,
1335 Vt. Ave. N. W., Wash , D. C.

Demoss, W. R.............M. D , '63

Denby, Hon. Charles........LL D , '85
Deceased, Jan. 13, 1904,
Jamestown, N. Y.

Deneen, John.............LL B , '98
Lawyer,   LL. M , '99
Elmira, N. Y.

Denegre, Charles...........LL. B , '01
Lawyer,
Birmingham, Ala.

Denman, Hampton Y........LL. M.,'96
Deceased, 1904.

Dennis, William Henry......A. B., '74
Lawyer,   LL. B., '76, A. M., '83
416 5th St. N. W., Washington, D. C.

Denton, John S............LL. B., '95
Vice-Pres. So. Lumber Mfg. Co.,
Nashville, Tenn.

Denu, Albert R.............LL. B., '03
Lawyer,   /
Rapid City., S. D.

Denver, Hon. Matthew Rombach,
Bank President,   A. B.,   '92
Mem. Cong., Wilmington, Ohio.

Denvir, William J..........A. B. '58
H. C., Mass. Deceased, Sept. 1, 1885,
Charlestown, Mass.

Dermody, John C...........LL. B., '89
Deceased,   LL. M.,'90
Washington, D. C.

Desaulniers, Rev. Francis L..A. M., '34

desGarennes, Jean Felix Poulain,
Lawyer,   A. B., '94, A. M., '96
            LL. B., '95, LL. M.,'97
63 Wall St., N. Y. City.

desGarennes, Poulain Jean...A. M., '92
Professor,
U. S. Naval Academy, Annapolis, Md.

Desloge, George Thatcher...A. M., '02
Lawyer,   .
Liggett Bldg., St. Louis, Mo.   "

Deslonde, Maj. Edmund A..A. B., '49
Deceased, April 5, 1886.

Deslonde, Edward L........A. B., '52

Desmond, Daniel I..........A. M , '31
Deceased.

Desmond, Stephen William..A. B., '04
31 Robert St., New Bedford, Mass.

Desmond, Walter Patrick...D D. S ,'03

Dessaulles, Casimir.........A. B., '48

Dessez, Paul Tonnel........M. D., '97
Ass't Surgeon, U. S. Navy,
Naval Hospital, Chelsea, Mass.

Dessez, Theodore H........LL. B , '98
            LL. M , '00

Detrick, R. Baxter.........M. D , '58
Deceased, Nov. 7, 1904,
Kensington, Md.

Devereux, Anthony John Antello,
Stock Broker,   A. B., '98
Arcade Bldg , Philadelphia, Pa.

Devereux, Frederick L......LL. B , '06
Traffic Mgr. The C. & P. Tel. Co.,
1232 Irving St. N. W., Wash., D. C.

Devereux, James Ashton.....A. B., '96
Lawyer,   ,
1326 Land Title Bldg., Phila., Pa.

Devine Harry J.............LL. B., '09
Milwaukee, Wis.

Devine, James..............LL. B , '90
Lawyer,   LL. M.,'91
Whitefield, Me.

Devine, John.....A. B., '95, LL. B., '97
Lawyer,
500 First St., Brooklyn, N. Y.

Devine, Patrick H..........LL. B., '85

Devine, Thomas Farrell.....A. M., '94
Principal, Grammar School,
Waterbury, Conn.

Devlen, John E...A. B., '40, A. M , '53
Deceased, March, 1888, N. Y. City.

Devlin, Daniel J............A. B., '02
Vice-President, Carrollton Land Co,
906 Gravier St., New Orleans, La.

Devlin, Hugh M...........LL. B., '07
Lawyer,
Berkley, R. I.

Devlin, William H.........A. B., '50
H. C, Mass ,
Deceased, Boston, Mass.

De Ycaza, Y. Moratinos Ignacio,
      A. M.,'03, Ph. S.,'05, LL. B., '06
Lawyer,   Ph. D , '07, LL. M.,'07
2 Uli Uli St., Manila, P. I.

Dial, Joseph A..............LL. B , '06
Lawyer,
Sulphur Springs, Tex.

Diamond, William Carrell...A. B , '98
Lawyer,
120 Broadway, New York City.

Dick, Ewell A..............LL. B , '77

Dickey, Raymond B........LL B, '99
  Lawyer,   LL. M, '00
  1416 F St. N. W, Washington, D. C.
Dickinson, Dwight, Jr......M. D., '09
  Intern G. U. Hospital,
  1806 R St. N. W, Washington, D. C.
Dickson, Martin Thomas....A. B., '71
Dielman, Prof Henry....Mus Doc., '49
Digges, Daniel C............A. B., '33
  Deceased,   A. M., '37
Digges, Eugene.............A. B., '57
  Deceased, June 29, 1899.
Digges, John Henry........M. D., '03
  Physician,
  805 First St N. W, Wash, D C.
Digges, John T.............M D., '69
  Physician,
  La Plata, Md.
Diggs, Charles F............LL. B, '02
  Lawyer,
  412 5th St N. W., Wash, D. C.
Dilkes, James Alphonsus....A. B., '09
  1912 Arch St, Philadelphia, Pa.
Dillard, James Edwin, Jr....LL. B, '04
  Lawyer,   LL. M, '06
  Memphis Trust Bldg, Memphis, Tenn.
Dillard, Joseph P...........LL. B, '08
  Lawyer,
  Spokane, Wash.
Dillon, George W..........A. B, '58
  H. C, Mass,
  Deceased.
Dillon, Hon John..........A. M, '96
  Lawyer, County Attorney,
  Lander, Wyoming
Dillon, Rev. Patrick........Ph. D, '89
  Priest,
  St Mary's, Peru, Ill.
Dillon, Paul...............A. M, '97
  Lawyer,
  1106 Fullerton Bldg, St Louis, Mo.
Dimitry, Alexander......... A M, '32
  Deceased, 1883,   LL D, '59
  New Orleans, La.
Dimitry, Charles Patton.....A. M., '67
  Journalist and Author,
  852 Camp St, New Orleans, La
Dimitry, John B............A. M, '67
  Deceased.
Dimitry, Michael Draco.....A. M., '56
  Deceased, Feb, 1883.
Dimitry, Theodore J........A. M, '92
  Deceased, May 31, 1904,
  New Orleans, La

Dinnies, Charles............A. B, '17
  Deceased.
Dinnies, George............A. B, '17
  Deceased.
Dixon, William S...........M. D, '68
  Medical Director, U. S. N,
  Care U. S. Navy Dept., Wash., D. C.
Dixon, William Wirt, Jr....LL. B, '99
  Deceased.
Doar, W. Thomas..........LL. B, '06
  Lawyer,
  New Richmond, Wis.
Dodge, Clarence............LL. B, '05
  Real Estate,
  1416 F St. N. W., Washington, D. C.
Dodge, Robert H..........M. D, '93
  Deceased, Mar 11, 1907, Bethesda, Md.
Dohan, Joseph M..........A. B., '86
  Lawyer,   A. M, '89
  1012 Stephen Girard Bldg, Phila, Pa.
Doherty, Michael L........A. B., '63
  H. C., Mass, Clergyman,
  Deceased, Aug. 28, 1886.
Doing, Charles H..........LL. B, '08
  Clerk,
  Wash. Loan & Trust Co., Wash, D. C
Doing, Robert B...........LL B, '08
  Clerk,
  District Bldg., Washington, D C.
Dolan, John J..............LL. B., '93
  Deceased, Aug, 1900   LL. M., '94
Dolan, P. V...............LL. B., '85
  Physician,   M. D, '90
  1434 Newton St. N. W., Wash, D. C.
Dolloway, Louis Marsh......M. D, '00
  Physician,
  323 Spitzer Bldg, Toledo, Ohio
Dolmage, Mihran M.......D. D S.,'03
  Dentist,
  825 Vermont Ave., Washington, D. C.
Dominguez, Virgil F........A. B., '63
Donahoe, Alphonsus Rich ...A M, '05
  Ecclesiastical Student,
  27 S. Park St., Halifax, N S.
Donahue, Charles Louis.....A. B, '00
  Lawyer,
  390 Congress St., Portland, Me.
Donahue, Francis William ..A B, '97
  Physician and Surgeon,
  Greenfield, Mass.
Donaldson, Glenn R........LL. M.,'06
  Lawyer,
  Boston Bldg, Kansas City, Mo.

Donaldson, R Newton......LL. B , '90
Lawyer, LL. M.,'91
McGill Bldg., Washington, D. C.

Donaldson, Robert Golden ..LL. B , '95
Lawyer,
611 14th St , Washington, D. C.

Donaldson, Walter A........A B., '75
Deceased, May 15, 1906, A. M ,'91
Bloomfield, N. J.

Donaldson, Walter Franklin..LL. B., '05
Lawyer,
611 14th St , Washington, D. C.

Donch, Wm. A..LL. B , '91, LL. M ,'92

Donegan, James H.........A B., '47

Donegan, Maurice Francis...A. M., '98
Masonic Temple Bldg , Ph. D , '99
Davenport, Iowa.

Donegan, Patrick J.........LL B , '97
LL. M.,'98

Donlon, Rev. Alphonsus J , S. J,
Jesuit Priest, A. B., '88
Woodstock, Md.

Donnelly, Charles....⌐.......LL. B., '96

Donnelly, Edward C........A. B., '44
Deceased, Jan. 4, 1891, N. Y. City.

Donnelly, Horace J.........LL. B , '09
1026 8th St. N. W., Washington, D. C.

Donnelly, James P.........A. B., '53

Donnelly, Joseph Patrick....A. M , '98
322 So. Excelsior Ave., Butte, Mont.

Donnelly, Richard J.. ......LL. B , '89
Chf. of Div , War Dept., LL. M ,'90
The Wyoming, Washington, D. C.

Donnelly, William J........A. B., '91
Real Estate and Notary Public,
1403 H St. N. W , Washington, D. C.

Donoghue, James Kiernan...M. D., '09
Intern,
Monroe Co. Hospital, Rochester, N. Y.

Donohoe, Clarence F.......LL. B , '97
Real Estate Broker, LL. M.,'98
314 Penn. Ave. S. E., Wash., D. C.

Donohue, Florence.........M. D., '72
Physician and Surgeon,
1134 8th St N. W., Washington, D. C.

Donovan, Dennis D........LL. B , '95
Lawyer,
Napoleon, Ohio.

Donovan, George Timothy...A. B., '05
Shoe Manufacturer,
Liberty Sq , Lynn, Mass.

Donovan, Joseph M........LL B , '89

Donovan, Michael R........A. B., '80
Physician,
128 S. Common St., Lynn, Mass.

Donovan, Thomas J........LL. B , '95
Real Estate,
108 I St. N. W , Washington, D. C.

Donworth, Hon. George.....A. B , '81
Judge, U. S. Circuit Court,
Burke Bldg , Seattle, Wash.

Dooley, Francis X..........M. D., '65
Physician,
1346 F St., Washington, D. C.

Dooley, James H............A. B., '60
Lawyer, A. M., '65
922 E. Main St , Richmond, Va.

Doran, Charles M. Cantwell, LL. B , '98
Lawyer, LL. M.,'99
Norfolk, Va.

Dorman, John Edward.. ..:D. D. S ,'04

Dorsey, Roscoe J. C.........LL. B , '02
Lawyer, LL. M ,'03
701 12th St. N. W , Wash., D C.

Dougherty, Francis P..... ..LL. B , '05
Lawyer,
Pittsfield, Mass.

Dougherty, Ja es D........A B , '57
Deceased, April 2, 1878. A. M , '60

Dougherty, Very Rev. James J,
Deceased, D. D , '89, LL. D , '97

Dougherty, John Francis....A. B , '04
Deputy County Auditor,
Grafton, N. Dak.

Dougherty, Philip Joseph. .A.M., '98
Ph. D., '99, LL. B , '99, LL. M ,'00
Lawyer,
412 Sloan St., Philadelphia, Pa.

Douglas, R. V.... .... .A B., '96
Lawyer,
Greensboro, N. C.

Douglas, Hon. Robert M....A. B., '67
Lawyer, A. M.,'70, LL. D., '97
Greensboro, N. C.

Douglas, Stephen Arnold....A. B , '01
Deceased.

Douglas, George...........A. B , '73
Deceased, Mar. 8, 1888, A. M., '77
Washington, D. C.

Douglass, John J...........LL. B., '96
Lawyer,
252 Webster St , East Boston, Mass.

Douglass, Henry J..........M. D., '73
Deceased.

Douglass, Will W..........LL. B., '87

Douglass, Wm. B...........LL. M., '88

Dowd, Dennis P., Jr........A. B., '08
Law Student,
169 W. 18th St., N Y. City, N. Y.

Dowd, Ed. F................A. B, '94
Physician,
26 Common St, Waltham, Mass.

Dowd, Patrick..............A. B, '53

Dowling, Patrick V........LL B, '04
Lawyer,

Downey, Richard J..........LL. B., '09
1106 16th St. N. W., Wash, D. C.

Downing, Augustine H......LL. B, '05
Lawyer,
16 Comstock Ave., Providence, R. I.

Downing, George E.........LL. B., '01
Lawyer,
324 Wilcox Bldg, Los Angeles, Cal.

Downing, Mortimer A.......LL B, '88

Downing, Rossa F...........LL B, '89
Lawyer,   LL. M, '90
Stewart Bldg, Washington, D. C.

Downing, Thomas R......Phar. B., '73
Deceased

Downs, N. Carroll..........LL. B, '99
Lawyer,
1420 N. Y. Ave N. W., Wash., D. C.
170 Broadway, N. Y. City.

Downs, Thomas Charles....LL. B., '99
Lawyer,   LL. M., '00, A. M., '00
Fon du Lac, Wis.

Doyle, Edw. F...A B, '35, A. M, '39

Doyle, Francis Joseph.......M. D., '01
Physician,
611 E. Fort Ave., Baltimore, Md.

Doyle, J. Herbert...........A. B., '07
Care W. R. Grace & Co.,
Hanover Square, N. Y. City, N. Y.

Doyle, John T....A. B., '38, A. M., '42
Deceased, Dec. 23, 1906,   LL. D., '89
Menlo Park, Cal.

Doyle, Michael M...........LL. B., '08
Lawyer,
705 6th St N. W., Washington, D. C.

Doyle, Robert Emmet.......A. B., '46
Deceased, Mar. 18, 1898,
San Francisco, Cal.

Doyle, W. T. Sherman......A B, '97
718 14th St., N. W.,   LL B., '99
Washington, D. C.

Dragicsevics, Alex. O.......M D., '90

Drake, Otis Branch.........LL. B., '03
Lawyer,
Century Bldg., Washington, D. C.

Dreaper, Edward Bernard...A. B., '03

Drennan, Lawrence M......M. D., '06
Intern, Gov. Hospital for Insane,
Washington, D. C.

Dresbach, H. V.............M D., '94
Physician,
Iola, Kan.

Drew, Harry C...............M. D., '09
Intern, St. John's Hospital,
Long Island City, N Y.

Drew, Walter...............LL B., '09
Madison, Wis

Drill, Lewis L...............LL B , '03
Lawyer,
New York Life Bldg., St Paul, Minn.

Driscoll, Thomas A.........A B, '96
Lawyer,   LL. B., '97
Hibernia Bank Bldg, San Franc., Cal.

Drown, J. H................M D., '94

Drum, John William.........LL B, '95
Lawyer,
Marble Hill, Mo

Drum, Joseph C............LL. B., '99
Lawyer,
1115 Tremont Bldg., Boston, Mass

DuCharme, Alfred Joseph...A. B., '91
Lawyer,
34 Buhl Block, Detroit, Mich.

Dudley, John Gurney.......LL M.,'02
Lawyer,
7th St & Penn. Ave N.W , Wash.,D.C.

Duff, Edwin H.............LL. B, '97
Lawyer,
1306 F St N. W, Washington, D. C.

Duffey, Arthur Francis......LL. B., '03
Editor Boston Post,
Boston, Mass.

Duffey, H. C...............M. D., '91
Physician,
929 O St. N. W, Washington, D. C

Duffy, Bernard F..........A B., '01
788 Broadway, So Boston, Mass.

Duffy, Charles Hugh......LL. B, '98
                         LL. M., '99

Duffy, Francis............A. B., '79
Deceased,   A. M., '89

Duffy, Jas. Patrick Bernard..A. B., '01
Lawyer,
Roch. Sav. Bk. Bldg., Rochester, N Y.

Duffy, Joseph..............LL. B., '08
Lawyer,
393 Perkins St., Akron, Ohio.

Duffy. Joseph T......... ...LL B , '93
Railway Mail Clerk,   LL. M.,'94
930 4th St N. E., Washington, D. C.

Dufour, Rev. Alphonse, S. J., A. M.,   '96
Jesuit Priest,
Deceased, 1907.

Dufour, Clarence R........M D,   '90
Physician, G. U. Med. Fac.,
1343 L St., Washington, D. C.

Dufour, Everett............LL. B.,   '02
Lawyer,   LL. M., '03
Munsey Bldg., Washington, D. C.

Dufour, J. F. R............M. D,   '73

Dugan, James Henry........A. B.,   '96
Deceased, Mar. 2, 1903, La Salle, Ill.

Duggan, Jeremiah R........A. B.,   '02
Druggist,
254 Asylum St., Hartford, Conn

Duggan, John, Jr............LL. B.,   '06
Lawyer,   LL. M., '07
Connellsville, Pa.

Duke, Douglas William......M. D.,   '90
Physician,
England.

Duke, Thomas.............LL. B,   '76
Deceased, Feb, 3, 1888.

Dulin, Edgar A............M. D.,   '65
Physician and Surgeon,
Nevada, Mo.

Dumont, Very Rev. Francis L. M., SS.,
Catholic University,   D. D,   '89
Brookland, D. C.

Duncan, James M..........M. D,   '69

Duncan, John K............D. D. S.,'06
Dentist,
320 Mass. Ave. N. E., Wash., D. C.

Duncan, Rev. Wm. H., S. J., A. B,   '53
Deceased, Dec. 20, 1894,   A. M.,   '60
Georgetown College, D. C.

Dunn, Charles Aloysius......LL. B.,   '91
Clerk,   LL. M., '92
Sec.'s Office, Navy Dept., Wash., D. C.

Dunn, Charles Clark........LL. B.,   '07
U. S. Land Office, Denver, Colo.

Dunn, John Thomas Francis, M. D.,   '01
Physician,
1625 Retuer St., Philadelphia, Pa.

Dunn, L. B................M. D.,   '58

Dunn, Wood Gilmer.........LL. B.,   '99
Lawyer,
Charlottesville, Va.

Dunne, James P............LL. M.,'04

Dunne, William G., Jr.......LL. B.,   '91
                         LL. M.,'92

Dunnigan, John Patrick.....M. D.,   '01
Physician,
214 2nd St S. E., Washington, D. C

Dunphy, John F.............M. D.,   '73
Deceased,
Newburgh, N. Y.

Dunton, John F.............LL. B.,   '94
U. S. Chinese Inspector,   LL. M.,'95
Rouses Point, N. Y.

Durant, Horace B............LL. B.,   '97
Lawyer,
Miami, Okla.

Durfee, Raphael Burke......M. D.,   '00
1814 K St. N. W., Washington, D. C.

Durkee, Robert A...........A. M.,   '31

Durkin, Martin J............LL. B.,   '07
Lawyer,
Parkersburg, W. Va.

Durney, Charles Paul......M. D.,   '09
Intern,
G. U. Hospital, Washington, D. C.

Durnin, Rev. James A.......A. B.,   '51
H. C, Mass.,
Deceased, April 15, 1873.

Duross, Charles E...........A. B.,   '90
Real Estate,
155 W. 14th St, New York City.

Duross, James Edward......A. B.,   '91
Lawyer,
20 Vesey, New York City

Dutcher, George C.........LL. B.,   '08
Lawyer,
526 Caswell Blk., Milwaukee, Wis.

Duvall, Charles..............A. B.,   '30
Deceased.

Duvall, Edward S., Jr.......LL. B.,   '93
Lawyer,   LL. M.,'94
902 F St. N. W., Washington, D. C.

Duvall, William H..........LL. B.,   '91
Lawyer,
Martinsburg, W. Va.

Duvall, William S...........LL. B.,   '93
Lawyer and Patent Expert,
902 F St. N. W., Washington, D. C.

Duvall, William T. S.......M. D.,   '65
Physician,
1718 U St. N. W., Wash., D. C.

Dwight, Thomas............LL. D.,   '89
Physician, Howard U. Med. Fac.,
235 Beacon St., Boston, Mass.

Dwyer, William A..........B. S.,   '88
Vice-President and Genl. Manager.
The Art Stove Co., Detroit, Mich.

Dyer, Rev. David Marcus...A. B.,   '92
Priest,   A. M.,   '93
510 W. 165th St., New York City

Dyer, Dr. George A.........A. M., '56
Deceased, Jan. 12, 1879,
Washington, Indiana.

Dyer, Joseph T., Jr.........LL. B., '04
Lawyer,
715 14th St. N. W., Wash., D. C.

Dyer, Philip Eugene........A. B, '96
Deceased.

Dyer, Richard Nott.........LL. B, '78
LL. M., '79

Dykers. Francis H., A. B, '44, A. M, '45

Eagan, Sylvester Broezel....A. B, '03
Pres. Hotel Broezel Co,
Hotel Broezel, Buffalo, N. Y.

Earl, Charles................LL. B., '95
Solicitor,   LL. M., '96
Dept. of Com and Labor, Wash., D. C.

Earle, Henry Montague......LL. B., '93
Lawyer,
1 Nassau St., N. Y. City.

Earls, Michael, S. J.........A. M., '97
Jesuit Scholastic,
Woodstock College, Woodstock, Md.

Easby-Smith, James Stanislaus,
Lawyer,   A. B., '91, A M, '92
              LL B, '93, LL. M., '94
Century Bldg., Washington, D C.

Easterday, George J.........LL. B., '86
Real Est. Dealer and Stock Broker,
1410 G St. N. W., Washington, D. C.

Easterling, Horace V........LL. B, '94
Clerk,   LL. M., '95
Treasury Dept, Washington, D. C.

Easterling, J. Morgan.......LL M., '85

Eastman, Joseph A..........M. D, '65
Deceased, June 5, 1902, Indianap., Ind.

Easton, Edw. D..LL. B., '88, LL M., '89

Eccleston, Charles' A........LL B, '92
Deceased, Jan. 24, 1901,   LL M, '93
Washington, D. C.

Eccleston, G. Malcolm.......LL. B., '99
District Bldg.,   LL. M., '00
Washington, D. C.

Eckenrode, John W.........A. B, '09
351 W. Orange St., Lancaster, Pa.

Eckfeldt, Frederick .. ..M. D., '82

Eckhardt, Charles H.......M. D., '71
Deceased.

Eckstein, Otto G...........LL. M., '87

Edelen, E. Gardiner........LL. B, '90
Deceased, Mar. 18, 1891,
Baltimore, Md.

Edmonds, Dean Sockett.....LL. B., '99
Lawyer,   LL. M., '00
32 Liberty St., N. Y. City.

Edmondston, Preston Paul..A. B., '02
Care The Crowell Pub. Co,
New York City, N. Y.

Edmondston, Raphael Augustine,
Deceased, 1900,   M. D., '97
Philippine Islands.

Edmundson, James P..... .A. B, '35
Deceased

Edwards, Joseph F.........A. M; '82
Deceased.

Edwards, Richard Lee......LL. B, '02
Asst. Supt,   LL. M, '03
Treasury Dept, Washington, D. C.

Edwards, Robert H........M. D, '68

Edwards, William A........LL. B., '92
Covington, Ga.   LL. M, '93

Edwards, W. Walton........LL. B, '91
Lawyer,   LL. M, '92
Equity Bldg, Washington, D. C.

Effler, Erwin R.. .... A. M., '06
Lawyer,   LL. B., '08
829 Huron St., Toledo, Ohio.

Egan, Gerald M.............A. B, '06
Correspondent,
1322 F St. N. W, Washington, D C.

Egan, Dr. Maurice Francis..LL. D, '89
U. S Minister to Denmark,
Copenhagen, Denmark.

Eggleston, James Denslow.. M. D., '95

Elbridge, William A........LL. B., '76

Eldridge, Stuart ....M. D, '68
Physician,
Yokohama, Japan.

Elia, Ezechiel de............A. B., '74

Eline, Francis M..LL B, '94, LL. M, '95
Lawyer,   A B, '95
Milwaukee, Wis.

Eliot, Thomas Johnson..   M. D, '90
Physician,
718 H St. N. E, Washington, D. C.

Eliot, J. Llewellin........ . M. D., '74
Physician, G U. Med Fac,
1106 P St. N. W., Washington, D. C.

Eliot, Johnson, A. M, '69, Phar. B, '71
Deceased, Dec. 30, 1883, Phar. D, '72
Washington, D. C.

Elliot, John J...............A. B, '61

Elliott, Charles A, A. B., 72, LL. B, '74
Deceased, Aug. 1, 1894,   A. M, '89
Washington, D. C

Elliott, Jerre B .... M. D., '93
Physician,
Brooklyn, N. Y.

Ellis, Don Carlos .... A B., '04
Care Sec. Education,   LL. B., '08
Forest Service, Washington, D. C.

Ellsworth, Goodwin D ...... LL. B., '97
LL. M, '99

Elston, Arthur G .... LL. B., '08
Lawyer,
428 Peyton Bldg., Spokane, Wash.

Emery, William H .... LL. B, '96

Emmons, Charles M .... M. D., '93
Physician,
1100 Pa. Ave. S. E, Wash, D. C.

English, Charles Henry ...... LL B, '05
Lawyer,   LL M, '07
Erie, Pa.

English, John J .... A B, '00
Broker,
First Nat. Bank Bldg., Chicago, Ill.

Ennis, Charles H .... LL B, '94
LL M., '95

Ergood, Clarence Elmo ...... LL B, '96
Retail Grocer,   LL. M, '97
Lancaster, Pa.

Eriksson, Leonard .... LL. B., '04
Lawyer,
Fergus Falls, Minn.

Errazurez, Senor Don Ysidoro,
Deceased, Mar. 12, 1898,   A. B., '52
Rio Janeiro, Brazil.

Erskine, Harlow L .... LL M., '86

Ervine, Artemus J., Jr ...... LL. B, '96
LL. M. '97

Escobar, J ...... A B, '60 A. M., '62

Esling, Charles H .... A. M., '89
Deceased, Feb. 1, 1907,
Stuttgart, Germany.

Eslin, James F .... M. D., '91
Physician,
1717 14th St. N. W., Wash., D. C.

Estabrook, Leon M .... LL B., '97
Record Officer,
Dept. of Agriculture, Wash, D. C

Estabrook, Watts T .... LL. B., '07
Patent Lawyer,
802 F St. N. W., Washington, D. C.

Etchison, Howard M .... LL. B., '04
1820 Mintwood Place, Wash., D C.

Ethridge, Bell W .... A. B., '76
Deceased, March 26, 1901,
Dresden, Tenn

Etty, Robert A .... LL. B., '91
LL. M., '92

Evans, John M .... M. D., '61

Evans, Paul Warrington .... A. B , '94
Dentist,   LL B., '98
Bond Bldg., Washington, D. C.

Evans, W. Warrington ...... A. B., '91
Dentist,
Bond Bldg, Washington, D. C.

Evans, Warwick .... M. D, '52
Physician,
1105 9th St. N. W., Wash., D. C.

Eve, Oswell R .... LL. B, '99
Lawyer,
Augusta, Ga

Evert, Henry C.. .... ∴ LL. B, '91
Patent Lawyer,   LL M., '92
100-108 Smithfield St, Pittsburg, Pa.

Ewing, John K. M , ... LL. B, '06
Lawyer,
60 Wall St., New York City.

Ewing, Thomas, Jr .... LL. B., '90
Lawyer,
67 Wall St., New York City.

Ewing, Thomas, Jr .... LL. D, '70
Deceased

Fague, Joseph R .... LL. B, '97
Lawyer,   LL M, '98
504 E St. N. W., Washington, D. C.

Fairclough, Rev. John ...... A. M, '21
Deceased.

Fairfax, John Wheeler, Jr ... A. B., '04
Stocks and Bonds,
218 Hennen Bldg, New Orleans, La.

Falconer, Balivar Lang ...... M. D , '95
Asst Director Civil Service,
Manila, P. I.

Fallon, Frederick B .... LL. B, '92
Lawyer,
406 Security Bldg., Bridgeport, Conn.

Fallon, James ....∴ .... LL. B., '96
Lawyer,
21 North St., Pittsfield, Mass

Fallon, John T.. LL. B, '78 LL. M, '79

Fallon, Joseph D .... A. B., '58
H. C, Mass.,   A. M, '64
Lawyer, and Justice of the Municipal
Court of South Boston District,
56 Pemberton Square, Boston, Mass.

Fallon, Joseph P .... LL. B., '81

Falls, Alexander J .... LL. B, '73

Farish, John Hamilton .... A. B., 79
Real Estate and Loans,
119 N. 8th St., St. Louis, Mo

Farr, Richard R...............LL. B., '07
Lawyer,
Fairfax, Va.

Farr, Wilson M...............LL. B. '07
Lawyer,
Fairfax, Va.

Farrell, Edward G.........LL. B., '97
Deceased,   LL. M., '98

Farrell, Ed. P...............A.B., '83
Deceased, Louisville, Ky.

Farrell, Emmet Lee.........A. M , '93
Deceased, Feb. 23, 1895. LL. B , '94

Farrow, Patillo.............LL B., '97
Lawyer,
Charleston, S. C.

Faulkner, James Burton.....LL. B , '05
Lawyer,
Security Tr. Co. Bldg., Lexington, Ky.

Faulkner, Charles James F..A. B., '22
Deceased, Nov. 1, 1884,
Martinsburg, W. Va.

Favis, Asterio...............LL B., 07
Deputy District Attorney,
Island of Negros, P. I.

Fay, Andrew Edwin.........LL. B., '98

Fay, John Baptist, Jr........A. B., '02
                           A. M., '03

Fegan, Edward John........A M., '03
Lawyer,   LL. B., '05
538 Tremont Bldg., Boston, Mass.

Fegan, Hugh J., Jr.........A. B., '01
Law Clerk,   A. M., '02
Office of the Solicitor,   LL. B., '07
Agricultural Dept., Washington, D. C.

Fellows, Harry A...........LL. B., '91
Clerk, War Dept ,   LL. M., '92
East Falls Church, Va.

Fenton, David H.............LL. B., '96
Lawyer,   LL. M., '97
Colorado Bldg., Washington, D. C.

Fenwick, George............A. B., '32
Deceased, Nov., 1857, Wash , D. C.

Fergell, J. A...............D. D. S.,'02

Ferguson, Abner H.........LL. B., '04
Lawyer,
611 14th St. N. W., Washington, D. C.

Ferguson, Daniel John.......A. B., 98
Lawyer, New O'Hara Theatre Bldg.,
Shenandoah, Pa.

Ferguson, S. Colfax.........LL. M.,'02
Lawyer,
Prestonburg, Ky.

Ferguson, Arthur W........LL. B., '85
Deceased, 1908,   LL. M.,'86
Manila, P. I.

Fernandez, Benigno.........LL. B , '08
Lawyer,
33 Allen St , San Juan, Porto Rico.

Ferneding, Thomas A.......A. B., '01
President and General Manager, Dayton, Springfield & Xenia So. Ry. Co.,
Dayton, Ohio.

Ferry, Joseph T ....LL. B , '91
Clerk, P. O. Dept ,   LL M , '92
The Hillside, Washington, D. C. ·

Ferry, Lemuel A...........M. D , '79
Physician,
Geneseo, Ill.

Fetterman, Wilfred B.......A. B., '52
Deceased.

Ficklin, Col. Theodore Hamilton,
Principal, G. W. H. School, A. M , '69
714 Duke St., Alexandria, Va.

Fields, Frank H.............LL. B , '92
Clerk,
Treasury Dept., Washington, D C.

Fillette, St. Julian...........LL B , '86
Deceased,   LL. M ,'87

Finch George A.,............LL. B , '07
Clerk, War Dept ,
617 Kenyon St , Wash., D C

Fink, Rev. Edward X., S. J ,A. B., '73
Jesuit Priest,
Leonardtown, Md.

Finke, Alvin J..............A. B , '96
Numismatist,
P. O. Dept., Dayton, Ohio.

Finn, William T.............LL. B , '01
Lawyer,   LL. M., '02
Bond Bldg , Washington, D. C.   ·

Finnegan, John J............LL. B., '01

Finnerty, Wm. M............LL. B , '08
Lawyer,
Denver. Colo.

Finney, Frank ....M. D., '82
Physician,
La Junta, Colo.

Finney, Robert Gordon......LL. B , '98
Lawyer,   LL. M , '99
The Shannon 30th and P Sts.,
Washington, D. C.

Finney, William Brantner...A M , '98
Advertising,
Care Kastor & Co , Kansas City, Mo.

Finning, Rev. Thomas James, A. B , '95
Priest,
St. Helena's Church, Enfield, N. H.

Fisher, C Henry............M. D, '91
Medical Corps, U. S. A,
War Dept, Washington, D. C.

Fisher, Charles.............LL. B., '99
Clerk, Chf. Clk's Office, LL. M., '00
Treasury Dept, Washington, D. C.

Fisher, George P, Jr.....¬...A. B, '74
LL. B., '76

Fisher, George W...........M. D., '70
Deceased, Anacostia, D. C.

Fisher, Hugh Conniff........LL. B., '06
Lawyer,
Shreveport, Pa.

Fisher, Samuel P...........LL. B., '95
LL. M., '96

Fisher, Wm. J...............LL. B., '07
Lawyer,
Lohrville, Iowa.

Fitch, George A............M. D., '68
Deceased, Nov. 30, 1875. A. M., '69

Fitch, William S...........LL. B, '95
U. S. Spec Pen. Ex., LL. M., '97
Fl Paso, Texas.

Fitnam, Thomas H........¬.LL. B., '84
Lawyer, LL. M., '85
432 Q St. N. W., Wash., D. C.

Fitzgerald, Edmund A........A. B, '08
Student,
505 G St. S. W., Washington, D. C.

Fitzgerald, Edmund, Jr......A. B., '09
206 3d St., Troy, N. Y.

Fitzgerald, Edward ....A. B., '32
Deceased.

Fitzgerald, Edward H.......A. M., '50

Fitzgerald, George W........LL. B, '88

Fitzgerald, John J...........LL. B, '95
Lawyer, LL. M, '96
255 Main St, Pawtucket, R. I.

Fitzgerald, Joseph S........M. D, '70
New York City.

Fitzgerald, Maurice.........LL. B, '09
508 6th St. S. W., Washington, D. C.

Fitzgerald, Thomas J.......LL. B., '96
Lawyer, LL. M., '97
Dudley St, Roxbury, Mass.

Fitzgerald, William Joseph, A. B, '98
Lawyer,
Mears Bldg, Scranton, Pa.

Fitzmaurice, Rt. Rev. John E,
D. D., '89
924 Sassafras St., Erie Pa.

Fitzpatrick, Clarence Edm...A. B, '04
Probation Officer Juvenile Court,
Boston, Mass.

Fitzpatrick, Francis Percival.A. B., '09
96 Pleasant St., Malden, Mass.

Fitzpatrick, James F........A. B, '65

Fitzpatrick, Joseph Paul.....LL. B., '01

Fitzpatrick, Thos. Costello..B. S., "88
Lawyer,
N. Y. Life Ins. Bldg., St. Paul, Minn.

Fitzpatrick, Rev. William H..A. B, '62
H. C., Mass, Priest,
2221 Dorchester Ave., Boston, Mass.

Fitzsimmons, James I........LL. B., '97
Lawyer,
Wells Bldg, Milwaukee, Wis.

Flaherty, John E...........M. D., '08
Physician,
58 Hammond St., Rockville, Conn.

Flanagan, John J............LL. B, '06
Lawyer,
1944 Calvert St. N. W., Wash., D. C.

Flanagan, Roy Chetwynd....LL. B., '03
Lawyer, and Postmaster,
Greenville, N. C.

Flannery, John Spalding....LL. B., '94
Lawyer, LL. M., '95
Hibbs Bldg., 723 15th St., Wash., D.C.

Flannery, Martin Markham..LL. B., '95
Spec. Atty., Bureau of Corporations,
Dept. of Com. and Labor, Wash., D. C.

Flannery, Rev. William.....D. D., '92
Deceased, London, Ont.

Flatley, Thomas..A. B., '77, LL. B., '79
Deceased, Feb. 25, 1892. LL. M., '89

Fleharty, Ralph B..........LL. B., '09
Galesburg, Ill.

Fleharty, Ward W..........LL. B., '08
Lawyer,
Columbian Bldg., Washington, D. C.

Flick, Cyrus P.............LL. B, '88

Flood, Dr. P. H...........M. D., '74
San Francisco, Cal.

Flood, Thomas Arthur......M. D., '97
Physician,
McCormick Bldg., Salt Lake Cy., Utah.

Flora, W. Kirkwood.......LL. B., '94
Lawyer,
Bisbee, Ariz.

Floyd, Benjamin R..........A. B., '32
Deceased. A. M., '36

Floyd, William P...........A. B., '30
Deceased. A. M., '36

Flueck, Edwin Henry.......LL. B., '03
Lawyer, LL. M., '04
517 Mutual Life Bldg, Seattle, Wash.

Flynn, Caryl Bernard......M. D , '03
Physician,
Nepperhan Ave., Yonkers, N. Y.

Flynn, Very Rev. D. J.......LL. D., '06
President Mt. St. Mary's College,
Emmittsburg, Md.

Flynn, David J..............A. B , '00
Physician,
58 W. 91st St., N. Y. City.

Flynn, James Augustine.....M D., '98
Physician,
1333 Q St N. W., Washington, D. C.

Flynn, Joseph B............LL B , '07
Lawyer,
Bond Bldg , Washington, D. C.

Flynn, Thomas Donovan....LL B , '02
Lawyer,
Hibernia Bk. Bldg., New Orleans, La

Focke, Bernard M.........LL. B., '09
Dayton, Ohio.

Fogle, John L...LL. B , '97, LL. M.,'98

Foley, John F..............LL. B., '09
So. Manchester, Conn

Follens, Alphonse James....A. M., '98
817-18 N. Y. Life Bldg, Kan City, Mo

Foote, John Ambrose.......M. D., '06
Physician,
1219 Conn. Ave , Washington, D. C.

Ford, Bernard Joseph..... A. M., '01
Lawyer,   Ph. D , '03, LL B., '03
Cooper Bldg., Denver, Colo.

Ford, Horace................LL. B., '96

Ford Hon Rob't..A. B , '38, A M ,   '42
Deceased, 1884.   LL. D., '68
St Mary's County, Md.

Ford, William F............LL. B., '96

Forman, Sands W ....A B ,   '69
Deceased,   A M ,   '71

Forney, Edward O ....LL B , '77
Ass't Examiner Patent Office,
Washington, D. C.

Forrest, Bladen.............A B ,   '67

Forrest, Joseph............. A B ,   '65

Forscuth, Clarence S........LL. B., '09
Manchester, N. H.

Forstall, Henry J...........A B ,   '48

Forwood, William Henry....LL D , '97
Brig. Sur Genl U. S A. Retired,
1425 Euclid Pl., Washington, D C

Fosselman, John J..........LL B , '09
Donnally Mills, Pa

Foster, Daniel S........ .. M D , '68

Foster, F. J.................M. D., 71
Physician,
942 S St. N. W., Washington, D. C.

Foster, John J..............LL. B , '97
Lawyer,
Del Rio, Texas.

Fournet, Gabriel A.........A. B., '61
Deceased, Killed in Civil War.

Fouts, Francis A............LL. B , '80

Fowler, Allen L..............LL B , '91

Fowler, Harry Brightwell...LL. B , '98

Fowler, W. C...............M D., '88
Physician,
1812 1st St N W , Wash., D C.

Fox, Edmond K.............LL B , '97
Real Estate,
14th St and N. Y. Ave , Wash , D. C

Fox, George H..............A. B., '67

Fox, James C...............LL. B , '91
Lawyer,   LL. M.,'94
39 Exchange St., Portland, Me

Fox, Paul.................LL. B , '02
Lawyer,
Lompoc, Cal.

Fox, W Tazewell, A B , '66, A. M , '68

Foy, Francis Martin........A B , '04
Lawyer,   A M , '06, LL. B , '07
68 William St., Pittston, Pa.

Franc, Herbert L............LL. B , '99
Lawyer,   LL. M ,'00
Pacific Bldg , Washington, D C.

France, J. M Duncan.. . . M D., '65
Deceased, May 9, 1906,
St. Joseph, Mo

Francis, Claude de la Roche, LL. B , '92
Lawyer,   LL. M ,'93
1518 Pine St , Philadelphia, Pa

Freeman, Joseph E... .. ..LL B , '01
Lawyer,
60 Wall St , New York City.

Freeman, Joseph H..........LL B , '98
                          LL M ,'99

French, Edmund R........ .LL B , '98
Lawyer,
231 9th St. S. E , Wash., D C.

French, George K   .LL B , '89

French, George N   .. .. ..M D , '68

French, James H .. . .   .A B , '39

French, Lawrence Eugene ..A M , '91
Lawyer,   LL B , '92
41 Park Row, New York City

French, Ricardo D Del.....M D , '67
Deceased, 1890, Washington, D C.

Frey, Clarence E............LL B., '05
Clerk,
3010 P St. N. W., Wash, D. C.

Frey, Joseph Louis.........M. D., '07
Post Graduate Student in Medicine,
Berlin, U., Germany,
59 S. Wash. Sq., N. Y. City, N. Y.

Friedrich, Alexander E......LL. B., '07
Wisconsin.

Frost, John W.............M. D., '91
Deceased, May 17, 1906.

Frye, George R.............A. B., '06
Law Student,
14 4th St N. E, Washington, D. C.

Fuchs, William R ....LL B., '05
District Fiscal Agent,
Dept. of Agriculture, Wash, D. C.

Fuhrman, William J........LL. B, '97

Fuller, Edward A. .... LL M.,'95

Fuller, George E ....M. D, '65
Physician,
1 Green St, Monson, Mass.

Fuller, Walter M ....LL. B, '04

Fullerton, James B.........LL B, '80

Fulmer, George W.........A. B, '53
Deceased,   A. M., '55

Fulton, Creed M............LL.B., '90
Lawyer,   LL M., '91
Colorado Bldg., Washington, D. C.

Furbershaw, Walter S......LL. M.,'07
Lawyer,
713 14th St, Washington, D. C.

Furlong, Francis Mohun....M D., '95
U. S S Vermont,
Care Navy Dept,,Washington, D. C.

Gaddis, Edgar T...........LL. B., '92
Lawyer,   LL. M.,'93
1017 E Capitol St., Washington, D. C.

Gaffney, John L............ LL. B., '08
Lawyer.
54 Gaffney Place, Waterbury, Conn.

Gaither, Harris E...........D D S ,'06
Deceased, 1908, Washington, D. C.

Galiher, Samuel S..........LL. B., '91

Gall, John Camden ....LL B, '99

Gallagher, Anthony J.......LL M ,'87
Lawyer,
Devon, Pa

Gallagher, John Martin......B S, '96
Instructor, English, High School,
Worcester, Mass

Gallagher, Joseph Aloysius..A. M., '97
Devon, Pa

Gallagher, Lawrence J......LL. B., '09
Troy, N. Y.

Gallagher, M. F...........M. D., '89
Physician,
512 A St. S. E., Washington, D. C.

Gallagher, Nicholas A......M. D., '09
Intern St. Francis Hospital,
Jersey City, N. J.

Gallagher, P. J............M. D., '91
U. S. Bu. of Pensions, Wash, D. C.

Gallagher, Thomas D. J.....A B., '84
402 S. 22d St, Philadelphia, Pa.

Gallaher, E McHenry.......LL B, '08
Lawyer,   LL M ,'09
514 C St. S W, Washington, D. C.

Gallatin, Daniel B...........LL B, '76

Gallen, William J. A.......LL. B., '03
Lawyer,
4823 Lancaster Ave., Philadelphia, Pa.

Galligan, John H...........A B., '72
Deceased, Sept. 8, 1893.

Gallinger, William Henry Augustine,
Lawyer,   LL. B., '93
The Normandie, Washington, D. C.

Ganahl, Alphonse E.........A M., '07
Law Student,
3843 Cleveland Ave., St. Louis, Mo

Gandarillas, Rev. Joaquin Larrain Y.,
Deceased,   D. D., '52

Gannon, James A...........M. D, '06
Physician and Surgeon,
1219 Conn. Ave, Washington, D C.

Gantt, Daniel J.............LL. B., '95
Clerk,   LL. M ,'96
Treas'ry Dept., Washington, D. C.

Gantt, Robert Joseph.........LL. B, '96
Lawyer,
Spartanburg, S. C

Gapen, Nelson...............M D, '00
Asst. Sur. Gen'l, U. S Navy,
Navy Dept, Washington, D. C.

Garabedian, Aram L ... . D D. S ,'03
Dentist,
607 13th St. N. W., Washington, D. C.

Gardiner, Ge r e ....A B, '24
Deceased. o g

Gardiner, John B........ ..A B, '59
Deceased.

Gardiner, Richard A...... A B, '55
Deceased,   A. M, '56

Gardiner, W. Gwynn ....LL B, '99
Lawyer,   LL M ,'00
Fendall Bldg, Washington, D C.

Gardner, W H............M. D , '61
Deceased, June 3, 1908

Gardner, R. Bennett........LL. B , '96

Garesche, Lieut. Julius P , U. S. A.,
Deceased, Dec. 13, 1862, A. M., '42
Was appointed Chief of Staff to General Rosecrans, commanding the Department of Cumberland, and served
in that capacity from Nov. 9, 1862,
until his death. He fell in the battle
of Stone River.

Garesche, William A........A B., '71

Garland, Hon. Augustus H..LL. D., '89
Deceased.

Garland, Rufus Cummings...Ph. B , '87
Deceased, Mar. 11, 1901, LL. B., '91
Fort Worth, Tex.

Garnett, Dr. Algernon S....A. M., '75
Physician,
Hot Springs, Ark.

Garnett, Leslie C.. ....LL B , '99
Lawyer,   LL. M., '00
Mathews, Va.

Garnett, Robert Stanislaus. .M. D., '03
Physician,
324 E. 26th St , Tacoma, Wash.

Garrison, F. H............M. D., '93
Asst. Librarian, War Dept ,
1437 R St , Washington, D. C.

Garrott, Frank H..........LL. B., '09
Shenandoah Junction, W. Va.

Garvey, Thomas Q..........M. D., '94
Physician,
Lancaster, Pa.

Garvy, Wm J...LL. B., '94, A. M., '94
Pres and Treas., The Garvy Co.,
51st and Grand Ave , Chicago, Ill.

Gaston, Hugh J............A B., '55
Killed at Fredericksburg, Dec., 1862.

Gately, M. J..............M. D., '72
Physician,
11 S. Broadway, Baltimore, Md.

Gates, Charles J..........LL. B., '04
Lawyer.
Treasury Dept , Washington, D. C.

Gauss, John J............LL. B , '08

Gavan, Joseph W..........LL B , '04
Lawyer,
80 Wall St , New York City

Gaynor, Hubert Edward.....M. D., '09
Intern,
G U Hospital, Washington, D. C.

Gaynor, Hugh Augustine, S. J.,
Jesuit,   A. B , '95, A. M , '96,
Woodstock College, Woodstock, Md.

Geary, Daniel J......... ...A B , '89
Manufacturer,
Oil City, Pa.

Gelpi, Maurice Joseph.......A B , '05
Intern, Charity Hospital
3720 Canal St., New Orleans, La

Geneste, Leonard F ..... .A B., '07
Law Student,
936 22d St. N. W , Washington, D. C.

Gengler, Adam C.... ....LL. B , '09
Chicago, Ill.

Gentsch, Charles........ ...M. D., '73
Physician,
2822 Franklin Ave , Cleveland, Ohio.

Gentsch, Daniel C...........M. D, '89
Physician,
New Philadelphia, Ohio.

Geoghan, Wm F X.........LL B , '06
Lawyer,
302 Broadway, New York City.

George, Isaac Stewart.......A M , '04
Lawyer,   LL B , '06, LL. M , '07
Calvert, Bldg , Baltimore, Md

George, John M..LL. B , '92, LL. M , '93

Gering, Matthew LL B , '83, LL M , '84

Geringer, Emil J............LL. B , '03
630 West 12th St , Chicago, Ill.

Gery, Raymond E...........LL. B , '93
                               LL. M , '94

Gettinger, Wm Malcolm ...LL B , '09
1000 E St. S W., Washington, D C.

Gibbon, D. J ....M. D , '69
Deceased, Mar. 5, 1907, Wash., D. C.

Gibbs, Alexander C...... . LL. B , '06
Lawyer,   LL M , '07
Union City, Tenn

Gibbs, Thomas F............M. D , '70
Deceased, Jan. 30, 1906, Wash', D. C.

Gibson, Frederick P.........LL. B., '98

Gibson, T. Catlett..........M..D , '93
Physician,
Scott Bldg , Salt Lake City, Utah.

Gibson, Werner....... ....LL. B , '06
Stephenville, Tex

Gieseking, Henry N.........M. D., '76
Deceased, Washington, D C.

Gilchrist, Walter Schell......A B., '02
Clerk,
Dept of Com and Labor, Wash., D. C.

Gill, James Edward.........M. D., '01
P. A. Surg, U. S. Navy,
Navy Dept., Washington, D. C.

Gillan, Edward Francis......LL. B., '01
Clerk,   LL. M., '02
Bureau of Census, Washington, D. C.

Gillespie, John B............LL. B., '89
Lawyer,   LL. M., '90
37 W. Market St, Scranton, Pa.

Gillespie, Robert K.........LL. B., '94

Gillis, Lieut. J. Merville, U. S. N.,
Deceased, Feb. 9, 1865.   M. A., '43

Gilluly, John Francis.......M. D., '03
Deceased, June 21, 1905.

Gilmore, William T.........LL. B, '04
Lawyer,
Danville, Ill.

Ginther, Cyril Francis......A. B, '03
Brewer,
Buffalo, N. Y.

Girard, Charles............M. D., '56
Deceased, Jan. 29, 1895.

Given, Ralph...............LL. B, '99
Asst. U S. Dis. Atty.,   LL. M, '00
City Hall, Washington, D. C.

Gleason, Aaron R..........M. D., '64

Gleeson, John K...........A. B., '52

Glennan, Charles P.........A. B, '78
Physician,
420 Fla. Ave. N. W., Wash, D. C.

Glennan, John Walter......LL. B., '91
Lawyer,   LL. M., '92
420 Fla. Ave. N. W., Wash., D. C.

Gloetzner, Prof. Anton..Mus. Doc, '89
1228 M St. N. W., Washington, D. C.

Gloetzner, Herman Francis..A. B., '99
Clerk,
Pension Office, Washington, D. C.

Glover, Mervin Wilbur......M. D, '98
1539 9th St.; Washington, D. C.

Glueck, Bernard............M. D., '09
Intern,
Providence Hospital, Wash., D. C.

Goddard, W. H.............LL. B., '72
1630 Conn. Ave. N. W., Wash, D. C.

Goff, George Paul..........LL. B., '74
Deceased, Dec., 1896.   A. M., '80

Goff, Hon. Nathan.........LL. D., '89
Lawyer,
Clarksburg, W. Va

Golden, Paul Emmet.......A. B., '09
214 Fairview Ave., Scranton, Pa.

Goldsborough, John A.......LL. B, '86
Patent Lawyer,
McGill Bldg., Washington, D. C.

Gonzaga, Isais P...........LL. B., '07
Lawyer,
Cebu, P. I.

Gooch, Dr. Philip C........A. M, '49
Deceased.

Goodman, William R., Jr....M. D, '70
Physician,
1332 12th St. N. W., Wash, D. C.

Goodwin, Wm. D...........LL. B., '08
Clerk,
Office of Indian Affairs, Wash, D.C .

Gorham, Newton B.........LL B, '92
Lawyer,
Rochester, N. Y.

Gorman, Charles Edmund...LL. D, '96
Lawyer,
906 Banigan Bldg., Providence, R I.

Gorman, Edward Aloysius...M. D, '98

Gorman, George E.........LL. B, '95
Lawyer,
Ashland Block, Chicago, Ill

Gough, Henry............. A. B, '18
Deceased.

Gough, Stephen H. ....A. M., '31
Deceased.

Gould, Hon, Ashley Mulgrave, LL. B, '84
Jus. Sup. Court, G. U. Law Fac.,
Court House, Washington, D. C.

Gouldston, John C...... ...M D, '54

Gouley, Louis G............A. B, '66
Deceased, Oct. 17, 1879,   A. M., '71
New York City.

Gove, Frank E.............LL. B, '91

Govern, Charles J.........LL. B, '96
                            LL M, '97

Govern, Frank.............LL B, '93
Clerk,   LL. M. '94
Indian Office, Washington, D C.

Govern, Hugh, Jr..........LL. B, '91
Asst. U. S. Atty.,   LL. M., '92
7 Beekman St., New York City.

Gow, Edwin R.............LL. B, '96
Deceased, Feb. 29, 1908, Wash, D. C.

Gow, James R.............LL. B., '93

Gower, Henry Ryan.........A B, '98
Lawyer,
412 5th St. N. W., Wash. D. C.

Grace, Albert L............LL. B, '99
Lawyer,   LL. M., '00
Plaquemine, La.

Grace, Pierce Joseph........A. M, '92
Lawyer,
36 Crawford St., Dorchester, Mass.

Gracie, Asa Creede..........A. B., 'o1
Lawyer,   A. M, '02 LL. B, '04
Sou. Trust Bldg., Little Rock, Ark.

Gracie, John Pierce........A. B., 'o1
Planter,
Rob Roy, Ark.

Grady, James Aloysius......M. D, '03
Physician,
325 E Main St., Waterbury, Conn

Graff, Carl J F............LL B, '92
Lawyer,   LL. M, '93
472 La Ave. N. W, Wash., D. C.

Graham, Harry C ....LL. B, '06
Lawyer,
Marshall, Ill.

Graham, John W............A. B, '52

Graham, William Henry, Jr..A. B, '05
Jesuit Scholastic,
Woodstock College, Woodstock, Md.

Grant, Rev James A........A. B., '89
Priest,
Burlingame, Cal.

Grant, John H.............M. D, '90
Physician,
136 Virginia St., Buffalo, N. Y.

Grant, Thomas..LL. B, '96 LL. M., '97
Sec. of Wash. Cham of Com.,
1202 F St N. W., Washington, D. C.

Grau, Philip A.............A. M., 'o1
        LL. B, '03 LL M, '04
Sec'y Allied Tob. Trades Asso.,
1st Nat Bank Bldg., Chicago, Ill.

Gray, James Aloysius.......A. B, '88
        A. M., '91

Grayson, William W........LL. B., '96

Green, Andrew Jordan......LL. B, '88
Legal Reviewer,   LL. M, '89
U S Bu of Pensions, Wash, D C.

Green, Augustine de Yturbide,
Provident Bldg,   M. D, 'o1
Prosser, Wash.

Green, Benjamin E........A. B, '38
Deceased, May 13, 1907, Dalton, Ga.

Green, Benjamin G.........LL. B, '77
Lawyer,
Warrentown, N. C.

Green, Burton R.. ....LL B, '09
1259 Irving St, Washington, D C.

Green, Francis Key.........LL B, '98
Crier,   LL. M.,'99
U S Supreme Court, Wash., D. C.

Green, George Chancellor...A. B., 'o1
Lawyer,
Weldon, N. C.

Green, James B............LL. B, '92
Lawyer,   LL. M., '93
1425 N. Y. Ave. N. W., Wash., D. C.

Green, Joel C..............M. D., '68

Green, John H.............A. M., '70

Green, John J.............LL. B, '08
Lawyer,
Thomaston, Conn

Green, John Matthew.......M. D., '75
Deceased, Oct., 1881, Key West, Fla.

Green, Lawrence H.........LL B, '09
1259 Irving St., Washington, D. C.

Green, Richardson ....A. B., '33
Deceased

Green, Robert Joseph ....M D., '04
Physician,
120 Aisquith St, Baltimore, Md.

Green, Virgil R............LL. B, '06
Lawyer,
Petersburg, Ind.

Green, Wallace ....LL. B., '90

Green, William G..........M. D., '68

Green, William R...... ....A. B., '33
Deceased.

Greene, J. Gardiner.........LL. B., 'o1
Lawyer,   LL. M., '02
Pell City, Ala.

Greene, Warren Earl........LL. B., '02

Greenfield, William E........LL. B., '89
Proofreader,
The Sun, Baltimore, Md.

Gregg, William S..........LL. B., '05

Griffin, Dennis Peter........LL. B., '99
        LL. M.,'00

Griffin, James H............LL. B, '94
Patent Lawyer,   LL M., '95
277 Broadway, N. Y. City.

Griffin, John Charles ... ...M D., '09
Physician,
Towanda, Pa.

Griffin, John J.............D. D. S.,'04
Dentist,
110 Central St, Waltham, Mass.

Griffin, William Yancey .....LL. B, '88
Clerk,   LL. M,'90
Treasury Dept, Washington, D. C.

Griffiss, Edward J..........A. B., '74

Griffiss, John I ....A. B, '76
Deceased, Feb 19, 1904, Wash, D. C.

Griffith, James E........·.....LL. B, '77

Griffith, Monte J............M. D., '69
G. U. Med. Fac.,
The Farragut, Washington, D. C.

Grima, Alfred.............A B, '04
Lawyer,
1604 4th St, New Orleans, La.

Grimes, Junius D...........LL. B., '02
Lawyer.

Grimes, William H.........LL B, '92
LL. M., '93

Grinstead, John R...........LL.B, '09
Cantril, Iowa

Grogan, Stephen Sylvester...A M, '03
Editor,   LL B, '06, LL. M, '07
1422 33rd St. N. W., Wash, D. C.

Grogan, Thomas J..........LL. B, '96
LL. M, '97
Care Peter Grogan & Sons Co.,
Baltimore, Md

Grogay, Patrick J..........LL. B., '96
LL..M., '97

Gross, Alfred Gregory.......M. D., '00
Physician,
1722 17th St N. W, Wash., D. C.

Grymes, James W..........M D, '53
Deceased, 1862

Guidry, Onesimus..........A. B., '36

Guinan, Joseph P..........M. D., '08
Physician,
Lima, N. Y.

Gulentz, Charles............LL. B, '90
Lawyer,   LL. M., '92
Berger Bldg, Pittsburg, Pa.

Gunnell, Francis M.........A. B, '44
Deceased, Wash., D. C.   A M, '46

Gwinn, Chester A..........LL. B., '09
Slator, Mo.

Gwynn, Raphael N.,.......LL. B, '98
LL. M., '99

Gwynn, William Clarence...M. D., '98
Physician,
3336 O St. N. W., Washington, D. C.

Gwynn, William............LL. D, '31

Gwynn, Dr. William H......A. B., '55
A. M, '57

Haag, Harry O.............LL. B., '97
Lawyer,
Pottsville, Pa.

Haag Jackson D.. ....LL. B, '90
Lawyer, Dramatic Writer, LL. M, '91
The Post, Pittsburg, Pa.

Haas, Carlton Daniels.......M D, '97
Soldiers Home, Elizabeth City, Va

Hagan, Christopher J........A. B., '00
General Insurance Agent,
52 Central St, Lowell, Mass

Hahn, Harry William ...,...LL. B, '03
Shoe Dealer,
7th and K Sts, Washington, D. C.

Haines, Walter S...........M D, '91

Hainner, Edward D.........LL B, '88
Lawyer, State Senator,   LL M., '89
Attalla, Etowah Co., Ala.

Hainner, George W...... ..LL. M., '87
Deceased, May, 1908.

Hale, William .... M D, '67

Hall, Arthur A......... ...LL. B, '93
Credit Man,   LL M, '95
L S Baumgardner & Co, Toledo, O.

Hall, Henry S..............M D, '71
Deceased, Hyattsville, Md

Hall, Harry Thomas.. .... A B, '05

Hall, John Dillan............LL. B., '99
Lawyer,   LL M, '01
Tensaw, Baldwin County, Ala

Hall, John H..............A B, '53

Hall, Joseph Edward. . . . LL. B, '98

Hall, Ross C...............LL. B, '88
Lawyer,
Seattle, Wash.

Hall, Walter D.............LL. B, '09
Southwest City, Mo.

Hallahan, John William... A B, '99
Real Estate Trust Bldg, A. M, '00
Philadelphia, Pa.

Hallam, Paul L.............LL. B, '09
Cold Water, Mich.

Halstead, Thomas.. .   .. LL. B, '89
Lawyer,   LL. M, '90
4611 Wayne Ave, Philadelphia, Pa.

Haltigan, Patrick J....... LL. B, '97
Editor and Publisher,
614 La. Ave. N. W, Wash, D. C.

Ham, Henry H.............LL. B, '05
Lawyer,
California, Mo.

Hamby, Louis L............LL. B, '06
Lawyer,
Bond Bldg, Washington, D. C

Hamersly, Lewis Randolph..LL. B., '96
Publisher,
1 W. 34th St, N. Y. City.

Hamill, James H...........LL. B, '06
Accountant Auditor's Office,
District Bldg, Washington, D. C

Hamilton, Edward J........M. D., '95
Physician,
616 McGowan Ave., Houston, Tex.

Hamilton, Charles William..B. S, '81
Banker,
1112 Park Ave., Omaha, Neb

Hamilton, George E........A. B., '72
LL. B., '74 A. M., '82
Lawyer,   LL. D., '89
Century Bldg, Washington, D C.

Hamilton, Hon Harper.....LL. B., '83
Judge, Floyd City Court,
Rome, Ga.

Hamilton, John B..........LL. B, '89
Deceased

Hamilton, John C. C.......A. B, '51

Hamilton, John J...........LL. B, '91
Lawyer,   LL. M., '92
Century Bldg., Washington, D. C.

Hamilton, Patrick H........A. B, '35
Deceased, Dec 24, 1898, Elgin, Ill.

Hamilton, Ralph Alexander..M. D, '04
Physician, G. U. Med. Fac.,
924 15th St., Washington, D. C.

Hamlet, William............M. D., '69

Hammett, C M.............M. D, '56
Deceased, Nov. 22, 1898, Wash, D. C.

Hammett, Charles Maddox..M. D., '92
Physician,
The Brunswick, Washington, D. C.

Hammond, William A......,A. B., '68
Deceased, Sept, 1892,   A. M., '71
Ellicott City, Md.

Hampson, Thomas..........LL. B, '82
Deceased, 1888.

Hampton, George R.......M. D, '09
Intern,
St. Francis Hosp, Jersey City, N. J.

Hampton, J. Rodolph........LL. B, '89
LL. M., '90

Hanawalt, George P.......M. D., '64
Physician and Surgeon,
Des Moines, Iowa.

Hanger, Hugh H...........LL. B., '03
Sales Manager,
1312 Penn. Ave. N. W., Wash., D. C.

Hanger, McCarthy...........LL. B., '08
General Manager,
1312 Pa Ave N. W., Wash, D. C.

Hanigan, Harry A..........A. B., '06
Engineering Student,
119 W. 70th St., New York City.

Hanley, Bernard T.........LL. B, '73
Deceased, 1882

Hanna, John F............A. M., '70
Deceased, Oct. 31, 1885, Wash., D. C.

Hannegan, Edward A......LL. B., '90

Hanrahan, Rev. James Vincent,
Priest,   A M., '96
Fitchburg, Mass.

Hanretty, Lawrence Michael, Jr.,
78 Carpenter Ave.,   A. B, '04
Newburg, N. Y.

Harbin, George Francis, Jr..A. B., '02
Elec. Eng
11 7th St. S. E., Washington, D. C.

Hardie, Joseph Cuyler.......LL. B., '92
Clerk, Freight Trans,   LL. M., '93
War Dept, Washington, D C

Hardin, Palmer..............LL. B., '92

Hardin, Thomas B., Jr......LL. B, '84
LL. M., '85

Harding, W. R.............A. B, '36
Deceased

Hardisty, John T...........LL. B., '04

Hardy, Calvin S...........LL. B, '96
Clerk,   LL. M., '97
Pension Bureau, Washington, D. C.

Hare, William C...........LL. B, '95
Lawyer,
Upper Sandusky, Ohio.

Harker, Charles O.........LL. B., '99

Harley, Richard Joseph......A. B., '96
Hotel Business,
1842 Market St., Philadelphia, Pa.

Harlow, Leo P..............LL. B., '98
Lawyer,   LL. M.,'99
412 5th St, Washington, D. C.

Harmon, John Oregon.......LL. B., '99

Harmon, Monton C.........LL. B., '08

Harper, B. E...............D. D. S,'02

Harper, James E............LL. B., '97
Clerk and Auditor,
P. O. Dept., Washington, D. C.

Harper, Robert W..........A. B, '52
Deceased, Killed at Chickamauga.

Harr, William R............LL. B, '95
Lawyer,   LL. M.,'96
Dept. of Justice, Washington, D. C.

Harrington, Edward P......LL. B., '86
Clerk,   LL. M.,'87
Treasury Dept., Washington, D. C.

Harris, Hon. Charles N.....A. B, '71
Lawyer,   A M., '89
89 Madison Ave., New York City.

Harris, Edward F..........LL. M.,'88

Harrison, John C..........M. D., '60

Harrison, Walton..........LL. B., '97
Harrison, William Barnett...M. D, '05
Physician,
Starkville, Miss.

Harrison, William Clinton...LL. B., '99
Harrison, Wilham H.......LL B., '81
Bank President,
Tutwiler, Miss

Harroun, William S........M D., '65
Physician,
234 W. Palace Ave, Santa Fe, N. M.

Hart, Harry L..............LL B., '03
Hart, James H... ....D D S ,'05
Dentist,
Everett, Mass

Hart, John T... ....LL. B , '95
Clerk,   LL. M , '96
Pension Office, Washington, D C.

Hart, Timothy J............LL. B , '09
Brooklyn, N. Y.

Hartigan, James F.........M D, '68
Deceased, Jan 31, 1894,
Trieste, Austria

Hartnett, Daniel J•.........LL B , '03
Hartnett, Francis J.........A B , '09
Reporter,
1332 Eye St. N. W., Wash., D. C.

Hartsfield, Augustus M.....LL. B , '95
Clerk,
Interstate Com Com , Wash, D. C

Harvey, A Thomas ....A. B , '76
Deceased, Oct. 6, 1882, Wash, D C.

Harvey, George E.........,...M. D , '84
Deceased.

Harvey, Levin Allen........M. D., '75
Deceased, Washington, D. C

Harvey, Richard E.........LL. B , '05
Lawyer,
Portland, Me.

Harvey, Thomas M.........A. B , '89
Journalist,
U. S. Court House, City Hall,
Washington, D. C.

Harvey, William F.........M. D , '68

Harveycutter, Austin........LL B , '05
Clerk,
Dept. of Justice, Washington, D C.

Hasbrouck, Edwin Marble...M. D., '95
Physician,
1819 Adams Mill Road, Wash., D. C.

Haskell, Lewis W..........LL B , '94
Lawyer,
Columbia, S. C.

Hassan, Dudley T... ....LL. B , '96
                                LL. M.,'97
Hassler, Alpha M..........LL. B., '95
Hastings, Edward..........A. B., '36
Haswell, John H............LL. B., '73
Hatch, William B..........LL. B., '94
Lawyer,
11 Huron St., Ypsilanti, Mich.

Haven, Charles L..........M. D., '65
Hawes, John B............M. D., '86
Deceased, Aug. 20, 1907, Denver, Colo.

Hawken, Samuel McComas..LL. B., '05
Tennallytown, Md.

Hawkes, Dr. William H....A. M., '90
Deceased, Mar. 13, 1904.

Hawley, Cornell S..........LL. B., '97
Vice Pres. and Gen'l Manager,
Con. Car Heating Co., Albany, N. Y.

Haycock, Ira C.............LL. B., '07
Lawyer,   LL M., '08
Chevy Chase, Md.

Hayden, Dan'el B..........M. D., '04
Hayden, Joseph E..........LL. B., '7
Deceased, 1902, Washington, D. C.

Hayden, Reynolds..........M D., '05
Haydon, William Thomas...A. B., '94
Lawyer,
209 St. Paul St., Baltimore, Md.

Hayes, Edward.............LL. B., '72
Hayes, Henry L............M. D., '90
Physician,
Hilo, Hawaii.

Hayes, Noah...............M. D., '76
Physician,
Seneca, Kas.

Hayes, Stephen H..........LL. B., '89
                                LL. M.,'90
Hayes, Stephen Quentin.....A. B., '92
Electrical Engineer,
4 Brushton Ave., Pittsburg, Pa.

Hayes, T. Frank...........A. B , '06
Manager,
48-56 E. Main St., Waterbury, Conn.

Hays, Melville Ambrose.....M. D., '00
Physician,
Care of Army and Navy Journal,
New York City.

Hays, W. W................M. D., '61
Deceased, July 3, 1901, Obisco, Cal.

Hayward, William H........M. D., '69
Deceased, 1896, Cal.

Hazard, Daniel C..........M. D., '71

Hazen, David H...........M. D., '73
Deceased, Nov. 7, 1906, Wash , D C.

Hazen, William P. C.... ...M. D, '77
Physician,
511 E Capitol St , Washington, D. C.

Head, Paul Jones...........A. B, '00
Lawyer,
Greensburg, Pa.

Head, Morris William.......A B., '98
Greensburg, Pa.

Healy, Charles B.. ....M D, '08
Physician,
46 Curve St , W. Newton, Mass.

Healy, Hugh C............ A B, '49
H C , Mass ,
Deceased, Sept. 23, 1852

Healy, Rt. Rev. James Augustine,
H. C , Mass ,   A. B., '49 A. M , '51
R. C. Bishop,   D D, '74
Deceased, Aug. 5, 1900

Healy, James M..A B , '72, A. M , '89

Healy, Patrick F.. .., ...A. B , '50
H C , Mass , Jesuit Priest,
Georgetown Univ , Washington, D. C

Healy, Thomas F............LL B , '99
Reader,   LL M ,'00
Gov. Printing Office, Wash , D C.

Heard, John M..A B , '42, A M , '47

Hearst, William, T ....LL. B , '92
Clerk,   LL. M ,'95
War Dept , Washington, D. C.

Heaton, John Harry.........LL. B , '03
Lawyer,
American Bank Bldg , Seattle, Wash.

Heberle, John J.............LL. B., '09
Olean, N. Y.

Hechtman, Henry J.........LL B , '73

Hedrick, Charles Joseph.....LL. B., '84
Lawyer,
606 F St. N. W., Washington, D C.

Hedrick, John T., S. J......A. B , '71
Jesuit Priest,   A. M., '74
G. U. Observatory, Washington, D. C.

Heffernan, Bernard J.......LL. B , '06
Clerk,
Interstate Com. Com , Wash., D. C.

Heffernan, John Francis.....LL. B , '04
Lawyer,   LL. M ,'05
90 Wall St , New York City.

Hegarty, Harry A...........LL. B , '01
Lawyer,
612 F St N W , Washington, D. C.

Heideman, Ivan.. ...... LL. B , '01
Lawyer,
Stewart Bldg , 402 6th St N. W.,
Washington, D. C.

Heimler, Rev. Alphonsus, O S B ,
Priest,   A M , '60
St. Benedict, Cambria Co , Pa

Heintzelman, Joseph A , Jr. M D , '02
Druggist,
2000 Ridge & N. Col Ave , Phila , Pa.

Heiskell, Raymond Angelo ..A. B , '91
Lawyer,   LL. B , '93, LL M , '94
Century Bldg , Washington, D. C.

Heitmuller, H. Anton ......LL. B , '97
Lawyer,   LL M ,'98
458 La. Ave. N. W , Wash , D C.

Heizman, Col. Charles L....A. B , '64
U. S. A , Retired,
Care U. S A , Adjt. Gen Wash , D C.

Heller, Joseph Milton.......M D , '96
Physician,
The Farragut, Washington, D C.

Heller, P. H..............Phar B , '71
Physician,   M D , '74
801 Santa Fe Ave , Pueblo, Colo.

Helm, Dr. Charles J....... A B , '83

Helm, Gratz W...... ....LL B , '01
Hotel Leighton, Los Angeles, Cal

Helmer, Burton K.. . LL B , '91
Lawyer,
Herkimer, N. Y

Helmick, William J... .. ..A B , '00

Helmus, John...............LL. B , '08
Lawyer,   LL. M., '09
House of Representatives, Wash , D C.

Helton, A S............. M D , '90
Pension Office, Washington, D C.

Hemler, William Francis....M. D , '04
Physician,
613 15th St , Washington, D. C.

Henderson, James Abby ....LL B , '93
Lawyer,
Rockville, Md.

Henderson, John M.. . ... LL B , '90
Real Estate,
1418 F St N. W , Washington, D. C.

Hendler, Charles T ....LL. B , '96
Lawyer,   LL. M ,'97
Fendall Bldg , Washington, D C.

Hendrick, David S.... . ...LL. B , '09
1378 Harvard St , Washington, D. C.

Hennessy, John F...........LL. B., '06
Lawyer,
Florence, Mass.

Hennessy, Vincent D.. ....A. M , '06
Lawyer, LL B , '08
Majestic Bldg, Milwaukee, Wis

Henning, R. E.... ... M D, '85
Physician,
Cheriton, Va.

Hennon, John Francis... . A B , '93
A M , '94

Henry. Charles T...........LL B , '92
Deceased, Dec 16, 1908, LL M , '93
Colonial Beach, Va.

Henry, Thomas Stanhope . LL B , '99
Lawyer,
Dept of Justice, Washington, D C

Henry, William J...........M. D, '66

Herbert, J Wells...........M D, '59
Deceased, Oct. 21, 1903

Hermesh, Harry R.........M D, '07
Asst. Surgeon U. S N,
U. S. Navy Dept., Washington, D C

Hernitz, Stanislaus .... M D, '53

Heron, Alexander P........LL. B , '99

Heron, Benjamin F. L.... ..LL B , '07
Lawyer, LL M , '08
Columbian Bldg, Washington, D. C

Herran, Hon. Thomas.... .A B , '63
A. M., '68, LL. D , '99
Deceased, Aug. 10, 1904, Liberty, N. Y.

Herring, Carl E.............LL. M , '89

Herring, James L.......... LL B , '
,38

Herron, W. Francis D.'......LL B , '99
Auditor, LL M., '00
Union Trust Co , Washington, D C.

Hickcox, John Howard, Jr. LL B , '79

Hickey, Harry K ....LL. B , '08
Sec'y to Pres. So. Ry. Co..LL M ,'09
1817 16th St N W, Wash , D C.

Hickling, D. Percy.........M D, '84
Physician, G. U. Med. Fac,
1304 R I. Ave, Washington, D C.

Hickling, Daniel Percy.... Phar B ,'71
Phar. D ,'72, M D, '84
Deceased, 1906, Washington, D. C.

Hickman, G. W. Vinton....M D., '72
Physician,
Texas.

Hicks, Frederick Charles....LL. B., '01
Librarian Pub Library,
Brooklyn, N. Y.

Hicks, Jesse Addison........LL B , '99
Lawyer,
306 Bond Bldg., Washington, D C.

Hicks, L. Richard..........A. B , '05
Capitalist,
Los Gatos, Cal.

Higgins, Andrew J.... ...LL. B , '09
Drifton, Pa.

Higgins, Hon. James H......LL B ,'99
Lawyer, LL M ,'00, LL. D , '09
Pawtucket, R. I.

Higgins, Reginald H........LL. B , '90
Lawyer, LL. M ,'91
Standish, Me.

Higgins, William Lawrence Denis,
A. B., '97

Hill, Eugene F.............A. B., '70
4423 Campbell St., Kansas City, Mo.

Hill, Ezra N..............'. .LL. B , '09
Ouachita, Co., Kansas

Hill, F. Snowden..........A. B., '73
Lawyer,
Fendall Bldg., Washington, D. C.

Hill, G. W......'.........M. D, '59

Hill, Henderson F........LL. B., '08
326 B St. S. E , Washington, D. C.

Hill, J. Chambers..........M. D., '91
Physician,
78 Middle St., Rockland, Me.

Hill, Joshua................LL. B , '93
Lawyer,
Madison, Ga.

Hill, Major Nicholas S......A. B., '58
The Albion, A. M.,'60
Baltimore, Md.

Hill, Raymond J............A. B., '60
H. C , Mass.,
Deceased, California.

Hill, Richard S.............M. D., '86
Upper Marlborough, Md.

Hill, William Costilo........M. D, '97

Hill, William J.............A. B., '57
Deceased. A. M., '60

Hillen, Solomon.............A. B., '27
Deceased

Hilliard, Patrick R..........LL B , '93
Lawyer, LL. M ,'94
Century Bldg., Washington, D C

Hillyer, Charles S..........LL. B , '07
Lawyer,
Colorado Bldg., Washington, D. C,

Hillyer, Clair Richards......LL. B , '99
Special Atty., LL. M ,'00
Bureau of Corporations, Wash., D C.

Hilman, Joseph G. ....LL B , '06
Lawyer,
Epes, Ala

Hilton, James Franklin......M D, '0{
Physician,
The Susquehanna, Washington, D. C

Hilton, Wm. A.... ....LL B, '09
Salt Lake City, Utah.

Hindmarsh, Walter B........LL. B, '96
Chf. Clk L. House Bd, LL M,'97
719-21 13th St. N. W., Wash., D C

Hine, Oliver C...LL. B., '92, LL M.,'93

Hines, J. Arthur ....M D, '69
Physician,
Van Wert, Ohio.

Hinton, John R.... ....LL B, '08
Dept. of Justice, Washington, D C

Hipkins, William A........LL B, '89
LL. M, '90

Hird, John Denby...........LL. B., '01
Chemist,
305 T St. N. E., Washington, D C

Hirschman, Morris..........LL. M., '05
Lawyer,
Columbian Bldg., Washington, D. C.

Hirst, Anthony A...........M. A., '71
Lawyer, LL. D., '01
211 S. 6th St., Philadelphia, Pa.

Hirst, William L............A. B., '63

Hitchcock, Thomas D.......LL. B., '90
LL. M., '91

Hitz, William Henry.......LL. B., '98
Lawyer, LL. M., '99
Hibbs Bldg, Washington, D. C.

Hoard, Francis De V.......M. D., '79

Hoban, James ....A. B, '60
Lawyer,
Kellogg Bldg, Washington, D. C.

Hodge, Edwin R............M. D, '92
Chemist,
Army Med. Museum, Wash., D. C.

Hodge, Howard B.... .....LL B, '96
LL. M., '97

Hodges, Benjamin F........M. D., '58

Hodges, E. F..............A. M., '83
Physician,
2 West N Y. St, Indianapolis, Ind

Hodges, E. F.......... ... M D, '74

Hodges, Henry W. .... LL B, '92
Clerk, Court of Appeals, LL M, '93
City. Hall, Washington, D C

Hodges, William S.. ....LL B, '93
Patent Lawyer, LL M, '94
90? F St. N. W., Washington, D C.

Hodgkins, Chester Lyman.. M D, '00
Surgeon, U. S A,
War Dept., Washington, D. C.

Hodgson, Telfair ....LL B, '89

Hof, Charles R ....LL. B, '93
Clerk, LL M, '94
General Land Office, Wash, D C.

Hoffar, Noble S. A B, '66, A M, '67

Hogan, Frank J.............LL. B, '02
Lawyer,
Colorado Bldg, Washington, D C

Holcombe, E Prosser........LL B, '95

Holden, Raymond T........M. D., '81
Physician,
802 6th St. S W., Wash, D. C

Holder, Willis B............LL B, '90
LL. M, '91

Holland, G West ....LL B., '08
Special Agent Gen'l Land Office,
Quincy Bldg, Denver, Colo

Holland, William Joseph....M D, '03
Physician,
Maplewood, Mass.

Hollander, Harry H........LL B, '99
Lawyer, LL M, '00
Columbian Bldg, Washington, D C.

Hollinger, Frank S..........LL M, '98

Hollingsworth, John S......A B, '73
Deceased, Jan. 14, 1895.

Holt, George A...............M D, '80

Holt, John Henry............LL. B, '97
Patent Lawyer,
McGill Bldg, Washington, D. C.

Holt. John Herrimon....... LL B, '81

Holt, Robert Oscar.........LL B, '91
LL. M, '92
Lorton Valley, Fairfax Co, Va

Holtzman, Ernest............LL. B, '93
LL. M., '94

Homer, Charles C..........A B, '67
President, A. M, '96
Second Nat. Bank, Baltimore, Md.

Hood. Col Arthur.......A. B, '77
Deceased, Feb. 24, 1901, Cuthbert, Ga.

Hood, Edward........... ..LL B, '07
Cecelia, Ky.

Hood, John H. P....... ..A B, '08
Sudent,
2812 N St. N. W., Washington, D. C.

Hootec, Louis C............M. D '61

Hoover, George Rendelton ..LL B, '97
Lawyer,
Com Nat. Bank Bldg., Wash, D. C.

Hoover, William D ....LL B, '88
Pres Nat. Sav & Tr Co, LL M, '89
15th St. and N. Y Ave., Wash., D. C.

Hopewell, Edward N........LL. B , '06
Lawyer,
Fendall Bldg , Washington, D C

Hopkins, Alfred Francis....D. D. S.,'03
Dentist,
1730 I St., Washington, D. C

Hopkins, Francis A..........LL B , '90

Hopkins, Louis M...........LL B., '87
Lawyer,
225 Dearborn St., Chicago, Ill

Hopkins, Ralph.............A. B , '95

Hopkins, William A.........LL. B , '05

Horah, James H..LL B , '89. LL M , '93

Horgan, John C.............LL. B , '84

Horgan, John J..LL B , '88. LL. M , '89

Horgan, William............LL B , '08
Lawyer,
Met. Bank Bldg., Washington, D. C.

Horigan, James Bernard....A. B., '01
Lawyer,   A. M., '02. LL. B , '04
3601 O St. N. W., Washington, D. C.

Horigan, Dr. William D.....LL. B., '99
Librarian,
Naval Observatory, Wash., D. C.

Horkan, George Augustus...LL. B., '02
Lawyer,
Forsyth, Mont.

Horn, Elihu................LL. B , '07
Merchant Tailor,
7th and F Sts., Washington, D. C.

Horrigan, James J..........LL. B , '92
Pension Examiner,   LL. M., '93
Bloomington, Ill.

Horsey, Charles C. L........A. B , '01
                          LL. B., '04

Horsey, Outerbridge, Jr.....A. B , '96
Asst. Treas. Ind. Light Co.,
56 W. 10th St., New York City.

Horton, William Ed.........LL. B., '92
Captain, U. S. A.,   LL. M., '93
Quartermaster's Dept., Wash , D. C.

Hough, J. Spencer..........M. D., '93

Hough, William Hite...:...M. D., '04
G. U. Med. Fac.,
Insane Asylum, Washington, D. C.

Houghton, Percy Francis....M. D., '01
Physician,
220 Brooklyn Ave., Brooklyn, N. Y.

Houston, Charles James.....LL. B , '05
Lawyer,
1st Nat. Bk. Bldg., San Francisco, Cal.

Houston, Harry J..........LL. B , '09
Princeville, Ill.

Houston, Samuel...... ....M D , '68

Howard, A. Clinton.........LL. B , '95

Howard, Arcturus L........M D , '93
G. U. Med. Fac.,
124 L St. N. W., Washington, D. C.

Howard, Flodoardo....... Phar. B ,'71
Deceased, Jan , 1888,   Phar D , 72
Rockville, Md.

Howard, John Chalmers.....LL. B., '01
Lawyer,
Fendall Bldg., Washington, D C

Howard, Joseph T.........M. D, '59
Physician,
1126 9th St. N. W , Washington, D. C.

Howard, Joseph T. D......M D , '89
Physician,
Falls Church, Va.

Howard, Leland O.........Ph. D., '96

Howard, Robert..M. D., '67. A. M , '70
Deceased, Dec. 1, 1899,   LL. B., '74
St. Paul, Minn.

Howard, Stanton Wren.....M. D., '03
G. U. Med. Fac.,
2725 13th St. N. W., Wash., D. C.

Howe, Franklin Theodore...M. D , '67
Deceased, 1908.   A. M., '89
Washington, D. C.

Howe, Theodore Gilman....M. D., '03
Physician,
Sandy Hill, N. Y.

Howell, Rev. R............LL. B., '75

Howle, Peter C............A B., '45
Deceased, Nov. 24, 1865.

Hoyt, Allen G.............LL. B., '02
Banker,
49 Wall St., N. Y. City.

Hoyt, Charles A...........A. B , '57
Deceased, April 18, 1903, A M , '60
Pasadena, Cal.

Hubachek, Francis R.......LL M ,'87

Hubbard, Oliver P.........LL. B , '91
Lawyer,
Newcastle, Ind.

Hubbell, Santiago F........LL B , '74

Hudson, Arthur J..........LL B , '07
Patent Lawyer,
1028 Soc. for Savings Bldg., Cleveland, Ohio.

Huff, Thomas S............LL M ,'06
New York City.

Hughes, Arthur J..........LL. B., '07
Fargo, N. D.

Hughes, Arthur L..........LL. B , '88
                          LL. M., '89

Hughes, Charles L.........LL. B , '73

Hughes, Cornelius E.......LL B , '09
Poolesville, Md

Hughes, Ellis................LL. B , '99

Hughes, Harry Canby.   ...LL B , '99

Hughes, William J ... . ..LL B , '91
Lawyer,   LL M , '92
Dept of Justice, Washington, D C

Hull, Marion McHenry......M D , '95
Physician,
502 Prudential Bldg , Atlanta, Ga

Hullihen, Alfred F.........A B , '55

Hullihen, Manfred F . . ...A B , '55
A M , '70

Hummer, Harry R.........M D , '99
Physician,
Asy. for Insane Indians, Canton, S D

Humrichouse, Harry H......LL B , '07
Lawyer,
Hagerstown, Md.

Hunt, Granville M.........LL B , '89
Sup. of Registry,   LL M , '90
Post Office, Washington, D. C

Hunt, Presley C ....M. D , '91
Physician,
815 M St. N W , Washington, D C

Hunter, Edwin Clarence.....M. D , '03
G. U. Med Fac,
707 4th St. N. E , Wash, D. C

Huntoon, Andrew J........M D , '67
Deceased.

Huselton, William S.......M. D , '65
Physician and Surgeon,
Fifth Ave , Pittsburg, Pa.

Hussey, John Patrick......M D , '03
Physician,
156 Cranston St , Providence, R I.

Hutchins, Frank W.. . . ... LL B , '99
LL M , '00

Hutchinson, Claudius P.. ...M D , '99
Physician,
Arcola, Va.

Hutchinson, Edmund Archus, LL B , '03

Hutchinson, Edwin B ......LL. B , '08
Lawyer,
Herndon, Va

Huyck, Thomas B ....LL B , '92
Real Estate and Lawyer, LL M , '93
1505 Penn Ave., Washington, D C

Hyams, William Washington, LL B , '03
Lawyer,
Tulsa, Okla

Hyatt, P F ..   ... M D , '65

Hyatt, William A. ....LL M., '88

Hynson, N. Thornton......LL. B , '07
Lawyer,
Century Bldg , Washington, D. C.

Iglehart, James Alexis . . .A B , '45
Deceased, May 1, 1908,
Davidsonville, Md

Igoe, Michael L.............LL. B , '08
Lawyer,
Title and Trust Bldg , Chicago, Ill.

Illman, Harold...... . .....LL. B , '75

Ingalls, Ellsworth...........LL. B , '88

Ingalls, Ralph.. . . . .LL B , '91
Lawyer,
Atchison, Kansas

Ironside, Charles Norton....LL. B , '82
Newspaper Man,
Box 646, Springfield, Mass.

Ironside, George E...... ...LL D., '22
Deceased, May 7, 1827, Wash , D C.

Irwin, John, Jr...............LL M , '94

Irwin, John W...............LL. B , '82

Isbell, John B...............LL. B , '01
Lawyer,
Fort Payne, Ala.

Israeli, Baruch........ . ... M D., '97
Clerk, War Dept ,
476 F St. S W , Washington, D. C.

Ittig, Henry . ...LL. B , '03 LL M., '04

Ives, Eugene S..............A. B , '78
Lawyer,   A. M , '88 Ph D , '89
Tucson, Ariz.

Jackson, Albert L.... ....M. D., '89
Deceased, Oct 16, 1899,
Herkimer, N. Y

Jackson, George E.........LL B , '09
San Francisco, Cal.

Jackson, John Joseph........A.M , '97
Head Master Newman School,
Hackensack, N. J.

Jackson, Wm A..LL. B , '94 LL M , '96

Jackson, William C ....LL B , '98

Jackson, Wm. S..LL B., '80, LL. M., '81

Jaffe, Saul Sydney..........D D S.,'05
G U Dental Fac ,
1415 K St N. W., Washington, D. C.

James, C Clinton.............LL B , '97
Lawyer,   LL. M.,'98
416 5th St N. W , Washington, D. C.

James, Grover Cleveland....LL B , '09
Bentonville, Ark

James, Judge Charles P.... .LL D., '70
Deceased

James, Howard...........M. D , '93
Jamison, Albion B.........M. D., '67
Jamison, Alexander........LL. B , '09
Philadelphia, Pa.
Jaranilla, Delfin...........LL. B , '07
Lawyer,
Care Court of First Inst., Iloilo, P. I
Jeffs, Benjamin.............A. B., '08
Rockland, Mich.
Jenal, Frank P.............LL. B., '07
Lawyer,
503 Douglas Bldg., Los Angeles, Cal.
Jenkins, Charles............LL. B., '03
Clerk,
Dept. of Justice, Washington, D C
Jenkins, Lewis W...........A. B., '22
Deceased.   A. M., '31
Jenkins, T. Robert.........A. B., '40
Deceased.
Jenkins, Theodore........,..A. B., '26
Deceased
Jenner, Norman R.........M. D , '91
Physician,
1110 R. I. Ave. N. W., Wash., D. C.
Jennings, David E.........LL. B , '91
Lawyer,   LL. M., '92
Nashville, Tenn.
Jennings, Edward James.....LL. B., '80
LL. M., '80
Jennings, John W...........LL. B., '03
Druggist and Lawyer,   LL. M., '04
1142 Conn. Ave , Washington, D. C.
Jennings, Raymond S........LL. B, '08
Jennings, Robert W........LL B , '87
Lawyer,   LL. M., '88
Port Townsend, Wash.
Jerrell, Herbert P..........LL. B , '90
Jessup, Wilfred.............LL. M., '01
Lawyer,
Richmond, Ind.
Jewell, J. Gray.............M. D., '55
Deceased, Sept. 17, 1894.
Jewell, William R., Jr.......LL. B., '92
Lawyer,
209 Daniel Bldg., Danville, Ill.
Jewett, Nelson J............LL. B., '08
Asst. Examiner Patent Office,
Patent Office, Washington, D. C.
Jirdinston, William C........LL. B., '80
Johnson, Benjamin R........LL. B., '01
Patent Lawyer,
605 7th St. N. W., Washington, D. C.
Johnson, Dallas............M. D., '68

Johnson, Frank G..........M D., '91
Deceased, April 16, 1906,
Kensington, Md.
Johnson, Hayden............LL. B., 95
Lawyer,   LL. M.,'96
416 5th St. N. W., Washington, D. C.
Johnson, Jeremiah..........LL. B , '85
LL. M , '86
Johnson, John Altheus......LL. B , '82
Lawyer,   LL. M ,'87
408 5th St. N. W., Washington, D. C.
Johnson, John D....:.......LL. B , '08
Clerk Consular Bureau,
Dept. of State, Washington, D C
Johnson, John Lewis........LL. B , '04
Lawyer,
500 5th St. N. W., Washington, D. C.
Johnson, Joseph..A. B., '42, A. M , '46
Johnson, Joseph Taber......M. D , '65
Physician,   Ph. D., '89
Vice Pres G. U. Med. Fac.,
926 17th St , Washington, D. C.
Johnson, Loren Bascom Taber,
Physician,   M. D., '00
1211 Conn. Ave. N. W., Wash., D. C
Johnson, Louis Alward.....M. D., '92
Physician,
711 C St. S. W., Washington, D. C.
Johnson, Paul Bowen Alden..M. D., '05
Physician,
2460 6th St. N. W., Washington, D. C.
Johnson, Paul E...........LL B , '90
Lawyer,   LL. M ,'91
512 F St. N. W., Washington, D. C.
Johnson, Richard W........LL. B , '89
Johnson, Robert............LL. B , '80
Lawyer,
98 Commercial Place, Norfolk, Va.
Johnson, Stuart Clarke.....M. D , '97
Physician,
1616 9th St. N. W., Washington, D C.
Johnson, Titian W..........LL. B , '94
Lawyer,
McGill Bldg., Washington, D. C.
Johnson, Walter A.........A. B., '91
Deceased, Dec. 16, 1899
Johnson, William A........LL. M ,'87
Lawyer,
1406 G St. N. W., Washington, D. C.
Johnson, William Carey.....LL. B , '99
Deceased, Wash , D. C.   LL. M.,'00
Johnson, William H........LL. M , '86
Johnston, James A.........LL. B , '92

Johnston, James M..........LL. B , '95
Lawyer,
Waupun, Wis.

Johnston, Leslie J..........LL. B., '09
Galesburg, Ill.

Johnston, Robert D., Jr......LL. B , '01
Patent Lawyer,
Brown-Marx Bldg , Birmingham, Ala.

Joliat, Albert L. F.........D D S ,'07
Dentist,
Canton, Ohio.

Jones, Alvah W ....M D, '91
Physician,
Red Wing, Minn

Jones, Benjamin C ....M D, '68
Deceased, May, 1898,
Popular Bluff, Mo.

Jones, Bennett S............LL B , '89
Lawyer,   LL. M , '90
611 7th St., Washington, D. C.

Jones, Charles M............LL. B , '97

Jones, Charles S., LL. B , '91, LL. M , '92

Jones, Senator Charles W...LL D., '82
Deceased.

Jones, E. S................M. D, '72
Deceased.

Jones, Edward..............M. D, '70

Jones, Edwin C............LL. B , '95
Deceased, April 7, 1908,   LL M , '96
Long Beach, Cal.

Jones, Elcon...............A. M , '32

Jones, Elwyn Thornton......LL B , '03
Care D. W. Baker, Colorado Bldg ,
Washington, D. C.

Jones, Frank A..LL. B , '96, LL M , '97

Jones, George Wilson ....M D, '05
Physician,
1730 N. Fulton Ave., Baltimore, Md

Jones, Grosvenor M.........LL. B , '09
Cleveland, Ohio.

Jones, Jacobus S............LL. M , '98

Jones, James K.............LL. B., 89
Lawyer,
621 Colorado Bldg , Wash , D C.

Jones, John B..............LL B , '88

Jones, Richard Henry.......LL. B , '98

Jones, Richard J...........LL B , '03
Care D. W. Baker, Colorado Bldg,
Washington, D. C.

Jones, Thomas.............LL B , '05

Jones, William E...........LL B , '77

Jones, William J..........LL. B , '02
Lawyer,
416 Liggett Bldg , St Louis, Mo.

Jones, Winfield P..........A B , '01
Lawyer,
331 Equitable Bldg , Atlanta, Ga.

Jordan, Edward L..........LL. B , '96
Deceased, Jan. 8, 1907, Wash , D C

Jordan, James Hammer ....M. D, '56

Jordan, Llewellyn, LL. B , '89, LL. M , '90

Jorrin, Leonardo Sorzaro ...A. B , '99
Calle 5-A 31 Velado St ,
Havana, Cuba.

Joslin, Philip C............LL. B , '08
Lawyer,
42 Westminster, Providence, R. I.

Jourdan, Arthur J..........A. B , '52
H. C., Mass.,
Deceased, 1853.

Jourdan, Charles A.........Ph. D, '81

Jouy, Joseph...............M. D., '69
Deceased, Jan. 5, 1901.

Joyce, J. Williamson........M. D, '73
Deceased, Dec. 16, 1890.

Joyce, Joseph I.............LL. B., '81

Joynt, Martin E.............LL. B., '09
Oil City, Pa

Judd, Sylvester D..........M S., '97
Deceased, 1905.   Ph. D., '98

Judd, Theodore Mann.......LL. B., '05
Real Estate,
617 E St N. W., Washington, D. C.

Julihn, Magnus L...........M. D, '66
Physician and Druggist,
1423 5th St. N. W., Washington, D. C.

Jullien, Cyrus S.............LL. B , '04
Lawyer,   LL. M., '05
90 Wall St., N. Y. City.

Junghans, John Henry......A. B , '88
Physician,   A. M., '91
417 D St. N. E., Washington, D. C.

Jurney, Chesley W..........LL. B , '08
Private Secretary,
U. S Senate P. O., Washington, D. C.

Kalbfus, Samuel T..........LL B., '01
Asst. Assessor,
1727 De Sales St. N. W., Wash., D. C.

Kalussowski, H. Corwin.....M. D, '52
Deceased.

Kanaley, Rev. Francis Thomas,
Priest,   A B , '02
1974 Seneca St., Buffalo, N. Y.

Kane, Charles J.... .... . .LL B , '05
South Bend News, LL. M , '07
South Bend, Ind.
Kane, Denis D.......... ...LL. B , '75
Kane, Frank Anthony, Jr....A B , '03
Lawyer, LL. B , '05
Minooka, Pa
Kane, Henry Victor.. ..... A M , '05
Lawyer, Ph. D , '01, LL. B , '02
802-808 Wells Bldg , Milwaukee, Wis
Kane, John J............. LL B , '09
Worcester, Mass
Kappler, Charles J.... .....LL B , '95
Lawyer, LL. M , '97
Bond Bldg , Washington, D. C
Karch, Charles M.......... LL. B , '01
Karicofe, W. H. A.........LL B., '87
Kathman, James A.......... A M , '00
Lawyer, LL. B , '02
New Orleans, La
Kauffman, Harry B.. . ....A B , '91
Physician, M. D , '94
New Mexico.
Kaveney, Joseph James , M D , '04
G U Med. Fac.
The Elkton, Washington, D C
Keables, Dr. T. A., ...M D , '72
Deceased, Mar. 2, 1902
Keach, Le Roy............LL M , '09
Indianapolis, Ind.
Kean, Thomas J............M D , '93
Keane, Michael Aloysius . ..LL B., '01
Merchant,
1109 K St N. W , Washington, D. C.
Keane, Michael J............LL B , '97
Lawyer, LL M., '98
Century Bldg , Washington, D C
Kearney, George..A B , '88, LL B , '90
Librarian, LL M , '91, A. M., '91
Dept. of Justice, Washington, D. C
Kearney, Richard F..... ..M D , '66
Keating, J. Percy ....A B , '75
Lawyer, A M., '91
701 Arcade Bldg., Philadelphia, Pa
Keating, John Joseph........LL. B , '03
Keaton, James R..........LL B , '90
Lawyer,
Oklahoma City, Okla.
Keegin, William C.........LL B., '91
Lawyer, LL M., '92
McGill Bldg , Washington, D. C
Keene, P. T...............M. D., '70
Physician,
Portland, Ore

Keene, Walter Prince......M. D , '00
Keith, Robert Lee.........A. M., '97
Keleher, Michael Joseph:...A. B , '04
Kellogg, Daniel M.... .... ..LL. B , '93
Examiner, LL. M., '94
Patent Office, Washington, D C
Kelly, Charles B...........LL. B , '96
Kelly, Rev. Charles F, S J..D. D., '89
Jesuit Priest,
Deceased, 1906, Philadelphia, Pa.
Kelly, Charles M............LL. B., '97
Lawyer,
519 N Schroeder St , Baltimore, Md.
Kelly, Daniel J.............A. M., '73
Physician, M. D., '75
1314 13th St. N. W , Washington, D.C.
Kelly, Howard Ignatius.....A B , '96
Theatrical,
National Theatre, Philadelphia, Pa.
Kelly, James F............LL. B., '08
Lawyer,
Care Washington Post Wash , D. C.
Kelly, James Vincent.......LL B , '99
Sec.-Treas Bd. Park Com. LL M , '00
Druid Hill Park, Baltimore, Md
Kelly, John J..............LL. B., '97
Lawyer,
Tam, Nat. Bk. Bldg. Tamaqua, Pa
Kelly, Peter A ... .A B , '70
Traveling Salesman,
23 So. Hanover St , Baltimore, Md
Kelly, Walter E.... ....LL B., '09
Cincinnati, Ohio
Kelly, William E.... ... ...LL. B., '97
Kelso, Felix A....... .....A B , '89
Magnolia, Ark.
Kelso, Paul............. . LL. B , '97
Kemp, James Finley........M. D , '98
Kendall, William Converse .M D , '96
Kengla, Bernard A.........LL B , '87
Deceased, Feb 18, 1891, Wash., D C.
Kengla, Louis A B S , '82, A. B , '83
Deceased, 1904, M D , '86
San Francisco, Cal.
Kenna, Edward B.... .....A. B , '99
Charlestown, W Va
Kennedy, Beverly C........A. B , '58
Kennedy, Charles T........M D , '92
Physician,
Greenville, Tex.
Kennedy, Rev. Daniel B.. ..A. B , '62
H C , Mass ,
Mt. Hope Ret,, Baltimore, Md

Kennedy, Duncan A........A B, '34
Kennedy, Frank P..........LL B, '97
Pres Newark Trust Co,
Newark, Ohio
Kennedy, George S..........A B., '34
Kennedy, John A............A B, '40
Kennedy, John M .. .. LL B, '07
Lawyer,
Scarritt Bldg, Kansas City, Mo
Kennedy, Judge Thomas H..A. B, '32
Kennedy, Robert Joseph .. LL B, '06
Lawyer,
326 So. Linden Ave, Pittsburg, Pa
Kennedy, William E........A M, '32
Kennedy, Wm J.. .... .M D, '05
Physician,
Newark, Ohio
Kennelly, James........ .LL B, '88
Pension Office, LL M, '90
Washington, D C.
Kenney, Alfred E ....LL B, '94
Lawyer, LL M, '95
Parkersburg, W Va.
Kenney, John P .... .LL B, '08
Lowell, Mass
Kennon, J C W. ....M D, '57
Deceased
Kenny, Charles Borromeo...A B, '58
Lawyer,
Frick Bldg Annex, Pittsburg, Pa
Kenny, Lawrence.. ... A B, '60
H C, Mass,
Deceased, 1886
Kent, Otis B .... LL B, '07
Law Clerk, LL M, '08
Interstate Com Com, Wash, D C
Kernan, Senator Francis ...LL D, '80
Deceased, Sept. 8, 1892, Utica, N Y
Kernan, Leslie Warnick A B, '86
Deceased, 1903, Utica, N Y
Kernan, Nicholas Edward A B, '03
5 Nassau St, N. Y. City
Kernan, Thomas P..:.... . A B, '78
Utica, N Y
Kernan, Walter N.... .... .A B, '85
Lawyer,
527 5th Ave, N Y. City
Kernan, Warnick Joseph A B, '01
Lawyer,
Utica, N. Y.
Kernan, William J.:........A B, '80
Deceased, Dec 8, 1900, Utica, N Y.

Kerns, Francis Joseph ..... M. D, '03
Physician,
6 Wyman St, Worcester, Mass
Kerr, Denis......LL B, '81 LL M, '82
Kerrigan, George Edward.. A M., '96
Lawyer, LL B, '97, LL M, '98
Pine and Trinity Sts, Redding, Cal.
Ketcham, Orlando E. ......M D, '71
Deceased, July 30, 1890, Wash, D. C.
Kett, Michael C..... .. .. M D, '04
Deceased, August 6, 1909
Glenwood Springs, Colo.
Kettler, Milton A ....LL B, '04
Manager, Wash Bill Posting Co.,
513 13th St N W, Wash, D C
Keyes, Dr Edward L, Jr. .A B, '92
Physician, Ph D, '01
109 E 34th St, New York City
Keyes, Francis Corey.. . ...A B, '93
Keys, Frank R . LL. B, '90, LL M, '91
Kidwell, Edgar . A B, '86, A M, '89
Mechanical Engineer, Ph D, '97
3002 Hobart Boulevard,
Los Angeles, Cal
Kidwell, John W, A B, '60, A. M, '66
Kieckhoefer, Francis J .. A B, '68
LL B, '87, LL M, '88, A M, '89
63 West 96th St, New York City
Kiernan, Cortland A ... A B, '01
Kiggins, F M...LL B, '85, LL M, '86
Kilcullen,, P E ..... . .LL B, '99
Lawyer,
506 Dime Bank Bldg, Scranton, Pa.
Kilkenny, Francis J .. . LL B, '02
Conf Clerk, Comp Currency,
Treasury Dept, Washington, D C
Killeen, Thomas . ... A B, '58
Kilroy, Dr James Joseph . M D, '98
Physician,
2 I St N. E, Washington. D C
Kimball, Charles O .. LL B., '92
Lawyer, LL M, '93
Charlestown, N. H
Kimball, E S .... M D, '66
Teacher of Singing,
1010 F St N. W, Washington, D C.
Kincaid, Douglas Howard.. .M. D, '91
Physician,
Danville, Ky.
King, Alexius S. ... LL B, '78
King, Claude F..LL B, '89, LL M, '90
King, Edwin F .A B, '51, A M, '55

King, George Sherman.......LL. B, '99
　　　　　　　　LL. M, '00
King J. T.................M. D., '94
Physician,
Quitman, Ga

King, John F..............A. B, '52
Deceased, Mch 25, 1873, Wash', D. C

King, Michael H...........LL. B., '97

King, Thomas B...........A. B, '52
Deceased, 1868,　　　A. M., '60
Charleston, S. C.

Kingsbury, Albert D.......M. D, '69
Physician,
291 Great Plain Ave, Needham, Mass

Kingsley, Hiram A....... ...LL B, '93
U. S. Special Pension Examiner,
1410 W. 6th St, Topeka, Kans.

Kingston, A. T. V.........M D., '02
Physician,
1409 Prospect Ave, New York City

Kinsell, Tyson.............. LL. B, '05

Kinyoun, Joseph J.........Ph. D, '96
G U. Med Fac,
1423 Clifton St. N. W, Wash, D. C.

Kirby, Elmer L.............LL. B., '08
Mechanical Expert,
The Elsmere, Washington, D. C.

Kirby, John Joseph........A M, '98
Lawyer,　　　LL. B, '99, LL. M, '00
41 Wall St, New York City.

Kirby, Maurice Brown ......A B, '98
Journalist,
Care Henry W. Savage, N. Y. City

Kirby, Thomas, Jr.........'..LL. B, '05
Journalist,
203 I St. N. W., Washington, D. C

Kirby, William P..........M. D., '06
Physician,
492 K St. S. W., Washington, D C

Kirkpatrick, John L.........A. B., '43

Kirtland, Michael...........LL. B, '92
Lawyer,
Montgomery, Ala.

Kitch, James Barbour.......LL. B, '05
Clerk, Census Office,
1827 18th St. N. W., Wash, D C

Kitchin, Edgar M..........LL. B, '99
Lawyer,
805 G St N. W., Washington, D- C

Klein, Anthony Eller........M. D., '00
Physician and Surgeon,
168 National Ave., Corona, N. Y.

Kleinschmidt, Charles H. A..M. D., '62
Deceased, May 20, 1895,　Ph. D, '89
Washington, D. C.

Kleinschmidt, Harry C......LL B., '02
Treasurer,
3068 M St. N. W., Washington, D. C.

Klinger, David B...........LL. B, '93
Pension Officer,　　　LL. M., '94
229 12th St. N. E., Washington, D. C.

Klopfer, Walter H..........LL. B., '91
Prin. Ex. Pen Bureau,　LL. M., '92
1346 Howard St. N. W., Wash., D. C.

Knight, Henry E..LL. B., '84, LL. M., '85

Knight, Hervey S..........LL. B., '88
Patent Lawyer,
McGill Bldg., Washington, D. C.

Knight, Joseph Sheridan.....LL. B, '03
Jesuit Scholastic,
St. Andrew on Hudson, Poughkeepsie,
N. Y.

Knight, William E..........LL B.,' '91

Knighton, Nicholas S.......A. B, '45
Deceased.

Knowlan, Dominic F.........A. B, '90
Deceased, July, 1899.

Kober, George Martin.......M. D, '73
　　　　　　　　LL D.,'06
Dean G. U. Medical Department,
920 H St. N. W, Washington, D C

Koch, Adolph A............LL B, '02
1327 5th St. N. W, Washington, D. C.

Kolipinski, Louis............M. D, '83
Physician,
631 I St. N. W., Washington, D C.

Koonce, Claude J..........M D, '95

Koontz, Clarke..............A B, '51

Kopmeier, Norman J........LL. B, '05
Ice Merchant,
234 Wells Bldg, Milwaukee, Wis.

Kram, Charles A............LL. B., '92
Law Clerk,　　　　　LL. M., '93
Office of Auditor of P. O. Dept.,
Washington, D. C.

Kratz, John A., Jr..........LL. B., '04
Lawyer,
Met. Bank Bldg., Washington, D. C.

Krebs, Conrad..............LL. B., '92
Merchant,
Salem, Oreg.

Krichelt, Frederick W.......LL. B, '99
Clerk, Adjt Gen Office,　LL M.,'00
War Dept., Washington, D. C.

Kroll, Wm. A.............LL B, '08
Clerk,
Takoma Park, D. C

Kuehn, Otto Frederick......D D S,'05

Kuhn, James O'Reilly.... ..A B, '99
Law Clerk   ,   LL. B, '02
3334 N St. N. W, Washington, D C.

Kuhn, John Frederick,......M. D, '01
Physician
iii W. 9th St, Oklahoma City, Okla.

Kuhn, Joseph Aloysius......A. B, '02
3334 N St. N. W, Washington, D C.

La Bossiere, Edward A......LL B., '08
Boston, Mass   LL M, '09

Laboule, John F............LL. B, '85

Lacey, Anderson B........LL B, '98
Lawyer,
Pacific Bldg, Washington, D C

Lacson, Roman J.........Ph L, '02
Lawyer,   Ph D, '03, LL B, '04
53 Palacio, Manila, P. I

Lacy, Eugene B ....LL. B, '93
Lawyer,   LL. M, '94
Montgomery, Ala.

Lafferty, Daniel L.........A. B, '64
Deceased, 1866.

Lafferty, Francis P. S.......A B, '65

Lagarde, Ernest............A B, '66
Prof Eng Lit,   A M, '69
Mt. St Mary's Col, Emmitsburg, Md.

LaGrange, Ernest H........LL B, '88
                        LL M., '89

Lamar, George H.. ....LL B, '89
Lawyer,   LL M, '90
Fendall Bldg, Washington, D C

Lamar, Lucius Q. C........LL B, '95
Lawyer,
Oxford, Miss.

Lamar, William H, Jr......LL B, '84
Lawyer,   LL M, '85
Dept. of Justice, Washington, D C

Lamb, Daniel S. ....M D, '67
Physician,
Army Med. Museum, Wash, D C

Lamb, William James Charles,
Physician,   M D, '03
311 Amber St, Pittsburg, Pa

Lambert, Wilton J........ LL B, '93
Lawyer,   LL M, '94
410 5th St N. W, Washington, D C.

Lambert, Tallmadge A......A B, '62
    A. M, '71, LL. D, '94
2209 Mass. Ave, Washington, D. C.

Lamkin, Griffin ....LL M, '01
Lawyer,
Title Guar Bldg, Birmingham, Ala.

Lancaster, C. C.... .   ..A B, '74
Lawyer,   LL B, '76
Corcoran Bldg, Washington, D C.

Lancaster, Rev. Clement S, S J,
Jesuit Priest,   A B, '59
St Aloysius Church, Wash., D. C.

Lancaster, Dr. F. M ......A. B, '51
Deceased,   A. M, '57, M D., '57

Lancaster, Francis A.... . .A B., '57
Col, Killed at Chancellorsville,
May 3, 1863.

Lancaster, George D . .: LL B, '86
Lawyer,   LL M, '87
Chattanooga, Tenn

Landa, Gabriel M..... ....A B, '77
Cienfuegos, Cuba.

Landry, Anatole........ .:..A. B, '60

Landry, John C...........A. M., '06
Law Student,
Dorchester, New Brunswick, Canada.

Landry, L. Valery..........A. B., '48

Landry, Prosper R...... ...A. B., '46

Lang, Charles J........ ...M D, '87
Deceased, April 9, 1900, Wash., D. C.

Lang, Henry J.. ...   A B, '40
Deceased.

Langan, Raymond Charles ..LL B, '95
Lawyer,
Clinton, Iowa.

Langley, Hon John W...: .LL M, '94
Lawyer and Member of Congress,
Pikeville, Ky.

Lannon, John David........A B, '94
2 Rector St, New York City

Lanston, Aubrey............LL B., '99
Novelist and Playwright,
Care Tolbert Lanston,
3012 O St. N W, Washington, D C.

Lantry, Thomas B... . .A B, '89
Lawyer,
807-809 The Rookery, Chicago, Ill

Lantz, Ira................LL B, '08
Clerk, G. L. O.,   LL M., '09
1010 Mass Ave. N. W., Wash, D. C.

Laphen, James S...........A B, '37

Laplace, Albert J...........A B, '79

Laplace, Dr Ernest . .. A B, '80
Surgeon,   A. M, '87, LL. D, '95
1828 S. Rittenhouse Sq, Phila, Pa.

La Plante, J. B. Edmund....A B, '09
523 Broadway, Vincennes, Ind.

Lapretre, J. B. Adrien......A. B , '49

Larcombe, James A........LL. B , '88
LL M., '89

Larkin, P. Edward ....M. D ,' '08
Intern,
. Providence Hospital, Wash , D. C

LaRoche, Dr. C. Percy de.. A. B., '53
Deceased, Mar. 12, 1907,. A M , '61
Rome, Italy. '

Lastrappes, Ludger..........A. B , '51
H. C , Mass , Retired Merchant,
Natchitoches, La.

Latham, Benjamin F.......M. D., '76

Latham, Charles L.........LL. B., '04
U. S. Consul Carthagena,
. U. S. of Colombia, South America.

Latham, Samuel B.........LL. B ,"85
LL. M.,'87

Lathrop, John P...........LL. B , '74

Latimer, E. F..............D. D. S ,'02
Merchant,
. Lowndesville, S. C.

Latshaw, Henry J..........Ph. B., '85
Lawyer,
. 1010 Scarritt Bldg., Kansas City, Mo.

Latshaw, Ralph S..........A. B , '85

Laughborough, L. H.......Ph. B., '87
Agriculturist,
. Bethesda, Md.

Laughlin, John Edward .....A B , '00
Lawyer,
. Berger Bldg., Pittsburg, Pa.

Laumont, Henry B..........A. B , '48

Lauve, Louis L.............A. B , '01

Lavalle, Don Jose Antonio de, A. M., '69

Lavelle, Thomas Eugene....A. B , '09
301 West St., Butte, Mont.

Lavin, James P.............LL. B., '94
U. S. Immigrant Insp., LL. M ,'96
Seattle, Wash

Lawler, Hon Daniel W.....A. B , '81
. Lawyer,, A. M., '89, LL. D., '97
N. Y. Life Bldg , St Paul, Minn.

Lawler, Francis J..........A. B., '85
Deceased, May, 1890,
Prairie du Chien, Wis.

Lawler, Joseph C......... A B , '85

Lawler, Joseph H..........A. B , '06
.Lawyer,
79 Farmington Ave., Hartford, Conn.

Lawler, Thomas C.........A. B , '79
Deceased, Apr. 17, '08, Dubuque, Iowa.

Lawrence, James B........M. D., '73

Lawton, John M..LL B ,'86, LL M ,'87

Leach, Hamilton E........M D , '72
Deceased, May 19, 1893, Wash, D. C.

Leahy, Edw. L..............LL. B., '08
. Lawyer,
704 Banigan Bldg , Providence, R. I.

Leahy, John Stephen........A M , '95
Lawyer, LL. B , '96
Carleton Bldg , St. Louis, Mo

Leahy, Rev. Michael David..A B , '92
Priest,
1346 Gladys Ave., Cleveland, Ohio.,

Leahy, Michael J...........LL. B , '06
Deceased, Aug 12, 1909, Wash , D. C.

Leary, Francis Paul........LL. B , '04
Lawyer,
1201 11th St N. W., Wash , D C

Leary, Robert J............LL. B., '99

LeBoeuf, Peter George......A. B., '96
Chippewa Falls, Wis

Leckie, A. E. Lloyd........LL B , '94
Lawyer, LL M ,'95
Colorado Bldg , Washington, D C.

Leckie, Richard.............LL B , '92

LeCompte, S. B.............M. D , '68

LeCouteulx, Louis..........A B , '49

Lee, Albert James..........LL B , '03
Lawyer,
Oklahoma City, Okla.

Lee, Arthur.................A. B , '67
Deceased, April 12, 1899, St Louis, Mo.

Lee, Chapman .... M D , '66
Deceased

Lee, F. D..................M. D., '94
Pension Office, Washington, D. C

Lee, Henry.......LL B , '08, LL. M ,'09
498 Md Ave S W., Wash , D C

Lee, Orr W......LL. B., '89, LL M ,'90

Legare, George S.. ..... LL B , '92
Lawyer,
Columbia, S C.

Legendre, Adolphus........ A. B , '25
Deceased.

Lehmann, Frederick A.... ..LL B , '75

Lenahan, William D.........LL B , '06
Lawyer, LL. M.,'07
612 F St. N. W., Washington, D. C.

Lennon, Joseph Arthur......A. M., '03
Lawyer, LL. B., '07
29 Broadway, New York City.

Lennon, Leo Camillo........A. M., '00
Lawyer, . Ph. D , '01
660 Market St , San Francisco, Cal.

Lennon, Maurice F.........LL. B., '07
Lawyer,
Joliet, Ill.

Lennon, Milton Byrne ... ..A M., '98
Physician,
802 Butler Bldg , San Francisco, Cal

Leonard, John D ....LL B, '92
Lawyer, LL M, '93
1006 F St N. W, Washington, D. C.

Leonard, Richard B.........D D S,'03
Dentist,
1320 L St N. W, Washington, D C.

Lesh, Paul E.................LL B, '06
Lawyer, LL M., '07
Pacific Bldg, 622 F St. N. W,
Washington, D. C

Lethert, Charles A.........LL. B., '09
St Paul, Minn.

Lett, Frederick R... ....A. B, '86
Deceased, Sept. 14, 1900

Lever, Hon Asbury Frank..LL B, '99
Member of Congress
103 Md. Ave N. E, Wash., D C

Levey, A L................M D, '94

Lewis, Fielding ....LL B, '89
Deceased, Nov 12, 1908, LL. M, '90
McAlester, Okla.

Lewis, J. Edward.............LL B, '97
Lawyer, Real Estate Brok, LL. M, '98
617 E St. N. W, Washington, D. C.

Lewis, James P.............M D, '78
Deceased, Dec 22, 1901, Wash, D C

Lewis, William H ....LL B, '87
Law Examiner, LL M, '88
General Land Office, Wash, D C

Lewis, William H...........A B, '40

Liebermann, Charles D.....LL B, '77

Lieuallen, William Grant ....LL. B., '99
Moscow, Idaho.

Light, Given Addison.......M. D, '06
Physician,
Salt Lake City, Utah.

Lilly, Samuel M ....A. B, '42

Lincoln, John Ledyard .....A. B, '81
Lawyer, A. M, '89
First Nat. Bk Bldg., Cincinnati, Ohio

Lindsay, David R...........M. D, '60

Linn, Samuel F.............M. D, '76

Linnehan, George Albert....M. D, '04
Physician,
16 Union Ave, Jamaica, N Y.

Linney, Romulus Zachariah .M. D, '01
Physician,
Hopeton, Okla.

Little, John J..............M. D, '71
Deceased, Washington, D C

Littlewood, James B........M. D, '68
Deceased, Feb 7, 1906.

Litzinger, Lewis P.........LL. B., '02
LL. M., '03

Lloyd, George H.............A. B, '50
H. C., Mass, Merchant,
74 W. Cottage St, Boston, Mass

Lobit, Joseph, Jr.............A. B, '99
Galveston, Texas

Lochboehler, George J.......M. D, '89
Physician,
55 K St. N. W, Washington, D C

Locke. Herbert M..........LL. B., '94
LL. M., '95
Berryville, Va.

Loeffler, Louis...............LL. B., '07
1813 14th St, Washington, D. C.

Logan, Alonzo T..LL. B., '88, LL. M., '89

Logan, Eugene Adolphus....LL. B., '98
Bureau of Labor, LL. M., '99
Dept. of Com. & Labor, Wash, D. C.

Long, Carlos A.............LL. B, '01
Lawyer,
Honolulu, Hawaii

Long, Elia A. C... ....LL. B, '01
Lawyer, LL. M., '02
Honolulu, Hawaii

Long, William..............M D, '87

Longshaw, Luther M........LL. M., '87
Keyser Bldg, Baltimore, Md.

Longstreth, John Cook......A. B, '47
Deceased, Dec. 29, 1891. A. M., '51

Longuemare, Eugene.......A. B., '54

Looby, Patrick W . ...LL. B., '03

Loomis, Silas L.............M. D, '57
Deceased, June 22, 1896

Loomis, L. C................M.D, '63
Deceased, October 17, 1905.

Loos, John G...............LL B, '06
Lawyer, LL M, '07
Omaha, Neb

Lordan, John J...LL. B., '95, LL. M, '96

Loughborough, Alex. H.....A B., '55
A. M., '58 LL. D., '89
Deceased, Jan. 28, 1897, San Fran, Cal.

Loughborough, L. N........Ph B, '87
Agriculturist,
Bethesda, Md.

Loughran John M..........LL B, '05
Lawyer, LL. M., '06
50 Eye St. N. E., Washington, D. C.

Loughran, Joseph E.........LL B, 'o1
Lawyer,
6 Hildreth Bldg., Lowell, Mass

Loughran, Patrick H........LL B, '96
Lawyer,
Columbian Bldg, Washington, D C.

Lovelace, Robert............A B, '59
Deceased.

Lovett, John W.......... .LL B, '72

Lowe, E. Louis.......... LL D, '53
Ex-Governor of Maryland

Lowe, Enoch M.............A B, '52
Deceased, June 11, 1879, Alex, Va

Lowe, Francis M...........LL. B, '93
Lawyer,   LL. M, '98
First National Bank Building,
Birmingham, Ala.

Lowe, Louis.............. .LL B., '05

Lowe, Thomas F...........M. D., '02
Physician,
205 H St. N. W., Washington, D. C.

Lowrie, H. H.......... ...M·D, '63
Physician,
Plainfield, N. J.

Lozano, Chas. I..LL. B.,.'99, LL M.,'oo

Luby, Emanuel S...........LL B., '98
Lawyer,   LL. M, '99
1336 N. Y. Ave. N. W., Wash, D C.

Lucas, Charles............M. D., '93
Physician,
Shelton, Nebr

Luce, Dr. Charles Roscoe....M. D., '85
Physician,
215 2d St. S. E., Washington, D. C.

Luckett, Oliver A..........A. B., '39
Deceased, Mar. 30, 1900

Luckey, Nelson E..LL B, '94, LL. M.,'95

Lucy, Daniel J.............LL B, '07
Lawyer,
536 Main St., Melrose, Mass.

Lusk, Addison Knox........A. B, '08
Surveyor,
1322 12th St. N. W, Wash., D. C

Lusk, Hall Stoner... ....A B., '04
Lawyer,   LL. B, '07
303 So. Idaho St., Butte, Mont·

Luthy, John H...... ......LL. B, '97
Clerk,
P. O. Dept, Washington, D C.

Luttrell, Walter McM.......M D, '93
Physician,
Knoxville, Tenn.

Lyden, Michael J. .... LL. B., '95
Deceased, Aug 2, 1901.   LL. M, '96

Lyles, D C.....A B, '68, A. M., '71

Lynch, Anthony Vincent....A. B., '09
77 Rutger St., Utica, N. Y.

Lynch, Edw. A..A B, '22, A. M., '31

Lynch, Rev. James.........A. M, '28

Lynch, James D............A. M., '93
129 E 21st St, N. Y. City.

Lynch, John G.............A. B, '24
Deceased.

Lynch, Rt Rev. Mgr. James S. M.,
St John's Church,   D. D., '89
Utica, N. Y.

Lynch, Rev Joseph Thomas..A B., '02
Priest. Deceased, May, 8, 1908,
Northampton, Mass.

Lynch, Patrick H..........A B., '77

Lynch, Patrick Michael......M. D., 'o1
Physician,
39 Main St, Springfield, Mass.

Lynch, Thomas.............LL B, '08
Lawyer,
N. Y. Life Bldg, Omaha, Neb

Lynch, William D..........A. B., '86
Deceased, 1888.

Lynch, Capt. W. F.........A. M., '44
U S Navy,
Deceased, Oct. 17, 1865.

Lynch, William Francis.....A. B., '04
House Physician,
St. Vincent's Hosp, Worcester, Mass

Lyon, Frank................LL. B, '89
Special Examiner,   LL. M, '90
Interstate Com. Com, Wash, D C

Lyon, Rutherford B. H.....LL B., '99
Lawyer,   LL. M, 'oo
1416 F St. N. W., Washington, D. C

Lyon, Simon................LL B, '90
Lawyer,   LL M, '91
1416 F St. N. W., Washington, D C.

Lyon, William B............M. D, '67

Lyons, Hilary Herbert......A. M, 'oo

Lyons, Thomas H...........A. B, '85

McAleer, John Hugh........A. B, '98
Flour Merchant,
211 Bainbridge St., Phila., Pa

McAleer, Joseph Leo........A. B., 'oo
Lawyer,   A. M, 'o1, Ph D, '05
509 W. End, Trust Bldg, Phila, Pa

McAleer, William, Jr.. ....A B, '98
213 Bainbridge St., Philadelphia, Pa

McAllister, Richard, Jr......LL. B., '73
Deceased

McAnerney, Frank Bernard..A. B , '98
Real Estate,
500 5th Ave , N. Y. City.

McArdle, Thomas E........M. D., '79
Physician,
1826 Columbian Road, Wash., D. C.

McAuley, John..............A. B , '55
St. F. X , N. Y.

McBlair, J. Hollins, Jr......M. D., '69
Deceased, Dec. 13, 1899.

McBride, Charles R........LL. B , '92
U S. Special Examiner, LL. M., '95
U. S. Court and P. O. Bldg.,
Chicago, Ill.

McBride, Parks R..........LL. B., '94
Lawyer,   LL. M , '95
Martinsville, Ind.

McCabe, John..............A. B., '49
H. C , Mass ,
Deceased, Providence, R. I.

McCahill, Edwin............A. B., '65
Deceased, Oct. 23, 1878,   A. M., '67
New Brunswick, N. J.

McCall, Robert S............LL. B , '89
Interior Dept ,.   LL. M , '90
Land Office, Washington, D. C

McCandlish, F. S..........LL B., '06
Lawyer,
Fairfax Court House, Va.

McCann, Thomas A........A. B , '07
Wholesale Lumber Salesman,
1730 Com. Nat. Bank Bldg,
Chicago, Ill.

McCannel, Alexander J.....M. D , '06
Physician,
Minot, N. D.

McCardle, Battle..........LL B , '94
Lawyer,   LL. M , '96
Vicksburg, Miss.

McCarthy, Charles A......LL. B , '06
Sec'y and Treas...........LL M., '07
The E. Wash Sav. Bank, Wash , D.C.

McCarthy, Charles C.......A. B , '05
Lawyer,
141 Milk St., Boston, Mass.

McCarthy, Daniel Joseph....A. B , '95
Physician,   A. M , '99, M D., '99
Davenport, Iowa.

McCarthy, James C.........A. B., '52

McCarthy, John J..........LL. B , '99,
                           LL M., '00

McCarthy, John Linus .....D D. S ,'03
Dentist,
Barrister's Hall, Brockton, Mass.

McCarthy, Joseph J.........A B , '07
Medical Student,
923 R St. N. W , Washington, D C.

McCarthy, William T.......LL B., '93
Lawyer,
Newberne, N. C.

McCauley, Francis Harney ...A. M., '99
Lawyer,
325 Clinton Ave , W Hoboken, N J.

McCauley, Joseph A ....M D , '72

McChesney, Charles E......M. D '67

McClellan, Frederick F.....LL B., '04
Lawyer and City Attorney,
507-9 Wyson Bldg , Muncie, Ind

McCloskey, Felix R........LL B , '92

McCloskey, Very Rev. George,
Deceased, Aug. 3, 1890,   D D, '89

McCloskey, Very Rev. John, D D, '75
Deceased Dec. 24, 1880.

McCloskey, Joseph J.........LL. B , '85

McCloskey, William C......LL B., '93
                           LL. M., '94

McCluskey, William J.......A. B , '89
Lawyer,
Kirk Block, Syracuse, N. Y.

McClure, James............A. B., '85
Physician,   M D., '99
Williamstown, N. J.

McCole, Thomas A ....LL B , '02
Lawyer,
170 Broadway, New York City

McComas, Hon. Louis E... LL. D , '02
Deceased, 1907, Washington, D. C.

McConnell, Frank Stevenson, D. D. S.,'04

McConnell, James C .... M. D., '68
Deceased, July 25, 1904

McCormick, Charles...... . M D., '61
Deceased, July, 1868.

McCormick, John Joseph ...M D , '04
Physician,
60 Montvale Ave., Woburn, Mass

McCormick, Michael A......LL B , '09
700 N. Capitol St , Washington, D. C.

McCoy, Edward A..........A B , '00

McCoy, George....... ......M. D., '57
Deceased, Oct. 8, 1880.

McCoy, Joseph S........ ...LL B , '93
Govt. Actuary,   LL. M , '94
Treasury Dept., Washington, D. C.

McCoy, Washington J .....M D , '80

McCreedy, Dr. Jeremiah ....A. B , '24
Deceased.   A. M., '32

McCullough, Charles E......LL. B , '06

McCullough, Frisby H .... .LL B, '89

McCullough, Henry L ... ..A B, '63
Deceased, 1873.

McDermid, Claude E.... ..M D., '08
Physician,
619 Fallowfield Ave, Charleroi, Pa

McDermott, Francis Borgia, A. B, '96
Stockport, Ohio.

McDermott, John A .... ..A. B, '84

McDermott, Rev. Thomas Joseph,
Priest,   A M., '96
St Patrick's Rectory, Jersey City, N. J

McDevitt, William M... ..LL. B, '94
                             LL M, '95

McDonald, Allen C.........LL B, '96
Lawyer,   LL. M, '97
Callahan Block, Dayton, Ohio.

McDonald, James C. ......LL M, '92

McDonald, James E.......:.LL. M., '06
Real Estate Broker,
San Benito, Texas.

McDonald, Richard Francis, D. D. S, '05
Dentist,
Manchester, N. H.

McDonald, Thomas Benton..M. D., '95
Physician,
Cumberland, Md.

McDonnel, Thomas F......LL. B., '07
Lawyer,
75 Goddard St., Providence, R. I.

McDonnell, Rev. Eugene de L., S J.,
Jesuit Priest,   A. B, '85
Gonzaga College, Washington, D C.

McDonogh, James S........LL. B., '01
Lawyer,
80 Wall St, New York City

McDonough, Francis Patrick, A B, '93

McDonough, Francis Xavier, LL B, '05
Lawyer,   LL. M, '06
80 Wall St, New York City.

McDonough, James A......:A. B, '63
H. C Mass., Deceased,
Austin Farms, Mass

McDowell, James Evans....LL B., '99

McElhinney, James W......A. B., '77
Lawyer,
120 Broadway, N. Y. City.

McElhone, James F........A. B., '86

McElhone, John J.........A.M., '83
Deceased, 1890.

McElmell, Com. J Jackson..A. M., '72
1931 Spring Garden St., Phila, Pa.

McElroy, Bernard W........LL B., '01
Lawyer,
4 Market St., Providence, R I.

McElroy, James Aloysius....A B, '02
Civil Engineer,
307 Golden Hill, Bridgeport, Conn

McElroy, James P.........A. B., '64
Deceased, 1866

McEniry, William Patrick ..A B, '03

McFarlan, Walter... ....A. B., '62
Clerk, War Dept,   A. M., '65
2905 13th St. N. W, Wash., D. C.

McFaul, John B...........A B, '87
Deceased, Dec. 23, 1890, N. Y. City.

McGahan, Charles F.......B. S., '81
Physician,
Bethlehem, N. H.; Aiken, S C

McGarrell, Andrew P.......:.LL. B., '92
Lawyer,   LL. M., '93
Benwood, W. Va.

McGary, Peter J..A. B., '53, A. M., '57

McGill, Grafton L...:.......LL. B., '99
Patent Lawyer,   LL. M., '00
15 William St., N. Y. City.

McGill, J. Nota..:.......LL. B, '87
Lawyer,   LL. M., 88
McGill Bldg., Washington, D. C.

McGirr, Joseph B..LL. B., '92, LL. M., '93

McGlue, George Percy......LL. B., '97
Lawyer,   LL. M., '98
643 La. Ave. N. W., Wash., D. C.

McGovern, Edward M...,..A. M., '64

McGovern, Thomas F......LL. B., '97

McGowan, Daniel F.........LL. B, '07
Claims Clerk, U. S. Forest Service,
Beck Bldg, Portland, Ore.

McGowan, Edward...:......A. B., '52
H. C. Mass.

McGowan, Louis A.........LL B, '09
Providence, R. I.

McGrath, Bernard F........A. B., '94
Physician,   M. D., '95
23 Bow St., Beverly, Mass.

McGrath, Rev. John B......A M., '94
Priest,
262 W. 118th St, N. Y. City.

McGrath, William V., Jr....B. S., '87
Real Estate,
712 Walnut St., Philadelphia, Pa.

McGuire, James C.........A. B, '96
Physician,   A M., '97
G. U. Med. Fac,
1725 H St, Washington, D. C.

McHenry, Philip J., Jr.. . . .A B, '87
A M., '91, LL B, '96
McIntire, Douglas...........M D, '01
McIntire, Hugh Henry.. .M D, '68
Deceased, Aug 13, 1906, Barnard, Vt.
McIntyre, T. C.............M D., '54
Deceased, 1862.
McIntyre, Andrew J.... . M D, '02
Physician,
3013 Cambridge Pl. N.W , Wash , D C.
McKaig, Dr Joseph F .. A B, '90
Physician, M D, '93
2420 Penn. Ave N. W., Wash , D. C.
McKay, Augustus Francis...M D, '72
Retired,
Colorado Springs, Colo
McKechnie William G.. ..A B., '90
Lawyer,
366 Elm St., Springfield, Mass
McKee, Fred..............LL B, '95
Lawyer, LL M, '96
610 13th St. N. W., Washington, D C.
McKenna, Bernard Charles..A B, '03
Lawyer,
41 Wall St , N. Y. City
McKenna, Daniel P. J... ..LL B, '07
Lawyer, LL M, '08
406 5th St. N. W., Washington, D C.
McKenna, Henry C...... ..LL B, '08
Clerk,
Treasury Dept , Washington, D C
McKenna, Royal T.... LL B, '08
Lawyer, LL M, '09
1446 R. I. Ave. N. W , Wash , D C.
McKeon, Frank H . ...M D, '02
Physician,
Westerly, R. I.
McLaughlin, D. J...........A B, '88
Deceased, June, 1905,
San Francisco, Cal
McLaughlin, Francis J A B, '83
Real Estate,
43 Tremont St , Boston, Mass.
McLaughlin, Hugh E A M , '96
Civil Engineer,
949 Pelham Ave , New York City
McLaughlin, James A . . . LL M ,'05
McLaughlin, James F A B, '60
Deceased, 1903, A M , '62, LL D., '89
New York City.
McLaughlin, James W. ...M D, '08
Physician,
Mercy Hospital, Pittsburg, Pa

McLaughlin, John D. .. A B, '83
Lawyer, A M, '89
730 Tremont Bldg , Boston, Mass
McLaughlin, Joseph I.......A B, '08
Agent,
Care Ginn & Co , 29 Beacon St ,
Boston, Mass
McLaughlin, William L . A B, '82
Lawyer, A M, '84, LL B, '84
Deadwood, S. Dak
McLeod, James M. ...... A B, '57
Deceased, Feb 11, 1897, A M, '60
Texas.
McLeod, Wilfred M........M D, '76
McLoughlin, Peter J.......LL B, '97
Lawyer, LL M,'98
340 Main St , Worcester, Mass
McLoughlin, William I......LL B, '95
Lawyer,
340 Main St , Worcester, Mass
McMahon, John J...........LL B, '04
Lawyer,
918 F N. W , Washington, D C.
McMahon, John J...........LL B, '09
Lawyer,
1212 N. Capitol St , Washington, D C.
McMahon, Rev. John W.....D D, '89
Priest,
St Mary's Church, Charlestown, Mass.
McMahon, Richard.........LL B, '07
Lawyer,
918 F St. N. W., Washington, D C
McMannus, Joseph..........LL B., '07
Lawyer,
McManus, Francis Patrick..A B, '80
Lawyer,
Davidson Bldg , Jersey City, N J.
McManus, Joseph .... .LL B, '04
LL M,'05
McMullen, F. P......... ...LL B, '81
McNally, Col Valentine, U. S A,
M. D, '67, A M , '69, LL D, '89
The Hamilton, Washington, D C
McNamara, Frank B.......D D S ,'03
Dentist,
26 Thomas Park, So. Boston, Mass.
McNamara, Robert Emmett, LL B, '05
Lawyer, LL M,'06
416 5th St , Washington, D C
McNamara, Stuart...... A B, '97
Lawyer, A. M, '98, LL B, '01
2409 18th St , Washington, D C
McNamara, William F ......LL B, '04
Lawyer,
53 State St , Boston, Mass

McNeal, Rev. Mark J., S. J. A. B., '93
Jesuit Priest,
Georgetown College, Wash, D C

McNeir, Charles S.........LL B, '92
LL M, 93

McNeir, George..LL. B, '81· LL M, '82
Vice-President, W. & J Sloane,
Broadway and 18th St, N. Y. City.

McNeirny, Michael J........LL B, '77
Lawyer,
132 Main St., Gloucester, Mass

McNish, Alvin M..........LL. B, '95
LL M, '96

McNulty, Alexander C.....LL M, '88

McNulty, Frederick J........M. D, '60
Deceased, June 14, 1897, Boston, Mass.

McQuaid, George J.........LL. B., '94
Lawyer,
Fort Scott, Kansas.

McQuaid, William P........A. B, '64
H. C., Mass., Priest,
9·Whitmore St., Boston, Mass

McQuillan, Francis.........M. D, '03
Physician,
204 Penn. Ave. S. E, Wash, D C

McQuirk, Rev. John.........D D, '84
Priest,
113 E. 117th St., New York City.

McRae, Irwin C........\...LL. B, '96
Timberman,
Calvert, Ala.

McSheehy, Thomas......... LL. B, '84

McSherry, James...........A B, '33

McSherry, William D.......A B, '42

McSorley, Charles D........LL. B, '92
LL M., '93

McTarnaghan, Arthur.......LL. B, '09
Dansville, N. Y.

McVary, Stephen A.......·..M D, '80

Mabrey, Richard L..........LL. B., '96

Maclay, Joseph P..........M. D, '08
Physician,
Chambersburg, Pa.

Macdonald, Alexander A....M. D., '95
Physician,
125 Blue Hill Ave., Boston, Mass.

Macdonald, Clarence J......A. M., '97

Macdonald, Martin A.......LL. B, '93
LL. M., '94

MacDonald, Michael R......M. D., '95
Physician,
Lourdes, Nova Scotia·

Macdonald, T Howard ....A M, '97
Physician,
Port Hawkesburg, Nova Scotia.

Machen, Francis Stanislaus..M D, '01
G U. Med Fac,
1314 16th St. N. W, Wash, D C.

Mackall, Bruce McVean.....M. D., '03
Physician,
1041 Lunalilo St., Honolulu, Hawaii.

Mackall, James McV .. .. A B, '70
A. M., '74, M D., '74
Deceased, June 25, 1909, Wash, D. C.

MacKaye, Harold Steele ....LL B., '91
Patent Lawyer, LL M., '91
2 Rector St., N. Y. City

Mackey, Beekford..........LL. B, '83

Mackey, Crandal............LL. B., '89
Lawyer and Commonwealth Atty., Va.
416 5th St. N. W., Washington, D. C.

Mackin, Very Rev. Dean Thomas, V. G.,
A B, '71· A M, '89
Deceased Feb. 15, 1905, Rock Is., Iowa.

Mackley, Arthur R.........LL. B, '04
Clerk, LL. M, '05
Interstate Com. Com, Wash, D C.

MacMahon, Paul William Arthur,
Manuf. and Exporter, A. B, '98
Room 1012, 8 Bridge St. N Y. City.

MacMahon, Thomas, Jr.....A. B, '00
Business, 8 Bridge St. N. Y. City.

Macnair, Augustine W.... LL B, '08
Lawyer,
622 Citizens Bk. Bldg, Norfolk, Va

Macnamee, Arthur Munson .M. D., '98
Physician, G. U. Med. Fac
938 P St. N. W., Wash., D. C.

MacShane, Col James. .....A. M, '58

Maddox, George Edmondson, LL B., '99
Lawyer,
Rome, Ga.

Madeira, Francis P..........LL B, '96

Madigan, Albert W..,......A B, '72
Houlton, Me. A M., '89

Madigan, James C..........A. M., '50

Madigan, Hon John B......A. B., '83
Lawyer, A. M., '89
Houlton, Me

Madigan, John J..........M D, '09
Intern, Garfield Hospital, Wash., D. C.

Madigan, Patrick S..........A. B, '08
Medical Student,
432 Nichols Ave., Wash., D. C.

Madison, B. F.............M. D, '84
Physician,
417 B St S. E, Washington, D. C.

Magale, Joseph F..........A. B, '91
Deceased.

Magee, M. D'Arcey........M. D, '96
1355 Corcoran St., Wash, D. C.

Magie, Edward R..........LL. M.,'99
Law Clerk,
Dept. of Com. and Labor, Wash, D. C.

Maginnis, Charles B........A B., '62
H. C., Mass., Deceased, July 6, 1867.

Maginnis, Charles H........LL. B, '92

Magruder, Caleb C., Jr.....LL. B, '97
Clerk,
U. S. Treasury Dept., Wash, D. C.

Magruder, Caleb C.........A. M., '34
Deceased.

Magruder, Caleb Clarke......A. B, '58
Lawyer,   A. M, '61
Clerk of Maryland Court of Appeals,
Com. Nat. Bank Bldg, Wash, D. C.

Magruder, George Lloyd.....M. D, '70
Physician, G. U. Med. Fac., A. M, '71
Stoneleigh Court, Washington, D C

Magruder, Mercer Hampton, LL. B, '98
Lawyer,
Upper Marlboro, Md.

Maguire, Charles F., Jr.....LL B, '05
Lawyer,   LL. M, '06
Hornell, N. Y.

Maguire, Dominic..........A. B., '52
H. C, Mass., Deceased.   A. M, '58

Maguire, Dominic..........A. M, 58

Maguire, Francis S.........LL B, '04
Lawyer,   LL. M.,'05
908 G St. N. W., Washington, D C.

Maguire, Joseph I..........LL. B, '05
1376 V St., Washington, D. C.

Maguire, Robert F.........LL B, '09
, Toledo, Ohio.

Maher, Benedict F..........A. B, '97
Augusta, Me.

Mahoney, Ed. Joseph.......A. M, '93
Physician,   M D, '95
250 Maple St, Holyoke, Mass.

Mahoney, John J...........LL B, '03

Mahoney, Matthew P.......A. B., '06
Medical Student.
46 Butterfield St, Lowell, Mass.

Mahony, Daniel W.........LL B, '02
Lawyer,
505 Bay State Bldg, Lawrence, Mass.

Mahony, William F........LL. B., '96
Patent Lawyer,
1203 Girard St. N W., Wash, D. C.

Major, Daniel G...........A. M., '59
Deceased.

Major, Henry..............A. B, '64
Lawyer,   A. M., '66
45 Broadway, New York City.

Major, John J.............A. B., '64
Deceased, 1889.   A. M., '72

Malabre, Alfred L.........M. D., '08
Physician,
603 West 184th St, New York City.

Malcom, Dr. Granville.....M. D., '67
Real Estate and Loans,
700 Ernest-Cranner Bldg, Denver, Col.

Mallan, Thomas F.........M. D, '80
Physician,
820 Conn. Ave. N. W., Wash., D. C.

Mallory, Hon. Stephen R....A. B, '69
                      A. M, '71, LL. D, '04
Deceased, Dec. 23, 1907, while U. S.
Senator from Fla.....Pensacola, Fla.

Malone, E. Halsey..........LL. B, '08
Lawyer,
24 Broad St, New York City.

Malone, Henry D., A. B., '85, LL. B., '87
Lawyer,   LL. M.,'88, A. M., '88
336 Adams St. N. E, Wash, D. C.

Malone, James B...........LL. B., '06
Lawyer,
Fairbanks Bldg, Springfield, Ohio.

Malone, John..............M. D., '56
Physician,
Dundee, N. Y.

Maloney, John M..........M. D., '07
Physician and Surgeon,
559 Liberty St., Springfield, Mass.

Malony, John M...........M. D., '70

Malony, William Redfield Proctor,
Lawyer,   LL B, '03, LL. M., '04
47 Cedar St, New York City.

Mandan, Philip A.........A. B., '58

Mangan, Michael F.........LL. B., '03
Lawyer,   LL. M., '05

412 5th St. N. W., Washington, D. C.

Mangan, William J.........LL. B., '97

Manly, Clement............A. B., '76
Lawyer,
Winston, N. C.

Mann, George M..........LL. B, '07
Lawyer,
612 F St. N. W, Wash, D. C.

Mann, Harry E.............A M, '89
Lawyer,
100 E. Lexington St., Baltimore, Md.

Manning, John N..........LL M, '86
Clerk,
War Dept., Washington, D. C

Manogue, William H.......LL B, '86
Lawyer,
509 E Capitol St, Washington, D C.

Mansell, Edward R, Hon...M D., '88
England.

Manson, C. Farraud.........LL. B., '09
Canton, So. Dak.

Marble, John O.............M. D, '68
Physician,
16 Murray Ave, Worcester, Mass.

Marbury, Charles C.........M. D, '93
Physician, G. U. Med. Fac.,
1015 16th St. N. W., Wash, D. C.

Marbury, William..........A. B, '43
Deceased, Dec. 18, 1879.

Marcy, William L...........LL B, '85
                        LL. M., '86

Markey, James F............LL. B, '01
Clerk,
1413 5th St. N. W., Wash, D. C.

Markriter, John J..........M. D., '82
Deceased, July 13, 1891, Wash, D. C.

Marmion, William Vincent..A. M, '83
Physician,
1211 13th St. N. W., Wash, D. C.

Maroney, Edward B........LL M., '92

Marple, Raleigh W.........LL. B., '95

Marr, Samuel S.............M. D, '76
1318 Corcoran St., Wash., D. C.

Marsden, Francis Thomas....A. B., '09
472 E St. S. W., Washington, D. C.

Marshall, Cary A.......... LL. B., '07
Lawyer,
Markham, Va.

Marshall, George............A. B., '44

Marshall, John P...........A B., '59
Deceased.

Marshall, P. J..............D. D. S,'02

Marshall, Percival H.......LL B., '95
Lawyer,
Columbian Bldg, Wash., D. C.

Marshall, T. W. M.........LL. D, '72
Deceased, Dec. 14, 1877, Surrey, Eng.

Marshell, Cloud ....LL B, '08
Special Agent,
Interstate Commerce Commission,
Wash, D. C.

Marstelleo, Massillon H.....LL B, '74

Martell, Charles J..........LL. B., '99
Lawyer,   LL. M, '00
1101-2 Barrister's Hall, Boston, Mass.

Martell, Leon Alphonse.....M. D., '08
Physician,
389 Front St., Weymouth, Mass.

Martin, F. P., Jr...........LL. B., '83
Lawyer,
Johnstown, Pa.

Martin, Frederick R........LL. B., '09
Anniston, Ala.

Martin, James J.............A. B, '01

Martin, James O............A. B., '59
Deceased.

Martin, John H.............LL. B, '90
Lawyer,   LL. M., '91
Fendall Bldg., Washington, D. C.

Martin, Hon. John M.......A. M., '91
Deceased.   LL. D., '94

Martin, John T.............LL. B., '82
Lawyer,
Williams Bldg, Scranton, Pa.

Martin, Robert H..........LL. B., '94
Clerk,   LL. M., '95
U. S. Treasury Dept., Wash., D. C.

Martin, Villard.............LL. B., '08
Lawyer,
Muskogee, Okla.

Martin, Walter Stanislaus...A. B., '96
Claus Spreckels Bldg.,
San Francisco, Cal.

Martinson, Joseph E........LL. B., '96
                          LL. M., '97

Martyn, Francis G..........LL. B., '90
                          LL. M., '91

Mason, E.....................A. B., '23
Deceased.

Mason, Hugh L.............LL. B., '73

Mason, John E.............M. D., '68

Masterson, Daniel Stephen...LL. B., '02
Private Secretary,   LL. M., '03
The Rochambeau, Wash., D. C.

Matthews, William.........LL. B., '05
Law Clerk,   LL. M., '07
Treasury Dept., Wash., D. C.

Mattingly, Charles M.......LL. B., '07
Lawyer,
Columbian Bldg, Wash., D. C.

Mattingly, Francis Carroll...LL. B., '97
Deceased, Mch. 5, 1908,   LL. M., '98
Washington, D. C.

Mattingly, Joseph Carbery...A. B., '93
Lawyer,   LL. B., '95, LL. M., '96
Fendall Bldg, Washington, D. C.

Mattingly, Leonard H.......LL B , '98
Public Accountant,   LL. M , '00
740 15th St. N. W., Wash., D C.

Mattingly, Robert E........LL. B., '91
Lawyer,   LL. M., '92
472 La. Ave N. W , Wash., D. C

Maurer, Robert A...........LL B , '06
Teacher,
Central High School, Wash., D C

Maury, Matthew F , U S. N., A. M , '45
Deceased, Jan. 31, 1873, Lexington, Va.

Mauss, Richard G...........M D , '72
Deceased, April 30, 1891.

Maxey, James H............LL. M., '02
Lawyer,
Shawnee, Okla.

Mayer, Robert Daniel.......M. D., '95

Mayo, George Upshur.......A. M , '89
Deceased, Feb. 3, 1896.

Mayock, Peter P....:.......M. D , '08
Physician,
Miners Mills, Pa.

Mayock, Thomas J.....:....D. D. S ,'09
Dentist,
Miners Mills, Pa.

Mead, F. W................M D., '58
Public Health, U. S. Marine Hospital
Service, Wash., D. C.

Mead, Theodore............M. D., '69
Med. Exam Bureau of Pensions,
928 23d St , Washington, D. C.

Mellen, Edward L..........B. S., '81

Melling, George............LL. B., '09
Greensboro, N. C.

Melville, George Wallace....LL. D , '99
Rear Admiral U. S. N.,
615 Walnut St , Philadelphia Pa.

Mercer, Claude.............LL. B , '96
Lawyer,
Hardinsburg, Ky.

Mercier, Hon Honore......LL. D., '89
Deceased, Oct. 30, 1894

Meredith, Edward C , Jr.....LL. B , '99

Menke, John R .. .. M D , '80
Deceased Sept 30, 1882.

Merrick, Richard T.........LL. B , '96
Chicago, Ill.   LL. M ,'97

Merrick, Richard T.........LL. D , '73
Deceased, June 23, 1885.

Merrick, Col William D....A M., '31
Deceased 1870,
U. S. Senator from Maryland.

Merrick, Hon. William M...LL. D., '75
Deceased, Feb 4, 1889.

Merrill, H Clay...LL B , '91' LL. M., '92

Merritt, Addis D , LL B , '87' LL M., '88

Merritt, Edgar Bryant.......LL. B , '98

Merritt, Frank C...........LL B , '09
Houlton, Me

Merrow, David W..........LL B , '87
Lawyer,   LL. M , '90
Omaha, Nebr.

Metzger, Percy..LL. B., '88' LL M., '89
Lawyer,
472 La. Ave. N. W., Wash , D. C.

Meyer, Robert ....LL B , '01
Lawyer,
1233 Pa. Ave , Wash, D C.

Meyerhardt, Louis ....LL. B , '86

Meyers, William F.........LL. B , '91
Assistant Secretary,   LL M , '92
District Commission, Wash., D C

Michener, Algeron S.......LL. B , '93
Lawyer,   LL M., '94
Brownsville, Pa.

Middleton, Johnson V. D....M D., '55
Deceased, January 29, 1907.

Milburn, Joseph W..........LL B , '09
Hagerstown, Md.

Miles, Matthew James.......A M , '98
Lawyer,
305 1st Ave , Cedar Rapids. Iowa

Millard, Edward M........A. B , '32
Deceased, 1882, at Grand Coteau, La.

Miller, Charles A...........LL B , '96

Miller, Charles Colden......A. B , '04
Lawyer,   LL. B , '06
Colorado Bldg , Wash , D C.

Miller, Charles H.......... M. D., '72

Miller, James ....M. D , '99
Physician,
Corning, Perry County, Ohio

Miller, James E............LL B , '75

Miller, James H , LL. B , '97' LL. M ,'98

Miller, John S ....M D , '65
Deceased, Mch. 1, 1908, Redlands, Cal.

Miller, Jozach...............A. B , '04
Banking,
Belton, Tex.

Miller, Samuel F...........LL. D., '72

Miller, W. W..............M. D., '69

Miller, Wilbur G. ..:......LL B , '04

Millott, Augustus F........LL B , '08
Secretary,   LL M.,'09
1403 R. I. Ave , Washington, D. C.

Millot, Eugene.............LL. B , '09
Chicago, Ill.

Millrick, Daniel A.........:....LL B, '04
Clerk, LL M, '05
526 12th St. N. E, Wash, D. C.

Mills, Charles A..... .. ...LL. B, '89
Lawyer, LL M, '90
1415 R I. Ave, Washington, D C.

Mills, Ellis.. ...LL. B, '87, LL M, '88

Miner, Francis Hannibal....M D, '95
Physician,
300 E. Capitol St, Washington, D C

Minnick, W. H. H ....M D, '73
Deceased, Aug. 24, 1904, Wash, D. C.

Minor, Louis J.............LL B, '99
Lawyer,
N. W. Corner Pub Sq, Aurora, Mo

Mitchell, Charles Piquette. .A. B., '93
LL B, '95

Mitchell, George D.........LL B, '89
LL. M, '90

Mitchell, Herbert Francis .LL. B, '04
Examiner,
Civil Service Com, Wash, D C.

Mitchell, Paul V............LL B, '09
120 W. St N. W., Washington, D C

Mitchell, Richard Clarke....A M, '97
Draftsman,
Care Robert Mitchell Furniture Co,
Cincinnati, Ohio

Mitchell, William Ansel . ..LL B, '94
Editor and Publisher,
Columbus, Kans.

Mitchell, William M .. .. .M. D, '70
Deceased, June 15, 1908, Ferndale, Cal

Mock, James K.............LL. B., '97
Law Examiner,
General Land Office, Wash, D. C

Mohrman, Henry Joseph....A. M, '02
Real Estate,
216 Wainwright Bldg, St Louis, Mo

Mohun, Barry..............LL B, '96
Lawyer, LL M, '97
1414 F St. N. W, Washington, D. C

Mohun, Philip V...........LL B, '93
U. S. N. Retired,
New Rochelle, N. Y

Molloy, John..............LL. B, '06
LL. M, '07

Monaghan, Hugh I.........LL. B., '05
Law Student,
533 N 25th St, Philadelphia, Pa.

Monaghan, Joseph Patrick...A. B, '96
Lawyer,
Wilkinson Bldg, Shenandoah, Pa.

Monaghan, Martin M ....LL. B., '98

Monohan, Edward Sheehan, Jr,
Stock Farmer, A B, '05, A M, '06
St Matthews, Ky.

Montgomery, Charles P.....LL B., '97
Lawyer, Chief of Customs Division,
U. S. Treasury Dept, Wash, D C

Montgomery, Denny . ....LL B, '96
LL M '98

Montgomery, Francis Stanton, A M, '05
Lawyer, Ph D, '07, LL. B, '07
Los Angeles Tr. Bldg, Los Angeles,Cal.

Montgomery, George C... ..LL. B., '94
Lawyer,
Alexandria, Va.

Montgomery, James P . .B S, '88
LL. B, '89

Montgomery, Joseph W.....A. B, '09
Lake Providence, La.

Montgomery, Hon Zachariah,
Deceased, LL D, '89

Moon, John B..............LL. B, '95
Lawyer, LL. M, '97
Fenton Bldg, Portland, Ore.

Mooney, Henry F..... . . LL. B, '95
Real Estate, LL. M., '96
707 G St N W, Washington, D C.

Mooney. Paul..............A B, '21
Deceased,

Moore, Charles T ... . LL B, '83
Inventor,
31 E. 17th St, New York City.

Moore, J B . .. . . M D, '71
Deceased, Oct 1908, Wash, D C.

Moore, J Hall...... ...M D, '54
Deceased, Dec 28, 1905, Richmond, Va.

Moore, John Edward. .. .. A B., '00
Woburn. Mass

Moore, Samuel Broder.. M D, '97
Physician,
811 Prince St, Alexandria, Va

Morales, Aug Jose ....LL. D, '59
Deceased,

Moran, Charles Vincent A B, '02

Moran, Rev. Dennis C . . A B, '62
H C, Mass, Deceased, July 23, 1889.

Moran, James Linus.... ...A B, '08
318 Hutchinson Ave, Swissvale Sta,
Pittsburg, Pa

Moran, John F...... ....M D, '87
Physician, A B., '94
2426 Pa Ave, Washington, D. C.

Moran, John J..............M. D, '08
Physician,
Lyons, N. Y.

Moran, Timothy J.........A. B, '01
Oculist,
628 Fulton Bldg, Pittsburg, Pa.

Morgan, Cecil...........LL. B, '87
Lawyer,   LL. M, '88
Macon, Ga.

Morgan, D. Oswald.......LL. B., '96
                          LL. M., '97

Morgan, Daniel H.... ...LL. B, '95
Lawyer,
Cookeville, Tenn.

Morgan, Daniel P....... .LL B, '93
                          LL M, '94

Morgan, Ethelbert C........Ph. D., '89
Deceased, May 5, 1891, Wash. D. C.

Morgan, Haze.............LL B., '99
Lawyer,
Clarksburg, W. Va.

Morgan, J. Dudley.........A B., '81
Physician, G. U. Med. Fac, M. D, '85
919 15th St. N. W., Wash, D. C.

Morgan, James E..........A B, '05
Banker,
Neola, Iowa

Morgan, J. Felix..........M. D, '58
Physician,
Leonardtown, Md

Morgan, James LaMotte.....A. B, '78
Deceased, Jan. 30, 1904, New York.

Morgan, Joseph V.........LL. B., '09
Leonardtown, Md.

Morgan, William M........LL. M, '99
Lawyer,
Commercial Block, Moscow, Idaho

Morgan, Zachariah R.......M D, '80
Physician,
Mechanicsville, Md.

Moroney, Edward B........LL. B, '91
Lawyer,
Pontiac, Mich.

Moross, W. Paul Dwight....A B, '88
Manager Cement Mfg. Co,
Chattanooga, Tenn.

Morrill, Charles P.........M. D., '66
Physician,
62 Elm St, North Andover, Mass.

Morrill, Chester............LL B., '09
The Willson, Washington, D. C.

Morris, Ballard.............LL. M., '87

Morris, James L...........A. B, '82
Lawyer,
403-404 Hollenback Coal Ex. Bldg,
Wilkesbarre, Pa.

Morris, John Penn.........A. B, '82

Morris, Hon. Martin F......LL. D., '77
Asso. Jus. of the Court of Appeals,
Retired, Washington, D. C.

Morris, P. Pemberton.......A. B., '36
Deceased, 1888,   A. M., '40
Philadelphia, Pa.

Morse, Alexandria Porter...LL. B., '72
Lawyer and Author,
1505 Pa. Ave. N. W, Wash, D. C.

Morthrop, George...........LL. B, '87

Mortimer, Charles G........LL. B., '95
1st Lieut. Art, U. S. A,   LL. M., '96
War Dept., Washington, D. C.

Morton, Joseph F..........LL. B., '07
Lawyer,
Spokane, Wash.

Moulton, Charles L.........M. D, '87

Moulton, Clarence E........LL. B, '88
Lawyer,
Board of Trade Bldg, Portland, Ore.

Moulton, Irwin B..........LL. B., '91
Assistant Chief,
Bureau of Engraving and Printing,
Washington, D. C.

Moynihan, Dennis L.........LL. B, '02

Mudd, Jeremiah ....A. M, '24
Deceased. ,

Mudd, Sydney E, Jr........A. B., '06
La Plata, Md.   LL. B., '09

Mueller, Carl C............LL. B., '08
Merchant,   LL. M, '09
2621 13th St N. W., Wash., D C.

Mueller, J. Max........Mus. Doc., '82

Mulcahy, Daniel D.........M D., '99
Physician,
1216 N. Capitol St, Wash, D. C

Mulcare, James H..........LL. B, '09
North Adams, Mass

Mulhall, Francis J ....LL B, '99
Asst. to Finance Clerk,   LL. M., '00
Bureau of Medicine and Surgery,
Navy Dept, Washington, D. C.

Mulhearn, Charles E........LL. B., '02
Lawyer,
75 Westminster St, Providence, R. I.

Mulhearn, F. Richard......D D S,'04
Dentist,
25 Aborn St., Providence, R. I.

Mullaly, James F...........LL. B., '93
Lawyer,   LL. M., '94
National Union Bldg., Wash, D. C.

Mullaly, James P..........A. B, '73
Deceased, Spokane Falls, Wash.

Mullally, George LeGuere....A. B , '03
Actor, A. M., '04
Care Klaw and Erlanger, N. Y. City.

Mullan, Frank Drexel......A. B., '93
Journalist,
1 Madison Ave., New York City.

Mullan, Horace E..........LL. B., '86

Mullen, Charles Vincent.....A. M., '05
Lawyer, Ph. D., '07, LL. B., '07
Exchange Bldg., Denver, Colo.

Mulligan, Rev. John.........A. B., '50
H. C., Mass , A. M., '52
Deceased, Dec. 16, 1861.

Mullins, Geo. Holland.......A. B., '09
North Yakima, Washington.

Mulloney, Daniel C..........LL. B., '09
Portland, Me.

Mulvanity, Albert F.........M. D., '06
Physician,
123 Palm St., Nashua, N. H.

Mulvihill, John Aloysius.....A. B., '96
LL. B., '98

Muncaster, Alexander........LL. B , '91
Lawyer, G.W.U.Med.C.Fac, LL. M., '92
482 La. Ave., Washington, D. C.

Muncaster, Stewart B......M. D., '85
Physician,
907 16th St. N. W. Wash, D C.

Mundell, Joseph Joshua......M. D., '03
. Physician,
302 Nichols Ave., Anacostia, D. C.

Munger, M. J..............M. D., '65

Munhall, Herbert Nicholas..A. B., '09
701 S. Linden Ave., Pittsburg, Pa.

Munson, Leonard Walter....M. D., '96
Physician,
Stamford, Conn.

Murchison, Kenneth S.......LL. B , '86
Lawyer, LL. M., '99
320 Fifth Ave., New York City.

Murdock, Edwin F..........LL. B., '89

Murnigham, Richard J......D. D. S.,'07
Dentist,
9 Elk St., Amsterdam, N. Y.

Murphey, John J...........LL. B., '92
Superintendent,
Station D, City P. O., Wash., D. C.

Murphy, Charles J.........LL. B , '92
Lawyer, LL. M., '93
Century Bldg., Washington, D. C.

Murphy, Charles J..........LL. B , '99
LL. M , '00

Murphy, Cornelius A........A. B , '04
6 Jacques St., Somerville, Mass.

Murphy, Daniel..LL. B , '96, LL. M., '97

Murphy, Daniel A.........D. D. S.,'07
Dentist,
309 Hanover St., Fall River, Mass.

Murphy, Daniel C., Hon.....LL. B., '90
Lawyer, LL. M., '91
Mut. Sav. Bk. Bldg., San Franc., Cal.

Murphy, Edward II.........A. B , '90
Lawyer,
Keenan Bldg., Troy, N. Y.

Murphy, Edward V., Jr......LL. B., '05
Special Agent General Land Office.
2511 Penn. Ave., Washington, D C.

Murphy, James R............A. B , '72
Lawyer, B. C., Mass ,
27 School St., Boston, Mass.

Murphy, James A., A. B., '63, A. M., '66

Murphy, James Wilmot......LL. B., '99
Official Reporter, LL. M., '00
U. S. Senate, Washington, D. C.

Murphy, John A............LL. B., '06
Lawyer, LL. M., '07
Newport, R. I.

Murphy, John A............LL. B , '09
Clerk,
3268 P. St. N. W., Washington, D. C.

Murphy, John F.............LL. B., '04
Lawyer,
227 Colman Bldg., Seattle, Wash.

Murphy, John J............LL. B , '94
Lawyer, LL. M , '95
Scranton, Pa.

Murphy, John Maxwell......A. B , '02
Suburb, N. C.

Murphy, Hon. Lester T......LL. B., '06
Probate Judge,
4 Welyhasset St., Providence, R. I.

Murphy, Martin.............A. B , '95

Murphy, Patrick J.........M. D , '73
Deceased, Oct. 3, 1891, A. M , '73
Washington, D. C.

Murphy, Richard...........LL. B., '91
Englewood, N. J.

Murphy, Thomas J.........LL. B., '74

Murphy, William A.........A. M , '92
2 Ainsly St., Ashmont, Mass.

Murphy, William Joseph.....LL. B., '97

Murray, George F..........A. B , '61
Lawyer,
20 Nassau St., New York City.

Murray, Lawrence O........LL. M., '95
Comptroller of Currency,
Treasury Dept., Washington, D. C.

Murray, Neal T.............A. B, '73
Deceased, 1898   LL. B, '76
Murray, Thomas...........LL B, '76
Murray, Thomas J.........LL. B, '94
Murrin, Joseph S..........M. D, '07
Physician,
Carbondale, Pa.
Muruaga, Hon Emiliode....LL D, '89
Deceased.
Nadeau, Arthur J..........LL. B., '04
Lawyer,
Fort Kent, Me.
Nally, Charles F............M D, '68
Deceased, Mch. 4, 1876, Wash, D. C.
Nally, Denis...............A. B., '27
Deceased.
Nash, John A...............LL B, '08
Law Clerk, Office Asst., Att'y Gen'l,
P. O. Dept., Washington, D. C.
Nast, Conde Montrose.......A. B. '94
Pres of Vogue Co.,   A. M, '95
Vice-Pres. of Home Pattern Co,
6206 Metropolitan Tower, N Y. City.
Naylor, Levi W.............LL. M, '87
Naylor, Van Denson........M D, '60
Neale, Augustine W.........A B, '60
105 I St. N. W., Wash., D. C.
Neale, Francis..............A. M, '69
Neale, James Pye...........A B, '59
Deceased, Philadelphia, Pa.
Neale, R A.................M. D, '70
Physician,
417 La Salle Ave, Chicago, Ill
Neas, William H., LL. B, '88, LL M, '89
Nee, Festus J..............D. D S, '06
Dentist,
317 Butler Exchange, Providence, R I.
Neel, William J., LL. B, '87, LL. M., '88
Neely, Edgar A.... ....LL. B, '05
Lawyer,
Atlanta, Ga.
Neely, John R....... .....M. D, '91
Physician,
2159 Clarendon Ave, Chicago, Ill
Neill, Charles P............A. B, '91
U. S. Commissioner of Labor,
1429 N. Y. Ave, Washington, D. C.
Neill, Thomas E...........M D., '08
Intern,
G. U. Hospital, Washington, D. C.
Neilson, Frederick K........LL. M., '07
Office of the Solicitor,
State Dept, Washington, D. C.

Neis, Claudius J............LL. B., '99
Nelligan John J............LL. B, '92
Lawyer,
Olathe, Kansas.
Nelms, William H ....LL M., '98
Special Examiner,
Bureau of Pensions, Montpelier, Vt.
Nelson, Cyrus W...........M. D, '09
Physician,
Stillwater, Okla.
Nelson, James Edward......M. D, '95
Physician,
10 B St. N. E, Washington, D C.
Nelson, Thomas Clement....A. B.; '96
Bank Auditor,
Kearney Co. Bk. Bldg, Lakin, Kansas
Nemmers, Erwin Plein......A M., '99
Ph. D., '00, LL. B; '01 LL. M., '02
Lawyer,
506 Germania Bldg., Milwaukee, Wis.
Netherland, Thomas H......LL. B., '95
Special Counsel, P. O Dept.,
Wash., D. C.
Neubeck, Francis L.........LL. B., '03
Lawyer and Notary,
422 Bond Bldg, Wash., D. C
Neuhaus, Paul Immanuel....LL. B., '83
LL. M., '84
Nevins, John C.............A. B, '46
Nevins, Joseph D...........LL. B, '92
Law Clk., Secretary Office, LL. M., '93
Treas. Dept., Wash., D. C
Newbern, John Melvin......M. D, '98
Physician,
Jarvisburg, N. C.
Newberne, R L. E.........M. D., '93
Newman, Charles R....... .A. B, '77
Lawyer,   LL. B., '80, LL. M, '81
902 F St N. W., Wash, D. C.
Newman, Enos S ....LL. B, '92
Lawyer,
1465 Harvard St, Wash, D C.
Newman, Henry M..........M. D., '76
Physician,
2403 Pa. Ave, Wash., D. C.
Newton, James Thornwell...LL. B., '95
Principal Examiner, Patent Office,
Wash, D. C.
Newton, Louis E............M. D., '68
Deceased, Feb. 3, 1899.
Niblack, William Caldwell....A. B., '74
Lawyer, V. Pres. Chicago Title & Trust
Co, 100 Washington St, Chicago, Ill.
Nichols, Edmund L...........LL. B., '87

Nichols, Henry J............A B., '89
277 Nichols St., Brooklyn, N. Y.

Nichols, John L.............LL B, '95

Nichols, Joshua.............A B, '39

Nicholson, John T..........LL. B, '78

Nicodemus, Bvt. Maj. William Joseph
Leonard, U. S. A.........A. M, '65
Deceased, Jan. 1879.   M D., '67

Nishio, Shohaku............M. D., '94

Noeker, Joseph John, Jr.....A. M., '98
Physician,   M. D, '02
Mullett St., Detroit, Mich.

Nolan, John M.............LL B, '01
25 Broad St., New York City.

Nolan Joseph A.............A. M., '65

Nolan, Lawrence F.........LL. B, '06
Lawyer,
Care Higgins & Fitzgerald, Paw-
tucket, R. I.

Nolan, Thomas J...........A. B., '02
Seminarian,
St. Bonaventure's Seminary,
Allegany, N. Y.

Noonan, Louis T., A. B., '95 LL. B, '97
Lawyer,   LL. M.,'98
146 Broadway, N. Y. City., N. Y.

Norcross, Frank H.........LL. B, '94
Chief Jusice of Supreme Court,
Carson City, Nev.

Norcross, George J.........M. D., '65

Nordlinger, Isaac W.........A. B., '83
Lawyer,   LL. B., '85, LL. M., '86
Stewart Bldg., Wash., D. C.

Normile, Judge James C....A. M, '67
Deceased, 1892.

Normoyle, John D..........LL. B, '98
Real Estate and In. Agt., LL. M., '99
Alex. Nat Bk. Bldg, Alexandria, Va.

Norris, Ralph W......   ..LL. B, '08
Lawyer,
New Windsor, Colo.

Norton, Frank P...........LL. B, '98
Lawyer,   LL. M., '99
Detroit, Mich.

Norton, John M..... ......LL. B.,'94
Lawyer,
Newton, Kansas.

Nourse, C. H..............M. D., '69
Physician,
Darnestown, Md.

Nourse, Upton Darby.......M. D., '00
Physician
Dawsonville, Md.

Nowlin, Homer Edgar......M. D., '96
Clerk,
War Dept, Washington, D C.

Noyes, George F ....LL. B, '86
Lawyer,   LL M., '86
98 Exchange St, Portland, Me

Nunez, Manuel I ....M. D, '05
Physician,
Arequipa, Peru, South America.

Nussa, Rafael Lopez.......M. D, '06
Physician,
San Juan, Porto Rico

Nye, Edwin B............ .LL B, '09
936 O St. N. W., Washington, D. C.

Obenchain, Charles Austin ..LL B, '99
Clerk,   LL. M.,'00
General Land Office, Wash., D. C.

Ober, George C............M. D, '82
Physician,
210 B St S. E, Washington, D. C.

Oblinger, Edward Vincent...A. B., '05
Finished Cotton Goods,
Care Grinnell, Willis & Co.,
44 Leonard St, New York City.

O'Brien, Hon. Denis....... LL D, '93
Deceased.

O'Brien, Dennis F........ LL. B, '01
Lawyer,
Times Bldg. Times Sq, N. Y. City.

O'Brien, Gen. Edward C....LL. D., '97

O'Brien, Edward D ....A. B, '90
Lawyer,
120 Broadway, New York City.

O'Brien, Edward M........LL. B, '09
Waterbury, Conn.

O'Brien, John Lawrence ... LL B., '99
Lawyer,   LL. M, '00

O'Brien, John.............A B, '55
St. F. X., New York.

O'Brien John F.............A. B., '96
Lawyer,
Hall of Records, New York City

O'Brien, John Henry........A. B, '04
Lawyer,   ,
128 School St, Clinton, Mass.

O'Brien, John P..A. M., '95, LL B, '97
Asst. Corp Counsel, City of N. Y.,
44 E. 23rd St., New York City.

O'Brien, Joseph P...........A. B, '80
Deceased, 1904, LL B., '82, A. M., '89
Adirondacks, N. Y.

O'Brien, Michael C..........LL. B, '06
Lawyer, Bur. Ptg,   LL M.,'07
610 3d St. N. W., Wash., D. C.

O'Brien, Michael J.........D. D. S.,'08
Dentist,
Warren, R I.

O'Brien, Miles M., Jr.......LL B., '99
Lawyer,   LL. M., '00
38 Park Row, New York City.

O'Brien, Thomas W........LL. B., '07
Lawyer,   LL M, '08
406 5th St. N. W., Washington, D. C.

O'Bryan, John Duross.......A. B, '62
Deceased, Mch. 1, 1904, A. M, '64
Paris, France.

O'Byrne, Dominic A........A. B, '51
Deceased, Feb. 17, 1896, Savannah, Ga.

O'Connell, Daniel...........LL. B., '86
Lawyer,
840-841 Pacific Bldg.,
San Francisco, Cal.

O'Connell, Jeremiah D......LL B, '80
                          LL M., '81

O'Connell, John J...........LL M, '87
The Revere, 1201 M St. N. W.,
Washington, D. C.

O'Connell, Ralph T.........LL. B., '07
Bangor, Me.

O'Connell, Richard F.......M. D, '94
Physician,
Wellston, Ohio.

O'Connor, F J..............M. D., '77
Deceased, Washington, D. C.

O'Connor, Charles E........A. B, '78
Deceased, 1899.

O'Connor, Charles Emmet..M. D, '95
Physician,
1309 13th St. N. W., Wash, D. C.

O'Connor, Jeremiah I.......A. B, '92
Dramatist,   LL. B, '94 LL. M, '95
101 2d St. N. E., Washington, D. C.

O'Connor, Joseph T.........M. D, '67
Physician, Retired,
Garden City, N. Y.

O'Connor, Michael F........A. B, '98
                          LL. B, '01
1811 35th St. N. W., Wash, D C.

O'Connor, Patrick J........LL. B, '80

O'Day, Charles F..........Ph. B, '89

O'Day, Daniel E............A. B, '89
Rye, N. Y.

O'Dea, Patrick H..........LL B., '94
Clerk,   LL M, '95
Navy Dept., Washington, D. C.

Odell, Willmot Mitchell.....LL. M., '00
Lawyer,
Cleburne, Tex.

O'Doherty, George..........LL. B., '84
                          LL. M., '85

O'Doherty, John D.........M. D, '88
Physician,
5 Locust St., Dover, N. H.

O'Donnell, Daniel J.........A. B., '89
Deceased, Mch. 3, 1893,   LL B., '92
Scranton, Pa.

O'Donnell, Edward Pius.....A. B., '02
Heckschersville, Pa.

O'Donnell, Patrick Henry...A. B, '92
Lawyer,   A. M., '93, LL. B., '94
911 Ashland Block, Chicago, Ill.

O'Donnell, Rev. William Aloysius,
Priest,   A. B., '94
48th St. and Lancaster Ave., Phila., Pa.

O'Donoghue, Daniel William, A. B., '97
           A. M., '98, Ph. D, '99, LL. B., '99
Lawyer,   LL. M., '00
412 5th St. N. W., Washington, D. C.

O'Donoghue, John Alphonso, A. M., '97
Physician,   M. D., '00
3311 N St. N. W., Washington, D. C.

O'Donovan, Charles........A. B., '78
Physician,   A. M., '88
5 E. Read St, Baltimore, Md.

Offutt, George W...........M. D., '74
Deceased, Sept. 13, 1878, Wash., D. C.

O'Flynn, Cornelius John.....A. B., '58
Lawyer,
Buhl Block, Detroit, Mich.

Ogden, Herbert Gouverneur, LL. M., '00
Patent Lawyer,
2 Rector St., New York City.

Ogden, Warren Greene......LL. B., '05
Patent Lawyer,
53 State St., Boston, Mass.

O'Gorman, Maurice J. C....A. B., '00
Real Estate and Builder,
Willis Ave. and 140th St., N. Y. City.

O'Halloran, Thomas M......LL. B., '92
Lawyer,
Braddock, Pa.

O'Hanlon, Michael..........LL. B, '99
Business,   LL. M, '00
1325 7th St. N. W., Wash., D. C.

O'Hara, Francis James......A. M., '01
Physician,   M. D., '04
15 N. Holden St, N. Adams, Mass.

O'Hara, James F...........M. D., '06
Physician,
Wilkesbarre, Pa.

O'Hara, John J.............LL. B., '04
Lawyer,
Hancock Chambers, Quincy, Mass.

O'Hara, The Very Rev. William Louis,
Priest, LL. D., 'o1
104 Greenwich St, Hempstead, N. Y.

O'Keefe, Rev. Charles M....D. D., '89
Deceased, Sept. 28, 1892.

O'Keeffe, Lawrence E. A....LL. B, '05
LL. M., '06

O'Laughlin, James P.......LL. B, '95
Lawyer, LL. M., '96
Clearfield, Clearfield Co., Pa.

O'Leary, Charles R.........LL. B., '98
Paymaster,
U. S. N. Dept., Washington, D. C.

O'Leary, Charles W........M. D., '72
Deceased.

O'Leary, John G............A. B., '95
Broker,
17 Battery Place, New York City.

O'Leary, Timothy S.........LL. B, '93
LL. M., '94

O'Leary, William Joseph....A. M., '94

Olesen, Robert............M. D., '05
Quarantine Officer,
Iloilo, P. I.

Oller, George E............LL. B, '05
Clerk, LL. M., '06
Census Office, Wash, D. C.

Olmsted, Edwin B..........M. D., '87
Special Pension Examiner,
Pension Office, Washington, D. C

O'Malley, Austin, A. M., '88, Ph. D., '89
Physician, M. D., '93
2228 S. Broad St., Phila., Pa.

O'Malley, Joseph...........M. D, '93
Physician,
2228 S. Broad St., Phila, Pa.

O'Neil, Albert Murray.......A. B., '04
Lawyer, A. M., '05, LL. B, '08
Binghamton, N. Y.

O'Neill, Eugene J. B........LL. B, '83
LL. M, '89

O'Neill, Francis J..........LL. B, '88
LL. M., '89

O'Neill, Ignatius P..........A. B. '80
Deceased, Aug. 8, 1898. A. M., '89
Summerville, S. C.

O'Neill, James F............A B, '83
A. M., '89

O'Neill, John B.............LL. B, '87
LL. M., '88

O'Neill, John H............A. B, '41
Deceased, Dec. 1890, Chicago, Ill.

O'Neill, John H............A M., '55

O'Neill, John Joseph........A. B., '94
Lawyer,
77 Bank St., Waterbury, Conn.

O'Neil, Joseph H...........A. B., '08
Law Student,
122 Seaver St., Boston, Mass.

O'Neill, Rev. Thomas Jeremiah Lantry,
C. S. P., Priest, A. B, '99
2630 Ridge Road, Berkeley, Cal.

O'Neill, William M. A.......LL. B., '99
Lawyer, Highland Falls, N. Y., and
188 Montague St., Brooklyn, N. Y

O'Neill, William E.........LL. B., '88
LL. M. ,'89

Ongley, A. Hugh...........LL. B, '97
Deceased, 1898.

Opisso, Antonio M.........LL. B., '03
Lawyer, Bar Examiner, LL. M., '04
31 Plaza Moraga, Manila, P. I.

Oppenheimer, Bernard ....A. B., '72
Deceased, Feb. 26, 1882.

O'Reilly, J................A. B., '36

O'Reilly, John Boyle........LL. B., '89
Deceased, Aug. 10, 1890.

O'Reilly, Thomas...........M. D., '89
Physician,
41 M St. N. W., Washington, D C

Orleman, Carl S............LL. B, '91
Chapin, Sacks Mfg, Co., LL. M., '95
Wash., D. C.

Orleman, Louis H., Jr.......LL. B., '94

Osborn, Harry S...........LL. B, '03

Osborne, Henry G..........LL. B., '88

Osburn, Alexander.........M. D., '68

Osenton, Charles W........LL. B., '95
Lawyer, LL. M, '95
Fayetteville, W. Va.

O'Shea, James Aloysius.......A. B, '99
A. M., '00, Ph. D., '01, LL. B., '02
Lawyer, Century Bldg., Wash, D. C

Osterman, Albert H.........LL B., '06
Bell Telephone Co., Philadelphia, Pa.

Osterman, Oscar H.........LL. B., '09
161 Maple St., Washington, D. C.

O'Sullivan, Rev. Florence T..A. B., '43
Jesuit Priest,
Deceased, Apr. 2, '07, Santa Clara, Cal.

O'Toole, Rev. Lawrence J...A. B, '72
B. C., Mass., Rector of St. Bernard's
Church, W. Newton, Mass.

Ourdan, Vincent L.........LL. B., '95

Owen, Frederick Wooster ...M. D., '67
Physician,
Morristown, N. J.

Owen, James W.............LL B , '08
Owens, Samuel Logan.......M D., '03
Physician, G. U. Med Fac,
2418 Pa. Ave N. W., Wash , D C.

Owens, William Dunlop .....M D, '01
Surgeon, U S Navy,
Navy Dept , Wash , D. C.

Owens, Winter.............LL. B., '98
Owings, William Randall.....A B , '01
A. M., '02, LL B , '04, Ph. L., '04
Lawyer,   LL M., '05, Ph. D , '05
6 Beacon St , Boston, Mass

Oxnard, George C...........B S., '79
Pace, Charles F.............LL B., '94
Lawyer, Starke, Fla.

Pace, Louis D, LL., B , '90, LL M.,'91
Principal Examiner,
Gen'l Land Office, Wash , D C.

Packard, Harry M..........LL. B , '97
Lawyer,   LL M , '98
412 5th St. N. W., Wash., D. C.

Paddock, Le Roy M........LL. B , '07
Lawyer,   LL M., '08
Lee Bldg., Oklahoma City, Okla.

Page, R. A ....M. D., '71
Deceased, 1898.

Paine, A. Elliot .... .M D , '65
Physician,
13 Clinton Ave., Brockton, Mass.

Painter, John Isaac.........LL. B , '98
Lawyer,   LL. M ,'99
Davenport, Iowa.

Paladoni, Frank S..........LL. B., '07
Lawyer,
Colorado Bldg., Washington, D C

Pallen, Conde Benoist ....A. B.,   '80
A. M., '83, LL D., '96
Author and Editor,
39 West 38th St , New York City.

Palmer, Dennis ...LL. B , '98, LL M , '99
3215 13th St. N. W., Wash , D. C.

Palmer, Oscar.... ....M. D., '64
Palmer, Theodore Sherman..M. D , '95
Palms, Charles Louis........Ph. B , '89
Trustee, Estate of Francis Palms,
Campau Bldg , Detroit, Mich.

Palms, Francis ....A. B , '04
Michigan Stove Co , Detroit, Mich.

Pardee, Dr. Edmund W.....D. D. S.,'06
Dentist,
317 Butler Exch., Providence, R. I.

Pardee, Munson D ....LL B , '98
Lawyer,   LL. M., '99
So. Norwalk, Conn.

Pargon, Augustine Joseph A , M. D ,   '05
Parke, Clarence Le Roy.....LL. B., '07
Library of Congress,   LL M., '08
Washington, D. C.

Parkhurst, Lincoln A ....LL B , '91
Lawyer,
Wampsville, N Y.

Parkinson, Clinton ....M. D , '69
Parks, Charles J........ .. ..LL. B , '04
Lawyer,
Goldfield, Nev.

Parrott, John, Jr...... .....A. B , '05
Law Student,
Parrott Bldg , San Francisco, Cal.

Parrott, P. Bishop...........LL B., '96
Parsons, Isaac...............A. B , '61
Parsons, John...............M. D , '70
Physician,
246 65th Pl , Chicago, Ill.

Paschal, George............LL. B , '76
Paschal, George............LL B , '06
Clerk, Pension Office,
413 4th St. N. W., Washington, D. C.

Paschal, Hon. George W.... LL. D , '75
Deceased, Feb. 16, 1878, Texas.

Pater, Alphonse J...........A. M , '06
603 S. 4th St , Hamilton, Ohio.

Patterson, Herbert Stewart...A. B , '98
Patterson, John C. C........LL B , '94
Lawyer,   LL M , '95
Interstate Commerce Commission,
Washington Grove, Md

Patterson, John Scott.......M. D , '70
Patterson, Rev. Richard J. A B , '63
H. C., Mass , Deceased, Dec. 31, 1900

Patterson, Thomas H........LL. B , '06
Lawyer,
Columbian Bldg., Wash., D C.

Pattison, Allen S....... ...LL. B., '89
Patent Lawyer,   LL M.,'90
629 F St. N. W., Washington, D. C.

Payn, Abbott Smith..........M. D , '95
Physician,
542 West 148th St , New York City.

Payne, Howard T....... ...M. D , '70
Deceased, Washington, D C.

Payne, James G..........LL D , '85
2112 Mass. Ave., Washington, D. C.

Payne, John Carroll.........A. B , '76
Lawyer,
Atlanta, Ga

Payne, Lewis A.............LL. B., '08
Insurance and Real Estate, LL. M.,'09
700-706 14th St. N. W., Wash. D C

Payne, Rev. W. Gaston.....A B, '79
Priest,
Clifton Forge, Va

Peabody, James H.. ... ...M D, '60
Deceased, Sept. 11, 1906, Omaha, Neb.

Pearman, Silas D..........LL. B, '09
Anderson, S. C.

Pearson, John Maxwell... .M D, '07
Physician,
Camp Verde, Ariz.

Pearson, Joseph W.... .....LL. B, '97
LL. M, '98

Pease, Harlow F..........A. B., '05
Law Student,
700 Clyman St, Watertown, Wis.

Peck, C. W.................M. D, '63

Peck, Hurbert E............LL. B, '90
Patent Lawyer, LL. M, '91
629 F St. N. W, Washington, D. C.

Peck, William D... ....LL. B, '95
Lawyer,
Milton, Ky.

Pell, George Pierce.........:.LL. B., '96
Lawyer,
Winston-Salem, N. C.

Pendergast, Robert Joseph ..A. B, '05
Lawyer,
59 S. 1st St, Fulton, N. Y.

Pendelton, Forrest C........LL. B., '08
Cambridge, Mass.

Penichet, J. Marion.........M. D., '09
Intern,
Providence Hospital, Wash., D. C.

Pennington, Polk K.........LL. B, '95
Clerk, A G. O., LL. M., '96
War Dept, Washington, D C

Pennybacker, Isaac S........LL B., '97
Clerk,
Dept of Agriculture, Wash, D. C

Pennybacker, James Edmund, LL. B, '99
Chief of Road Management, Office of
Public Roads,
Agriculture Dept, Washington, D. C.

Pentecost, William Chester..LL. B., '02
Lawyer,
Knox, Ind.

Perkins, Edward Dyer.......M. D., '95
Deceased, Aug 24, 1906, Wash, D C.

Perkins, Louis L............LL. B, '90
Spec. Rep, Ill. Surety Co., LL. M., '91
Bond Bldg., Washington, D. C.

Perry, David B.............LL. B, '98
Clerk, LL. M, '99
Pension Office, Washington, D. C.

Perry, Frank Sprigg........LL. B, '02
Lawyer,
Bond Bldg., Washington, D. C.

Perry, Frederick Charles ...D D. S,'05

Perry, R. Ross, Jr..........LL. B., '94
Lawyer, LL. M, '95
Fendall Bldg, Washington, D. C.

Perry, Richard Ross........A. B, '64
Lawyer, A. M, '65, LL D, '92
Fendall Bldg, Washington, D. C.

Perry, Walter S............A. B, '74

Perskin, Israel..............LL. B., '07
New York.

Petteys, C. V..............M. D, '73
Physician,
1822 12th St. N. W., Wash., D. C.

Pettijohn, J. W.............M. D, '64

Peyser, Julius I.............'....LL. B, '99
Lawyer,
705 G St. N. W, Washington, D C.

Pfirman, Franklin..........LL. M., '04
Lawyer,
Wallace, Idaho.

Phelan, Francis M..........A. M., '95
Lawyer,
73 Tremont St., Boston, Mass.

Phelan, William J.....:.....LL B., '08
Lawyer,
New Britain, Conn.

Philbin, Edw. T.............LL. B., '08
Lawyer,
Archbald, Pa.

Phillips, Bennett............LL. B, '89

Phillips, Edmund Lawrence, A. B, '97

Phillips, Frederick E........LL. B, '98
Lawyer, LL. M., '99
Tuscola, Ill.

Phillips, Lewis H...........LL. M, '94

Phillips, Robert L...........LL M, '95

Pickens, Alvin H...........LL B, '87

Pickett, Theodore J.........LL. B, '87
Lawyer, LL M, '88
Bond Bldg, Washington, D. C

Pierce, Albert S............M. D, '67
Physician and Surgeon,
611 North 20th St, Omaha, Neb.

Pierce, Henry Fletcher......LL B, '04
1315 Meridian St. N. W., Wash, D C.

Pierce, Thomas Murray, Jr., A. B, '98
Lawyer,
Care Boyce & Priest, 1207 Bank of
Commerce Bldg, St. Louis, Mo.

Pierce, William P..........LL. B, '73

Pierce, William Percy.......LL M,'80

Pierson, Henry C.......... M D, '68
Physician,
Roselle, N. J.

Piks, Albert H..............LL B, '07
Lawyer,   LL. M., '08
Evans Bldg., Wash., D. C

Pilon, Joseph A........... .A M, '06
Priest,
St. Viateur's Sem., Bourbounais, Ill.

Pimper, Harry K...........LL B, '09
1302 30th St. N. W., Wash, D. C.

Pirtle, William J...........LL. B, '99
Lawyer,   LL M, '00
Topeka, Kansas.

Pise, Rev. Charles Constantine,
Deceased, May 26, 1866, A. M., '30
Brooklyn, N. Y.

Pitts, George B....,...........LL. B, '04
Patent Attorney,
Ouray Bldg, Washington, D C

Pitts, W. Stanley..........M. D, '92
Physician,
East Providence, R. I.

Pizzini Juan A.............A B, '65
Deceased, Nov., 1891, A. M, '82
Richmond, Va.

Pless, William A....,.....LL M, '95

Poland, John A.............A M, '92
Lawyer,   LL. B., '92
Chillicothe, Ohio.

Poland, Nicholas Albert. .. LL B, '98
Lawyer,   LL. M., '99
Chillicothe, Ohio.

Polk, James K.............LL B, '90
Lawyer,   LL. M., '91
1407 F St. N. W, Washington, D. C.

Pollock, George F........ ..LL. M, '87
Lawyer,
Bond Bldg, Washington, D C

Pool, Solomon C...........LL. B, '97
                           LL. M., '98

Pope, Francis........... ...LL B, '90
Deceased,   LL. M, '91

Porrata, Nestor Rivera......D. D. S,'06
Surgeon Dentist,
San German, Porto Rico.

Porter, Henry C...........M. D, '69

Porter, Henry R......... ..M D, '72

Porter, Horace T....... M D, '70
Deceased, Aug. 14, 1879.

Porter, J .H............. ..M D, '61
Deceased, Feb. 5, 1908

Porter, John Waterman... M. D, '68

Posey, Fabian..............LL B, '01
Lawyer and Editor of the Examiner,
Frederick, Md.

Posey, G. Gordon.. ... ... A B, '71
Deceased, May 29, 1891,
Silver City, New Mexico

Posey, Richard B..........LL B, '95

Pospispel, Joseph..........M D, '94
Deceased, June 7, 1908, Wash, D C.

Postley, Charles E..........M D, '91
Physician,
Bureau Indian Affairs, Wash, D. C.

Potbury, Edwin, Jr........M D, '00
Deceased, Feb. 18, 1901, Wash, D. C

Potbury, Jesse E..........LL. B, '96
Lawyer,   LL M, '97
Columbian Bldg, Wash., D. C.

Potts, Louis Joseph..........A M, '98
Lawyer,   Ph. D., '99 LL. B, '99
180 Montague St.,   LL. M, '00
New York City, N. Y.,

Poulton, William E..........M. D., '64
Physician,
227 4½ St. S. W., Wash., D. C.

Poulton, William F..........LL. B, '92
                           LL M., '93

Powell, Benjamin F..........LL. B., '97

Powell, James L............LL. B., '07
Belmont, Va.   LL. M., '08

Power, Charles Benton.......A B., '88
Land and Live Stock Investments,
Helena, Mont.

Power, Edmund Murray .....M. D., '00

Power, James D'Alton.......LL. B, '80
                           LL. M., '81

Power, James...............A. M, '93
Broker,
University Club, Albany, N. Y.

Power, J. Neal, A. B., '95, LL. B, '97
Lawyer,
250 Montgomery St, San Franc., Cal.

Power, Very Rev. John......D D., '33
Deceased, April 14, 1849.

Power, Rev. John J.........A. B, '51
H. C, Mass., Deceased, Jan. 27, 1902.

Power, Dr. Maurice A......A. M., '31
Deceased.

Powers, Edward Parnell.....M. D., '05
Asst Physician, Kings Park State Hospital, Kings Park, L. I.

Powers, William............LL. D., '22
Deceased.

Pratz, Frederick C..........LL B, '91
Lawyer,   LL M.,'92
445 Q St. N. W., Washington, D. C.

Prendergast, Very Rev. P. J, D. D., '89
Deceased Oct. 1, 1899.

Prendergast, Rev. Jere M., S J., A. B, '89
Jesuit Priest,   A M., '92
Boston College, Boston, Mass

Prentiss, Charles E..........M D.,   '68
Deceased, March 19, 1908

Prescott, Charles C..........LL. B, '91
                      LL M,'92

Preston, Thomas........A. B.,   '37
Deceased.

Preston, Rt. Rev. Mgr. Thomas S.,
Deceased, Nov. 4, 1891,   D D, '89

Price, John G.............LL B, '05

Prince, Sydney R..........LL. B, '98

Pritchard, Henry T........:LL. B, '99

Pritchard, Howard Dallas....LL. B., '02
Lawyer,
Garfield Bldg., Cleveland, Ohio.

Pryal, Andrew D., Jr........LL. B, '88
Deceased, June 2, 1892, Wash, D. C.

Puebla, Luis de.............A. B., '68
Deceased, July 24, 1893,   A. M., '69
Coatzacoalcin, Mex.

Pugh, Henry L...........LL. B., '90
Clerk, Mount Vernon Flat,
Wash., D. C.

Pugh, James L., Jr., ...LL. B:, '84
Asst. District Atty.,   LL. M.,'85
3402 Mt. Pleasant St, Wash, D. C.

Pugh, John C ....LL. B., '88
Lawyer,
Brown-Mark Bldg., Birmingham, Ala.

Pugh, Ronald W...........LL. B., '09
Vanceburg, Ky.

Pulskamp, Bernard........M. D., '90
Physician,
Kneipp Sanatarium, Rome City, Ind.

Purcell, Rev. John B........A. B., '64
H. C., Mass., Deceased, Mar. 24, 1873.

Purman, Louis C.........M D, '91

Putman, William D.........M D, '68

Pye, James B.............A. M., '67

Quay, John B.............M. D, '93
Physician,
273 N St. N. W., Washington, D. C

Queen, Charles R..........M. D, '55

Quicksall, William F........A B, '61
Lawyer,   · LL B., '72, A. M, '72
1426 N Y. Ave, Washington, D C.

Quigley, Edward T.........LL. B, '05
Chief Clerk, Solicitor's Office,
Dept. Com and Labor, Wash, D C.

Quigley, Francis Leo.......M. D, '04
Physician,
Wallace, Idaho.

Quinlan, George Austin.....A. B., '02
Houston, Texas.

Quinlan, Richard J........A. B, '63
H. C, Mass, Priest,
St. Mary's Church, Holliston, Mass

Quinn, Edwin L............LL. B., '02

Quinn, Harry I............LL. B, '04
Lawyer,   LL. M,'05
Century Bldg, Washington, D C

Quinn, James Henry........M. D, '07
Physician,
52 E. Quincy St., Nor. Adams, Mass.

Quinn, John............LL. B, '93
Lawyer,
31 Nassau St., New York City.

Quinn, John A.............LL. B, '09
806 E St. S. W, Wash., D. C.

Quinn, Joseph Gray........A. B, '04
523 West 3rd St., Little Rock, Ark.

Quinter, Ralph De Shields...LL. B, '08
Lawyer, Fendall Bldg.,   LL. M.,'09
3422 14th St. N. W., Wash, D. C.

Rabbett, James Aloysius.....M. D., '00
Physician,
Elkins, W. Va.

Radcliffe, Samuel J........M. D, '52
Deceased, July 9, 1903,   A. M., '66
Washington, D. C.

Ragan, Gillum T...........M. D., '66
Physician,
Neoga, Ill.

Rager, Wm. H.............LL. M,'07
Lawyer,
Maryland.

Rague, Charles W. S.......LL. B, '03
Lawyer,
41 Wall St., New York City.

Raines, Benjamin R.......M. D, '67

Rainey, Francis H........A. B, '63
Chief Clk, M. O. Division, LL. B, '74
Post Office Dept, Washington, D. C.

Ralston, Jackson Harvey.....LL. B, '76
Lawyer,
Bond Bldg, Washington, D C.

Ramage, Joseph C ....LL. B, '99
Supt. of Tests, Sou. Ry, LL M.,'00
Alexandria, Va.

Ramos, Joaquin .... LL B , '07
Lawyer,
Tarlac, P I.

Ramsdell, George P ....M. D., '69

Rand, Charles F. ....M D , '73
Deceased, Oct 13, 1908, Wash·, D C

Randall, Thomas G..........LL. B , '89

Randle, Edward'Thomas.....LL B , '03
Lawyer,
Wilson Bldg , Dallas, Texas

Raney, Roscoe J .. .. .LL. B , '04
Clerk,
Census Office, Washington, D C

Rankin John M..LL B , '85, LL. M , '87

Ransom, Stacy A..........:...M. D , '93
Physician,
221 Seaton Place N. E , Wash·, D. C.

Ransom, Thomas R.........A. B., '85
Deceased, Nov 14, 1896,
Northampton Co , N. C.

Rask, Harry George .... ..LL B , '96
Lawyer,
Frewsburg, N Y

Rauterberg, Louis E ..... .M. D , '67
Physician,
, The Farragut, Washington, D C

Rawlings, Carroll M.........M. D., '84
Deceased, 1894.

Ray, Charles B ....A B , '72

Ray, Hon J. Enos, Jr . LL B , '96
Lawyer,   LL M ,'97
Speaker of the House of Delegates of
Maryland, 416 Fifth St , Wash , D C

Ray, Hon Robert....... . .A. B., '54
Deceased, Oct. 25, 1899, A. M , '59
Monroe, La

Rea, George W...... .... .LL B , '90
Patent Lawyer,   LL M ,'91
McGill Bldg., Wash , D C

Read, William G .... .. LL D , '42
Deceased.

Ready, Michael J...........A. B , '01
Physician,   M D , '05
3325 N St., Wash , D C.

Reagan, Francis Charles.....A M , '01
Lawyer,   LL B., '03
911 Lowman Bldg., Seattle, Wash.

Reavis, Wade ...:..........LL B., '02

Reddy, Anthony Cosgrove....A. M , '94
Lawyer,
94 Pleasant St., Malden, Mass.

Redmond, Edward J........LL B., '90
Lawyer,   LL. M ,'91
McGill Bldg , Wash , D. C.

Redrow, Walter L..........LL B , '04
Asst Examiner, Patent Office,
Washington, D. C.

Reedy, Frank H..... ..... .LL B , '07
Law Clerk,
Long Meadow, Mass

Reese, Henry F.............LL B , '85
State Senator,   LL M ,'88
Selma, Ala.

Reeside, Frank Palton........LL B , '94
Secretary, Equitable Co-operative Bldg.
Asso , 1003 F St N. W., Wash , D C.

Reeve Jesse N.............M. D , '93
Physician,
926 17th St , N. W , Wash , D C

Reeves, Isaac Stockton K ....M D , '03
Pass. Asst Surgeon U. S Navy, U S.
F. S. Marietta, care Postmaster, N Y.
City.

Reeves, John R. T..........LL B , '05
Clerk, Dept. of the Interior,
Wash , D. C

Reeves, William P.........:...M D , '99
Physician,
The Congressional, 100 E. Capital St ,
Wash , D. C.

Regan, Ralston Byrnes ......D D. S.,'04

Regli, J. A. S ....M D , '02
Physician,
Warburton Bldg., Tacoma, Wash

Reid, George Conrad .... A B , '02
Lawyer,   LL. B , '05
Century Bldg., Wash., D C.

Reid, John........A. B., '49, A M', '51

Reid, Louis Henry .... M. D , '70
Deceased, June 25, '08, Atlanta, Ga

Reidt, Urban H·......... . M D , '06
Physician,
Jeanette, Pa.

Reiley, Harold Aloysius .. ...A B , '03
Jesuit Scholastic Gonzaga College,
Spokane, Wash.

Reilly, Ellsworth F. J.... ..A. B , '08
Stockman,
204 N. 34th St., Billings, Mont.

Reilly, Henry Francis ....A M., '96
Ph. D , '97, LL B., '97, LL M., '98
Lawyer,
389 Broadway, Milwaukee, Wis.

Reilly, John V.............M. D., '06
Physician,   .
33 Tremont St., Rochester, N. Y.

Reilly, Joseph A ....D. D. S., '05
Kansas City Athletic Club,
Kansas City, Mo.

Reilly, William B...........LL B , '92
Lawyer,   LL. M., '93
486 La. Ave. N. W., Wash , D C.

Reisinger, Emory William....M D., '93
Physician,
1424 K St. N. W., Wash , D. C.

Remus, Ramon Eduardo.... A M., '98

Repetti, Frederick Francis ...M. D., '95
Physician,
149 B St. S. E., Wash., D. C

Repetti, Frederick F , Jr.....LL B , '07
Real Estate and Insurance,
149 B St S E , Washington, D. C.

Repetti, John Joseph........M. D , '97
Physician,
404 Seward Square, Wash , D. C.

Rex, Thomas A.............M. D , '65
Physician,
1423 St. Andrews Pl., Los Angeles, Cal

Reyes, Pio.................LL. B., '09
Manila, P. I.

Reynard, Walter A.........M D , '
Reynolds, Edward C ....LL M , '86
Lawyer,
31 1-2 Exchange St , Portland, Me.

Reynolds, George E........M D , '06
Physician,
334 North St., Pittsfield, Mass.

Reynolds, Walter B........M D , '74
Physician,
13 Trinity Place, Williamsport, Pa.

Reynolds, William C.......LL. B , '88
Merchant,   LL M , '89
Mesilla, N. Mex.

Reynolds, William E........LL. B , '92
Montgomery Co , Md.   LL. M , '93

Rhoads, Wm. L.............LL. M., '07
Clerk,
P. O. Dept., Washington, D. C.

Rhodes, Eugene............LL. M , '94

Rice, Charles Edward.......LL. B., '80

Rice, James Willie..........A. M., '53

Rice, Joseph A.............A. B , '63
Deceased, Oct. 1901,   A. M., '64
Alexandria, Va.

Rice, Nathan E............M. D., '80

Rice, William J.............A. B., '50

Rice, Wm R.............LL. B., '08
Lawyer,
60 Wurts St., Kingston, N. Y.

Rice, Thomas C............M. D., '69

Rich, William James........LL B , '98
Principal Examiner,   LL. M., '99
U S Patent Office, Wash , D. C.

Rich, John S...............LL. M., '87

Richards, Alfred...........M. D , '97
Physician,
The Seward, Seward Sq , Wash., D. C.

Richards, F. P.............M. D., '63

Richardson, Frederick D....LL. B., '08
Lawyer,
Fairfax, Va.

Richardson, John Robert....LL. B., '96

Richardson, William A......LL. D , '81
Deceased

Richmond, Charles Wallace, M. D., '97

Richmond, Elbert E........LL. B., '96
Clerk,   LL. M., '97
Treasury Dept , Washington, D. C.

Richmond, James A........LL. B , '03
Lawyer,
520 E St. N. E., Washington, D. C.

Richmond, John Albert......A. M., '05
Lawyer,
1303 Bank Lick St , Covington, Ky.

Richmond, Paul............M. D , '92
Treasury Dept ,
3146 O St. N. W., Washington, D. C.

Riddelle, Philip S..........M D., '79

Ridgely, Harry S ....LL. B , '96
Law Clerk,   LL. M., '97
Dept. of Justice, Washington, D C.

Ridgway, Albert B..........A. B , '07
Law Student,
Grafton St., Chevy Chase, Md.

Ridgway, Frank H.........LL B , '01
Lawyer,
11th St N. W., Wash , D. C.

Rieckelmann, John.........A. B., '56
                          A. M.; '59

Riehle, Charles F...........LL. B , '93
Deceased, 1894

Riley, Ambrose Joseph......A. M., '98

Riley, Benjamin C.........M. D , '52

Riley, Harry B.............D. D. S.,'07
Dentist,
4509 Wis. Ave. N. W., Wash., D. C.

Riley, John C............A. B., '48
Deceased, Feb 22, 1879, A. M., '51
Washington, D. C.

Riley, John F..............LL. B., '73

Riley, Edward S............A. B, '64
Deceased, 1882, LL. B.,'72, A. M., '76
Conewago, Pa

Rindge, Joseph B..........A. B, '40

Ring, John................LL. B., 'o1
Bookbinder,
Care Harper Bros, New York City.

Riordon, J. Allen..........LL. B., '04
Gen Claim Agt ,N.& W. Steamboat Co·,
Washington, D. C.

Risque, F. W..............A. B., '71

Ritchie, Abner Cloud.......A B., '98
Lawyer,
400 5th St. N. W., Washington, D. C.

Ritchie, Joshua A.........A. B, '35
Deceased, 1887.   A. M., '40

Ritchie, Louis W..........M. D, '63
Deceased, Sept. 9, 1901.

Rivera-Pagan, Pedro M.....M. D., '04
Physician,
San Germain, Porto Rico.

Rix, Carl B................LL. B., '03
Lawyer,   LL M., '04
833 Wells Bldg , Milwaukee, Wis.

Roach, Charles Edward.....A. B, '95
Lawyer,   LL. B., '97' LL. M., '98
Century Bldg , Washington, D. C.

Roach, Francis de Sales.....A. B., '07
Law Student,
1761 Willard St. N. W., Wash., D. C.

Roach, William Nathaniel, Jr,
          A. B., '96' LL. B , '98
Lawyer, Patents and Patent Causes,
Metzerott Bldg , Washington, D. C.

Roane, James..............M. D, '82
Physician,
Yankton, S. Dakota.

Roane, Samuel B..........LL. M., '86
Lawyer,
Yankton, S. Dakota.

Robbins, A. J............M. D, '91
Physician,
Jamestown, N. Y.

Robbins, Thomas A.........LL. M., '87

Roberts, Charles Francis ....LL. B., '94
Notary and Insurance,   LL. M., '95
706 14th St. N. W., Wash., D. C.

Roberts, E E. ....M. D., '94
Physician,
125 Maple Ave , Anacostia, D. C.

Roberts. Thomas W...... . LL B, '91
Tuscola, Ill   LL M., '92

Roberts, William........ M D, '94
Physician,
Fort Myer, Va

Robertson, Frederick C.. LL B , '89

Robertson, J Caldwell.......A B., '75
Capitalist,   A M , '77
Loan and Exc. Bk., Columbia, S C·

Robertson, Samuel A.... .A. M , '70

Robinson, Samuel A. .... A B , '58
Deceased, Dec , 1894.

Robinson, Thomas .... .M. D, '76

Robinson, Thomas Somerset, M D., '58

Roche, Charles H..........A B, '86

Roche, Peter A. ....A M , '91

Rochford, Richard ....A B, '47

Rodgers, Charles H........LL. B., '08
Clerk,
Dept. of Com. & Labor, Wash , D. C.

Rodrique, A................M. D., '71

Roebuck, Jarvis H...... . A B, '20
Deceased.

Rogers, Frank Leo..........A. B., '03
Lawyer,
69 Borden St , New Bedford, Mass.

Rogers, Hamilton............LL B , '02
Lawyer,
Northport, N. Y.

Rogers, James Charles ......LL. B , '86
Lawyer,
344 D St. N. W , Washington, D. C.

Rogers, Joseph Sebastian .. Ph B , '92
Deceased, Aug. 20, 1898 LL B , '94

Rogers, Thomas Mitchell....LL. B , '98

Rogers, William Elwin. .. .M D , '04
Deceased, Nov. 22, 1908, Wash , D. C.

Romadka, Charles Aloysius ...A B , '95
Mining,   A M.,'96
Care Globe Mine, Nacozari, Senora,
Mexico.

Romadka, Francis Joseph .. ..A. M.,'o1
Manufacturer,
32d & Center Sts., Milwaukee, Wis.

Romaine, Frank William.....M. D., '05
Physician,
935 H St. N. W., Wash., D. C.

Rudge, William H...........A. B , '93
Pres and Mgr. of the Forsyth Pattern
Co., Youngstown, Ohio.

Ruff, John A................M. D., '64

Ruffin, Thomas.............LL. B , '96
Lawyer,   LL. M., '97
U. of N. C. Law School Faculty,
Chapel Hill, N. C.

Ruffner, Charles E.........LL. B , '09
Manassas, Va.

Rupli, J. Theodore..........LL. B , '94
Lawyer,   LL. M., '95
1405 F St., Wash., D. C.

Russel, Bert................LL. B , '06
Asst. Examiner of Patents,
Patent Office, Washington, D. C.

Russell, Charles W ....LL. B , '83
                             LL. M., '84

Russell, Edward O , A. B., '79, LL. B., '81
Lawyer,   LL. M , '82, A. M , '89
244 Equitable Bldg , Denver, Colo.

Russell, George M..........LL. B., '87

Russell, Henry M...........A. B., '69
Lawyer,   A. M., '71
Wheeling, W. Va.

Russell, Murray Alfred......A. B , '03
Physician,   M. D , '08
2307 Wash. Circle, Wash , D. C.

Ruth, Charles H...........LL. B , '95

Rutherford, Robert Gedney, Jr.,
1st Lieut. 24th U. S. Inf , LL. B , '99
Madison Barracks, N. Y.

Ryan, James A.............LL. B , '96
Lawyer,   LL. M., '97
Nashville,' Tenn.

Ryan, James H.............LL. B , '04
Chamber of Commerce, Chicago, Ill.

Ryan, John McNulty.......A. B., '93

Ryan, Patrick J............LL. B., '94

Ryan, Thomas J., LL. B., '85, LL. M., '86

St. Clair, Francis Alphonzo, M. D., '90
Physician,
1319 T St. N. W, Washington, D. C.

St. Clair, F. O...... ......:.M. D., '69
Deceased, April 7, 1908,   A. M., '89
Washington, D. C.

Sakurai, Elchi.............D. D. S.,'07
Dentist,
Tokio, Japan.

Salomon Joseph.............LL. B , '97
Lawyer,   LL. M ,'98
416 5th St. N. W., Washington, D. C.

Salten, George W..........LL. B., '72
Salter, George W...........LL. B, '79
Clerk,
War Dept, Washington, D. C

Sanders, William ....A. B, '57

Sands, Francis P. B ....A. B, '61
Lawyer,   A. M, '68
1416 F St N. W. Washington, D. C.

Sands, William Franklin....A B, '96
                           LL B, '96
U. S Legation, Panama, R. P.

Sanford. Joseph L..........M. D., '92

Saul, John Aloysius.........LL B, '91
·Lawyer,   LL. M, '92
Fendall Bldg, Washington, D. C.

Saunders, Joseph N.........LL. B., '91
Lawyer,   LL. M, '92
412 5th St. N. W., Washington, D. C.

Sawtelle, Henry W........M D, '68
Surgeon, Marine Hospital Service,
3917 14th St., Washington, D C.

Sawyer, Glen R ....LL. B, '03
Lawyer,
504 S. Main St, Elkhart, Ind

Saxton, Francis G..........LL B, '73

Scaggs, James F...........LL. B, '84
Deceased, Dec 19, 1907, LL M, '85
Washington, D. C.

Scanlan. Andre Christie.....A M, '95
Agriculturalist,
Richmond, Ky.

Scanlan, Rev. Michael James,
Priest,   A M, '96
Cathedral, Boston, Mass.

Scanlon, Edward..........:.LL. B., '98
Journalist,   LL. M., '99
408 9th St. N. W., Washington, D C.

Schaake, Frederick W......D. D S.,'06
Dentist,
23 Bradford St., Lawrence, Mass.

Schade, Frederick..........LL B, '98
Lawyer,   LL. M, '99
Herndon, Va.

Schade, Herman R.........LL B, '99
Deceased, Washington, D. C

Scharf, J Thomas, A. M., '81' LL. B, '85

Schaus, James Peter........A M, '93
                           LL. B., '94

Scheib, Prof. Edward E.....A. B, '71

Scheller, Thomas K., Jr....A B, '06
·Lawyer,   LL. B., '09
·North Point, Chambersburg, Pa.

Schick, James P............LL. B., '09
1405 15th St. N. W., Wash., D. C.

Schildroth, Henry T........M. D., '93

Schlafly, James Joseph......A. M., '07
4532 ·Westminster Pl.,   LL. B., '09
St. Louis, Mo.

Schleimer, David...........M. D., '73
Elizabeth, N. J.

Schley, Winfield Scott.......LL. D., '99
Rear Admiral, U. S. N.,
1826 I St. N. W, Washington, D. C.

Schmaltz, Oscar J...........LL. B., '07
Stenographer,
P. O. Dept., Washington, D. C.

Schmidt, Oscar P...........LL. B., '90
                           LL. M., '91

Schneider, Elwin Carl.......M. D., '05
Physician,
1724 21st St, Washington, D C.

Schneider, Ferdinand Turton, LL. B, '99
Architect,
1314 F St N. W., Washington, D. C.

Scholz, Wm J..............LL. B, '06
Lawyer,   LL. M., '07
Saginaw, Mich.

Schoolfield, Charles S.......A. B, '78
Deceased

Schott, G J. VanVerbeck...M. D, '89

Schreiber, Henry R.........M. D., '07
Physician,
657 H St. N. E., Washington, D C.

Schreiner, Edmund..........LL. B, '04

Schubert, Bernhard F ......LL. B., '99
Clerk,   LL. M, '00
Pension Office, Washington, D. C

Schuler, Harry R ....LL B, '02
Lawyer,   LL. M., '03
Galion, Ohio.

Schulteis, Herman J ....LL. M, '02

Scott, Edgar B.............LL. M.,'09
Lawyer,
Norfolk, Va.

Scott, Thomas Edward......A. B.,- '97

Scott, Thomas W..........LL. B, '96

Searcy, Reuben Martin......M. D., '92

Sears, Fulton H ....LL. B., '96
Lawyer,
500 Journal Bldg, Chicago, Ill.

Seaton, Charles H..........LL. B, '91
                           LL M., '92

Seawell, Charles W........A. B., '85
                 LL. B, '86' LL. M., '87

Seay, Hon. Harry L.........LL. B , '94
Lawyer, Police & Fire Commissioner,
Trust Bldg , Dallas, Tex.

Se Legue, C. Albert.........LL. B., '09
Logansport, Ind.

Sibiakin, Ross W..........M. D., '81

Sefton, Edwin..............LL. B , '96
Lawyer,
63 Wall St., New York City.

Seger, William Thomas.....A. B , '94
Pianos and Sheet Music,
237 W. 142nd St., New York City.

Seitz, Charles J.............LL. B , '05
Mining,   LL. M., '06
P. O. Box, 492 Goldfield, Nev.

Seitz, Joseph William.......A. B., '03
Mining,   A. M , '04
P. O. Box 492 Goldfield, Nev.

Semmes, Alexander Harry...A. B., '81
Lawyer,
Dept. of Justice, Washington, D. C.

Semmes, Rev. Alexander J..A. B , '50
Deceased, Sept , 1898,   A. M , '52
New Orleans, La.

Semmes, Alphonso T........A. B , '50
                          A. M , '53

Semmes, Benedict I.........A. B., '53
                          A. M , '55

Semmes, Francis Joseph.....A. B , '90

Semmes, P. Warfield ....A. B , '60

Semmes, Thomas J., A. B., '42, A. M., '45
Deceased, June 23, 1899, LL. D., '80
New Orleans, La.

Senn, Hon. Charles A.......LL B , '83
Senior Judge City Court,
Birmingham, Ala.

Sessford, Charles E.........LL. B , '95
Real Estate,
Am. Security & Tr. Co., Wash., D. C.

Sessford, Joseph S. F.......M. D , '85
Clerk,
The Adjutant Gen. Office, Wash , D. C.

Settle, Tecumseh Gore ......LL. B., '97
                           LL. M., '98

Sewall, Eugene D ....LL. B , '89
                           LL. M., '90
Prin. Examiner, U. S. Patent Office,
Wash., D. C.

Shannon, Andrew C.........LL. B , '95
General Manager,
1305 Kenyon St., Wash , D. C.

Sharbaugh, Frank C........LL. B , '95
Lawyer,
Ebensburg, Pa.

Sharp, DeHaven ....M. D , '04
Deceased, Feb 4, '06, Wash , D. C

Sharp, Edwin H.............LL. B., '98

Shaw, Charles O............LL. B , '09
Prince George Co , Md.

Shaw, Clarence..............LL. B., '99
Deceased,   LL M , '00

Shaw, Clarence Edward .....M. D , '01
Physician,
342 West 4th St , Williamsport Pa.

Shaw, Kenneth A...........LL. B., '08
Law Clerk,   LL. M., '09
Gen. Land Office, Washington, D. C.

Shea, Charles Augustus ......A. B., '97
Lawyer,
4 and 5 Peoples Bldg., Wilkesbarre, Pa.

Shea, Rev. Edward Maurice, A. B., '98
Priest,
Bayou La Batre, Ala.

Shea, John Gilmary ....LL. D , '89
Deceased, Feb. 23, 1892,
Elizabeth, N. J.

Shea, Michael Ignatius ....M D., '04
Physician,
112 Belcher St , Chicopee Falls, Mass.

Shea, Thomas J ....A. B , '86
Commercial Traveller,
12 Florida Ave., Wash. D C.

Shealey, Robert Preston .....LL. B., '97
Lawyer,   LL. M , '98
Equity Bldg., Wash , D. C.

Sheean, John A. Rawlins.....LL. B., '99
Lawyer, Law Dept., U. P R. R. Co.,
Omaha, Nebr.

Sheehan, Dennis John.......M. D , '04
Physician,
Lowell, Vt.

Sheehan, John D ....LL B., '95

Sheehy, Francis Patrick......A. B , '93
Lawyer,   LL. B , '95, LL. M., '96
406 5th St. N. W., Wash., D. C.

Sheehy, Joseph C............LL. B., '02
Lawyer,
Colorado Bldg , Wash., D. C.

Sheehy, Vincent Alphonsus, ..A. B., '93
Lawyer,   LL. B , '95, LL. M., '96
406 5th St. N. W., Wash., D. C.

Sheibley, Sinclair B........ LL. B., '86
                           LL. M., '87

Shekell, Abraham B.........M. D., '63
Physician,
1529 Wisconsin Ave., Wash., D. C.

Shekell, Ben R ....A. B., '59

Shenners, Martin Joseph.....LL. B., '03
Lawyer,
378 National Ave., Milwaukee, Wis.

Shepard, Hon Seth ....LL. D , '95
Associate Justice Court of Appeals,
1447 Mass Ave. N. W., Wash., D. C.

Shepard, Seth, Jr.............A. B., '04
Lawyer,
319 Wilson Bldg , Dallas, Texas.

Sheppard, Walter W.........LL. M.,'94
Lawyer,
Savannah, Ga.

Sheridan, Denis..............A B , '71

Sheridan, Denis R..........A. B , '64
H. C , Mas⁵   A M , '66

Sheriff, A. Rothwell ....LL. B., '92

Sherman, Henry C.,   Mus. Doc., '89

Sherman, Rev. Thomas Ewing, S. J.,
Jesuit Priest,   A. B , '74
Missionary Apostolic,
413 W. 12th St., Chicago, Ill.

Sherrett, William L.........LL. B., '88
Deceased, Dec. 9, 1890,   LL. M.,'89
DeLand, Fla.

Sherrill, Edgar Beverly......LL B., '98
Lawyer,   LL. M.,'00
1318 12th St. N. W., Wash , D. C.

Shinn, George Curtis .....LL. B , '03
Lawyer,
Nat. Met. Bank Bldg , Wash , D. C.

Shipley, Charles E.........LL B , '04
Deceased, June 14, 1904

Shipman, Andrew J....... A. B , '78
Lawyer,   A. M., '87
37 Wall St , New York City.

Shipman, J. Bennett Carroll, A B , '92
Continental Bldg., Baltimore, Md.

Shipp, E. Richard..........LL. B , '95
Lawyer,   LL. M , '96
Casper, Natrona Co , Wyo.

Shoemaker, Albert Edwin...B. S, '88
Lawyer,   LL. B., '92, LL. M ,'93
Columbian Bldg., Washington, D C.

Shoemaker, F..............M. D , '91
Physician,
Carlisle, Pa.

Shoemaker, Louis P........LL. B , '80
Real Estate,   LL. M ,'81
612 14th St. N. W., Wash., D. C.

Sholes, William H..........LL. B., '87
Lawyer,   LL. M., '88
Columbian Bldg , Washington, D. C.

Shomo, Harvey L..........LL. B., '86
LL. M , '87

Short, Francis Jerome.......M. D., '04
Physician,
738 E. 31st St., Brooklyn, N. Y.

Short, William Henry.......M. D., '04
Physician,
307 Lexington, Ave., Brooklyn, N. Y.

Short, William O...........LL. B., '03
Clerk,
1000 M St. N. W., Washington, D. C.

Shoulters, George H........M D , '83
Deceased, Dec. 14, 1906.

Shreve, Benjamin..........LL. B., '09
Sterling, Va.

Shriver, Joseph N..........A. B., '06
Care B. F. Shriver Co.,
Union Mills, Md.

Shugrue, Patrick...........LL. B., '09
1233 Mass. Ave. N. W., Wash., D. C.

Shyne, Michael R..........M. D., '55

Sigur, Lawrence S.........A. B , '37

Sillers, Albert.............LL. B , '88
Lawyer,
472 La Ave. N W., Wash , D. C.

Sillers, Robert Fry.........M. D , '90
Physician,
313 H St. N. W., Washington, D. C.

Simmons, Leo..............LL. B , '90
Lawyer,   LL. M.,'91
1416 F St. N. W , Washington, D C.

Simon, Gerhard............A. B., '06
1320 Main St.,   LL. B., '09
Buffalo, N. Y.

Simons, H. N..............LL. B., '85

Simonton, John P..........LL. B , '78
Clerk,
War Dept , Washington, D. C.

Simonton, Vincent DePaul ..LL. B., '01

Sims, Charles....LL. B., '83, LL. M., '84

Sims, Erskine K............LL. B., '08
Clerk, House of Representatives,
Linden, Tenn.

Sims, Grant...:.............LL. M., '91

Sinclair, A. Leftwich........LL. B., '93
Lawyer, LL. M., '94
Columbian Bldg., Washington, D. C.

Sinclair, J McDonald........LL. B., '02

Singleton, Joseph W.......LL. B, '88
Lawyer, Ph B, '88
16-17 Ingram Block, Eau Claire, Wis.

Sizer, Adrian..............LL. B, '01
Lawyer, LL M, '02
Colorado Bldg., Washington, D. C.

Skerrett, Robert Gregg......LL. B, '91
Engineering, LL. M, '92
1₅ William St., New York City.

Skinner, George............M D, '68
Physician,
Fort Yellowstone, Wyoming.

Slattery, Daniel J..........LL. B., '02
1710 N. J Ave., Washington, D. C.

Slattery, Francis Edward....A. B., '96
43 Tremont St., Boston, Mass.

Slattery, John R............A. B., '85
Physician,
520 Broadway, So. Boston, Mass.

Slattery, Philip A..........LL. B., '06
St. Joseph, Mo.

Slaughter, William D.......LL. B, '93
LL. M., '94

Slinder, Michael E.........LL. B., '09
Lawlor, Iowa.

Sloan, J. G..............M. D., '69
Deceased, Nov. 2, 1897.

Sloan, Robert Neale........A. B., '85
Capitalist,
Stevenson, Md.

Sloane, James H............A. B., '81
Deceased, Oct. 23, 1884, Balt., Md.

Slough, Martin............LL. B., '84

Smart, Robert..............M. D., '96
Asst. Surgeon, U. S. A.,
War Dept, Washington, D. C.

Smart, William M..........M. D., '02

Smith, Andrew T..........LL. B., '06
Clerk,
Treasury Dept., Washington, D. C.

Smith, Antonio Justinian.....A. B., '96
A. M, '97, LL. B., '98, LL. M, '99
Lawyer,
609 Law Bldg, Plume St, Norfolk, Va.

Smith, Augustine P........LL. B, '88

Smith, Benjamin............M. D, '73
Physician,
Doncaster, Md

Smith, Charles J., Jr........LL. B., '07
Lawyer,
Milford, Mass.

Smith, Charles P...........LL. B., 82

Smith, Dexter A............M. D., '84
Physician,
3856 N. 42nd Ave., Chicago, Ill.

Smith, E. Vincent..........A. B., '95
Dry Goods,
298 Main St, Norfolk, Va.

Smith, Edward D..........LL B., '98
Lawyer,
Birmingham, Ala.

Smith, Edward J ....A. B., '01
Lawyer,
Frederick, Md

Smith, Edward Joseph......A B., '01
1706 West End Ave., Nashville, Tenn.

Smith, Edmund L..........A. B., '49

Smith, Edmund R...........A. B., '48

Smith, Ernest Renard.......A. B., '91
39 Driennason St., Norfolk, Va.

Smith, Francis T..........A. M., '89

Smith, Frank E.............LL. B., '98
Lawyer, LL. M., '99
Hall of Records, New York City.

Smith, Fred L.............A. B., '54
Deceased, 1898, A. M., '58

Smith, Giles W. L..........LL. B, '93
Lawyer,
Brewton, Ala.

Smith, Harlan S............M. D., '67
Physician,
Schoolcraft, Mich.

Smith, Howard T..........A. B., '08
Law Student,
96 Plymouth Ave., Buffalo, N. Y.

Smith, Hugh M.............M. D., '68
Dep. Commissioner,
Bureau of Fisheries, Wash, D. C.

Smith, James Alexander.....LL. B., '99
Deputy Tax Collector, 2d District,
Parish of Orleans,
2504 Ursuline Ave., New Orleans, La.

Smith, James F.............LL. B, '89
Lawyer, LL. M., '90
1339 K St. N. W., Wash., D. C.

Smith, John E ....M. D., '67
Deceased, Jan. 22, 1907, N. Y. City.

Smith, John Francis........A. B., '94
Lawyer,
Frederick, Md.

Smith, Joseph A...........M. D., '55

Smith, Joseph Edward......M. D, '00
Deceased, Aug. 14, 1909,
Bardstown, Ky.

Smith, Joseph Ernest.......D. D. S.,'03
Dentist,
631 Pa. Ave. N. W., Wash., D. C.

Smith, Joseph S ....M. D, '57

Smith, L. A.....LL B, '82, LL. M , '84

Smith, Lauria E.............LL. B., '07
Lawyer, and Sec'y of the Credit Exc.,
Durango, Colo.

Smith, Lawrence Dick.......A. B., '09
1020 Kentucky St., Quincy, Ill.

Smith, Lloyd ....M. D., '70

Smith, Lucius,.............M. D , '59

Smith, Peter M.............M. D , '94
Physician,
758 Tremont St , Boston, Mass

Smith, P. W................LL. B , '87

Smith, Peter D.............A. B., '84
Lawyer,
222½ 4th St., Logansport, Ind

Smith, Peter Xavier ....A. B., '82
A. M., '84, LL B., '84
Deceased, Feb. 3, 1896.

Smith, Philip...............A. B., '18
Deceased.

Smith, Robert E. L.........LL. B., '95
Lawyer,   LL. M., '96
Columbian Bldg., Wash., D. C.

Smith, Thomas C .....-....M. D., '64
Physician,
1133 12th St. N. W., Wash., D. C.

Smith, Thomas W..........A. B , '01
1706 West End Ave., Nashville, Tenn.

Smith, Walter ....A. B., '43

Smith, William F...........A. B., '78
LL. B , '80

Smith, William M., A. B., '53, A. M., '57
Deceased, May 4, 1892.

Smith, William Meredith ....A. B., '00
Physician,   M. D , '04
Frederick, Md.

Smyth, James J ....LL B , '92
Lawyer,   LL. M., '93
Grand Junction, Tenn.

Snider, C. Vernon..........LL. B., '09
Sterling, Va.

Snow, Roswell W...........LL. B. '09
3401 Holmead Ave., Wash., D. C.

Snow, William S...........A B , '61

Snyder, Harold C ....LL. B., '96

Sohon, Frederick.......... M. D , '88
Physician,
512 I St. N. W., Wash , D. C

Sohon, Henry W...........LL. B., '84
Lawyer,   LL. M., '85, A. M., '89
Fendall Bldg., Washington, D. C.

Solignac, Gustave L .... LL. B , '92

Solis, Frederico ....A. M , '01

Somers, Paul Joseph ....A M , '99
Lawyer,   LL. B., '01-
27 Cawker Bldg , Milwaukee, Wis.

Sonnenschmidt, C. W ....M. D , '67
Deceased, Feb. 1908, Wash , D C.

Soper, Julius S., A. B., '66, A M , '67

Sothoron, James J ....M. D., '65
Deceased, Sept. 27, 1897, Wash , D. C.

Sothoron, Levin Johnson....M D., '96
927 20th St., Wash., D. C

Sour, Louis................M. D , '55
Physician,
Lansing, Mich.

Spalding, Hughes..........A. B., '08
Law Student,
Empire Bldg., Atlanta, Ga.

Spalding, Samuel E ....M. D., '58

Spangler, William A........LL B , '88
LL M.,'90

Sparks, Augustus R ....M. D , '59

Spear, J. M ....LL. B., '91
Lawyer, Solicitor of Patents,
1003 F St. N. W., Wash., D. C.

Speiden, Clarence E........LL. B., '09
525 9th St. N. E , Washington, D. C.

Spellacy, Thomas J.........LL. B., '01
Lawyer,
756 Main St., Hartford, Conn

Spellissy, James M.......... A. B., '55
Deceased, June, 1875,   A. M., '56
New York City.

Spellissy, Joseph H ....A. B., '85
Physician,   A M , '90
110 S. 18th St., Phila , Pa

Spier, Alexander M........LL. B., '91
LL M.,'92

Spiess, Louis A.............LL. B., '07
Clerk,
Dept. of Com. & Labor, Wash , D. C.

Spiller, James.............LL. B., '09
Jacksboro, Tex.

Spratt, Maurice Charles .....A. B., '88
Lawyer,
77 W. Eagle St., Buffalo, N. Y.

Springer, Ruter W ....LL. B , '89
LL. M., '90
Chaplain, U. S. A., Care War Dept.,
Wash , D. C.

Sprinkle, Thomas H ....LL. M., '93

Sproules, Joseph Aloysius...A. B., '95
Physician,
1615 Tremont St , Boston, Mass.

Squier, Algernon Marble....M. D , '67
Deceased.

Stack, John B..............LL. B., '87

Stack Joseph C..............LL. B., '04
Patent Lawyer,
115 I St. N. W., Wash., D. C.

Stack, Maurice J............M. D., '76
Physician,
Gov't Hospital for the Insane,
Washington, D. C.

Stackhouse, George M ....LL. B., '98

Stafford, Rev. Denis J.......D. D. '90
Deceased, Jan. 3, 1908, Wash., D. C.

Stafford, James Raymond....LL. B., '98

Stafford, John J ....M. D., '85
Deceased, Mch. 17, 1902. A. M , '86

Stafford, Hon. Wendell P...LL. D., '07
Asso. Justice Sup. Court D. C.,
1603 Irving St. N. W., Wash., D. C.

Stagg, John Alfred ....LL. B., '97
LL. M., '98

Staggers, John W...........LL. M., '08
Lawyer,
118 McGill Bldg., Washington, D. C.

Staley, Charles Melrose......LL. B., '87
U. S. Patent Office, Wash., D. C.

Staley, William F ....LL. B., '92
Dept. of Agriculture,   LL. M., '93
411 Beck Bldg , Portland, Ore.

Stallings, Thomas B.........LL. B., '05
Private Secretary, U. S. Senate,
Washington, D. C.

Stang, Rt. Rev. William......D. D., '89
Deceased.

Stanion, Ralph P ....LL. B., '05
Superintendent Indian School,
Rosebud, S. D

Stansell, Wallace K.........LL. B., '90
Lawyer,   LL. M., '91
Cartersville, Ga.

Stanton, Lemuel J....... ...LL. M , '87

Starek, Emil ....LL. B , '89
LL. M., '90

Starkweather, Carlton Lee...M. D., '98
Physician,
Occoquan, Va.

Starr, Joseph A ....M. D., '02

Stead, Mark Aloysius ....A. M., '98
Deceased,
St. Louis, Mo.

Stearman, Mark.............LL. M., '06
Lawyer,
Columbian Bldg., Washington, D. C.

Stearns, John Sargent.......M. D , '94
Physician,
1425 R. I Ave. N. W., Wash., D. C.

Stearns, Dr. S. S...........M. D., '68
Physician,
1425 R. I. Ave. N. W., Wash., D. C.

Stein, Joseph B.............LL. B , '09
454 D St. N. W., Washington, D. C.

Stein, Robert...............M. D., '86
Bur. of Statistics, Dept. of C. and L.,
1335 F St. N. W., Wash , D. C.

Steinmertz, William R.......M. D , '65
Deceased, Jan. 26, '08, Walbrook, Md.

Stelzner, Robert H..........LL. B , '09
Milwaukee, Wis.

Stephan, Anton.............LL. B , '91
Treasurer and Manager,   LL. M., '92
Messrs. Wm. H. McKnew Co.
Wash , D. C.

Stephens, F. Wilson,.........LL. B., '01
Lawyer,
Huntington, W. Va.

Stephens, John J ....M. D , '68

Stephens, Thomas A ....A. B., '74
Merchant,
709 12th St., Wash., D. C.

Stephenson, Joseph Gwynn..M. D , '75

Sterling, Hugh M...........LL. B , '91
LL. M., '92

Stern, Samuel B............LL. B., '07
Lawyer,
Roden Bldg , Birmingham, Ala.

Stetson, Charles W.........LL. B , '90
Lawyer,   LL. M , '92
412 5th St. N. W., Washington, D. C.

Stevens, Eugene E.........LL. B , '88
Patent Lawyer,   LL M., '89
817 14th St. N. W., Wash., D. C.

Stevens, Frank L........... LL B , '92
Clerk,   LL. M., '93
220 Ind. Ave. N. W., Wash , D C

Stevenson, Charles..........LL. B., '08
Clerk,
Treasury Dept., Washington, D. C.

Stewart, Fenwick Joseph....A. B., '91
Electrical Engineer,
46 Cedar St., New York City

Stewart, John Frew........LL. M., '96

Stewart, William Walter....LL. B., '97
LL. M., '98

Stier, Henry Clay, Jr.......LL. B., '98
Deceased LL. M., '00

Stirewalt, Jacob P..........LL. B., '06
Clerk,
25 Iowa Circle N. W., Wash., D. C.

Stitt, Frederick S...........LL. B., '98

Stockbridge, Virgil D........LL. B., '75
Assistant Examiner,
Patent Office, Washington, D C.

Stockly, Charles Daniel......LL. B., '04
Lawyer,
715 Market St., Wilmington, Del.

Stockman, Charles W.......M. D., '65
Physician,
121 Payson St., Portland, Me.

Stockstill, Francis W.......LL. B., '83

Stone, Addison G ....LL. B., '75

Stone, Charles ....A. B., '59
H. C., Mass., Journalist,
Deceased, 1867, New Orleans, La

Stone, George H............M. D., '68
Deceased, Feb. 19, 1899,
Savannah, Ga.

Stone, Ralph W............A B., '95
Lawyer, LL. B., '95, LL. M., '96
Warren, Pa.

Stone, Warren C.........'...LL. B., '73

Stonebraker, Samuel E......LL. B., '04
Law and Real Estate,
1413 H St N. W., Wash, D. C.

Stonestreet, Rev. Charles H, S. J.,
Jesuit Priest, A B., '33
Pres. of G. U., Deceased, July 3, 1885.

Stonestreet, Nicholas........A. B., '36
Deceased, 1889. A M., '40

Storer, Hon. Bellamy.......LL D., '02
164 Marlboro St., Boston, Mass.

Story, Leon Ellery..........M. D. '01

Stout, Alexander M.........M. D., '80
Physician,
304 Wash Boulevard, Chicago, Ill.

Stout, Stanley S ....LL B., '74

Stoutenbergh, J. A.........M. D., '91
Physician,
116 2nd St. N. E., Washington, D. C.

Strasburger, Milton.........LL. B., '96
Lawyer, LL. M., '98
705 G St. N. W., Washington, D. C.

Strass, Henry...............A. B., '26
Deceased.

Stratton, John T...........M. D., '73

Strawbridge, Henry........A. B., '37

Streator, Wallace...........LL. B., '93
Lawyer, LL. M., '94
Columbian Bldg, Washington, D. C.

Street, Daniel B.............M. D., '74
Physician,
1102 9th St. N. W., Wash, D. C.

Street, Garfield A...........LL. B, '04
Lawyer,
Com Nat. Bank Bldg, Wash, D. C.

Street, H. R................M. D., '91
Physician,
641 E. Capitol St., Washington, D. C.

Strickland, Reeves T........LL. B, '97
Clerk, Dept. of Justice, LL. M., '98
309 E St. N. W., Washington, D. C.

Stringfield, Francis M.......M. D., '70
Deceased, Sept. 12, 1903,
Chicago, Ill

Strittmatter, Thomas P......LL. B., '95

Strong, Michael R..........A. B., '60
Deceased. A. M., '62

Strong, Shepard...........LL. B., '06
Real Estate Broker,
1226 Williamson Bldg, Cleveland, O.

Stuart, Benjamin R ....LL. B., '96

Stuart, Daniel D. V., Jr....M. D., '08
Physician,
Garfield Hospital, Washington, D. C.

Stuart, John M..............A. B., '07
Care C. M. Stuart Coal Co.,
Albany, N. Y.

Styll, Harry H..............LL. B., '09
Philadelphia, Pa.

Sudbrink, John T...........LL. B, '99
Lawyer,
Terre Haute, Ind.

Sudler, Oden Rochester.....M. D, '03
Physician and Surgeon,
462 H St. N. W, Washington, D. C.

Sullivan, Francis Paul.......A. B., '04
1823 U St. N. W., Washington, D. C.

Sullivan, Francis W.........A. B., '87
512 1st Nat. Bank, Duluth, Minn.

Sullivan, George E.........LL. B., '02
Lawyer,
Fendall Bldg., Washington, D. C.

Sullivan, George N.........LL. B., '74
Clerk,
Bur. of Eng and Ptg, Wash, D C.

Sullivan, James F...........A B., '52
H. C., Mass., Deceased, July 26, 1905.

Sullivan, Jere A.............LL. B., '05
Lawyer,
Realty Bldg, Wash. Sq, Newport, R I.

Sullivan, J. H...............A. B, '93
Stockman,
Temple, Tex.

Sullivan, John Joseph.......A. B, '98

Sullivan, John K............LL. B, '76

Sullivan, Joseph Daniel......A. B, '97
Lawyer,   LL. B, '99, LL. M., '00
Columbian Bldg, Washington, D. C.

Sullivan, Joseph David.....D D. S, '03

Sullivan, Michael William ..LL. B, '03
Lawyer,   LL M, '05
Century Bldg., Washington, D. C.

Sullivan, Patrick Thomas ...M. D, '95

Sullivan, Simon E..........LL. B, '96
                       LL. M, '97

Sullivan, Thomas J.........LL B, '85
Deceased, May 4, 1908,   LL. M., '86
Washington, D C

Sullivan, Thomas V........A B, '00
Chemist,
1823 N St. N. W., Washington, D. C.

Sullivan, Timothy Joseph....M. D., '04
Physician,
512 6th St., Washington, D C.

Sullivan, W. L..............M. D., '94

Sullivan, William Cleary.....LL. B., '01
Lawyer,
410 5th St. N. W., Washington, D C.

Sullivan, William D......LL. B, '01
Real Estate, Loans and Insurance,
1408 G St. N. W., Washington, D. C.

Summey, B W ....M. D, '86
Physician and Examiner, War Dept,
920 19th St., Washington, D. C.

Swank, Walter.............LL. B., '09
Denver, Colo.

Swayne, Noah H., Jr........LL. B, '73

Swayze, S Courtland ....A. B, '53

Sweeney, Harry J..........LL. B., '04

Sweeney, John A............LL. B, '89
                       LL. M., '90
Hampshire Arms, Minneapolis, Minn.

Sweeney, Matthew J.......D. D. S.,'07
Dentist,
54 Lowell St., N. Weymouth, Mass.

Sweeney, Michael T.......M. D., '06
Physician,
381 Broadway, So. Boston, Mass.

Sweetman, James T........M. D, '72

Swetnam, Charles R. Keith..M. D., '04
Physician,
Swetnam P. O., Fairfax Co, Va.

Swetnam, Ford H.........M. D., '07
Physician,
Woodstock, Va.

Sylvester, George...........M. D., '64
Deceased.

Sylvester, J. Henry.........M. D., '71

Taggart, Hugh Fairgreave...LL. B, '02
Lawyer,   ..   LL. M.,03
400 5th St. N. W., Washington, D. C.

Talbot, J. Theodore.........A. M., '47
U. S. A., Deceased, April 22, 1862.

Talbott, Edward Melville....M. D., '01
Asst. Surgeon, U. S A,
War Dept, Washington, D C.

Taggart, George R.........LL. B., '08
Clerk,
P. O. Dept., Washington, D. C.

Taggart, Richard J..........LL. B., '06
Law Clerk,   LL. M.,'07
3249 N St. N. W., Washington, D. C.

Talmadge, Theodore........LL. M., '89

Tarkington, J. A............M. D., '70
Deceased, May 1, 1902.

Tastet, Joseph M............M. D., '53

Tatum, Thomas H........ ..LL. B, '02
Lawyer,
Bishopville, S C.

Tauzin, Emile M...... .....A. B, '55

Taylor, A. S...............LL. B., '81
Lawyer, U. S. Com,   LL M., '82
1407 N. Y. Ave, Washington, D. C.

Taylor, Charles B..........LL. B., '99

Taylor, Charles Benjamin...M. D., '05
Physician,
Amador City, Cal.

Taylor, George W..........LL B, '90
                       LL. M, '91

Taylor, James A.... ... ...Ph B, '88
Supt. Trans, N. Y. Edison Co,
149 Clifton Place, Brooklyn, N. Y.

Taylor, Judge John Lewis...LL. D, '28
Sup. Court, Deceased, Jan 29, 1829,
Raleigh, N. C.

Taylor, John Louis..........LL. D., '22
Deceased.

Taylor, J. Waldo............LL. B., '08
Lawyer,
Findlay, Ohio.

Taylor, Leroy M............M. D, '60
Deceased, Sept. 27, 1905.

Taylor, Dr J. Archibald ....M. D, '85
Deceased, 1898,
Washington, D. C.

Taylor, Thomas............M. D., '82
Physician,
238 Mass. Ave N E., Wash, D. C.·

Taylor, Walter I...........LL. M, '91

Taylor, William C..........LL. B, '91
Deputy Reg. of Wills,   LL. M. '93
City Hall, Washington, D. C.

Teeling, Very Rev. John ....D. D., '54
Priest,
8 S. Common St., Lynn, Mass.

Teicher, John G..... ......LL. B., '88
U. S. Spec. Ex of Pens, LL. M., '89
Dept. of Interior, Washington, D. C.

Telford, Erastus Dalson.....LL. B, '99
Lawyer,   LL. M, '00
Salem, Ill.

Tempes, Frederick W.......LL. B, '07
Lawyer,
Schofield Block, Vancouver, Wash.

Tepper, Joseph L...........LL. B, '04
Lawyer,
503 E St. N. W., Washington, D. C.

Test, Frederick Cleveland ...M. D, '95
Physician,
103 State St, Chicago, Ill.

Tete, Leo Frederick..........B. S., '83
61 Front St., Philadelphia, Pa.

Thatcher, John.............M. D., '68

Thian, Louis R.............A. B, '75
Lawyer,
Minneapolis, Minn.

Thian, Prosper E..........A. B, '81

Thomaides, George Th... ..LL. B, '05
Lawyer,   LL. M., '07
Columbián Bldg, Washington, D. C.

Thomas, Adolf A ....LL. B., '06
Patent Lawyer,
1550 Monadnock Block, Chicago, Ill.

Thomas, Charles Theodore .LL B, '94
                          LL M, '95

Thomas, Edward H. ......LL B, '77
Lawyer,
Hibbs Bldg, Washington, D C

Thomas, Edward J.........LL B, '76

Thomas, Edw. W..... ...LL B, '08
Rodman,
D. C. Engineer Dept., Wash, D C.

Thomas, Richard W........ LL B, '09
Boston, Mass.

Thomas, Roy.............. LL B, '97
Electrotyper,
Navy Dept, Washington, D C

Thomas, William B.........LL. B, '07
Wash. Ry. & Elec. Co., Wash, D.C.

Thompson, Charles F.......LL B, '02

Thompson, Edwin S ....LL B, '91
                          LL M, '92

Thompson, Frederic M......LL B, '91
Physician,
Albion, N. Y.

Thompson, Granville S..·... .M D, '67

Thompson, John C :........A B, '42
Deceased, May, 1895.

Thompson, John H..........A. M., '65
Deceased, Rome, Italy.

Thompson, John H., Jr......M. D, '75
Ophthalmic Surgeon,
Kansas City, Mo.

Thompson, John S..........M. D., '95
Physician,
1529 Cambridge St., Cambridge, Mass.

Thompson, Michael Joseph ..A. M., '01
Teacher,
Washington College, Chestertown, Md.

Thompson, Smith, Jr........LL. B., '96
                          LL. M., '97

Thorn, Charles Edwin.......LL M., '94

Thorne, Walter W.........LL. B, '09
Lowell, Mass.

Thornton, Richard H........LL. B., '78

Thurn, George A...........M. D, '70

Tibbals, W. F..............M D., '65

Tibbitts, Orlando O........ .LL B., '05
Lawyer,
Oklahoma City, Okla·

Tierney, Rev. John J........D. D , '93
Professor, Mt. St. Mary's College,
Emmitsburg, Md.

Tierney, Matthew D........LL. B., '88
LL. M., '89

Tierney, Michael V.........LL. B., '86
Deceased, Sept. 12, 1906, LL. M., '87
Wash , D C.

Tierney, Myles Joseph.......A. B., '95
Physician,
143 W. 74th St , New York City.

Tighe, Alvin..............LL. B., '08
Lawyer,
Milwaukee, Wis.

Tilden, William C..........M. D., '67
Deceased

Tillman, Lloyd Montgomery..LL. B., '99
Natl. Bank Examiner, LL. M., '00
413 P. O. Bldg., Phila., Pa.

Timmes, John W............A. B , '01
Lawyer,
Shamokin, Pa.

Timmins, Dr. P. J..........M. D., '78
Physician,
487 Broadway, S. Boston, Mass

Timmins, Thomas J.........A. B., '78

Tindall, William ....M. D , '69
LL. B., '82
Secy. Board of Commissioners,
Municipal Bldg , Wash., D. C.

Tinley, John A.............LL. B., '97

Tobin, Clement P...........LL. B., '93
Lawyer,
Hibernia Bk Bldg , San Francisco, Cal.

Tobin, Edward James......A. B., '95
A. M., '96, Ph. D., '97, LL. B, '97
Lawyer,
Hibernia Bk Bldg , San Francisco, Cal.

Tobin, James H ....LL. B., '93
Clerk, LL. M., '94
U. S. Pension Agency, Milwaukee, Wis.

Tobin, Joseph E., Jr........LL. B., '90

Tobin, Richard Francis......M. D., '05
Physician,
731 22d St. N. W., Wash., D. C.

Todd, William G...........LL B, '08
Scottdale, Pa. LL. M , '09

Toner, John E ....M. D., '91
Physician,
214 14th St. N. E., Wash., D. C.

Toner, Joseph M...........A. M., '67
Deceased, July 30, 1896. Ph. D., '89

Tonry, Prof. William P.....Ph. D., '75
Deceased, Baltimore, Md

Toohey, Frank.............LL. B, '07
Examiner,
Patent Office, Wash., D. C.

Toomey, James A...........A. B , '96
Lawyer, A. M , '97, LL B , '01
Fendall Bldg., Wash., D. C.

Torrey, Earl G., LL. B , '92, LL M , '93
Lawyer,
Lansing, Mich.

Torrey, Turner............M. D , '73
Deceased, Dec. 3, 1895, Wash., D. C.

Totten, Howe ....LL. B., '95
Lawyer, LL. M., '96
Room 306 Pope Bldg., Wash , D. C.

Touart, Tisdale Joseph......A. M., '02
Lawyer,
Mobile, Ala.

Toumay, Francis...........LL B , '82

Tower, Frederick W........LL. B , '90
LL. M , '91

Towsend, Charles G ....LL B , '92
Lawyer, LL M., '93
Kalamazoo, Mich.

Towsend, Samuel D ......LL B , '05
Lawyer,
104 St. Charles St , Baltimore, Md.

Tracey, James F...........A. B., '74
Lawyer,
25 N. Pearl St , Albany, N. Y.

Tracey, Luke Louis.........A. M , '96
Lawyer, Ph D., '97
Union Trust Bldg., Detroit, Mich

Tracy, Francis M...........LL. B., '07
Care N. Y. & N. J. Telephone Co ,
184 Eldridge St , Univ. Settlement,
New York City.

Tracy, James ....A. B , '59
H. C , Mass , Clergyman,
Deceased, July, 1866.

Tralles, George Edward.....LL. B , '97
Lawyer, LL. M., '98
Nave Block, Tucson, Ariz.

Trautman, B..............M. D , '74
Deceased, Philadelphia, Pa.

Tree, Charles M...........M. D., '67
Deceased, Dec. 3, 1881.

Trembly, Royal H..........LL. B., '99
LL. M., '00

Tremoulet, Joseph Sydney...A. B , '97
New Orleans Manager, The Grasselli
Chemical Co., Cleveland, Ohio.

Trenholm, Frank............LL. B, '92
Lawyer,   LL. M., '93
141 Broadway, New York City.

Trenholm, W. de Saussure..LL B, '90

Triplet, Caius E, LL. B, '88, LL M., '89

Trott, Thomas H...........M.D, '67
Deceased, April 23, 1896.

Trowbridge, George E......LL. B., '08
Asst. Law Officer, Forest Service,
Bick Bldg., Portland, Ore.

Troy, Robert P ....LL. B, '99
Lawyer,
1101-3-5-7 Claus, Spreckels and Call
Bldg., San Francisco, Cal.

Tschiffely, Stuart Aloysius...A. B, '02
Pharmacist,
1900 N St N. W, Washington, D C

Tuason, Pedro.... ....LL. B, '08
Lawyer,
Balanga, P. I.

Tucker, Maurice ....M D, '62

Tuomy, Rev. John...........LL D, '21
Deceased.

Tureaud, Benjamin .. ..A. B, '88

Turner, Emmett, LL B, '90, LL. M,'91

Turner, Henry V........A. B, '80

Turner, John F.......... ...LL B, '05
Lawyer,
Grafton, W. Va.

Turner, Lawrence J... . . M.D, '64

Turner, O. C............:... .. M. D, '64

Turner, S S................M.D, '63
Deceased, Dec. 11, 1904.

Turpin, Henry W...........M.D, '64

Turton, William E.........M D, '08
Physician,
1216 12th St. N. W., Wash, D. C

Twibill, Aloysius Holland...A. M., '01
Commonwealth Tr. Bldg, Phila, Pa.

Tyler, Frederick S..........LL. B, '05
Lawyer,   LL M,'06
Colorado Bldg, Washington, D. C.

Tyler, George W............LL. B, '09
Malcolm, Iowa.

Ucker, Clement S, LL B, '98, LL. M.,'99
Chf. of Div. of Private Contests and
Administrative Officer,
General Land Office, Wash, D. C.

Underwood, Fred Rutan.....M. D., '97
Physician,
Oriental Block, Seattle, Wash.

Underwood, Robert L ......LL B, '99
Clerk,
Pension Bureau, Washington, D. C.

Vale, Frank P . ...M D, '92
Physician,
The Toronto, Washington, D C.

Valentine, Charles Francis. A. B, '96
Money Order Division,
Post Office, New York City.

Van Arnum, John W.. . M D, '67
Deceased, Nov. 9, 1884, Wash., D. C.

Van Bibber, Claude.........A B, '74
Physician and Surgeon,
9 E Read St, Baltimore, Md.

Van Casteel, Gerald.. ......LL. B, '99
Lawyer, and Editor,   LL M, '00
80 Wall St, New York City

Vander Chatten, Baron .....A. M, '45

Vanderhoff, George ....A M, '58

Vandeventer, Braden.........LL. B., '99

Van Duzer, Clarence... ...LL. B, '93
Lawyer,   LL. M, '94
Reno, Nev.

Van Dyne, Frederick........LL B, '90
U. S. Consul,   LL. M., '91
Kingston, Jamaica.

Vanel, Andrew V. .... A B, '39

Van Emon, Walter C........LL. B., '09
Yorkville, Ill.

Van Gieson, Henry C......M D, '64
Deceased, Mch 7, 1905, Omaha, Neb.

Van Nest, Raymond H......LL. B., '06
Asst. Examiner,
Patent Office, Washington, D. C.

Van Sant, Frank............LL. B, '07
Lawyer,
Colorado Bldg., Washington, D. C.

Varnell, Malcolm K.........LL B, '09
1529 Vermont Ave., Wash., D. C.

Van Vranken, Frederick.....LL B, '92
Clerk,   LL. M, '93
War Dept, Washington, D C.

Vaughan, Daniel C..........LL B, '95
Clerk,   LL. M, '96
Dept of Com and Labor, Wash, D. C.

Vaughan, Walter J... ..... .LL. B, '96
Journalist and Publisher, LL M, '97
Griffin, Ga.

Verbrycke, J. Russell, Jr....M. D., '06
Physician,
2307 1st St., Washington, D. C.

Verrill, Charles H ....LL. B., '90
Statistician,
1429 N. Y Ave, Washington, D C.
Vest, Hon George Graham, LL D, '00
Deceased.
Via, Lemuel R.............LL B, '98
Vierbuchen, Julius.......... LL. B, '05
Secy of German American Bldg Asso.,
300 B St. S. E, Washington, D C.
Vincent, Thomas Norris... .A. B, '85
G U. Med Fac., A. M, '91
1221 N St, Washington, D. C.
Vlymen, Henry T,.........A. B., '06
Teacher,
379 Front St., Hempstead, N. Y.
Vlymen, William J.........A. B., '06
Teacher,
379 Front St., Hempstead, N. Y.
Von Rosen, Ferdinand G....LL. B, '87
LL. M.,'93
Von Rosenberg, Fred C.....LL. B., '89
Voorhees, Charles S........A. B, '73
Hyde Block, Spokane, Wash.
Wadden, John Joseph.......A. B, '04
Commercial Traveller,
Care V R. Wadden & Son,
Madison, S. Dak.
Wade, Edward Julius........A. B., '04
Student,
1410 N Broad St., Philadelphia, Pa.
Wade, John Douglas........LL. B., '06
Electrical Engineer,
325 E. North Ave., Baltimore, Md.
Waggaman, Samuel John, Jr., A. B, '98
Wagner, G. Henry.........M. D., '85
Physician,
728 9th St. N. E, Washington, D. C.
Wagner, R. B ....M. D., '70
Deceased.
Wagner, Warren H.........LL. B., '08
Private Secretary,
Interstate Com. Com., Wash., D. C.
Waguespeck, William J......A. B., '82
Lawyer,
300 Perrin Bldg, New Orleans, La.
Wahly, William H.........LL. B, '96
LL. M.,'97
Wainscott, George...........LL. B., '74
Waite, George W. C.. .... LL. B., '74
Walace, Hamilton S........LL. B, '84
Waldo, G. S........... D D. S,'02

Wales, Orlando G..........LL. B, '87
Walker, Charles M.........LL. B, '93
Secretary, Monroe Cotton Mills,
Monroe, Ga.
Walker, Francis B ....LL. B, '89
LL. M,'90
Walker, James S............LL. B, '83
Walker, John Brisben ......Ph D, '89
Writer and Business Manager,
Care Cosmopolitan Mag, N. Y. City.
Walker, John B. Fuller......LL B, '98
Walker, Lewis Albert, Jr....M D, '98
Physician,
622 N. J. Ave., Washington, D. C
Walker, Ralph Elliott...... LL B, '01
Lawyer,
416 5th St. N. W., Washington, D. C.
Walker, Reginald Redford...M D., '00
Physician,
1710 H St N. W., Washington, D C.
Walker, Robert H..........LL. B, '07
Law and Real Estate,
458 La. Ave., Washington, D. C.
Walker, W. Henry.........LL B, '88
LL. M, '89
Walker, William A.....:....A. B, '60
H. C, Mass., Deceased,
New Orleans, La.
Walker, William Gillespie ...LL B, '97
Clerk,
Treasury Dept, Washington, D. C.
Walker, William H.........M. D, '02
Physician,
493 Hudson St. New York City.
Walker, Gen. William Stephen,
A. B, '41
Wall, Joseph Stiles.........M. D., '97
Physician, G. U. Med. Fac,
1232 14th St. N. W., Wash, D. C.
Wall, Maurice J.............LL. B., '05
Examiner,
U. S. Patent Office, Wash., D. C.
Wall, Michael...............A. M., '66
Wall, Very Rev. Stephen V. G,
Deceased, Aug 21, 1894. D. D, '89
Wallace, Elliot L............LL. B., '09
Birmingham, Ala.
Wallace, Joseph F.... ......M. D., '99
Modern Woodmen Sanitorium,
Colorado Springs, Colo.
Wallace, M. T . .. .M D, '73

Wallis, Samuel B . . . . A. B, '84
Wallis, Samuel T . . . . A M , '87
Walsh,. Edward F . . . . LL. B , '02
Walsh, Ed. J . . . . LL B , '93, LL M , '94
Manager Northwestern Nat In Co ,
1302 F St N. W, Washington, D. C
Walsh, Francis . . . . M. D , '66
Walsh, Henry Collins . . . . . . A M , '88
Editor of The Travel Magazine,
331 4th Ave , New York City
Walsh, John H . . . . A. B , '73
Asst Supt Schools, N. Y., A. M , '89
8502 Hamilton Ave., Brooklyn, N. Y.
Walsh, John K . . . . M D , '65
Deceased, Jan. 4, 1894
Walsh, Julius Sylvester, Jr. . A B , '98
V. Pres Royal Typewriter Co ,
364 Broadway, New York City.
Walsh, Michael James . . . . A B., 'oi
Lawyer,
Mayfield, Pa.
Walsh, Ralph S. L . . . . M D , '63
Physician,
1807 H St. N. W., Wash , D. C.
Walsh, Redmond D . . . . A. B , '78
Walsh, Thomas, Ph. B., '92, Ph. D., '99
Author,
227 Clinton St., Brooklyn, N Y.
Walsh, Thomas J., A. B., '94, A. M., '96
Culebra, Canal Zone,
Central America
Walsh, William A . . . . LL. B., '97
Lawyer,
2-8 Hudson St., Yonkers, N. Y.
Walsh, William S . . . . A M., '89
Walshe, Patrick J . . . . LL. B , '98
LL. M., '99
Walter, Dr. John, Jr . . . . M. D., '68
Deceased, Nov. 17, 1906.
Walter, William Francis . . . . M. D., '92
Physician,
487 H St S. W., Washington, D. C.
Walters, Harris A . . . . LL. B., '99
V. Pres. Hydraulic Press Brick Co.,
Chicago Div., Chamber of Commerce,
Chicago, Ill.
Walters, Harry F . . . . LL. B., '06
Clerk,
W. S. G L O., Alliance, Neb.

Walters, Henry,. . . A. B., '69, A. M., '71
LL D.,. '09
President, Atlantic Coast Line,
5 South St , Baltimore, Md
Walthall, Wilson J . . . . A. B., '54
Wanamaker, William H . . . . . LL. B., '99
Chief of Division, Office of P. O. Dept.
Auditor, Wash., D. C.
Wand, Arthur J . . . . LL B , '05
Ward, Elijah J . . . . M D , '80
Ward, Francis M . . . . M. D , '81
Ward, Francis X , A. B., '59, A. M , '67
Lawyer,
2417 Spruce St., Philadelphia, Pa.
Ward, George A . . . . LL B , '98
Law Clerk, LL M., '99
Indian Office, Wash , D. C.
Ward, Samuel B . . . . . . ,. . . . M. D , '64
Physician,
281 State St , Albany, N. Y.
Ward, Samuel R . . . . M. D., '68
Physician,
Richmond, Ill.
Ward, William L . . . . M. D., '71
Deceased, April 12, 1909
Wardwell, Eugene McC . . . . . LL B , '93
LL M., '94
Ware, Edward H . . . . M D , '65
Warfield, Ralph Sturtevant . . . LL B , '98
Patent Lawyer, LL. M., '99
501 Eddy Bldg , Saginaw, Mich.
Warman, Philip C . . . . LL. B., '80
Deceased, Nov. 25, '08, Wash , D. C.
Warner, Richard Ambrose . . . M. D , 'oi
Passed Assistant Surgeon, U. S N ,
Care Navy Dept , Wash , D C
Warren, Bates . . . . LL. B., '92
Lawyer, LL. M., '93
Columbian Bldg., Wash , D. C
Warren, Charles . . . . M D , '68
Warren, John L . . . . LL B , '99
LL. M., '00
Warriner, William F . . . . LL. M., '87
Washburn, Albert H . . . . LL. B., '95
Lawyer,
12 Broadway, New York City, N. Y.
Washington, Joseph E . . . . . . A B , '73
Planter, A. M., '89
Wessyngton, Tenn.
Wasner, Wendell H . . . . LL B , '09
Batavia, Ohio.

Wasser, Henry R...........LL. B , '09
Williamsport, Pa.

Wasson, Robert Bingham....LL B , '99
Lawyer,
Cadiz, Ohio.

Waters, Bowie F...........LL. B., '93
Lawyer,
Rockville, Md.

Waters, David C........... M. D , '67

Waters, Elkhanah N........LL. B , '76
Deceased, Oct 26, 1908,
Frederick, Md.

Waters, Eugene H.........LL. B , '08
Germantown, Md.   LL. M.,'09

Waters, Francis..A. B , '55, A M., '56

Waters, Thomas B.........LL. B , '91

Watkins, John C...........M. D , '65

Watkins, Richard James ....A B , '97
Lawyer,   LL B , '99, LL. M ,'00
506 E St. N W., Washington, D. C.

Watkins, Samuel Evans.....M. D , '92
Physician,
The Alabama, 11th and N Sts. N W ,
Washington, D. C.

Watkins, Victor E. ....M D , '94
Medical Reserve Corps, U S. A ,
War Dept , Washington, D. C.

Watson, Frank E , Jr.......LL B., '09
Cadott, Wis.

Watson, James A...........M. D , '90
Physician,
201 Monroe St , Anacostia, D. C.

Watson, James M...........LL B , '02
Penitentiary, Moundsville, W. Va.

Watson, Joseph Twichell....LL M.,'03
-Lawyer,
344 A Central Bldg , Seattle, Wash.

Watson, Martin M..........LL. B., '05
Fancy Grocer,
113 4th St. N E , Washington, D. C.

Watson, Richard F ....LL. B , '05
-Lawyer,
Greenville, S. C.

Watson, Robert............ LL B , '95
Patent Lawyer,
Nat. Union Bldg , Washington, D. C.

Watt, Alexander...........LL B , '09
Burke, Va.

Watterson, George W... ...A. B , '32
          A. M., '43, LL D , '59
Watterson, Rt Rev. John Ambrose,
Deceased, April 7, 1899   D. D , '78

Watts, Frederick, Jr........LL. B., '09
New York City.

Watts, Reuben Benjamin.....LL. B , '98
Lawyer,
410 Title Guar. Bldg , Birmingham, Ala.

Wayland, Confucius L.......LL. M.,'89

Weaver, Alfred S...........D. D. S.,'02
Dentist,
410 10th St S. E , Washington, D. C.

Webb, Daniel Aphonsus.....A M , '95
Surgeon,   M D., '96
310 Wyoming Ave , Scranton, Pa.

Weber, Casper C...........LL. B., '90
          LL. M ,'91
Care Pension Office, Wash , D. C.

Weber, Julius Henry........LL. B., '99
U. S. A , Retired.

Webster, Ben ....M D , '00
Physician,
Washington, Pa.

Webster, Ben Temple........LL. B., '98

Webster, Charles S.........LL. B., '89

Wedderburn, George C......LL. B., '92
          LL. M.,'96

Weed, Chester A............LL. M.,'92

Weikert, Clyde B..........LL. B., '07
Lawyer,
1446 R. I. Ave. N. W., Wash., D. C.

Welch, Benjamin T.........LL. B., '90

Welch, Thomas Francis.....M. D., '04
Physician,
356 Windsor Ave , Hartford, Conn.

Welch, Timothy J. ....A. B , '97

Welch, Williams............LL. B;, '09
Newberry, S C.

Wellenreiter, Otto Francis...M. D., '01
Physician,
Perry, Ill.

Weller, Joseph I............A. B , '93
Real Estate Broker,   LL. B., '95
602 F St. N. W., Washington, D. C.

Wellman, George M ....M. D., '68
Deceased, Jan. 13, 1902.

Wellman, George T.........LL. B., '91
Lawyer,   LL. M., '92
930 3rd Ave., Sheldon, Iowa.

Wells, George M..........Phar. B , '72

Wells, John Bernard........A. M., '05
Lawyer,
108 E. Madison St., Baltimore, Md.

Wells, Walter A..........:.M D., '91
Physician,
The Rochambeau, Washington, D. C.

Wells, Walter H.. ..   M D, '68
Physician and Surgeon,
Coffeyville, Kansas.

Welsh, John Joseph ....LL. B, '03
Lawyer,
309 Broadway, New York City.

Wendell, Robert Paine ......M. D, '92
Physician,
Aberdeen, Miss.

Werle, Charles M ....LL B, '96

Wertenbacker, C. I ....M. D, '94
U. S Army Medical Service,
Care Surg. Genl U. S. A., Wash., D. C.

Wessel, John Frederick......A. B, '96
Electrical Engineer,
Gen Electric Co, Baltimore, Md.

West, Bertram H ....LL. B, '75

West, Vernon E............LL. B., '08
1364 Harvard St,   LL M., '09
Washington, D. C.

Westenhaver, David C ......LL. M, '84
Lawyer,
929 Garfield Bldg, Cleveland, Ohio.

Westfall, Harry M.........:.LL. B, '90
Lawyer,
Tuscola, Ill.

Wetmore, James A... ......LL. B, '96
Chief of Law and Records Division,
Supervising Architect's Office,
Treasury Dept, Washington, D. C

Weyrich, John Raymond.....LL B, '04
U. S. Attorney's Office,   LL. M, '05
City Hall, Washington, D. C.

Wheatly, J Walter....... ..LL. B, '89
Special U S. Agent,   LL. M, '90
Treasury Dept, Galveston, Texas

Wheaton, Henry ....M D, '66

Wheaton, Isaac S....... ....LL B, '85

Wheeler, Arthur M, Jr.. ..LL B, '94
Stenographer,
3 B St S. E, Washington, D. C.

Wheeler, General Joseph, U. S A,
Deceased, Jan 1906.   LL. D, '99

Wheeler, Laban Homer . ..LL. M., '87
Lawyer,
656-7 N. Y. Block, Seattle, Wash.

Wheeler, William D.... ...LL B, '04
Lawyer, U. S Forest Service,
Albuquerque, New Mexico.

Wheelock, George L ....LL. B., '89
Patent Lawyer.   LL. M., '90
45 Broadway, New York City.

Whelan, Benjamin L........A. M., '57

Whelan, John A...../.........LL. B., '03
                        LL. M., '04
Care Bank Cor. 7th and Penn. Ave.,
Washington, D. C.

Whilley, William H.........A. M., '85

Whipple, Ulysses V..........LL. B., '89
                        LL. M., '90

White, Charles Albert.......A. B, '90
Lawyer,   LL. B, '92, LL. M., '93
Bond Bldg., Washington, D. C.

White, Columbus J..........M. D., '66

White, Hon. Edward Douglass,
                        LL. D, '92
Associate Jus. U. S. Supreme Court,
1717 R. I. Ave. N. W., Wash., D. C.

White, Edward H..........A. B, '68

White, Francis P............LL. B., '87
Clerk,   LL. M., '88
Bureau of Pensions, Wash., D. C.

White, Guy Harris.........:.D. D. S.,'02
Dentist,
1523 Lamont St. N. W., Wash., D. C.

White, James R.............LL. B, '89
                        LL. M.,'90

White, John W.............M. D., '70

White, Louis C..............B. S., '87
            LL. B., '89, LL. M,'90

White, Robert R., LL. B., '99, LL. M.,'00

White, Thomas J............LL. B, 82
Lawyer,   LL. M, '83
Com. Nat. Bk. Bldg., Kansas City, Kans.

White, Walter N...........LL B, '09
Muskogee, Okla.

White, William Henry.......LL. B., '97
Lawyer,
715 Columbian Bldg., Wash., D. C.

Whitefoot, R. M............M. D., '66
Deceased, July 25, 1906,
Bozeman, Mont.

Whitehouse, Joseph S.......LL. M., '87
Real Estate and Financial Agent,
Tacoma, Wash.

Whiteley, Richard Peyton...A. B., '01
Lawyer,   LL. B., '04
1419 G St. N. W., Washington, D. C.

Whiting, Wm. H. C, U. S. A., A. B, '40
Confederate General, A. M, '50
Deceased, Mch. 10, 1865.

Whitley, W. H..........M D, '66
Deceased, Paterson, N. J.

Whitney, C F.............M. D., '90
Medical Referee,
U. S. Pension Bureau, Wash., D. C.

Whitten, John L...........LL. M, '91
Lawyer,
Point Pleasant, W. Va.

Whitthorne, Washington C, LL. B, '88
Lawyer,
Columbia, Tenn.

Wibirt, William C..........LL B, '89

Wickham, Edward E........LL. B., '08
'Care J. F. Murtaugh, Elmira, N. Y.

Wiecker, Otho..............LL. B, '86
Antiquarian and Geneologist,
587 Tremont St., Boston, Mass.

Wiggenhorn, Edwin C......LL. B., '89
LL. M., '90

Wiggin, Augustus W.......M. D, '65

Wikle, Douglas.............LL. B, '80

Wikoff, William............A. B., '27
Deceased.

Wilcox, Adolphus D........LL. B., '94
Chief Clerk,
Bureau of Insular Affairs, War Dept,
Washington, D. C.

Wilcox, John A............M. D. '57

Wilcox, John H.........Mus Doc., '64

Wilder, A. M...............M. D., '63

Wildman, Joseph C.........LL B., '73

Wilkerson, Oliver D........LL. B, '95
Deceased, 1908. LL. M., '96

Wilkinson, A. D............M. D., '93
Pension Office,
455 Mass. Ave., Washington, D. C.

Wilcox, James M..........A. B, '81
A. M, '89
V. Pres. of the Phila. Sav. Fund Soc.,
700 Walnut St., Philadelphia, Pa.

Wilcox, William J..........A. B., '76
Deceased, 1895. A. M, '89

Willett, Archibald M.........LL. B., 95
Deceased, Oct. 19, 1905.

Willett, J. Edward.........M. D., '55
Deceased, Jan. 21, 1887.

Willey, Harry P .... LL B, '92
Lawyer, LL. M, '93
Law Division, Bureau of Pensions,
Wash, D. C.

Williams, A. Roy.......... LL. B, '04

Williams, C Fuller..........LL B, '05
Lawyer,
35 Wall St, New York City, N. Y.

Williams, George Francis,....LL. M, '89
Lawyer,
Nat'l Met. Bank Bldg, Wash, D. C.

Williams, Hugh H.......·....LL B, '96
LL M, '97

Williams, James R..........LL B, '09
Brooke, Va.

Williams, John G. .. .. LL B, '97
Auditor, Norfolk & Washington Steamboat Co, 7th St. Wharf, Wash., D C.

Williams, Dr. R. E. ....M D., '70

Williams, Sherman..........M D, '98
Physician,
405 California Bldg, Denver, Colo.

Williams, W. Mosby... ... .LL B, '90
Lawyer, LL M, '91
Columbian Bldg, Wash, D C.

Williams, William F. .... .A B, '63
Deceased, Sept. 9, 1892

Williamson, Frank E........LL. B, '03
Lawyer, LL. M., '04
Urbana, Ill

Williamson, George M......LL M., '93

Williamson, Hugh C ....A. B, '66
A M, '72

Williamson, Joseph A ....LL B, '05
Champagne, Ill. LL. M, '06

Willige, Louis C.............LL. B, '90

Willis, Thomas C..........LL. B., '06
Lawyer,
Munsey Bldg., Washington, D. C.

Wills, Joseph W.............LL. B., '93
Lawyer, LL. M., '94
Arlington, Va.

Wills, William Xavier ....A. B., '51
Deceased, June 25, 1865, A. M., '59
Charles County, Md.

Willson, Prentiss...........M. D., '05
Physician,
The Toronto, Wash., D. C.

Willson, S. C ...:...........M. D., '88
Physician,
2033 Meridian St., Anderson, Ind.

Wilson, Andrew............LL. B., '90
Lawyer,   LL M., '91
504 E St. N. W., Wash., D. C.

Wilson, Augustus ....A. B , '60
Deceased, Sept, 1903.

Wilson, Calvert ....A B , '86
Lawyer,   A M , '90
300 Wilcox Bldg , Los Angeles, Cal

Wilson, Clarence R..........LL. M., '99
G. U. Law Faculty,
1707 R. I. Ave , Washington, D C.

Wilson, Daniel J............LL. B., '05
Lawyer,
Galveston, Tex.

Wilson, Edwin L...........:...LL. B , '95
Lawyer,
Fendall Bldg , Wash , D. C.

Wilson, Eliel Soper ....A B , '46
Deceased, Sept, 1860,   A. M , '48
Anne Arundel County, Md.

Wilson, Henry O...........LL B, '89
                         LL M', '90

Wilson, Henry Peter .... .A. B , '91
Deceased.

Wilson, Hon. Jeremiah M ...LL D., '83
Deceased, 1903.

Wilson, John Chamberlain....A B , '65

Wilson, John E..............A. B , '45
Deceased, 1909,   A. M , '47
Wakefield, Va.

Wilson, Joseph S............LL B , '07
Iron Ore Business,
Rockefeller Bldg , Cleveland, Ohio.

Wilson, Lawrence...........M D , '70

Wilson, Nelson.......... ...LL B, '04
Lawyer,   LL. M., '05
1417 G St. N. W , Washington, D. C

Wilson, Thomas J ....LL B , '92

Wimberly, Warren W.......M. D , '92
Deceased, April 27, 1908.

Wing, George C.............LL. B., '73

Wingard, Edward V........M. D , '80
Physician,
Deadwood, S. Dak.

Wimsatt, William Kurtz.....A. B., '00
Wholesale Lumber,Johnson & Wimsatt,
1212 Water St. S.W , Wash , D C.

Winter, Frank E............M. D., '06
Physician,
Payson, Utah.

Winkle, Douglas.............LL. B , '80

Winter, John T .. . .M D , '70
Deceased, June 22, 1902, Wash , D. C

Winthrop, William.... .....LL. D , '96

Wirt, Richard W., Jr........LL. B , '08
Stenographer,   LL. M., '09
Alexandria, Va.

Wise, James A... ....A B , '58
Deceased, Feb. 23, 1875 Austin, Tex.

Wise, Thomas W ....M. D , '65
Deceased, Feb. 17, 1891.

Wissner, Frank J .. .. LL B , '01
Lawyer, Editor and Publisher,
1264 Wis. Ave., Washington, D C.

Woerner, Otto E............LL. B , '04
Clerk, Gov. Dept ,
734 6th St. N. W , Washington, D. C.

Wolf, Alexander.............LL B , '92
Lawyer,   LL M , '93
Jenifer Bldg , Washington, D. C

Wolf, Dr. J S ....M. D , '67
Deceased, Dec. 7, 1898

Wolfe, John Loyola....,.....A M , '02
Lawyer,   LL. B , '04
302-4-6 Weston Bldg , Clinton, Iowa.

Wolfe, John Magruder......A B , '01

Wolfe, William Lloyd. :. . A B , '92

Wolhanpter, William E... ..M. D , '90
Deceased, Jan 21, 1896.

Wollard, Paul D............LL B , '07

Wollenberg, Robert A C....M D , '05
Physician,
736 Dix Ave., Detroit, Mich

Wood, Elmer C.............LL B , '08
Clerk,   LL. M., '09
U. S. Dept. of Agric , Wash , D. C.

Wood, George F...........M. D., '65

Wood, George William......M. D , '94
Physician,
2906 P St. N. W , Washington, D. C.

Wood, Leonard C..........LL. B , '85
Lawyer,   LL. M , '85
617 La. Ave., Washington, D. C.

Wood, William C..........LL. B , '89
                        LL. M., '90

Woodburn, William, Jr....LL B , '03

Woodbury, Edward C.......M. D , '63
Deceased, Jan 15, 1905.

Woodbury, H. E............M. D , '63

Woodley, Robert D..........A. B , '25
Deceased.

Woodley, Thomas A........M. D , '57

Woods, Clifton F..........A. B., '08
Editor,
303 S. Idaho St., Butte, Mont.

Woods, Joseph..............A. B, '55
St F. X., New York.

Woodson, L. C........ ....M D, '91

Woodward, Herbert E.......LL. B, '85
Clerk,   LL. M., '87
Assessor's Office, District Building,
Washington, D. C.

Woodward, Rigual Duckett..A B, '85
Lawyer,
5 Nassau St, New York City.

Woodward, Roland E........M. D, '64

Woodward, Thomas Pursell, LL. B, '89
Lawyer,
322 Blair Road, Takoma Park, D. C.

Woodward, William Creighton,
M. D., '89, LL. B, '99, LL. M., '00
Physician,
Health Dept, Washington, D C.

Woolf, Oliver P ....LL B, '89
Clerk,   LL M., '90
P. O. Dept, Washington, D C.

Wootton, Edward..........A B., '58

Worthington, A. Saunders...LL. B, '97
Lawyer,   LL. M, '00
31 Am. Nat. Bk. Bldg, Wash, D. C.

Wright, A Clarke. ....A. B, '82
Deceased,   A. M, '84, LL. B., '84

Wright, Arthur..............LL. B, '06
Patent Attorney,
220 Broadway, New York City.

Wright, Arthur W... ......LL. B, '92
Advertising,
811 Great Northern Bldg, Chicago, Ill.

Wright, J. Henry..........M. D., '67

Wright, Joseph D..........LL. B, '97
Lawyer,   LL. M, '98
Evans Bldg, Washington, D. C.

Wright, Wilbur L..........M. D, '94
Physician,   .
1658 Park Road, N. W., Wash, D. C.

Wrightman, Charles J.......LL. B., '90
Lawyer,
Tulsa, Okla.

Wynn, Frederick S..........LL. B., '06
Asst. Secretary So. Ry. Co.,
Washington, D. C.

Wynne, Robert F..........LL B, '97

Yancey, G. Earle.......... .LL. B., '99
Clerk,
Navy Dept, Washington, D. C.

Yeatman, Charles R..... ...LL B, '98
                          LL. M, '99
Columbia Phonograph Co., N. Y. City.

Yeatman, Rudolph H........LL. B., '06
Lawyer,   LL. M, '07
410 5th St. N. W., Washington, D. C.

Yeatman, Samuel M........LL B, '83
Deceased, Dec., 1905,   A. M, '89
Washington, D. C.

Yoder, Frank W.... ..... LL B, '05
1337 22nd St. N. W., Wash, D C.

Yoshida, C................D. D S, '02

Young, Noble.....:........A. M, '76
Deceased, 1883,
Sacketts Harbor, N. Y.

Young, Parke G............M. D, '72
Deceased, July 20, 1906.

Youngblood, Robert K......LL B, '87

Yount, Clarence Edgar ......M D, '96

Yount, Marshall H.... ... LL. B, '97
Lawyer,
Hickory, N. C.

Yrarrazabal, Manuel.... ....A. B, '52

Yturbide, Augustine de......Ph D, '84
G U. Hospital, Washington, D. C.

Zabel, John H..............LL. B., '06
Lawyer,   LL. M., '07
412 5th St. N. W., Washington, D. C.

Zane, Edmund P..A B, '55, A. M., '60

Zappone, A .. ..M. D, '60
Deceased, Washington, D C.

Zegarra, Felix Cypriano.. . A B, '64
                 A. M, '65, LL D, '77
Deceased, April, 1897, Lima, Peru.

Zepp, Jesse................M. D., '70

Ziegler, Eugene M..........LL. B, '06
Lawyer,
Orangeburg, S. C.

Zimmerman, Harvey J.......LL. B., '05
Clerk,
Census Office, Washington, D. C.

Zuniga, Manuel G. de... ...A. B., '55
                          A. M., '56

TRIENNIAL LIST OF GRADUATES

1912

GEORGETOWN UNIVERSITY

WASHINGTON, D. C.

PUBLISHED BY

GEORGETOWN UNIVERSITY
QUARTERLY
[JULY TO SEPTEMBER, 1912]

Entered May 16, 1904, at Washington, D. C., as second-class matter, under
Act of Congress, July 16, 1894

Contents

Directory

GEORGETOWN UNIVERSITY

WASHINGTON, D. C.

Rev. Alphonus J. Donlon, S.J., President:
    Georgetown University.

The Secretary:
    North Building, Georgetown University.

The Treasurer and Bursar:
    Healy Building, Georgetown University.

The College (Graduate and Undergraduate Schools):
    The Registrar, 37th and O Sts. N. W.

The School of Medicine:
    The Dean, 920 H St. N. W.

Georgetown University Hospital:
    35th and N Sts. N. W.

The Training School for Nurses:
    Georgetown University Hospital.

The School of Dentistry:
    The Dean, 920 H St. N. W.

The School of Law:
    The Dean, 506 E St. N. W.

The Astronomical Observatory:
    The Director, Georgetown University.

The Riggs Library:
    The Librarian, Georgetown University.

The Seismograph Observatory:
    The Director, Georgetown University.

Foreword

After a lapse of three years this revised and corrected List of Graduates from all departments of Georgetown University has again been prepared and is herewith presented to the Alumni.

The purpose of the publication is two-fold: 1st, to strengthen the union already auspiciously existing between the Alumni and their Alma Mater; and, 2d, to strengthen union and fraternity among the Alumni themselves by thus furnishing a reliable means of intercommunication, with a view to mutual aid and recommendation. A lawyer in Massachusetts, or a doctor in New York may have professional dealings with parties in distant regions—be it California, New Mexico, or Michigan—which he is unable to attend to in person; by consulting his Triennial Catalogue he is sure to find some reliable brother alumnus to whom he can with confidence entrust his case. And the same may be said of commercial, mercantile and other business interests.

The Triennial List thus enables the officers of the University, as well as the graduate body, to maintain a live interest in the whereabouts, the work, and the progress of each individual who has passed through the institution. From information thus gathered, records are kept which are a distinct advantage when, as not infrequently happens, the Faculty is requested to recommend a suitable man for a given position.

It must be remembered, however, that in a body of over five thousand individuals, absolute accuracy is well nigh impossible. A most extensive correspondence must be instituted and maintained; in many cases, a second, a third, and a fourth letter became necessary, because the graduate in question, either through negligence or press of business, failed to reply; while in other cases every trace of the person sought for had vanished and laborious correspondence with friends and classmates has ended, not infrequently, with the one disappointing word "missing."

Even as these pages go to press, new information, changes of address, new occupations, etc., are at hand.

In order, therefore, to attain the original purpose of this Directory and to maintain it at the highest possible efficiency, the continued co-operation of every loyal alumnus is earnestly requested. Notify the Director of the Graduate List regarding any. change, be it in personal occupation or in residence; forward information regarding classmates and fellow alumni—their successes, honors or new distinctions that may come to them—for Alma Mater will rejoice with her sons rejoicing; and finally, endeavor, as far as possible, to locate those missing graduates whose names were included in a list recently mailed from the University.

The Secretary takes this opportunity of extending his gratitude to the secretaries of the various Alumni Associations, and to all the other Alumni who, in devotion to Alma Mater, rendered him the most cordial and thorough assistance in preparing the Graduate List, and he again urges on every alumnus the necessity of forwarding to him information regarding any graduates whose names or addresses have been omitted from this list.

JOHN B. CREEDEN, S.J., Secretary,
Georgetown University,
Washington, D. C.

The Presidents of Georgetown University

The list of the Presidents of Georgetown University is worthily headed by the illustrious Founder of the University:

The Most Rev. John Carroll, (S.J.),
Prefect Apostolic of the Catholic Church in the U. S.,
First Archbishop of Baltimore.

The Presidents

Rev. Robert Plunkett.............................1791-1793
Deceased, January 15, 1815, Prince George's Co., Md.

Rev. Robert Molyneux, S.J........................1793-1796
Deceased, February 9, 1809' Georgetown, D. C.   1806-1808

Most Rev. William L. Dubourg, (S.S.).............1796-1799
Bishop of New Orleans, Bishop of Montauban in
France, and Archbishop of Besancon, France.
Deceased, December 12, 1833, Besancon, France.

Most Rev. Leonard Neale, (S.J.)..................1799-1806'
Second Archbishop of Baltimore.
Deaceased, June 15, 1817, Georgetown, D. C.

Rev. William Matthews...........................1808-1810
Vicar Apostolic and Administrator of Philadelphia.
Pastor of St. Patrick's Church, Washington, D. C.
Deceased, April 30, 1854, Washington, D. C.

Rev. Francis Neale, S. J........................1810-1812
Deceased, December 20, 1837, St. Thomas's Manor,
Md.

Rev. John A. Grassi, S. J.......................1812-1817
Deceased, December 12, 1849, Rome.

Rt. Rev. Benedict J. Fenwick, (S. J.)...........1817-1818
Bishop of Boston, 1825.   1822-1825
Deceased, August 11, 1846, Boston, Mass.

Rev. Anthony Kohlmann, S.J......................1818-1820
Deceased, April 10, 1836, Rome.

Rev. Enoch Fenwick, S.J........................1820-1822
Deceased, November 25, 1827, Georgetown, D. C.

Rev. Stephen L. Dubuisson, S.J...............1825-1826
Deceased, August 14, 1864, Pau, France.
Rev. William Feiner, S.J...................1826-1829
Deceased, June 9, 1829, Georgetown, D. C.
Rev. John William Beschter, S.J................1829
Deceased, January 4, 1842, Paradise, Pa.
Rev. Thomas F. Mulledy, S.J..................1829-1837
Deceased, July 20, 1860, Georgetown, D. C.   1845-1848
Rev. William McSherry, S.J.....-.............1837-1840
Deceased, December 18, 1839, Georgetown, D. C.
Rev. Joseph A. Lopez, S.J.....................1840
Deceased, October 5, 1841, St. Inigoes, Md.
Rev. James Ryder, S.J.......................1840-1845
Deceased, January 12, 1860, Philadelphia, Pa.   1848-1851
Rev. Samuel A. Mulledy, S.J..................1845
Deceased, January 8, 1866, New York.
Rev. Charles H. Stonestreet, S.J...............1851-1852
Deceased, July 3, 1885, Holy Cross College, Worces-
ter, Mass.
Rev. Bernard A. Maguire, S.J.................1852-1858
Deceased, April 26, 1886, Philadelphia, Pa.   1866-1870
Rev. John Early, S.J........................1858-1866
Deceased, May 24, 1873, Georgetown, D. C.   1870-1873
Rev. Patrick F. Healy, S.J....................1873-1882
Deceased, January 10, 1910, Georgetown University,
Washington, D. C.
Rev. James A. Doonan, S.J....................1882-1888
Deceased, April 12, 1911, Georgetown University,
Washington, D. C.
Rev. J. Havens Richards, S.J..................1888-1898
Church of St. Ignatius, 84th St., New York City.
Rev. John D. Whitney, S.J....................1898-1901
Loyola College, Baltimore, Md.
Rev. Jerome Daugherty, S.J...................1901-1905
Woodstock College, Woodstock, Md.
Rev. David H. Buel, S.J......................1905-1908
Gonzaga College, Washington, D. C.
Rev. Joseph J. Himmel, S.J...................1908-1912
Keyser Island, South Norwalk, Conn.
Rev. Alphonus J. Donlon, S.J..................1912

Prefects of Studies, College Department

Rev. Daniel Lynch, S.J............................1850-1855
Deceased, April 1, 1884, Washington, D. C.
Rev. George Fenwick, S.J.........................1855-1857
Deceased, November 27, 1857, Georgetown, D. C.
Rev. Joseph O'Callaghan, S.J.....................1857-1858
Deceased, January 21, 1869, at sea.   1867-1868
Rev. J. Robert Fulton, S.J........................1858-1860
Deceased, September 4, 1895, San Francisco, Cal.
Rev. Charles H. Stonestreet, S.J..................1860-1862
Deceased, July 3, 1885, Holy Cross College,   1863-1864
Worcester, Mass.
Rev. Edward McNerhany, S.J...................1862-1863
Deceased.
Rev. James A. Ward, S.J..........................1864-1867
Deceased, May 29, 1895, Georgetown, D. C.
Rev. Patrick F. Healy, S.J........................1868-1879
Deceased, January 10, 1911, Georgetown University,
Washington, D. C.
Rev. William T. Whiteford, S.J....................1879-1881
Deceased, April 16, 1883, Georgetown, D. C.
Rev. James A. Doonan, S.J........................1881-1882
Deceased, Georgetown University, Washington, D. C.
Rev. James B. Becker, S.J.........................1882-1883
Georgetown University, Washington, D. C.
Rev. Edward I. Devitt, S.J........................1884-1886
Georgetown University, Washington, D. C.
Rev. Edward H. Welch, S.J........................1888-1890
Deceased, December 2, 1904, Georgetown, D. C.
Rev. Edward Connolly, S.J........................1890-1891
Deceased, Boston, Mass.
Rev. Thomas E. Murphy, S.J......................1891-1893
Brooklyn College, Brooklyn, N. Y.
Rev. Jerome Daugherty, S.J.......................1893-1894
Woodstock College, Woodstock, Md.

Rev. Francis P. Powers, S.J......................1894-1895
    Boston College, Boston, Mass.
Rev. William J. Ennis, S.J.......................1895-1897
    President, Loyola College, Baltimore, Md.
Rev. John A. Conway, S.J........................1897-1899
    Georgetown University, Washington, D. C.   1901-1903
Rev. James B. Fagan, S. J.......................1899-1901
    Deceased, April 28, 1906, New York City.
Rev. W. G. Read Mullan, S.J......................1903-1905
    Deceased January 25, 1911, Baltimore, Md.
Rev. Charles Macksey, S.J.......................1905-1909
    Gregorian University, Rome, Italy.
Rev. John B. Creeden, S.J........................1909

Founders of the School of Medicine

Joshua A. Ritchie, A.M., '40, M.D.; Noble Young, M.D.; Flodoardo Howard, M.D.; Charles H. Lieberman, M.D., and Johnson Eliot, M.D.

Deans of the School of Medicine

Flodoardo Howard, M.D.........................1851-1855
    Deceased, January, 1888, Rockville, Md.
Johnson Eliot, M.D.............................1855-1876
    Deceased, December 30, 1883, Washington, D. C.
Robert Reyburn, M.D...........................1876-1878
    Deceased, March 25, 1909, Washington, D. C.
Francis A. Ashford, M.D........................1878-1883
    Deceased, May 18, 1883, Washington, D. C.
J. W. H. Lovejoy, M.D..........................1883-1888
    Deceased, March 18, 1901, Washington, D. C.
G. L. Magruder, M.D., A.M......................1888-1900
    Stoneleigh Court, Washington, D. C.
George M. Kober, M.D., LL.D....................1900
    1600 T Street, Washington, D. C.

Dean of the Dental School

William N. Cogan, D.D.S.........................1901
920 H Street N. W., Washington, D. C.

Founders of the School of Law

Hon. Martin F. Morris, Hon. Charles W. Hoffman and Dr. Joseph M. Toner.

Deans of the School of Law

Hon. Charles P. James, LL.D.....................1870-1875
Deceased.
Hon. George W. Paschal, LL.D...................1875-1876
Deceased, February 16, 1878.
Hon. Charles W. Hoffman, LL.D..................1876-1890
Deceased.
Hon. Martin F. Morris, LL.D....................1890-1895
Deceased, September 12, 1909, Washington, D. C.
Hon. Jeremiah M. Wilson, LL.D..................1895-1900
Deceased, October, 1901, Washington, D. C.
Hon. George E. Hamilton, LL.D..................1900-1903
Lawyer and President of the Capital Traction Co.,
Union Trust Co., Washington, D. C.
Hon. Harry M. Clabaugh, LL.D...................1903
Chief Justice of the Supreme Court of the District
of Columbia.

Alumni Societies of Georgetown University

NATIONAL SOCIETY OF ALUMNI

OFFICERS

George E. Hamilton, Washington, D. C.............President
William F. Quicksall, Washington, D. C....First Vice-President
Dr. S. S. Adams, Washington, D. C......Second Vice-President
Charles A. DeCourcy, Lawrence, Mass... Third Vice-President
Robert J. Collier, New York City........Fourth Vice-President
J. Percy Keating, Philadelphia, Pa.........Fifth Vice-President
Henry R. Gower, Union Trust Bldg., Washington,
    D. C. ....Secretary

EXECUTIVE COMMITTEE

Rev. Alphonsus J. Donlon, S.J....................Ex-Officio
George E. Hamilton.............................Ex-Officio
Raymond A. Heiskell, Washington, D. C.
Joseph I. Weller, Washington, D. C.
Charles J. Murphy, Washington, D. C.
Dr. Roy D. Adams, Washington, D. C.
Dr. C. P. Neil, Washington, D. C.
Clarence E. Fitzpatrick, Boston, Mass.
Grafton L. McGill, New York City.
William V. McGrath, Philadelphia, Pa.
C. Moran Barry, Norfolk, Va.

New York Society

J. Lynch Pendergast, 32 Liberty Street, N. Y. City....President
Andrew J. Shipman, 37 Wall Street, N. Y. City...Vice-President
James A. MacElhinny, 120 Broadway, N. Y. City......Treasurer
Jas. S. McDonogh, 80 Wall Street, N. Y. City........Secretary
Joseph Healy, 57 Fulton St., N. Y. City....Executive Committee
John G. Agar, 31 Nassau St., N. Y. City..Executive Committee
Martin Conboy, 27 Pine St., N. Y. City....Executive Committee

Philadelphia Society

Anthony A. Hirst...........................President
William V. McGrath, Jr...................Vice-President
Joseph L. McAleer........................Secretary
Edward J. Wade....................Executive Committee
William L. Hirst ....Executive Committee
William McAleer, Jr...............Executive Committee

Northeastern Pennsylvania Society

. John O'D. Mangan, Pittston, Pa...................President
James L. Morris, Wilkesbarre, Pa..............Vice-President
Francis M. Foy, Pittston, Pa.........Secretary and Treasurer

Pacific Coast Society

James V. Coleman...............................President
Walter S. Martin..............................Vice-President
J. Neal Power.....................Secretary and Treasurer
Dr. J. Dennis Arnold............................Director
Joseph S. Tobin................................Director
Thomas A. Driscoll.............................Director

Wisconsin Society

Erwin Plein Nemmers, Milwaukee..................President
Thomas C. Downs, Fond du Lac...............Vice-President
Harry V. Kane, Milwaukee.......................Secretary
James T. Fitzsimmons, Milwaukee.................Treasurer
Henry F. Reilly, Milwaukee....Chairman Executive Committee
Joseph W. Singleton, Eau Claire.........Executive Committee
Otto Bosshard, La Crosse...............Executive Committee
Francis X. Boden, Milwaukee,
     Wisconsin Correspondent Georgetown College Journal

Georgetown University Club of New England

John M. Madigan, Houlton, Me....................President
Hon. Charles A. DeCourcy, Lawrence, Mass......Vice-President
Hon. John D. McLaughlin, Boston, Mass.......Vice-President
Hon. William G. McKechnie, Springfield, Mass...Vice-President
B. A. Doherty, Boston, Mass..................Vice-President
Charles J. Martell, Boston, Mass...................Treasurer
Clarence E. Fitzpatrick, Boston, Mass..............Secretary

Georgetown University Club of Western Pennsylvania

Albert E. Murphy, Pittsburgh, Pa..............Vice-President
Herbert N. Munhall, Pittsburgh, Pa...........Vice-President
J. Linus Moran, Pittsburgh, Pa........Secretary and Treasurer

Georgetown University Club of Chicago

Patrick H. O'Donnell............................President
Clifton F. Woods.........................Vice-President
Vincent F. Corcoran................Secretary and Treasurer

GEORGETOWN UNIVERSITY
Alphabetical List of Living Graduates

The sign (*) indicates that the address is the last known, though it has not been verified.

When two addresses are given, the first is the present address; the second, the permanent home address.

Abbaticchio, Raymond J., LL.B., '05. Lawyer, Trust Building, Fairmont, W. Va.

Abbott, Joseph F., LL.B., '11; LL.M., '12. Secretary to Chief Justice, Court of Appeals, D. C., 1422 Rhode Island Ave. N. W., Wash., D. C.

Abel, Joseph, LL.B., '96; LL.M., '97. Dept. of Agriculture, 1454 Clifton St., Washington, D. C.

Abell, Enoch B., A.B., '77; LL.M., '89. Lawyer and Editor, Leonardtown, Md.

Acker, Albert E., M.D., '07. Physician, Jacksonville, Fla.

Abrahams, Horatio Ely, M.D., '03. Physician, Trinidad, Colo.

Adair, George Fitzpatrick, M.D., '00. Physician, Fort Wood, N. Y.

Adams, Hon. Alfred A., LL.B., '89; LL.M., '90. Lawyer, Lebanon, Tenn.

Adams, Edward H., M.D., '76. Physician, McLean Hospital, Waverly, Mass.

Adams, Francis J., M.D., '81. Physician, 1008 Third Ave., Great Falls, Mont.

Adams, J. Ray, LL.B., '97; LL.M., '98. Lawyer, 1009 Fifth St. S. E., Washington, D. C.

Adams, Jesse Lee, Jr., M.D., '98. Physician, Tacoma Park, D. C.

Adams, John Warren, LL.B., '02. Lawyer, Alturas, Cal.

Adams, Roy Delaplaine, M.D., '04. Physician, G. U. Med. Fac., 926 17th St. N. W., Washington, D. C.

Adams, Samuel Shugert, M.D., '79. Physician, G. U. Med. Fac., 1 Dupont Circle, Washington, D. C.

Adams, William W., LL.B., '10. Gen. Land Office, 1423 S St. N. W., Washington, D. C.

Addison, Francis G., Jr., LL.B., '11. 1339 Q St. N. W., Washington, D. C.

Addison, Joseph, LL.B., '08; LL.M., '09. Lawyer, 207 N. Calvert St., Baltimore, Md.

Adkins, Jesse Corcoran, LL.B., '99; LL.M., '00. Lawyer, G. U. Law Fac., Columbian Bldg., Washington, D. C.

Adler, Leon, LL.B., '91; LL.M., '92. Lawyer, U. S. Pension Office., Washington, D. C.

Agar, John G., A.B., '76; A.M., '88; Ph.D., '89; LL.D., '10. Lawyer, 31 Nassau St., New York City.

Ahlgren, William B., LL.B., '10; LL.M., '11; L.D.M., '11. Civil Service Com., Atlanta, Ga.

Aikin, William E., LL.B., '96; LL.M., '97. Lawyer, 607 4th St. N. W., Washington, D. C.

Aimone, Victor A., M.D., '12. N. Y. Lying-in Hospital, New York City.

Albertsen, Walter F., LL.B., '08. Vice-Pres. Mechan. & Metals. Nat'l Bank, 33 Wall St., New York City.

Albrecht, Joseph A., LL.B., '09. Lawyer, Robey, East Falls Church, Va.

Alexander, Arthur A., A.B., '97; LL.B., '02. Lawyer, 412 5th St. N. W., Washington, D. C.

Alexander, Charles W., LL.B., '89; LL.M., '90. Lawyer, Title Ins. and Trust Co., 5th and Spring Sts., Los Angeles, Cal.

Alexander, Frank C., LL.B., '12. Duluth, Minn.

Alexander, George W., M.D., '08. Physician, 53 Main St., Orono, Maine.

Alexander, John C., LL.B., '10; LL.M., '11; L.D.M., '11. Pros. Atty. Wayne County, 462 Jefferson Ave., East, Detroit, Mich.

Alford, James R., LL.B., '99. Lawyer, *Nashville, Tenn.

Algue, Rev. Jose, S.J., Ph.D., '04. Director, Weather Bureau, Manila Observatory, Manila, P. I.

Alicoate, John W., LL.B., '12. Ashtabula, Ohio.

Allain, Louis Bush, A.B., '87. Manufacturer, Seattle, Wash.

Allee, John G., LL.B., '05. Lawyer, Wibaux Bldg., Miles City, Mont.

Alleger, Walter W., M.D., '90. Physician and Prof. Bacter., U. S. Col. Phys. and Surg., 143 U St., Washington, D. C.

Allen, Albert R., LL.B., '88. Lawyer, 326 Chester St., Anacostia, D. C.

Allen, Edward, LL.B., '90. Lawyer, *Norwalk, Conn.

Allen, Rt. Rev. Edward P., D.D., '89. Bishop, Diocese of Mobile, Cathedral, Mobile, Ala.

Allen, Harlan C., LL.M., '94. Clerk, Coast and Geodetic Survey, 1460 Monroe St., Washington, D. C.

Allen, John, M.D., '08. Physician, Wye, Ark.

Allen, Joseph B., LL.B., '94; LL.M., '95. Lawyer, 2011 12th St. N. W., Washington, D. C.

Allen, Thomas B., LL.B., '91; LL.M., '92. Lawyer, St. Joseph, Mo.

Allen, William, A.B., '75. Lawyer, 51 E. 65th St., New York City.

Allison, George Wm., LL.B., '98; LL.M., '99. Lawyer, *Elberton, Ga.

Altman, John W., LL.B., '01. Reg. in Chancery, Court House, Birmingham, Ala.

Anderson, George M., LL.B., '99. Lawyer, 705 G St. N. W., Washington, D. C.

Anderson, Herbert L., LL.B., '10. Special Agent, Bureau of Corporations, 1223 12th St. N. W., Washington, D. C.

Anderson, James W., LL.B., '04. Principal Examiner, U. S. Patent Office, Washington, D. C.

Anderson, Joseph W., LL.B., '89; LL.M., '90; M.D., '94. Real Estate, Manette, Kitsap Co., Wash.

Anderson, Lindley S., LL.B., '87; LL.M., '88. Asst. Examiner, Patent Office, Washington, D. C.

Anderson, Richard T., LL.B., '05. Dept. Com. and Labor, Washington, D. C.

Anderson, Dr. Sam H., A.B., '67. Physician, Woodwardville, Md.

Andrews, Burt W., LL.M., '99. Treasury Department, Washington, D. C.

Andrews, Marshall V., LL.M., '93. Pension Office, Washington, D. C.

Andrews, Oliveira T., A.B., '47; A.M., '70. 621 St. Paul St., Baltimore, Md.

Andrews, Wm. A., LL.B., '94; LL.M., '95. Lawyer, Fendall Bldg., Washington, D. C.

Andrews, Wm. Robert, LL.B., '97; LL.M., '98. Lawyer, 344 D St. N. W., Washington, D. C.

Andrews, Wm. T., LL.B., '88; LL.M. '89. P. O. Dept., Washington, D. C.

Angulo, Charles, A.B., '11. Law Student, 509 W. 121st St., New York City.

Ansart, Louis L., LL.B., '10. Patent Office, 1400 Chapin St., Washington, D. C.

Aplin, Alfred, M.D., '88. Physician, England.

Applegarth, Wm. F., Jr., A.B., '99. Lawyer, Golden Hill, Md.

Appleman, Frank S., LL.B., '92. Patent Lawyer, 16 Warder Bldg., Washington, D. C.

Archer, James B., Jr., LL.B., '97. Lawyer, 458 La. Ave. N. W., Washington, D. C.

Archer, John W., A.B., '45; A.M., '51. *Virginia.

Armstrong, John D., LL.B., '02. Inventor, 311 Gay St., Phoenixville, Pa.

Armstrong, Stanley Everton, D.D.S., '10. 1778 Nostrand Ave., Brooklyn, N. Y.

Armstrong, Wm. J., M.D., '70. Physician, 1620 Conn. Ave. N. W., Washington, D. C.

Armstrong, Wm. P., LL.B., '88. U. S. Envelope Agent, Hartford, Conn.

Arnold, Eugene F., LL.M., '79; A.M., '90. 1633 31st St. N. W., Washington, D. C.

Arnold, Francis S., LL.B., '91; LL.M., 92. Lawyer, Bemidji, Minn.

Arnold, Dr. J. Dennis, A.B., '73; A.M., '77. Physician, *San Francisco, Cal.

Arnold, J. DeWitt, LL.B., '93; LL.M., '94. Secretary and Treasurer, Vapor Heating Co., 503 North American Bldg., Philadelphia, Pa.

Arnold, T. J., M.D., '69. *New York City.

Arth, Charles Woodbury, LL.B., '03; LL.M., '04. Corcoran Bldg., Washington, D. C.

Ashfield, John M., M.D., '73. *Ohio.

Ashford, Bailey Kelly, M.D., '96; Sc.D., '11. Maj. U. S. Med. Corps, San Juan, Porto Rico.

Ashford, Francis Asbury, M.D., '01. U. S. Immigration Service, Montreal, Canada.

Ashford, Mahlon, M.D., '04. Capt. Med. Corps, U. S. A., 1763 P St. N. W., Washington, D. C.

Ashley, Wm. F., Jr., LL.B., '99; LL.M., '00. Lawyer, 40 Exchange Pl, New York City.

Ashmore-Noakes, S. S., M.D., '88. Physician, England.

2

Ashton, John Thornton, D.D.S., '11. 210 S. Washington St., Alexandria, Va.

Aspern, Henry T., LL.B., '86; LL.M., '87. Lawyer, 822 1st National Bank Bldg., Chicago, Ill.

Atherton, Leland T., LL.B., '12. Atlanta, Ga.

Athey, Thomas Franklin, LL.B., '01. Lawyer, Larned, Kansas.

Atkins, John W. G., LL.B., '87. *Fayetteville, Ark.

Atkins, Paul N., M.D., '12. Georgetown University Hospital, Washington, D. C.

Atkinson, Charles D., LL.M., '04. Lawyer, Pocahontas, Iowa.

Atkinson, Lawrence C., A.B., '04. 1329 St. Mary's St., New Orleans, La.

Atkinson, Wade H., M.D., '89. Physician, 1402 M St. N. W., Washington, D. C.

Atkisson, Horace L. B., LL.B., '94; LL.M., '95. Counsel, Banking and Currency Com., House of Rep., Washington, D. C.

Augenstein, Melvin M., D.D.S., '12. 1343 Fairmont St., Washington, D. C.

Austin, Walter F., LL.M., '00. Editor and Publisher, 34 Union Sq., New York City.

Ayer, David E., LL.B., '95. *Oakland, Cal.

Ayer, F. Carleton, M.S., '05. Professor, Tempe, Arizona.

Ayer, Richard B., LL.M., '92. Bates, Boland & Ayer, General Contractors, Oakland, Cal.

B

Babcock, Henry J., Jr., LL.B., '06. Govt. Printing Office, Washington, D. C.

Babcock, Louis A., LL.B., '11. 215 Eighth St. S. E., Washington, D. C.

Babendreier, Louis Milius, M.D., '10. Physician, 1110 F St. N. W., Washington, D. C.

Baby, Michael W., A.M., '60. *Canada.

Baby, Raymond Francis, A.B., '95. 830 Land Title Bldg., Philadelphia, Pa.

Bach, Edmund J., A.M., '97; LL.B., '98; LL.M., '99. Manufacturer, 2500 Grand Ave., Milwaukee, Wis.

Backes, Edward H., LL.B., '06. Lawyer and Broker, 135 William St., New York City.

Bacon, Wm. J., Jr., LL.B., '09; LL.M., '10. Washington Dime Savings Bank, 7th and E Sts., Washington, D. C.

Badeaux, Thomas A., A.B., '71; A.M., '73. Lawyer, Thibodeaux, La.

Baden, James H., LL.B., '02. Sec. U. S. Trust Co., 29 S St., Washington, D. C.

Baden, Wm. H., LL.B., '91; LL.M., '92. Lawyer, Colorado Bldg., Washington, D. C.

Bailey, Frederick J., LL.B., '10. Wells River, Vermont.

Bailey, Lorenzo Alton, LL.B., '76. Lawyer, 452 D St. N. W., Washington, D. C.

Baker, Alfred B., LL.B., '11. 130 Bryant St. N. W., Washington, D. C.

Baker, Daniel Wm., LL.B., '92; LL.M., '93. Lawyer, G. U. Law Faculty, Evans Bldg., Washington, D. C.

Baker, Francis B., LL.B., '85; LL.M., '86. Asst. Chief, Pension Office, 1619 17th St. N. W., Washington, D. C.

Baker, Dr. Frank, A.M., '88; Ph.D., '90. (G. U. Med. and Den. Fac.), Supt. Nat. Zoological Park, Washington, D. C.

Baker, Frank C., M.D., '99. Maj., U. S. A., Camp Overton, Mindanao, P. I.

Baker, Gibbs Latimer, LL.B., '99. Lawyer, Colorado Bldg., Washington, D. C.

Baker, Henry A., LL.B., '10. Clerk, 1300 Pa. Ave. N. W., Washington, D. C.

Baker, J. Newton, LL.B., '04; LL.M., '05. Lawyer, Interstate Commerce Com., Washington, D. C.

Baker, Jason E., LL.B., '94. *Covington, Ind.

Baker, John G., LL.B., '93. Lawyer, Eschol, Pa.

Baker, Ril T., LL.B., '97; LL.M., '98. Manager Union Central Life Ins. Co., 812-15 U. B. Bldg., Dayton, Ohio.

Baker, Samuel S., LL.B., '94. *326 F St. N. E., Washington, D. C.

Baker, Wm. W., M.D., '91. P. O. Dept., Washington, D. C.

Ball, Walter J., A.B., '74. Sec. Lafayette Loan and Trust Co., Lafayette, Ind.

Ballard, Thomas V., LL.B., '96. Navy Yard, Portsmouth, Va.

Ballentine, John G., A.B., '87. Pulaski, Tenn.

Balzer, Henry J., LL.B., '11. 27 Adams St., Washington, D. C.

Bandel, George E., LL.B., '04; LL.M., '05. Asst. Supt. Div. Ry. Adj., P. O. Dept., Washington, D. C.

Banfield, Charles P., M. D., '09. Physician, *1407 S. Michigan Ave., Chicago, Ill.

Bangs, Roscoe E., LL.B., '09. Lawyer, 1768 Willard St., Washington, D. C.

Bankert, Robert F., LL.B., '12. Altoona, Pa.

Bankhead, John H., Jr., LL.B., '93. Lawyer, Jasper, Ala.

Bankhead, Wm. B., LL.B., '95. Lawyer, Jasper, Ala.

Barbee, Robert A., LL.B., '08. Lawyer, Prospect Hill, Va.

Barber, Horace W., LL.B., '08. Dept. of Agriculture, Washington, D. C.

Barber, James H. Morgan, M.D., '88. 918 E St. N. W., Washington, D. C.

Barker, Harry A. L., LL.B., '10. The Royal, 14th and Girard Sts. N. W., Washington, D. C.

Barnard, Clarence, LL.B., '99. Automobile Sales Manager, 17th and U Sts., Washington, D. C.

Barnard, Ralph P., LL.B., '92; LL.M., '93. Lawyer, Columbian Bldg., Washington, D. C.

Barnes, Robert L., LL.B., '11. Lawyer, 225 Federal Bldg., San Antonio, Texas.

Barney, J. W., M.D., '71. *San Francisco, Cal.

Barnhart, Wm. P., LL.B., '03. Automobile Business, 1707 14th St. N. W., Washington, D. C.

Barnitz, Harry D., M.D., '80. Physician, E. Houston and Losoya Sts., San Antonio, Texas.

Barr, Hugh W., LL.B., '10. Lawyer, 219 8th St. N. E., Washington, D. C.

Barrett, George T., M.D., '08. Physician, Erie, Pa.

Barrett, John Michael, A.B., '99. Asst. Corp. Counsel, 10 W. 90th St., New York City.

Barrett, Park Mitchell, M.D., '11. Chief Res. Physician, Garfield Hospital, Washington, D. C.

Barrie, George, M.D., '92. Surgeon, 601 W. 110th St., New York City.

Barrington, Richard L., M.D., '89. Physician, 208 Old Custom House, St. Louis, Mo.

Barron, Clement Laird, M.D., '98. Physician, St. Mary's, W. Va.

Barrow, Wylie M., LL.B., '97. Asst. Atty. Gen. of La., Baton Rouge, La.

Barrows, Frederick I., LL.B., '01. Cashier, Cent. State Bank, Connersville, Ind.

Barry, Cheevers Moran, A.B., '01; LL.B., '04. Real Estate and Ins., 58 Mariner St., Norfolk, Va.

Barry, James D., LL.B., '12. 928 14th St. N. W.; Washington, D. C.; Chicago, Ill.

Barry, John A., M.D., '91. Physician, 45 Monument Square, Charlestown, Mass.

Barry, Wm E., LL.B., '96. Pawtucket, R. I.

Barry, Wm. Foley, LL.B., '95. Lawyer, Cranston, R. I.

Bartlett, George A., LL.B., '94. Lawyer, Reno, Nevada.

Barton, Frederick Rae, M.D., '04. *Nova Scotia.

Barton, McKinney, Jr., LL.B., '07. Lawyer, 600 Memphis Trust Bldg., Memphis, Tenn.

Barton, Wilfred M., M.D., '92. Physician, (G. U. Med. and Den. Fac.) 1730 Conn. Ave., Washington, D. C.

Bastion, Joseph Edward, M.D., '06. Lieut., U. S. A., Manila, P. I.

Bates, John Savage, A.B., '98. St. Louis, Mo.

Baukhages, Frederick E., Jr., LL.B., '97. Lawyer, Berwyn, Md.

Baumgardner, Ray, LL.B., '07. Journalist, Indianapolis Star, Indianapolis, Ind.

Bayly, Charles B., LL.B., '92. Manager, John F. Ellis Co., 1333 Eleventh St. N. W., Washington, D. C.

Bayne, Joseph Breckenridge, M.D., '03. Physician, 1141 Conn. Ave. N. W., Washington, D. C.

Beach, S. Edward, LL.B., '10; LL.M., '11; L.D.M., '11. Bureau of Eng. and Ptg., 303 N. Alfred St., Alexandria, Va.

Beale, J. F., LL.B., '72. Lawyer, 303-4 Com. Nat. Bank Bldg., Washington, D. C.

Beall, Benjamin M., M.D., '73. Physician, 417 H St. N. E., Washington, D. C.

Beary, John V. H., A.B., '04. Planter, Thibodeaux, La.

Beaven, Rt. Rev. Thomas D., D.D., '89. Bishop of Diocese of Springfield, 260 State St., Springfield, Mass.

Beck, Henry K., LL.B., '95; LL.M., '96. Lawyer, Lancaster, Ohio.

Beck, John A., LL.B., '12. Sec. U. S. S., Salt Lake City, Utah.

Becker, George Heilmann, D.D.S., '10. Dentist, G. U. Den. Fac., 927 S St., Washington, D. C.

Becker, Joseph, LL.B., '88; LL.M., '89. Patent Atty., 1315 Fairmont St. N. W., Washington, D. C.

Beckman, John J, LL.B., '10. 1403 Marlowe Ave., Indianapolis, Ind.

Beckman, John J., LL.B., '10. Lawyer, Beckman & Smith, 422-3-4 Yeon Bldg., Portland, Oregon.

Becnel, Alphonse, A.B., '55. *Louisiana.

Beegan, Joseph Francis, LL.B., '80. *Bergan, Ind.

Behrend, Adajah, M.D., '66. Physician, 1214 K St. N. W., Washington, D. C.

Behrend, Ed. B., M.D., '94. Physician, (G. U. Med. and Den. Fac.), 1214 K St. N. W., Washington, D. C.

Behrend, Rudolph B., LL.B., '97; LL.M., '98. Lawyer, 416 5th St. N. W., Washington, D. C.

Belew, Russell P., LL.B., '07. Supt. of City Hall, Washington, D. C.

Belisle, George E., LL.B., '97; LL.M., '98. Lawyer, 340 Main St., Worcester, Mass.

Bell, Charles, M.D., '02. Physician, Old P. O. Bldg., Detroit, Mich.

Bell, David Wilkinson, LL.M., '05. Treas. Dept., 4318 9th St. N. W., Washington, D. C.

Bell, Henry, M.D., '74. *New York.

Bell, James Fisher, A.B., '99. Lawyer, 1310 N. Washington Ave., Scranton, Pa.

Beller, Frederick F., LL.B., '11; LL.M., '12; L.D.M., '12. P. O. Dept., 235 First St. N. W., Washington, D. C.

Benfer, James P., LL.B., '99. Lawyer, Dundee, Ohio.

Benham, Wm. R., LL.B., '97. Lawyer, 319 John Marshall Place, Washington, D. C.

Benjamin, Charles F., LL.B., '76. Lawyer, 506 11th St. N. W., Washington, D. C.

Bennett, Hilary F., LL.B., '95. *Austin, Texas.

Bennett, Wm. Aloysius, M.D., '95. Physician, 2810 Wentworth Ave., Chicago, Ill.

Bennewitz, John A., LL.B., '04. Lawyer, Creighton Law Fac., 303 First Nat. Bk. Bldg., Omaha, Neb.

Benson, Charles J., LL.B., '91. Lawyer, Shawnee, Okla.

Bergin, Frank J., LL.B., '10. Gen. Land Office, 11 L St. N. E., Washington, D. C.

Bernhard, Eugene J., LL.B., '92; LL.M., '93. 720 A St. S. E., Washington, D. C.

Bernstein, Hyman, M.D., '04. Physician, 1008 Wylie Ave., Pittsburg, Pa.

Bernstein, I. Isadore, LL.B., '09. Lawyer, 3920 Northampton St., Chevy Chase, Md.

Berry, Albert E., LL.B., '03; LL.M., '04. Division Manager, Bell Telephone Co. of Penna., 6708 McCallum St., Germantown, Pa.

Berry, Washington, R., LL.B., '93; LL.M., '94. Lawyer, 1416 Meridian Pl. N. W., Washington, D. C.

Best, Johnson V., LL.B., '10; LL.M., '11; L.D.M., '11. Govt. Clerk, P. O. Dept., 1823 Holland Ave., New York City.

Betts, Albert P., M.D., '94. Physician, Woodburn, Ind.

Bevington, Morris R., LL.M., '09. Chief Naturalization Examiner, Federal Bldg., St. Louis, Mo.

Bierer, A. G. Curtin, LL.M., '86. Lawyer, Guthrie, Okla.

Bilbrey, Joseph H., LL.B., '12. Vale, Tenn.

Binckley, J. M., M.D., '61. *Ohio.

Bingham, Goundry W., LL.B., '98. *Birmingham, Ala.

Binley, Walter S., LL.B., '06. Lawyer, Newburyport, Mass.

Birckhead, Edward, LL.B., '01. Lawyer, 1810 First St. N. W., Washington, D. C.

Birckhead, Oliver W., LL.B., '08. Treasury Dept., Washington, D. C.

Birge, Harry C., LL.B., '91; LL.M., 92. Lawyer, Woodland, Falls Church, Va.

Birgfeld, Frank A., LL.B., '01. Lawyer, Linden P. O., Montgomery Co., Md.

Birgfeld, Wm. Edward. LL.B., '03. Isthmian Canal Com., Washington, D. C.

Birkby, Wm. T., LL.B., '11. 1228 Mass. Ave., Washington, D. C.

Biscoe, Frank L., M.D., '01. Physician, (G. U. Med. and Den. Fac.), The Farragut, Washington, D. C.

Bishop, Arthur Garnett, LL.B., '98; LL.M., '99. Vice-Pres. Dist. and Wash. Title Companies, 610 13th St., Washington, D. C.

Bittenbender, John H., LL.B., '12. Bloomsbury, Pa.

Bivins, James Daniel, LL.B., '98. Atty and Editor, Albemarle, N. C.

Black, Paul S., LL.B., '94; LL.M., '95. Asst. Atty., Dept. Interior, Washington, D. C.

Black, Richard R., LL.B., '98. *Waterboro, S. C.

Blackburn, James W., Jr., LL.B., '86. Lawyer, Gunton Bldg., 472 La. Ave. N. W., Washington, D. C.

Blackburn, Samuel E., LL.B., '91. Dist. Judge, Ancon, Canal Zone, Pan.

Blackistone, Frank D., LL.B., '94. Lawyer, Southern Bldg., Washington, D. C.

Blackistone, Julien C., M.D., '06. Physician, (G. U. Med. Fac.), Wash. Asylum Hospital, Washington, D. C.

Blackmon, Henry C., LL.B., '97. Lawyer, *Anadasko, Okla.

Blackwell, Samuel, LL.B., '95; LL.M., '96. Lawyer, New Decatur, Ala.

Blaine, Robert G., M.D., '97. Physician, 133 C St. S. E., Washington, D. C.

Blake, Thomas C., A.B., '79; A.M., '89. Lawyer, 90 W. Broadway, New York City.

Blanchard, Edwin C., LL.B., '08. Lawyer, 811 Colorado Bldg., Washington, D. C.

Blanford, E. Murray, LL.B., '11. The Plymouth, Washington, D. C.

Blanford, Joseph H., A.B., '54; A.M., '56. Agriculturist, T. B., Prince George County, Md.

Blease, Hon. Coleman L., LL.B., '89. Governor of South Carolina, Columbia, S. C.

Blease, Henry H., LL.B., '87. *Newbury, S. C.

Blewett, Robert L., LL.B., '02. Lawyer, 426 Coleman Bldg., Seattle, Wash.

Bliss, George R., LL.B., '09. Lawyer, 1923 15th St., Washington, D. C.

Block, Emil H., LL.B., '93; LL.M., '93. War Dept., 1917 I St. N. W., Washington, D. C.

Block, Leon A., LL.B., '10. Real Estate, 155 11th St. N. E., Washington, D. C.

Block, Theodore L., LL.B., '12. Muskogee, Okla.

Bloomer, G. Beale, LL.B., '11. 2008 Hilyer Pl. N. W., Washington, D. C.

Blount, Julian W., LL.B., '12. Pierre, S. D.

Bobst, Alfred E., LL.B., '10. Asst. Examiner, Patent Office, 102 13th St. N. E., Washington, D. C.

Bocock, James B., LL.B., '06. Director of Athletics, Univ. of N. C., Chapel Hill, N. C.

Boden, Francis Xavier, A.M., '98; LL.B., '99; LL.M., '00; Ph.D., '00. Lawyer, 504 Majestic Bldg., Milwaukee, Wis.

Boe, Edward J., D.D.S., '12. 656 Morris St. N. E., Washington, D. C.

Boehs, Charles J., M.D., '09. Physician, Fort Banks, Winthrop, Mass.

Bogan, Joseph A., LL.B., '05. P. O. Dept., 1138 6th St. N. W., Washington, D. C.

Boggs, Walter J., A.B., '98. Lawyer, 215 St. Paul St., Baltimore, Md.

Bogue, A. P., M.D., '72. Bureau of Education, Washington, D. C.

Boiseau, Louis T., LL.B., '90; LL.M., '91. Capt. Art. U. S. A., Fort Riley, Kan.

Bolan, Herbert A., A.B., '92. Physician, 3827 Spring Garden St., Philadelphia, Pa.

Boland, J. Bernard, LL.B., '08. Lawyer and Broker, North Adams, Mass.

Boland, Joseph Emmet, A.B., '09. Carbondale, Pa.

Boldrick, Samuel J., LL.B., '92. Lawyer, 408-9 Walker Bldg., Louisville, Ky.

Bolen, Hon. Hubert L., LL.B., '05. Lawyer, Member of Legislature, Amer. Nat. Bank Bldg., Oklahoma City, Okla.

Bomberger, Lincoln, LL.B., '99; LL.M., '00. Prin. Examiner, Pension Bureau, 1607 7th St. N. W., Washington, D. C.

Bond, George J., LL.B., '72. Lawyer, 623 F St. N. W., Washington, D. C.

Boone, Rev. Ed. D., S. J., A.B., '51. Loyola College, Baltimore, Md.

Boone, Nathan F., LL.B., '96; LL.M., '97. Lawyer, Mulberry, Tenn.

Booth, Clarence M., LL.B., '06. *Boise City, Idaho.

Booth, Edward H., LL.B., '93. War Dept., 717 21st St. N. W., Washington, D. C.

Booth, John F., LL.B., '92; LL.M., '93. *Rutledge, Tenn.

Borchardt, Herbert, D.D.S., '11. 912 French St., Washington, D. C.

Borden, Frank Wheeler, M.D., '95. Physician, 904 E. Capitol St., Washington, D. C.

Borden, Joseph A., LL.B., '88; LL.M., '89. *Dunkirk, Ind.

Borger, Bernard L., LL.B., '12; L.D.M., '12. 1832 Biltmore St., Washington, D. C.

Borger, George I., LL.B., '12. 647 7th St. N. E., Washington, D. C.

Borroughs, Dent, M.D., '59. *Maryland.

Bosshard, Otto, LL.B., '00. Lawyer and Pres., Bank of Holmen, Batavian Nat. Bank Bldg., La Crosse, Wis.

Bossidy, John C., M.D., '85. Physician, 419 Boylston St., Boston, Mass.

Bounds, Edgar W., LL.B., '93. Lawyer, Marlin, Texas.

Bouic, Wm. Garner, LL.B., '97. Lawyer, Hot Springs, Garland Co., Ark.

Bourgeois, Sidney J., LL.B., '12. Jeanerette, La.

Bourne, Caleb P., LL.M., '87. Chief of Division, Stamps and Supplies, Manila, P. I.

Bowen, H. Morton, M.D., '93. Physician, Aquasco, Md.

Bowen, Ivan, LL.B., '11. Lawyer, Mankato, Minn.

Bowen, John M., LL.B., '10. Lawyer, 35 Everton St., Dorchester, Mass.

Bowen, Thomas, M.D., '63. *West Indies.

Bower, S. W., M.D., '86. *New York.

Bowie, George Calvert, LL.B., '10. Real Estate, 17 R St. N. W., Washington, D. C.

Bowles, Benjamin A., LL.B., '08. Cashier, Potomac Savings Bank, Washington, D. C.

Bowles, Norman S., LL.B., '09. Lawyer, 1814 G St. N. W., Washington, D. C.

Boyd, Carl Bainbridge, M.D., '98. 1st Lieut. U. S. A., Campo Indian Agency, Campo, Cal.

Boyd, Howard, LL.B., '95; LL.M., '96. Lawyer, (G. U. - Law Fac.), Columbian Bldg., Washington, D. C.

Boyd, John Aloysius, A.M., '97; LL.B., '99. Lawyer, 713 N. Calvert St., Baltimore, Md.

Boyd, Wm. H., LL.B., '08. Army War College, Washington, D. C., 4438 Kansas Ave. N. W., Washington, D. C.

Boykin, Lester E., LL.B., '08. Expert Public Roads, Dept. of Agriculture, Washington, D. C.

Boyle, Frank A., LL.B., '09. Lawyer, *1211 Euclid Pl. N. W., Washington, D. C.

Boyle, Thomas Maurice, A.B., '09. Shenango House, Sharon, Pa.

Brabant, Louis J., LL.B., '12. Madison, Wis.

Braden, Frank Wheeler, M.D., '95. Physician, 628 E. Capitol St., Washington, D. C.

Bradenbaugh, Claude C., A.B., '89. *Fendall Bldg., Washington, D. C.

Bradfield, Jefferson Davis, M.D., '91. Physician, 1506 N. Capitol St., Washington, D. C.

Bradley, Very Rev. Bernard J., LL.D., '12. Pres. Mt. St. Mary's College, Emmitsburg, Md.

Bradley, Howard Alnsen, D.D.S., '04. *Morrison, Ill.

Bradley, James F., D.D.S., '11. 317 C St. S. E., Washington, D. C.

Bradley, John N., LL.B., '12. Kensington, Md.

Bradley, Thomas Henry, LL.B., '74. *Missouri.

Bradshaw, Aaron, LL.B., '77. Lawyer, 901 C St. N. E., Washington, D. C.

Bradshaw, Leonard, LL.B., '94; LL.M., '95. Asst. Dist. Atty., Chevy Chase, Md.

Bradshaw, Moses, LL.B., '77. Atty. and Postmaster, Aspen, Colo.

Bradshaw, Thomas G., LL.B., '11. 2575 14th St. N. W., Washington, D. C.

Brady, Edmund, LL.B., '04. Lawyer, (G. U. Law Fac.), Union Trust Bldg., Washington, D. C.

Brady, Edward J., A.B., '98. Broker, Riverdale, Md.

Brady, Eugene D. F., A.B., '70; A.M., '72; LL.B., '72. Lawyer, Bond Bldg., Washington, D. C.

Brady, George M., A.M., '01; Ph.L., '02; Ph.D., '03; LL.B., '03. Lawyer, 804 St. Paul St., Baltimore, Md.

Brady, James T., LL.B., '92; LL.M., '93. Lawyer, 515 Ashland Block, Chicago, Ill.

Brady, John Stanley, A.B., '01. Physician, 40 W. 68th St., New York City.

Brady, Joseph P., LL.B., '96. Clerk U. S. Circuit and Dist. Courts, Richmond, Va.

Bragaw, George Driver, M.D., '11. 911 O St., Washington, D. C.

Bragg, Charles G., LL.B., '12. Oklahoma City, Okla.

Branagan, Francis A., LL.B., '89. Philippine Commissioner, Manila, P. I.

Brand, Carl Martin, LL.B., '03. *Pittsburg, Pa.

Brand, Edward A., LL.B., '09. Manassas, Va.

Brand, J. Stewart, LL.B., '10. Bureau Im. and Nat., 3411 Holmead Pl., Washington, D. C.

Brantley, A. Augustus, LL.B., '96. U. S. Commissioner of Dist. Court, Orangeburg, S. C.

Brantley, Thomas F., LL.B., '94; LL.M., '95. Lawyer, Orangeburg, S. C.

Brapley, James F., D.D.S., '11. Delaware.

Brashears, John W., Jr., LL.B., '03; LL.M., '04. U. S. Geol. Survey, Winthrop Heights, Washington, D. C.

Brashears, Shipley, Jr., LL.B., '99; LL.M., '00. Ins. Broker and Not. Pub., Woodward Bldg., Washington, D. C.

Braud, Peter S., A.B., '59. *Louisiana.

Brawley, Wm. C., LL.B., '96. Lawyer, Warsaw, Wis.

Bray, Wm. J., LL.B., '12. Bridgeport, Conn.

Brearton, John L., LL.B., '02. Lawyer, Savanna, Ill.

Breck, Gen. Samuel, U. S. A., M.D., '67. 1651 Beacon St., Brookline, Mass.

Breckenridge, Scott Dudley, M.D., '07. Physician, Columbia Hospital, Washington, D. C.

Breckons, Robert W., LL.B., '90. U. S. Dist. Atty., Dist of Hawaii, Honolulu, Hawaii.

Breece, Abner B., LL.B., '12. Fayetteville, N. C.

Breen, James, M.D., '71. *Massachusetts.

Breese, Edmund C., LL.B., '12. Treas. Dept., Toledo Apts., Washington, D. C.

Breitenbucher, Ed. E., LL.B., '03. Lawyer, Lodi, Cal.

Bremner, Vincent Aloysius, A.M., '03. Manufacturer, 901 Forquer St., Chicago, Ill.

Brennan, Frederick J., LL.B., '09; LL.M., '10. Lawyer, 1405 G St. S. E., Washington, D. C.

Brennan, James Joseph, A.B., '05. 70 Oxford St., Somerville, Mass.

Brennan, James Smith, A.B., '83. Banker, 1011 Delaware Ave., Wilmington, Del.

Brennan, John C., LL.B., '10. 75 U St. N. W., Washington, D. C.

Brennan, John E., M.D., '05. Physician, 153 E. Main St., Waterbury, Conn.

Brennan, John P., LL.B., '04. Lawyer, 16 Weybosset St., Providence, R. I.

Brennan, Leslie W., A.B., '06. Cotton Business, Seneca Bldg., Utica, New York.

Brennan, Michael F., LL.B., '99; LL.M., '00. *District of Columbia.

Brennan, Rev. Patrick H., S. J., M.D., '67. Trinity Church, Washington, D. C.

Brenner, Charles F., LL.B., '00. Merchant, 229 Worth Ludlow, Dayton, Ohio.

Brent, George, LL.B., '90; LL.M., '92. Lawyer, 118 Van Buren St., Brooklyn, N. Y.

Brent, Henry W., A.B., '52. *Baltimore, Md.

Brent, Wm. M., A.B., '74. *Maryland.

Bresnahan, Francis J., LL.B., '03; LL.M., '04. Real Estate, 424 M St. N. W., Washington, D. C.

Brez, Selig C., LL.B., '12. 908 N. Y. Ave. N. W., Washington, D. C.

Briant, Lassaline P., A.B., '61. Lawyer, *138 S. White St., New Orleans, La.

Brice, Charles H., LL.B., '87. *Washington, D. C.

Brick, George Joseph, M.D., '11. Fanwood, N. J.

Brickenstein, John H., LL.B., '91. Lawyer, 1603.19th St., Washington, D. C.

Brickley, Bartholomew A., LL.B., '04. Lawyer, 18 Tremont St., Boston, Mass.

Bride, Wm. W., LL.B., '04. Lawyer, Century Bldg., Washington, D. C.

Bridges,Walter S., LL.B., '87. U. S. Special Examiner, U. S. Court, P. O. Bldg., Chicago, Ill.

Brien, L. Tiernan, A.B., '46. Urbanna, Frederick Co., Md.

Briggs, Edmund B., LL.B., '75. Lawyer, *Washington, D. C.

Brisbane, Howard P., M.D., '82. Physician, Pearl Lagoon, Nicaragua, C. A.

Brisboe, Arthur, LL.B., '91; LL.M., '92. P. O. Dept., 143 T St. N. W., Washington, D. C.

Brock, Fenelon B., LL.B., '96; LL.M., '97. Washington Loan & Trust Bldg., Washington, D. C.

Brockbank, Senes T., LL.M., '88. Lawyer, *Clearfield, Pa.

Broderick, Dr. John Kern, A.M., '97. Sales Manager, 809 N. Main St., St. Louis, Mo.

Broe, Wm. B., LL.B., '84. *Pittsburg, Pa.

Brogan, Francis Albert, A.B., '83. 548 Bee Bldg., Omaha, Neb.

Bromson, Solomon, LL.B., '10. Lawyer, 87 Weybossett St., Providence, R. I.

Bronson, Charles E., M.D., '83. Physician, 936 T St., Washington, D. C.

Brooke, John Cook, LL.B., '05. Lawyer, Evans Bldg., Washington, D. C.

Brooks, J. Henry, M.D., '65. Physician, 3737 Michigan Ave. N. E., Brookland, D. C.

Brooks, John Dosher, M.D., '95. Physician, Sturgis, S. D.

Brosnan, John J., LL.B., '01. Lawyer, 482 La. Ave. N. W., Washington, D. C.

Brosseau, Leonard A., A.B., '12. 1950 Barry Ave., Chicago, Ill.

Brown, Bernard C., LL.B., '10. Lawyer, Colorado Bldg., Washington, D. C.

Brown, C. F., M.D., '65. *Connecticut.

Brown, Charles F., LL.B., '12; L.D.M., '12. Frankfort, Ind.

Brown, Charles J., LL.B., '90; LL.M., '92. Sec. and Treas. Arcade Co., 3435 Oakwood Terrace, Washington, D. C.

Brown, Charles O., LL.B., '73. *Washington, D. C.

Brown, Charles Orton, LL.B., '94. *Washington, D. C.

Brown, Rev. Edward Howard, S. J., A.B., '79. Pastor, Juneau, Alaska.

Brown, Everard C., LL.B., '88; LL.M., '89. Pension Bureau, 1361 Oak St. N. W., Washington, D. C.

Brown, Dr. Francis E., A.B., '87. Physician, 917 St Paul St., Baltimore, Md.

Brown, Frank I., LL.B., '12. Calvin Run, Va.

Brown, Harry S., LL.B., '99. Lawyer, 1502 Meridian St. N. W., Washington, D. C.

Brown, Henry Hagerty, A.B., '11. Law Student, 2087 Fifth Ave., New York City.

Brown, James C., LL.B., '76. *Pennsylvania.

Brown, Joe C., LL.B., '12. Battle Creek, Mich.

Brown, Joseph Richard, M.D., '11. (G. U. Med. Fac.), Napa City, Cal.

Brown, Leo Joseph, M.D., '11. St. John's Hospital, Long Island City, L. I., N. Y.

Brown, Oliver P. Morton, LL.B., '95. Lawyer, 409 Commercial Bank Bldg., Washington, D. C.

Brown, Orlando, A.B., '52 *Tennessee.

Brown, Paul J., A.B., '03. 45 E. Willis Ave., Detroit, Mich.

Brown, Samuel K., LL.B., '12. 911 N. H. Ave., Washington, D. C.

Brown, Thomas H., LL.B., '92. *District of Columbia.

Brown, Walter N., LL. B., '08. Lawyer, Interstate Com. Commission, Washington, D. C.

Brown, Walter S., LL.B., '09. Lawyer, 515 E. Pike St., Seattle, Wash.

Brown, Wm. Arthur, A.M., '00. Merchant, C. H. Brown & Co., Fitchburg, Mass.

Brown, Wm. E., LL.B., '10. Dist. Govt., 315 H St. N. W., Wash., D. C.

Brown, Wm. H. J., LL.B., '98. *Chevy Chase, Md.

Brownell, Henry B., LL.B., '90; LL.M., '91. Lawyer, 41 Park Row, New York City.

Browning, A. G., M.D., '60. Physician, Third and Sutton Sts., Maysville, Ky.

Browning, George L., LL.B., '95. Lawyer, Rediviva, Va.

Browning, Wm. Livingston, LL.M., '01. Lawyer, 416 5th St. N. W., Washington, D. C.

Brownson, Henry Francis, A.B., '52; A.M., '55. Lawyer, 243 E. Larned St., Detroit, Mich.

Bruder, Andrew Joseph, M.D., '10. Physician, 1024 Baxter Ave., Superior, Wis.

Bruhl, Charles Emil, M.D., '00. Physician, 502 Scanlon Bldg., Houston, Texas.

Brumbaugh, Gaius Marcus, M.D., '88. Physician, 905 Mass. Ave. N. W.. Washington, D. C.

Brummett, Randolph Breese, M.D., '93. Navy Dept., 103 5th St. N. E., Washington, D. C.

Bryan, Henry L., LL.B., '88; LL.M., '89. Lawyer, 604 E. Capitol St., Washington, D. C.

Bryan, Paul S., LL.B., '92. *Middleport, Ohio.

Bryan, Richard H., A.B., '50. *Maryland.

Bryant, Frank W., LL.B., '04. Nat. Bank Examiner, 1410 S. Baltimore St., Tulsa, Okla.

Brylawski, Fulton, LL.B., '08; LL.M., '09. Lawyer, Fendall Bldg., Washington, D. C.

Buard, Louis A., A.B., '60. *Louisiana.

Buckley, John J., LL.B., '09; LL.M., '10. Lawyer, 1719 S St. N. W., Washington, D. C.

Buckley, J. T., LL.B., '08. Lawyer, 319-21 Arcade Bldg, Utica, N. Y.

Budlong, Orsemus, M.D., '80. Physician, Belford, N. J.

Buie, Walter A., LL.B., '92. Kimball Bldg., Boston, Mass.

Bullock, Edmund Cooper, LL.B., '03; LL.M., '04. Lawyer, Lewisburg, Tennessee.

Burbank, Caryl, M.D., '03. Physician, 2147 F St. N. W., Wash., D. C.

Burchmore, J. S., LL.B., '09. Evanston, Ill.

Burdick, Hon. Morton H., LL.B., '10. Mass. State Senator, Adams, Mass.

Burdine, Elbert F., LL.B., '95; LL.M., '96. *District of Columbia.

Burg, Hon. John B., LL.B., '97; LL.M., '98. Member of Legislature, Albuquerque, N. M.

Burg, Joseph P., LL.B., '94. U. S. Vice and Deputy Consul, Reichenberg, Austria.

Burger, John C. S., LL.B., '73. War Dept., 1412 Delafield Place, Washington, D. C.

Burger, Leopold C. E., LL.B., '99. Legal Reviewer, 507 6th St. N. W., Washington, D. C.

Burk, James W., A.B., '95; LL.B., '97 Lawyer, Canton, Pa.

Burke, Francis Hunter, LL.B., '03. Lawyer, Louisville Trust Co. Bldg., Louisville, Ky.

Burke, Frank H., A.B., '12. The Clermont, Kent Ave., Pittsfield, Mass.

Burke, Frederick B., M.D., '06. Physician, 121 Willis Ave., Detroit, Michigan.

Burke, John C., LL.B., '96; LL.M., '97. Lawyer, 115 Gibbs Ave., Newport, R. I.

Burke, Thomas W., M.D., '84. Pension Bureau, 800 L St. N. W., Washington, D. C.

Burlingame, Harry, LL.B., '11. Riverdale, Md.

Burnam, Harry E., LL.B., '87; LL.M., '88. Corporation Counsel, 303 City Hall Bldg., Omaha, Neb.

Burns, James Philip, A.B., '05. Hyde Park, Mass.

Burns, James W., LL.B., '08; LL.M., '10. Lawyer, Stanton Place, Washington, D. C.

Burton, Clarence F., LL.B., '07. Lawyer and Miner, Reno, Nev.

Burton, Hiram Ralph, LL.B., '08. Lawyer, Union Trust Bldg., Washington, D. C.

Burton, Linnoir, LL.B., '83. *North Yamhill, Oregon.

Busick, Adrian F., LL.B., '11. Sec. Com. of Corp., 3013 Dent Place, Washington, D. C.

Butcher, C. Tyson, LL.M., '86. *Virginia.

Bute, James H., M.D., '99. Physician, Houston, Texas.

Butler, A. Jeter, LL.B., '01. Lawyer, *Union, S. C.

Butler, Bartholomew W., LL.B., '07. Govt. Service, 10 Britton St., Worcester, Mass.

Butler, Francis J., M.D., '08. Physician, 10 Britton St., Worcester, Mass.

Butler, Henry, A.B., '87. *Omaha, Neb.

Butler, John A., LL.B., '88; LL.M., '89. Lawyer, 520 Rhode Island Ave. N. E., Washington, D. C.

Butler, John H., LL.B., '02. The Montgomery, N. Capitol and M Sts. Washington, D. C.

Butler, Patrick J., LL.B., '88; LL.M., '89. *Minneapolis, Minn.

Butler, Ulysses, LL.B., '01. Interstate Commerce Com., Wash., D. C.

Byrne, Arthur L., LL.B., '12. Everson, Pa.

Byrne, Edward Louis, A.B., '01. Brooklyn Un. Gas Co., 455 5th St., Brooklyn, N. Y.

Byrne, Francis Joseph, A.B., '99. Journalist, The Evening Times, Philadelphia, Pa.

Byrne, John F., LL.B., '04. Patent Attorney, 1814 N. Capitol St., Washington, D. C.

Byrne, John J., LL.B., '09; LL.M., '10. Dept. of Justice, 1902 H St. N. W., Washington, D. C.

Byrne, Walter C., M.D., '92. Physician, 168 Madison Ave., Elmira, N. Y.

Byrne, William L., A.B., '10. 151 6th Ave., Brooklyn, N. Y.

Byrne, Hon. Wm. M., A.B., '87. Lawyer, 220 Broadway, New York City.

Byrnes, Charles W., A.B., '07. Lawyer, 734 5th St., San Rafael, Cal.

Byrnes, J. C., M.D., '70. Med. Dir. and Capt., U. S. N., Washington, D. C.

Byrnes, Wm. Henry, Jr., A.B., '08. Lawyer, 305 Camp St., New Orleans, La.

Byrns, William F., M.D., '73. Physician, 1923 Calvert St., Wash., D. C.

C

Cabanis, E. Gerry, LL.B., '95; LL.M., '96. *Atlanta, Ga.

Cahill, Joseph Henry, A.B., '98. 57 Colony St., Meriden, Conn.

Cahill, Michael H., LL.B., '11. 2034 I St. N. W., Washington, D. C.; Corning, N. Y.

Cahill, Wm. Ambrose, B.S., '82. Physician, 1310 N. Salina St., Syracuse, N. Y.

Cain, James P., LL.B., '08. Lawyer, Dickinson, N. D.

Cain, William S., M.D., '02. Health Commissioner, 358 N. Main St., Elmira, N. Y.

Caldwell, George H., M.D., '65. *Massachusetts.

Calhoun, Charles A., LL.B., '96; LL.M., '97. Lawyer, 837 First Nat'l Bank Bldg., Birmingham, Ala.

Calkins, Thomas Joseph, A.M., '99; M.D., '00. Physician, 2512 Superior St., Cleveland, Ohio.

Callaghan, D. O'C., LL.B., '73; A.M., '89. Lawyer, 616 18th St. N. W., Washington, D. C.

Callaghan, William J., M.D., '01. Physician, Chevy Chase, Md.

Callahan, Charles J., LL.B., '11. Interstate Commerce Com., Washington, D. C.; Lowell, Mass.

Callahan, James Edward, A.B., '80. Law Book Pub., 114 Monroe St., Chicago, Ill.

Callan, Guida C., LL.B., '94; LL.M., '96. Patent Office, Wash., D. C.

Callander, William F., LL.B., '12. Dept. Agr., Wash., D. C.; Chicago, Ill.

Calvert, Clarence W., LL.B., '09. Lancaster, Wis.

Calvin, Claude W, LL.B., '12. P. O. Dept., Wash., D. C.; Joplin, Mo.

Camalier, Hon. Benj. Harris, A.M., '84. Sup. Court of Md., Leonardtown, Md.

Camalier, Franklin A., A.B., '04; M.D., '08. Physician, Leonardtown, Md.

Cammerer, Arno B., LL.B., '11; L.D.M., '11. Janesville, Wis.

Camp, Ernest W., LL.B., '12. Priv. Sec. H. R., Washington, D. C.; Saginaw, Mich.

Campbell, Charles B., M.D., '94. Pharmacist, 17th and Park Sts. N. W., Washington, D. C.

Campbell, Daniel G., LL.B., '89; LL.M., '90. Lawyer, San Antonio, Tex.

Campbell, J. Percy, LL.B., '11; L.D.M., '11. 940 S St. N. W., Washington, D. C.

Campbell, Louis J., LL.B., '10. Govt. City Office, Washington, D. C.; LaCrosse, Wis.

Campbell, Hon. Richard, LL.B., '99. Judge of Supreme Court, Manila, P. I.

Cannario, Lawrence Vergil, A.B., '05. Olla Sugar Co., Mt. View, Hawaii.

Cannon, Walter D., M.D., '90. Physician, The Alabama, Wash., D. C.

Cantwell, Edward J., LL.B., '04. Sec. Nat. Assn. of Letter Carriers, 945 Penna. Ave. N. W., Washington, D. C.

Cantwell, Thomas, A.B., '08. 471 I St. S. W., Washington, D. C.

Carleton, Hon. Robert P., LL.B., '95; LL.M., '96. County Judge, Fernandina, Fla.

Carlin, Frederick A., A.B., '02. Metropolitan Life Bldg., New York City.

Carlin, Frederick Theodore, A.B., '05. Contractor, Metropolitan Life Bldg., New York City.

Carlin, Harry Vincent A.B., '04. Contractor, Metropolitan Life Bldg, New York City.

Carlin, John Francis, A.B., '10. Law Student, 270 Washington Ave., Brooklyn, N. Y.

Carman, Louis D., M.D., '89. Med. Exam., U. S. Pension Office, 1351 Q St. N. W., Washington, D. C.

Carmody, John Doyle, LL.B, '11 Lawyer, 1614-16 Southern Bldg., Washington, D. C.

Carnahan, Joseph H., LL.B., '09. Lawyer, Keamath Falls, Oregon.

Carnes, Edward I., LL.B., '11. Jersey City, N. J.

Carney, Patrick Joseph, M.D., '04. Physician, School Committee, 626 Southbridge St., Worcester, Mass.

Carpenter, Matthew Hale, A.M., '04. Manufacturer, 325 35th St., Milwaukee, Wis.

Carr, Edward Quintin, A.B., '10. Law Student, 831 Carroll St., Brooklyn, N. Y.

Carr, Hon. John McAuliffe, A.B., '97; A.M., '98; LL.B., '99; LL.M., '00. Judge of City Courts, 548 Spitzer Bldg., Toledo, Ohio.

Carr, W. Saunders, A.M., '88. 9 E. Lexington St., Baltimore, Md.

Carr, Wilbur John, LL.B., '94. Chief of Consular Bureau, Dept. of State, Washington, D. C.

Carroll, Augustine Levins, A.B., '98. R. F. D. No. 2, Edgewater, Colo.

Carroll, J. Camillus, LL.B., '07. Lawyer, 1108 Hanna St., Fort Wayne, Indiana.

Carroll, Lafayette J., A.M., '82. *Arkansas.

Carroll, Michael James, M.D., '10. 29 Arbor St., Springfield, Mass.

Carroll, Stephen W., A.B., '12. Law Student, 285 Ashland Ave., Buffalo, N. Y.

Carroll, Timothy A., LL.B., '93; LL.M., '94. Bureau of Corporations, 1329 Mass. Ave., Washington, D. C.

Carroll, Vincent Levins, A.B., '01. Mining, Elko, Nev.

Carroll, Walton C., D.D.S., '10. 1408 L St. N. W., Washington, D. C

Carson, Frederick D., LL.B., '82. *Minneapolis, Minn.

Carter, Charles T., LL.B., '95. *Portland, Ore.

Carter, Edward Vivian, A.B., '11. Broker, Sharp & Irvine Co., Seattle, Wash.

Carter, G. William, Jr., LL.B., '09. Markham, Va.

Carter, J. Barrett, LL.B., '05; LL.M., '06. Lawyer, Evans Bldg., Washington, D. C.

Carter, Paul, LL.B., '06. Lawyer, Marianna, Fla.

Carusi, Thornton A., LL.B., '74. Lawyer, 1214 F St., Wash., D. C.

Carusi, Charles Francis, A.B., '94. Lawyer, Nat. Metro. Bank Bldg., Washington, D. C.

Cary, Frederick, D.D.S., '10. Stewart Bldg., Washington, D. C.

Cary, Joseph M., LL.B., '91; LL.M., '92. *Montgomery, Ala.

Cary, William G., LL.B., '90. Lawyer, 513 L St. N. W., Wash., D. C.

Casares, Erneste Espinosa, M.D., '10. Calle 56, No. 474, Merida, Yucatan, Mexico.

Casey, Daniel E., LL.B., '09. Lawyer, 1244 10th St., Washington, D. C.

Casey, John J., LL.B., '11. Lawyer, Webster, Mass.

Casey, Rev. John Thomas, A.B., '99. 192 School St., Athol, Mass.

Casey, Stephen J., LL.B., '96; LL.M., '97. Lawyer, 731 Bannigan Bldg., Providence, R. I.

Cashell, Joseph, LL.B., '77. *Wisconsin.

Cashman, Joseph T., LL.B., '02. Lawyer, 51 Chambers St., New York.

Cashman, Thos. F., M.D., '02. Physician, Slater Bldg., Washington, Pa.

Cassidy, Charles W., A.B., '12. 104 Washington St., Norwich, Conn.

Cassidy, Francis W., LL.B., '10. Lawyer, 411-12 Berkshire Life Ins. Bldg., Pittsfield, Mass.

Cassidy, John Hughes, A.B., '97. Lawyer, 95 Bank St., Waterbury, Conn.

Cassidy, Louis T., A.B., '04; M.D., '08. Physician, 32 Willow St., Waterbury, Conn.

Cassin, John Leo, LL.B., '01. Lawyer, Southern Bldg., Wash., D. C.

Casteel, Frank A., D.D.S., '08. Dentist (G. U. Den. Fac.), Philippi, W. Va.

Catlin, Benj. Rush, LL.B., '73. Patent Lawyer, 622 F St. N. W., Washington, D. C.

Caulfield, John, Mus.Doc., '65. Klopper's Station, B. & O. R. R., Md.

Cauthorne, Robert Gabriel, A.B., '99. Lawyer, 911 Lowman Bldg., Seattle, Wash.

Cavanagh, Richard B., LL.B., '01. Lawyer, *New York City, N. Y.

Cavanaugh, Thos. Ed., M.D., '00. Physician, 245 Maple St., Holyoke, Mass.

Chalmers, Nills, LL.B., '09. Imm. Insp., Hidalgo, Texas.

Chamberlin, Frank T., M.D., '85. Physician, 1323 M St. N. W., Washington, D. C.

Chamberlin, Justin Morrill, LL.B., '97; LL.M., '98. Lawyer, 482 La. Ave., Washington, D. C.

Chamberlin, Wm. L., M.D., '91. Physician, Poland, Ind.

Chambers, J. Paul, M.D., '84. 530 Media St., Philadelphia, Pa.

Chapin, Harry Bailey, M.D., '08. Physician and Surgeon, Torrington, Conn.

Charles, Garfield, LL.B., '04; LL.M., '05. Senate Bldg., Wash., D. C.

Chauveau, Lieut.-Col. Charles Auguste, A.B., '95; A.M., '96. Advocate, Quebec Bar, 75 Peter St., Quebec, Canada.

Cheney, Archie W., LL.B., '09. Lawyer, 525 Atlas Block, Salt Lake City, Utah.

Chew, John Paul, A.B., '82; LL.B., '84; LL.M., '85. Editor-in-Chief "The Church Progress," 520 Fullerton Bldg., St. Louis, Mo.

Chew, Philemon W., LL.B., '93; LL.M., '94. Lawyer, 612 F St. N. W., Washington, D. C.

Chewning, Alexander C., LL.B., '09. Postal Savings Bank, 1344 Vermont Ave. N. W., Washington, D. C.

Chez, Joseph, LL.B., '97. Lawyer, First Nat. Bank Bldg., Ogden, Utah.

Chick, Henry S., LL.B., '12. 1646 32d St. N. W., Washington, D. C.

Chisholm, Joseph L. B., LL.B., '12. Cambridge, Mass.

Choate, Rufus, M.D., '67. Physician, The Farragut, Washington, D. C.

Choice, William, A.B., '57; A.M., '60. *South Carolina.

Christiancy, George A. C., LL.B., '92. Lawyer, 141 Broadway, New York City.

Church, J. B., LL.B., '75. Lawyer, 908 G St. N. W., Washington, D. C.

Clabaugh, Hon. Harry M., LL.D., '08. Dean, G. U. Law Fac., Chief Justice of Supreme Court D. C., Washington, D. C.

Clagett, Henry William, A.B., '60. Agriculturist, Rosaryville, Prince George County, Md.

Clapp, Harry M., LL.B., '93; LL.M., '94. Sec. U. S. Appraiser, Custom House, New York City.

Clapp, Woodbridge, LL.B., '09; LL.M., '10. Lawyer, U. S. Senate, Washington, D. C.

Clark, Elroy Newton, LL.B., '92. Lawyer, Gen. Attorney Denver & Rio Grande Railway, 429 Equitable Bldg., Denver, Col.

Clark, Eugene B., M.D., '72. Patents, 724 9th St. N. W., Wash., D. C.

Clark, Henry Clyde, LL.B., '12. Bu. of Immig., Wash., D. C.; Carmi, Ill.

Clark, John Alexander, M.D., '98. Capt. and Asst. Surgeon, U. S. A., Plattsburg Barracks, Plattsburg, N. Y.

Clark, J. Nelson, M.D., '67. Physician, 306 Broad St., Harrisburg, Pa.

Clark, John Francis, A.B., '93. New York City.

Clark, Julius S., M.D., '69. Physician, 109 Maple St., Melrose, Mass.

Clark, Leon A., LL.B., '03. Dist. Atty. Alameda Co., 651 Boulevard Way, Oakland, Cal.

Clark, Manley J., LL.B., '09. Dep. Dist. Atty., 651 Boulevard Way, Oakland, Cal.

Clark, Roland Eugene, LL.B., '04. Lawyer, Houlton, Maine.

Clark, Thomas R., LL.B., '12. 463 Luray Place, Washington, D. C.

Clark, Thomas Russell, LL.B., '12; L.D.M., '12. New Orleans, La.

Clarke, Daniel E., LL.B., '10; LL.M., '11. Edge Hill P. O., King George, Virginia.

Clarke, Harold H., LL.B., '09; LL.M., '10. 627 E St. N. W., Wash., D. C.

3

Clarke, Joseph C. B., M.D., '55. *Missouri.

Clarke, Walter S., A.B., '80. 49 and 51 Chambers St., New York City.

Clay, Wm. Rogers, LL.B., '88; LL.M., '89. Commissioner of Appeals of Kentucky, Frankfort, Ky.

Clayson, H., LL.B., '00. *Buffalo, N. Y.

Cleary, Francis J., LL.B., '06. Dept. of Agriculture, 45 Randolph Pl. N. W., Washington, D. C.

Clary, Thomas J., M.D., '08. Surgeon, 369 1st St., Brooklyn, N. Y.

Clements, Elmer E., LL.M., '12. McHenry County, N. D.

Clements, James E., LL.B., '81. Lawyer, 1321 F St. N. W., Washington, D. C.

Cleveland, Jesse F., A.B., '53; A.M., '55. *South Carolina.

Clevenger, Oliver Blaine, D.D.S., '11. 2411 Pa. Ave., Washington, D. C.

Cleverdon, J. S., M.D., '72. *Ohio.

Cline, Roy R., LL.B., '11; LL.M., '12; L.D.M., '12. Patent Office, Washington, D. C.; White Heath, Ill.

Clothier, Albert J., LL.B., '11. Somerset, Ky.

Coad, Wm. James, A.M., '00 Lawyer, 407 First Nat. Bk. Bld., Omaha, Neb.

Cobb, James S., M.D., '93. Physician, Clayton, Del.

Cobb, Norville H., LL.B., '07. Merchant, 1713 G St. N. W., Washington, D. C.

Cockran, Hon. W. Bourke, LL.D., '99. Lawyer, 31 Nassau St., New York City.

Cockrell, Alston, A.B., '06. Lawyer, 703 Laura St., Jacksonville, Fla.

Cody, John K. I., LL.B., '98. Nat. Cash Register Co., 64 N. Clinton Ave., Trenton, N. J.

Coflin, Charles B., LL.M., '09. Lawyer, 1116 15th St. N. W., Washington, D. C.

Cogan, Wm. J., A.B., '12. Med. Stu., 98 Avenue C, Bayonne, N. J.

Cogswell, Julius E., LL.B., '88. Lawyer, Charleston, S. C.

Cohen, Girard M., LL.B., '10. Savannah, Ga.

Cohen, Morris, LL.B., '11. 624 4½ St. S. W., Washington, D. C.

Cohen, Nathan, LL.B., '10. Patent Lawyer, 154 Nassau St., New York City.

Cohnan, Ed. J., LL.B., '07. Treasury Dept., 433 10th St. N. E., Washington, D. C.

Colbert, Michael J., A.B., '83; A.M., '89; LL.B., '85; LL.M., '86. Attorney-at-Law, 1809 R St. N. W., Washington, D. C.

Cole, Halbert Denton, LL.B., '04. Lawyer, Black River Falls, Wis.

Cole, John T., M.D., '91. Physician, 820 H St. N. E., Washington, D. C.

Cole, Peter L., LL.B., '92; LL.M., '93. Pension Bureau, New York City.

Coleman, David Charles, M.D., '04. Physician, 377 Cabot St., Beverly, Mass.

Coleman, James Valentine, A.B., '69; A.M., '71; LL.B., '73. Lawyer, 711 Balboa Bldg., San Francisco, Cal.

Coleman, Watson E., LL.B., '94. Lawyer, Pacific Bldg., Washington, D. C.

Colfer, John T., LL.B., '10; L.D.M., '11. 18 16th St. N. E., Wash., D. C.

Colgin, Edward Broadnax, A.M., '00; LL.B., '01. Lawyer, 65-66 Theater Bldg., Houston, Texas.

Collier, Hon. C. Needham, A.B., '68; A.M., '95; LL.D., '98. Associate Justice of the Supreme Court, New Mexico.

Collier, Robert Joseph, A.B., '94. Publisher and Editor, 752 Park Ave., New York City.

Colliere, George Riggs, A.B., '04; LL.B., '07. Real Estate and Ins., 1410 G St. N. W., Washington, D. C.

Colliflower, Charles E., Jr., LL.B., '05. Stenographer, 156 Tenn. Ave. N. E., Washington, D. C.

Colliflower, James Edward, A.B., '06; LL.B., '10; LL.M., '11. 220 First St. S. E., Washington, D. C.

Collins, J. Harry, M.D., '06. Physician, 308 Collins Ave., Pittsburg, Pa.

Collins, James Marshall, LL.B., '96; LL.M., '97. Lawyer, 216 Court St., Marysville, Ky.

Collins, Joseph Francis, A.B., '97; A.M., '98; LL.B., '99; LL.M., '00. Lawyer, 43 Cedar St., New York City.

Collins, Lawrence M., M.D., '12. St. Francis Hospital, Jersey City, New Jersey.

Collins, Robert L., LL.B., '91. Lawyer, Wellington, Kansas.

Collins, Walter Homer, LL.B., '01. Clerk U. S. Soldiers' Home, Washington, D. C.

Collins, Wm. Granville, LL.B., '05. Law and Real Estate, Clarendon, Alexandria County, Va.

Columbus, Wm. F., LL.B., '07; LL.M., '08. Lawyer, 452 D St. N. W., Washington, D. C.

Combs, Robert Cornelius, A.B., '55; A.M., '59. Lawyer, Leonardtown, Maryland.

Comerford, Peter Patrick, Ph.B., '93. 480 8th Ave., New York City.

Conant, Thomas, M.D., '67. Physician, Addison Gilbert Hospital, 38 Pleasant St., Gloucester, Mass.

Conaty, Rt. Rev. Thomas James, D.D., '89. Bishop of Monterey and Los Angeles, 114 E. 2nd St., Los Angeles, Cal.

Conboy, Martin, LL.B., '98; LL.M., '99. Lawyer, 27 Pine St., New York City.

Condon, Wm. F., A.M., '03; LL.B., '06; LL.M., '07. Lawyer, Fort Dodge, Iowa.

Coneby, Wm. H., LL.B., '04. Lawyer, 34 Warder Bldg., Washington, D. C.

Coniff, John J., LL.B., '89. Lawyer, 1421 Chaplain St., Wheeling, West Virginia.

Conley, Francis, A.B., '53. *Massachusetts.

Conley, Martin S., A.B., '08; LL.B., '11; LL.M., '12. Lawyer, 40 Brackett St., Portland, Maine.

Conley, Maurice J., D.D.S., '12. 24 West Green St., Somersworth, N. H.

Conlon, Charles F., LL.B., '98. Lawyer, New Britain, Conn.

Connelan, James A., LL.B., '96. Lawyer, Portland, Maine.

Connelly, Benjamin M., LL.B., '97; LL.M., '98. Govt. Service, Takoma Park, Md.

Connelly, Denis J., LL.B., '98. Lawyer, Elmira, N. Y.

Connelly, Martin F., LL.B., '09. Lawyer, 8 Congress St., Boston, Mass.

Conner, Wm. Wallace, LL.B., '02. Sec. and Counsel, Con. Sales Co., 1410 H St. N. W., Washington, D. C.

Connolly, Anthony A., LL.M., '90. Lawyer, 1219 13th St. N. W., Washington, D. C.

Connolly, Arthur L., LL.M., '06. Lawyer and Professor, 6 Beacon St., Boston, Mass.

Connolly, J. Edward, A.B., '04; LL.B., '07. Special Agent G. L. O., 712 E. & C. Bldg., Denver, Colo.

Connolly, John E., LL.B., '01. Lawyer, Banigan Bldg., Providence, Rhode Island.

Connolly, John W., A.B., '04. Broker, Nahant, Mass.

Connolly, Joseph B., LL.M., '90. Lawyer, 1219 13th St. N. W., Washington, D. C.

Connolly, Timothy Stanislaus, A.B., '97. Care of Charles Libby, Portland, Maine.

Connor, George A., LL.B., '02. Lawyer, 604 21st St. N. W., Washington, D. C.

Connor, John Edward, M.D., '04. Physician, Holmesdale, Pittsfield, Mass.

Connor, Wm P., M.D., '08. Physician, 913 Belmont Ave., Youngstown, Ohio.

Connors, George Robert, D.D.S., '04. Dentist, 331 Main St., Patterson, N. J.

Conover, J. C., M.D., '71. *New Jersey.

Conrad, Thomas K., M.D., '98. Physician, Chevy Chase, Md.

Conradis, Charles, LL.B., '90; LL.M., '91. Gen. Counsel, Traffic Serv.; The Ontario, Washington, D. C.

Constas, John N., M.D., '04. Physician, (G. U. Med. Fac.), 925 N. Y. Ave. N. W., Washington, D. C.

Conway, John Joseph, M.D., '01. Physician, Warren, R. I.

Conway, Wm. O., LL.B., '76. *Maryland.

Conigisky, Joseph Perl, D.D.S., '04. *Peoria, Ill.

Cony, Robert A., Jr., LL.B., '11. Lawyer, Augusta, Maine.

Cook, Ansell B., A.B., '75; LL.B., '77. *Georgia.

Cook, James C., LL.B., '97; LL.M., '98. Atty., Coweta, Okla.

Cook, Joseph P., LL.B., '10. Asst. Gen. Counsel, So. R. R. Co., 1502 Meridian Place, Washington, D. C.

Cook, Robert M., LL.B., '05. *West Philadelphia, Pa.

Cook, Wilson E., LL.B., '95. V.-Pres. Corydon Nat. Bank, Corydon, Ind.

Cookerow, Martin W., LL.B., '10. Special Agt. Bu. of Corpor., Com. and Labor, 1477 Newton St. N. W., Washington, D. C.

Cooksey, Ferdinand Cash, LL.B., '04. States Attorney for Charles Co., La Plata, Md.

Coon, John B., LL.B., '12. War Dept., Washington, D. C.; Woodville, Mississippi.

Cooney, James J., LL.B., '98; LL.M., '99. *Philadelphia, Pa.

Cooney, Matthew D., LL.B., '12. Dubuque, Iowa.

Cooper, John S., M.D., '69. Physician, *Louisville, Ky.

Cooper, Moses, M.D., '74. England.

Cooper, Sam Bronson, LL.B., '99; LL.M., '00. Lawyer, Beaumont, Texas.

Copeman, Wm. H., LL.M., '87. . *Nashville, Tenn.

Copp, Zed H., LL.B., '09. 1675 Wisconsin Ave., Washington, D. C.

Coppinger, Conor Walter Blaine, A.B., '07. 820 18th St. N. W., Washington, D. C.

Coppinger, J. G. Blaine, A.B., '07; LL.B., '10. Lawyer, 820 18th St. N. W., Washington, D. C.

Corbett, Edwin P., LL.B., '11; L.D.M., '11. Patent Attorney, Columbus, Ohio.

Corbett, Rev. John Walter Healy, A.M., '99. 177 Ashland St., W. Roxbury, Mass.

Corbin, E. Lyon, M.D., '59. *New York.

Corbin, Wm. E., M.D., '91. *1005 23d St. N. W., Washington, D. C.

Corcoran, Henry E., LL.B., '11. G. L. O., Washington, D. C.

Corcoran, James A., LL.B., '12. 2618 13th St. N. W., Washington, D. C.

Corcoran, Richard P., LL.B., '94; LL.M., '95. Mining, *Tonopah, Nev.

Corcoran, Vincent, A.B., '09. 6554 Stewart Ave., Chicago, Ill.

Corgan, Charles E., LL.B., '07. Lawyer, Nanticoke, Pa.

Cornell, Martin C., LL.B., '11. Asst. City Solicitor, 480 W. 5th St., Erie, Pa.

Cortelyou, Hon. George Bruce, LL.B., '95; LL.D., '08. Pres., Consolidated Gas Co., New York City.

Costello, John F., LL.B., '08. Hutchins Bldg., Washington, D. C.

Costello, M. F., LL.B., '08. Lawyer, 376 Weeden St., Pawtucket, R. I.

Costigan, Ignatius J. J., A.B., '02; LL.B., '04. Lawyer, 77 Fendall Bldg., Washington, D. C.

Cotterill, Charles E., LL.B., '11. Interstate Commerce Commission, 1348 Fairmont St., Washington, D. C.

Cottrell, Samuel, Jr., LL.B., '96. War Dept., 422 Belair Rd., Takoma Park, D. C.

Coughlan, J. Vincent, LL.B., '01. Special Agt., Gen. Land Office, Cheyenne, Wyo.

Coughlin, John T., LL.B., '81; LL.M., '82. Bu. Lat. Am. Af., State Dept., 1010 Otis Pl. N. W., Washington, D. C.

Coulthurst, John A., A.M., '93. Boston City Council, Lawyer, 1 Beacon St., Boston, Mass.

Cowhig, John J., LL.B., '09; LL.M., '10. Casanova, Va.

Cowles, A. E., D.D.S., '02. Dentist, Victor Bldg., Washington, D. C.

Cox, Charles Robert, LL.B., '04. Lawyer, 3422 O St. N. W., Washington, D. C.

Cox, Enoch M., LL.B., '11. Census Bureau, 444 M St. N. W., Washington, D. C.

Cox, Frank B., LL.B., '96; LL.M., '97. Lawyer, 7 Yankee Pl., Ellenville, N. Y.

Cox, Harry C., LL.B., '12. San Francisco, Cal.

Coyle, Dennis J., D.D.S., '08. Dentist, 4th and U Sts. South Bethlehem, Pa.

Coyle, Dr. Wm. E., M.D., '08. Physician, 45 Hawkins St., Waterbury, Conn.

Craig, Albert E., M.D., '06. Physician, 3125 O St. N. W., Washington, D. C.

Craighill, G. D., LL.B., '06. Lawyer, 723 15th St. N. W., Washington, D. C.

Cramer, Dick, LL.B., '90; LL.M., '91. Pension Office, Washington, D. C.

Cramer, Herman W., LL.B., '97. Lawyer, Junction City, Kansas.

Cranch, Dr. Edward, M.D., '73. Physician, 813 Sassafras St., Erie, Pa.

Crandall, Samuel B., LL.B., '06. Asst. U. S. Atty., Independence, N. Y.

Crane, Hon. G. Wm., LL.B., '09. Judge, Municipal Court, Aberdeen, S. D.

Crane, Wm. L., LL.B., '09. Lawyer, Union Trust Co., Washington, D. C.

Craven, Charles A., LL.B., '93. Highland Milling Co., 1122 Empire Bldg., Birmingham, Ala.

Craven, Thomas J., A.B., '87. 958 26th St. N. W., Washington, D. C.

Crawford, Charles A., LL.B., '05. Lawyer, U. S. Trust Co. Bldg., Terre Haute, Ind.

Crawford, James C., LL.B., '98; LL.M., '99. Dept of Justice, Washington, D. C.

Crawford, Wm. A., LL.B., '07. Lawyer, 128 C St. N. E., Washington, D. C.

Crawford, Wm. Gordon, LL.B. '98. Lawyer, 1407 F St. N. W., Washington, D. C.

Creecy, Donald B., LL.B., '11. Lawyer, Ilchester, Md.

Crittenden, Thomas B., M.D., '95. Physician, Horton, W. Va.

Croker, John Howard, LL.B., '12. Bu. Indian Affairs, Washington, D. C.; Stillwater, Okla.

Croghan, Francis E., M.D., '08. Physician, 1634 Westminster St., Providence, R. I.

Cromelin, Paul B., LL.B., '12. 526 6th St. S. E., Washington, D. C.

Crook, Harrison, M.D., '78. Physician (G. U. Med. Fac.), The Sherman, 15th and L Sts. N. W., Washington, D. C.

Crosby, John F., A.B., '12. Law Student, 117 Sheboygan St., Fond du Lac, Wis.

Crossfield, Hon. Amasa S., LL.B., '83; LL.M., '84. Justice, Sup. Court, Army and Navy Club, Manila, P. I.

Crossfield, Clare B., LL.B., '11; LL.M., '12; L.D.M., '12. Lawyer, 412 15th St. N. W., Washington, D. C.; Berkley, Cal.

Crosson, Henry J., M.D., '90. Physician, 1746 M St. N. W., Washington, D. C.

Crouch, Ralph W., LL.B., '12. Johnson City, Tenn.

Crow, Hon. Philip M., LL.B., '88; LL.M., '89. Judge, Circuit Court, Kenton, Ohio.

Crowe, John W., M.D., '97. Physician, 704 T St. N. W., Washington, D. C.

Crowley, Leo Francis, M.D., '09. Physician, 666 Jersey Ave., Jersey City, N. J.

Crowley, Robert E., LL.B., '06; LL.M., '07. Lawyer, Conrad Bk. Bldg., Great Falls, Montana.

Crozier, St. George B., Mus. Doc., '70. *Canada.

Cruikshank, Thomas Antisell, LL.B., '96; LL.M., '97. City P. O., 3125 11th St. N. W., Washington, D. C.

Crummey, Edward J., A.B., '08. Lawyer, 7 Madison Pl., Albany, N. Y.

Crump, C. Edward, LL.B., '11. Alexandria, Va.

Cruse, George E., LL.B., '96. Patent Atty., 141 Broadway, New York City.

Cuddy, M. Frank, LL.B., '10. 802 D St. N. E., Washington, D. C.; Baltimore, Md.

Cuddy, Stephen A., LL.B., '95. Law Clerk, 701 12th St. N. E., Washington, D. C.

Cudlipp, Malcolm A., M.D., '90. Physician, *Denver, Colo.

Cuenco, Jose Maria, A.M., '05; Ph.D., '07; LL.B., '07. Student, Seminario de San Carlos, Cebu, P. I.

Culkin, Wm. Purcell, A.B., '09. 245 Wabash Ave., Carthage, Ill.

Cull, Abner H., M.D., '68. *District of Columbia.

Cullen, Livingston James, A.B., '99. Lawyer, 105 S. La Salle St., Chicago, Ill.

Cullen, Rev. Thomas Francis, A.B., '99. St. Patrick's Church, Providence, R. I.

Cullinen, Alexander A., A.B., '86. Moncton, New Brunswick.

Culver, Ira J., M.D., '68. Physician, Knox City, Texas.

Cummings, George W., M.D., '65. *Minnesota.

Cummins, J. Wm., LL.B., '07. Lawyer and Referee in Bankruptcy, 1425 Chapline St., Wheeling, W. Va.

Cummisky, Edward Francis, M. D., '96. Physician, 1342 U St. N. W., Washington, D. C.

Cunniff, Michael M., Ph.B., '12. 1032 Beacon St., Boston, Mass.

Cunniff, Patrick S., LL.B., '99; LL.M., '00. Lawyer, 12 Pemberton Sq., Boston, Mass.

Cunningham, Francis Aloysius, A.B., '72; A.M., '74. Civil Engineer, 508 W. Maple Ave., Merchantville, N. J.

Curley, Charles Fallon, A.B., '97. Lawyer, Ford Bldg., Wilmington, Delaware.

Curran, John D. J., M.D., '03. Physician, 1418 S. Broad St., Philadelphia, Pa.

Curran, John L., LL.B., '10. Lawyer, 10 Burnside St., Providence, R. I.

Curran, Joseph J., LL.B., '05. Lawyer, 38 Auburndale Ave., W. Newton, Mass.

Curran, Robert J., LL.B., '11. Dept. Commerce and Labor, 18 Congress St., Boston, Mass.

Curriden, Samuel W., LL.B., '77. Lawyer, Office of Centre Market, Washington, D. C.

Curry, Daniel, LL.B., '01. Insurance Dept., Dist. Govt., Washington, D. C.

Curry, Frank L., D.D.S., '07. Dentist, 92 Shelton Ave., Jamaica, L. I.

Curtin, Richard A., LL.B., '04. Lawyer, Southern Bldg., Washington, D. C.

Curtis, George F., LL.B., '89; LL.M., '90. Lawyer, Shanghai, China.

Curtis, Maury, LL.B., '10. Dept. of Agr., 1225 1st Nat. Bk. Bldg., San Francisco, Cal.

Cuttle, Ignatius X., LL.B., '07; LL.M., '08. Lawyer, 56 N. Main St., Fall River, Mass.

D

Daiker, Fred. H., LL.B., '07; LL.M., '08. Bureau of Pensions, Washington, D. C.

Dailey, Vincent, A.B., '12. Grain and Produce Business, 48 South Ave., Brockport, N. Y.

Daily, B. E., M.D., '74. *Pennsylvania.

Daish, John Broughton, LL.B., '99; LL.M., '00. Lawyer, 723 15th St. N. W., Washington, D. C.

Dallas, Everett Jerome, LL.B., '73. *Kansas.

Dalton, Alfred S., LL.B., '97. Manager, Montgomery Mut. Bldg. and Loan Assn. of Montgomery Co., Kensington, Md.

Daly, J. Harry, LL.B., '92; LL.M., '93. 2924 E. 78th Pl., Chicago, Ill.

Daly, Joseph T., LL.B., '95; LL.M., '97. Stenographer, Navy Dept., Washington, D. C.

Daily, Louis J., A.B., '12. Law Student, 507 S. Broad St., Philadelphia, Pa.

Daly, Walter F., LL.B., '91; LL.M., '92. Lawyer, Denver, Colo.

Dammann, Milton, LL.B., '99. Lawyer, 141 Broadway, New York City.

Danforth. R. Foster, M.D., '86. Physician, 919 12th St., Washington, D. C.

Daniels, John W., LL.B., '01. Lawyer, Pawtucket, R. I.

Daniels, Rees P., LL.M., '86. Lawyer, Monadnock Bldg., San Francisco, Cal.

Daniels, Richard D., LL.B., '11. Special Clerk Amer. Nat. Red Cross, 1033 Newton St. N. E., Washington, D. C.

Darby, John J., M.D., '83. Physician, 311 A St. N. E., Washington, D. C.

Darby, Samuel E., LL.B., '90; LL.M., '91. Patent Lawyer, 220 Broadway, New York City.

Darlington, Joseph James, LL.D., '86 Lawyer, (G. U. Law Fac.), 410 5th St. N. W., Washington, D. C.

Darr, Charles W., LL.B., '94; LL.M., '95. Lawyer, 705 G St. N. W., Washington, D. C.

Darrah, John R., LL.M., '94. *Washington, Pa.

Dartt, James F., LL.B., '77. *New York.

Davenport, Henry B., LL.B., '05; LL.M., '06. Office Comt. Currency, Washington, D. C.

David, Edward, LL.B., '91; LL.M., '92. Lawyer, 944 Engineers' Bldg., Cleveland, Ohio.

David, Frederick E., LL.B., '87; LL.M., '88. *Carlinville, Ill.

Davidson, Edwin R., LL.B., '05; LL.M., '07. Govt. Ptg. Office, 915 H St. N. W., Washington, D. C.

David, Levi, LL.B., '98; LL.M., '99. Lawyer, Fendall Bldg., Washington, D. C.

Davies, Gomer, M.D., '88. Physician, England.

Davila, Alfonzo Ortiz, M.D., '10. Surgeon and Professor, Morelos, 420 Guadalajara (Jal), Mexico.

Davis, Beverly A., LL.B., '91. *Snow Creek, Va.

Davis, Bliss N., LL.B., '97. P. O. Dept., Rochambeau, Washington, D. C.

Davis, Charles Sands, LL.B., '96; LL.M., '97. Special Exam. Bu. of Pension, Mulvane, Sumner Co., Kansas.

Davis, Daniel Grant, M.D., '97. Clerk, House of Rep., 1979 Biltmore St., Washington, D. C.

Davis, Eugene A., LL.B., '93; LL.M., '94. *Fall River, Mass.

Davis, George M., M.D., '71. *District of Columbia.

Davis, Harry N., LL.B., '12. Huntington, W. Va.

Davis, John G., M.D., '68. *Kentucky.

Davis, John.H., LL.B., '93; LL.M., '94. Prin. Exam., Gen. Land Office, Washington, D. C.

Davis, Brig. Gen. John M. K., U. S. A., A.B., '62. 133 Washington St., Hartford, Conn.

Davis, John N., M.D., '60. *Indiana.

Davis, Robert H., LL.B., '12. Rochester, N. Y.

Davis, Warren J., LL.B., '11. Commissioner for Panama-California Expos., U. S. Grant Hotel, San Diego, Cal.

Davis, Wm. James, D.D.S., '11. Dentist, 300 E. Capitol St., Washington, D. C.

Davison, Ferdinand D., LL.B., '12; L.D.M., '12. Richmond, Va.

Davison, John Webster, LL.B., '93. Lawyer, 521 2nd St. S. E., Washington, D. C.

Dawley, Wm. J., LL.B., '03. Lawyer, 25 Broad St., New York City.

Dawson, Andrew D., LL.B., '09. Waterbury, Conn.

Day, Ewing W., M.D., '89. Physician, 1005 Westinghouse Bldg., Pittsburg, Pa.

Dear, W. Thomas, LL.B., '06. Lawyer, New Richmond, Wis.

Decker Arthur J., LL.M., '12; L.D.M., '12. 1334 Harvard St., Washington, D. C.

DeCourcy, Hon. Charles A., A.B., '78; A.M., '89; LL.D., '04. Justice, Mass. Supreme Judicial Circuit, Lawrence, Mass.

Deery, James P., A.B., '95. P. O. Box 605, Ware, Mass.

Degges, Addison B., LL.B., '95; LL.M., '96. Ship Draftsman, 141 N St. N. W., Washington, D. C.

DeKnight, Edward W., LL.B., '92; LL.M., '93. *District of Columbia.

Delacroix, Jules D., A.B., '54. *Louisiana.

Delacroix, Peter D., A.B., '49. *Louisiana.

DeLacy, Hon. Wm. Henry, LL.B., '83; LL.M., '84. Justice, Juvenile Court, Washington, D. C.

Delaiplaine, Patrick H., LL.B., '07. Train Director, 1010 6th St. N. E., Washington, D. C.

Delaney, Martin Donohue, M.D., '98. Physician, 131 Washington St., Alexandria, Va.

Delany, Rev. Francis Xavier, S. J., A.B., '97. Professor, St. George's College, Kingston, Jamaica, W. I.

DeLashmutt, Donald Ayres, LL.B., '10. Dept. of State, Washington, D. C.

Del Pica, Sergio, LL.B., '12. Santa Clara, Cuba.

DeMerritt, J. Henry, M.D., '68. Navy Dept., 1333 Vermont Ave. N. W, Washington, D. C.

Demoss, W. R., M.D., '63. *Indiana.

Deneen, John, LL.B., '98; LL.M., '99. 26 Chestnut St., Elmira, N. Y.

Denegre, Charles M., LL.B., '01. Lawyer, Birmingham, Ala.

Dennis, Wm. Henry, A.B., '74; LL.B., '76; A.M., '83. U. S. Commissioner, 2207 K St. N. W., Washington, D. C.

Denton, John S., LL.B., '95. Real Estate Operator and Mfgr., 1318 St. Charles St., Birmingham, Ala.

Denue, Albert R., LL.B., '03. State Atty., Rapid City, Pennington Co., South Dakota.

Denver, Hon. Matthew Rombach, A.B., '92. Member of Congress, Wilmington, Ohio.

DeRiemer, Arthur H., LL.B., '12. Aurora, Ill.

Des Garennes, Jean Felix Poulain, A.B., '94; A.M., '96; LL.B., '96; LL.M., '97. Professor of Law, Fordham Univ., New York City.

Des.Garennes, Jean Poulain, A.M., '92. Professor, 611 W. 141st St., New York City.

Desloge, George Thatcher, A.M., '02. Lawyer, 621 Liggett Bldg., St. Louis, Mo.

Des Londe, Edward, A.B., '52. *Louisiana.

Desmond, Stephen Wm., A.B., '04. 31 Roberts St., New Bedford, Mass.

Desmond, Walter Patrick, D.D.S., '03. Dentist, 49 Farragut Ave., Medford, Mass.

Dessaulles, Casimir, A.B., '48. Editor, St. Hyacinthe, Canada.

Dessez, Paul Tonnel, M.D., '97. P. Asst. Surg., U. S. N., Hongkong, China.

Dessez, Theodore H., LL.B., '98; LL.M., '00. Lawyer, 85 Liberty St., New York City.

Devereux, A. J. Antello, A.B., '98. Stock Broker, Arcade Bldg., Philadelphia, Pa.

Devereux, Ashton, A.B., '96. Lawyer, 1018 Real Estate Trust Bldg., Philadelphia, Pa.

Devereux, Frederick L., LL.B., '06. Gen. Aud. Amer. Tel. Co., 15 Dey St., New York City.

Devine, Harry Joseph, LL.B., '09. Lawyer, Quarles, Spence & Quarles, Sentinel Bldg., Milwaukee, Wis.

Devine, James, LL.B., '90; LL.M., '91. 1306 R St., St. N. W., Washington, D. C.

Devine, John, AB., '95; LL.B., '97. Lawyer, 41 Wall St., New York City.

Devine, Thomas Farrell, A.M., '94. Lawyer, Milford Bldg., Waterbury, Conn.

Devlin, Arthur Joseph, A.B., '10. Law Student, 1721 Lanier Pl., Washington, D. C.

Devlin, Daniel Joseph, A.B., '02. V.-Pres Carrollton Land Co., 906 Gravier St., New Orleans, La.

Devlin, Hugh M., LL.B., '07. Lawyer, Berkely, R. I.

De Ycaza, Y. Moratinos, Ignacio, A.M., '03; P.H.S., '05; LL.B., '06; Ph.D., '07; LL.M., '07. Lawyer, 2 Uli Uli St., Manila, P. I.

Dial, Joseph A., LL.B., '06. Lawyer, Muskogee, Okla.

Diamond, Wm. Carrell, A.B., '98. Lawyer, 165 Broadway, New York City.

Dickey, Raymond B., LL.B., '99; LL.M., '00. Lawyer, 1702 Kilbourne Pl., Washington, D. C.

Dickinson, Dwight, Jr., M.D., '09. Act.-Asst. Surg. U. S. N., U. S. Marine Recruiting Office, Cincinnati, Ohio.

Dickson, Martin Thomas, A.B., '71. St. Louis, Mo.

Digges, John Henry, M.D., '03. Physician, 805 1st St. N. W., Washington, D. C.

Digges, John T., M.D., '69. Physician, La Plata, Md.

Diggs, Charles F., LL.B., '02. Lawyer, 9th and G Sts. N. W., Washington, D. C.

Dilkes, Charles Edward, A.B., '10. Manufacturer, 219 E. Biddle St., Philadelphia, Pa.

Dilkes, James Alphonsus, A.B., '09. Lawyer, 56 Pine St., New York City.

Dillard, James Edwin, LL.B., '04; LL.M., '06. Lawyer, 600 Memphis Trust Bldg., Memphis, Tenn.

Dillard, James Pitt, LL.B., '08. Lawyer, 607-8-9 Rookery Bldg., Spokane, Wash.

Dillon, John, A.M., '96. County Atty., Lander, Fremont Co., Wyo.

Dillon, John R., LL.B., '12. 8 I St. N. E., Washington, D. C.

Dillon, Rev. Patrick, Ph.D., '89. St. Mary's Parish, Peru, Ill.

Dillon, Paul, A.M., '97. Lawyer, 600 Fullerton Bldg., St. Louis, Mo.

Dimitry, Charles Patton, A.M., '67. Journalist and Author, 852 Camp St., New Orleans, La.

Dismer, Louis C., LL.B., '11; LL.M., '12. Real Estate, 1327 Euclid St. N. W., Washington, D. C.

Dixon, Wm S., M.D., '68. Medical Director, U. S. N. Dept., Washing-ington, D. C.

Dodge, Clarence, LL.B., '05. Real Estate, 735 15th St. N. W., Washington, D. C.

Dodge, James E., LL.B., '11; LL.M., '12; L.D.M., '12. 717 Mass. Ave. N. W., Washington, D. C.

Dohan, Joseph M., A.B., '86; A.M., '89. Lawyer, 1012 Stephen Girard Bldg., Philadelphia, Pa.

Doing, Charles H., LL.B., '08. Clerk, Wash. Loan and Trust Co., Washington, D. C.

Doing, Robert B., LL.B., '08. Lawyer, 422 5th St. N. W., Washington, D. C., Beltsville, Md.

Dolan, Henry F., LL.B., '10. P. O. Dept., 1434 Newton St., Washington, D. C.

Dolan, P. V., LL.B., '85; M.D., '90. 1453 W St., Washington, D. C.

Dollaway, Louis Marsh, M.D., '00. Physician, 120 Nasby Bldg., Toledo, Ohio.

Dolmage, Mihran M., D.D.S., '03. Dentist, 825 Vermont Ave., Washington, D. C.

Dominguez, Virgil, A.B., '63. *Cuba.

Donahue, Alphonsus Richard, A.M., '05. Halifax, N. S.

Donahue, Charles Lewis, A.B., '00. Lawyer, 390 Congress St., Portland, Maine.

Donahue, Francis Wm., A.B., '97. Physician and Surgeon, Greenfield, Mass.

Donaldson, Glenn R., LL.M., '06. Lawyer, 1002 Gloyd Bldg., Kansas City, Mo.

Donaldson, R. Newton, LL.B., '90; LL.M., '91. Lawyer, 1639 13th St. N. W., Washington, D. C.

Donaldson, Robert Golden, LL.B., '95. Lawyer, 611 14th St., Washington, D. C.

Donch, Wm. A., LL.B., '91; LL.M., '92. Lawyer, 614 4th St. N. E., Washington, D. C.

Donegan, James H., A.B., '47. *Alabama.

Donegan, Morris Francis, A.M., '98; Ph.D., '99. City Atty., 630 E. 14th St., Davenport, Iowa.

Donegan, Patrick J., LL.B., '97; LL.M., '98. Lawyer, *Baltimore, Md.

Donlon, Rev. Alphonsus J., S.J., A.B., '88. President of Georgetown University, Washington, D. C.

Donnelly, Charles, LL.B., '96. *Minneapolis, Minn.

Donnelly, Horace J., LL.B., '09; LL.M., '10. Law Clerk, 1430 V St. N. W., Washington, D. C.

Donnelly, Joseph P., A.M., '98. State Mgr. Nat. Surety Co., Helena, Montana.

Donnelly, Richard J., LL.B., 89; LL.M., '90. Chief of Div., Water Dept., The Wyoming, Washington, D. C.

Donnelly, Wm. J., A.B., '91. Real Estate and Not. Pub., 1403 H St. N. W., Washington, D. C.

Donoghue, James Kiernan, M.D., '09. 551 Culver Road, Rochester, New York.

Donohoe, Clarence F., LL.B., '97; LL.M., '98. Real Estate Broker, 314 Pa. Ave. S. E., Washington, D. C.

Donovan, Dennis D., LL.B., '95. Lawyer, Napoleon, Ohio.

Donovan, Edward Patrick, A.B., '11. 108 I St. N. W., Washington, D. C.

Donovan, George Timothy, A.B., '05. Shoe Mfgr., Liberty Sq., Lynn, Mass.

Donovan, Joseph M., LL.B., '89. *Littleton, N. H.

Donovan, Michael R., A.B., '80. 128 S. Common St., Lynn, Mass.

Donovan, Thomas J., LL.B., '95. Real Estate, 108 I St. N. W., Washington, D. C.

Donworth, Hon. George, A.B., '81. Lawyer, Seattle, Wash.

Dooley, Francis X., M.D., '65. Physician, 1346 T St., Washington, D. C.

Dooley, James E., LL.B., '11. Sec. and Lawyer, 34 Cedar St., Manton, Rhode Island.

Dooley, James H., A.B., '60; A.M., '65. Railroad Business, 922 Main St., Richmond, Va.

Doonan, George W., LL.B., '12. Bu. Manfrs., Washington, D. C.; Greenville, N. H.

Doran, Charles M. Cantwell, LL.B., '98; LL.M., '99. Lawyer, Norfolk, Va.

Dorman, John Edward, D.D.S., '04. Dentist, Fayette, Iowa.

Dorsey, Roscoe J. C., LL.B., '02; LL.M., '03. Lawyer, The Sherman, Washington, D. C.

Dougherty, Daniel N., LL.B., '12. Indian Office, Washington, D. C.; West Elkton, Ohio.

Dougherty, Francis P., LL.B., '05. Lawyer, Pittsfield, Mass.

Dougherty, John Francis, A.B., '04. Deputy County Aud., Walsh Co., Grafton, N. D.

Dougherty, Leo J., LL.B., '12. Baltimore, Md.

Dougherty, Philip Joseph, A.M., '98; Ph.D., '99; LL.B., '99; LL.M., '00. Lawyer, 412 Sloane St., Philadelphia, Pa.

Douglas, R. D., A.B., '96. Lawyer, Greensboro, N. C.

Douglas, Hon. Robert Martin, A.B., '67; A.M., '70; LL.D., '97. Lawyer, Greensboro, N. C.

Douglas, John J., LL.B., '96. Lawyer, 252 Webster St., E. Boston, Mass.

Douglass, Will W., LL.B., '87. Lawyer and Real Estate, Ballston, Fairfax, Co., Va.

Douglass, Wm. B., LL.M., '88. *Corydon, Ind.

Dowd, Dennis P., Jr., A.B., '08. Lawyer, 169 W. 18th St., New York City.

Dowd, Ed. F., A.B., '94. Physician, 26 Common St., Waltham, Mass.

Dowling, Patrick V., LL.B., '04. Automobile Salesman, care Houston & Merton, Los Angeles, Cal.

Downey, Richard J., LL.B., '09. Lawyer, 1106 16th St. N. W., Washington, D. C.

Downing, Augustine H., LL.B., '05. Lawyer, Banigan Bldg., Providence, R. I.

Downing, Geo. E., LL.B., '01. Lawyer, 324 Wilcox Bldg., Los Angeles, Cal.

Downing, Mortimer A., LL.B., '88. Lawyer, 1028 Golden Gate Ave., San Francisco, Cal.

Downing, Rossa F., LL.B., '89; LL.M., '90. Lawyer, 6th and D Sts. N. W., Washington, D. C.

Downs, N. Carroll, LL.B., '99. Lawyer, 1420 N. Y. Ave., Washington, D. C.

Downs, Norman Lee, D.D.S., '11. 908 14th St., Washington, D. C.

Downs, Thomas Charles, LL.B., '99; LL.M., '00; A.M., '00. Lawyer, Fond du Lac, Wis.

Doyle, Francis Joseph, M.D., '01. Physician, 611 E. Fort Ave., Baltimore, Md.

Doyle, J. Herbert, A.B., '07. Care R. G. Barthols & Co., 2-4 Stone St., New York City.

Doyle, Michael M., LL.B., '08. Lawyer, Second National Bank Bldg., Washington, D. C.

Doyle, W. T. Sherman, A.B., '97; LL.B., '99. State Dept., Chf. Div. Lat. Am. Af., 1347 Park Road, Washington, D. C.

Dragicsevics, Alex. O., M.D., '90. France.

Blake, Otis Branch, LL.B., '03. Lawyer, Century Bldg., Washington, D. C.

Dreaper, Edward Bernard, A.B., '03. Physician, 154 Government St., Mobile, Ala.

Drennan, Lawrence M., M.D., '06. Sanitation Physician, Ancon Hospital, Canal Zone, Panama.

Dresbach, H. V., M.D., '94. Physician, Iola, Kansas.

Drew, Harry C., M.D., '09. Lieut. Constab. Service, P. I., 1279 Pacific St., Brooklyn, N. Y.

Drew, Walter, LL.B., '09. Lawyer, Madison, Wis.

Drill, Lewis L., LL.B., '03. Lawyer, 216 New York Life Bldg., St. Paul, Minn.

Driscoll, Thos. A., A.B., '96; LL.B., '97. Lawyer, Hibernia Bank Bldg., San Francisco, Cal.

Drown, J. H., M.D., '94. Special Agent Treasury Dept., 406 U. S. Custom House, New York City.

Drum, Joseph C., LL.B., '99. Care Cleveland Leader, Cleveland, Ohio.

Drun, John Wm., LL.B., '95. Lawyer, Marble Hill, Mo.

DuCharme, Alfred Joseph, A.B., '91. Lawyer, 22 Buhl Block, Detroit, Mich.

Dudeck, Joseph, LL.B., '11; LL.M., '12; L.D.M., '12. Rolling Prairie, Ind.

Dudley, John Gurney, LL.M., '02. Lawyer, 2004 Bond Bldg., Washington, D. C.

Duehring, Frank E., M.D., '12. Georgetown Hospital, Washington, D. C.

Duff, Edwin H., LL.B., '97. Lawyer, 1306 F St., Washington, D. C.

Duff, Valentine Stephen, D.D.S., '11. 18 Cameron St., Dorchester, Mass.

Duffey, Arthur Francis, LL.B., '03. Editor, Boston Post, Boston, Mass.

Duffey, Hugh C., M.D., '91. Physician, 929 O St. N. W., Washington, D. C.

Duffy, Bernard F., A.B., '01. 788 Broadway, South Boston, Mass.

Duffy, Chas. Alphonsus, M.D., '10. Physician, 3417 Ward St., Pittsburgh, Pa.

Duffy, Chas. Hugh, LL.B., '98; LL.M., 99. Lawyer, 612 F. St. N. W., Washington, D. C.

Duffy, James Patrick Bernard, A.B., '01. Lawyer, 1011 German Ins. Bldg., Rochester, N. Y.

Duffy, Joseph, LL.B., '08. 393 Perkins St., Akron, Ohio.

Duffy, Joseph T., LL.B., '93; LL.M., '94. Railway Mail Clerk, 930 4th St. N. E., Washington, D. C.

Dufour, Clarence R., M.D., '90. Physician (G. U. Med. Fac.), 1343 L St., Washington, D. C.

Dufour, Everett, LL.B., '02; LL.M., '03. Lawyer, 53-54 Munsey, Bldg., Washington, D. C.

Dufour, J. F. R., M.D., '78. Physician, Mitchellville, Md.

Dugan, Chas. Leo., M.D., '12. 3421 Dent Place N. W., Washington, D. C.

Dugan, J. Cotter, LL.B., '10. Lawyer, Kenton, Ohio.

Duggan, Jeremiah Richard, A.B., '02. 254 Asylum St., Norwich, Conn.

Duggan, John, Jr., M.D., '06; LL.M., '07. Lawyer, Connelsville, Pa.

Duke, Douglas William, M.D., '89. Physician, England.

Dulin, Edgar A., M.D., '65. Physician and Surgeon, Nevada, Mo.

Dumont, Very Rev. Francis, L.M., S.S., D.D., '89. Professor Catholic University, Washington, D. C.

Duncan, Jas. M., M.D., '69. Physician, *Kansas City, Mo.

Duncan, John J. K., D.D.S., '06. Dentist, 320 Massachusetts Ave. N. E., Washington, D. C.

Dunn, Chas. Aloysius, LL.B., '91; LL.M., '92. Forest Service, Aspen, Colo.

Dunn, Chas. Clark, LL.B., '07. Department of Interior, Washington, D. C.. Friendship Heights, Md.

Dunn, Frank T., LL.B., '12. Goldfield, Nevada.

Dunn, John Thos. Francis, M.D., '01. Physician, 1625 Reteur St., Philadelphia, Pa.

Dunn, L. B., M.D., '58. Physician, *Arkansas.

Dunn, Wood Gilmer, LL.B., '99. Lawyer, Charlottesville, Va.

Dunne, J. Paul, LL.M., '04. Lawyer, 710 Title and Trust Bldg., Chicago, Ill.

Dunne, Wm. G., LL.B., '91; LL.M., '92. Col. Real Est. & Title Co., 727 10th St. N. E., Washington, D. C.

Dunnigan, John Patrick, M.D., '01. Physician, 214 2d St. S. E., Washington, D. C.

Dunnington, Clyde C., LL.B., '10. Salesman, 624 North Carolina Ave. S. E., Washington, D. C.

Dunsworth, Martin J., LL.B., '11; L.D.M., '11. Bureau Corporations, Washington, D. C., Carrollton, Ill.

Dunton, John F., LL.B., '94; LL.M., '95. U. S. Immigration Service, Vancouver, B. C.

Durant, Horace B., LL.B., '97. Lawyer, Miami, Okla.

Durfee, Raphael Burke, M.D., '00. Physician, 1814 K St. N. W., Washington, D. C.

Durkin, Martin J., LL.B., '07. Lawyer, Parkersburg, W. Va.

Durney, Chas. Paul, M.D., '09. Physician, Honolulu, Hawaii.

Duross, Chas. E., A.B., '90. Real Estate, 2850 Marion Ave., Bronx, New York City.

Duross, Jas. Edward, A.B., '91. Lawyer, American Surety Bldg., New York City.

Duryee, Joseph B., LL.B., '12; L.D.M., '12. 1915 14th St., Washington, D. C.

Dutcher, George C., LL.B., '08. Lawyer, 15-24 Cawker Bldg., Milwaukee, Wis.

Duvall, Edward S., Jr., LL.B., '93; LL.M., '94. Lawyer, Washington Loan and Trust Bldg., Washington, D. C.

Duvall, Wm. H., LL.B., '91. Lawyer, 977 Edgecomb Place, Chicago, Ill.

Duvall, Wm. S., LL.B., '93. Lawyer and Patent Expert, 914 Washington Loan and Trust Bldg., Washington, D. C.

Duvall, William T. S., M.D., '65. Physician, 1718 U St. N. W., Washington, D. C.

Dwyer, Wm. A., B.S., '88. President of Art Stove Co., Detroit, Mich.

Dyer, Rev. David Marcus, A.B., '92; A.M., '93. 510 W. 165th St., New York City.

Dyer, Jesse F., LL.B., '12. Minneapolis, Minn.

Dyer, Joseph T., Jr., LL.B., '04. Lawyer, Hyattsville, Md.

Dyer, Richard Nott, LL.B., '78; LL.M., '79. Lawyer, 31 Nassau St., New York City.

Dykes, John W., LL.B., '10. Department of Forestry, Albuquerque, N. M.

E

Eagan, Sylvester Broezel, A.B., '03. President, Hotel Broezel Co., Buffalo, N. Y.

Earl, Chas., LL.B., '95; LL.M., '96. Solicitor, Dept. Commerce and Labor, Washington, D. C.

Earle, Henry Montague, LL.B., '93. Lawyer, 1 Nassau St., New York City.

Earls, Rev. Michael, S.J., A.M., '97. Woodstock College, Woodstock, Md.

Earnshaw, Frank L., LL.B., '11. Bu. Biol. Surv., Washington, D. C., Earnshaw, W. Va.

Easby-Smith, James Stanislaus, A.B., '91; A.M., '92; LL.B., '93; LL.M., '94. G. U. Law Fac., Lawyer, 426 5th St. N. W., Washington, D. C.

Easterday, Geo. J., LL.B., '86. Real Estate Broker, 1410 G St. N. W., Washington, D. C.

Easterling, Horace V., LL.B., '94; LL.M., '95. Treasury Dept., Washington, D. C.

Easton, Edward D., LL.B., '88; LL.M., '89. President American Phonograph Co., New York City.

Eckenrode, John W., Jr., A. B., '09. General Agent Penn Mut. Life Ins. Co., 48 N. Queen St., Lancaster, Pa.

Eckstein, Otto G., LL.M., '87. *Washington, D. C.

Eddy, Richard T., LL.B., '11.. Interstate Com., Los Angeles, Cal.

Edmonds, Dean Stockett, LL.B., '99; LL.M., '00. Lawyer, 32 Liberty St., New York City.

Edmonston, Preston Paul, A.B., '02. Care Crowell Publishing Co., 381 4th Ave., New York City.

Edwards, Keith W., LL.B., '10. Lawyer, Fort Sumner, New Mexico.

Edwards, Richard Lee, LL.B., '02; LL.M., '03. 38 Rhode Island Ave. N. E., Washington, D. C.

Edwards, Robert H., M.D., '68. *Ohio.

Edwards, W. Walton, LL.B., '91; LL.M., '92. Lawyer, 9-11 Equity Bldg., Washington, D. C.

Edwards, Wm. A., LL.B., '92; LL.M., '93. Lawyer, Covington, Ga.

Effler, Edwin R., A.M., '06; LL.B., '08. Lawyer and Professor, Smith & Baker Bldg., Toledo, Ohio.

Egan, Gerald M., A.B., '06. Copenhagen, Denmark.

Egan, Dr. Maurice Francis, LL.D., '89.. Envoy Extraordinary and Minister Plenipotentiary, Copenhagen, Denmark.

Eggleston, Jas. Denslow, M.D., '95. *Denver, Col.

Eldridge, Wm. A., LL.B., '76. *Wisconsin.

Elia, Ezechiel de, A.B., '74. Buenos Ayres, Argentina.

Eline, Francis M., LL.B., '94; LL.M., '95; A.M., '95. Lawyer, *Milwaukee, Wis.

Eliot, J. Llewellyn, M.D., '74. Physician, 1106 P St., Washington, D. C.

Eliot, Thos. Johnson, M.D., '90. Physician, 718 H St. N. E., Washington, D. C.

Elliott, Jere B., M.D., '93. *Brooklyn, N. Y.

Elliott, Stuart H., LL.B., '11. Law Clerk, 1616 Kilbourne Place N. W., Washington, D. C.

Ellis, Don Carlos, A.B., '04; LL.B., '08. Forest Service, Washington, D. C.

Ellsworth, Goodwin D., LL.B., '97; LL.M., '99. Treasury Department, 1248 Girard St. N. W., Washington, D. C.

Elston, Arthur G., LL.B., '08. Lawyer, 428 Peyton Bldg., Spokane, Wash.

Elwell, Chas. B., LL.B., '12. Salem, Mass.

Emch, George H., LL.B., '12. Woodville, Ohio.

Emery, William H., LL.B., '96. Treasury Department, 1505 12th St. N. W., Washington, D. C.

Emmons, Chas. M., M.D., '93. Physician, 1100 Pennsylvania Ave. S. E., Washington, D. C.

English, Chas. Henry, LL.B., '05; LL.M., '07. Lawyer, City Solicitor, 722 State St., Erie, Pa.

English, John J., A.B., '00. Broker, 4129 Michigan Ave., Chicago, Ill.

4

Ennis, Chas. H., LL.B., '94; LL.M., '95. Lawyer, Burke Bldg., Seattle, Wash.

Ergood, Clarence Elmo, LL.B., '96; LL.M., '97. Grocer, Lancaster, Pa.

Eriksson, Leonard, LL.B., '04. Lawyer and Alderman, Fergus Falls, Minn.

Erskine, Harlow L., LL.M., '86. *Omaha, Neb.

Ervine, Artemus J., Jr., LL.B., '96; LL.M., '97. *Crawford, Miss.

Erwin, Frank, Jr., LL.B., '11; L.D.M., '11. Bureau Commerce and Labor, Washington, D. C., Tullytown, Pa.

Escobar, J., A.B., '60; A.M., '62. *Mexico.

Esher, Albert D., LL.B., '11; LL.M., '12; L.D.M., '12. Lawyer, 263 N St. N. W., Washington, D. C.

Eslin, Jas. F., M.D., '91. Physician, 1717 14th St., Washington, D. C.

Estabrook, Leon M., LL.B., '97. Record Officer, Department Agriculture, Washington, D. C.

Estabrook, Watts T., LL.B., '07. Patent Lawyer, 635 F St. N. W., Washington, D. C.

Etchison, Howard M., LL.B., '04. Lawyer, 1820 Mintwood Place, Washington, D. C.

Etty, Robert A., LL.B., '91; LL.M., '92. Bureau of Pensions, Eau Claire, Ohio.

Evans, Paul Warrington, A.B., '94; LL.B., '98. Dentist, Bond Bldg, Washington, D. C.

Evans, W. Warrington, A.B., '91. Dentist, Bond Bldg., Washington, D. C.

Evans, Warwick, M.D., '52. Physician, 1105 9th St. N. W., Wash., D. C.

Eve, Oswell R., LL.B., '99. Lawyer, Augusta, Ga.

Evert, Henry C., LL.B., '91; LL.M., '92. Patent Lawyer, Jenkin's Arcade, Pittsburgh, Pa.

Ewing, John K. M., LL.B., '06. Lawyer, 30 Church St., New York City.

Ewing, Thos., Jr., LL.B., '90. Lawyer, 67 Wall St., New York City.

F

Fague, Joseph R., LL.B., '97; LL.M., '98. Lawyer, 503 E St. N. W., Washington, D. C.

Fain, Jesse C., LL.B., '12. Neely, Miss.

Fairbanks, Leigh Cole, D.D.S., '12. 911 New York Ave. N. W., Washington, D. C.

Fairfax, John Wheeler, A.B., '04. Broker, 218 Hennen Bldg., New Orleans, La.

Falconer, Balivar Lang, M.D., '95. Physician, Director, Civil Service, Manila, P. I.

Fallon, Frederick B., LL.B., '92. Lawyer, 406 Security Bldg., Bridgeport, Conn.

Fallon, James, LL.B., '96. Lawyer and City Solicitor, Savings Bank Bldg., Pittsfield, Mass.

Fallon, John T., LL.B., '78; LL.M., '79. *Washington, D. C.

Fallon, Joseph D., A.B., '58; A.M., '64. Lawyer and Judge, Municipal Court, 789 Broadway, South Boston, Mass.

Fallon, Joseph P., LL.B., '81. Lawyer, Omaha, Neb.

Fanning, William Michael, D.D.S., '10. Dentist, 433 Westminster St., Providence, R. I.

Farish, John Hamilton, A.B., 79. Real Estate and Loans, 5221 Westminster Place, St. Louis, Mo.

Farley, Frank P., LL.B., '12. Flat Lick, Ky.

Farr, Richard R., LL.B., '07. Lawyer, Fairfax, Va.

Farr, Wilson M., LL.B., '07. Lawyer, Fairfax, Va.

Farrell, Chas. H., LL.B., '12. Newport, Vt.

Farrell, Frank C., LL.B., '11. Courtland, N. Y.

Farrow, Patillo, LL.B., '97. Lawyer, Charleston, S. C.

Faulkner, James Burton, LL.B., '05. Lawyer, 718 First National Bank Bldg., Cincinnati, Ohio.

Favis, Asterio, LL.B., '07. City Attorney, Bagino, P. I.

Fay, John Baptist, Jr., A.B., '02; A.M., '03. 1432 New York Ave. N. W., Washington, D. C.

Feeley, Wm. G., LL.B., '11. Providence, R. I.

Feenan, Arthur Michael, A.B., '11. 91 Essex St., Salem, Mass.

Fegan, Edward John, A.M., '03; LL.B., '05. Lawyer, 916 Tremont Bldg., Boston, Mass.

Fegan, Hugh, Jr., A.B., '01; A.M., '02; LL.B., '07. Secretary and Treasurer G. U. Law Dept., Washington, D. C.

Fellows, Harry A., LL.B., '91; LL.M., '92. War Dept., East Falls Church, Va.

Felten, Albert L., LL.B., '11. Care Y. M. C. A., Washington, D. C.

Felter, Herman, LL.B., '10. Interstate Commerce Commission, 211 Morgan St. N. W., Washington, D. C.

Fennell, Robert B., LL.B., '11. Culpeper, Va.

Fergell, J. A., D.D.S., '02. Dentist, The Victor Bldg., Washington, D. C.

Ferguson, Abner H., LL.B., '04 Lawyer, Southern Bldg., Washington, D. C.

Ferguson, Daniel John, A.B., '98. Lawyer, New O'Hara Theatre Bldg., Shenandoah, Pa.

Ferguson, S. Colfax, LL.M., '02. Lawyer, Prestonsburg, Ky.

Fernandez, Benigno, LL.B., '08. Lawyer, 33 Allen St., San Juan, P. R.

Ferneding, Thos. A., A.B., '01. Vice-President and General Manager The Dayton, Springfield & Xenia Southern Ry., Dayton, Ohio.

Ferris, Nathan Sherwood, M.D., '10. 2417 Ontario Road, Washington, D. C.

Ferry, Jos. T., LL.B., '91; LL.M., '92. P. O. Dept., The Hillside, Washington, D. C.

Ferry, L. A., M.D., '79. Physician, Geneseo, Ill.

Fickling, Col. Theo. Hamilton, A.M., '69. Principal George Washington High School, 714 Duke St., Alexandria, Va.

Field, Earl R., LL.B., '10. Civil Service Examiner, 224 Federal Bldg., Seattle, Wash.

Fields, Frank H., LL.B., '92. Treasury Dept., Washington, D. C.

Finch, Geo. A., LL.B., '07. Manager American Journal of International Law, 1313 Emerson St. N. W., Washington, D. C.

Fink, Rev. Edw. X., S.J., A.B., '73. 30 W. 16th St., New York City.

Finke, Alvin J., A.B., '96. Numismatist, Dayton, Ohio.

Finn, Wm. T., LL.B., '01; LL.M., '02. Lawyer, Bond Bldg., Washington, D. C.

Finnegan, John J., LL.B., '01. U. S. Court Com., Probate Judge and City Attorney, Seward, Alaska.

Finnerty, Wm. N., LL.B., '08. Lawyer, Denver, Col.

Finney, Frank, M.D., '82. Physician, La Junta, Col.

Finney, Harry W., LL.B., '10. American Secur. & Trust Co., 2204 Q St. N. W., Washington, D. C.

Finney, Robert Gordon, LL.B., '98; LL.M., '99. Lawyer, Clarendon, Va.

Finney, Wm. Brantner, A.M., '98. Adver. Bus., 417-418 Keith & Perry Bldg., Kansas City, Mo.

Finning, Rev. Thos. Jas., A.B., '95. Rector, St. Helena's, Enfield, N. H.

Fisher, Henry C., M.D., '91. Lieut. Col. U. S. Army, Columbus, Ohio.

Fisher, Chas., LL.B., '99; LL.M., '00. Treasury Dept., 3768 McKinley St. (Chevy Chase), Washington, D. C.

Fisher, Clarence Geo., LL.B., '10; LL.M., '11; L.D.M., '11. Land Office, 1425 Ames Place N. E., Washington, D. C.

Fisher, Hugh Coniff, LL.B., '06. Lawyer, Shreveport, La.

Fisher, Samuel P., LL.B., '95; LL.M., '96. Corp. Counsel, Alexandria, Va.

Fisher, Wm. J., LL.B., '07. Lawyer, Lohrville, Iowa.

Fitch, Wm. S., LL.B., '95; LL.M., '97. Attorney Inter. Dept., Custom House, New Orleans, La.

Fitman, Thos. H., LL.B., '84; LL.M., '85. Lawyer, 432 Q St. N. W., Washington, D. C.

Fitts, Harrison F., LL.B., '12. Buffalo, N. Y.

Fitzgerald, Edmund A., A.B., '08. 212 8th St. S. W., Washington, D. C.

Fitzgerald, Edmund, Jr., A.B., '09. Manufacturer, 206 Third St., Troy, N. Y.

Fitzgerald, Geo. W., LL.B., '88. *Chicago, Ill.

Fitzgerald, John F. L., LL.B., '11. Attorney for Land Tit. Abs. Co., 1914 E. 66th St., Cleveland, Ohio.

Fitzgerald, John J., LL.B., '95; LL.M., '96. Lawyer, 255 Main St., Pawtucket, R. I.

Fitzgerald, Joseph S., M.D., '70. *New York City, N. Y.

Fitzgerald, Morris, LL.B., '09. Lawyer, 508 6th St. S. W., Washington, D. C.

Fitzgerald, Thos. J., LL.B., '96; LL.M., '97. Lawyer, Dudley St., Roxbury, Mass.

Fitzgerald, Thomas J., LL.B., '11; LL.M., '12; L.D.M., '12. Brooklyn, N. Y.

Fitzgerald, Thomas R., LL.B., '10. Lawyer, Iroquois Apartments, Washington, D. C.

Fitzgerald, Wm. Eugene, A.B., '11. Manufacturer, 206 3d St., Troy, N. Y.

Fitzgerald, Wm. Joseph, A.B., '98. Lawyer, 510 Mears Bldg., Scranton, Pa.

Fitz-Gibbon, James E., LL.B., '10; LL.M., '11. Lawyer, 920 Massachusetts Ave. N. W., Washington, D. C.

Fitzmaurice, Rt. Rev. John E., D.D., '89. 924 Sassafras St., Erie, Pa.

Fitzpatrick, Clarence Edmond, A.B., '04. Quincy Dept. Store, Quincy, Mass.

Fitzpatrick, Francis Percival, A.B., '09. Med. Stu., 96 Pleasant St., Walden, Mass.

Fitzpatrick, Joseph Paul, LL.B., '01. Pittston, Pa.

Fitzpatrick, Thos. Costello, B.S., '88. Lawyer, 310-313 Germania Life Bldg., St. Paul, Minn.

Fitzpatrick, Rev. Wm. H., A.B., '62. 2221 Dorchester Ave., Boston, Mass.

Fitzsimmons, Jas. I., LL.B., '97. Lawyer, 802 Wells Bldg., Milwaukee, Wis.

Flaherty, John E., M.D., '08. Physician, 75 Union St., Rockville, Conn.

Flanagan, John J., LL.B., '06. Lawyer, 1944 Calvert St., Washington, D. C.

Flanagan, J. Lewiston, LL.B., '10. Lawyer, 9 William St., Mechanicsville, N. Y.

Flanagan, Leo Joseph, M.D., '11. Physician, St. Mary's Hospital, San Francisco, Cal.

Flanagan, Roy Chetwynd, LL.B., '08. Lawyer and Postmaster, Greenville, N. C.

Flannery, John Spalding, LL.B., '94; LL.M., '95. Lawyer, 2017 O St. N. W., Washington, D. C.

Flannery, Martin Markham, LL.B., '95. Special Attorney, Bureau of Corporations, Washington, D. C.

Flather, Alfred C., LL.B., '11. 612 8th St. N. E., Washington, D. C.

Flavin, Philip T., D.D.S., '11. Concord, Mass.

Fleharty, Ralph B., LL.B., '09. Lawyer, 426 5th St. N. W., Washington, D. C.

Fleharty, Ward W., LL.B., '08. Banker, 637 5th Ave., San Francisco, Cal.

Flett, John H., LL.B., '12. Atlantic City, N. J.

Flick, Cyrus P., LL.B., '88. *Cleveland, Ohio.

Flood, P. H., M.D., '74. Physician, 1219 Page St., San Francisco, Cal.

Flood, Thos. Arthur, M.D., '97. Physician, 510 McCormick Bldg., Salt Lake City, Utah.

Flora, W. Kirkwood, LL.B., '94. Assistant Attorney E. P. & S. W. System, Bisbee, Ariz.

Flores, Placido, D.D.S., '11. Manila, P. I.

Flueck, Edwin Henry, LL.B., '03; LL.M., '04. Lawyer, 517 Mutual Life Bldg., Seattle, Wash.

Flume, Albert Geo., A.B., '11. Palatine Bridge, N. Y.

Flynn, Caryl Bernard, M.D., '03. Physician, Nepperhan Ave., Yonkers, N. Y.

Flynn, Chas. T., LL.B., '11. Fitchburg, Mass.

Flynn, David J., A.B., '80. Physician, 202 Fair St., Kingston, N. Y.

Flynn, Jas. Augustus, M.D., '98. Physician, G. U. Med Fac., 1333 Q St. N. W., Washington, D. C.

Flynn, John A., LL.B., '10. 42 Trask St., Providence, R. I.

Flynn, Joseph B., LL.B., '07. Lawyer, Bond Bldg., Washington, D. C.

Flynn, Thos. Donovan, LL.B., '02. Lawyer, *New Orleans, La.

Flynn, Wm. S., LL.B., '10. Lawyer, 42 Trask St., Providence, R. I.

Focke, Bernard M., LL.B., '09. Lawyer and Assistant City Solicitor, 3 City Bldg., Dayton, Ohio.

Fogle, John L., LL.B., '97; LL.M., '98. Lawyer, Harris Trust Bldg., Chicago, Ill.

Foley, John D., A.B., '12. Med. Student, The Cairo, Washington, D. C.

Foley, John F., LL.B., '09. South Manchester, Conn.

Follens, Alphonse Jas., A.M., '98. 817-18 New York Life Bldg., Kansas City, Mo.

Foote, John Ambrose, M.D., '06. Physician, 1726 M St. N. W., Washington, D. C.

Forbes, Daniel R., LL.B., '10; LL.M., '12; L.D.M., '12. Assistant, Bureau of Chem., 1211 Girard St., Washington, D. C.

Ford, Bernard Joseph, A.M., '01; Ph.D., '03; LL.B., '03. Lawyer, 2821 Tremont Place, Denver, Col.

Ford, Horace, LL.B., '96. *Fifes, Va.

Ford, Wm. F., LL.B., '96. *Salt Lake City, Utah.

Fornaris, Ferdinand, LL.B., '12. Ponce, Porto Rico.

Forney, Edward O., LL.B., '77. Assistant Examiner, Patent Office, 1436 Fairmont St. N. W., Washington, D. C.

Forrest, Bladen, A.B., '67. 1115 Euclid St., Washington, D. C.

Forscuth, Clarence S., LL.B., '09. Lawyer, Manchester, N. H.

Fort, J. Carter, LL.B., '11. 1613 30th St. N. W., Washington, D. C.

Fortune, Thos. L., LL.B., '11; LL.M., '12. 3134 13th St. N. W., Washington, D. C.

Forwood, Wm. Henry, LL.D., '97. Brig. Gen. Ret., 1425 Euclid Place, Washington, D. C.

Fosselman, J. J., LL.B., '09. Donally Mills, Pa.

Foster, Daniel S., M.D., '68. Dept. of Justice, 19 Iowa Circle, Washington, D. C.

Foster, John J., LL.B., '97. Lawyer, Del Rio, Texas.

Foster, Walter C., LL.B., '10. Lib. of Congress, 942 S St. N. W., Washington, D. C.

Fournet, Gabriel A., A.B., '61. Rigmaiden Bldg., Lake Charles, La.

Fouts, Francis A., LL.B., '80. *Illinois.

Fowler, Allen L., LL.B., '91. *Chicago, Ill.

Fowler, W. E., M.D., '88. Physician, 1812 1st St. N. W., Washington, D. C.

Fox, Edmund K., LL.B., '97. Real Estate, 1311 H St. N. W., Washington, D. C.

Fox, Geo. H., A.B., '67. *New York.

Fox, Jas. C., LL.B., '91; LL.M., '94. Lawyer, 39 Exchange St., Portland, Me.

Fox, Paul, LL.B., '02. Lawyer, Lompoc, Cal,

Fox, W. Tazewell, A.B., '66; A.M., '68. *New York City, N. Y.

Foy, Francis Martin, A.B., '04; A.M., '06; LL.B., '07. Lawyer, 68 William St., Pittsburgh, Pa.

Franc, Herbert L., LL.B., '99; LL.M., '00. Lawyer, Pacific Bldg., Washington, D. C.

Francis, Claude De La Roche, LL.B., '92; LL.M., '93. Lawyer, 1518 Pine St., Philadelphia, Pa.

Frank, Morton E., LL.B., '10. War Dept., 128 C St. N. E., Washington, D. C.

Frederick, Alexander E., LL.B., '07. Preacher, Methodist Episcopal Church, 16 N. Hancock St., Madison, Wis.

Freeman, Albert M., LL.B., '11. Lawyer, 123½ S. Phillips Ave., Sioux Falls, S. D.

Freeman, Joseph E., LL.B., '01. Lawyer, 117 Wall St., New York City.

Freeman, Joseph H., LL.B., '98; LL.M., '99. Expert in Patent Law, 45 Broadway, New York City.

Freeman, Joseph E., LL.B., '01. *Aurora, Ill.

French, Edmund R., LL.B., '98. Lawyer, *Washington, D. C.

French, Edwin Spence, LL.B., '10; L.D.M., '11. War Dept., 1802 G St. N. W., Washington, D. C.

French, Geo. K., LL.B., '89. Lawyer, *Nogales, Ariz.

French, Lawrence Eugene, A.M., '91; LL.B., '92. Lawyer, 41 Park Row, New York City.

Frey, Clarence E., LL.B., '05. Int. Dept., 3010 P' St. N. W., Washington, D. C.

Frey, Joseph Louis, M.D., '07. Physician, 59 Washington Square South, New York City.

Frye, Geo. R., A.B., '06; LL.B., '10; L.D.M., '11. Examiner U. S. Patent Office, 408 A St. S. E., Washington, D. C.

Fuchs, Wm. R., LL.B., '05. Lawyer, 3226 N St. N. W., Washington, D. C.

Fuhrman, Wm. J., LL.B., '97. Lawyer, 83 H St. N. W., Washington, D. C.

Fuller, Edward A., LL.M., '95. Editor, Hyattsville Independent, Hyattsville, Md.

Fuller, Geo. E., M.D., '65. Physician, 1 Green St., Monson, Mass.

Fuller, Walter M., LL.B., '04. Patent Lawyer, 715 Monadnock Bldg., Chicago, Ill.

Fullerton, Reese P., LL.B., '11; LL.M., '12; L.D.M., '12. Denton, Md.

Fulton, Creed M., LL.B., '90; LL.M., '91. Colorado Bldg., Washington, D. C.

Furbershaw, Thos. L., D.D.S., '12. 80 R St. N. W., Washington, D. C.

Furbershaw, Walter S., LL.M., '07. Lawyer, 713 14th St., Washington, D. C.

Furlong, Francis Mohun, M.D., '95. Medical Officer, Naval Hospital, Chelsea, Mass.

G

Gaddis, Edgar T., LL.B., '92; LL.M., '93. Lawyer, 1017 E. Capitol St.,
Washington, D. C.

Gaffney, John L., LL.B., '08. Sec. and Agt. Milford Land and Cottage
Co., 51 Leavenworth St., Waterbury, Conn.

Gagien, Thomas Reed, M.D., '12. St. Francis Hospital, Jersey City, N. J.

Galiher, Samuel S., LL.B., '91. Bureau of Immigration, 436 6th St.
N. E., Washington, D. C.

Gall, John Camden, LL.B., '99. *Philippi, W. Va.

Gallagher, Anthony J., LL.M., '87. Lawyer, *Pottsville, Pa.

Gallagher, John Martin, B.S., '96. Instructor, 10 Frank St., Watertown, Mass.

Gallagher, Joseph Aloysius, A.M., '97. Devon, Pa.

Gallagher, Lawrence J., LL.B., '09. Lawyer, Wagoner, Okla.

Gallagher, Nicholas A., M.D., '09. Physician, 221 Highland Ave., Malden, Mass.

Gallagher, P. J., M.D., '91. U. S. Bureau of Pensions, Washington, D. C.

Gallagher, Thos. D. J., A.B., '84. Physician, 2826 Harrison Ave., Camden, N. J.

Gallaher, E. McHenry, LL.B., '08; LL.M., '09. County Attorney, Wagoner, Okla.

Gallatin, Daniel B., LL.B., '76. Bureau of Patents, 24 Q St. N. W.,
Washington, D. C.

Gallen, Wm. J. A., LL.B., '03. Lawyer, 4823 Lancaster Ave., Philadelphia, Pa.

Galliett, Harold H., LL.B., '12. Mowrystown, Ohio.

Ganahl, Alphonse E., A.M., '07. Lawyer, 621 Liggett Bldg., St. Louis, Mo.

Gannaway, Thos. D., LL.B., '11. Dayton, Tenn.

Gannon, Jas. A., M.D., '06. Physician and Surgeon (G. U. Med. Fac.),
The Dresden, Washington, D. C.

Gantt, Daniel J., LL.B., '95; LL.M., '96. Treasurer Department, 3532
11th St. N. W., Washington, D. C.

Gantt, Robert Joseph, LL.B., '96. Lawyer, Spartanburg, S. C.

Gapen, Nelson, M.D., '00. Capt. Med. Corps, U. S. A., Boston, Mass.

Garabedian, Aram L., D.D.S., '03. Dentist, 1404 H St., Washington, D. C.

Garcia, B. Fernandez, LL.B., '08. Lawyer, Cayey, P. R.

Gardiner, W. Gwynn, LL.B., '99; LL.M., '00. Lawyer, Fendall Bldg.,
Washington, D. C.

Gardner, Frank D., LL.B., '12. 623 E. Capitol St., Washington, D. C.

Gardner, R. Bennett, LL.B., '96. Clarendon, Va.

Garnett, Dr. Algernon S., A.M., '75. Physician, Hot Springs, Ark.

Garnett, Leslie Coombs, LL.B., '99; LL.M., '10. Attorney for Mathews
Co., Va., 717-718 Mutual Bldg., Richmond, Va.

Garnett, Robert Stanislaus, M.D., '03. Physician, 1008 Fidelity Bldg.,
Tacoma, Wash.

Garrison, F. H., M.D., '93. Librarian, Army Med. Library, 1437 R St.,
Washington, D. C.

Garrot, Frank H., LL.B., '09. Lawyer, Rogers, Ark.

Garvey, Thos. Q., M.D., '94. Physician, Lancaster, Pa.

Garvy, Wm. J., LL.B., '94; A.M., '94. President and Treasurer The Garvy Co., 51st and Grand Ave., Chicago, Ill.

Gately, M. J., M.D., '72. Physician, 11 S. Broadway, Baltimore, Md.

Gates, Chas. J., LL.B., '04. Lawyer, Treasury Dept., Washington, D. C.

Gauss, John J., LL.B., '08. Sp. Agt. Census Bureau, St. Louis, Mo.

Gavan, Joseph W., LL.B., '04. Author and Journalist, 256-7 Broadway, New York City.

Gaynor, Hubert Edward, M.D., '09. Physician, 323 8th St., Parkersburg, W. Va.

Gaynor, Rev. Hugh Augustine, S.J., A.B., '95; A.M., '96. Professor of Poetry, Boston College, Boston, Mass.

Geary, Daniel J., A.B., '89. Manufacturer, Oil City, Pa.

Geis, Homer E., LL.B., '11; LL.M., '12; L.D.M., '11. Lawyer, 2100 First St. N. W., Washington, D. C.

Gelpi, Maurice Joseph, A.B., '05. Physician, 3720 Canal St., New Orleans, La.

Geneste, Elmon A., LL.B., '10; LL.M., '11; L.D.M., '12. City Attorney, Bay City, Ore.

Geneste, Leonard F., A.B., '07; LL.B., '11. Lawyer, 1507 3d St. N. W., Washington, D. C.

Gengler, Adam C., LL.B., '09; LL.M., '10. War Department, Washington, D. C.

Gentsch, Charles, M.D., '73. Physician, 2822 Franklin Ave., Cleveland, Ohio.

Gentsch, Daniel C., M.D., '89. Physician, 164 East Ave., New Philadelphia, Ohio.

Geoghan, Wm. F. X., LL.B., '06. Lawyer, 302 Broadway, New York City.

George, Isaac Stewart, A.M., '04; LL.B., '06; LL.M., '07. Lawyer, 1009-1021 Calvert Bldg., Baltimore, Md.

George, John M., LL.B., '92; LL.M., '93. Assistant Corp. Counsel, 1521 Monroe St. N. E., Washington, D. C.

Gerald, Herbert P., LL.B., '90. Patent Office, Washington, D. C.

Gering, Matthew, LL.B., '83; LL.M., '84. Lawyer, Plattsmouth, Cass Co., Neb.

Geringer, Emil J., LL.B., '03. Lawyer, 1518 W. 12th St., Chicago, Ill.

Gerrity, Harry J., LL.B., '12. Scranton, Pa.

Gery, Raymond E., LL.B., '93; LL.M., '94. U. S. Forest Service, Ogden, Utah.

Gettinger, Wm. Malcolm, LL.B., '09. Lawyer, Barrister Bldg., Washington, D. C.

Gibbs, Alexander C., LL.B., '06; LL.M., '07. Lawyer, 2904 13th St. N. W., Washington, D. C.

Gibbs, Frederick R., A.B., '11. Law Student, 1323 30th St. N. W., Washington, D. C.

Gibson, Frederick P., LL.B., '98. Lawyer, 1602 19th St. N. W., Washington, D. C.

Gibson, T. Catlett, M.D., '93. Physician and Surgeon, Scott Bldg., Salt Lake City, Utah.

Gibson, Thos. Werner, LL.B., '06. Attorney, Roswell, N. M.

Gilchrist, Walter Schell, A.B., '02. Dept. of Commerce and Labor, Washington, D. C.

Gilday, Alfred L., LL.B., '11. Lawyer, Erie, Mich.

Gill, Jas. Edward, M.D., '01. P. A. Surg., U. S. Navy, Navy Dept., Washington, D. C.

Gillan, Edward Francis, LL.B., '01; LL.M., '02. Bureau of Census, Washington, D. C.

Gillen, Chas. Frederick, Ph.D., '12. Professor, St. Boniface College, Winnipeg, Manitoba, Canada.

Gillespie, John B., LL.B., '89; LL.M., '90. Lawyer, 37 Market St., Scranton, Pa.

Gilmore, Wm. T., LL.B., '04. Lawyer, Danville, Ill.

Ginther, Cyril Francis, A.B., '03. Treasurer Phoenix Brewery, Buffalo, N. Y.

Given, Ralph, LL.B., '99; LL.M., '00. Assistant U. S. District Attorney, Fendall Bldg., Washington, D. C.

Gleeson, John K., A.B., '52. *Jackson, La.

Glennan, Chas. P., A.B., '78. Physician, 420 Florida Ave. N. W., Washington, D. C.

Glennan, John Walter, LL.B., '91; LL.M., '92. Lawyer, The Damariscotta, Washington, D. C.

Gloetzner, Prof. Anton, Mus. Doc., '89. 1228 M St. N. W., Washington, D. C.

Gloetzner, Arnulf Anthony, A.B., '11. 1228 M St. N. W., Washington, D. C.

Gloetzner, Herman Francis, A.B., '99. Pension Office, Washington, D. C.

Glover, Marvin Wilbur, M.D., '98. P. A. Surg., U. S. Quarantine Station, Angel Island, Cal.

Glueck, Bernard, M.D., '09. Physician, Government Hospital for the Insane, Washington, D. C.

Goddard, W. H., LL.B., '72. Lawyer, 1630 Connecticut Ave. N. W., Washington, D. C.

Goff, Hon. Nathan, LL.D., '89. Lawyer, Clarksburg, W. Va.

Goggin, Geo. F., LL.B., '11. 1755 Kilbourne Place, Washington, D. C., Gardner, Mass.

Golden, Paul Emmet, A.B., '09. 214 Fairview Ave., Scranton, Pa.

Golden, Wm. P., LL.M., '11. War Dept., San Francisco, Cal.

Goldsborough, John A., LL.B., '86. Patent Lawyer, McGill Bldg., Washington, D. C.

Golladay, J. Emmerson, LL.B., '12. 1254 Irving St., Washington, D. C.

Goodman, Wm. R., Jr., M.D., '70. Physician, 1332 12th St. N. W., Washington, D. C.

Goodwin, Wm. D., LL.B., '08. Indian Office, Hailey, Idaho.

Gorham, Newton B., LL.B., '92. *Rochester, N. Y.

Gorman, Chas. Edmund, LL.D., '96. Lawyer, 906 Banigan Bldg., Providence, R. I.

Gorman, Edward Aloysius, M.D., '98. Health Officer, 321 Duke St., Alexandria, Va.

Gorman, Geo. E., LL.B., '95. Lawyer, 30 N. La Salle St., Chicago, Ill.

Gorman, Jas. Francis, M.D., '11. 166 Main St., S. Manchester, Conn.

Gottbrath, Norbert J., M.D., '12. St. Francis Hospital, Jersey City, N. J.

Gould, Hon. Ashley Mulgrave, LL.B., '84. Justice of Supreme Court (G. U. Law Fac.), Washington, D. C.

Gouldston, John C., M.D., '54. England.

Gove, Frank E., LL.B., '91. Lawyer, Yeaman & Gove, 411 Ernest & Cranmer Bldg., Denver, Colo.

Govern, Chas. J., LL.B., '96; LL.M., '97. *1133 Broadway, New York City.

Govern, Frank, LL.B., '93; LL.M., '94. Indian Office, Washington, D. C.

Govern, Hugh, Jr., LL.B., '91; LL.M., '92. Assistant U. S. Attorney, 7 Beekman St., New York City.

Gower, Henry Ryan, A.B., '98. Lawyer, Secretary G. U. Al. Ass., Union Trust Bldg., Washington, D. C.

Grace, Albert L., LL.B., '99; LL.M., '00. Lawyer, Plaquemine, La.

Grace, Pierce Joseph, A.M., '92; Mus. B., '92. Lawyer, 36 Crawford St., Dorchester, Mass.

Gracie, Asa Creed, A.B., '01; A.M., '02; LL.B., '04. Lawyer, 503 E. 6th St., Little Rock, Ark.

Gracie, John Pierce, A.B., '01. Planter, Rob Roy, Ark.

Grady, Jas. Aloysius, M.D., '03. Physician, 325 E. Main St., Waterbury, Conn.

Graff, Carl J. F., LL.B., '92; LL.M., '93. Lawyer, 472 Louisiana Ave., Washington, D. C.

Graham, Harry C., LL.B., '06. Lawyer, Marshall, Ill.

Graham, John W., A.B., '52. *Virginia.

Graham, Wm. Henry, Jr., S.J., A.B., '05. Professor of Greek, Georgetown University, Washington, D. C.

Grant, Rev. James A., A.B., '89. St. Catherine's Church, Burlingame, Cal.

Grant, John H., M.D., '90. Chief of Accounts, State Dept. of Agr. of N. Y., 195 Madison Ave., Albany, N. Y.

Grant, Thos., LL.B., '96; LL.M., '97. Secretary of Washington Chamber of Commerce, 1201 F St. N. W., Washington, D. C.

Grau, Philip A., A.M., '01; LL.B., '03; LL.M., '04. Lawyer, 67 Bellevue Place, Chicago, Ill.

Gray, Jas. Aloysius, A.B., '88; A.M., '91. Lawyer, 627-629 Southern Trust Bldg., Little Rock, Ark.

Grayson, William W., LL.B., '96. Auditor, Stone & Webster Bldg., Boston, Mass.

Green, Andrew J., LL.B., '88; LL.M., '89. Legal Reviewer, U. S. Bureau of Pensions, Washington, D. C.

Green, Augustine de Yturbide, M.D., '01. Physician, Provident Bldg., Proesser, Wash.

Green, Benjamin G., LL.B., '77. Lawyer, Warrentown, N. C.

Green, Burton R., LL.B., '09. 1259 Irving St., Washington, D. C.

Green, Francis Key, LL.B., '98; LL.M., '99. Officer U. S. Supreme Court, Washington, D. S.

Green, G. Marvin, LL.B., '12. War Department, Denver, Colo.

Green, Geo. Chancellor, A.B., '01. Lawyer, Weldon, N. C.

Green, Jas. B., LL.B., '92; LL.M., '93. Lawyer, 1425 New York Ave. N. W., Washington, D. C.

Green, Joel C., M.D., '68. *Kansas.

Green, John H., A.M., '70. *Ohio.

Green, John J., LL.B., '08. Lawyer, Thomaston, Conn.

Green, Lawrence H., LL.B., '09. 1259 Irving St., Washington, D. C.

Green, Robert Joseph, M.D., '04. Physician, 120 Aisquith St., Baltimore, Md.

Green, Virgil R., LL.B., '06. Lawyer, Petersburg, Ind.

Greene, J. Gardner, LL.B., '01; LL.M., '02. Lawyer, Pell City, Ala.

Greene, Wallace, LL.B., '90. Patent Attorney, McGill Bldg, Washington, D. C.

Greene, Warren Earl, LL.B., '02. Assistant Pros. Attorney, Court House, Duluth, Minn.

Greenfield, Wm. E., LL.B., '89. The Sun, Baltimore, Md.

Gregg, Wm. S., LL.B., '05. Special Assistant Attorney General, 1450 Clifton St., Washington, D. C.

Griffin, James H., LL.B., '94; LL.M., '95. Patent Lawyer, 277 Broadway, New York City.

Griffin, John Chas., M.D., '09. Physician, Towanda, Pa.

Griffin, John J., D.D.S., '04. Dentist, 110 Central St., Waltham, Mass.

Griffin, Wm. Yancey, LL.B., '98; LL.M., '90. Treasury Department, 3109 Wisconsin Ave., Washington, D. C.

Griffith, E. Colville, LL.B., '10. Coal Dealer, 1446 Rhode Island Ave., Washington, D. C.

Griffith, Jas. E., LL.B., '77. *Washington, D. C.

Griffith, Monte J., M.D., '69. Physician (G. U. Med. Fac.), The Farragut, Washington, D. C.

Grima, Alfred, A.B., '04. Lawyer, 1604 4th St., New Orleans, La.

Grimes, Junius D., LL.B., '02. Lawyer, Washington, N. C.

Grimes, Wm. H., LL.B., '92; LL.M., '93. Treasurer Commercial Credit Co., 1006 Keyser Bldg., Baltimore, Md.

Grinstead, John R., LL.B., '09. Lawyer, Cantril, Iowa.

Groden, Peter F., D.D.S., '12. Dentist, 240 W. 136th St., New York City.

Grogan, Stephen Sylvester, A.M., '03; LL.B., '06; LL.M., '07. Journalist, The Post, Washington, D. C.

Grogan, Thomas J., LL.B., '96; LL.M., '97. Care Peter Grogan & Sons Co., Baltimore, Md.

Grogay, Patrick J., LL.B., '96; LL.M., '97. *Baltimore, Md.

Gross, Alfred Gregory, Jr., M.D., '00. Physician, 1722 17th St., Washington, D. C.

Gross, Frank C., LL.B., '12. 3326 Prospect Ave., Washington, D. C.; Lockhaven, Pa.

Grove, Selbie D., LL.B., '11. Lawyer, 1332 B St. S. E., Washington, D. C.; Detroit, Mich.

Guilfoile, Joseph C., LL.B., '11. Lawyer, Waterbury, Conn.

Guinan, Joseph P., M.D., '08. Physician, Lima, N. Y.

Gulentz, Chas., LL.B., '90; LL.M., '92. Lawyer, 1109 Park Bldg., Pittsburgh, Pa.

Gunnell, Dr. Francis M., A.B., '44; A.M., '46. U. S. Navy, Surgeon General, Ret., 600 20th St. N. W., Washington, D. C.

Gurnett, John M., LL.B., '12. 1917 G St. N. W., Washington, D. C.; Omaha, Neb.

Gwinn, Chester A., LL.B., '09; LL.M., '10. Lawyer, Slator, Mo.

Gwynn, Raphael N., LL.B., '98; LL.M., '99. Lawyer, Denver, Col.

Gwynn, Wm. Clarence, M.D., '98. Physician and Surgeon, G. U. Med. Fac., 1514 30th St. N. W., Washington, D. C.

H

Haag, Harry O., LL.B., '97. Lawyer, Pottsville, Pa.

Haag, Jackson D., LL.B., '90; LL.M., '91. Dramatic Editor, Editorial Rooms, The Post, Pitsburgh, Pa.

Haas, Carlton Daniels, M.D., '97. Physician, 3018 13th St., Washington, D. C.

Hackworth, Green H., LL.B., '12. 120 6th St. N. E., Washington, D. C.; Willard, Ky.

Hagan, Christopher J., A.B., '00. General Ins. Agt., 52 Central St., Lowell, Mass.

Haggerty, Louis C., A.B., '12. 50 South St., New York City.

Hahn, Harry William, LL.B., '03. Shoe Dealer, 7th and K Sts., Washington, D. C.

Haines, Walter S., M.D., '91. *Kentucky.

Hainner, Hon. Edward D., LL.B., '88; LL.M., '89. Lawyer, State Senator, Attalla, Etowah Co., Ala.

Hale, William, M.D., '67. *New York.

Hall, Arthur A., LL.B., '93; LL.M., '95. Credit Man, L. S. Baumgardner & Co., Toledo, Ohio.

Hall, Frank L., LL.B., '11. Burton Harbor, Mich.

Hall, Harry Thomas, A.B., '05. Organist, St. Mary's Church, 1911 New Hampshire Ave., Washington, D. C.

Hall, John Dillan, LL.B., '99; LL.M., '01. Chief Identification Bureau, Navy Department, Washington, D. C.

Hall, John H., A.B., '53. *Tennessee.

Hall, Joseph Edward, LL.B., '98. *Mancato, Minn.

Hall, Ross C., LL.B., '88. Seattle, Wash.

Hall, Walter D., LL.B., '09. Lawyer, South West City, Mo.

Hallam, Paul L., LL.B., '09. Indian Office, 326 5th St. S. E. Washington, D. C.

Halley, John H., LL.B., '12. 3023 Cambridge Place, Washington, D. C.; Morristown, Tenn.

Halpin, James A., M.D., '12. Alescian Hospital, Elizabeth, N. J.

Halstead, Thomas, LL.B., '89; LL.M., '90. Lawyer, 4611 Wayne Ave., Philadelphia, Pa.

Haltigan, Patrick J., LL.B., '97. Editor and Publisher, 614 Louisiana Ave., Washington, D. C.

Ham, Henry H., LL.B., '05. Fayetteville, Ark.

Hamby, Louis L., LL.B., '06. Lawyer, Bond Bldg., Washington, D. C.

Hamersly, Lewis Randolph, LL.B., '96. Publisher, 1 W. 34th St., New York City.

Hamill, James H., LL.B., '06. Auditor's Office, District Bldg., Washington, D. C.

Hamilton, Charles Wm., B.S., '81. Banker, 1112 Park Ave., Omaha, Nebraska.

Hamilton, Edward J., M.D., '95. Physician, 616 McGowan Ave., Houston, Texas.

Hamilton, George E., A.B., '72; LL.B., '74; A.M., '82; LL.D., '89. G. U. Law Fac., Pres. G. U. Al. Assn., Pres. Capital Tract Co., Union Trust Bldg., Washington, D. C.

Hamilton, Hon. Harper, LL.B., '83. Judge, City Court, Rome, Ga.

Hamilton, John J., LL.B., '91; LL.M., '92.. Lawyer, Hamilton, Yerkes & Hamilton, G. U. Law Fac., Union Trust Bldg., Washington, D. C.

Hamilton, Ralph Alexander, M.D., '04. Physician, G. U. Med. and Den. Fac., 924 15th St., Washington, D. C.

Hammett, Charles Maddox, M.D., '92. Eye and Ear Specialist, The Brunswick, 1330 I St. N. W., Washington, D. C.

Hammer, Edward D., LL.B., '88; LL.M., '89. Lawyer, Attalla, Etowah County, Ala.

Hampton, George R., M.D., '09. St. Francis Hospital, Jersey City, N. J.

Hampton, J. Rodolph, LL.B., '89; LL.M., '90. Clifton, Arizona.

Hanawalt, George P., M.D., '64. Physician and Surgeon, Des Moines, Iowa.

Haney, Leonard T., LL.B., '11; L.D.M., '11. Patent Office, Washingtton, D. C.

Hanger, Hugh H., LL.B., '03. Sales Mgr. Nat. Bank Cash Register, 1312 Pa. Ave. N. W., Washington, D. C.

Hanger, McCarthy, LL.B., '08. Manufacturer, 1312 Pa. Ave. N. W., Washington, D. C.

Hanigan, Harry A., A.B., '06. Merchant, 119 W. 70th St., New York City.

Hanrahan, Rev. James Vincent, A.M., '96. S. H. Church, W. Fitchburg, Mass.

Hanretty, Lawrence Michael, Jr., A.B., '04. Business, 78 Capenter Ave., Newburgh, N. Y.

Harbin, George Francis, Jr., A.B., '02. In charge of Electrical Engineering Dept., G. U. of Amer., 11 7th St. S. E., Washington, D. C.

Hardie, Joseph Cuyler, LL.B., '92; LL.M., '93. War Dept., Washington, D. C.

Hardin, Palmer, LL.B., '92. *Springfield, Ky.

Hardin, Thomas B., Jr., LL.B., '84; LL.M., '85. *Seattle, Wash.

Hardisty, John T., LL.B., '04. Lawyer, Collington, Prince George Co., Maryland.

Hardy, Calvin S., LL.B., '96; LL.M., '97. Pension Bureau, 664 E St. N. W., Washington, D. C.

Hare, Wm. C., LL.B., '95. Lawyer, Upper Sandusky, Ohio.

Hargis, Samuel O., LL.B., '11. Secretary, House of Representatives, Washington, D. C.; St. Louis, Mo.

Hargrove, Karl A., LL.B., '12. 5431 Conn. Ave. N. W., Washington, D. C.; Little Rock, Ark.

Harker, Charles O., LL.B., '99. *Grand Junction, Iowa.

Harley, Richard Joseph, A.B., '96. Hotel Business, 1842 Market St., Philadelphhia, Pa.

Harlow, Leo P., LL.B., '98; LL.M., '99. Lawyer, 412 5th St., Washington, D. C.

Harman, Walter P., LL.B., '11. Dept. of Commerce and Labor, 425 Manor Pl., Washington, D. C.; Rutland, Vt.

Harmon, John Oregon, LL.B., '99. Cashier, 615 Rock Creek Church Rd. N. W., Washington, D. C.

Harmon, Morton C., LL.B., '08. Mt. Rainier, Md.

Harper, B. E., D.D.S., '02. *Washington, D. C.

Harper, James E., LL.B., '97. P. O. Dept., Washington, D. C., Chevy Chase, Md.

Harr, Wm. R., LL.B., '95; LL.M., '96. Lawyer, Assistant Atty. General in Dept of Justice, Union Trust Bldg., Washington, D. C.

Harrington, Edward P., LL.B., '86; LL.M., '87. U. S. Revenue Cutter Service, 816 13th St. N. W., Washington, D. C.

Harris, Charles N., A.B., '71; A.M., '89. Lawyer, Judge of Domestic Relations Court, New York City, 31 E. 49th St., New York City.

Harris, Edward F., LL.M., '88. *Cambridge, N. Y.

Harrison, Floyd R., LL.B., '12. Dept. Agr., 818 A St. S. E., Washington, D. C.; Petersburg, Va.

Harrison, John C., M.D., '60. *Virginia.

Harrison, Walton, LL.B., '97. *Washington, D. C.

Harrison, Wm. Barnett, M.D., '05. Physician, Starkville, Miss.

Harrison, Wm. Clinton, LL.B., '99. Sec., Elmore Cotton Mills, Sol. 1st Jud. Circuit Alabama, Demopolis, Morengo, Ala.

Harrison, Wm. H., LL.B., '81. Bank President, Tutwyler, Miss.

Harrison, Wilson Allyn, Jr., D.D.S., '10. Dentist, 1616 I St., Washington, D. C.

Harroun, Wm. S., M.D., '65. Physician, 234 W. Palace Ave., Sante Fe, New Mexico.

Hart, Harry L., LL.B., '03. Philipsberg, N. J.

Hart, Harry L., LL.B., '12. War Dept., 1759 Willard St. N. W., Washington, D. C.; Westmoreland, Kansas.

Hart, James Henry, D.D.S., '05. 134 Hancock St., Everett, Mass.

Hart, John T., LL.B., '95; LL.M., '96. Pension Office, Washington, D. C.

Hart, Ringgold, LL.B., '11. 621 Md. Ave. N. E., Washington, D. C.

Hart, Timothy J., LL.B., '09. Bu. Ins. Affairs, 712 20th St. N. W., Washington, D. C.

Hartley, Wilbur, LL.B., '11. Treasury Dept., 444 M St. N. W., Washington, D. C.; Mankato, Minn.

Hartnett, Daniel J., LL.B., '03. U. S. Census Bureau, 417 N. J. Ave. N. W., Washington, D. C

Hartnett, Francis J., A.B., '09. Journalist, Washington Times, 421 10th St. N. W., Washington, D. C.

Hartsfield, Augustus M., LL.B., '95. Interstate Commerce Commission, Washington, D. C.

Harvey, Harry Edward, D.D.S., '12. 2216 1st St. N. W., Washington, D. C.

Harvey, Richard E., LL.B., '05. Lawyer, City Solicitor, Portland, Maine.

Harvey, Thomas M., A.B., '89. Journalist, U. S. Court House, City Hall, Washington, D. C.

Harvey, Wm. F., M.D., '68. *Vermont.

Harveycutter, Austin, LL.B., '05. Assistant Attorney, Dept. of Justice, 1368 Harvard St., Washington, D. C.

Hasbrouck, Edwin Marble, M.D., '95. Physician, 1819 Adams Mill Rd., Washington, D. C.

Haskell, Lewis, LL.B., '94. Lawyer, U. S. Consul, Hull, England.

Hassan, Dudley T., LL.B., '96; LL.M., '97. 3255 M St. N. W., Washington, D. C.

Hassler, Alpha M., LL.B., '95. *Forest City, S. D.

Hatch, Wm. B., LL.B., '94. Lawyer and Journalist, 11 Huron St., Ypsilanti, Mich.

Haven, Charles L., M.D., '65. *Maine.

Hawken, Samuel McComas, LL.B., '05. Tennallytown, Md.

Hawley, Cornell S., LL.B., '97. Vice-President and Manager, Consolidated Car Heating Co., Albany, N. Y.

Haycock, Ira C., LL.B., '07; LL.M., '08. Lawyer, Wilburton, Okla.

Hayden, Daniel B., M.D., '04. Surgeon, Inst. in Otology, Rush Med. College, 122 S. Mich. Ave., Chicago, Ill.

Hayden, Reynolds, M.D., '05. P. A. Surgeon, U. S. N., Washington, D. C.

Haydon, Wm. Thomas, A.B., '94. Lawyer, 209 St. Paul St., Baltimore, Maryland.

Hayes, Edward, LL.B., '72. Bureau of Fisheries, 107 I St. N. W., Washington, D. C.

Hayes, Henry L., M.D., '90. Thomas Cook & Sons, Berlin, Germany.

Hayes, Noah, M.D., '76. Physician, Seneca, Kansas.

Hayes, Stephen H., LL.B., '89; LL.M., '90. *Cleaves, Ohio.

Hayes, Stephen Quentin, A.B., '92. Elec. Eng., 410 East Ave., Pittsburg, Pa.

Hayes, T. Frank, A.B., '06. Merchant. 347 N. Main St., Waterbury, Connecticut.

Hays, Melville Ambrose, M.D., '00. Physician, Army and Navy Journal, New York City.

Hazen, Wm. P. C., M.D., '77. Physician, 511 E. Capitol St., Washington, D. C.

Head, Morris Wm., A.B., '98. Greensburg, Pa.

Head, Paul Jones, A.B., '00. Lawyer, Greensburg, Pa.

Healy, Charles B., M.D., '08. Physician, The Montana, Washington, D. C.

Healy, Charles L. M.D., '12. Emergency Hospital, Buffalo, N. Y.

Healy, Edward Charles, A.B., '11. Commercial National Bank, 46 I St. N. E., Washington, D. C.

Healy, George L., LL.B., '10. Lawyer, 46 Curve St., West Newton, Mass.

Healy, James M., A.B., '72; A.M., '89. *Pennsylvania.

Healy, Thomas F., LL.B., '99; LL.M., '00. Government Printing Office, Washington, D. C.

Hearst, Wm. T., LL.B., '92; LL.M., '95. War Dept., Washington, D. C.

Heaton, Harry John, LL.B., '03. Lawyer, American Bank Bldg., Seattle, Wash.

Heberle, John J., LL.B., '09. Immigrant Inspector, Cattarangus, Fla.

Hedrick, Charles Joseph, LL.B., '84. Patent Attorney, 606 F St. N. W., Washington, D. C.

Hedrick, Rev. John T., S.J., A.B., '71; A.M., '74. Director Georgetown Astronom. Observ., Georgetown Univ., Washington, D. C.

Heffernan, Bernard J., LL.B., '06. Interstate Com. Comm., Washington, D. C.

Heffernan, John Francis, LL.B., '04; LL.M., '05. Lawyer and U. S. Attorney, 90 Wall St., New York City.

Hegarty, Harry A., LL.B., '01. Lawyer, 612 F St. N. W., Washington, D. C.

Heideman, Ivan, LL.B., '01. Lawyer, Columbian Bldg., 416 5th St. N. W., Washington, D. C.

Heintzelman, Joseph A., Jr., M.D., '02. Druggist, 2000 Ridge and N. College Ave., Philadelphia, Pa.

Heiskell, Raymond Angelo, A.B., '91; LL.B., '93; LL.M., '94. Lawyer, Century Bldg., Washington, D. C.

Heitmuller, H. Anton, LL.B., '97; LL.M., '98. Lawyer, 458 La. Ave. N. W., Washington, D. C

Heizman, Col. Charles L., A.B., '64. (Retired), Care of Adjutant General, U. S. A., 37 Praesidio Ave., San Francisco, Cal.

Heller, Joseph Milton, M.D., '96. Physician and Surgeon, The Marlborough, 917 18th St. N. W., Washington, D. C.

Heller, P. H., Phar.B., '71; M.D., '74. Physician, 801 Sante Fe Ave., Pueblo, Cal.

Helm, Dr. Charles J., A.B., '83. Physician, 153 W. 3d St., Peru, Ind.

Helm, Gratz W., LL.B., '01. Hotel Leighton, Los Angeles, Cal.

5

Helmick, Wm. J., A.B., '00. P. O. Dept., 1533 Wis. Ave., Washington, D. C.

Helmus, John, LL.B., '08; LL.M., '09. Lawyer, House of Representatives, Washington, D. C.

Helton, A. S., M.D., '90. Pension Office, Washington, D. C.

Hemler, Wm. Francis, M.D., '04. Physician, G. U. Med. Fac., 613 15th St., Washington, D. C.

Hemphill, Joseph C, LL.B., '12; L.D.M., '12. 1025 Vermont Ave., Washington, D. C.; Paris, Ill.

Henderson, James Abby, LL.B., '93. Lawyer, Rockville, Md.

Henderson, John M., LL.B., '90. Real Estate, 1418 F St. N. W., Washington, D. C.

Hendler, Charles T., LL.B., '96; LL.M., '97. Lawyer, Fendall Bldg., Washington, D. C.

Hendrick, David S., LL.B., '09. Automobile Business, 1317 H St. N. W., Washington, D. C.

Henkel, Solomon D., LL.B., '10; LL.M., '11; L.D.M., '11. Boiling Spring Farm, Quicksbury, Va.

Hennessy, John F., LL.B., '06. Lawyer, Third Assistant Postmaster General, Division of Classification, Majestic Bldg., Milwaukee, Wis.

Hennessy, Vincent B., A.M., '06; LL.B., '08. Lawyer, Majestic Bldg., Milwaukee, Wis.

Henning, R. E., M.D., '85. Physician, Cheriton, Va.

Hennon, John Francis, A.B., '93; A.M., '94. Manufacturer, Jewett City, Conn.

Henry, Thomas Stanhope, LL.B., '99. Lawyer, Dept. of Justice, Washington, D. C.

Henry, Wesley, D.D.S., '11. Dentist, Nezperce, Idaho.

Henry, Wm. J., M.D., '66. Physician, *Connecticut.

Hermesch, Harry R., M.D., '07. Past Assistant Surgeon, U. S. N., Bureau of Navigation, Navy Dept., Washington, D. C.

Hernitz, Stanislaus, M.D., '53. Poland.

Heron, Alexander P., LL.B., '99. *Washington, D. C.

Heron, Benjamin F. L., LL.B., '07; LL.M., '08. Lawyer, Columbian Bldg., Washington, D. C., Mt. Rainier, Md.

Herrero, Juan, LL.B., '11; LL.M., '12; L.D.M., '12. Professor, 11 Grant Place, Washington, D. C.; Humacao, P. R.

Herring, Carl E., LL.M., '89. 417 Omaha National Bank Bldg., Omaha, Nebraska.

Herring, Hon. James L., LL.B., '98. Judge, Probate Court, St. Clair Co., Ashville, Ala.

Herron, W. Francis, LL.B., '99; LL.M., '00. Assistant Treas., Union Trust Co., Washington, D. C.

Hickey, Andrew I., LL.B., '11; LL.M., '12; L.D.M., '12. 1300 W St. N. W., Washington, D. C.

Hickey, Harry K., LL.B., '08; LL.M., '09. Sec. to the President of the So. Railway Co., 1817 16th St. N. W., Washington, D. C.

Hickling, D. Percy, M.D., '84. Physician, G. U. Med Fac., 1304 R. I. Ave. N. W., Washington, D. C.

Hickman, G. W. Vinton, M.D., '72. Physician, Smithville, Texas

Hicks, Frederick Charles, LL.B., '01. Librarian, Columbia University, New York City.

Hicks, Jesse Addison, LL.B., '99. Lawyer, 310-311 Bond Bldg., Washington, D. C.

Hicks, Leo Richard, A.B., '05. Capitalist, Los Gatos, Cal.

Higgins, Andrew J., LL.B., '09. Lawyer, Higgins and Ambrose, Mackay, Idaho.

Higgins, Hon. James H., LL.B., '99; LL.M., '00; LL.D., '09. 114 Prospect St., Pawtucket, R. I.

Higgins, Reginald H., LL.B., '90; LL.M., '91. Lawyer, Standish, Maine.

Higgins, Rev. Wm. Lawrence Denis, A.B., '97. Pastor, Manley Neb.

Hildreth, Arthur Lander, D.D.S., '11. Dentist, 1616 I St. N. W., Washington, D. C.

Hill, Eugene F., A.B., '70. Kansas City, Mo.

Hill, Ezra N., LL.B., '09. Bureau of Engraving and Printing, 2145 K St. N. W., Washington, D. C.

Hill, F. Snowden, A.B., '73. Lawyer, 512 Fendall Bldg., Washington, D. C. and Upper Marlboro, Md.

Hill, G. W., M.D., '59. *Ohio.

Hill, Henderson F., LL.B., '08; L.D.M., '11. Lawyer, 605 7th St. N. W., Washington, D. C.

Hill, J. Chambers, M.D., '91. Physician, 78 Middle St., Rockland, Maine.

Hill, Richard S., M.D., '86. Physician, Upper Marlboro, Md.

Hilliard, Patrick R., LL.B., '93; LL.M., '94. Dept. of Justice, 956 West Garfield Boul., Chicago, Ill.

Hillyer, Charles S., LL.B., '07. Lawyer, Colorado Bldg., Washington, D. C.

Hillyer, Clair Richards, LL.B., '99; LL.M., '00. Attorney, Interstate Com. Comn., Washington, D. C.

Hilman, Joseph G., LL.B., '06. Special Agent, U. S. Land Office, Epes, Alabama.

Hilton, Edward J., LL.B., '10; LL.M., '11. Interior Dept., 1736 G St. N. W., Washington, D. C.

Hilton, James Franklin, M.D., '04. Physician, The Susquehanna, Washington, D. C.

Hilton, Wm. A., LL.B., '09. Lawyer, Salt Lake City, Utah.

Hine, Oliver C., LL.B., '92; LL.M., '93. Manager, 437 Fulton St., Brooklyn, N. Y.

Hines, J. Arthur, M.D., '69. Physician, Van Wert, Ohio.

Hinton, John R., LL.B., '08. Dept. of Justice, 3632 13th St., Washington, D. C.

Hipkins, Wm, A. LL.B., '89; LL.M., '90. Lawyer, District Bldg., 3514 10th St. N. W., Washington, D. C.

Hird, John Denby, LL.B., '01. Chemist, G. U. Med. and Den. Fac., 1806 Lamont St., Washington, D. C.

Hirst, Anthony A., A.M., '71; LL.D., '01. Lawyer, 1200 Chestnut St., Philadelphia, Pa.

Hitchcock, Thomas D., LL.B., '90; LL.M., '91. Atty-at-Law, 518 Fidelity Bldg., Takoma, Washington, D. C.

Hitz, Wm. Henry, LL.B., '98; LL.M., '99. Lawyer, Hibbs Bldg., Washington, D. C.

Hoard, Francis De V., M.D., '79. Physician, *Illinois.

Hodge, Edwin R., M.D., '92. Chemist, Army Med. Museum, Washington, D. C.

Hodge, Howard B., LL.B., '96; LL.M., '97. Attorney, Fidelity and Deposit Co. of Maryland, 2945 Macomb St:, Cleveland Park, D. C.

Hodges, Benjamin F., M.D., '58. Physician, *Maryland.

Hodges, E. F., M.D., '74; A.M., '88. Physician, Emer. Professor, Indianapolis Medical College, 2 W. N. Y. St., Indianapolis, Ind.

Hodges, Henry W., LL.B., '92; LL.M., '93. G. U. Law Fac., Clerk Court of Appeals, City Hall, Washington, D. C.

Hodges, Wm. S., LL.B., '93; LL.M., '94. Patent Lawyer, Judge Adv. D. C. Militia; Washington Loan and Trust Co., Washington, D. C.

Hodgkins, Chester Lyman, M.D., '00. Physician, *Waterville, Vt.

Hodgson, Reginald M., LL.B., '11; LL.M., '12; L.D.M., '12. Treasury Dept., 1812 G St. N. W., Washington, D. C., Falls Church, Va.

Hodgson, Telfair, LL. B., '89. *Mobile, Ala.

Hof, Charles R., LL.B., '93; LL.M., '94. General Land Office, Washington, D. C.

Hoffar, Noble S., A.B., '66; A.M., '67. *Washington, D. C.

Hoffman, Joseph O., LL.B., '12. 100 I St. N. W., Washington, D. C.; Washington, Ind.

Hogan, Frank J., LL.B., '02. Lawyer, G. U. Law Fac., Evans Bldg., Washington, D. C.

Holcombe, E. Prosser, LL.B., '95. Inspector, Indian Office, R. R. Bldg., Denver, Collo.

Holden, Raymond T., M.D., '81. Physician, 802 6th St. S. W., Washington, D. C.

Holder, Willis B., LL.B., '90; LL.M., '91. Treasury Dept, 3018 F' St. N. W., Washington, D. C.

Holland, G. West, LL.B., '08. Interior Dept., 622 Rock Creek Church Rd., Washington, D. C.

Holland, T. Stanley, LL.B., '12. 1737 17th St. N. W., Washington, D. C.

Holland, Wm. Joseph, M.D., '03. Physician, 780 Salem St., Malden, Mass.

Hollander, Harry H., LL.B., '99; LL.M., '00. Lawyer, Columbian Bldg., Washington, D. C.

Holliger, Frank S., LL.M., '98. War Dept., 1346 Newton St. N. W., Washington, D. C.

Holmes, Wm. C., LL.B., '12. Sec. and Treas., J. Louis Willage Co., 3539 13th St. N. W., Washington, D. C.; Nashville, Tenn.

Holt, George A., M.D., '80. Physician, *New York.

Holt, John Henry, LL.B., '97. Patent Lawyer, McGill Bldg., Washington, D. C.

Holt, John Herrimon, LL.B., '81. Lawyer, Huntington, W. Va.

Holt, Robert Oscar, LL.B., '91; LL.M., '92. Real Estate, Lorton, Fairfax Co., Va.

Homer, Charles C., A.B., '67; A.M., '96. Pres., 2nd National Bank, Baltimore, Md.

Hood, Edward, LL.B., '07. Lawyer, Seattle, Wash.

Hood, John H. P., A.B., '08. Lieut. U. S. Coast Art., Fort Ward, Wis., care of Adj. Gen. U. S. Army.

Hooper, Lionel Elcan, M.D., '11. Physician, Covington, Va.

Hoote, Louis C., M.D., '61. Physician, *Missouri.

Hoover, George Pendleton, LL.B., '97. Lawyer, Com. Nat. Bank Bldg., Washington, D. C.

Hoover, Wm. D., LL.B., '88; LL.M., '89. President of National Savings and Trust Co., 1428 Euclid St., Washington, D. C.

Hopewell, Edward N., LL.B., '06. Lawyer, Fendall Bldg., Washington, D. C.

Hopkins, Alfred Francis, M.D., '03. Physician, 1730 I St., Washington, D. C.

Hopkins, Francis A., LL.B., '90. Patent Attorney, 1124 Monadnock Bldg., Chicago. Ill.

Hopkins, Louis M., LL.B., '87. Lawyer, 225 Dearborn St., Chicago, Ill.

Hopkins, Ralph, A.B., '95. Physician, 1524 Harmony St., New Orleans, La.

Hopkins, Willam A., LL.B., '05. Lawyer, Seattle, Wash.

Horah, James H., LL.B., '89; LL.M., '93. Lawyer, Salisbury, N. C.

Horan, John S., LL.B., '11. Lawyer, Charleston, W. Va.

Horgan, John C., LL.B., '84. Lawyer, *Minneapolis, Minn.

Horgan, John J., LL.B., '88; LL.M., '89. Lawyer, *Boston, Mass.

Horgan, William, LL.B., '08. Lawyer, Met. Bank Bldg., Washington, D. C.

Horigan, James Bernard, A.B., '01; A.M., '02; LL.B., '04. G. U. Law Fac., 3601 O St. N. W., Washington, D. C.

Horigan, Dr. William D., LL.B., '99. Librarian, Naval Observatory, Washington, D. C.

Horkan, George Augustus, LL.B., '02. Lawyer, County Attorney, Forsyth, Rosebud County, Montana.

Horn, Elihu, LL.B., '07. Merchant Tailor, 7th and F Sts., Washington, D. C.

Horrigan, J. J., LL.B., '92; LL.M., '93. Special Examiner U. S. Bureau of Pensions; Chariton, Iowa.

Horsey, Chas. C. L., A.B., '01; LL.B., '05. Maryland.

Horsey, Outerbridge, Jr., A.B., '96. Treasurer Light Co., 153 E. 37th St., New York City.

Horton, William Ed., LL.B., '92; LL.M., '93. Major and Quartermaster, U. S. Army, War Department, Washington, D. C.

Hough, J. Spencer, M.D., '93. Act. Asst. Surgeon, Hongkong, China.

Hough, William Hite, M.D., '04. Physician, Insane Asylum, Washington, D. C.; G. U. Med. Fac., Washington, D. C.

Houghton, Alfred M., LL.B., '11; L.D.M., '11. Lawyer, 2011 Kalorama Road, Washington, D. C.

Houghton, Percy Francis, M.D., '01. Physician, 195 Leonard St., Brooklyn, N. Y.

Houston, Chas. James, LL.B., '05. Attorney-at-Law, 1363 Third Ave., San Francisco, Cal.

Houston, Harry I., LL.B., '09. Patent Office, 1248 Irving St., Washington, D. C.

Howard, A. Clinton, LL.B., '95. Pension Bureau, Washington, D. C.

Howard, Arcturus L., M.D., '93. Professor in Business High School, 124 S St. N. W., Washington, D. C.

Howard, John Chalmers, LL.B., '01. Lawyer, Hibbs Bldg., 1916 F St. N. W., Washington, D. C.

Howard, Joseph T. D., M.D., '89. Physician, Falls Church, Va.

Howard, Leland O., Ph.D., '96. Chief Bureau of Entomology, 2026 Hillyer Place, Washington, D. C.

Howard, Stanton Wren, M.D., '03. Physician, 1945 Calvert St. N. W., Washington, D. C.

Howe, Theodore Gilman, M.D., '03. Sandy Hill, N. Y.

Howell, John H., LL.B., '10. Interstate Commerce Commission, 1832 Biltmore St., Washington, D. C.

Howell, Bev. R., LL.B., '75. Lawyer, *Ohio.

Howell, Shrader P., LL.B., '12. Secretary, 422 House Office Bldg., Washington, D. C.

Howick, Tom, LL.B., '12. Private Secretary, 637 E. Capitol St., Washington, D. C.; Celina, Ohio.

Hoyt, Allen G., LL.B., '02. Banker, 49 Wall St., New York City, N. Y.

Hubachek, Francis R., LL.M., '87. Lawyer, *Racine, Wis.

Hubbard, Oliver P., LL.B., '91. Lawyer, *Valvez, Alaska.

Hubbell, Santiago F., LL.B., '74. Lawyer, *New. Mexico.

Hudson, Arthur J., LL.B., '07. Patent Lawyer, 1228 Citizens' Bldg., Cleveland, Ohio.

Hudson, William E., LL.B., '12. Lawyer, 1304 30th St. N. W., Washington, D. C.

Huff, Thomas Salisbury, LL.M., '06. Stocks and Bonds, 427 Fort Washington Ave., New York City, N. Y.

Hughes, Arthur J., LL.B., '07. Lawyer, International Bank Bldg., Los Angeles, Cal.

Hughes, Arthur L., LL.B., '88; LL.M., '89. Lawyer, *Dayton, Ohio.

Hughes, Charles L., LL.B., '73. Lawyer, *Washington, D. C.

Hughes, Cornelius E., LL.B., '09; LL.M., '10. Clerk, 1413 Q St. N. W., Washington, D. C.

Hughes, Ellis, LL.B., '99. Merchant, care Dorsey & Co., Dallas, Texas.

Hughes, Harry Canby, LL.B., '99. Lawyer, *Lincoln, Va.

Hughes, William J., LL.B., '91; LL.M., '92. Lawyer, Department of Justice, Washington, D. C.

Hull, Marion McHenry, M.D., '95. Physician, Prof. Mat. Med. and Ther. Atl. Col., P. & S., 502 Grant Bldg., Atlanta, Ga.

Hullihen, Manfred S., A.B., '55; A.M., '70. *West Virginia.

Hummer, Harry R., M.D., '99. Physician, Asylum for Insane Indians, Canton, S. D.

Humrichouse, Harry H., LL.B., '07. Lawyer, Hagerstown, Md.

Hunt, Bert L., LL.B., '12. State Department, 1232 10th St. N. W., Washington, D. C.; Olean, N. Y.

Hunt, Granville M., LL.B., '89; LL.M., '90. Superintendent of Registry, Postoffice, Washington, D. C.

Hunt, Leo J., M.D., '12. Physician, 4322 Jefferson St., Bellaire, Ohio.

Hunter, Edwin Clarence, M.D., '03. Physician, 107 4th St. N. E., Washington, D. C.

Hurney, Thomas J., LL.B., '11; LL.M., '12. Attorney, 2207 13th St. N. W., Washington, D. C.

Hussey, John Patrick, M.D., '03. Physician, 156 Cranston St., Providence, R. I.

Hutchings, Frank W., LL.B., '99; LL.M., '00. Care National Founders, Detroit, Mich.

Hutchinson, Claudius P., M.D., '99. Physician, Arcola, Va.

Hutchinson, Edmund Archus, LL.B., '03. Government Printing Office; 127 W St. N. W., Washington, D. C.

Hutchinson, Edwin B., LL.B., '08. Lawyer, Herndon, Va.

Huyck, Thos. B., LL.B., '92; LL.M., '93. Real Estate and Lawyer, 1504 H St., Washington, D. C.

Hyams, William Washington, LL.B., '03. Lawyer, Tulsa Okla.

Hyatt, William A., LL.M., '88. Lawyer, *Little Rock, Ark.

Hynson, N. Thornton, LL.B., '07. Lawyer, Century Bldg., Washington, D. C.

I

Igoe, Michael L., LL.B., '08. Lawyer, Room 1209, 69 W. Washington St., Chicago, Ill.

Illman, Harold, LL.B., '75. Lawyer, *New York.

Ingalls, Ellsworth, LL. B., '88. Lawyer, 1040 Santa Fe St., Atchison, Kans.

Ingalls, Ralph, LL.B., '91. Lawyer, Atchison, Kans.

Ironside, Charles Norton, LL.B., '82. Journalism, 771 Central Ave., Cleveland, Ohio.

Irvin, John, LL.M., '94. Lawyer, *Portland, Ore.

Irwin, John W., LL.B., '82. Lawyer, *Washington, D. C.

Isbell, John B., LL.B., '01. Lawyer, Fort Payne, Ala.

Israeli, Baruch, M.D., '97. War Department; 476 F St. S. W., Washington, D. C.

Ittig, Henry, LL.B., '03; LL.M., '04. Lawyer, Seattle, Washington.

Ives, Eugene S., A.B., '78; A.M., '88; Ph.D., '89. Lawyer, Tuscon, Ariz.

J

Jackson, George E., LL.B., '09. Lawyer, 345 Neilson Ave., Fresno, Cal.

Jackson, John Joseph, A.M., '97. Newman School, Hackensack, N. J.

Jackson, William A., LL.B., '94; LL.M., '96. Lawyer, 521 Monadnock Bldg., San Francisco, Cal.

Jackson, William S., LL.B., '80; LL.M., '81. Lawyer, *Washington, D. C.

Jacobson, Benjamin L., LL.B., '11. Isthmian Canal Commission, Canal Zone, Panama.

Jaffe, Saul Sydney, D.D.S., '05. G. U. Dental Fac.; 1415 K St. N. W., Washington, D. C.

James, C. Clinton, LL.B., '97; LL.M., '98. Lawyer, 416 5th St. N. W., Washington, D. C.

James, Grover Cleveland, LL.B., '09. Lawyer, 419 Main St., Joplin, Mo.

James, Howard, M.D., '93. Physician, retired, 98 Pembroke St., Boston, Mass.

Jamieson, Thomas, LL.B., '12. Lawyer, 100 I St. N. W., Washington, D. C.; Omaha, Nebr.

Jamison, Albion B., M.D., '67. U. S. Treasury Department, Washington, D. C.

Jamison, Alexander, LL.B., '09. Lawyer, Drew & Jamison, Madison, Wis.

Jaranilla, Delfin, LL.B., '07. Lawyer, care Court of First Inst., San Jose, Province of Antique, P. I.

Jeffs, Benjamin, A.B., '08. Merchant, Rockland, Mich.

Jenal, Frank P., LL.B., '07. Lawyer, Montgomery & Jenal, 421 American Bank Bldg., Los Angeles, Cal.

Jenkins, Charles, LL.B., '03. Department of Justice, Washington, D. C.

Jenner, Norman R., M.D., '91. Physician, 1110 Rhode Island Ave., Washington, D. C.

Jennings, David E., LL.B., '91; LL.M., '92. Lawyer, Nashville, Tenn.

Jennings, Edward James, LL.B., '80; LL.M., '80. Steel Business, care Carpenter Steel Co., 100 Broadway, New York City, N. Y.

Jennings, John K., A.B., '12. Medical Student, 203 W. Maine St., Grafton, W. Va.

Jennings, John W., LL.B., '03; LL.M., '04. Druggist and Lawyer, 1142 Connecticut Ave., Washington, D. C.

Jennings, Raymond S., LL.B., '08. Lawyer, New London, Wis.

Jennings, Robert W., LL.B., '87; LL.M., '88. Lawyer, Juneau, Alaska.

Jessup, Wilfred, LL.M., '01. Lawyer, Richmond, Ind.

Jewell, William R., Jr., LL.B., '92. Lawyer, 209 Daniel Bldg., Danville, Ill.

Jewett, Nelson J., LL.B., '08. Assistant Examiner, Patent Office, Washington, D. C.

Jirdinston, William C., LL.B., '80. Lawyer, Washington, D. C.

Johnson, Benjamin R., LL.B., '01. Patent Lawyer, 605 7th St. N. W., Washington, D. C.

Johnson, Ernest M., LL.B., '12. Lawyer, St. Paul, Minn.

Johnson, Everett A., LL.B., '10. Assistant U. S. District Attorney, Fenton Bldg., Portland, Ore.

Johnson, Hayden, LL.B., '95; LL.M., '96. Lawyer, 416 5th St. N. W., Washington, D. C.

Johnson, John Altheus, LL.B., '82; LL.M., '87. Lawyer, Seat Pleasant, Md.

Johnson, John D., LL.B., '08. Consular Bureau, Department of State, Washington, D. C.

Johnson, Joseph, A.B., '42; A.M., '46. *Mississippi.

Johnson, Joseph Taber, M.D., '65; Ph.D., '89. Physician, Vice-President G. U. Med. Fac., 926 17th St., Washington, D. C.

Johnson, Loren Bascom Taber, M.D., '00. Physician, 2108 16th St. N. W., Washington, D. C.

Johnson, Louis Alward, M.D., '92. Physician, 711 C St. S. W., Washington, D. C.

Johnson, Paul Bowen Alden, M.D., '05. Physician, 3208 17th St. N. W., Washington, D. C.

Johnson, Paul E., LL.B., '90; LL.M., '91. Lawyer, 512 F St. N. W., Washington, D. C.

Johnson, Stuart Clarke, M.D., '97. Physician, G. U. Med. Fac., 1133 Girard St. N. W., Washington, D. C.

Johnson, Titian W., LL.B., '94. Lawyer, McGill Bldg., Washington, D. C.

Johnson, William A., LL.M., '87. Lawyer, 1406 G St., Washington, D. C.

Johnson, William H., LL.M., '86. Lawyer, *Springfield, Mo.

Johnston, James A., LL.B., '92. Lawyer, *Milwaukee, Wis.

Johnston, James M., LL.B., '95. Lawyer, *Waupun, Wis.

Johnston, Leslie J., LL.B., '09. Auditor, Postoffice Department; 155 Adams St. N. W., Washington, D. C.

Johnston, Richard W., LL.B., '89. Lawyer, *Arlington, Va.

Johnston, Robert, LL.B., '80. President, Old Dominion Paper Co., 98 Commercial Place, Norfolk, Va.

Johnston, Robt. D., Jr., LL.B., '01. Patent Lawyer, 835 Brown-Marx Bldg., Birmingham, Ala.

Joliat, Albert L. F., D.D.S., '07. Dentist, 1048 S. Arch St., Canton, Ohio.

Joliat, Leo Francis, A.B., '11. Manager Goodrich Co., Auto Tires, 429 S. 20th St., Birmingham, Ala.

Jones, Alva W., M.D., '91. Physician, Red Wing, Minn.

Jones, Bennett S., LL.B., '89; LL.M., '90. Patent Lawyer, Victor Bldg., 9th and Grant Place, Washington, D. C.

Jones, Charles M., LL.B., '97. Attorney, 1502 H St., Washington, D. C.

Jones, Edward, M.D., '70. Physician, *Pennsylvania.

Jones, Frank A., LL.B., '96; LL.M., '97. 617 E St. N. W., Washington, D. C.

Jones, George Wilson, M.D., '05. Physician, 1730 N. Fulton Ave., Baltimore, Md.

Jones, Grosvenor M., LL.B., '09. Statistician, American Paper and Pulp Association, 2415 20th St. N. W., Washington, D. C.

Jones, Jacobus S., LL.M., '98. Law Examiner, General Land Office; The Brunswick, Washington, D. C.

Jones, James K., LL.B., '89. Lawyer, 621 Colorado Bldg., Washington, D. C.

Jones, James R., LL.B., '12. Dept. Com. and Labor; 1601 15th St. N. W., Washington, D. C.; Scranton, Pa.

Jones, John B., LL.B., '88. Lawyer, Pensacola, Fla.

Jones, Richard Henry, LL.B., '98. Lawyer, *Andalusia, Ala.

Jones, Hon. Richard J., LL.B., '03. Mayor, Editor and Proprietor of Sebring Times, Sebring, Mahoning County, Ohio.

Jones, Thomas, LL.B., '05. Lawyer, Rockwall, Texas.

Jones, William E., LL.B., '77. Lawyer, *Ohio.

Jones, William J., LL.B., '02. Lawyer, 416 Liggett Bldg., St. Louis, Mo.

Jones, Winfield P., A.B., '01. Lawyer, 331 Equitable Bldg., Atlanta, Ga.

Jordan, Llewellyn, LL.B., '89; LL.M., '90. Treasury Department; 607 4th St. N. W., Washington, D. C.

Jorrin-Sorzano, Leonardo, A.B., '99. Lawyer, Professor of Eng., University of Havana, Calle 217, Vedado, Havana, Cuba.

Joslin, Philips E., LL.B., '08. Lawyer, 49 Westminster St., Providence, R. I.

Jourdan, Charles H., Ph.D., '81. Professor, Mt. St. Mary's College, Emmitsburg, Md.

Joyce, Joseph I., LL.B., '81. Lawyer, *Washington, D. C.

Joynt, Martin E., LL.B., '09; LL.M., '10. Lawyer, Oil City, Pa.

Judd, Theodore Mann, LL.B., '05. Real Estate, 617 E St. N. W., Washington, D. C.

Julihn, Magnus L., M.D., '66. Physician and Druggist, 1423 5th St., Washington, D. C.

Jullien, Cyrus S., LL.B., '04; LL.M., '05. Lawyer, 189 Montague St., Brooklyn, N. Y.

Junghans, John Henry, A.B., '88; A.M., '91. Physician, 417 D St. N.E., Washington, D. C.

Journey, Chesley W., LL.B., '08. Private Secretary U. S. Senate P. O., Washington, D. C.

K

Kage, H. William, LL.B., '10. Treasury Department; 610 2d St. N. W., Washington, D. C.

Kalbfus, Samuel T., LL.B., '01. Assistant Assessor; 1727 De Sales St., N. W., Washington, D. C.

Kanaley, Rev. Francis Thos., A.B., '02. Angelica, N. Y.

Kane, Chas. J., LL.B., '06; LL.M., '07. Editor, 4804 S. Atlantic Ave., Pittsburgh, Pa.

Kane, Frank Anthony, Jr., A.B., '08; LL.B., '09. Lawyer, Minnooka, Pa.

Kane, Henry Victor, A.M., '00; Ph.D., '01; LL.B., '02. Lawyer, Lecturer on Law, Marquette University, 802 Wells Bldg., Milwaukee, Wis.

Kane, John F., M.D., '11. Physician, Minnooka, Pa.

Kane, John J., LL.B., '09. Patent Office, 1320 12th St. N. W., Washington, D. C.

Kappler, Chas. J., LL.B., '96; LL.M., '97. Lawyer, Bond Bldg., Washington, D. C.

Karch, Chas. M., LL.B., '01. Lawyer, *Ohio.

Karicofe, W. H. A., LL.B., '87. Lawyer, *Martinsburg, W. Va.

Kathman, James A., A.M., '00; LL.B., '02. Lawyer, New Orleans, La.

Kauffman, Harry B., A.B., '91; M.D., '94. Physician, Grant Bldg., Albuquerque, N. M.

Kaveney, Jos. James, M.D., '04. Physician (G. U. Med. Fac.), The 'Elkton, Washington, D. C.

Keach, Le Roy, LL.M., '09. Lawyer, Indianapolis, Ind.

Kean, Thos. J., M.D., '93. Physician, *Philadelphia, Pa.

Keane, Michael Aloysius, LL.B., '01. Merchant, care T. T. Keane Beef Co., Washington, D. C.

Keane, Michael J, LL.B., '97; LL.M., '98. Lawyer, Century Bldg., Washington, D. C.

Kearney, George, A.B., '88; LL.B., '90; LL.M., '91; A.M., '91. Librarian, Department of Justice, Washington, D. C.

Kearney, Richard F., M.D., '66. Physician, *Washington, D. C.

Keating, J. Percy, A.B., '75; A.M., '91. Lawyer, 1833 De Lancey Place, Philadelphia, Pa.

Keating, John Joseph, LL.B., '03. Lawyer, Lima, N. Y.

Keaton, Jas. R., LL.B., '90. Lawyer, 600 Terminal Bldg., Oklahoma City, Okla.

Keegin, Wm. C., LL.B., '91; LL.M., '92. Lawyer, 301 McGill Bldg., Washington, D. C.

Keene, Walter Prince, M.D., '00. Physician, Grapeland, San Bernardini County, Cal.

Keith, Robert Lee, A.M., '97. *St. Louis, Mo.

Kelleher, Geo. E., LL.B., '10. Special Agent, Department of Justice, Washington, D. C.

Keleher, Michael Joseph, A.B., '04. *Lawrence, Mass.

Kelly, Chas. B., LL.B.,' 96. Lawyer, *Baltimore, Md.

Kelly, Chas. N., LL.B., '97. Lawyer, 519 N. Schroeder St., Baltimore, Md.

Kelly, Daniel J., A.M., '73; M.D., '75. Physician, 1314 13th St. N. W., Washington, D. C.

Kelly, Frank, D.D.S., '11. Dentist, Harean, Ky.

Kelly, Howard Ignatius, A.B., '96. Theatrical Business, National Theatre, Philadelphia, Pa.

Kelly, James F., LL.B., '08. Lawyer, 825 Vermont Ave., Washington, D. C.

Kelly, James Vincent, LL.B., '99; LL.M., '00. Secretary and Treasurer Park Comm., Edgecombe Park, Baltimore, Md.

Kelly, John J.,LL.B., '97. Lawyer, 40 W. Broad St., Tamaqua, Pa.

Kelly, Joseph Dominic, M.D., '12. Interne, St. John's Hospital, Long Island City, New York

Kelly, Joseph J., LL.B., '11. 3273 Prospect Ave., Washington, D. C.

Kelly, Leo J., LL.B., '10. Lawyer, Doane Bldg., Rockville, Conn.

Kelly, Peter A., A.B., '70. Travelling Salesman, Baltimore, Md.

Kelly, Walter E., LL.B., '09. P. O. Dept., 1418 Webster St. N. W., Washington, D. C.

Keelly, Wm. E., D.D.S., '12. Dentist, 1433 S St. N. W., Washington, D. C.

Kelson, Felix A., A.B., '89. Magnolia, Arkansas

Kemp, James Finley, M.D., '98. Secretary, Univ. of Manila, Manila, P. I.

Kendall, Wm. Converse, M.D., '96. Bureau of Fisheries, 1404 11th St. N. W., Washington, D. C.

Kennedy, Charles T., M.D., '92. Physician, Greenville, Texas

Kennedy, Harry F., LL.B., '11. Lawyer, 112-117 Columbian Bldg., Washington, D. C.

Kennedy, John M., LL.B., '07. Lawyer, 728 New York Life Bldg., Kansas City, Mo.

Kennedy, Robert Joseph, LL.B., '06. Lawyer, *Baltimore, Md.

Kennedy, Wm. Clement, M.D., '11. Physician, 20 South St., Waterbury, Conn.

Kennedy, Wm. J., M.D., '05. Physician, Newark, Ohio

Kennelly, James, LL.B., '88; LL.M., '90. Lawyer, *Ohio

Kenney, Alfred E., LL.B., '94; LL.M., '95. Lawyer, Parkersburg, W. Va.

Kenney, John E., LL.B., '12. Lawyer, Clinton, Mass.

Kenney, John P., LL.B., '08. Lawyer, Lowell, Mass.

Kent, Otis B., LL.B., '07; LL.M., '08. Interstate Commerce Comm.; The Carolina, 706 11th St. N. W., Washington, D. C.

Kernan, Nicholas Edward, A.B., '03. Lawyer, 5 Nassau St., New York City

Kernan, Thomas P., A.B., '78. Lawyer, 144 Steuben St., Utica, N. Y.

Kernan, Walter N., A.B., '85. Lawyer, 527 5th Ave., New York City.

Kernan, Warnick Joseph, A.B., '01. Lawyer, 57 Elizabeth St., Utica, New York.

Kerns, Francis Joseph, M.D., '08. Physician, 17 Fairmount Ave., Newar,k N. J.

Kerr, Denis, LL.B., '81; LL.M., '82. Pension Office; 1436 Clifton St. N. W., Washington, D. C.

Kerrigan, George Edward, A.M., '96; LL.B., '97; LL.M., '98. Lawyer, 18 Elm St., Haverhill, Mass.

Kettler, Milton A., LL.B., '04. Manager, Washington Bill-Posting Co., Washington, D. C.

Keyes, Dr. Edward L., Jr., A.B., '92; Ph.D., '01. Physician and Surgeon, Prof. Urology, Cornell Med. College, 109 E. 34th St., New York City.

Keyes, Francis Corey, A.B., '93. *Nice, Italy.

Keys, Mark Butler, LL.B., '11. Lawyer, Los Angeles, Cal.

Kidwell, Edgar, A.B., '86; A.M., '89; Ph.D., '97. Consulting Mech Engineer, 2011 Channing Way, Berkely, Cal.

Kidwell, John W., A.B., '60; A.M., '66. *Washington, D. C.

Kiernan, Cortland A., A.B., '01. Sag Harbor, N. Y.

Kilcullen, P. E., LL.B., '99. Lawyer, 506 Dime Bank Bldg., Scranton, Pennsylvania.

Kilgour, Robert Mortimer, M.D., '10. Physician, 708 Mass. Ave. N. E., Washington, D. C.

Kilkenny, Francis J., LL.B., '02. Treasury Dept.; 951 Mass Ave. N. W., Washington, D. C.

Killeen, Thomas, A.B., '55. *New York City, N. Y.

Kilroy, Dr. James Joseph, M.D., '98. Physician, 103 I St. N.E., Washington, D. C.

Kimball. Charles O., LL.B., '92; LL.M., '93. Lawyer, P. O. Dept.; 2641 Myrtle Ave. N. E., Washington, D. C.

Kimball, E. S., M.D., '66. Vocal Instructor, 1010 F St. N. W., Washington, D. C.

Kimmel, George P., LL.B., '10. Dept. of Commerce and Labor, Washington, D. C.;Leavenworth, Kansas.

Kincaid, Douglas Howard, M.D., '91. Physician, Danville, Ky.

King, Alexius S., LL.B., '78. Lawyer, *Washington, D. C.

King, Carl C., LL.B., '10. P. O. Dept.; 1454 Fairmont St. N. W., Washington, D. C.

King, Claude F., LL.B., '89; LL.M., '90. File Clerk, Carnegie Institue; 587 Columbia Rd., Washington, D. C.

King, George Sherman, LL.B., '99; LL.M., '00. Lawyer, *Washington, D. C.

King, James Lewin Gibbs, D.D.S., '11. Dentist, 911 New York Ave., Washington, D. C.

King, J. T., M.D., '94. Physician, Quitman, Ga.

King, Michael H., LL.B., '97. Lawyer, Elkins, W. Va.

Kingsbury, Albert D., M.D., '69. Physician, 291 Great Plain Ave., Needham, Mass.

Kinksley, Hiram A., LL.B., '93. U. S. Special Pension Exam., 1410 W. 6th St., Topeka, Kansas.

Kingsley, John M., A.B., '12. Medical Student, 571 Main St., Hartford, Conn.

Kinkston, A. T. Y., M.D., '02. Physician, 1409 Prospect Ave., New York City.

Kiningham, Robert B., LL.B., '10. Danville, Ill.

Kinsell, Tyson, LL.B., '05. Lawyer, 433 Worcester Bldg., Portland, Oregon.

Kinyoun, Joseph J., Ph.D., '96. Physician, 1423 Clifton St. N. W., Washington, D. C.

Kirby, Elmer L., LL.B., '08. Lawyer, First Nat. Bank Bldg., Wagoner, Oklahoma.

Kirby, John Joseph, A.M., '98; LL.B., '99; LL.M., '00. Lawyer, 41 Wall St., New York City.

Kirby, Thomas, Jr., LL.B., '05. Journalist, The Washington Times, Washington, D. C.

Kirby, Wm. P., M.D., '06. Physician, 492 K St. S. W., Washington, D. C.

Kirtland, Michael, LL.B., '92. Lawyer, *Montgomery, Ala.

Kitch, James Barbour, LL.B., '05. Census Bureau; 1827 18th St. N. W., Washington, D. C.

Kitchin, Edgar M., LL.B., '99. Patent Lawyer, 805 G St. N. W., Washington, D. C.

Klein, Anthony Eller, M.D., '00. Physician and Surgeon, 166 46th St., Corona, N. Y.

Kleinschmidt, Harry C., LL.B., '02. Lawyer, 3068 M St. N. W., Washington, D. C.

Klinger, David B., LL.B., '93; LL.M., '94. Pension Office; 229 12th St. N. E., Washington, D. C.

Klopfer, Norman, LL.B., '11. Lawyer, 1348 Harvard St. N. W., Washington, D. C.

Klopfer, Walter H., LL.B., '91; LL.M., '92. Prin. Exam., Pension Bureau; 1346 Howard St. N. W., Washington, D. C.

Knight, Henry E., LL.B., '84; LL.M., '85. Patent Lawyer, 2 Rector St., New York City, N. Y.

Knight, Hervey S., LL.B., '88. Patent Lawyer, McGill Bldg., Washington, D. C.

Knight, Joseph Sheridán, S.J., LL.B., '03. Jesuit Scholastic, Woodstock College, Woodstock, Md.

Knight, William E., LL.B., '91. Lawyer, 2 Rector St., New York City.

Knode, Thomas Edson, LL.B., '10. Private Secretary, Hibbs Bldg., Washington, D. C.

Kober, George Martin, M.D., '73; LL.D., '06. Dean of G. U. Med. Dept., 1819 Q St. N. W., Washington, D. C.

Koch, Adolph A., LL.B., '02. Secretary of Local Board of Civil Service Examiners, 8th and Ill. Ave., Fresno, Cal.

Koch, Rev. Joseph, D.D., '89. Pastor of St. Edward's Church, Shamokin, Pa.

Koebel, William J., LL.B., '12; L.D.M., '12. Interstate Commerce Comm., 1440 W St. N. W., Washington, D. C.; Philadelphia, Pa.

Kolbe, Lawrence A., LL.B., '12. Dept. of Agriculture, 418 F St. N. E., Washington, D. C.; Lorain, Ohio.

Kolipinski, Louis, M.D., '83. Physician, 631 I St. N. W., Washington, D. C.

Konigsberg, Morris H., LL.B., '11. Interstate Commerce Comm., 1230 8th St. N. W., Washington, D. C.; Augusta, Ga.

Koonce, Claude J., M.D., '96. Physician, *West Virginia.

Koontz, Clarke, A.B., '51. *Frederick, Md.

Kopmeier, Norman J., LL.B., '05. Treas., Kopmeier Motor Co., Vice-pres., Wisconsin Lakes Ice and Cartage Co., 234 Wells Bldg., Milwaukee, Wis.

Korn, Louis L., LL.B., '12. P. O. Dept., Newark, N. J.

Kram, Charles A., LL.B., '92; LL.M., '93. Office of Auditor of P. O., Chevy Chase, Md.

Kratz, John A., Jr., LL.B., '04. Lawyer, Met. Bank Bldg., Washington, D. C.

Krebs, Conrad, LL.B., '92. Merchant, Salem, Oregon.

Krichelt, Frederick W., LL.B., '99; LL.M., '00. U. S. Weather Bureau, Washington, D. C.

Kroll, William A., LL.B., '08. Clerk, Takoma Park, D. C.

Kuehn, Otto Frederick, D.D. S., '05. *Indiana.

Kuhn, James O'Reilly, Jr., A.B., '99; LL.B., '02. 3334 N St. N. W., Washington, D. C.

Kuhn, John Frederick, M.D., '01. Physician, 1125 N. Shartel Ave., Oklahoma City, Okla.

Kuhn, Joseph Aloysius, A.B., '02. Claims Dept. Penna. R. R., 3334 N St. N. W., Washington, D. C.

L.

La Bossiere, Edward A., LL.B., '08; LL.M., '09. Ass't U. S. Dist. Att'y, Dist. of Mont., Conrad Bank Bldg., Great Falls, Mont.

LaBoule, John F., LL.B., '85. Lawyer, St. Lawrence, Wis.

Lacey, Anderson B., LL.B., '98. Lawyer, Barrister Bldg., Washington, D. C.

Lacson, Roman J., Ph.L., '02; Ph.D., '03; LL.B., '04. Lawyer, 53 Palacio, Manila, P. I.

Lacy, Eugene B., LL.B., '93; LL.M., '99. Lawyer, Ass't U. S. Att'y, Federal Bldg., Denver, Colorado.

Lagarde, Ernest, A.B., '66; A.M., '69. Prof. Eng. Lit., Mt. St. Mary's College, Emmitsburg, Md.

Lainhart, John W., Jr., LL.B., '11; LL.M., '12. Lawyer, 923 19th St. N. W., Washington, D. C.

Lally, John J., D.D.S., '12. Dentist, 12 Lincoln St., North Adams, Mass.

Lamar, George H., LL.B., '89; LL.M., '90. Lawyer, Fendall Bldg., Washington, D. C.

Lamar, William H., Jr., LL.B., '84; LL.M., '85. Lawyer, Dept. of Justice, Washington, D. C.

Lamason, Orville B., LL.B., '12. State Dept., 5 Iowa Circle, Washington, D. C.; Elizabeth, N. J.

Lamb, Daniel S., M.D., '67. Acting Ass't Surgeon, U. S. A., Pathologist, 2114 18th St. N. W., Washington, D. C.

Lamb, William James Charles, M.D., '03. Physician, 311 Amber St., Pittsburg, Pa.

Lambert, Tallmadge A., A.B., '62; A.M., '71; LL.D., '94. Lawyer, 2209 Mass. Ave., Washington, D. C.

Lambert, Wilton J., LL.B., '93; LL.M., '94. Lawyer, 410 5th St. N. W., Washington, D. C.

Lamkin, Griffin, LL.M., '01. Lawyer, 507-10 Title Guar. Bldg., Birmingham, Ala.

Lancaster, C. C., A.B., '74; LL.B., '76. Lawyer, Corcoran Bldg., Washington, D. C.

Lancaster, Rev. Clement S., S.J., A.B., '59. St. Aloysius Church, Washington, D. C.

Lancaster, Fred H., LL.B., '12. Lawyer, Pittsfield, Maine.

Lancaster, George D., LL.B., '86; LL.M., '87. Lawyer, James Bldg., Chattanooga, Tenn.

Landa, Gabriel M., A.B., '77. Physician, Paseo 190, Vedado, Havana, Cuba.

Landers, Eugene, LL.B., '10. Ass't Examiner, U. S. Patent Office; 4115 Fessenden St. N. W., Washington, D. C.

Landry, Anatole, A.B., '60. *Louisiana.

Landry, John C., A.M., '06. Lawyer, Alberta, Canada.

Landry, Prosper R., A.B.,''46. *Louisiana.

Lane, Charles E., LL.B., '11; LL.M., '12; L.D.M., '12. 710 E. 16th St., Cheyenne, Wyoming.

Lang, John Ridgley, LL.B., '11; LL.M., '12. 3331 P St. N. W., Washington, D. C.

Langan, Raymond Charles, LL.B., '95. Lawyer, Clinton, Iowa.

Langley, Hon. John W., LL.M., '94. Member of Congress, Pikesville, Kentucky.

Lannon, John David, A.B., '94. 2 Rector St., New York City.

Lansdale, Arthur L., LL.B., '12. Lawyer, 1128 25th St. N. W., Washington, D. C.

Lanston, Aubrey, LL.B., '99. Novelist and Playwright, 24 Bryant St. N. W., Washington, D. C.

Lantry, Thomas B., A.B., '89. Lawyer, Chicago Athletic Club, Chicago, Illinois.

Lantz, Ira, LL.B., '08; LL.M., '09. Special Agent, Dept. of Interior, Helena, Mont.

Laplace, Albert J., A.B., '79. Pharmacist, 3708 Canal St., New Orleans, La.

Laplace, Dr. Ernest, A.B., '80; A.M., '87; LL.D., '95. Surgeon, 1828 South Rittenhouse Sq., Philadelphia, Pa.

La Plante, J. B. Edmund, A.B., '09. Lawyer, 304 La Plante Bldg., Vincennes, Ind.

Lapretre, J. B. Adrien, A.B., '49. *Louisiana.

Larcombe, James A., LL.B., '88; LL.M., '89. Lawyer, *New York City.

Larkin, P. Edward, M.D., '08. Physician, 1716 M St. N. W., Washington, D. C.

Larzelere, Charles La Verne, LL.B., '12. Lawyer, 1864 Park Rd., Washington, D. C.; Fenton, Mich.

Lastrappes, Ludger, A.B., '51. Retired Merchant, *Louisiana.

Latham, Benjamin F., M.D., '76. Physician, *Aurora, W. Va.

Latham, Charles L., LL.B., '04. U. S. Consul, Punta Arenas, Chile, South America.

Latham, Samuel B., LL.B., '85; LL.M., '87. Lawyer, *Troy, S. C.

Latimer, E. F., D.D.S., '02. Merchant, Lowndesville, S. C.

Latshaw, Henry J., Ph.B., '85. Lawyer, 1010 Scarritt Bldg., Kansas City, Mo.

Latshaw, Hon. Ralph S., A.B., '85. Judge, 840 N. Y. Life Bldg., Kansas City, Mo.

Laughlin, John Edward, A.B., '00. Lawyer, Oliver Bldg., Pittsburg, Pennsylvania.

Laumont, Henry B., A.B., '48. *Louisiana.

Lauve, Louis L., A.B., '01. Armour & Co., Pearl St., New York City.

Lavalle, Don Jose Antonio de, A.M., '69. *Spain.

Lavelle, Thomas Eugene, A.B., '09. Medical Student, 301 West St., Butte, Mont.

Lavin, James P., LL.B., '94; LL.M., '96. Special Agent, Gen. Land Office, 512 Custom House, San Francisco, Cal.

Lawler, Hon. Daniel W., A.B., '81; A.M., '89; LL.D., '97. Lawyer, New York Life Bldg., St. Paul, Minn.

Lawler, Joseph C., A.B., '85. Spencer, Iowa.

Lawler, Joseph H., A.B., '06. Lawyer, 79 Farmington Ave., Hartford, Conn.

Lawler, William K., LL.B., '12. Lawyer, Waterbury, Conn.

Leahy, Daniel F., LL.B., '11. Pension Office, 36 R St. N. E., Washington, D. C.

Leahy, Edward L., LL.B., '08. Probate Judge of Bristol Co., Member of Legislature, Bristol, R. I.

Leahy, John Stephen, A.M., '95; LL.B., '96. Lawyer, Nat. Bank of Commerce Bldg., St. Louis, Mo.

Leahy, Rev. Michael David, .17514 Detroit Ave., Cleveland, Ohio.

Leahy, William E., LL.B., '12. Lawyer, Monson, Mass.

Leary, Francis Paul, LL.B., '04. Lawyer, 1201 11th St. N. W., Washington, D. C.

Leary, Robert J., LL.B., '99. U. S. Immigration Inspector, Pensacola, Fla.

LeBoeuf, Peter George, A.B., '96. Chippewa Falls, Wis.

Leckie, A. E. Lloyd, LL.B., '94; LL.M., '95. Lawyer, Southern Bldg., Washington, D. C.

Lecomte, Ralph Michael, M.D., '10. Army Med. Museum, 911 16th St. N. W., Washington, D. C.

Lecouteulx, Louis, A.B., '49. *New York.

Lee, Albert James, LL.B., '03. Lawyer, *Oklahoma City, Okla.

Lee, F. D., M.D., '94. Pension Office, Washington, D. C.

Lee, Henry, LL.B., '08; LL.M., '09. Lawyer, 498 Md. Ave. S. W., Washington, D. C.

Lee, Orr W., LL.B., '89; LL.M., '90. Lawyer, *Oelwein, Iowa.

Legare, Hon. George S., LL.B., '92. Member of Congress from S. C., House of Rep., Washington, D. C.; Columbia, S. C.

Legaspi, Villaflor, LL.M., '10. Lawyer, 34 Alcala St., Santa Cruz, Manila,, P. I.

Lehman, Hugo, D.D.S., '11. Dentist, 31 Smith St., Brooklyn, N. Y.

Lenahan, Wm. D., LL.D., '06; LL.M., '07. Lawyer, 612 F St. N. W., Washington, D. C.

Lennon, Leo Camillo, A. M., '00; Ph.D., '01. Lawyer, Foxcroft Bldg., San Francisco, Cal.

Lennon, Maurice F., LL.B., '07. Lawyer, 504 Joliet Nat. Bank Bldg., Joliet, Ill.

Lennon, Milton Byrne, A.M., '98. Physician, 802 Butler Bldg., San Francisco, Cal.

Leonard, John D., LL.B., '92; LL.M., '93. Lawyer, 1006 F St. N. W., Washington, D. C.

Leonard, Richard B., D.D.S., '08. Dentist, 910 F St. N. W., Washington, D. C.

Lesh, Paul E., LL.B., '06; LL.M., '07. Lawyer, Pacific Bldg., 622 F St. N. W., Washington, D. C.

Lethert, Charles A., LL.B., '09. Lawyer, Globe Bldg., St. Paul, Minn.

Lever, Hon. Asbury Frank, LL.B., '99. Member of Congress from S. C., 218 North Capitol St., Washington, D. C.

Levy, Michael A., LL.B., '11. Lawyer, 1632 French St., Washington, D. C.; Philadelphia, Pa.

Lewis, Geary W., LL.B., '10. Lawyer, 919 N. Main St., Fort Wayne, Indiana.

Lewis, J. Edward, LL.B., '97; LL.M., '98. Lawyer and Real Estate Broker, 617 E St. N. W., Washington, D. C.

Lewis, William H., LL.B., '87; LL.M., '88. Law Examiner, Gen. Land Office, Washington, D. C.

Lieberman, Charles D., LL.B., '77. Real Estate, 1303 F St. N. W., Washington, D. C.

Lieuallen, Grant, LL.B., '99. Clerk in Senate, 3008 17th St. N. E., Washington, D. C.

Light, Given Addison, M.D., '06. Physician, Salt Lake City, Utah.

Lincoln, John Ledyard, A.B., '81; A.M., '89. Lawyer, First Nat. Bank Bldg., Cincinnati, Ohio.

Lindsay, David R., M.D., '60. Physician, *Alabama.

Lingamfelter, Newton S., L.D.M., '12. Lawyer, 431 M St. N. W., Washington, D. C.

Linke, F. Otto, LL.B., '12. Lawyer, Plainfield, New Jersey.

Linn, Samuel F., M.D., '76. Physician, *Baltimore, Md.

Linnehan, George Albert, M.D., '04. Physician, 16 Union Ave., Jamaica, New York.

Linney, Romulus Zachariah, M.D., '01. Physician, Hopeton, Okla.

Linton, Howard, D.D.S., '11. Dentist, 800 N. Capitol St., Washington, D. C.

Linton, William C., LL.B., '12. Lawyer, 532 4th St. N. E., Washington, D. C.

Lipscomb, Milledge B., LL.B., '12. Lawyer, Columbia, South Carolina.

Little, Arthur B., M.D., '12. Providence Hospital, Washington, D. C.

Litzinger, Lewis P., LL.B., '02; LL.M., '08. Lawyer, Chicora, Pa.

Lloyd, George H., A.B., '50. Merchant, 74 W. Cottage St., Boston, Mass.

Lobit, Joseph, Jr., A.B., '99. Banker, Galveston, Texas.

Lochboehler, Dr. George J., M.D., '89. Physician, 55 K St. N. W., Washington, D. C.

Loeffler, Louis, LL.B., '07. Lawyer, 212 Ziegler Bldg., Oklahoma City, Oklahoma.

Logan, Alonzo T., LL.B., '88; LL.M., '89. Lawyer, *Austin, Texas.

Logan, Eugene Adolphus, LL.B., '98; LL.M., '99. Dept. of Commerce and Labor, Washington, D. C.

Lohr, Vernon J., D.D.S., '12. Dentist, Timberville, Va.

Long, Carlos A., LL.B., '01· Lawyer, Honolulu, Hawaii.

Long, Elia A. C., LL.B., '01; LL.M., '02· Lawyer, Honolulu, Hawaii.

Longan, John M., LL.B., '12· Lawyer, Gloucester, Mass.

Longshaw, Luther M., LL.M., '87· Lawyer, Keyser Bldg., Baltimore, Maryland.

Looby, Patrick W., LL.B., '03· Lawyer, 54 Broad St., Plattsburg, N. Y.

Loos, John G., LL.B., '06; LL.M., '07· Lawyer, 615 Bee Bldg., Omaha, Nebraska.

Lordan, John J., LL.B., '95; LL.M., '96· Lawyer, 115 Broadway, New York City.

Loughborough, Ludwell H., Ph.B., '87· Agriculture, Bethesda, Md.

Loughran, John M., LL.B., '05; LL.M., '06· Lawyer, 408 5th St. N. W., Washington, D. C.

Loughran, Joseph E., LL.B., '01· Lawyer, 6 Hildreth Bldg., Lowell, Mass.

Loughran, Leo D., LL.B., '12· Lawyer, 310 L St. N. W., Washington, D. C.

Loughran, Patrick H., LL.B., '96· Lawyer, Barrister Bldg., Washington, D. C.

Lovett, John W., LL.B., '72· Lawyer, *Indiana.

Lowe, Francis M., LL.B., '93; LL.M., '98· Lawyer, First Nat. Bank Bldg., Birmingham, Ala.

Lowe, Louis, LL.B., '05· Lawyer, 1313 Potomac St. N. W., Washington, D. C.

Lowe, Thomas F., M.D., '02· Physician, (G. U. Med. Fac.), 205 H St. N. W., Washington, D. C.

Lowe, Victor L., LL.B., '12· Lawyer, 1333 Belmont St., Washington, D. C.

Lowrie, H. H., M.D., '63· Physician, Plainfield, N. J.

Lozane, Charles I., LL.B., '99; LL.M., '00· Lawyer, *Washington, D. C.

Luby, Emanuel S., LL.B., '98; LL.M., '99· Lawyer, Kalamazoo, Mich.

Lucas, Charles, M.D., '93· Physician, Shelton, Neb.

Luce, Charles Roscoe, M.D., '85· Physician, 215 2nd St. S. E., Washington, D. C.

Lucey, Daniel J., LL.B., '07· Lawyer, 533 Main St., Melrose, Mass.

Lusk, Addison Knox, A.B., '08· Beckwith Mercantile Co., St. Ignatius, Mont.

Lusk, Hall Stoner, A.B., '04; LL.B., '07· Lawyer, 303 Mohawk Bldg., Portland, Oregon.

Luthy, John H., LL.B., '97· P. O. Dept., Washington, D. C.

Luttrell, Walter McM., M.D., '93· Physician, Knoxville, Tenn.

Lyles, D. Clinton, A.B., '68; A.M., '71· Prof., McDonough Institute, McDonough Station, Md.

Lyman, William F., LL.B., '10· Commercial Teacher, 2539 Caithness Place, Denver, Colorado.

Lynch, Anthony Vincent, A.B., '09· Lawyer, 608 W. 113th St., New York City.

Lynch, James D., A.M., '93· 129 E. 21st St., New York City.

Lynch, James K, A.B., '12. Law Student, care Lynch & Day, Canton, Ohio.

Lynch, Rt. Rev. Mgr. James, S.M., D.D., '89. Rector of St. John's Church, Utica, New York.

Lynch, Patrick H., A.B., '77. *Pennsylvania.

Lynch, Thomas, LL.B., '08. Lawyer, 511 City Nat. Bank Bldg., Omaha, Nebraska.

Lynch, William Francis, A.B., '04. Resident Surgeon, St. Vincent's Hospital, Worcester, Mass.

Lyon, Frank, LL.B., '89; LL.M., '90. Special Att'y, Interstate Commerce Comm., Washington, D. C.

Lyon, John Francis, A.B., '10. care J. B. Lyon & Co., Albany, N. Y.

Lyon, Rutherford B. H., LL.B., '99; LL.M., '00. Lawyer, Evans Bldg., Washington, D. C.

Lyon, Simon, LL.B., '90; LL.M., '91. Lawyer, Evans Bldg., Washington, D. C.

Lyons, Hilary Herbert, A.M., '00. Vice-Pres. Alabama Corn Mills Co., 1312 Dauphin St., Mobile, Ala.

Lyons, Thomas H., A.B., '85. *Baltimore, Md.

M.

McAleer, John Hugh, A.B., '98. Flour Merchant, 820 Lafayette Bldg., Philadelphia, Pa.

McAlleer, Joseph Leo, A.B., '00; A.M., '01; Ph. D., '05. Lawyer, 509 W. End Trust Bldg., Philadelphia, Pa.

McAleer, William, Jr., A.B., '98. Merchant, 213 Brainbridge St., Philadelphia, Pa.

McAnerney, Frank Bernard, A.B., '98. Real Estate, 500 5th Ave., New York City.

McArdle, Thomas E., M.D., '79. Physician, 1826 Columbia Rd., Washington, D. C.

McAuliffe, Maurice J., LL.B., '11; LL.M., '12; L.D.M., '12. 2211 M St. N. W., Washington, D. C.; St. Paul, Minn.

McBride, Charles R., LL.B., '92; LL.M., '95. U. S. Special Exam., U. S. Court and P. O. Bldg., Chicago, Ill.

McCabe, Herbert F., LL.B., '12. Interior Dept., Dubuque, Iowa.

McCandlish, Howard S., LL.B., '12. Lawyer, Saluda, Va.

McCall, Robert S., LL.B.,,, '89; LL.M., '90. Land Office, Interior Dept., Lemmon, S. D.

McCandlish, F. S., LL.B., '06. Lawyer, Fairfax Court House, Va.

McCann, Daniel Francis, Jr., A.B., '10. Medical Student, 312 Ave. C., West Brooklyn, N. Y.

McCann, Thomas A., A.B., '07. Mgr. Crookstown Lumber Co., Bemidji, Minn.

McCanna, George F., LL.B., '11. Auditor of P. O. Dept. of Washington, D. C.; Providence, R. I.

McCannel, Alexander J., M.D., '96. Physician, Pres. N. D. State Med. Society, Minot, N. D.

McCardle, Battle, LL.B., '94; LL.M., '96. Att'y, Bell Tel Co., N. Y. Life Bldg., Kansas City, Mo.

McCarron, John F., LL.B., '12. Lawyer, Farmersville, Ill.

McCarthy, Charles A., LL.B., '06; LL.M., '07. Sec'y and Treas., East Wash. Sav. Bank, Washington, D. C.

McCarthy, Charles C., A.B., '05. Lawyer, 141 Milk St., Boston, Mass.

McCarthy, Daniel Joseph, A.B., '95; A.M., '99; M.D., '99. Physician, Davenport, Iowa.

McCarthy, James C., A.B., '52. *Washington, D. C.

McCarthy, John Linus, D.D.S., '03. Dentist, Barristers' Hall, Brockton, Mass.

McCarthy, Joseph J., A.B., '07; M.D., '11. Physician, 923 R St. N. W., Washington, D. C.

McCarthy, William T., LL.B., '93. Lawyer, Newberne, N. C.

McCarthy, Albert E., LL.B., '10. Lawyer, 115 Lincoln St., Lewiston, Maine.

McCauley, Francis Harney, A.M., '99. Lawyer, 325 Clinton Ave., West Hoboken, N. J.

McChesney, Charles E., M.D., '67. Title Supervisor, U. S. Indian Service, 219 Federal Bldg., Spókane, Wash.

McClellan, Frederick F., LL.B., '04. Lawyer and City Att'y, Bennett Block, Muncie, Ind.

McCloskey, Felix R., LL.B., '92. *New York City.

McCloskey, William C., LL.B., '93; LL.M., '94. *San Francisco, Cal.

McClure, James, A.B., '85; M.D., '99. Physician, Williamstown, N. J.

McCluskey, William J., A.B., '89. Lawyer, Kirk Block, Syracuse, N. Y.

McCole, Thomas A., LL.B., '02. Lawyer, 170 Broadway, New York City.

McConnell, Frank Stevenson, D.D.S., '04. Dentist, Somerville, N. J.

McCormick, John Joseph, M.D., '04. Sanitation Physician, Canal Zone.

McCormick, Michael A., LL.B., '09; LL.M., '10. Navy Dept., 700 n. Capitol St., Washington, D. C.

McCoy, Edward A., A.B., '00. *Brooklyn, N. Y.

McCoy, Joseph S., LL.B., '93; LL.M., '94. Govt. Actuary, Treas. Dept., Washington, D. C.

McCoy, Washington J., M.D., '80. *Indiana.

McCue, Thomas E., LL.B., '10. Lawyer, 272 Willow Ave., Long Branch, New Jersey.

McCullough, Charles E., LL.B., '06. Lawyer, *New York City.

McCullough, Frisby H., LL.B., '89. Lawyer, Edina, Mo.

McCullough, Harry E., LL.B., '11. Treas. Dept., Washington, D. C.; Santa Fe, N. M.

McDermid, Claude E., M.D., '08. Physician, Sunnyside, Utah.

McDermott, Francis Borgia, A.B., '96. Stockport, Ohio.

McDermott, Rev. Thomas Joseph, A.M., '96. St. Patrick's Rectory, Jersey City, N. J.

McDevitt, William M., LL.B., '94; LL.M., '95. Lawyer, *San Francisco, California.

McDonald, Allen C., LL.B., '96; LL.M., '97. Lawyer, 222 Linwood St., Dayton, Ohio.

McDonald, James C., LL.M., '92. Lawyer, *Huntsville, Ala.

McDonald, James E., LL.M., '06. Real Estate Broker, San Benito, Texas.

McDonald, Morten Q., LL.B., '11. Lawyer, Hudson, N. Y.

McDonald, Richard Francis, D.D.S., '05. Dentist, Manchester, N. H.

McDonald, Thomas Benton, M.D., '95. Physician, Cumberland, Md.

McDonnell, Rev. Eugene De L., S.J., A.B., '85. Pres. of Conzaga College, Washington, D. C.

McDonnell, John J., LL.B., '10; LL.M., '11. Treas. Dept., Washington, D. C.; Bloomington, Ill.

McDonnell, Thomas F., LL.B., '07. Lawyer, 75 Goddard St., Providence, R. I.

McDonough, James S., LL.B., '01. Lawyer, Sec. G. U. Alum. Assn. of N. Y., 80 Wall St., New York City.

McDonough, Francis Patrick, A.B., '93. Brattle St., Providence, R. I.

McDonough, Francis Xavier, LL.B., '05; LL.M., '06. Lawyer, 80 Wall St., New York City.

McDowell, James Evans, LL.B., '99. Publisher, 1225 Foster Ave., Chicago, Ill.

McElhone, James F., A.B., '86. Journalist, N. Y. Herald, New York City.

McElroy, Bernard W., LL.B., '01. Lawyer, 4 Market St., Providence, Rhode Island.

McElroy, James Aloysius, A.B., '02. Div. Engineer, Conn. Highway Dept., 307 Golden Hill, Bridgeport, Conn.

McEniry, William Patrick, A.B., '03. Lawyer, 127 Ten Broeck St., Albany, N. Y.

McFarlan, Walter S., A.B., '62; A.M., '65. War Dept., 16th and Decatur Sts. N. W., Washington, D. C.

McFarland, Walter R., LL.B., '11. Lawyer, 653 E. Capitol St., Washington, D. C.

McFarland, William B., LL.B., '10. Lawyer, Coeur d'Alene, Idaho.

McGarrell, Andrew P., LL.B., '92; LL.M., '93. Lawyer, Benwood, West Virginia.

McGary, Peter J., A.B., '53; A.M., '57. *Virginia.

McGauley, William G., D.D.S., '12. Dentist, 23 Stoneland Rd., Worcester, Mass.

McGill, Grafton L., LL.B., '99; LL.M., '00. Patent Lawyer, 15 William St., New York City.

McGill, J. Nota, LL.B., '87; LL.M., '88. Lawyer, (G. U. Law Fac), McGill Bldg., Washington, D. C.

McGirr, Joseph B., LL.B., '92; LL.M., '93. Patent Lawyer, 69 Pineapple St., Brooklyn, N. Y.

McGlone, Albert V., D.D.S., '12. Dentist, Jackson Court, Natick, Mass.

McGlue, George Percy, LL.B., '97; LL.M., '98. Lawyer, 643 La. Ave. N. W., Washington, D. C.

McGovern, Thomas F., LL.B., '07. Lawyer, 410 Symes Bldg., Denver, Colorado.

McGowan, Daniel F., LL.B., '07. Lawyer, Albuquerque, N. M.

McGowan, Louis A., LL.B., '09. Lawyer, 10 Weybosset St., Providence, R. I.

McGrath, Bernard F., A.B., '94; M.D., '95. Physician, St. Mary's Hospital, Rochester, Minn.

McGrath, Rev. John B., A.M., '94. 262 West 118th St., New York City.

McGrath, William V., Jr., B.S., '87. Real Estate, 712 Walnut St., Philadelphia, Pa.

McGuire, James C., A.B., '96; A.M., '97. Physician, The Rochambeau, Washington, D. C.

McIntyre, Andrew J., M.D., '02. Physician, 3013 Cambridge Pl., Washington, D. C.

McIntyre, Douglas, M.D., '01. Physician, St. John, Wash.

McKaig, Joseph F., A.B., '90; M.D., '93. Physician, 511 13th St. N. W., Washington, D. C.

McKay, Augustus Francis, M.D., '72. Retired Physician, Colorado Springs, Colo.

McKechnie, Wm. G., A.B., '90. Lawyer, Pres. G. U. Club of New England, 366 Elm St., Springfield, Mass.

McKee, Edwin J., LL.B., '11. City Hall, 1729 Corcoran St., Washington, D. C.

McKee, Frederick, LL.B., '95; LL.M., '96. Lawyer, 610 13th St. N. W., Washington, D. C.

McKenna, Bernard Chas., A.B., '03. Lawyer, 654 West End Ave., New York City.

McKenna, Daniel P. J., LL.B., '07; LL.M., '08. Lawyer, 406 5th St. N. W., Washington, D. C.

McKenna, Henry C., LL.B., '08. Lawyer, 35 Congress St., Boston, Mass.

McKenna, Royal T., LL.B., '08; LL.M., '09. Lawyer, 1446 Rhode Island Ave. N. W., Washington, D. C.

McKeon, Frank H., M.D., '02. Physician, P. A. Surgeon, U. S. M. H. S., care Surgeon-General, Washington, D. C.

McKernan, Nelson M., LL.B., '11. Instructor, 714 20th St. N. W., Washington, D. C.

McLachlen, John M., LL.B., '12. Lawyer, 2800 Ontario Road, Washington, D. C.

McLarin, Howard M., LL.B., '12. War Dept., D. C.; Atlanta, Ga.

McLaughlin, Francis J., A.B., '83. Real Estate, Boston, Mass.

McLaughlin, Hugh E., A.M., '96. Civil Engineer, 949 Pelham Ave., New York City.

McLaughlin, James A., LL.M., '06. Lawyer, Norwich, Conn.

McLaughlin, James W., M.D., '08. Physician, Mercy Hospital, Pittsburgh, Pa.

McLaughlin, Hon. John D., A.B., '83; A.M., '89. Justice, Supreme Court, Court House, Boston, Mass.

McLaughlin, Joseph L., A.B., '08. Sec. G. U. Club of New England, care Ginn & Co., 29 Beacon St., Boston, Mass.

McLoughlin, Edward, LL.B., '12. Lawyer, Jamaica, New York.

McLoughlin, Peter J., LL.B., '97; LL.M., '98. Law Professor, Catholic University, Washington, D. C.; Worcester, Mass.

McLoughlin, Wm. I., LL.B., '95. Lawyer, Chairman License Commissioners, 340 Main St., Worcester, Mass.

McMahon, John J., LL.B., '04. Lawyer, 918 F St. N. W., Washington, D. C.

McMahon, John J., LL.B., '09; LL.M., '10. Lawyer, 1212 N. Capitol St., Washington, D. C.

McMahon, Rev. John W., D.D., '89. St. Mary's Church, Charlestown, Mass.

McMahon, Raymond J., LL.B., '12. Lawyer, Pawtucket, R. I.

McMahon, Richard W., LL.B., '07. Lawyer, 236 Southern Bldg., Washington, D. C.

McManus, Joseph, LL.B.,'0 4; LL.M., '05. Lawyer, Old South Bldg., Boston, Mass.

McManus, Joseph, LL.B., '07. Lawyer, Mexico City, Mexico.

McMeal, B. Campbell, A.B., '78. *Pittsburgh, Pa.

McMullen, F. P., LL.B., '81. Investments, Tacoma, Wash.

McNally, Valentine, M.D., '67; A.M., '69; LL.D., '89. Lieutenant-Colonel, U. S. A., Retired, The Hamilton, Washington, D. C.

McNamara, Frank B., D.D.S., '03. Dentist, 26 Thomas Park, South Boston, Mass.

McNamara, John G., A.B., '12. 15 Slater Ave., Norwich, Conn.

McNamara, Martin J., LL.B., '12. Lawyer, Clinton, Mass.

McNamara, Robert Emmett, LL.B., '05; LL.M., '06. Lawyer, 416 5th St. N. W., Washington, D. C.

McNamara, Stuart, A.B., '97; A.M., '98; LL.B., '01. Lawyer, New York City, N. Y.

McNamara, Wm. F., LL.B., '04. Lawyer, 53 State St., Boston, Mass.

McNaught, Archibald, LL.B., '11. Agricultural Department, Washington, D. C.; Baraboo, Wis.

McNeal, Rev. Mark J., S.J., A.B., '93. Professor of Rhetoric, G. U., Washington, D. C.

McNeir, Geo., LL.B., '81; LL.M., '82. Vice-President W. & J. Sloane Co., 575 5th Ave., New York City.

McNeir, Chas. S., LL.B., '92; LL.M., '93. Lawyer, Hibbs Bldg., Washington, D. C.

McNish, Alvin M., LL.B., '95; LL.M., '96. Examiner, 608 H St. N. W., Washington, D. C.

McNulty, Joseph Davis, A.B., '10. Contractor, 627 Melrose St., Chicago, Ill.

McQuaid, Geo. J., LL.B., '94. Lawyer, *Fort Scott, Kansas.

McQuaid, Rt. Rev. Wm. P., A.B., '64. 9 Whitmore St., Boston, Mass.

McQuillan, Francis, M.D. Physician, 204 Pennsylvania Ave. S. E., Washington, D. C.

McQuirk, Rev. John, D.D., '84. 113 E. 117th St., New York City, N. Y.

McRae, Irwin C., LL.B., '96. Lumber Business, Calvert, Ala.

McSheehy, Thomas, LL.B., '84. Lawyer, *Indianapolis, Ind.

McSorley, Chas. D., LL.B., '92; LL.M., '93. Special Examiner, Bureau of Pensions, 23 Adams St., Dorchester, Mass.

McTarnaghan, Arthur, LL.B., '09. Apartment 3, The Seville, St. Paul, Minn.

Macdonald, Alexander A., M.D., '95. Physician, 119 Washington St., Dorchester, Mass.

Macdonald, Clarence J., A.M., '97. Newfoundland.

MacDonald, Howard, A.M., '97. Physician, Port Hawkesburg, Nova Scotia.

Macdonald, Michael R., M.D., '95. Physician, Lourdes, Nova Scotia.

Macdonald, Morten Q., LL.B., '11. Special Agent, Bureau of Corporations, Department of Commerce and Labor; Hudson, N. Y.

MacElhinney, Jas. A., A.B., '77. Lawyer, 43 Cedar St., New York City.

Machen, Francis Stanislaus, M.D., '01. Physician (G. U. Med. Fac.), 3141 Mt. Pleasant St. N. W., Washington, D. C.

Mackall, Bruce McVean, M.D., '03. Physician and Surgeon, Kalispell, Mont.

MacKaye, Harold Steele, LL.B., '91; LL.M., '91. Patent Lawyer, 2 Rector St., New York City.

Mackey, Crandal, LL.B., '89. Lawyer and Commonwealth Attorney, Alexandria, Va.

Mackey, Wm. T., D.D.S., '12. Dentist, Lenox, Mass.

Mackley, Arthur R., LL.B., '04; LL.M., '05. Interstate Commerce Commission, Washington, D. C.

Maclay, Joseph P., M.D., '08. Physician, Coroner, Franklin Co., Chambersburg, Pa.

MacMahon, Paul Wm. Arthur, A.B., '98. Manufacturer and Exporter, Room 1012, 8 Bridge St., New York City.

MacMahon, Thos., Jr., A.B., '00. Business, 8 Bridge St., New York City.

Macnamee, Arthur Munson, M.D., '98. Physician (G. U. Med. Fac.), 938 P St. N. W., Washington, D. C.

Macnair, Augustine W., LL.B., '08. Lawyer, 419 Citizens' Bank Bldg., Norfolk, Va.

Macnulty, Alexander C., LL.M., '88. Assistant Coropration Counsel, New York City, Law Dept., Hall of Records, New York City.

Maddox, Geo. Edmonson, LL.B., '99. Lawyer, Rome, Ga.

Madeira, Francis P., LL.B., '96. Life Insurance, care Equitable Life Insurance Co., 165 Broadway, New York City.

Madigan, Albert W., A.B., '72; A.M., '89. Lawyer, Houlton, Me.

Madigan, Hon. John B., A.B., '83; A.M., '89. Lawyer, Maine Board, Legal Examiners, Houlton, Me.

Madigan, John J., M.D., '09. Physician, 2302 Nicholas Ave. S. E., Washington, D. C.

Madigan, Joseph P., A.B., '12. Medical Student, 2302 Nicholas Ave., Washington, D. C.

Madigan, Patrick S., A.B., '08; M.D., '12. Physician, 2302 Nicholas Ave., Washington D. C.

Madison B. F., M.D., '84. Physician, 417 B St. S. E., Washington, D. C.

Magee, M. D'Arcy, M.D., '96. Physician (G. U. Med. Fac.), 1623 Connecticut Ave., Washington, D. C.

Magie, Edward R., LL.M., '99. Department of Commerce and Labor, Washington, D. C.

Maginnis, Chas. H., LL.B., '92. Lawyer, *Duluth, Minn.

Magruder, Caleb Clarke, A.B., '58; A.M., '61. Lawyer, Clerk of Maryland Court of Appeals, Commercial Natl. Bank Bldg., Washington, D. C.

Magruder, Caleb C., Jr., LL.B., '97. Lawyer, The Cecil, Washington, D. C.

Magruder, Geo. Lloyd,M. D., '79; A.M., '71. Physician (G. U. Med. Fac., Dean Emeritus), Stoneleigh Court, Washington, D. C.

Magruder, Mercer Hampton, LL.B., '98. Lawyer, Upper Marlboro, Md.

Magruder, R. A. C., LL.B., '12. Lawyer, 712 22d St. N. W., Washington, D. C.

Maguire, Chas. F., Jr., LL.B., '05; LL.M., '06. Lawyer, Hornell, N. Y.

Maguire, Francis S., LL.B., '04; LL.M., '05. Patent Lawyer, 908 G St. N. W., Washington, D. C.

Maguire, Jered A., LL.B., '12. Navy Department, Washington, D. C.; Wilmington, Del.

Maguire, Joseph T., LL.B., '05. Civil Engineer, 1483 Newton St. N. W., Washington, D. C.

Maguire, Robert F., LL.B., '09. Assistant U. S. Attorney for Oregon, Postoffice Bldg., Portland, Oregon.

Mahan, Chas. J., LL.B., '11. Treasury Department; Bordentown, N. J.

Maher, Hon. Benedict F., A.B., '97. Judge of the Municipal Court, Augusta, Me.

Mahoney, Ed. Joseph, A.M., '93; M.D., '95. Surgeon, 4 Mattoon St., Springfield, Mass.

Mahoney, John J., LL.B., '03. Lawyer, Joliet, Ill.

Mahoney, Matthew P., A.B., '06. Physician, 46 Butterfield St., Lowell, Mass.

Mahony, Daniel W., LL.B., '02. Lawyer and Clerk of Court, 505 Bay State Bldg., Lawrence, Mass.

Mahony, Wm. F., LL.B., '96. Patent Lawyer, 1820 Park Road, Washington, D. C.

Major, Henry, A.B., '64; A.M., '66. Lawyer, 45 Broadway, New York City.

Major, Jas. Alexander, D.D.S., '12. Dentist, Watertown, N. Y.

Malabre, Alfred L., M.D., '08. Physician, 603 W. 184th St. New York City.

Mallan, Thos. F., M.D., '80. Physician, 820 Connecticut Ave. N. W., Washington, D. C.

Malone, E. Halsey, LL.B., '08. Lawyer, 24 Broad St., New York City.

Malone, Henry D., A.B., '85; LL.B., '87; LL.M., '88; A.M., '88. Lawyer, 336 Adams St. N. E., Washington, D. C.

Malone, Jas. B., LL.B., '06. Lawyer, Fairbanks Bldg., Springfield, Ohio.

Malone, John, M.D., '56. Physician, Ireland.

Maloney, John M., M.D., '07. Physician and Surgeon, 559 Liberty St., Springfield, Mass.

Maloney, Rupert L., LL.B., '12. Lawyer, Antwerp, New York.

Malony, John M., M.D., '70. Physician, Dundee, N. Y.

Malony, Wm. Redfield Proctor, LL.B., '03; LL.M., '04. Lawyer, 47 Cedar St., New York City.

Mangan, Michael F., LL.B., '03; LL.M., '05. Lawyer, 412 5th St. N. W., Washington, D. C.

Mangan, Wm. J., LL.B., '97. Law Examiner, Forest Service, 1908 15th St., Washington, D. C.

Manghum, Henry E., LL.B., '11. Lawyer, 1215 Rhode Island Ave. N. W., Washington, D. C.

Manghum, Mason, LL.B., '11. Lawyer, Columbian Bldg., Washington, D. C.

Manly, Clement, A.B., '76. Lawyer, Winston, N. C.

Mann, Geo. M., LL.B., '07. Assistant Vice-President Reliance Insurance Co., Pittsburgh, Pa.

Manning, John N., LL.M., '86. Chief of Division, Office of the Adjutant General, War Department, Washington, D. C.

Manogue, Wm. H., LL.B., '86. Lawyer, 509 E. Capitol St., Washington, D. C.

Mansell, Edward R., M.D., '88. Physician, England.

Manson, C. Farraud, LL.B., '09. Lawyer, White River, S. D.

Maple, Albert Henry, D.D.S., '11. Dentist, Ilo, Idaho.

Marble, John O., M.D., '68. Physician, 16 Murray Ave., Worcester, Mass.

Marbury, Chas. C., M.D., '93. Physician (G. U. Med. Fac.), 1015 16th St. N. W., Washington, D. C.

Marcy, Wm. L., LL.B., '85; LL.M., '86. Lawyer, *Old Forge, Pa.

Markey, Jas. F., LL.B., '01. Ism. Canal Com., Canal Zone.

Marks, Louis C., LL.B., '10. Government Clerk, 1314 5th St. N. W., Washington, D. C.

Marmion, Wm. Vincent, A.M., '83. Physician, 1211 13th St. N. W., Washington, D. C.

Marple, Raleigh W., LL.B., '95. Lawyer, *Fort Worth, Texas.

Marr, Samuel S., M. D., '76. Physician, 1318 Corcoran St., Washington, D. C.

Marsden, Francis Thos., A.B., '09. 701 E St. S. W., Washington, D. C.

Marshall, Cary A., LL.B., '07. Lawyer, Markham, Va.

Marshall, Cloud, LL.B., '08. Special Agent, Interstate Commerce Commission, Washington, D. C.

Marshall, Geo., A.B., '44. *Tennessee.

Marshall, Hunter, Jr., LL.B., '12. Lawyer, Lynchburg, Va.

Marshall, Pemberton John, D.D.S., '02. Dentist, 659 Maryland Ave. N. E., Washington, D. C.

Marshall, Percival H., LL.B., '95; LL.M., '96. Assistant Corporation Counsel, 416 5th St. N. W., Washington, D. C.

Marstellar, Ashbell C., LL.B., '12. Lawyer, Whitehaven, Pa.

Marstelleo, Massillon H., LL.B., '74. Lawyer, *California.

Martell, Chas. J., LL.B., '99; LL.M., '00. Lawyer, 1101-1102 Barrister's Hall, Boston, Mass.

Martell, Leon Alphonse, M.D., '08. Physician, 389 Front St., Weymouth, Mass.

Martin, F. P., Jr., LL.B., '83. Lawyer, Bank Bldg., Room 2, 128 Walnut St., Johnstown, Pa.

Martin, Frederick R., LL.B., '09. Special Agent, U. S. L. O., Custom House, San Francisco, Cal.

Martin, J. Wm., D.D.S., '12. Dentist, 71 Richmond St., Brockton, Mass.

Martin, Jas. J., A.B., '01. Care Martin & Martin, St. Martinsville, La.

Martin, John J., LL.B., '12. Lawyer, Johnstown, Pa.

Martin, John H., LL.B., '90; LL.M., '91. Lawyer, *Charlotte, N. C.

Martin, John T., LL.B., '82. Lawyer, *Williams Bldg., Scranton, Pa.

Martin, Robert H., LL.B., '94; LL.M., '95. U. S. Treasury Department, Washington, D. C.

Martin, Villard, LL.B., '08. Lawyer, Muskogee, Okla.

Martin, Walter Stanislaus, A. B., '96. Pacific Union Club, San Francisco, Cal.

Martinson, Joseph E., LL.B., '96; LL.M., '97. Lawyer, *Minneapolis, Minn.

Marye, Tench T., LL.B., '11. Lawyer, Hibbs Bldg., Washington, D. C.

Mason, Hugh L., LL.B., '73. Lawyer, *Kentucky.

Masterson, Daniel Stephen, LL.B., '02; LL.M., '03. Private Secretary The Rochambeau, Washington, D. C.

Matthews, Wm. LL.B., '05; LL.M., '07. Treasury Department, Washington, D. C.

Mattingly, Chas. M., LL.B., '07. Lawyer, Columbian Bldg, Washington, D. C.

Mattingly, Joseph Carbery, A.B., '93; LL.B., '95; LL.M., '96. Lawyer, Fendall Bldg., Washington, D. C.

Mattingly, Leonard H., LL.B., '98; LL.M., '00. Public Accountant, Woodward Bldg., Washington, D. C.

Mattingly, Robert E., LL.B., '91; LL.M., '92. Lawyer, 472 Louisiana Ave. N. W., Washington, D. C.

Maurer, Robert A., LL.B., '06; LL.M., '10. Teacher, Central High School, Washington, D. C.

Mawhinney, Raymond Joseph, A.B., '10. Patent Law, 38 M St. N. W., Washington, D. C.

Maxey, Chas. T., LL.B., '10. Room 226, Comp. of Currency, 516½ M St. N. E., Washington, D. C.

Maxey, Jas. H., LL.M., '02. Lawyer, Shawnee, Okla.

Mayer, Robert Daniel, M.D., '95. Physician, Germany.

Mayock, Peter P., M.D., '08. Physician, Miners Mills, Pa.

Mayock, Thos. J., D.D.S., '09. Dentist, 49 S. Washington St., Wilkesbarre, Pa.

Mead, F. W., M.D., '58. U. S. Marine Hospital, Vineyard Haven, Mass.

Mead, Theodore, M.D., '69. Medical Examiner, Bureau of Pensions; 923 23d St., Washington, D. C.

Melling, Geo., LL.B., '09; LL.M., '10. Lawyer, 114 V St. N. W., Washington, D. C.

Mercer, Claude, LL.B., '96. Lawyer, Hardinsburg, Ky.

Meredith, Edward C., Jr., LL.B., '99. Lawyer, Manassas, Va.

Merrick, Richard T., LL.B., '96; LL.M., '97. Lawyer, Chicago, Ill.

Merrill, H. Clay, LL.B., '91; LL.M., '92. Lawyer, Washington, D. C.

Merritt, Addis D., LL.B., '87; LL.M., '88. Principal Examiner, Patent Office; 3327 17th St. N. W., Washington, D. C.

Merritt, Edgar Bryant, LL.B., '98. Lawyer, 42 Seaton Place N. W., Washington, D. C.

Merritt, Frank C., LL.B., '09. House of Representatives, Washington, D. C.; Houlton, Me.

Merrow, David W., LL.B., '87; LL.M., '90. Lawyer, Omaha, Neb.

Mess, Henry Florence, D.D.S., '11. Dentist, 817 14th St. N. W., Washington, D. C.

Metzger, Percy, LL.B., '88; LL.M., '89. Lawyer, 472 Louisiana Ave. N. W., Washington, D. C.

Meyer, Anthony J., LL.B., '11. General Land Office, Washington, D. C.; Jersey City, N. J.

Meyer, Robert, LL.B., '01. Merchant, 1231 Pennsylvania Ave., Washington, D. C.

Meyers, Wm. F., LL.B., '91; LL.M., '92. Assistant Secretary, District Commission, Washington, D. C.

Michener, Algeron S., LL.B., '93; LL.M., '94. General Secretary, Stone & Webster Management Association, 147 Milk St., Boston, Mass.

Milburn, John R., LL.B., 11. U. S. Patent Office, Washington, D. C.

Milburn, Joseph W., LL.B., '09. Patent Office, 328 Massachusetts Ave., Washington, D. C.

Miles, Matthew Jas., A.M., '98. Financial Broker, 305 1st Ave., Cedar Rapids, Iowa.

Millard, Wm. J., LL.B., '10. War Department, Washington, D. C.; 1719 McKee St., Houston, Texas.

Miller, Chas. A., LL.B., '96. Lawyer, *Luray, Va.

Miller, Chas. Colden, A.B., '04; LL.B., '06. Lawyer (G. U. Law Fac.), Southern Bldg., Washington, D. C

Miller, Chas. H., M.D., '72. Chief of Division of Appropriations, Treasury Department; 1401 Girard St. N. W., Washington, D. C.

Miller, Edwin Lang, A.B., '10. Secretary of Lang Brewing Company, 1199 Main St., Buffalo, N. Y.

Miller, Jas., M.D., '99. Physician, Corning, Perry Co., Ohio.

Miller, Jas. E., LL.B., '75. Lawyer, *Washington, D. C.

Miller, James H., LL.B., '97; LL.M., '98. Government Printing Office; Room 208, The Ontario, Washington, D. C.

Miller, Jozach, A.B., '04. Globe Surety Co., care Commercial Bldg., Kansas City, Mo.

Miller, Wilbur G., LL.B., '04. Lawyer, *Washington, D. C.

Miller, W. W., M.D., '69. Physician, *Racine, Wis.

Milligan, Leo Patrick, M.D., '11. St. Francis Hospital, Jersey City, N. J.; Huntsville, Ala.

Millot, Eugene, LL.B., '09. Lawyer, 913 H St. N. W., Washington, D. C.

Millott, Augustus F., LL.B., '08; LL.M., '09. Lawyer, Kellogg, Idaho.

Milloy, Adolphus M., LL.B., '12. War Department, D. C.; Erie, Pa.

Millrick, Daniel A., LL.B., '04; LL.M., '05. Law Examiner, General Land Office, Washington, D. C.

Mills, Chas. A., LL.B., '89; LL.M., '90. Postoffice Inspector, 1013 Topeka Ave., Topeka, Kans.

Mills, Ellis, LL.B., '87; LL.M., '88. Lawyer, Honolulu, Hawaii.

Miner, Francis Hannibal, M.D., '95. Physician, 300 E. Capitol St., Washington, D. C. ·

Minor, Louis J., LL.B., '99. Lawyer and Railroad Tie Contractor, N. W. corner of Public Square, Aurora, -Mo.

Minor, Philip Edmund, D.D.S., '11· Dentist, 137 Alden Ave., New Haven, Conn.

Mitchell, Chas. Piquette, A.B., '93; LL.B., '96. Lawyer, Flanders' Manufacturing Co., Pontiac, Mich.

Mitchell, Curtis W., LL.B., '12· Interstate Commerce Commission, Washington, D. C.; Ava, Mo.

Mitchell, Geo. D., LL.B., '89; LL.M., '90. Editor of the 'Pathfinder,' 1812 Irving St. N. E., Washington, D. C.

Mitchell, Herbert Francis, LL.B., '04. Civil Service Commissioner, 806 Highland Ave., Philadelphia, Pa.

Mitchell, Paul V., LL.B., '09; LL.M., '10. Lawyer, 120 W St. N. W., Washington, D. C.

Mitchell, Richard Clarke, A.M., '97. Draftsman, care Robert Mitchell Furniture Co., Cincinnati, Ohio.

Mitchell, Wm. Ansel, LL.B., '94. Real Estate Dealer, 5420 Baltimore Ave., Kansas City, Mo.

Mock, Jas. J., LL.B., '97. Law Examiner, General Land Office, Washington, D. C.

Mohn, Earl J., LL.B., '10. Lawyer, 309 S. Rebecca St., East End, Pittsburgh, Pa.

Mohrmann, Henry Joseph, A.M., '02. Real Estate, 216 Wainwright Bldg., St. Louis, Mo.

Mohun, Barry, LL.B., '96; LL.M., 97. Lawyer, 340 Indiana Ave., Washington, D. C.

Mohun, Phillip V., LL.B., '93. Lieut., U. S. N., retired, New Rochelle, N. Y.

Molloy, John, LL.B., '06; LL.M., '07. Clerk, 941 M St N. W., Washington, D. C.

Moloney, Benjamin J. D., LL.B., '10. Lawyer, 226-227 Hildreth Bldg., Lowell, Mass.

Monaghan, Hugh I., LL.B., '05. Lawyer, 2102 Summer St., Philadelphia, Pa.

Monaghan, Joseph Patrick, A.B., '96. Lawyer, Wilkinson Bldg., Shenandoah, Pa.

Monaghan, Martin M., LL.B., '98. Claim Department, C. M. & St. P. Ry., St. Paul, Minn.

Monarch, J. Louis, LL.B., '12. Department of Agriculture, Washington, D. C.; Boston, Mass.

Money, John T., LL.B., '10. Interstate Commerce Commission; Lewinsville, Va.

Monohan, Edward Sheehan, Jr., A. B., '05; A.M., '06. Stock Farmer, St. Matthews, Ky.

Montgomery, Chas. P., LL.B., '97. Lawyer and Chief of Customs Division, U. S. Treasury Department, Washington, D. C.

Montgomery, Denny, LL.B., '96; LL.M., '98. Lawyer, *Oklahoma.

Montgomery, Francis Stanton, A.M., '05; Ph.D., '07; LL.B., '07. Lawyer, 421 American Bank Bldg., Los Angeles, Cal.

Montgomery, Geo. C., LL.B., '94. Lawyer, *Virginia.

Montgomery, Jas. P., B.S., '88; LL.B., '89. Lawyer, 1620 8th St., Oakland, Cal.

Montgomery, Joseph W., A.B., '09. Care Saunders, Dufour & Dufour, Louisiana Bank and Trust Bldg., New Orleans, La.

Moody, Leander J., LL.B., '12. General Land Office; Limington, Me.

Moon, John B., LL.B., '96; LL.M., '97. Lawyer, 1036 Chamber of Commerce, Portland, Ore.

Mooney, Henry F., LL.B., '95; LL.M., '96. Real Estate, 707 G St. N. W., Washington, D. C.

Moore, Everett F., LL.B., '11. 823 6th St. S. W., Washington, D. C., and Front Royal, Va.

Moore, John Edward, A.B., '00. Woburn, Mass.

Moore, Samuel Broder, M.D., '97. Physician, 811 Prince St., Alexandria, Va.

Moran, Chas. Vincent, A.B., '02. Census Bureau, 1342 Girard St., Washington, D. C.

Moran, Jas. Linus, A.B., '08. Lawyer, Secretary of G. U. Alum. of West Pennsylvania, Bullfield Dwel., Centre and Bullfield Ave., Pittsburgh, Pa.

Moran, John F., M.D., '87; A.B., '94. Physician, 2426 Pennsylvania Ave., Washington, D. C.

Moran, John J., M.D., '08. Physician, 24 Barnett Bldg., Albuquerque, New Mexico.

Moran, Johnson E., LL.B., '12. Lawyer, 1649 Newton St. N. W., Washington, D. C.

Moran, Timothy Joseph, A.B., '01. Oculist, Jenkins Bldg., Pittsburgh, Pa.

Morgan, Cecil, LL.B., '87; LL.M., '88. Lawyer, Vice-President Commercial National Bank, 501 College St., Macon, Ga.

Morgan, D. Oswald, LL.B., '96; LL.M., '97. Lawyer, New York City.

Morgan, Daniel H., LL.B., '95. Lawyer, Cookeville, Tenn.

Morgan, Daniel P., LL.B., '93; LL.M., '94. Lawyer, Bethesda, Md.

Morgan, Haze, LL.B., '99. Lawyer, Clarksburg, W. Va.

Morgan, J. Dudley, A.B., '81; M.D., '85. Physician, 919 15th St. N. W., Washington, D. C.

Morgan, Joseph V., LL.B., '09; LL.M., '10. Lawyer, Alabama Apartment, Washington, D. C.

Morgan, Nicholas G., LL.B., '10. Secretary U. S. Senate, Washington, D. C.; Salt Lake City, Utah.

Morgan, Wm. M., LL.M., '99. Lawyer, Commercial Block, Moscow, Idaho.

Morgan, Zachariah R., M.D., '80. Physician, Mechanicsville, Md.

Moriarty, Daniel J, LL.B., '12. Bureau of Standards, Washington, D. C.; Newport, R. I.

Moroney, Edward B., LL.B., '91; LL.M., '92. Lawyer, *Pontiac, Mich.

Moross, W. Paul Dwight, A.B., '88. Manager Cement Manufacturing Co., Chattanooga, Tenn.

Morrill, Chas. P., M.D., '66. Physician, 62 Elm St., North Andover, Mass.

Morrill, Chester, LL.B., '09. Lawyer, The Willson, Washington, D. C.

Morris, Ballard, LL.M., '87. Patent Office, Washington, D. C.

Morris, Jas. L., A.B., '82. Lawyer, 403-404 Hollenback Coal Exchange Bldg., Wilkesbarre, Pa.

Morris, John Penn, A.B., '82. *Louisa County, Va.

Morrison, John W., LL.B., '11. Census Department, Washington, D. C.; Harrisonburg, Va.

Morse, Alexander Porter, LL.B., '72. Lawyer and Author, 1505 Pennsylvania Ave. N. W., Washington, D. C.

Mortimer, Chas. G., LL.B., '95; LL.M., '96. Captain, 3d Art., U. S, A., Fort San Houston, Texas.

Morton, Joseph F., LL.B., '07. Lawyer, Rooms 403-4-5 Lindelle Block, Spokane, Wash.

Moser, Jas. Madison, M.D., '10. Physician, 1107 Massachusetts Ave., Washington, D. C.

Moulton, Chas. L., M.D., '87. Physician, *New Hampshire.

Moulton, Clarence E., LL.B., '88. Lawyer, Suite 1102 Wilcox Bldg., Portland, Ore.

Moulton, Irwin B., LL.B., '91. Assistant Chief, Bureau of Engraving and Printing, Washington, D. C.

Moynihan, Dennis L., LL.B., '02. The San Francisco Call, San Francisco, Cal.

Mudd, Sydney E., Jr., A.B., '06; LL.B., '09. Assistant District Attorney, Columbian Bldg., 416 5th St. N. W., Washington, D. C.

Mudd, W. Aubrey, LL.B., '10. Civil Service Comm., Waldorf, Md.

Mudd, W. Griffin, LL.B., '10. Lawyer, La Plata, Md.

Mueller, Carl C., LL.B., '08; LL.M., '09. 2621 13th St. N. W., Washington, D. C.

Mueller, J. Max, Mus. Doc., '82. *Pennsylvania.

Mulcahy, Daniel D., M.D., '99. Physician, 1216 N. Capitol St., Washington, D. C.

Mulcare, Jas. H., LL.B., '09. Lawyer, 310 Main St., Springfield, Mass.

Mulhall, Francis J., LL.B., '99; LL.M., '00. Amer. Nat. Red Cross Soc., 2125 H St. N. W., Washington, D. C.

Mulhearn, Chas. E., LL.B., '02. Lawyer, Grovesner Bldg., Providence, R. I.

Mulhearn, F. Richard, D.D.S., '04. Dentist, 23 Aborn St., Providence, R. I.

Mullaly, Jas. F., LL.B., '93; LL.M., '94. Lawyer, National Union Bldg., Washington, D. C.

Mullaly, Geo. LeGuere, A.B., '03; A.M., '04. Actor, The Lambs, New York City.

Mullan, Frank Drexel, A.B., '93. Journalist, 1 Madison Ave., New York City.

Mullan, Horace E., LL.B., '86. Lawyer, *Maryland.

Mullen, Chas. Vincent, A.M., '05; Ph.D., '07; LL.B., '07. Lawyer, 603-7 Ernest & Cramner Bldg., Denver, Colo.

Mulligan, Jas. A.B., '12. Banker, 25 W. South St., Wilkesbarre, Pa.

Mulligan, Tracy E., LL.B., '12. Navy Department, Woodley Lane Road, Washington, D. C.

Mullins, Geo. Holland, A.B., '09. North Yakima, Wash.

Mulloney, Daniel C., LL.B., '09; LL.M., '10. Lawyer, Portland, Me.

Mulvanity, Albert F., M.D., '06. Physician, 123 Palm St., Nashua, N. H.

Mulvey, Wm. Aloysius, M.D., '10. Physician, 145 Penn St., Providence, R. I.

Mulvihill, John Aloysius, A.B., '96; LL.B., '98. Wholesale Produce, 37 Walnut St., Cincinnati, Ohio.

Muncaster, Alexander, LL.B., '91; LL.M., '92. Lawyer, 482 Louisiana Ave., Washington, D. C.

Muncaster, Stuart B., M.D., '85. Physician (G. U. Med. Fac.), 907 16th St. N. W., Washington, D. C. /

Mundell, Joseph Joshua, M.D., '03. Physician, 8 Maple New Place, Anacostia, D. C.

Munger, M. J., M.D., '65. Physician, *New York.

Munhall, Herbert Nicholas, A.B., '09. Automobile Business, 701 S. Linden Ave., Pittsburgh, Pa.

Munson, Leonard Walter, M.D., '96. Physician, Stamford, Conn.

Murchison, Kenneth S., LL.B., '86; LL.M., '99. Lawyer, 320 5th Ave., New York City.

Murdock, Edwin F., LL.B., '89. Lawyer, *Washington, D. C.

Murnigham, Richard J., D.D.S., '07. Dentist, 128½ E. Main St., Amsterdam, N. Y.

Murphey, John J., LL.B., '92. Superintendent, Station D, City Postoffice, Washington, D. C.

Murphy, Chas. J., LL.B., '92; LL. M., '93. Lawyer (G. U. Law Fac.), Century Bldg., Washington, D. C.

Murphy, Chas. J., LL.B., '99; LL.M., '00. Milling, care N. W. Mills Co., Winona, Minn.

Murphy, Cornelius A., A.B., '04. 6 Jacques St., Somerville, Mass.

Murphy, Daniel, LL.B., '96; LL.M., '97. Care Underwood Typewriter Co., Elkhart, Ind.

Murphy, Daniel A., D.D.S., '07. Dentist, 309 Hanover St., Fall River, Mass.

Murphy, Daniel C., LL.B., '90; LL.M., '91. Lawyer, Mutual Saving Bank Bldg., San Francisco, Cal.

Murphy, Edward 2d, A.B., '90. Lawyer, 16 Second St., Troy, N. Y.

Murphy, Edward J., LL.B., '11. Department of Agriculture, Washington, D. C.; Auburn, Me.

Murphy, Edward V., Jr., LL.B., '05. Special Agent, General Land Office, 2511 Pennsylvania Ave., Washington, D. C.

Murphy, Harry L., M.D., '12. Georgetown University Hospital, Washington, D. C.

Murphy, Jas. A., A.B., '63; A.M., '66. *New York City.

Murphy, Jas. R., A.B., '72. Lawyer, 27 School St., Boston, Mass.

7

Murphy, Jas. Wilmot, LL.B., '99; LL.M., '00. Official Reporter, U. S. Senate, Washington, D. C.

Murphy, John A., LL.B., '06; LL.M., '07. State's Attorney, Seattle, Wash.

Murphy, John A., LL.B., '09. Clerk, 3268 P St. N. W., Washington, D. C.

Murphy, John F., LL.B., '04. Prosecuting Attorney for King County, 1116 Alaska Bldg., Seattle, Wash.

Murphy, John J., LL.B., '94; LL.M., '95. Lawyer, Troy, N. Y.

Murphy, John Maxwell, A.B., '02. Mining, Joplin, Mo.

Murphy, Hon. Lester T., LL.B., '06. Probate Judge, Providence, R. I.

Murphy, Martin, A.B., '95. *San Jose, Cal.

Murphy, Michael J., LL.B., '11. Treasury Department, Washington, D. C.; Providence, R. I.

Murphy, Richard, LL.B., '91. Lawyer, Englewood, N. J.

Murphy, Thos. J., LL.B., '74. Lawyer, *Ohio.

Murphy, Wm. A., A.M., '92. Journalist, 2 Ainsly St., Ashmont, Mass.

Murphy, Wm. Joseph, LL.B., '97. Department Correction, 123 W. 63d St., New York City.

Murray, Daniel Bradley, A.B., '10. Lawyer, 783 St. Mark's Ave., Brooklyn, N. Y.

Murray, Geo. F., A.B., '61. Lawyer, 20 Nassau St., New York City.

Murray, O. H., LL.B., '11; L.D.M., '11. 934 B St. S. W., Washington, D. C.

Murray, John Desmond, A.B., '10. Manufacturer, 200 S. College St., Grand Rapids, Mich.

Murray, Lawrence O., LL.M., '95. Comptroller of Currency, Treasury Department, Washington, D. C.

Murray, Louis J., A.B., '12. 200 College Ave., Grand Rapids, Mich.

Murray, Percy E., LL.B., '11; LL.M., '12. Treasury Department; 1477 Newton St., Washington, D. C.; Camden, Ohio.

Murray, Thos., LL.B., '76. Lawyer, *Missouri.

Murray, Thos. J., LL.B., '94. Care New York Law Book Co., 60 Wall St., New York City.

Murrin, Joseph S., M.D., '07. Physician, Carbondale, Pa.

Myers, Abram F., LL.B., 12. Department of Justice, Washington, D. C.; Fairfield, Iowa.

Myers, Stacy H., LL.B., '12. Interstate Commerce Commission, Washington, D. C.; Hagerstown, Md.

N

Nadeau, Arthur J., LL.B., '04. Lawyer, Fort Kent, Me.

Nash, John A., LL.B., '08. Lawyer, 505 5th St. N. E., Washington, D. C.

Nast, Conde Montrose, A.B., '94; A.M., '95. Vice-President of Home Pattern Co., 443 4th Ave., New York City.

Naylor, Levi W., LL.M., '87. Lawyer, *Racine, Wis.

Naylor, Van Denson, M.D., '60. Physician, *Maryland.

Neale, Augustine W., A.B., '60. Retired, 105 I St. N. W., Washington,

Neale, Francis, A.M., '69. *Texas.

Neale, R. A., M.D., '70. Physician, 1209 U St. N. W., Washington, D. C.

Neas, Wm. H., LL.B., '88; LL.M., '89. Lawyer, Greenesville, Tenn.

Nee, Festus J., D.D.S., '06. Dentist, 317 Butler Exchange, Providence, R. I.

Neely, Edgar A., LL.B., '05. Lawyer, 701 Equitable Bldg., Atlanta, Ga.

Neely, John R., M.D., '91. Physician, Spokane, Wash.

Neely, Wm. Clinton, D.D.S., '12. Dentist, Virgen, Ill.

Neff, Abner R., LL.B., '10. Lawyer, Erie, Pa.

Neill, Chas. P., A.B., '91. U. S. Commissioner of Labor, 1429 New York Ave., Washington, D. C.

Neill, Thos. E., M.D., '08. Physician, 1213 Connecticut Ave. N. W., Washington, D. C.

Neilson, Frederick K., LL.M., '07. Office of the Solicitor, State Department, Washington, D. C.

Neis, Claudius J., LL.B., '99. Forest Service, Albuquerque, N. M.

Nelligan, John J., LL.B., '92. Lawyer, *Olathe, Kans.

Nelms, Wm. H., LL.M., '98. Counsel for Reisch Indem. Co., 918 S. 5th St., Springfield, Ill.

Nelson, Carl Frederick, D.D.S., '11. Dentist, 6th and S St. N. W., Washington, D. C.

Nelson, Cyrus W., M.D., '09. Physician, Houston, Texas.

Nelson, Thos. Clement, A.B., '96. General Manager of Lakin Land and Immigration Co., Lakin, Kans.

Nemmers, Erwin Plein, A.M., '99; Ph.D., '00; LL.B., '01; LL.M., '02. Lawyer, 506 Germania Bldg., Milwaukee, Wis.

Neubeck, Francis L., LL.B., '03. Lawyer and Notary, 422 Bond Bldg., Washington, D. C.

Nevins, Joseph D., LL.B., '92; LL.M., 93. Secretary's Office, Treasury Department, Washington, D. C.

Newbern, John Melvin, M. D., '98. Physician, Co. Supt. Public Inst., Pres. O. & N. River S. S. Co., Jarvisburg, N. C.

Newberne, R. L. E., M.D., '93. Physician, Manila, P. I.

Newman, Chas. R., A.B., '77; LL.B., '80; LL.M., '81. Lawyer 902 F St. N. W., Washington, D. C.

Newman, Enos S., LL.B., '92. Lawyer, 26th and Tilden Sts., Washington, D. C.

Newsom, Herbert, LL.B., '12. Lawyer, St. Louis, Mo.

Newton, Jas. Thornwell, LL.B., '95. Principal Examiner, Patent Office, Washington, D. C.

Newton, Philip, M.D., '10. (G. U. Med. Fac.), Chevy Chase, Md.

Niblack, Wm. Caldwell, A.B., '74. Lawyer and Vice-President of the Chicago Title and Trust Co., 69 W, Washington St., Chicago, Ill.

Nichols, Edmund L., LL.B., '87. Lawyer, *Wapakoneta, Ohio.

Nichols, Henry J., A.B., '89. Tremont and Webster Ave., New York City.

Nichols, John L, LL.B., '96. Lawyer, *Washington, D. C.

Nicholson, John T., LL.B., '78. Lawyer, *Maryland.

Nishio, Shohaku, M.D., '94. Physician, Nagasaki, Japan.

Nixon, Cleon R., LL.B., '12. Census Department, Washington, D. C.; St. Paris, Ohio.

Noeker, Joseph John, Jr., A.M., '98; M.D., '02. Physician, Mullett St., Detroit, Mich.

Nolan, John M., LL.B., '01. 25 Broad St., New York City.

Nolan, Lawrence F., LL.B., '06. Lawyer, care Higgins & Fitzgerald, Pawtucket, R. I.

Nolan, Rev. Thos. J., A.B., '02. Loretto, Fla.

Noonan, Louis T., A.B., '95; LL.B., '97; LL.M., '98. Lawyer, 165 Broadway, New York City.

Noonan, Peter J., LL.B., '11. Lawyer, Housatonic, Mass.

Norcross, Hon. Frank H., LL.B., '94. Justice Supreme Court, Carson City, Nev.

Norcross, Geo. J., M.D., '65. Physician, *New Hampshire.

Nordlinger, Isaac W., A.B., '83; LL.B., '85; LL.M., '86. Lawyer, Stewart Bldg., Washington, D. C.

Normoyle, John D., LL.B., '98; LL.M., '99. Real Estate Agent, Alexandria National Bank Bldg., Alexandria, Va.

Norris, Ralph W., LL.B., '08. Lawyer, North Vernon, Ind.

Norris, Raymond S., LL.B., '11; L.D.M., '11. Treasury Department, Washington, D. C.; Boyd's, Md.

Northrop, Geo., LL.B., '87. Lawyer, *Charleston, S. C.

Norton, Frank P., LL.B., '98; LL.M., '99. Lawyer, *Detroit, Mich.

Norton, John M., LL.B., '94. Lawyer, *Newton, Kans.

Nourse, C. H., M.D., '69. Physician, Darnestown, Md.

Nourse, Upton Darby, M.D., '00. Physician, Dawsonville, Md.

Noyes, Geo. F., LL.B., '86; LL.M., '86. Lawyer, 98 Exchange St., Portland, Me.

Nunez, Manuel I., M.D., '05. Physician, Arequipa, Peru, South America.

Nussa, Rafael Lopez, M.D., '06. Physician, San Juan, Porto Rico.

Nye, Edwin B., LL.B., '09. Lawyer, 936 O St. N. W., Washington, D. C.

Nye, L. Frank, LL.B., '11; L.D.M., '11. War Department, Washington, D C.; Hummelston, *Pa.

O

Oakes, Raymond S., LL.B., '12. Com. Com., U. S. Senate, Washington, D. C.; Auburn, Me.

Obenchain, Chas. Austin, LL.B., '99; LL.M., '00. General Land Office, 1415 29th St. N. W., Washington, D. C.

Ober, Geo. C., M.D., '82. Physician, 210 B St. S. E. Washington, D. C.

Oblinger, Edward V., A.B., '05. Insurance Broker, 220 Broadway, New York City.

O'Brien, Dennis F., LL.B., '01. Lawyer, 125 Alta Ave., Park Hill, Yonkers, N. Y.

O'Brien, General Edward C., LL.D., '97. Union League Club, New York City.

O'Brien, Edward D., A.B., '90. Lawyer, 120 Broadway, New York City.

O'Brien, Edward M., LL.B., '09. Lawyer, Waterbury, Conn.

O'Brien, John, A.B., '55. *New York City, N. Y.

O'Brien, John F., A.B., '96. Lawyer, Hall of Records, New York City.

O'Brien, John Henry, A.B., '04. Lawyer, 128 School St., Clinton, Mass.

O'Brien, John Lawrence, LL.B., '99; LL.M., '00. Lawyer, *Washington, D. C.

O'Brien, John P., A.M., '95; LL.B., '97. Assistant Corporation Counsel, City of New York, 44 E. 23d St., New York City.

O'Brien, Michael C., LL.B., '06; LL.M., '07. Lawyer, 610 3d St. N. W., Washington, D. C.

O'Brien, Michael J., D.D.S., '08. Dentist, Warren, R. I.

O'Brien, Miles M., Jr., LL.B., '99; LL.M., '00. Lawyer, 38 Park Row, New York City.

O'Brien, Thos. W., LL.B., '07; LL.M., '08. Lawyer, 406 5th St. N. W., Washington, D. C.

O'Connell, Daniel, LL.B., '86. Lawyer, 942-6 Pacific Bldg., San Francisco, Cal.

O'Connell, John J., LL.M., '87. Lawyer, *Boston, Mass.

O'Connell, Ralph T., LL.B., '07. Lawyer, Bangor, Me.

O'Connell, Richard F., M.D., '94. Physician, 1157 Parsons Ave., Columbus, Ohio.

O'Connor, Charles B., LL.B., '12. Lawyer, Elmira, N. Y.

O'Connor, Chas. Emmet, M.D., '95. Physician, 1309 13th St. N. W., Washington, D. C.

O'Connor, Jeremiah I., A.B., '92; LL.B., '94; LL.M., '95. Dramatist, 101 2d St. N. E., Washington, D. C.

O'Connor, Joseph T., M.D., '67. Physician, Retired, 20 Bayard Lane, Princeton, N. J.

O'Connor, Michael, A.B., '98; LL.B., '01. Lawyer, 1811 35th St. N. W., Washington, D. C.

O'Day, Charles F., Ph.B., '89. 39 Courtland St., New York City.

O'Day, Daniel E., A.B., '89. Rye, N. Y.

O'Dea, Patrick H., LL.B., '94; LL.M., '95. Navy Department, Washington, D. C.

O'Dell, Wilmot Mitchell, LL.M., '00. Lawyer, Cleburne, Texas.

O'Doherty, John D., M.D., '88. Physician, 5 Locust St., Dover, N. H.

O'Donnell, David, LL.B., '12. Lawyer, Providence, R. I.

O'Donnell, Edward Pius, A.B., '02. Physician, Heckschersville, Pa.

O'Donnell, Patrick Henry, A.B., '92; A.M., '93; LL.B., '94. Lawyer, 1218-1219 Ashland Block, Chicago, Ill.

O'Donnell, Rev. William Aloysius, A.B., '94. 48th St. and Lancaster Ave., Philadelphia, Pa.

O'Donoghue, Daniel Wm., A.B., '97; A.M., '98; Ph.D., 99; LL.B., '99; LL.M., '00. Lawyer (G. U. Law Fac.), 1704 16th St. N. W., Washington, D. C.

O'Donoghue, John Alphonso, A.M., '97; M.D., '00. Physician (G. U. Med. Fac.), 909 16th St. N. W., Washington, D. C.

O'Donovan, Chas., A.B., '78; A.M., '88. Professor of Medicine, 5 E. Read St., Baltimore, Md.

Offutt, Armand, LL.B., '12. Lawyer, 901 B St. N. E., Washington, D. C.

Ogden, Herbert Gouverneur, LL.M., '00. Patent Lawyer, 2 Rector St., New York City.

Ogden, Warren Greene, LL.B., '05. Patent Lawyer, 53 State St., Boston, Mass.

O'Gorman, Hon. Jas. A., LL.D., '12. U. S. Senator from New York, New York City.

O'Gorman, Maurice J. C., A.B., '00. Real Estate and Builder, New York City.

O'Halloran, Thos. M., LL.B., '92. Lawyer, *Braddock, Pa.

O'Hanlon, Michael, LL.B., '99; LL.M., '00. Merchant, 1132 Lamont St. N. W., Washington, D. C. .

O'Hara, Francis Jas., A.M., '01; M.D., '04. Physician, 15 N. Holden St., North Adams, Mass.

O'Hara, Jas. F., M.D., '06. Physician, 723 S. Market St., Canton, Ohio.

O'Hara, Jas. J., LL.B., '10. Navy Department, Washington, D. C.; 902 E. Broadway, South Boston, Mass.

O'Hara, John J., LL.B., '04. Lawyer, Greenleaf Bldg., Quincy, Mass.

O'Hara, The Very Rev. Wm. Louis, LL.D., '01. 104 Greenwich St., Hempstead, N. Y.

O'Hearn, Hon. Wm. A., LL.B., '10. Lawyer, Massachusetts House of Representatives, North Adams, Mass.

O'Keefe, Lawrence E. A., S.J., LL.B., '05; LL.M., '06. Lecturer on Law, Santa Clara College, Santa Clara, Cal.

O'Laughlin, Jas P., LL.B., '95; LL.M., '96. Lawyer, Clearfield, Clearfield, County, Pa.

O'Leary, Chas. R., LL.B., '98. Paymaster, U. S. N. Dept., Washington, D. C.; Philadelphia, Pa.

O'Leary, Jas. J., LL.B., '11. Lawyer, 1211 L St. N. W., Washington, D. C.; Wheeling, W. Va.

O'Leary, John G., A.B., '95. Broker New York City.

O'Leary, Timothy S., LL.B., '93; LL.M., '94. Paymaster, U. S. N., Navy Department, Washington, D. C.; Boston, Mass.

O'Leary, Wm. J., LL.B., '11. Department of Agriculture, Washington, D. C.; Bellaire, Ohio.

O'Leary, Wm. Joseph, A.M., '94. *Connecticut.

Olesen, Robert, M.D., '05. Acting Surgeon, Public Health and Hospital Marine Service, Box 424, Manila, P. I.

Oller, Geo. E., LL.B., '05; LL.M., '06. Census Office, Washington, D. C.

Olmsted, Edwin B., M.D., '87. Special Pension Examiner, Pension Office, Washington, D. C.

O'Malley, Austin, A. M., '88; Ph.D., '89; M.D., 93. Physician, 2228 S. Broad St., Philadelphia, Pa .

O'Malley, Joseph, M.D., '93. Physician, 2228 S. Broad St., Philadelphia, Pa.

O'Neil, Albert Murray, A.B., '04; A.M., '05; LL.B., '08. Lawyer, Professor, Loyola School, N. Y.; Binghamton, N. Y.

O'Neil, Desmond J., LL.B., '10. County Attorney, Roundup, Mont.

O'Neill, Joseph H., A.B., '08. Manager of Massachusetts Bonding and Insurance Co., 238 Ind. Trust Bldg., Providence, R. I.

O'Neill, Eugene J. B., LL.B., '88; LL.M., '89. Lawyer, Phoenix, Ariz.

O'Neill, John B., LL.B., '87; LL.M., '88. Lawyer, *San Francisco, Cal.

O'Neill, John H., A.M., '55. *Ohio.

O'Neill, John Joseph, A.B., '94. Lawyer, 77 Bank St., Waterbury, Conn.

O'Neill, John J., LL.B., '11. Lawyer, Bennett Block, Muncie, Ind.

O'Neill, Rev. Thos. Jeremiah Lantry, C.S.P., A.B., '99. 2630 Ridge Road, Berkeley, Cal.

O'Neill, Wm. E., LL.B., '88; LL.M., '89. Lawyer, 1522 Harris Bldg., Chicago, Ill.

O'Neill, Wm. M. A., LL.B., '99. Lawyer, O'Neill Bldg., Highland Falls, N. Y.

Opisso, Antonio M., LL.B., '03; LL.M., '04. Lawyer, 412 5th St. N. W., Washington, D. C.

O'Regan, John, LL.B., '12. Lawyer, Jersey City, N. J.

O'Reilly, Thos., M.D., '89. Physician, 41 M St. N. W., Washington, D. C.

Orleman, Carl S., LL.B., '91; LL.M., '95. Chapin, Sacks Manufacturing Co., Washington, D. C.

Orleman, Louis H., Jr., LL.B., '94. Lawyer, *Austin, Texas.

O'Rourke, Leo W., LL.B., '10. 909 Board of Trade, Portland, Ore.

Osborn, Harry S., LL.B., '08. Lawyer, Darlington, Wis.

Osborne, Henry G., LL.B., '88. Lawyer, *Leaksville, N. C.

Osburn, Alexander, M.D., '68. Physician, *Virginia.

Osenton, Chas. W., LL.B., '95; LL.M., '96. Lawyer, Fayetteville, W. Va.

O'Shea, Jas. Aloysius, A.B., '99; A.M., '00; Ph.D., '01; LL.B., '02. Lawyer, Century Bldg., Washington, D. C.

Osterman, Albert H., LL.B., '06. Bell Telephone Co., Swarthmore, Pa.

Osterman, Oscar H., LL.B., '09; LL.M., '10. 161 Maple Ave., Washington, D. C.

Ottenburg, Louis, LL.B., '11. Lawyer, 323 Colorado Bldg., Washington, D. C.

Ourdan, Vincent L., LL.B., '95. Lawyer, *Washington, D. C.

Owen, Claude W., LL.M., '10. Lawyer, 301-6 Evans Bldg., Washington, D. C.; Gaithersburg, Md.

Owen, Frederick Wooster, M.D., '67. Physician, Retired, Morristown, N. J.

Owen, Jas. W., LL.B., '08. Lawyer, 111 E. 9th St., Cincinnati, Ohio.

Owens, Samuel Logan, M.D., '08. Physician (G. U. Med. Fac.), 2418 Pennsylvania Ave. N. W., Washington, D. C.

Owens, Wm. Dunlop, M.D., '01. P. A. Surgeon, U. S. Navy, Washington, D. C.

Owens, Winter, LL.B., '98. Lawyer, *The Plains, Va.

Owings, Wm. Randall, A.B., '01; A.M., '02; LL.B., '04; Ph.L., '04; LL.M., '05; Ph.D., '05. Lawyer, 126 Lincoln St., Newton Highlands, Mass.

Oxnard, Geo. C., B.S., '79. 175 W. 58th St., New City.

P

Pace, Chas. F., LL.B., '94. Lawyer, Starke, Fla.

Pace, Louis D., LL.B., '90; LL.M., '91. Principal Examiner, General Land Office, Washington, D. C.

Packard, Harry M., LL.B., '97; LL.M., '98. Lawyer, 412 5th St. N. W., Washington, D. C.

Paddock, LeRoy M., LL.B., '07; LL.M., '08. Lawyer, Lee Bldg., Oklahoma City, Okla.

Paine, A. Elliott, M.D., '65. Physician, 13 Clinton Ave., Brockton, Mass.

Painter, John Isaac, LL.B., '98; LL.M., '99. Department of Agriculture; 800 Taylor St. N. W., Washington, D. C.

Paladini, Frank S., LL.B., '07. Lawyer, 516 Evans Bldg., Washington, D. C.

Pallen, Conde Benoist, A.B., '80; A.M., '83; LL.D., '96. Editor of Cath. Encyc., 39 W. 38th St., New York City.

Pallen, Conde de Sales, A.B., '10. Medical Student, 197 Weyman Ave., New Rochelle, N. Y.

Palmer, Alfred C., LL.B., '12. Lawyer, City Hall, Washington, D. C.

Palmer, Dennis, LL.B., '98; LL.M., '99. Lawyer, 3215 13th St. N. W., Washington, D. C.

Palmer, Jas. A. C., LL.B., '11. Lawyer, 1401 Belmont St. N. W., Washington, D. C.

Palmer, Oscar, M.D., '64. Physician, *Michigan.

Palmer, Theodore Sherman, M.D., '95. Department of Agriculture; 1939 Biltmore St., Washington, D. C.

Palms, Chas. Louis, Ph.B., '89. Director of First National Bank, 890 Jefferson Ave., Detroit, Mich.

Palms, Francis A., A.B., '04. Michigan Stove Co., Detroit, Mich.

Pardee, Edmund W., D.D.S., '06. Dentist, Realty Bldg., Washington Square, Newport, R. I.

Pardee, Munson D., LL.B., '98; LL.M., '99. Lawyer, South Norwalk, Conn.

Pargon, Augustine Joseph A., M.D., '05. Physician, 688½ 5th St., Portland, Ore.

Parke, Clarence LeRoy, LL.B., '07; LL.M., '08. Library of Congress, Washington, D. C.

Parker, Benjamin H., LL.B., '10. Real Estate, 435 4½ St. S. W., Washington, D. C.

Parkhurst, Lincoln A., LL.B., '91. Lawyer, Wampsville, N. Y.

Parks, Chas. J., LL.B., '04. Lawyer, 57 Post St., San Francisco, Cal.

Parrott, John, Jr., A.B., '05. Diplomatic Service, San Mateo, Cal.

Parrott, P. Bishop, LL.B., '96. Lawyer, *Darlington, S. C.

Parsons, Harold K., LL.B., '11. Lawyer, Des Moines, Iowa.

Parsons, John, M.D., '70. Physician, 246 65th Place, Chicago, Ill.

Parsons, Lee L., LL.B., '11. Lawyer, 1443 Massachusetts Ave. N. W., Washington, D. C.

Paschal, Geo., LL.B., '76. Lawyer, *Texas.

Paschal, Geo., LL.B., '06. Lawyer, Tahlequah, Okla.

Pater, Alphonse J., A.M., '06. 603 S. 4th St., Hamilton, Ohio.

Patterson, Geo., D.D.S., '12. Dentist, Burke, N. Y.

Patterson, Herbert Stewart, A.B., '98. *Washington, D. C.

Patterson, John C. C., LL.B., '94; LL.M., '95. Lawyer, Interstate Commerce Commission, Washington Grove, Md.

Patterson, Thos. H., LL.B., '06. Lawyer, Columbian Bldg., Washington, D. C.

Pattison, Allen S., LL.B., '89; LL.M., '90. Patent Lawyer, 629 F St. N. W., Washington, D. C.

Paulson, Peter C., LL.B., '11. Interstate Commerce Commission, Washington, D. C.; Ashby, Minn.

Payn, Abbott Smith, M.D., '95. Physician, 536 W. 148th St., New York City.

Payne, John Carroll, A.B., '76. Lawyer, Atlanta, Ga.

Payne, J. Stanley, LL.B., '10; LL.M., '11. Interstate Commerce Commission; 818 North Carolina Ave. S. E., Washington, D. C.

Payne, Lewis A., LL.B., '08; LL.M., '09. Insurance and Real Estate, 708 14th St. N. W., Washington, D. C.

Payne, Rev. W. Gaston, A.B., '79. Clifton Forge, Va.

Pearce, Waldo Roberts, D.D.S., '10. Dentist, 723 14th St., Washington, D. C.

Pearman, Silas D., LL.B., '09. Lawyer, Anderson, S.C.

Pearman, John Maxwell, M.D., '07. Physician, Camp Verde, Ariz.

Pease, Harlow F., A.B., '06. Lawyer, Dillon, Mont.

Peck, C. W., M.D., '63. Physician, *New York.

Peck, Herbert E., LL.B., '90; LL.M., '91. Patent Lawyer, 708 Barrister Bldg., Washington, D. C.

Peck, Wm. D., LL.B., '95. Auditor, 619 14th St., Washington, D. C.

Peeples, A. McBride, LL.B., '11. Treasury Department, Washington, D. C.; Varnville, S. C.

Pell, Geo. Pierce, LL.B., '96. Lawyer, Winston-Salem, N. C.

Pelton, Chas. Rexford, D.D.S., '10. Dentist, Keith Bldg., Beaumont, Tex.

Pelzman, Frederick M., LL.B., '11. Lawyer, 723 6th St. N. W., Washington, D. C.

Pendergast, Robert Joseph, A.B., '05. Lawyer, 59 S. First St., Fulton, N. Y.

Pendleton, Forrest C., LL.B., '08. Department of Justice, Washington, D. C.

Penichet, J. Marion, M.D., '09. Oculist, Mercedes Hospital, Lealdad 81, Havana, Cuba.

Pennington, Polk K., LL.B., '95; LL.M., '96. A. G. O., War Department, Washington, D. C.

Pennybacker, Isaac S., LL.B., '97. Department of Agriculture, Washington, D. C.

Pennybacker, Jas. Edmund, LL.B., '99. Chief, Road Management, U. S. Office Public Roads, Department of Agriculture, 3151 17th St. N. W., Washington, D. C.

Pentecost, Wm. Chester, LL.B., '02. Lawyer, Knox, Ind.

Perkins, Louis L., LL.B., '90; LL.M., '91. Special Representative Empire State Surety Co., Bond Bldg., Washington, D. C.

Perrier, Casimir E., D.D.S., '10. Dentist, 186 Fountain St., Pawtucket, R. I.

Perry, David B., LL.B., '98; LL.M., '99. Pension Office, Washington, D. C.

Perry, Frank Sprigg, LL.B., '02. Lawyer, Bond Bldg., Washington, D. C.

Perry, Frederick Chas., D.D.S., '05. Dentist, *Washington, D. C.

Perry, R. Ross, Jr., LL.B., '94; LL.M., '95. Lawyer, Fendall Bldg., Washington, D. C.

Perry, Richard Ross, A.B., '64; A.M., '65; LL.D., '92. Lawyer, 1635 Massachusetts Ave., Washington, D. C.

Perskin, Israel, LL.B., '07. Lawyer, 189 Montague St., Brooklyn, N. Y.

Peters, Joseph W., LL.B., '12; L.D.M., '12. Bureau of Mines, Interior Department, Washington, D. C.; St. Louis, Mo.

Pettey, R. Moulton, LL.B., '12. Navy Department, Washington, D. C.; Alexandria, Va.

Petteys, C. V., M.D., '73. Physician, 1822 12th St. N. W., Washington, D. C.

Pettijohn, J. W., M.D., '64. Physician, Hoyt, Kans.

Pettis, Hugh S., LL.B., '10. Department of Commerce and Labor, 1724 Corcoran St. N. W., Washington, D. C.

Peyser, Julius I., LL.B., '99. Lawyer, 705 G St. N. W., Washington, D. C.

Pfirman, Franklin, LL.M., '04. Lawyer, Wallace, Idaho.

Phelan, Francis M., A.M., '95. Lawyer, 73 Tremont St., Boston, Mass.

Phelan, Wm. J., LL.B., '08. Lawyer, New Britain, Conn.

Philbin, Edw. T., LL.B., '08. Lawyer, 311 William St., Scranton, Pa.

Phillips, Edmund Lawrence, A.B., '97. Baltimore, Md.

Phillips, Frederick E., LL.B., '98; LL.M., '99. Lawyer, Tuscola, Ill.

Phillips, Lewis H., LL.M., '94. Lawyer, *Girard, Kans.

Phillips, Robert L., LL.M., '95. Lawyer, *Marshall, Ill.

Pickens, Alvin H., LL.B., '87. Lawyer, 708 Ernest & Cranmer Bldg., Denver, Colo.

Pickett, Theodore J., LL.B., '87; LL.M., '88. Lawyer, Bond Bldg., Washington, D. C.

Pierce, Albert S., M.D., '67. Physician and Surgeon, 611 N. 20th St., Omaha, Nebr.

Pierce, Henry Fletcher, LL.B., '04. Lawyer, 1315 Meridian St. N. W., Washington, D. C.

Pierce, Jas. Madigan, A.B., '11. Merchant, Houlton, Me.

Pierce, Thos. Murray, Jr., A.B., '98. Lawyer, Attorney for Terminal Co., care Boyce & Priest, 1207 Bank of Commerce Bldg., St. Louis, Mo.

Pierce, Wm. P., LL.B., '73. Lawyer, *Georgia.

Pierce, Wm. Perry, LL.B., '79; LL.M., '80. Lawyer, *Georgia.

Pierson, Henry C., M.D., '68. Physician, Roselle, N. J.

Pike, Albert H., LL.B., '07; LL.M., '08. Special Attorney, Department of Justice; 1106 Fidelity Bldg., Baltimore, Md.

Pilon, Rev. Joseph A., A.M., '06. Winter, Wis.

Pimper, Harry K., LL.B., '09. Southern Ry. Co., 1302 30th St. N. W., Washington, D. C.

Pirtle, Wm. J., LL.B., '99; LL.M., '00. Lawyer, Council Bluffs, Kans.

Pitts, Geo. B., LL.B., '04. Patent Lawyer, Ouray Bldg., Washington, D. C.

Pitts, W. Stanley, M.D., '92. Q. M. Dept., U. S. A., New York City.

Pless, Wm. A., LL.M., '95. Lawyer, Knoxville, Tenn.

Poland, John A., A.M., '92; LL.B., '92. Lawyer, Ross County Block, Chillicothe, Ohio.

Poland, Nicholas Albert, LL.B., '98; LL.M., '99. Lawyer, Chillicothe, Ohio.

Polk, Jas. K., LL.B., '90; LL.M., '91. Lawyer, 1406 Irving St., Washington, D. C.

Pollock, Geo. F., LL.M., '87. Lawyer, Bond Bldg., Washington, D. C.

Pool, Solomon C., LL.B., '97; LL.M., '98. New York City Ry., 21 Park Row, New York City.

Porrata, Nestor Rivera, D.D.S., '06. Surgeon Dentist, San German, Porto Rico.

Porter, Henry C., M.D., '69. Physician, *New York City.

Porter, John Waterman, M.D., '68. Physician, *Illinois.

Posey, Fabian, LL.B., '01. Lawyer and Editor of the Examiner, Police Magistrate, Frederick, Md.

Posey, Orlando J., M.D., '12. Physician, 516 Seward Square S. E., Washington, D. C.

Posey, Richard B., LL.B., '95. Meridian Life Ins. Co., Indianapolis, Ind.

Postley, Chas. E., M.D., '91. Physician, Bureau of Indian Affairs, Washington, D. C.

Potbury, Jesse E., LL.B., '96; LL.M., '97. Lawyer, 601-605 Evans Bldg., Washington, D. C.

Potts, Louis Joseph, A.M., '98; Ph.D., '99; LL.B., '99; LL.M., '00. Lawyer, 201 Montague St., Brooklyn, N. Y.

Poulton, Wm. E., M.D., '64. Physician, 227 4½ St. S. W., Washington, D. C.

Poulton, Wm. E., LL.B., '92; LL.M., '93. Lawyer, 307 C St. N. W., Washington, D. C.

Powell, Benjamin F., LL.B., '97. Lawyer, *Washington State.

Powell, Fred H., LL.B., '11. War Department, Washington, D. C.; Sehenectady, N. Y.

Powell, Jas. L., LL.B., '07; LL.M., '08. Lawyer, Muskogee, Okla.

Powell, Wm. F., LL.B., '10. Lawyer, 317 John Marshall Place N. W., Washington, D. C.

Powell, Wilson A., LL.B., '12. Census Department, Washington, D. C.; Tanners Creek, Va.

Power, Chas. Benton, A.B., '88. Land and Live Stock Investments, Helena, Mont.

Power, Jas. Harrison, A.M., '98. Broker, University Club, Albany, N. Y.

Power, John Merlin, A.B., '11. Rancher, Helena, Mont.

Power, J. Neal, A.B., '95; LL.B., '97. Lawyer, 250 Montgomery St., San Francisco, Cal.

Powers, Edward Parnell, M.D., '05. Physician, 1611 Tremont St., Boston, Mass.

Powers, John S., LL.B., '11; L.D.M., '11. Lawyer, 1421 Columbia Road, Washington, D. C.

Prendergast, Jere M., S.J., A.B., '89; A.M., '92. Professor, Brooklyn College, Brooklyn, N. Y.

Prescott, Chas. C., LL.B., '91; LL.M., '92. Broker, 1019 Linden Ave., Wilmette, Ill.

Price, John G., LL.B., '05. Assistant Prosecuting Attorney, Court House, Columbus, Ohio.

. **Price, Robert E., LL.B., '10.** Department of Commerce and Labor, 715 Gresham Place, Washington, D. C.

Prince, Sidney R., LL.B., '98. General Counsel, Mobile & Ohio Ry., Mobile, Ala.

Pritchard, Henry T., LL.B., '99. Westinghouse E. & M. Co., Pittsburgh, Pa,

Pritchard, Howard Dallas, LL.B., '02. Lawyer, Assistant Manager American Surety Co., Garfield Bldg., Cleveland, Ohio.

Pugh, Henry L., LL.B., '90. Lawyer, 1024 Bennett Block, Baltimore, Md.

Pugh, Jas. L., Jr., LL.B., '84; LL.M., '85. Judge Police Court, 3402 Mount Pleasant St., Washington, D. C.

Pugh, Hon. John C., L.B., '88. Lawyer, Judge, Tenth Judicial Circuit, 1011 Crescent Ave., Birmingham, Ala.

Pugh, Ronald W., LL.B., '09. Lawyer, Vanceburg, Ky.

Pulskamp, Bernard, M.D., '90. Physician, Kneipp Sanatarium, Rome City, Ind.

Purcell, Robert E., LL.B., '11; LL.M., '12; L.D.M., '12. War Department, Washington, D. C.; Monticello, N. Y.

Purman, Louis C., M.D., '91. Postoffice Department, Washington, D. C.

Pye, Jas. B., A.M., '67. *Texas.

Q

Quay, John B., M.D., '93. Physician, 273 N St. N. W., Washington, D. C.

Quicksall, Wm. F., A.B., '61; A.M., '72; LL.B., '72. Lawyer, 1426 New York Ave., Washington, D. C.

Quigley, Edward T., LL.B., '05. Chief Clerk, Solicitor's Office, Department of Commerce and Labor, Washington, D. C.

Quigley, Francis Leo., M.D., '04. Physician, Wallace, Idaho.

Quigley, Frank, LL.B., '12. Lawyer, Columbus, Ohio.

Quinlan, Edward S., LL.B., '12. Lawyer, 72 K St. N. W., Washington, D. C.

Quinlan, Geo. Austin, A.B., '02. Civil Engineer, Chicago, Ill.

Quinlan, Richard J., A.B., '63. St. Mary's Church, Holliston, Mass.

Quinn, Edwin L., LL.B., '02. Lawyer, *Cambridge, Mass.

Quinn, Fred A., LL.B., '10. Lawyer, 158 E. Bissell Ave., Oil City, Pa.

Quinn, Harry I., LL.B., '04; LL.M., '05. Lawyer, Century Bldg., Washington, D. C.

Quinn, Jas. Henry, M.D., '07. Physician, 52 E. Quincy St., North Adams, Mass.

Quinn, John, LL.B., '98. Lawyer, 31 Nassau St., New York City.

Quinn, John A., LL.B., '09; LL.M., '10. Lawyer, 806 E St. S. W., Washington, D. C.

Quinn, Joseph Gray, A.B., '04. Little Rock, Ark.

Quinter, Hubert R., LL.B., '12. Lawyer, 1313 Irving St. N. W., Washington, D. C.

Quinter, Ralph De Shields, LL.B., '08; LL.M., '09. Lawyer (G. U. Law Fac.), Century Bldg., Washington, D. C.

R

Rabbett, Jas. Aloysius, M.D., '00. Physician, Elkins, W. Va.

Raby, St. Geo. R., LL.B., '10. Lithographic Map Engraver, U. S. G. S., 1513 Meridian St. N. W., Washington, D. C.

Rafferty, William V., LL.B., '12. Lawyer, Plainfield, N. J.

Ragan, Gillum T., M.D., '66. Physician, Neoga, Ill.

Ragan, John J., LL.B., '11. Government Printing Office, 55 Randolph Place N. W., Washington, D. C.; Indianapolis, Ind.

Rager, Wm. H., LL.M., '07. Lawyer, *Frederick, Md.

Rague, Chas. W. S., LL.B., '08. Lawyer, 41 Wall St., New York City.

Rainey, Francis H., A.B., '63; LL.B., '74. Chief Clerk, M. O. Division, Postoffice Department, Washington, D. C.

Ralston, Jackson Harvey, LL.B., '76. Lawyer, Union Savings Bank, Washington, D. C.

Ramage, Joseph C., LL.B., '99. .LL.M., '00. Supt. of Tests, Southern Ry., Alexandria, Va.

Ramos, Joaquin, LL.B., '07. High School Teacher, Tarlac, P. I.

Ramsdell, Geo. P., M.D., '69. Physician, *Newton, Mass.

Randall, Thos. G., LL.B., '89. Lawyer, *Osage City, Kans.

Randle, Edward Thos., LL.B., '03. Lawyer, Wilson Bldg., Dallas, Tex.

Raney, Roscoe J., LL.B., '04. Statistician, 660 West 180th St., New York City.

Rankin, John M., LL.B., '85; LL.M., '87. Lawyer, Maryland Bldg., and 1903 Kalorama Road, Washington, D. C.

Ransom, Stacy A., M.D., '98. Physician, Medical Officer, U. S. Consulate General., Shanghai, China.

Rask, Henry Geo., LL.B., '96. Real Estate, Jamestown, N. Y.

Rasmussen, Clyde, LL.B., '12; L.D.M., '12. General Land Office, Washington, D. C.; Ephraim, Utah.

Rattigan, Michael A., LL.B., '11. General Land Office, Washington, D. C.; Providence, R. I.

Rauterberg, Louis E., M.D., '67. Physician, The Farragut, Washington, D. C.

Ray, Chas. B., A.B., '72. *Louisiana.

Ray, J. Enos, Jr., LL.B., '96; LL.M., '97. Lawyer, 416 5th St. N. W., Washington, D. C.; Chillum, Md.

Rea, Geo. W., LL.B., '90; LL.M., '91. Patent Lawyer, McGill Bldg., Washington, D. C.

Ready, Michael J., A.B., '01; M.D., '05. Physician, 3325 N St., Washington, D. C.

Reagan, Francis Chas., A.M., '01; LL.B., '03. Lawyer, Lowman Bldg., Seattle, Wash.

Reavis, Wade, LL.B., '02. Lawyer, *Hamptonville, N. C.

Reddington, Cornelius T., LL.B., '11. Lawyer, Jessup, Pa.

Reddy, Anthony Cosgrove, A.M., 94. Lawyer, 96 Pleasant St., Malden, Mass.

Redmond, Edward J., LL.B., '90; LL.M., '91. Lawyer, McGill Bldg., Washington, D. C.

Redrow, Walter L., LL.B., '04. Assistant Examiner, Patent Office, Washington, D. C.

Reedy, Frank H., LL.B., '07. Lawyer, Long Meadow, Mass.

Reese, Hon. Henry F., LL.B., '85; LL.M., '88. State Senator, Selma, Ala.

Reeside, Frank Palton, LL.B., '94. Secretary, Equitable Co-Operative Building Association, 915 F St. N. W., Washington, D. C.

Reeve, Jesse N., M.D., '93. Physician, 926 17th St.N. W., Washington, D. C.

Reeves, Isaac, Stockton K., M.D., '03. Assistant Surgeon, U. S. Navy, care Navy Department, Washington, D. C.

Reeves, John R. T., LL.B., '05. Department of Interior, Indian Affairs, Washington, D. C.

Reeves, Wm. P., M.D., '99. Physician, The Congressional, 100 E. Capitol St., Washington, D. C.

Regan, Ralston Byrnes, D.D.S., '04. Dentist, 601-602 City Bank, Mobile, Ala.

Regar, Robert S., LL.B., '12. Postoffice Department, Washington, D. C.; Lancaster, Pa.

Regli, J. A. S., M.D., '02. Physician, San Jose, Cal.

Reid, Chas. C., LL.B., '11. Examiner, Patent Bureau, Washington, D. C.; Hamilton, Ohio.

Reid, Geo. Conrad, A.B., '02.; LL.B., '05. Lawyer (G. U. Law Fac.), 2011 Columbia Road, Washington, D. C.

Reid, John, A.B., '49; A.M., '51. *Maryland.

Reidt, Urban H., M.D., '06. Physician, 402 Clay Ave., Jeanette, Pa.

Reiley, Harold Aloysius, S.J., A.B., '03. Los Gatos, Cal.

Reilly, Chas. Joseph, A.B., '11. G. U. Med. Student, The Alabama, Washington, D. C.; Wheeling, W. Va.

Reilly, Ellsworth F. J., A.B., '08. Stockman, 204 N. 34th St., Billings, Mont.

Reilly, Henry Francis, A.M., '89; Ph.D., '97; LL.B., '97; LL.M., '98. Lawyer, 389 Broadway, Milwaukee, Wis.

Reilly, J. Forrest, LL.B., '12. Lawyer, 1729 U St. N. W., Washington, D. C.

Reilly, John V., M.D., '06. Physician, 33 Tremont St., Rochester, N. Y.

Reilly, Joseph A., D.D.S., '05. Dentist, Kansas City Athletic Club, Kansas City, Mo.

Reisinger, Emory Wm., M.D., '93. Physician (G. U. Med. Fac.), 1228 16th St., Washington, D. C.

Remus, Ramon Eduardo, A.M., '98. Guadalajara, Mex.

Repetti, Frederick Francis, M.D., '95. Physician, 149 B St. S. E., Washington, D. C.

Repetti, Frederick F., Jr., LL.B., '07. Real Estate and Insurance, 149 B St. S. E., Washington, D. C.

Repetti, John Joseph, M.D., '97. Physician, 404 Seward Square, Washington, D. C.

Rex, Thos. A., M.D., '65. Physician, 1423 St. Andrew's Place, Los Angeles, Cal.

Reyes, Rio, LL.B., '09. Lawyer, 389 Calle Read, Paco, P. I.

Reynard, Walter A., M.D., '07. Physician, 347 Atlantic St., Stamford-Conn.

Reynolds, Edward C., LL.M., '86. Lawyer, 31½ Exchange St., Portland, Me.

Reynolds, Geo. E., M.D., '06. Physician and Surgeon, 334 North St., Pittsfield, Mass.

Reynolds, Walter B., M.D., '74. Physician, 13 Trinity Place, Williamsport, Pa.

Reynolds, Wm. C., LL.B., '88; LL.M., '89. Merchant, Mesilla, N. M.

Reynolds, Wm. E., LL.B., '92; LL.M., '93. Captain U. S. Revenue Service, Treasury Department, Washington, D. C., Montgomery Co., Md.

Rhoads, Wm. L., LL.M., '07. Postoffice Department, 3800 8th St. N. W., Washington, D. C.

Rhodes, Eugene, LL.M., '94. Lawyer, Nashville, Tenn.

Rice, Chas. Edward, LL.B., '80. Auditor's Office, Treasury Bldg., Winder Bldg., Kensington, Md.

Rice, Frederick J., LL.B., '10. .Lawyer, 313 John Marshall Place, Washington, D. C.

Rice, Jas. Willie, A.B., '50; A.M., '53. *Maryland.

Rice, Nathan E., M.D., '80. Physician, *California.

Rice, William R., LL.B., '08. Business, 17 Battery Place, New York City.

Rich, John S., LL.M., '87. Lawyer, *Rochester, N. Y.

Rich, Thos. C., M.D., '69. Physician, *Newcastle, Ind.

Rich, William Jas., LL.B., '98; LL.M., '99. Principal Examiner, U. S. Patent Office, Washington, D. C.

Richards, Alfred, M.D., '97. Physician (G. U. Med. Fac.), The Seward, Seward Square S. E., Washington, D. C.

Richardson, Frederick D., LL.B., '08. Lawyer, Fairfax, Va.

Richmond, Chas. Wallace, M.D., '97. Assistant Curator, Division Birds, U. S. Nat. Museum, Washington, D. C.

Richmond, Elbert E., LL.B., '96; LL.M., '97. Treasury Department; 202 12th. St. S. E., Washington, D. C.

Richmond, Jas. A., LL.B., '03. Lawyer, 520 E St. N. E., Washington, D. C.

Richmond, John Albert, A.M., '05. Lawyer, First Assistant City Solicitor, Covington, Ky.

Richmond, Paul, M.D., '92. Postoffice Department, Washington, D. C.

Ridgely, Harry S., LL.B., '96; LL.M., '97. Lawyer, Department of Justice, 1452 Newton St. N. W., Washington, D. C.

Ridgeway, Albert B., A.B., '07; LL.B., '10. Private Secretary, Department of Justice, Chevy Chase, Md.

Ridgway, Franz H., LL.B., '01. Assistant Secretary, Corcoran Fire Ins. Co., Pharmacist, 604 11th St. N. W., Washington, D. C.

Ridgway, Roscoe Allen, A.B., '10. Law Student, Chevy Chase, Md.

Rieckelmann, John, A.B., '56; A.M., '59. *Ohio.

Riley, Benjamin C., M.D., '52. Physician, *Washington, D. C.

Riley, Harry B., D.D.S., '07. Dentist, 4509 Wisconsin Ave. N. W., Washington, D. C.

Riley, John F., LL.B., '73. Lawyer, *Washington, D. C.

Ring, John, LL.B., '01. Lawyer, *407 Pearl St., New York City.

Riordon, J. Allen, LL.B., '04. General Claim Agent, Norfolk & Washington Steamboat Co., 627 7th St. N. E., Washington, D. C.

Risque, F. W., A.B., '71. Accountant, 4021 Morgan St., St. Louis, Mo.

Ristine, John C., LL.B., '12. War Department, Washington, D. C.; Philadelphia, Pa.

Ritchie, Abner Cloud, A.B., '98. Lawyer, Fairfax, Va.

Riverva, Pascual, M.D., '12. Physician, San German, Porto Rico.

Rivera, Rafael R., LL.B., '12. Lawyer, Coamo, Porto Rico.

Rivera-Pagan, Pedro M., M.D., '04. Physician, Morovis, Porto Rico.

Rix, Carl B., LL.B., '03; LL.M., '04. Lawyer (Law Fac. Marquette University), 833 Wells Bldg., Milwaukee, Wis.

Roach, Chas. Edward, A.B., '95; LL.B., '97; LL.M., '98. Lawyer (G. U. Law Fac.), Metzerott Bldg., Washington, D. C.

Roach, Francis deSales, A.B., '07; LL.B., '10. Real Estate and Col. Title Ins. Co., 1751 Willard St. N. W., Washington, D. C.

Roach, Wm. Nathaniel, Jr., A.B., '96; LL.B., '98. Patent Lawyer, Metzerott Bldg., Washington, D. C.

Roane, Jas., M.D., '82. Physician, Yankton, S. D.

Roane, Samuel B., LL.M., '86. Assistant Examiner, Patent Office, 29 Bryant St. N. W., Washington. D. C.

Robbins, Ansel Jerome, M.D., '91. Physician, 304 Main St., Jamestown, N. Y.

Robbins, Thos. A., LL.M., '87. Postoffice Department, 1015 N St. N. W., Washington, D. C.

Roberts, Chas. Francis, LL.B., '94; LL.M., '95. Notary and Insurance, 2253 Mount View Place, Anacostia, D. C.

Roberts, E. E., M.D., '94. Physician, 125 Maple Ave., Anacostia, D. C.

Roberts, Thos. W., LL.B., '91; LL.M., '92. Lawyer, *Tuscola, Ill.

Roberts, William, M.D., '94. Physician, England.

Robertson, Frederick C., LL.B., '89. Lawyer, Hyde Block, Spokane, Wash.

Robertson, Samuel A., A.M., '70. *Tennessee.

Robinson, Aquilla T., Jr., LL.B., '10. Lawyer, Brandywine, Md.

Robinson, Thos., M.D., '76. Physician, 1356 Emerson St., Washington, D. C.

Roche, Chas. H., A.B., '86. *St. Louis, Mo.

Roche, Peter A., A.M., '91. 701 James St., Syracuse, N. Y.

Rodgers, Chas. H., LL.B., '09. Accountant, Department of Commerce and Labor, 1348 Meridian Place N. W., Washington, D. C.

Rodrique, A., M.D., '71. Physician, *Pennsylvania.

Rogers, Francis Joseph, D.D.S., '10. Dentist, Kenois Bldg., Washington, D. C.

Rogers, Frank Leo., A.B., '03. Lawyer, 69 Borden St., New Bedford, Mass.

Rogers, Hamilton, LL.B., '02. Lawyer, 31 Nassau St., New York City.

Rogers, Jas. Chas., LL.B., '86. Lawyer, 344 D St. N. W., Washington, D. C.

Rogers, Jas. W., D.D.S., '12. Dentist, 5 Newbury St., Worcester, Mass.

Rogers, Thos. Mitchell, LL.B., '98. Lawyer, *St. Louis, Mo.

Romadka, Chas. Aloysius, A.B., '95; A.M., '96. Mining, Douglas, Ariz.

Romadka, Francis Joseph, A.M., '01. Manufacturer and Salesman, 132 20th St., Milwaukee, Wis.

Romaine, Frank Wm., M.D., '05. Physician, 2633 Adams Mill Road, Washington, D. C.

Roman, Richard, LL.B., '77. Lawyer, *Illinois.

Rondeau, Frederick P., LL.B., '10; LL.M., '11. Lawyer, 418-419 Yeon Bldg., Portland, Ore.

Ronning. Hon. Henry T., LL.M., '02. Judge of Probate Court, Pope County, Minn., Glenwood, Minn.

Rooney, Chas. Daniels, A.B., '87; A.M., '89; LL.B., '95; LL.M., '96. Editor, care Herald-Traveler, Boston, Mass.

Roosa, Frank M., LL.B., '10. Assistant U. S. Attorney Southern District of New York, 2049 7th Ave., New York City.

Rorke, Alexander I., LL.B., '04. Lawyer, 2 Rector St., 214 W. 82d St., New York City.

Rosell, Claude A., LL.B., '86. Patent Lawyer, 26 W. 27th St., New York City.

Rosenberg, Maurice D., LL.B., '96; LL.M., '97. Lawyer, Cor. 7th and E Sts., Washington, D. C.

Rosenthal, Sidney H., D.D.S., '12. Dentist, 3124 M St. N. W., Washington, D. C.

Ross, John R., A.B., '72; A.M., '89. Lawyer, Calle Cuba 24, Havana, Cuba.

Ross, Ralph H., M. D., '91. U. S. Indian Service, Pine Ridge, S. D.

Ross, Tenney, LL.B., '95. Instructor, Captain 3d Regiment U. S. Infantry, Manila, P. I.

Rost, Hon. Emile, A.B., '57; A.M., '60; LL.D., '89. Planter, 521 Godchaux Bldg., New Orleans, La.

Roth, Joseph A., LL.B., '04. Lawyer, 412 5th St. N. W., Washington, D. C.

Rothschild, David, LL.B., '02. Lawyer, 412 5th St. N. W., Washington, D. C.

Rover, Leo A., LL.B., '10. Lawyer, 49 I St. N. W., Washington, D. C.

Rowdybush, Chas. Reeves, LL.M., '10. Lawyer, Kensington, Md.

Rowland, Hugh B., LL.B., '97; LL.M., '98. Lawyer, 705 Colorado Bldg., Washington, D. C.

Roy, Rodolphe G., LL.B., '11. Lawyer, 240 Lisbon St., Lewiston, Me.

Roys, Chase, M.D., '67. Lawyer, 631 F St. N. W., Washington, D. C.

Royston, J. Perry, LL.B., '99. Lawyer, *Culpepper, Va.

Rudd, John S., A.M., '58. *Virginia.

Rudd, Thos. S., A.B., '64; A.M., '66. Louisville, Ky.

Rudge, William H., A.B., '93. 234 W. Wood St., Youngstown, Ohio.

Ruff, John A., M.D., '64. Physician, *Maryland.

Ruffin, Thos., LL.B., '96; LL.M., '97. Lawyer, Southern Bldg., Washington, D. C.

Ruffner, Chas. E., LL.B., '09. Lawyer, 330 Indiana Ave., Manassas, Va.

Rupli, J. Theodore, LL.B., '94; LL.M., '95. Lawyer, 1405 F St. N. W., Washington, D. C.

Russell, Alfred Murray, A.B., '03; M.D., '08. Physician, 1726 M St. N. W., and 1412 15th St. N. W., Washington, D. C.

Russell, Bert, LL.B., '06. Assistant Examiner of Patents, Patent Office, Washington, D. C.

Russell, Hon. Chas. W., LL.B., '83; LL.M., '84. Minister to Persia, Teheran, Persia.

Russell, Edward O., A.B., '79; LL.B., '81; LL.M., '82; A.M., '89. Lawyer, Nanzanola, Colo.

Russell, Geo. M., LL.B., '87. Lawyer, *Philadelphia, Pa.

Russell, Henry M., A.B., '69; A.M., '71. Lawyer, 300 S. Front St., Wheeling, W. Va.

Ruth, Chas. H., LL.B., '95. Lawyer, *District of Columbia.

Rutherford, Robt. Gedney, Jr., LL.B., '99. First Lieutenant, 24th U. S. Infantry, Madison Barracks, N. Y.

Ryan, Jas. A., LL.B., '96; LL.M., '97. Lawyer, *Nashville, Tenn.

Ryan, Jas. H., LL.B., '04. Chamber of Commerce, Chicago, Ill.

Ryan, John McNulty, A.B., '93. *Galena, Ill.

Ryan, Patrick J., LL.B., '94. Lawyer, 212 F St. N. W., Washington, D. C.

Ryan, Wm. D., Jr., LL.B., '10; LL.M., '11. Lawyer, 820 Commerce Bldg., Kansas City, Mo.

Ryder, Thos. J., LL.B., '85; LL.M., '86. Lawyer, Avenida Juarez, No. 94, Apartado 1203, Mexico, D. F.

S

Sacks, John, LL.B., '10. Government Clerk, 3318 N St. N. W., Washington, D. C.

Sage, Merton W., LL.B., '12; L.D.M., '12. Bureau of Patents, Washington, D. C.; Medford, Mass.

St. Clair, Francis Alphonzo, M.D., '90. Physician, 1319 T St., Washington, D. C.

Salomon, Joseph, LL.B., '97; LL.M., '98. Lawyer, 416 5th St. N. W., Washington, D. C.

Sanders, Charles H., M.D., '12. Garfield Hospital, Washington, D. C.

Sanders, Scott, LL.M., '12; L.D.M., '12. Lawyer, 714 18th St. N. W.; Washington, D. C.

Sanders, William A., A.B., '57. *Panama, R. P.

Sands, Francis P. B., A.B., '61; A.M., '68. Lawyer, 1416 F St. N. W., Washington, D. C.

Sands, William Franklin, A.B., '96; LL.B., '96. Care Apeyer & Co., 24 Pine St., New York City.

Sanford, Joseph L., M.D., '92. First Lieutenant U. S. Army, Medical Department, Clifton Station, Clifton, Va.

Sanger, Monie, LL.B., '12. 1710 U St. N. W., Washington, D. C.

Sargent, Lester L., LL.B., '10; LL.M., '11; L.D.M., '11. Lawyer, 21 Keeley St., Haverhill, Mass.

Saul, John Aloysius, L.L.B., '91; LL.M., '92. Lawyer, Fendall Bldg., Washington, D. C.

Saunders, Joseph N., LL.B., '91; LL.M., '92. Lawyer, 412 5th St. N. W., Washington, D. C.

Sawtelle, Henry W., M.D., '68. Surgeon, Marine Hospital Service, 3917 14th St. N. W., Washington, D. C.

Sawyer, Glen R., LL.B., '03. Lawyer and Prosecuting Attorney, 514 S. Main St., Elkhart, Ind.

Scanlan, Andre Christie, A.M., '95. Real Estate and Insurance, 2756 E. First St., Long Beach, Cal.

Scanlan, Rev. Michael James, A.M., '96. Director of Cath. Charities, Cathedral, Boston, Mass.

Scanlon, Edward, LL.B., '98; LL.M., '99. Journalist, 1340 8th St. N. W., Washington, D. C.

Schaake, Frederick W., D.D.S., '06. Dentist, 23 Bradford St., Lawrence, Mass.

Schade, Frederick, LL.B., '98; LL.M., '99. Lawyer, Spokane, Wash.

Schaus, James Peter, A.M., '93; LL.B., '94. Cor. West and Bird Ave., Buffalo, N. Y.

Schellberg, Leonard E., LL.B., '11. Interstate Commerce Commission, Washington, D. C.; Hawaii.

Scheller, Thomas K., A.B., '06; LL.B., '09. Lawyer, Trust Co. Bldg., 403 N. Main St., Chambersburg, Pa.

Schick, James P., LL.B., '09. Lawyer, Evans Bldg., Washington, D. C.

Schildroth, Henry T., M.D., '93. Physician, 1707 First St. N. E., Washington, D. C.

Schladt, Howard A.; LL.B., '12. Lawyer, Philadelphia, Pa.

Schlafly, James Joseph, A.M., '07; LL.B., '09. Com. Paper and Bond Business, 4532 Westminster Place, St. Louis, Mo.

Schleimer, David, M.D., '73. Physician, Elizabeth, N. J.

Schlosser, Frank B., LL.B., '11. Lawyer, 3489 Holmead Place, Washington, D. C.

Schmaltz, Oscar J., LL.B., '07. Postoffice Department, 1357 Meridian St. N. W., Washington, D. C.

Schmidt, Oscar P., LL.B., '90; LL.M., '91. Lawyer, 516 9th St. N. W., Washington, D. C.

Schneider, Elwin Carl, M.D., '05. Physician, G, U. Hospital Dispensary, 1742 U St. N. W., Washington, D. C.

Schneider, Ferdinand Turton, LL.B., '99. Architect, 1314 F St. and 1006 Massachusetts Ave. N. W., Washington, D. C.

Scholz, William J., LL.B., '06; LL.M., '07. Lawyer, Saginaw, Mich.

Schott, G. J. VanVerbeck, M.D., '89. Surgeon, Passaic General Hospital, 125 Lexington Ave., Passaic, N. J.

Schoyer, George Shiras, M.D., '10. Physician, 421 N. Highland Ave., Pittsburgh, Pa.

Schreiber, Henry R., M.D., '07. Physician, G. U. Med. Fac., 657 H St. N. E., Washington, D. C.

Schreiner, Edmund, LL.B., '04. Assistant Chief of Division, Bureau of Census, Washington, D. C.

Schubert, Bernard F., LL.B., '99; LL.M., '00. President U. S. Esperanto Association, 1505 N. Capitol St., Washington, D. C.

Schuler, Harry R., LL.B., '02; LL.M., '03. Lawyer, Schaffner Bldg., Galion, Ohio.

Schulteis, Herman J., LL.M., '02. Lawyer, 609-610 Munsey Bldg., 1519 R St. N. W., Washington, D. C.

Schwartz, Edward M., LL.B., '12. Lawyer, 604 Massachusetts Ave. N. W., Washington, D. C.

Scott, Edgar B., LL.M., '09. Treasurer P. H. & M, H. S., Washington, D. C.; Norfolk, Va.

Scott, Oliver H. P., LL.B., '12; L.D.M., '12. Navy Department, Washington, D. C.; Edgefield, S. C.

Scott, Thomas Edward, A.M., '97. 425 S. Spring, Los Angeles, Cal.

Scott, Thomas W., LL.B., '96. Lawyer, *Washington, D. C.

Sears, Fulton H., LL.B., '96. Lawyer, 500 Journal Bldg., Chicago, Ill.

Seaton, Charles H., LL.B., '91; LL.M., '92. Department of Agriculture; Glencarlyn, Va.

Seawell, Chas. Washington, A.B., '85; LL.B., '86; LL.M., '87. Agriculture, Roanes, Va.

Seay, Hon. Harry L., LL.B., '94. Lawyer, Police and Fire Commissioner, Trust Bldg., Dallas, Texas.

Sebiakin-Ross, W., M.D., '81. Physician, Wladimer, Russia.

Sefton, Edwin, LL.B., '96. Lawyer, 149 Broadway, New York City.

Seger, William Thomas, A.B., '94. Pianos and Sheet Music, 237 W. 142 St., New York City.

Seitz, Charles J., LL.B., '05; LL.M., '06. Mining Engineer, Goldfield, Nev.

Seitz, Joseph William, A.B., '03; A.M., '04. Mining, Mount Vernon, N. Y.

Se Legue, C. Albert, LL.B., '09. General Land Office, Washington, D. C.; Logansport, Ind.

Semmes, Alexander Harry, A.B., '81. Lawyer, Department of Justice, Washington, D. C.

Semmes, Francis Joseph, A.B., '90. Warrenton, Va.

Senn, Hon. Chas. A., LL.B., '83. Judge, City Court, Birmingham, Ala.

Sessford, Charles E., LL.B., '95. Real Estate, American Security and Trust Co., Washington, D. C.

Sessford, Joseph S., M.D., '85. Physician, 1738 F St. N. W., Washington, D. C.

Settle, Tecumseh Gore, LL.B., 97; LL.M., '98. Lawyer and Editor, State Capitol, Nashville, Tenn.

Sewall, Eugene D., LL.B., '89; LL.M., '90. Principal Examiner, Patent Office, Washington, D. C.

Seward, William Brown, D.D.S., '10. Dentist, 310 W. Main St., Springfield, Ohio.

Shannon, Andrew C., LL.B., '95. General Manager, Silver Spring, Md.

Sharbaugh, Frank C., LL.B., '95. Lawyer, Ebensburg, Pa.

Sharitz, Boyd C., LL.B., '10. Lawyer, Huntington, W. Va.

Sharp, Edwin H., LL.B., '98. Lawyer, *Leon, Iowa.

Shaw, Charles O., LL.B., '09. Lawyer, Prince George County, Md.

Shaw, Clarence Edward, M.D., '01. Physician, 342 W. 4th St., Williamsport, Pa.

Shaw, Frank L., LL.B., 11. Lawyer, 718 Bay State Building, Lawrence, Mass.

Shaw, Herschel, LL.B., '11; L.D.M., '11. U. S. Senate, Washington, D. C.; Houlton, Me.

Shaw, Kenneth A., LL.B., '08; LL.M., '09. General Land Office, Washington, D. C.

Shea, Charles Augustus, A.B., '97. Lawyer, Nanticoke, Pa.

Shea, Rev. Edw. Morris, A.B., '98. Bayou La Batre, Ala.

Shea, Michael Ignatius, M.D., '04. Physician, City Physician and Chairman Board of Health, 20 Walnut St., Chicopee Falls, Mass.

Shea, Thomas J., A.B., '86. Commercial Traveler, 12 Florida Ave., Washington, D. C.

Shealy, Robert Preston, LL.B., '97; LL.M., '98. Lawyer, Colorado Bldg., Washington, D. C.; Chevy Chase, Md.

Shearer, Norman Lee, D.D.S., '11. Dentist, Kenosha, Wis.

Sheean, John A. Rawlins, LL.B., '99. Lawyer, *Anamosa, Iowa.

Sheehan, Dennis John, M.D., '04. Physician, Lowell, Vt.

Sheehan, John D., LL.B., '95. U. S. Land Office, Washington, D. C.

Sheehy, Francis P., A.B., '93; LL.B., '95; LL.M., '96. Lawyer, 406 5th St. N. W., Washington, D. C.

Sheehy, Joseph C., LL.B., '02. Lawyer, Colorado Bldg., Washington, D. C.

Sheehy, Vincent Alphonsus, A.B., '93; LL.B., '95; LL.M., '96. Lawyer, 406 5th St. N. W., Washington, D. C.

Sheibley, Sinclair B., LL.B., '86; LL.M., '87. Assistant Attorney, Department of Justice, 815 Connecticut Ave. N. W., Washington, D. C.

Shekell, Abraham B., M.D., '63. Physician, 1529 Wisconsin Ave., Washington, D. C.

Shelse, Ronne C., LL.B., '12. War Department, The Balfour, Washington, D. C.

Shenners, Martin Joseph, LL.B., '03. Lawyer, 378 National Ave., Milwaukee, Wis.

Shepard, Hon. Seth, LL.D., '95. Chief Justice, Court of Appeals (G. U. Law Fac.), 1447 Massachusetts Ave. N. W., Washington, D. C.

Shepard, Seth, Jr., A.B., '04. Lawyer, 301 Wilson Bldg., Dallas, Texas.

Shepard, Hon. Walter W., LL.M., '94. Lawyer, Judge of Supreme Court, Atlantic Judicial Circuit of Georgia, Claxton, Ga.

Sheridan, Denis R., A.B., '64; A.M., '66. *Massachusetts.

Sheriff, A. Rothwell, LL.B., '92. Lawyer, *Washington, D. C.

Sherman, Rev. Thos. Ewing, S.J., A.B., '74. 413 W. 12th St., Chicago, Ill.

Sherman, Walter I., LL.B., '12. Census Bureau, Washington, D. C.; Mansfield, Mass.

Sherrill, Edgar Beverly, LL.B., '98; LL.M., '00. Lawyer, 1318 12th St. N. W., Washington, D. C.

Sherwood, Clarkson R., Jr., LL.B., '12. Deputy Marshal, Marshal's Office, Washington, D. C.

Shine, Henry L., LL.B., '11. Special Examiner, Department of Justice, Washington, D. C.; Needham Heights, Mass.

Shinn, George Curtis, LL.B., '03. Lawyer, 715 14th St. N. W., Washington, D. C.

Shipman, Andrew J., A.B., '78; A.M., '87; LL.D., '11. Lawyer, 37 Wall St., New York City.

Shipman, J. Bennett Carroll, A.B., '92. Atlas Bldg., San Francisco, Cal.

Shipp, E. Richard, LL.B., '95; LL.M., '96. Lawyer, Prosecuting Attorney, Natrona County, Casper, Natrona County, Wyo.

Shoemaker, Albert Edwin, B.S., '88; LL.B., '92; LL.M., '93. Lawyer, Columbian Bldg., Washington, D. C.; Bethesda, Md.

Shoemaker, F., M.D., '91. Physician, U. S. Indian Office, Railway Bldg., Denver, Colo.

Shoemaker, Louis P., LL.B., '80; LL.M., '81. Real Estate and Insurance, 220 Southern Bldg., Washington, D. C.

Sholes, Wm. H., LL.B., '87; LL.M., '88. Lawyer, Columbian Bldg., Washington, D. C.

Shomo, Harvey L., LL.B., '86; LL.M., '87. Lawyer, *Pennsylvania.

Short, Francis Jerome, M.D., '04. Physician, 738 E. 31st St., Brooklyn, N. Y.

Short, Wm. Henry, M.D., '04. P. A. Surgeon, U. S. Navy, Navy Department, Washington, D. C.; New York, N. Y.

Short, Wm. O., LL.B., '03. Clerk, 1000 M St. N. W., Washington, D. C.

Shreve, Benjamin, LL.B., '09. Lawyer, Sterling, Va.

Shriver, Joseph N., A.B., '06. With B. F. Shriver & Co., Westminster, Md.

Shugrue, Patrick, LL.B., '09; LL.M., '10. Lawyer, 1233 Massachusetts Ave. N. W., Washington, D. C.

Sibley, Geo. Julian, D.D.S., "11. Dentist, 816 14th St., Washington, D. C.

Sigmon, Jesse C., LL.B., '12. Lawyer, Newton, N. C.

Sillers, Albert, LL.B., '88. Lawyer, Stewart Bldg., Washington, D. C.

Sillers, Robert Fry, M.D., '90. Physician, 313 H St. N. W., Washington, D. C.

Simmons, Leo, LL.B., '90; LL.M., '91. Lawyer, 1416 F St. N. W., Washington, D. C.

Simon, Gerhard, A.B., '06; LL.B., '09. Manufacturer, 1320 Main St., Buffalo, N. Y.

Simons, H. N., LL.B., '85. Lawyer, *Lodi, Wis.

Simonton, John P., LL.B., '78. War Department, Washington, D. C.

Simonton, Vincent deP., LL.B., '01. Lawyer, 1774 Willard St. N. W., Washington, D. C.

Simpson, French C., LL.B., '10. Merchant, Alexandria, Va.

Sims, Chas., LL.B., '83; LL.M., '84. Lawyer, *New York City.

Sims, Erskine K., LL.B., '08. Lawyer, Indianola, Miss.

Sims, Grant, LL.M., '91. Lawyer, *Corydon, Ind.

Sinclair, A. Leftwich, LL.B., '93; LL.M., '94. Lawyer, Columbian Bldg., Washington, D. C.

Sinclair, J. McDonald, LL.B., '02. Isth, Can. Comm., Canal Zone.

Sincox, Glenn R., LL.B., '12. Lawyer, Garner, Iowa.

Singleton, Joseph Wilson, Ph.B., '88; LL.B., '88. Lawyer, 16-17 Ingram Block, Eau Claire, Wis.

Sink, Herbert O., LL.B., '12. Lawyer, Lexington, N. C.

Sisler, W. J. Lester, LL.B., '12. Lawyer, 1419 F St. N. W., Washington, D. C.

Sitterding, William H., A.B., '12. Lumber Business, 900 Floyd Ave., Richmond, Va.

Sizer, Adrian, LL.B., '01; LL.M., '02. Lawyer, Colorado Bldg., Washington, D. C.

Skerrett, Robert Gregg, LL.B., '91; LL.M., '12. Engineering, 15 William St., New York City.

Skinner, Geo. A., M.D., '68. Physician, *Indiana.

Slattery, Francis Edward, A.B., '96. Lawyer, 43 Tremont St., Boston, Mass.

Slattery, John R., A.B., '85. Physician, 520 Broadway, South Boston, Mass

Slattery, Philip A., LL.B., '06. Assistant City Counsellor, 1105 Henry St., St. Joseph, Mo.

Slaughter, Wm. D., LL.B., '93; LL.M., '94. Pension Office, 1428 Clifton St. N. W., Washington, D. C.

Slinder, Michael E., LL.B., '09; LL.M., '10. Lawyer, Y. M. C. A. Bldg., Washington, D. C.

Sloan, Robert Neal, A.B., '85. Capitalist, Stevenson, Md.

Slough, Martin, LL.B., '84. Lawyer, *Cincinnati, Ohio.

Smart, Arthur H., LL.B., '11. Lawyer, Council Grove, Kans.

Smart, Robert, M.D., '96. Physician, 307 Granger Bldg., San Diego, Cal.

Smart, Wm. M., M.D., '02. Captain, U. S. A., Fort Flagler, Wash.

Smith, Andrew T., LL.B., '06. Interstate Commerce Commission, 1343 Clifton St., Washington, D. C.

Smith, Antonio Justinian, A.B., '96; A.M., '97; LL.B., '98; LL.M., '99. Lawyer, 609 Law Bldg., Plume St., Norfolk, Va.

Smith, Augustine P., LL.B., '88. Lawyer, *Norwich, Conn.

Smith, B. Franklin, LL.M., '12; L.D.M., '12. War Department, Washington, D. C.; Biloxi, Miss.

Smith, Benjamin, M.D., '73. Physician, Doncaster, Md.

Smith, Chas. A., LL.B., '12; L.D.M., '12. Lawyer, 1416 Belmont St., Washington, D. C.

Smith, Chas. J., LL.B., '07. Lawyer, Milford, Mass.

Smith, Chas. P., LL.B., '82. Lawyer, *Washington, D. C.

Smith, Edward D., LL.B., '98. Lawyer, Birmingham, Ala.

Smith, E. Vincent, A.B., '95. Dry Goods, 298 Main St., Norfolk, Va.

Smith, Edmund R., A.B., '48. *New York.

Smith, Edward J., A.B., '01. Lawyer, Frederick, Md.

Smith, Edward Joseph, A.B., '01. Assistant City Attorney, 1706 West End Ave., Nashville, Tenn.

Smith, Ernest Renard, A.B., '91. 135 Freemason St., Norfolk, Va.

Smith, Francis T., A.M., '89. Editor, Pittsburgh, Pa.

Smith, Frank E., LL.B., '98; LL.M., '99. Lawyer, Hall of Records, New York City.

Smith, Giles W. L., LL.B., '93. Lawyer, County Attorney, Brewton, Ala.

Smith, Harlan S., M. D., '67. Physician, Schoolcraft, Mich.

Smith, Howard T., A.B., '08. Lawyer, 96 Plymouth Ave., Buffalo, N. Y.

Smith, Hugh F., LL.B., '12; L.D.M., '12. U. S. Senate Bldg., Washington, D. C.; Twin Falls, Idaho.

Smith, Hugh M., M.D., '88. Dep. Comm., Bureau of Fisheries, Washington, D. C.

Smith, Jas. Alexander, LL.B., '09. Deputy Tax Collector, Second District, Parish of New Orleans, 2504 Ursuline Ave., New Orleans, La.

Smith, Jas. F., LL.B., '89; LL.M., '90. Assistant Corporation Counsel, 1339 K St. N. W., Washington, D. C.

Smith, John Francis, A.B., '94. Lawyer, Frederick, Md.

Smith, Joseph Ernest, D.D.S., '08. Dentist, 631 Pennsylvania Ave. N. W., Washington, D. C.

Smith, Joseph S., M.D., '57. Physician, *Washington, D. C.

Smith, Jos. S. W., LL.B., '12. Lawyer, New Castle, Pa.

Smith, L. A., LL.B., '82; LL.M., '84. Attorney General, Minnesota, Montevideo, Minn.

Smith, Laurier E., LL.B., '07. Lawyer and Secretary of the Credit Exchange, Durango, Colo.

Smith, Lawrence Dick, A.B., '09. 1020 Kentucky St., Quincy, Ill.

Smith, Lucius, M.D., '59. Physician, *Ohio.

Smith, Peter D., A.B., '84. Lawyer, 222½ 4th St., Logansport, Ind.

Smith, Peter M., M.D., '94. Physician, 758 Tremont St., Boston, Mass.

Smith, Pinckney W., LL.B., '87. Lawyer, *Mattoon, Ill.

Smith, Robert E. L., LL.B., '95; LL.M., '96. Lawyer, Columbian Bldg., Washington, D. C.

Smith, Thos. C., M.D., '64. Physician, 1133 12th St. N. W., Washington, D. C.

Smith, Thos. S., A.B., '12. Merchant, 61 Green St., Hartford, Conn.

Smith, Thos. W., A.B., '01. Merchant, 1706 West End Ave., Nashville, Tenn.

Smith, Walter, A.B., '48. *Washington, D. C.

Smith, Will H., LL.B., '10. Lawyer, care Beckman & Smith, 422-424 Yeon Bldg., Portland, Ore.

Smith, Wm. Meredith, A.B., '00; M.D., '04. Physician, Frederick, Md.

Smithers, John T., LL.B., '10. Lawyer, Providence, R. I.

Smyth, Jas. J., LL.B., '92; LL.M., '93. Lawyer, Grand Junction, Tenn.

Snider, C. Vernon, LL.B., '09. Contractor and Builder, Carysbrook, Va.

Snider, Murray F., L.B., '12. Treasury Department, Washington, D. C.; Hamilton, Ohio.

Snow, Roswell W., LL.B., '09; LL.M., '10. Lawyer, 1323 Monroe St. N. W., Washington, D. C.

Snow, Wm. S., A.B., '61. *New Hampshire.

Snyder, Harold C., LL.B., '96. Captain, U. S. Marine Corps, care Headquarters, Washington, D. C.

Sohon, Frederick, M.D., '88. Physician, 512 I St. N. W., Washington, D. C.

Sohon, Henry W., A.M., '89; LL.B., '84; LL.M., '85. Lawyer, Fendall Bldg., Washington, D. C.

Solback, Leo Wm., D.D.S., '10. Dentist, 825 Vermont Ave. N. W., Washington, D. C.

Solignac, Gustave L, LL.B., '92. Lawyer, Santa Fe, N. M.

Solis, Frederic, A.M., '01. With Tropical Trading Co., 1002 Whitney Bldg., New Orleans, La.

Solomon, Chas. A., LL.B., '12. Department of Commerce and Labor, Washington, D. C.; Fall River, Mass.

Somers, Paul Joseph, A.M., '99; LL.B., '01. Lawyer, Milwaukee, Wis.

Soper, Julius S., A.B., '66; A.M., '67. *Washington, D. C.

Southoron, Levin Johnson, M.D., '96. Physician, Charlotte Hall, Md.

Sour, Louis, M.D., '55. Physician, *Washington, D. C.

Southerland, J. Julian, LL.B., '10. Office of Assistant Attorney General for Postoffice Department, Washington, D. C.

Spalding, Hughes, A.B., '08. Lawyer, Empire Bldg., Atlanta, Ga.

Spalding, Samuel E., M.D., '58. Physician, *Maryland.

Spangler, Wm. A., LL.B., '88; LL.M., '90. Lawyer, *Weatherford, Tex.

Sparks, Augustus R., M.D., '59. Physician, *Iowa.

Spear, Jas. M., LL.B., '91. Patent Lawyer, Victor Bldg., Washington, D. C.

Speiden, Clarence E., LL.B., '09; LL.M., '10. Navy Department, 525 9th St. N. E., Washington, D. C.

Speight, Jas. J., LL.B., '11. Jud. Com., Washington, D. C.; Eufaula, Ala.

Speer, Alexander M., LL.B., '91; LL.M., '92. General Land Office, Glenwood Springs, Colo

Spellacy, Thos. J., LL.B., '01. Lawyer and State Senator, 756 Main St., Hartford, Conn.

Spellisy, Dr. Joseph M., A.B., '85; A.M., '90. 110 S. 18th St., Philadelphia, Pa.

Spence, Gustavus B., LL.B., '12. Department of Agriculture, Washington, D. C.; Medway, Mass.

Spencer, Louis M., LL.B., '11; L.D.M., '11. Bureau of Patents, Washington, D. C.; Minica, Mich.

Spethman, Edward F., LL.B., '11; LL.M., '12; L.D.M., '12. Interstate Commerce Commission, Washington, D. C.; Omaha, Nebr.

Spiess, Louis A., LL.B., '07. Department of Commerce and Labor, Washington, D. C.

Spiller, Jas., LL.B., '09. Lawyer, 115 Broadway, New York City.

Spratt, Maurice Chas., A.B., '88. Lawyer, 77 W. Eagle St., Buffalo, N. Y.

Springer, Ruter W., LL.B., '89; LL.M., '90. Chaplain, U. S. A., Fort Caswell, N. C.

Sprinkle, Thos. H., LL.M., '93. Lawyer, *Charlotte, N. C.

Sproules, Dr. Joseph Aloysius, A.B., '95. .Physician, 1615 Tremont St., Boston, Mass.

Sprowls, Allen D., LL.B., '11. Treasury Department, Washington, D. C.; Washington, Pa.

Stack, Joseph C., LL.B., '04. Draftsman, 115 I St. N. W., Washington, D. C.

Stackhouse, Geo. M., LL.B., '98. Bureau of Navigation, Navy Department, Washington, D. C.

Stafford, Hon. Wendell P., LL.D., '07. Associate Justice of the Supreme Court, 1725 Lamont St., Washington, D. C.

Stagg, John Alfred, LL.B., '97; LL.M., '98. Lawyer, *New Orleans, La.

Staggers, John W., LL.M., '08. Lawyer, Montrose, Colo.

Staley, Chas. Melrose, LL.B., '87. U. S. Patent Office, Washington, D. C.

Staley, William F., LL.B., '92; LL.M., '93. Department of Agriculture, 411 Beck Bldg., Portland, Ore.

Stallings, Thos. B., LL.B., '05. Private Secretary, U. S. Senate, Washington, D. C.

Stanion, Ralph P., LL.B., '05. Superintendent Indian Reservation, Otoe, Okla.

Stansell, Wallace K., LL.B., '90; LL.M., '91. Lawyer, Cartersville, Ga.

Stanton, Lemuel J., LL.M., '87. U. S. Pension Bureau, Florida.

Stanton, Wm. Joseph, M.D., '11. G. U. Hospital, Washington, D. C.; West Barrington, R. I.

Starek, Emil, LL.B., '89; LL.M., '90. Patent Lawyer, 907 Chemical Bldg., St. Louis, Mo.

Starkweather, Carlton Lee, M.D., '98. Physician, Occoquan, Va.

Stearman, Mark, LL.M., '06. Lawyer, Columbian Bldg., Washington, D. C.

Stearns, Chas. P., LL.B., '12. Postoffice Department, Washington, D. C.; Culpepper, Va.

Stearns, John Sargent, M.D., '94. Physician, 1425 Rhode Island Ave. N. W., Washington, D. C.

Stebens, H. L., D.D.S., '12. Geesthacht a. d. Elbe, Bergedorferstr, Germany.

Stebbing, Ernest J., LL.B., '12. Lawyer, Congress Heights, Washington, D. C.

Stein, Joseph B., LL.B., '09; LL.M., '10. Lawyer, 454 D St. N. W., Washington, D. C.

Stein, Robert, M.D., '86. Chief of Bureau of Statistics, Department of Agriculture, 1335 F St. N. W., Washington, D. C.

Stelzner, Robert H., LL.B., '09. Indian Service, Shawnee, Okla.

Stephan, Anton, LL.B., '91; LL.M., '92. Lawyer, 816 14th St. N. W.,. Washington, D. C.

Stephens, F. Wilson, LL.B., '01. Lawyer, Huntington, W. Va.

Stephens, Jeremiah, LL.B., '12. Navy Department, Washington, D. C.; Havre de Grace, Md.

Stephens, John J., M.D., '68. Physician, *New York.

Stephens, Thos. A., A.B., '74. Merchant, 709 12th St., Washington, D. C.

Stephenson, Joseph Gwynn, M.D., '75. Physician, *Washington, D. C.

Sterling, Hugh M., LL.B., '91; LL.M., '92. Patent Lawyer, 1300 H St. N. W., Washington, D. C.

Stern, Samuel B., LL.B., '07. Lawyer, Roden Bldg., Birmingham, Ala.

Stetson, Chas. W., LL.B., '90; LL.M., '92. Lawyer, Vice-President Lawyers' Title Ins. Co., 3064 I St. N. W., Washington, D. C.

Stevens, Eugene E., L.B., '88; LL.M., '89. Patent Lawyer, 635 F St. N. W., Washington, D. C.

Stevens, Frank L., LL.B., '92; LL.M., '93. Lawyer, *Kansas City, Mo.

Stevenson, Chas., LL.B., '09. Lawyer, 826 Varnum St. N. W., Washington, D. C.

Stewart, Fenwick Joseph, A.B., '91. Fire Protection Engineer, 123 William St., New York City.

Stewart, John Frew, LL.M., '96. Lawyer, *Paintsville, Ky.

Stewart, William Walter, LL.B., '97; LL.M., '98. Lawyer, Stewart Bldg., Washington, D. C.

Stirewalt, Jacob P., LL.B., '06. Isth. Canal Commission, Canal Zone.

Stitt, Frederick S., LL.B., '98. Lawyer, 622 F St. N. W., Washington, D. C.

Stockbridge, Virgil D., LL.B., '75. Assistant Examiner, Patent Office, Washington, D. C.

Stockly, Chas. Daniel, LL.B., '04. Lawyer, Smyrna, Del.

Stockman, Chas. W., M.D., '65. Physician, 121 Payson St., Portland, Me.

Stockman, Frank J., D.D.S., '12. Army Medical Museum, Washington, D. C.

Stohlman, Frederick, A.B., '12. 3210 N St. N. W., Washington, D. C.

Stone, Addison G., LL.B., '75. Lawyer, *New York.

Stone, Fred N., LL.B., '11; L. D. M., '11. Bureau of Patents, Washington, D. C.; Auburn, Mass.

Stone, Ralph W., LL.B., '95; LL.M., '96. Lawyer, Warren, Pa.

Stone, Warren C., LL.B., '73. Lawyer, *New York.

Stonebraker, Samuel E., LL.B., '04. Law and Real Estate, 1413 H St. N. W., Washington, D. C.

Storer, Hon. Bellamy, LL.D., '02. Cincinnati, Ohio.

Story, Leon Ellery, M.D., '01. Physician, Corbett Bldg., Portland, Ore.

Stoutenbergh, J. A., M.D., '91. Physician, 116 Second St. N. E., Washington, D. C.

Strasburger, Milton, LL.B., '96; LL.M., '98. Lawyer, Columbian Bldg., Washington, D. C.

Streater, Wallace, LL.B., '93; LL.M., '94. Lawyer, 3160 18th St. N. W., Washington, D. C.

Street, Daniel B., M.D., '74. Physician, 1102 9th St. N. W., Washington, D. C.

Street, Garfield A., LL.B., '04. Lawyer, 200-1 Bond Bldg., Washington, D. C.

Street, H. R., M.D., '91. Physician, 641 E. Capitol St., Washington, D. C.

Strickland, Reeves T., LL.B., '97; LL.M., '98. Department of Justice, 309 E St. N. W., Washington, D. C.

Stritmatter, Thos. P., LL.B., '95. Manufacturer, Quaker City Cut Glass Co., Philadelphia, Pa.

Strong, Shepard, LL.B., '06. Real Estate Broker, 1226 Williamson Bldg., Cleveland, Ohio.

Stuart, Benjamin R., LL.B., '96. Lawyer, *Charleston, S. C.

Stuart, Daniel D. V., Jr., M.D., '08. Lieutenant, U. S. N., care Navy Department, Washington, D. C.; New York City.

Stuart, John M., A.B., '07. Journalist, The Times-Union, Albany, N. Y.

Stuart, Thos. Ambrose 2d., A.B., '10. Broker, care Horace Bell & Co., 100 State St., Albany, N. Y.

Styll, Harry H., LL.B., '09. Attorney for American Optical Co., Southbridge, Mass.

Sudbrink, John T., LL.B., '99. Lawyer, Terre Haute, Ind.

Sudler, Oden Rochester, M.D., '03. Physician and Surgeon, 462 H St. N. W., Washington, D. C.

Sullivan, Esmonde R., D.D.S., '12. Dentist, 41 Brooklyn St., North Adams, Mass.

Sullivan, Francis Paul, A.B., '04. Architect, 1823 U St. N. W., Washington, D. C.

Sullivan, Francis W., A.B., '87. Lawyer, 512 First National Bank, Duluth, Minn.

Sullivan, Geo. E., LL.B., '02. Lawyer (G. U. Law Faculty), Fendall Bldg., Washington, D. C.

Sullivan, Jere A., LL.B., '05. Lawyer and City Solicitor, 9 Realty Bldg., Washington Square, Newport, R. I.

Sullivan, J. H., A.B., '93. Stockman, Temple, Texas.

Sullivan, John K., LL.B., '76. Lawyer, *New Hampshire.

Sullivan, Joseph Daniel, A.B., '97; LL.B., '99; LL.M., '00. Lawyer (G. U. Law Faculty), Columbian Bldg., Washington, D. C.

Sullivan, Joseph David, D.D.S., '03. Dentist, 1122 Broadway, Toledo, Ohio.

Sullivan, Michael Wm., LL.B., '03; LL.M., '05. Lawyer, Century Bldg., Washington, D. C.

Sullivan, Simon E., LL.B., '96; LL.M., '97. Assistant Superintendent, Division Postmasters Appointments, Postoffice Department, Washington, D. C.; Friendship Heights, Md.

Sullivan, Thos. F., LL.B., '12. Interstate Commerce Commission, Washington, D. C.; Boston, Mass.

Sullivan, Thos. V., A.B., '00. Chemist, 1823 N St. N. W., Washington, D. C.

Sullivan, Timothy Joseph, M.D., '04. Physician, 512 6th St., Washington, D. C.

Sullivan, Welby Leslie, M.D., '94. Special Examiner, Pension Bureau, Memphis, Tenn.

Sullivan, Wm. Cleary, LL.B., '01. Lawyer (G. U. Law Fac.), President Catholic Young Men's Union, 410 5th St. N. W., Washington, D. C.

Sullivan, Wm. D., LL.B., '01. Real Estate, Loans and Insurance, 1408 G St. N. W., Washington, D. C.

Summey, B. W., M.D., '86. Physician and Examiner, War Department, 920 19th St., Washington, D. C.

Sutton, Richard Nevitte, M.D., '10. Physician, Clarendon, Va.

Swanberg, Alfred V., LL.B., '10. Lawyer, Kalispell, Mont.

Swank, Walter Ray, LL.B., '09. Lawyer, 328 Stapleton Bldg., Billings, Mont.

Swayne, Noah H., Jr., LL.B., '73. Lawyer, *Ohio.

Swayze, S. Courtland, A.B., '53. *Louisiana.

Sweeney, Harry J., LL.B., '04. Lawyer, Mt. Rainier, Md.

Sweeney, John A., LL.B., '89; LL.M., '90. Lawyer, Hampshire Arms, Minneapolis, Minn.

Sweeney, Matthew J., D.D.S., '07. Dentist, 54 Lowell St., North Weymouth, Mass.

Sweeney, Michael T., M.D., '06. Physician, 922 Hancock St., Atlantic, Mass.

Sweetman, Jas. T., M.D., '72. Physician, Ballston Lake, Ballston, N. Y.

Swetnam, Chas. R. Keith, M.D., '04. Physician, Swetnam Postoffice, Fairfax County, Va.

Swetnam, Ford H., M.D., '07. Physician, Fairfax Station, Va.

Swingle, Ernest A., LL.B., '11. Private Secretary, Fendall Bldg., Washington, D. C.

Sylvester, J. Henry, M.D., '71. Physician, *Washington, D. C.

T

Taggart, Geo. R., LL.B., '08. Postoffice Department, Washington, D. C.

Taggart, Richard J., LL.B., '06; LL.M., '07. Lawyer, 301 McGill Bldg., Washington, D. C.

Talbott, Capt. Edward Melville, M.D., '01. Physician, 1627 16th St. N. W., Washington, D. C.

Talmadge, Theodore, LL.M., '89. Special Examiner, Bureau of Pensions. 401 Federal Bldg., Pittsburgh, Pa.

Tastet, Joseph M., M.D., '53. Physician, *Washington, D. C.

Tatum, Thos. H., LL.B., '02. Lawyer, Bishopville, S. C.

Taylor, A.S., LL.B., '81; LL.M., '82. Lawyer, U. S. Comm., 1413 H St. N. W., Washington, D. C.

Taylor, Chas. B., LL.B., '99. Lawyer, *Richmond, Va.

Taylor, Chas. Benjamin, M.D., '05. Physician, Spencer, Okla.

Taylor, Frank Monroe, D.D.S., '12. Ontario, Cal.

Taylor, Geo. W., LL.B., '90; LL.M., '91. Lawyer, *Washington, D. C.

Taylor, J. Waldo, LL.B., '08. Lawyer, Buffalo, N. Y.

Taylor, Jas. A., Ph.B., '88. Superintendent Transportation New York Edison Co., 149 Clifton Place, Brooklyn, N. Y.

Taylor, Walter I., LL.M., '91. Lawyer, *New Orleans, La.

Taylor, Wm. C., LL.B., '91; LL.M., '93. Deputy Register of Wills, City Hall, Washington, D. C.

Teicher, John G., LL.B., '88; LL.M., '89. U. S. Special Examiner of Pensions, Bureau of Pensions, Washington, D. C.

Teller, Erastus Dalson, LL.B., '99; LL.M., '00. Lawyer, Salem, Ill.

Teller, S. Jay, LL.B., '11. Patent Lawyer, 1339 Fairmont St., Washington, D. C.

Tempes, Frederick W., LL.B., '07. Lawyer, Prosecuting County Attorney, Vancouver, Wash.

Tennent, Eugene Hunter, D.D.S., '11. Dentist, 747 Park Road N. W., Washington, D. C.

Tepper, Benjamin L., LL.B., '10. Census Bureau, 1244 Evarts St. N. E., Washington, D. C.

Tepper, Joseph L., LL.B., '04. Lawyer, 503 E St. N. W., Washington, D. C.

Test, Frederick Cleveland, M.D., '95. Physician, 103 State St., Chicago, Ill.

Tete, Leo Frederick, B.S., '83. 61 Front St., Philadelphia, Pa.

Thian, Louis R., A.B., '75. Lawyer, Minneapolis, Minn.

Thian, Prosper E., A.B., '81. *Washington, D. C.

Thomaides, Geo. Th., LL.B., '05; LL.M., '07. Lawyer, Columbian Bldg., Washington, D. C.

Thomas, Adolph A., LL.B., '06. Patent Lawyer, 200 5th Ave., New York City.

Thomas, Chas. Theodore, LL.B., '94; LL.M., '95. Lawyer, *Ridgeway, S. C.

Thomas, Chas. F., LL.B., '02. Lawyer, *Washington, D. C.

Thomas, Edward H., LL.B., '77. Lawyer, Corporation Counsel, Hibbs Bldg., 3225 18th St. N. W., Washington, D. C.

Thomas, Edward J., LL.B., '76. Lawyer, *Louisiana.

Thomas, Edward W., LL.B., '08. District of Columbia Engineer Department, Washington, D. C.

Thomas, J. Benson, LL.B., '11. Lawyer, 812 14th St. N. W., Washington, D. C.

Thomas, J. Edward, LL.B., '11; LL.M., '12; L.D.M., '12. Lawyer, 416 Fifth St. N. W., Washington, D. C.

Thomas, John T., LL.B., '12. Lawyer, Pittsburg, Pa.

Thomas, Richard W., LL.B., '09. Treasury Department, 1100 7th St. N. E., Washington, D. C.

Thomas, Roy, LL.B., '97. Electrotyper, Navy Department, Washington, D. C.

Thomas, Wm. B., LL.B., '07. Lawyer, 500 5th St. N. W., Washington, D. C.

Thompkins, Raymond S., LL.B., '11. Lawyer, Nyack, N. Y.

Thompson, Alexander Contee, M.D., '11. Intern, Garfield Hospital, Washington, D. C.; Gaithersburg, Md.

Thompson, Edwin St. Clair, LL.B., '91; LL.M., '92. Lawyer, Dewey Hotel, Washington, D. C.

Thompson, Frederick M., LL.B., '91. Lawyer, County Attorney, Albion, N. Y.

Thompson, Geo. F., LL.B., '11; LL.M., '12; L.D.M., '12. Lawyer, Manhattan, Kans.

Thompson, Granville S., M.D., '67. Physician, *New York.

Thompson, John H., Jr., M.D., '75. Ophthalmic Surgeon, Kansas City, Mo.

Thompson, John S., M.D., '95. Physician, 1529 Cambridge St., Cambridge, Mass.

Thompson, Michael Joseph, A.M., '01. Physical Director, Mt. St. Mary's College, Emmitsburg, Md.

Thompson, Smith, Jr., LL.B., '96; LL.M., '97. Lawyer, 1335 F St. N. W., Washington, D. C.

Thorn, Chas. Edwin, LL.M., '94. Lawyer, 165 Broadway, New York City.

Thorne, Walter W., LL.B., '09. Lawyer and Farmer, Galata, Hill County, Mont.

Thornton, Richard H., LL.B., '78. Lawyer and Author, Lancaster House, 36 Upper Bedford Place, Russell Sq., W. C., London, Eng.

Tibbals, W. F., M.D., '65. Physician, *Ohio.

Tibbitts, Orlando O., LL.B., '05. Lawyer, *Oklahoma City, Okla.

Tierney, Rev. John J., D.D., '93. Professor, Mt. St. Mary's College, Emmitsburg, Md.

Tierney, Myles Joseph, A.B., '95. Physician, 143 W. 74th St., New York City.

Tighe, Alvin, LL.B., '08. Lawyer, 1010 Majestic Bldg., Milwaukee, Wis.

Tighe, Joseph M., LL.B., '11. Customs Division, Treasury Department, Washington, D. C.; New Orleans, La.

Tillman, Lloyd Montgomery, LL.B., '99; LL.M., '00. National Bank Examiner, 413 Postoffice Bldg., Philadelphia, Pa.

Timmes, John W., A.B., '01. Lawyer, Shamokin, Pa.

Timmins, P. J., M.D., '78. Physician, President South Boston Medical Association, 487 Broadway, South Boston, Mass.

Timmins, Thomas J., A.B., '78. Easton, Pa.

Tindall, Wm., M.D., '69; LL.B., '82. Secretary, Board of Commissioners, The Stafford, Washington, D. C.

Tobin, Clement P., LL.B., '93. Lawyer, Hibernia Bank Bldg., San Francisco, Cal.

Tobin, Edward Jas., A.B., '95; A.M., '96; Ph.D., '97; LL.B., '97. Lawyer, Hibernia Bank Bldg., San Francisco, Cal.

Tobin, Jas. H., LL.B., '93; LL.M., '94. U. S. Pension Agency, Milwaukee, Wis.

Tobin, Joseph S., Jr., LL.B., '90. Lawyer, Hibernia Bank Bldg., San Francisco, Cal.

Tobin, Richard Francis, M.D., '05. Physician, 123 11th St. S. E., Washington, D. C.

Todd, Hugh C., LL.B., '10. Lawyer, 204-7 Collins Bldg., Seattle, Wash.

Todd, Wm. G., LL.B., '08; LL.M., '09. Lawyer, 77 Kilby St., Boston, Mass.

Toner, John E., M.D., '91. Physician, 214 14th St. N. E., Washington, D. C.

Toohey, Frank, LL.B., '07. Patent Lawyer, 35 Claremont Ave., New York City.

Toomey, Jas. A., A.B., '96; A.M., '97; LL.B., '01. Lawyer, Fendall Bldg., Washington, D. C.

Torbert, Frank P., LL.B., '12. War Department, Washington, D. C.; Berwyn, Md.

Torrey, Earl G., LL.B., '92; LL.M., '93. With Auditor for Treasury Department, 40 Randolph Place N. W., Washington, D. C.

Totten, Howe, LL.B., '95; LL.M., '96. Lawyer, Baldwin, Md.

Touart, Tisdale Joseph, A.M., '02. Lawyer and Assistant District Attorney, 1056 Spring Hill Ave., Mobile, Ala.

Townsend, James G., M.D., '12. G. U. Hospital, Washington, D. C.

Townsend, Chas. G., LL.B., '92; LL.M., '93. Lawyer, U. S, Pension Bureau, Mobile, Ala.

Townsend, Samuel D., LL.B., '05. Lawyer, Baltimore, Md.

Tracewell, Robert N., LL.B., '11; LL.M., '12; L.D.M., '11. Private Secretary to the Comptroller of Treasury, Washington, D. C.; Corydon, Ind.

Tracey, Luke Louis, A.M., '96; Ph.D., '97. Lawyer, Union Trust Bldg., Detroit, Mich.

Tracy, Francis M., LL.B., '07. Lawyer, New York City.

Tracy, Jas. F., A.B., '74; LL.D., '10. Lawyer, 25 N. Pearl St., Albany, N. Y.

Tralles, Geo. Edward, LL.B., '97; LL.M., '98. Lawyer, 420 Equitable Bldg., Denver, Colo.

Trembly, Royal H., LL.B., '99; LL.M., '00. Lawyer, 1419 Clifton St. N. W., Washington, D. C.

Tremoulet, Joseph Sydney, A.B., '97. Manager, The Grassselli-Chemical Co. of Cleveland, Ohio, New Orleans, La.

Trenholm, Frank, LL.B., '92; LL.M., '93. Lawyer, 141 Broadway New York City.

Trenholm, W. deSaussure, LL.B., '90. Secretary American Bridge Co., 30 Church St., New York City.

Triplett, Caius E., LL.B., '88; LL.M., '89. U. S. Pension Bureau, Bangor, Me.

Trott, Fred Pearson, LL.B., '10. Treasury Department, Washington, D. C.; Baring, Me.

Trowbridge, Geo. E., LL.B., '08. Assistant Solicitor, Forest Service, 1040 Josephine St., Denver, Col.

Troy, Robert P., LL.B., '99. Lawyer, 1101-3-5-7 Claus Spreckles Bldg., San Francisco, Cal.

Tschiffely, Stuart Aloysius, A.B., '02. Pharmacist, 1207 Connecticut Ave., Washington, D. C.

Tuason, Pedro, LL.B., '08. Lawyer, Balanga, P. I.

Tureaud, Benjamin, A.B., '88. *Hamilton, Ontario, Canada.

Turner, Emmett, LL.B., '90; LL.M., '91. Pension Bureau, Topeka, Kans.

Turner, Henry V., A.B., '80. *New York.

Turner, Lawrence J., M.D., '64. Physician, *Connecticut.

Turner, O. C., M.D., '64. Physician, *Massachusetts.

Turton, Wm. E., M.D., '08. Physician, 1216 12th St. N. W., Washington, D. C.

Twibill, Aloysius Holland, A.M., '01. Lawyer, 842 N. 19th St., Philadelphia, Pa.

Tyler, Frederick S., LL.B., '05; LL.M., '06. Lawyer 314 Evans Bldg., Washington, D. C.

Tyler, Geo. W., LL.B., '09; LL.M., '10. Lawyer, Malcolm, Iowa.

U

Ucker, Clement S., LL.B., '98; LL.M., '99. Chief Clerk, Department of Interior, 60 Bryant St., Washington, D. C.

Underwood, Fred Rutan, M.D., '97. Physician, A.A. Surg. P. H. & M. Hospital Service, 620 Leary Bldg., Seattle, Wash.

Upton, Edwin A., LL.B., '10. War Department, Washington, D. C.; Magnolia, Ark.

V

Vale, Frank P., M.D., '92. Physician, The Toronto, Washington, D. C.

Valentine, Chas. Francis, A.B., '96. Money Order Division, Postoffice, New York City.

Van Casteel, Gerald, LL.B., '99; LL.M., '00. Lawyer and Editor, 80 Wall St., New York City.

Vance, Henry M., LL.B., '10. General Land Office, Washington, D. C.; Muskogee, Okla.

Van Den Chatten, Baron, A.M., '45. *Washington, D. C.

Vandeventer, Braden, LL.B., '99. Lawyer, Norfolk, Va.

Van Duzer, Clarence, LL.B., '93; LL.M., '94. Lawyer, Navarre Hotel, New York City.

Van Dyne, Frederick, LL.B., '90; LL.M., '91. State Department, Office of Solicitor, Washington, D. C.

Van Emon, Walter C., LL.B., '09. Lawyer, Yorkville, Ill.

Van Horn, Robert L., LL.B., '11. Lawyer, Brentwood, Md.

Van Nest, Raymond H., LL.B., '06. Assistant Examiner, 105 Patent Office, 1770 Willard St., Washington, D. C.

Van Sant, Frank, LL.B., '07. Lawyer, 712-3 Southern Bldg., Washington, D. C.

Varnell, Malcolm K., LL.B., '09. Lawyer, 1529 Vermont Ave., Wash
ington, D. C.

Van Vranken, Frederick, LL.B., '92; LL.M., '93. War Departmen
Washington, D. C.

Vaughan, Daniel C., LL.B., '95; LL.M., '96. Department of Commerc
and Labor, Washington, D. C.

Vaughan, Walter J., LL.B., '96; LL.M., '97. Journalist and Publishe
Griffin, Ga.

Vaughan, Wm. V., M.D., '12. G. U. Hospital, Washington, D. C.

Verbrycke, J. Russell, Jr., M.D., '06. Physician, 2029 First St., Wash
ington, D. C.

Verrill, Chas. H., LL.B., '90; LL.M., '91. Statistician, 1429 New Yor
Ave., Washington, D. C.

Via, Lemuel R., LL. B., '98. Lawyer, *Huntington, W. Va.

Vierbuchen, Julius, LL.B., '05. Secretary of German American Buil
ing Association, 300 B St. S. E., Washington, D. C.

Vierbuchen, Raymond J., LL.B., '12. Lawyer, 114 11th St. N. E., Wash
ington, D. C.

Vilsack, Carl G., LL.B., '10. Real Estate Broker, Centre and Libert
Avs., Pittsburgh, Pa.

Vincent, Thos. Norris, A.B., '85; A.M., '91. Physician (G. U. Me
Fac.), Providence Hospital, 1730 M St., Washington, D. C.

Vlymen, Henry T., A.B., '06. Teacher, 379 Front St., Hempstead, N.

Vlymen, John Richmond, A.B., '12. Rancher, care H. F. Pease, Dillo
Mont.

Vlymen, Wm. J., A.B., '06. Teacher, 182 S. Jackson St., Janesville, Wi

Von Rosen, Ferdinand G., LL.B., '87; LL.M., '93. Lawyer, *Knoxvill
Tenn.

Von Rosenburg, Fred C., LL.B., '89. Lawyer, 2510 Whitis Ave., Austi
Texas.

W

Wadden, John Joseph, A.B., '04. Care Hart, Parr & Co., Gasolene an
Kerosene Tractors, Regina, Sask., Canada.

Wade, Edward Julius, A.B., '04. Contractor, 3915 Walnut St., Phila
delphia, Pa.

Wade, John Douglas, LL.B., '06. Electrical Engineer, Treasurer Balti
more Camera Club, 1111 Linden Ave., Baltimore, Md.

Waggaman, Samuel John, Jr., A.B., '98. Advertising Editor, Rich
mond Times Despatch, Richmond, Va.

Wagner, G. Henry, M.D., '85. Physician, 728 9th St. N. E., Washing
ton, D. C.

Wagner, Warren H., LL.B., '08; LL.M., '10. U. S. Immigrant and Na
tional Bureau, New York City.

Waguespack, Wm. J., A.B., '82. Lawyer, Louisiana Bank Bldg., Ne
Orleans, La.

Wahly, Wm. H., LL.B., '96; LL.M., '97. Lawyer, 317-319 John Mar
shall Place, Washington, D. C.

Wainscott, Geo., LL.B., '74. Lawyer, *Kentucky.

Wait, Chas. B., LL.B., '10; LL.M., '11; L.D.M., '11. Special Agent, Department of Commerce and Labor, Washington, D. C.; Muskogee, Okla.

Wait, Stanley S., LL.B., '10. Department of Justice, Washington, D. C.; Muskogee, Okla.

Waite, Geo. W. C., LL.B., '74. Lawyer, *Louisiana.

Waldo, G. S., D.D.S., '02. Dentist, Gainesville, Fla.

Wales, Orlando G., LL.B., '87. Lawyer, *Philadelphia, Pa.

Walker, Chas. M., LL.B., '93. Secretary, Monroe Cotton Mills, Monroe, Ga.

Walker, Francis, LL.B., '89; LL.M., '90. General Land Office, 1431 Newton St. N. W., Washington, D. C.

Walker, Jas. S., LL.B., '83. Lawyer, *New York City.

Walker, John B. Fuller, LL.B., '98. Lawyer, *New York City.

Walker, John Brisben, Ph.D., '89. Writer and Business Manager, care Cosmopolitan Magazine, New York City.

Walker, Lewis Albert, Jr., M.D., '98. Physician, 622 New Jersey Ave., Washington, D. C.

Walker, Ralph Elliott, LL.B., '01. Lawyer, 416 5th St. N. W., Washington, D. C.

Walker, Reginald Redford, M.D., '00. Physician, 1710 H St. N. W., Washington, D. C.

Walker, Robert H., LL.B., '07. Law and Real Estate, 458 Louisiana Ave., Washington, D. C.

Walker, Wm. Gillespie, LL.B., '97. Real Estate, 706 A St. S. E., Washington, D. C.

Walker, W. Henry, LL.B., '88; LL.M., '89. Lawyer, 729 15th St. N. W., Washington, D. C.

Walker, Wm. H., M.D., '02. Physician, 493 Hudson St., New York City.

Wall, Joseph Stiles, M.D., '97. Physician (G .U. Med. Fac.), 1232 14th St. N. W., Washington, D. C.

Wall, Maurice J., LL.B., '05. Examiner, U. S. Patent Office, Washington, D. C.

Wall, Michael, A.M., '66. *Ireland.

Wallace, Elliot L., LL.B., '09. Assistant in Copyright Office, The Roland, Washington, D. C.

Wallace, Hamilton S. Army Headquarters, Chronicle Bldg., San Francisco, Cal.

Wallace, Joseph F., M.D., '99. Physician, Modern Woodmen Sanitorium, Colorado Springs, Colo.

Wallis, Samuel B., A.B., '84; A.M., '87. Chemist, Leonardtown, Md.

Walls, Chas. A., LL.B., '10. Lawyer, Lonoke, Ark.

Walsh, Edward F., LL.B., '02. Lawyer, *Waterbury, Conn.

Walsh, Ed. J., LL.B., '93; LL.M., '94. Manager Northwestern National Ins. Co., 1302 F St. N. W., Washington, D. C.

Walsh, Francis, M.D., '66. Physician, *Washington, D. C.

Walsh, Henry Collins, A.M., '88. Editor, 29 W. 39th St., New York City.

Walsh, Jas. J., Lit.D., '10. Physician, Dean, Fordham University Medical School, New York City.

Walsh, John H., A.B., '73; A.M., '89; Ph.D., '12. Assistant Superintendent Schools New York, 8502 Hamilton Ave., Brooklyn, N. Y.

Walsh, Joseph J., LL.B., '11. Lawyer, Denver, Colo.

Walsh, Julius Sylvester, Jr., A.B., '98. Villa Clare, Kinloch, Mo.

Walsh, Michael Jas., A.B., '01. Lawyer, 603-4 Mears Bldg., Scranton, Pa.

Walsh, Ralph S. L., M.D., '63. Physician, Jerusalem, Harford County, Md.

Walsh, Thos., Ph.B., '92; Ph.D., '99. Author, 227 Clinton St., Brooklyn, N. Y.

Walsh, Thos. J., A.B., '94; A.M., '96. Frederick, Md.

Walsh, Wm. A., LL.B., '97. Lawyer, 2-8 Hudson St., Yonkers, N. Y.

Walsh, Wm S., A.M., '89. Sandy Hook, Conn.

Walshe, Patrick J., LL.B., '98; LL.M., '99. Lawyer, 1336 New York Ave., Washington, D. C.

Walter, Wm. Francis, M.D., '92. Physician, 487 H St. S. W., Washington, D. C.

Walters, Harris A., LL.B., '99. Vice-President Hydraulic Brick Co., Chicago, Ill.

Walters, Harry F., LL.B., '06. U. S. General Land Office, Alliance, Nebr.

Walters, Henry, A.B., '69; A.M., '71; LL.D., '09. President Atlantic Coast Line, 5 South St., Baltimore, Md.

Walthall, Wilson J., A.B., '54. *Alabama.

Wanamaker, Wm. H., LL.B., '99. Chief of Division, Office of Postoffice Department, Auditor, 2519 Ontario Road, Washington, D. C.

Wand, Arthur J., LL.B., '05. Secretary, The New Willard, Washington, D. C.

Ward, Elijah J., M.D., '80. Physician, *Maryland.

Ward, Francis M., M.D., '81. Principal Examiner, 527 6th St. N. W., Washington, D. C.

Ward, Francis X., A.B., '59; A.M., '67. Lawyer, 2417 Spruce St., Philadelphia, Pa.

Ward, Geo. A., LL.B., '98; LL.M., '99. Assistant Attorney, Interior Department, Washington, D. C.

Ward, Samuel B., M.D., '64. Physician, 281 State St., Albany, N. Y.

Ward, Samuel R., M.D., '68. Physician, Richmond, Ill.

Warder, Jas. F., LL.B., '11; LL.M., '12; L.D.M., '12. Lawyer, 620 Q St. N. W., Washington, D. C.

Warfield, Ralph Sturtevant, LL.B., '98; LL.M., '99. Patent Lawyer, care Adder Machine Co., Wilkesbarre, Pa.

Warner, Chas. S., D.D.S., '12. Lawyer, Forest Hill, Md.

Warner, Richard Ambrose, M.D., '01. Passed Assistant Surgeon, U. S. N., care Navy Department, Washington, D. C.

Warren, Bates, LL.B., '92; LL.M., '93. Lawyer, Columbian Bldg., Washington, D. C.

Warren, Claude E., LL.B., '11. Real Estate and Building, Riverdale, Md.

Warren, Henry B., LL.B., '12. Lawyer, Waukegan, Ill.

Warren, John L., LL.B., '99; LL.M., '00. Lawyer, Columbian Bldg., Washington, D. C.

Warriner, Wm. F., LL.M., '87. U. S. Patent Office, Washington, D. C.

Washburn, Albert H., LL.B., '95. Lawyer, 12 Broadway, New York City.

Washington, Joseph E., A.B., '73; A.M., '89. Planter, Cedar Hill, Tenn.

Wassell, Haverington E., LL.B., '12. Interior Department, Washington, D. C.; Pittsfield, Ill.

Wasner, Wendell H., LL.B., '09. Lawyer, Batavia, Ohio.

Wasser, Henry R., LL.B., '09; LL.M., '10. Department of Commerce and Labor, 709 6th St. N. W., Washington, D. C.

Wassen, Robert Bingham, LL.B., '99. Lawyer, Cadiz, Ohio.

Waters, Bowie F., LL.B., '93. Lawyer, State's Attorney, Rockville, Montgomery County, Md.

Waters, David C., M.D., '67. Physician, Covington, Tioga County, Pa.

Waters, Eugene H., LL.B., '08; LL.M., '09. Lawyer, Germantown, Md.

Waters, Francis, A.B., '55; A.M., '56. *Kentucky.

Watkins, Elton, LL.B., '12. Lawyer, Hattiesburg, Miss.

Watkins, Samuel Evans, M.D., '92. Physician, 1115 O St. N. W., Washington, D. C.

Watkins, Victor E., M.D., '94. Medical Reserve Corps, U. S. A., War Department, Washington, D. C.

Watsky, Jacob, LL.B., '12; L.D.M., '12. Lawyer, Richmond, Va.

Watson, Frank E., Jr., LL.B., '09; LL.M., '10. Lawyer, Cadott, Wis.

Watson, Jas. A., M.D., '90. Physician, 2101 Nicholas Ave., Anacostia, D. C.

Watson, Jas. M., LL.B., '02. Lawyer, *Louisville, Ky.

Watson, Joseph Twitchell, LL.M., '08. Lawyer, 344 A Central Bldg., Seattle, Wash.

Watson, Martin M., LL.B., '05. Fancy Grocer, 113 4th St. N. E., Washington, D. C.

Watson, Richard F., LL.B., '05. Lawyer, Greenville, S. C.

Watson, Robert, LL.B., '10. Department of Commerce and Labor, Washington, D. C.; Lowell, Mass.

Watson, Robert, LL.B., '95. Patent Lawyer, Hamilton Bldg., Washington, D. C.

Watt, Alexander, LL.B., '09. Lawyer, Burke, Va.

Watts, Frederick, Jr., LL.B., '09. Immigration Bureau, San Francisco, Cal.

Watts, Joseph F., M.D., '12. Physician, 64 Central Ave., Waterbury, Conn.

Watts, Reuben Benjamin, LL.B., '98. Lawyer, 410 Title Guarantee Bldg., Birmingham, Ala.

Wayland, Confucius L., LL.M., '89. Lawyer, *Seattle, Wash.

Wayman, Edgar H., LL.B., '12. Department of Commerce and Labor, Washington, D. C.; Trenton, N. J.

Weaver, Alfred S., D.D.S., '02. Dentist, 410 10th St. S. E., Washington, D. C.

Webb, Daniel Alphonsus, A.M., '95; M.D., '96. Surgeon, 310 Wyoming Ave., Scranton, Pa.

Webster, Ben, M.D., '00. Physician, Kingsbury, Ind.

Webster, Ben Temple, LL.B., '98. Real Estate Broker, 714 14th St., Washington, D. C.

Webster, Chas. S., LL.B., '89. Lawyer, *Troy, N. Y.

Wedderburn, Geo. C., LL.B., '92; LL.M., '96. Examiner, U. S. Patent Office, Chevy Chase, Md.

Weed, Chester A., LL.M., '92. Patent Lawyer, 1428 President St., Brooklyn, N. Y.

Weightman, R. Hanson, LL.B., '11. Weather Bureau, Washington, D.C.; Marysville, Cal.

Weikert, Clyde B., LL.B., '07. Lawyer, Southern Bldg., Washington, D. C.

Weinberger, Louis, LL.B., '12. Office of Adjutant General, War Department, Washington, D. C.; Brooklyn, N. Y.

Weinstein, David D., LL.B., '11. Government Printing Office, 20 N St. N. W., Washington, D. C.

Weiss, Thos. F., LL.B., '12. Lawyer, Oklahoma City, Okla.

Welch, Benjamin T., LL.B., '90. Conveyancer, Philadelphia, Pa.

Welch, Charles B., LL.B., '12. Department of Justice; 628 I St. N. E., Washington, D. C.

Welch, Thomas Francis, M.D., '04. Physician, 356 Windsor Ave., Hartford, Conn.

Welch, Timothy J., A.B., '97. *Washington, D. C.

Welch, Williams, LL.B., '09. Draftsman, No. 32 Grant Place, Washington, D. C.

Wellenreiter, Otto Francis, M.D., '01. Physician, Gessie, Ind.

Weller, Joseph Ignatius, A.B., '93; LL.B., '95. Real Estate Broker, 602 F St. N. W., Washington, D. C.

Wellman, Geo. T., LL.B., '91; LL.M., '92. Lawyer, 1001 7th St., Sheldon, Iowa.

Wells, Benjamin W., LL.B., '11; LL.M., '12. Navy Department, Washington, D. C.

Wells, George M., Phar.B., '72. *Havre de Grace, Md.

Wells, John Bernard, A.M., '05. Lawyer, 108 E. Madison St., Baltimore, Md.

Wells, Walter A., M.D., '91. Physician, G. U. Med. Fac, The Rochambeau, Washington, D. C.

Wells, Walter H., M.D., '68. Physician and Surgeon, Coffeyville, Kans.

Welsh, John Joseph, LL.B., '03. Lawyer, 164 Montague St., Brooklyn, N. Y.

Wentz, Herman T., LL.B., '10. Clerk, Colville, Wash.

Werner, G. Philip, LL.B., '12; L.D.M., '12. Interstate Commerce Commission, Brillian, Wis.

Wertenbacker, C. I., M.D., '94. Surgeon, P. H. & M. H. Service, Norfolk, Va.

Wessel, John Frederick, A.B., '96. Electrical Engineer, General Electric Co., Baltimore, Md.

West, Bertram H., LL.B., '75. Lawyer, *New York.

West, Vernon E., LL.B., '08; LL.M., '09. Lawyer and Instructor, G. U. Law School, The Octavia, Century Bldg., Washington, D. C.

Westenhaver, David C., LL.M., '84. Lawyer, 929 Garfield Bldg., Cleveland, Ohio.

Westfall, Harry M., LL.B., '90. Lawyer, Sioux Falls, S. D.

Wetmore, James A., LL.B., '96. Chief of Law and Records Division, Supervising Architect's Office, Treasury Dept., Washington, D. C.

Weyrich, John Raymond, LL.B., '04; LL.M., '05. U. S. Attorney's Office, City Hall, Washington, D. C.

Wheatley, J. Walter, LL.B., '89; LL.M., '90. Special Treasury Agent, in charge Port of New York, Custom House, New York City.

Wheaton, Henry, M.D., '66. Physician, *New York.

Wheaton, Isaac S., LL.B., '85. Lawyer, Poughkeepsie, N. Y.

Wheeler, Arthur M., Jr., LL.B., '94. Stenographer, 3 B St. S. E., Washington, D. C.

Wheeler, Laban Homer, LL.M., '87. Lawyer, 656, 7 New York Block, Seattle, Wash.

Wheeler, William D., LL.B., '04. Postoffice Department, 1358 Harvard St. N. W., Washington, D. C.

Wheeleck, George L., LL.B., '89; LL.M., '90. Patent Lawyer and Copyright, Room 1900, 2 Rector St., New York City.

Whelan, John A., LL.B., '03; LL.M., '04. Lawyer, Hotel Utah, Salt Lake City, Utah.

Whelan, Thomas A., LL.B., '12. War Department, Washington, D. C.; Jackson, Miss.

Whilley, William H., A.M., '85. *New Jersey.

Whipple, Ulysses V., LL.B., '89; LL.M., '90. Lawyer, Rome, Ga.

Whitaker, Walter Eugene, D.D.S., '11. Dentist, Centerville, Utah.

White, Chas. Albert, A.B., '90; LL.B., '92; LL.M., '93. Lawyer, Bond Bldg., Washington, D. C.

White, Charles H., LL.B., '11. Department of Agriculture, Washington, D. C.; Muskogee, Okla.

White, Columbus J., M.D., '66. Physician, *Washington, D. C.

White, Hon. Edward Douglass, LL.D., '92. Chief Justice U. S. Supreme Court; 1717 Rhode Island Ave., Washington, D. C.

White, Edward H., A.B., '68. *Maryland.

White, Francis P., LL.B., '87; LL.M., '88. Bureau of Pensions; 2501 14th St. N. W., Washington, D. C.

White, Guy Harris, D.D.S., '02. Sporting Goods, 1523 Lamont St. N. W., and 727 14th St. N. W., Washington, D. C.

White, Louis C., B.S., '87; LL.B., '89; LL.M., '90. Lawyer, Hotel San Remo, New York City.

White, James R., LL.B., '89; LL.M., '90. Treasury Department; 1331 Harvard St. N. W., Washington, D. C.

White, John W., M.D., '70. Physician, *Baltimore, Md.

White, Robert R., LL.B., '99; LL.M., '00. Lawyer, *Washington, D. C.

White, Thomas J., LL.B., '82; LL.M., '83. Lawyer, 202 Grossman Bldg., Kansas City, Kans.

White, Walter N., LL.B., '09. Lawyer, Muskogee, Okla.

White, William Henry, LL.B., '97. Lawyer, Assistant Corporation Counsel, Bond Bldg., Washington, D. C.

Whitehead, John C., D.D.S., '12. Dentist, 425 M St. N. W., Washington, D. C.

Whitehouse, Joseph S., LL.M., '87. Real Estate and Financial Agent, *Pottsville, Pa.

Whiteley, Richard Peyton, A.B., '01; LL.B., '04. Lawyer, 1419 G St. N. W., Washington, D. C.

Whitney, Chas. F., M.D., '90. Medical Referee, Pension Office, Washington, D. C.; Silver Spring, Md.

Whitney, Jay W., LL.B., '12. Office Indian Affairs, Washington, D. C.; Tacoma, Wash.

Whitten, John L., LL.M., '91. Lawyer, Point Pleasant, W. Va.

Whitthorne, Washington C., LL.B., '88. Lawyer, Columbia, Tenn.

Wibirt, William C., LL.B., '89. Treasurer, Alexandria County, Fort Myer, Va.

Wickham, Edward B., LL.B., '08. Lawyer, 501-506 Realty Bldg., Elmira, N. Y.

Wiecker, Otho, LL.B., '86. Antiquarian and Genealogist, 587 Tremont St., Boston, Mass.

Wiener, David, LL.B., '12. General Land Office, Washington, D. C.; Carlisle, Pa.

Wiggenhorn, Edwin C., LL.B., '89; LL.M., '90. Cashier, Farmers and Mechanics' Bank, Ashland, Neb.

Wikle, Douglas, LL.B., '80. Lawyer, *Georgia.

Wilcox, Adolphus D., LL.B., '94. Chief Clerk, Bureau of Insular Affairs, War Department; 2610 University Place, Washington, D. C.

Wilcox, James M., A.B., '81; A.M., '89. Vice-President Philadelphia Saving Fund Society, 700 Walnut St., Philadelphia, Pa.

Wilcox, John A., M.D., '57. Physician, *Washington, D. C.

Wilder, A. M., M.D., '63. Physician, *New Hampshire.

Wilkinson, A. D., M.D., '93. Pension Office; 455 Massachusetts Ave., Washington, D. C.

Wilkinson, Webster H., LL.B., '10. Immigrant Inspector, Department of Commerce and Labor; 1343 Clifton St., Washington, D. C.

Willey, Harry P., LL.B., '92; LL.M., '93. Lawyer, 49 S St. N. W., Washington, D. C.

Williams, A. Roy, LL.B., '04. Care Robert Tunstal, Norfolk, Va.

Williams, C. Fuller, LL.B., '05. Lawyer, care Tomlinson, Tompkins and Tomlinson, Mills Bldg., 35 Wall St., New York City.

Williams, George Francis, LL.M., '89. Lawyer, National Metropolitan Bank Bldg., Washington, D. C.

Williams, Hugh H., LL.B., '96; LL.M., '97. Lawyer, *Emporia, Kans.

Williams, James R., LL.B., '09. Department of Agriculture; 801 Webster Ave. N. W., Washington, D. C.

Williams, John G., LL.B., '97. Auditor, Norfolk and Washington Steamboat Co., 7th St. Wharf, Washington, D. C.

Williams, Sherman, M.D., '98. Physician, State Board of Health, 346 Metropolitan Bldg., Denver, Colo.

Williamson, Frank E., LL.B., '03; LL.M., '04. Lawyer, Urbana, Ill.

Williamson, George M., LL.M., '93. Lawyer, *Le Sueur, Minn.

Williamson, Hugh C., A.B., '66; A.M., '72. *Louisiana.

Williamson, Joseph A., LL.B., '05; LL.M., '06. Lawyer, 218 Danville Bldg., Danville, Ill.

Willis, J. Houston, LL.B., '12. Lawyer, Myersville, Md.

Willis, Stanley D., LL.B., '10. Attorney-at-Law, Union Savings Bank Bldg., 1483 Newton St., Washington, D. C.

Willis, Thomas C., LL.B., '06. Lawyer, Munsey Bldg., Washington, D. C.

Willo, John A., A.B., '12. Law Student, 244 E. Wood St., Youngstown, Ohio.

Wills, Joseph W., LL.B., '93; LL.M., '94. Lawyer, Arrington, Nelson County, Va.

Willson, Albert Burns, D.D.S., '11. Dentist, 918 14th St., Washington, D. C.

Willson, Harry A., LL.B., '10; LL.M., '11. U. S. Naturalization Examiner, 221 Federal Bldg., St. Louis, Mo.

Willson, Prentiss, M.D., '05. Physician, G. U. Med. Fac., The Toronto, Washington, D. C.

Willson, S. C., M.D., '88. Physician, 2033 Meridian St., Anderson, Ind.

Wilmeth, George M., LL.B., '10. Lawyer, 2307 Wisconsin Ave., Washington, D. C.

Wilmeth, John F., LL.B., '12. Lawyer, Prescott, Ark.

Wilson, Andrew, LL.B., '90; LL.M., '91. Lawyer, 301-306 Evans Bldg., Washington, D. C.

Wilson, Calvert, A.B., '86; A.M., '90. Lawyer, 350 Wilcox Bldg., Los Angeles, Cal.

Wilson, Clarence R., LL.M., '99. U. S. District Attorney, G. U. Law Faculty, 1707 Rhode Island Ave., Washington, D. C.

Wilson, Daniel J., LL.B., '06. Lawyer, City National Bank Bldg., Galveston, Texas.

Wilson, Edwin L., LL.B., '95. Lawyer, Fendall Bldg., Washington, D. C.

Wilson, Henry O., LL.B., '89; LL.M., '90. Secretary Trust Co., 1828 Phelps Place N. W., Washington, D. C.

Wilson, John Chamberlin, A.B., '65. Cosmos Club, Washington, D. C.

Wilson, Joseph S., LL.B., '07. Investment Bonds, American Trust Bldg., Chicago, Ill.

Wilson, Nelson, LL.B., '04; LL.M., '05. Lawyer, 1417 G St. N. W., Washington, D. C.

Wilson, Thomas Bernard, LL.B., '10. 239 Oakland Ave., Pittsburgh, Pa.

Wilson, Thomas J., LL.B., '92. Lawyer, 1227 G St. N. W.; 46 Bryant St. N. W., Washington, D. C.

Wimsatt, Walter T., LL.M., '10. Lawyer, 1125 Scarritt Bldg, Kansas City, Mo.

Wimsatt, William Kurtz, A.B., '00. Wholesale Lumber, Johnson & Wimsatt Co., 1212 Water St. S. W., Washington, D. C.

Windle, Charles T., LL.B., '10; LL.M., '11; L.D.M., '11. Lawyer, 3601 14th St. N. W., Washington, D. C.

Wing, George C., LL.B., '73. Lawyer, 1105 Citizens' Bldg., Cleveland, Ohio.

Wingard, Edward V., M.D., '80. Physician, *Deadwood, S. D.

Winter, Frank E., M.D., '06. Physician, Vienna, Austria.

Wirt, Richard W., Jr., LL.B., '08; LL.M., '09. Stenographer, Alexandria, Va.

Wise, Orville A., LL.B., '11. Lawyer, Carthage, Mo.

Wissner, Frank J., LL.B., '01. Lawyer, Editor and Publisher, 3293 M St. N. W., Washington, D. C.

Witman, Edward R., LL.B., '10. Patent Attorney, 318 McGill Bldg., Washington, D. C.

Wixon, Irving F., LL.B., '10. Bureau of Immigration; Dennisport, Mass.

Woerner, Otto E., LL.B., '04. Government Department, 734 6th St. N. W., Washington, D. C.

Woertendyke, Harold P., LL.B., '11. Pension Bureau, Washington, D. C.; Nyack, N. Y.

Wolf, Alexander, LL.B., '92; LL.M., '93. Lawyer, Jenifer Bldg., Washington, D. C.

Wolfe, Henry L., Jr., LL.B., '12. Lawyer, Chattanooga, Tenn.

Wolfe, John Loyola, A.M., '02; LL.B., '04. Lawyer, 302-4-6 Weston Bldg., Clinton, Iowa.

Wolfe, John Magruder, A.B., '01. Care Dr. G. Lloyd Magruder, Stoneleigh Court, Washington, D. C.

Wolfe, William Lloyd, A.B., '92. Lebanon, Lebanon County, Pa.

Wollard, Paul D., LL.B., '07; LL.M., '12. War Department, Office of Judge Advocate General, 601 N. C. Ave. S. E., Washington, D. C.

Wollenberg, Robt. A. C., M.D., '05. Dermatologist, Providence Hospital, 16 Harmon Ave. and 57 W. Foote St., Detroit, Mich.

Wood, Alfred E., LL.B., '11. Lawyer, 629 F St. N. W., Washington, D. C.

Wood, Elmer C., LL.B., '08; LL.M., '09. Department of Commerce and Labor, 902 B St. S. W., Washington, D. C.

Wood, George F., M.D., '65. Physician, *Massachusetts.

Wood, George William, M.D., '94. Physician, 2906 F St. N. W., Washington, D. C.

Wood, Leonard C., LL.B., '85; LL.M., '86. Lawyer, *Washington, D. C.

Wood, William C., LL.B., '89; LL.M., '90. Sup. Div. Class P O. D., 2902 14th St N. W., Washington, D. C.

Woodburn, William, Jr., LL.B., '03. District Attorney, Washoe County, Reno, Nevada.

Woodhouse, David R., LL.B., '12. Lawyer, Wethersfield, Conn.

Woodley, Thomas A., M.D., '57. Physician, *Virginia.

Woodruff, William A., LL.B., '11. Lawyer, Stilwell, Okla.

Woods, Clifton F., A.B., '08. President The Inland Advertising Agency, 505 McCormick Bldg., Chicago, Ill.

Woods, Joseph, A.B., '55. *New York City.

Woodson, L. G., M.D., '91. Physician, Woodward Bldg., Birmingham, Ala

Woodward, Herbert E., LL.B., '85; LL.M., '87. Assessor's Office, District Bldg., Washington, D. C.

Woodward, Rigual Duckett, A.B., '85. Lawyer, 5 Nassau St., New York City.

Woodward, Roland E., M.D., '64. Physician, *Illinois.

Woodward, William Creighton, M.D., '89; LL.B., '99; LL.M., '00. Health Officer, G. U. Med. and Dent. Fac., G. U. Law Fac., Washington, D. C.

Woolf, Oliver P., LL.B., '89; LL.M., '90. Postoffice Department, Washington, D. C.

Workman, Arthur C., LL.B., '12. Lawyer, Huntington, W. Va.

Worthington, A. Saunders, LL.B., '97; LL.M., '00. Lawyer, 31 American National Bank Bldg., Washington, D. C.

Wright, Arthur, LL.B., '06. Patent Attorney, 711 Broadway, New York City.

Wright, Arthur W., LL.B., '92. Advertising Manager National Druggist, 3426 Jackson Boulevard, Chicago, Ill.

Wright, Herbert Francis, A.B., '11. Instructor in Catholic University, 1103 P St., Washington, D. C.

Wright, Howard T., LL.B., '12; L.D.M., '12. Lawyer, 1733 Corcoran St., Washington, D. C.

Wright, J. Henry, M.D., '67. Physician, 64 Lake Ave., Worcester, Mass.

Wright, Joseph D., LL.B., '97; LL.M., '98. Lawyer, Clayton, Ala.

Wright, Wilbur L., M.D., '94. Physician, 1658 Park Road N. W., Washington, D. C.

Wrightsman, Charles J., LL.B., '90. Lawyer, Pioneer Bldg., Tulsa, Okla.

Wymard, Norman L., A.B., '12. 412 Todd St., Wilkinsburg, Pa.

Wynn, Frederick S., LL.B., '06. Purchasing Agent, Southern Railway Company, Washington, D. C.

Y

Yancey, Chas. L., LL.B., '12. Census Bureau, Washington, D. C.; McGaheysville, Va.

Yancey, G. Earle, LL.B., '99. Chief of Division, Bureau of Navigation, 5602 39th St., Chevy Chase, Md.

Yeatman, Chas. R., LL.B., '98; LL.M., '99. Lawyer, *New York City.

Yeatman, Rudolph H., LL.B., '06; LL.M., '07. Lawyer, 410 5th St. N. W., Washington, D. C.

Yoder, Frank W., LL.B., '05. U. S. Commissioner, Hoover, Butte County, S. D.

Young, Robert A., LL.B., '10. Lawyer, 1722 Kilbourne Place, Washington, D. C.

Youngblood, Robert K., LL.B., '87. Lawyer, *Columbus, Miss.

Yount, Clarence Edgar, M.D., '96. Physician and Surgeon, Prescott, Ariz.

Yount, Marshall H., LL.B., '97. Lawyer, Police Magistrate, Hickory, N. C.

Yturbide, Augustine de, Ph.B., '84. (G. U. Arts Fac.), 3325 O St. N. W., Washington, D. C.

Z

Zabel, John H., LL.B., '06; LL.M., '07. Lawyer, 412 5th St. N. W., Washington, D. C.

Zepf, Louis R., LL.B., '12. Lawyer, Nashville, Tenn.

Zepp, Jesse, M.D., '70. Physician, 60 Q St. N. E., Washington, D. C.

Ziegler, Eugene M., LL.B., '06. Lawyer, Orangeburg, S. C.

Zimmerman, Harvey J., LL.B., '05. Census Office, 1330 A St. S. E., Washington, D. C.

Zimmerman, Mervin, LL.B., '11. Department of Justice, Washington, D. C.

Zinkhan, Arthur M., M.D., '12. Emergency Hospital, Washington, D. C.

Zinkhan, Paul H., M.D., '12. Lawyer, Salem, Ore.

Zunigan, Manuel G. de, A.B., '55; A.M., '56. *Uraguay.

Zychowicz, John F., M.D., '11. Physician, 1315 Prospect Ave., Scranton, Pa.

Deceased Graduates

Abell, Charles S.............A.B., '68; A.M., '71· Dec. 3, 1876, Guilford, Baltimore Co., Md.

Abell, Walter R.............A.B., '69; A. M., '89· Jan. 3, 1891, Baltimore, Md.

Adams, Allen R.............LL.B., '01· Philadelphia, Pa.

Adams, Arthur W...........M.D., '78· 1898, St. Louis.

Adams, Benjamin B.........M.D., '76· Jan. 25, 1897, Washington, D. C.

Adams, C. B. S.............M.D , '86· May, 1896, Washington, D. C.

Adams, E. A...............M.D., '65· 1890.

Adams, J. Lee..............M.D., '68· April 16, 1905, Washington, D. C.

Aiken, Wm. E. A............LL.D., '45· 1880, Baltimore, Md.

Alexander, Walter O.........M.D., '67· May 23, 1904, Washington, D. C.

Allemong, Alex. A..........A.B., '48· Oct., 1864, Petersburg, Va.

Allen, Charles.............M.D., '61· Dec. 24, 1898, Washington, D. C.

Amery, Samuel A............M.D., '66· Aug., 1881, Cincinnati, O.

Andrade-Penny, Ed..........M.D., '94· Sept. 20, 1896, New York City.

Ansell, Aaron..............M.D., '62·

Antisell, Thomas...........Ph.D., '81· June 14, 1893, Washington, D. C.

Antisell, Thomas, Jr........M.D., '81· Nov. 26, 1896, Warm Spgs., Mont.

Appleby, J. F. R...........M.D., '68· Sept. 27, 1907, Washington, D. C.

Armant, Leopold L..........A.B., '55· Colonel, C. S. A., at battle of Mansfield, La.

Arnold, Paul...............LL.B., '83·

Ashton, Hon. J. Hubley......LL.D., '72· Mar. 14, 1907, Wash., D. C.

Babcock, Benjamin B........M.D., '67· Jan. 21, 1868.

Baby, Francis W............A.B., '53· Mar. 16, 1911, Paris.

Bailey, Geo. A.............M.D., '94·

Bailey, Thos. B............M.D., '86; A.M., '88·

Barbarin, Francis S........M.D., '56· March 29, 1900.

Barber, Rev. Samuel J., S.J..A.B., '30· Feb. 23, 1864, St. Thomas', Md.

Barbour, Clement C.........M.D., '64· Texas.

Bargy, Ludim Albert........A.B., '54· Killed in Mex. by Indians, 1860.

Barker, Howard H...........M.D., '70· Washington, D. C.

Barksdale, Noel W..........LL.B., '90; LL.M., '91· Feb. 27, 1911.

Barnard. W T...............M.D., '70·

Barnes, Benjamin F.........LL.B., '95· Oct., 1909, Washington D. C.

Barr, A. Jefferson.........LL.B., '90·

Barrett, Wm. H.............A.B., '61·

Barry, A. R................M.D., '61· Aug. 4, 1903, Weatherford, Tex.

Barry, Cornelius Neal.......M.D., '95· April 30, 1897.

Bawtree, Harvey............A.B., '54; A.M., '56· Lachine, Canada.

Baxter, Geo. T..............LL.M., '87·

Bayard, Hon. Thos. F.......LL.D., '89· Ex-Secretary of State, Sept.
                               28, 1898, Dedham, Mass.

Beahn Edward F...........A.B., '58· Died in California.

Beale, James S.............M. D., '69· Feb. 12, 1884, Wash., D. C.

Beall, John J..............A.B., '54· Feb. 18, 1898, Georgetown, D. C.

Becket, John J. A..........Ph.D., '87· Dec. 20, 1911, New York.

Beers, J...................M.D., '64· Dec. 5, 1901.

Bell, Ralph................M.D., '69·

Benet, Stephen V...........LL.D., '84· U. S. A. Brig. Gen., Jan. 22,
                               1895.

Bergen, James C...........A.B., '52· Died at sea.

Bergh, Edwin..............A.B., '19· 1876, New York.

Berry, Andrew.............A.B., '96·

Bevans, James H..........A.B., '42·

Binns, Douglass...........M D., '76· Aug. 31, 1910, New Holland, O.

Bird, Wm. E...............A.B., '44·

Birney, Theodore.Weld.....LL.B., '87· July 24, 1897.

Bitting, Louis C...........M.D., '65· Baltimore, Md.

Bittinger, Charles.........M.D., '73· Aug. 31, 1879, Wash., D. C.

Blackmon, John Powell.....LL.B., '95; LL.M., '96· Oct. 10, 1907, El
                               Reno, Okla.

Blake, George W...........M.D., '67· June, 1885, Lower Salem, O.

Blakely, Wm. J............A.M., '76· Jan. 7, 1877, Erie, Pa.

Blanc, Charles de..........A.B., '47; A.M., '50· Mar., 1891, Curacoa,
                               W. I.

Blandford, J. Walter.......LL.B., '88; LL.M., '89· Mar. 12, 1898,
                               Washington, D. C.

Boardman, Herbert.........M.D., '72·

Boardman, Myron..........M.D., '75· 1890.

Boarman, Chas. V..........M.D., '71· Nov. 2, 1901, Washington, D. C.

Boarman, Wm. T...........A.B., '52·

Bodisco, Waldemar de......A.B., '45; A.M., '48· Russian Consul Gen-
                               eral at New York. Died July 31, 1878,
                               Jordan Alum Springs.

Boernstein, Augustus S.....M.D., '73· June 21, 1901.

Bolan, T. V................A.B., '88; A.M., '92· Feb., 1908, Phila., Pa.

Bolway, Wm. J.............LL.B., '93; LL.M., '94·

Bond, Samuel S............M.D., '65· July 4, 1899, Washington, D. C.

Bonford, P. E.............A.B., '36·

Boone, John F.............A.B., '55· C. S. A. Killed crossing the
                               Potomac, Dec. 9, 1863.

Boone, Thos. B............A.B., '53· July, 1909, Brooklyn, N. Y.

Boothby, A................M.D., '63· Feb. 8, 1902, Boston, Mass.

Bossier, Paul.............A.B., '60· Killed in Civil War.

Bossier, Placide...........A.B., '60· C. S. A. Killed in battle of
                               Shiloh.

Boswell, E. V. B..........M.D., '65· Dec. 9, 1878, Washington, D. C.

Boughter, John Frazer......M.D., '67·
Bowling, Harry A...........A.B., '57· Killed in Civil War.
Bradford, John K...........A.B., '78; A.M., '89· July 6, 1901, Wilmington, Del.
Bradford, Wm. M...........A.B., '42·
Bradley, W. D..............A.B., '95· Nov. 16, 1906. Montana.
Bradshaw, Charles..........LL.B., '73. Washington, D. C.
Brennan, Geo. R............LL.B., '94; LL.M., '95· 1896, Wash., D. C.
Brennan, Patrick H. C.......LL.B., '93; LL.M., '94·
Brennan, Patrick J.........LL.B., '91· Aug 10, 1909, Wash., D. C.
Brent, Hon. Geo............A.B., '33; A.M., '37; LL.D., '68· Jan. 6, 1881, Charles County, Md.
Brent, Henry M............A.B., '63; A.M., '67· Oct. 16, 1892, Bay City, N. Y.
Brent, John Carroll.·........A.B., '33; A.M., '49· Feb. 10, 1876, Washington, D. C.
Brent, Robert J............LL.D., '54· Baltimore, Md.
Briscoe, Walter C...........M.D., '69· May 16, 1896.
Brooke, Albert.............LL.B., '90· Jan. 18, 1908, Benning, D. C.
Brooke, Wm. P.............A.B., '44· June 15, 1885, Washington, D. C.
Brosnan, Eugene, Jr........LL.B., '97; LL.M., '98· 1901, Elmira, N. Y.
Brower, Daniel Roberts.....M.D., '64; LL.D., '99· Mar. 1, 1909, Chicago, Ill.
Brown, Andrew Rothwell....M.D., '68· Dec. 16, 1900.
Brown, Robert Y...........A.B., '60· Major, 6th Miss. Cavalry.
Brown, Sevellon A..........LL.B., '73· Feb. 16, 1895.
Brown, Walter E...........LL.B., '98· Probably June, 1903.
Brown, William J..........LL.B., '08· Lawyer, Mar. 17, 1912, Washington, D. C.
Brownlow, J. H.............M.D., '65· Oct. 10, 1899, New York City.
Brownson, John H.........A.B., '49; A.M., '51· 1857, St. Paul, Minn.
Brownson, Orestes A., Jr....A.B., '55· April, 1892, Rockville, Iowa.
Buchanan, Edwin..........M.D., '85· Oct., 1895, Seattle, Wash.
Buck, Alonzo M............M.D., '66· Feb. 28, 1905.
Buck, Lewellyn A..........M.D., '66· Dec. 13, 1906, El Reno, Okla.
Buckley, Patrick...........A.B., '63· Halifax, N. S.
Burchard, Wm. M., Jr........M.D., '66· June 1, 1889, Montville, Conn.
Burche, John A. W.........LL.B., '87·
Burnett, Swan M...........Ph.D., '90· Jan. 18, 1906, Washington, D. C.
Burns, R. P. Miles..........A.B., '73· Feb. 28, 1875, Nashville, Tenn.
Busey, Samuel Clagett......LL.D., '99· Feb. 12, 1901, Wash., D. C.
Butts, Elias M.............LL.M., '95·
Byington, Francis..........M.D., '58· Jan. 14, 1905, Charlestown, W. Va.
Byrne, Rt. Rev. Wm........D.D., '81· Proth. Apost., 1912, Boston.
Byrnes, Thomas............M.D., '65· Walcott, Iowa.

Caine, David M..............LL.B., '87. 1888.
Caldwell, Samuel W........M.D., '67.
Callan, Cornelius Van Ness...M.D., '68. Jan. 28, 1911, Washington, D. C.
Callan, John F...............A.B., '56.
Callanen, Jos. P..............A.B., '53; A.M., '55. New York.
Campbell, Joseph Henry.....LL.B., '03. Feb. 24, 1905.
Camper, Capt. Charles.......LL.B., '73. Dec. 2, 1885, Washington, D C
Canfield, Andrew N........LL.B., '84; LL.M., '85. July 10, 1905.
Capehart, Poindexter W.....M.D., '98. June 29, 1907.
Caperton, Hugh.............A.B., '41. Sept. 14, 1877, Georgetown, D. C.
Carlon, Patrick Jos. F........A.B., '93. Washington, D. C.
Carmody, Francis Joseph....LL.B., '04. Feb. 16, 1907, Washington, D. C.
Carmody, Robert Francis....A.M., '93; M.D., '95. Dec. 31, 1899, Sayre,
                                        Pa.
Carne, Rev. Richard L.......A.M., '68. Feb. 18, 1911, Alexandria, Va.
Carney, Thomas Francis.....A.B , '91. Feb. 8, 1897, Lawrence, Mass.
Carr, Wm. Beresford........A.B., '61; A.M., '72. Nov., 1881.
Carraher, J. V..............M.D., '86. May 1, 1908.
Carriel, Lafayette J..........A.B., '51.
Carroll, John Lee...........LL.D., '89. Feb. 27, 1911, Wash., D. C.
Carroll, Philip..............M D., '79. Dec. 15, 1906, Manzanilla.
Carter, Hon. Thomas H......LL.D., '08. U. S. Senator from Montana.
                                        Sept. 16, 1911, Washington, D. C.
Carvill, William B.........A.B , '79. Dec. 9, 1890, St. John, N. B.
Cass, Philip H.............LL.B., '95; LL.M., '96. Mar. 20, 1912.
Casserly, Daniel A.........A.B., '62; A.M., '68. July 4, 1887, N. Y. City.
Casserly, Hon. Eugene.......A M., '56; LL.D , '72. June 14, 1883, San
                                        Francisco, Cal.
Caulfield, Bernard G.........A.B., '48; A.M., '50. Dec. 19, 1887, Dead-
                                        wood, Dak.
Cecil, Henry A..............A.M., '66. Jan. 23, 1893, Kentucky.
Chamberlin, J. A...........M.D., '63. Sept. 27, 1868.
Cheney, Jasper Edwin.......A.M., '68; M.D., '68.
Chism, Warren P...........A.B., '72. Nov., 1880, Patterson, La.
Choppin, Julius A..........A.B., '52; A.M., '53. Louisiana.
Christie, F. C..............M.D., '59. England.
Clagett, Howard C..........LL B., '79. May 9, 1893, Washington, D. C.
Clancy, John F.............A B., '63.
Clarke, Daniel Boone.......M.D., '57. Aug. 4, 1906, Washington, D. C.
Clarke, George B...........A.B , '41. Baltimore, Md.
Clarke, Joseph H...........A.M., '31. 1885, Washington, D. C.
Clarke, Richard H..........A.B., '46; A.M., '49; LL.D., '72. Lawyer,
                                        May 24, 1911, New York City.
Clarke, Rev. Wm. F., S.J.....A.B., '33. Oct. 17, 1890, Washington, D. C.
Clarke, Wm. H..............A.B., '75. July 13, 1876. Washington, D. C.
Clayson, Frederick H........LL M., '00. 1902.
Cleary, James T., Jr........LL.B., '05. Sept. 12, 1909, Ocean Pk., Cal.

Cleary, Reuben..............M.D., '59; A.M., '60· Feb. 12, 1898, Rio
 Janiero.

Cleary, Reuben..............A.B., '34· Novice, S.J. July 5, 1835,
 Frederick, Md.

Cleveland, Jeremiah.........A.B., '54; A.M., '60· Greenville, S. C.

Coffron, W. H...............M.D., '88· April 7, 1905, Grindstone City,
 Mich.

Cole, Hon. Charles C.........LL.D., '02· Mar. 17, 1905, Wash., D. C.

Colesberry, William H......M.D., '80·

Collins, William Joseph....:.A.B., '93· Feb., 1902, Dedham, Mass.

Collins, William T.........M.D., '65· Nov., 1906, Santa Monica, Cal.

Compton, Edmund...........LL.B., '92· 1906; Aquasco, Prince George
 County, Md.

Compton, Wm. P............M.D., '89· Feb. 1, 1910, Washington, D. C.

Concilio, Rt. Rev. Mon. J. da.. D.D., '89· Mar. 22, 1898, Jersey City, N. J.

Conlin, Charles Francis.....M.D., '04· Dec. 24, 1907, Worcester, Mass.

Conlin, Rev. John A.........A.B., '58· June 23, 1888, Bridgewater,
 Mass.

Conly, Francis..............A.B., '53·

Connolly, Rev. Ed. D.........A.M., '75· April 12, 1911, Norfolk, Va.

Contee, John D..............LL.B., '87· May 30, 1904.

Corcoran, Hon. John W.....LL.D., '95· 1905, Clinton, Mass.

Corcoran, Rev. Wm. J.......A.B., '63 Feb. 21, 1897, Boston, Mass.

Corey, Charles A.........·...LL.B., '95; LL.M., '96· Washington, D. C.

Costello, James F...........LL.B., '03· Dec. 24, 1910, Brookline, Mass.

Coumbe, J. T................M.D, '72· Mar. 7, 1895, Washington, D. C.

Cowan, Francis..............M.D., '69· Feb. 12, 1905. Pennsylvania.

Cowardin, Charles O'B......A.B., '74; A.M., '85· 1900.

Cowling, Wm. W............M.D., '72· 1900.

Cox, Francis Marcellus.....LL.B., '74· Oct., 1909, Washington, D. C.

Cox, Walter S...............A.B., '43; A.M., '47· 1903, Wash., D. C.

Croggon, Richard C........:..M.D., '60·

Cronin, Patrick W...........A.B., '64· Lawrence, Mass.

Cronin, Wm. Joseph.........LL.B., '94; LL.M., '95; A.M.; '95· Nov.,
 1899, Pawtucket, R. I. Mayor of Paw-
 tucket at death.

Crosby, Chas. F.............LL.B., '97; LL.M., '98· San Antonio, Tex.

Crowley, Jeremiah..........A.B., '64· Jan. 16, 1906, Chicago, Ill.

Cullinane, James A..........LL.B., '87; LL.M., '88·

Cummings, Francis J........A.M., '89· August, 1890.

Cummiskey, Eugene.........A.B., '44; A.M., '49· Philadelphia, Pa.

Cutts, Richard D............A.B., '35; A.M., '42· Dec. 14' 1883, Washington, D. C.

Cuyler, Geo. A..............A.B., '38; A.M., '42· June, 1867, Munich,
 Bavaria.

10

Dahlgren, John Vinton.......A.B., '89; A.M., '91; LL.B., '91; LL.M., '92·
Aug. 11, 1899, Colorado Spgs., Colo.
Dailey, Oliver A............M.D., '55· Jan. 5, 1896, Kansas City, Mo.
Daly, Francis J. M.........A.M., '75; LL.B., '75· Feb. 19, 1892, Macon, Ga.
Daly, Joseph Russell.......A.B., '09· Dec. 4, 1911, New York City.
Davenport, Benjamin........LL.B., '74·
Davidson, Falconer.........M.D., '93·
Deane, Julian W.'..........M.D., '68· May 6, 1905, Washington, D. C.
Deery, Rev. James P., S.J....A.B., '27· June 21, 1833, Washington, D. C.
Degni, Rev. Januarius M., S.J..Ph.D., '76· Jan. 31, 1909, Naples, Italy.
Deloughery, Edward........A.B., '26· Nov. 18, 1885, Baltimore, Md.
Denby, Hon. Charles........LL.D., '85· Min. to China, 1885-1898. Jan. 13, 1904, Jamestown, N. Y.
Denman, Hampton Y........LL.M., '96· 1904.
Denvir, William J...........A.B., '58· Sept. 1, 1885, Charlestown, Mass.
Dermody, John C...........LL.B., '89; LL.M., '90· Washington, D. C.
Desaulniers, Rev. Francis L..A.M., '34· St. Hyacinthe, P. Q., Canada.
Des Londe, Maj. Edmund A..A.B., '49· April 5, 1886.
Desmond, Daniel I..........A.M., '31·
Detrick, R. Baxter..........M.D , '58· Nov. 7, 1904, Kensington, Md.
Devine, Patrick H.........LL.B., '85· Washington, D. C
Devlen, John E.............A.B., '40; A.M., '53· Mar., 1888, N. Y. City.
Devlin, Wm. H.............A.B., '50· Boston, Mass.
Dick, Ewell A.............'..LL.B., '77· Oct. 19, 1903, Wash., D. C. ·
Dielman, Professor Henry...Mus. Doc., '49· Oct. 12, 1882, Emmitsburg, Md.
Digges, Daniel C..........A.B., '33; A.M., '37·
Digges, Eugene............A.B., '57· June 29, 1899, Austin, Tex.
Dillon, Geo. W.............A.B., '58·
Dimitry, Alexander.........A.M., '32; LL.D.; '59· 1883, New Orleans, La.
Dimitry, John B.............A.M., '67·
Dimitry, Michael Draco......A.M., '56· Feb., 1883.
Dimitry, Theodore J........A M., '92· May 31, 1904, New Orleans, La.
Dinnies, Charles...........A.B., '17·
Dinnies, Geo...............A.B., '17·
Dixon, Wm. Wirt, Jr........LL.B., '99· Mar. 30, 1900, Butte, Mont.
Dodge, Robert H...........M.D., '93· Mar. 11, 1901, Bethesda, Md.
Doherty, Rev. Michael L.....A.B., '63· Aug. 28, 1886, Milbury, Mass
Dolan, John J..............LL.B., '93; LL.M., '94· Aug., 1900.
Donaldson, Walter A.......A.B., '75; A.M., '91· May 15, 1906, Bloomfield, N. J.
Donaldson, Walter Franklin.LL.B., '05· Dec. 20, 1911. Wash , D. C.
Donnelly, Edward C........A.B., '44· Jan. 4, 1891, New York City.
Donnelly, James P....... ..A.B., '53· 1857, New Jersey.

Donahue, Florence.........∴..M.D., '72· June 24, 1908.

Dougherty, James D.......A.B., '57; A.M., '60· April 2, 1878, Harrisburg, Pa.

Dougherty, Very Rev. Jas. J..D.D., '89; LL.D.. '97. Feb.. 1906, New York City.

Douglas, Stephen Arnold....A.B., '01·

Douglass, Geo. M ..........A.B., '73; A.M., '77· Mar. 8, 1888, Washington, D. C.

Douglass, Henry J.........M.D., '73·

Dowd, Patrick.............A.B., '53· 1854.

Downing, Thos. R..........Phar.B., '73.

Doyle, Edward F...........A.B., '35; A.M., '39· Pennsylvania.

Doyle, John T .............A.B., '38; A.M., '42; LL.D., '89· Dec. 23, 1906, Menlo Park, Cal.

Doyle, Robert Emmet.......A.B., '46· Mar. 18, 1898, San Francisco, Cal.

Duffy, Francis............. A.B., '79; A.M., '89· Nov., 1900.

Dufour, Rev. Alphonse, S.J..A.M., '96· 1907, Alexandria, Egypt.

Dugan, James Henry..... ..A.B., '96· Mar. 2, 1903, La Salle, Ill.

Duke, Thomas.............LL.B., '76· Feb. 3, 1888.

Duncan, Rev. Wm. H:, S.J...A.B , '53; A.M., '60· Dec. 20, 1894, Georgetown College, D. C.

Dunphy, John F............M.D., '73· Newburgh, N. Y.

Durkee, Robert A..... ....A.M., '31· June, 1848, Baltimore, Md.

Durnan, Rev. James A..... .A.B., '51· April 15, 1873, Calais, Me.

Duvall, Charles........... A.B., '30·

Dwight, Thomas...........LL.D., '89· Sept., 1911, Nahant, Mass.

Dyer, Dr. Geo. A...........A.M., '56· Jan. 12, 1879, Washington, Ind.

Dyer, Philip Eugene........A.B., '96· April 7, 1897, Wash., D. C.

Dykers, Francis H..........A.B., '44; A.M., '45· New York.

Easterling, J. Morgan.......LL.M., '85·

Eastman, Joseph A........ M.D., '65. June 5, 1902. Indianapolis, Ind.

Eccleston, Charles A.......LL.B., '92; LL.M., '93· Jan. 24, 1901, Washington, D. C.

Eccleston, G. Malcolm...... LL.B., '99; LL.M., '00·

Eckfeldt, Frederick........M. D., '82·

Eckhardt, Charles H.......M.D., '71·

Edelen, E. Gardiner. .......LL.B., '90· Mar. 18, 1891, Baltimore, Md.

Edmonston, R. Augustine....M D., '97· 1900, Philippine Islands.

Edmundson, James P.......A.B., '35.

Edwards, Joseph F.........A.M., '82

Eldridge, Stuart............M.D., '68· Nov. 16, 1901, Yokohama.

Eliot, Johnson.............A.M., '69; Phar.B., '71; Phar.D., '72· Dec 30, 1883, Washington, D.·C.

Elliot, John J............ ..A.B., '61· Dec., 1867, Washington, D. C.

Elliott, Charles A..........A.B., '72; LL.B., '74; A.M., '89· Aug. 1, 1894, Washington, D. C.

Errazuriz, Senor DonYsidoro. A.B., '52.   Mar. 12, 1898, Rio Janier
                                      Brazil.
Esling, Charles H. A........A.M., '89. Feb. 1, 1907, Stuttgart, Ger.
Etheridge, Bell W..........A.B., '76· Mar. 26, 1901, Dresden, Tenn.
Ewing, Thomas, Jr.........LL.D., '70·

Fairclough, Rev. John....,...A.M., '21· Lancashire, England.
Falls, Alexander J..,......LL.B., '73·
Farrell, Edward G.........LL.B., '97; LL.M., '96·
Farrell, Edward P..........A.B., '83· Louisville, Ky.
Farrell, Emmet Lee.........A.M., '93; LL.B., '94· Feb. 23, 1895. -
Faulkner, Charles James F..A.B., '22· Nov. 1, 1884. Martinsburg
                                    W. Va.
Fay, Andrew Edwin........LL.B., '98· 1898. Old Orchard, Me.
Fenton, David H...........LL.B., '96; LL.M., '97· Kensington, Md.
Fenwick, Geo.............;A.B., '32· Nov. 18, 1857· Wash., D. C.
Ferguson, Arthur W........LL.B., '85; LL.M., '86· Jan. 30, 1908
                                Manila, P. I.
Fetterman, Wilfred B.......A.B., '52· Mar. 30, 1910, Philadelphia, Pa
Fillette, St. Julian..........LL.B., '86; LL.M., '87·
Fisher, George P., Jr.......A.B., '74; LL.B., 76.
Fisher, George W..........M.D.' '70· 1909, Anacostia, D. C.
Fitch, George A,...........M.D , '68; A.M., '69· Nov. 30, 1875.
Fitzgerald, Edward.........A.B., '32·
Fitzgerald, Edward H.......A.M., '50· Jan. 9, 1860.
Fitzpatrick, James F.......A.B., '65· Washington, D. C.
Flannery, Rev. Wm.........D.D., '92· London, Ontario,
Flatley, Thomas J...·.......A.B., '77; LL.B., '79; LL.M., '89· Feb. 25
                                1892, Boston, Mass.
Floyd, Benjamin R........A.B., '32; A.M., '36·
Floyd, Wm. P..............A.B., '30; A.M., 36.
Flynn, Very Rev. D. J......LL.D., '06· President Mt. St. Mary's Col
                                lege, July 7, 1911.
Folchi, Rev. Pietro, S.J.....D.Sc., '72· Sept. 13, 1890, Tivoli, Italy.
Ford, Hon. Robert..........A.B., '38; A.M., '42; LL.D., '68· 1884
                                St. Mary's County, Md.
Forman, Sands W..........A.B., '69; A.M., '71·
Forrest, Joseph I...........A.B., '65· 1901.
Forstall, Henry J..........A.B., '48·
Foster, F. J................M.D., '71· Feb. 5, 1911, Washington, D. C
Fowler, Harry Brightwell...LL.B., '98·
France, J. M. Duncan.......M.D., '65· May 9, 1906, St. Joseph, Mo.
French, George N..........M.D., '68· Arizona.
French, James H...........A.B., '39·
French, Richardo D. Del....M.D., '67· 1890, Washington, D. C.
Frost, John W..............M.D., '91· May 17, 1906.
Fullerton, James B.........LL.B., '80· Jan. 19, 1899, Wash., D. C.
Fulmer, Geo. W............A.B., '53; A.M., '55.

Gaither, Harris E..........D.D.S., '06· 1908, Washington, D. C.
Gallagher, M. F............M.D., '89· Nov. 25, 1910, Washington, D. C.
Galligan, John H...........A.B., '72· Sept. 8, 1893.
Gallinger, Wm. H. Augustine.LL.B., '93· 1910, Washington, D. C.
Gandarillas, Rev. Joaquin
   Larrain Y................D.D., '52·
Gardiner, Geo..............A.B., '24·
Gardiner, John B..........A.B., '59· 1861, Charles County. Md.
Gardiner, Richard H.......A.B., '55; A.M., '56· Charles County, Md.
Gardner, W. H....:.........M.D., '61· June 3, 1908, Washington, D. C.
Garesche, Lieut. Julius P....A.M., '42· Dec. 13, 1862, Battle of Stone
                              River.
Garesche, William A........A.B., '71· Mar. 17, 1905.
Garland, Hon. Augustus H...LL.D., '89· Jan. 26, 1899, Washington, D. C.
Garland, Rufus Cummings...Ph.B., '87; LL.B., '91· Mar. 11, 1901, Fort
                              Worth, Tex.
Gaston, Hugh J......:......A.B., '55· Dec., 1862. Killed at Battle of
                              Fredericksburg.
Gibbon, D. J...............M.D., '69· Mar. 5, 1907, Washington, D. C.
Gibbs, Thomas F....:.......M.D., '70· Jan. 30, 1906, Washington, D. C.
Gieseking, Henry N.........M.D., '76· Washington, D. C.
Gillespie, Robert K........LL.B., '94· Nov., 1894, Washington, D. C.
Gillis, Capt. J. Melvin, U.S.N..M.A., '43· Feb. 9, 1865.
Gilluly, John Francis......M.D., '03· June 21, 1905.
Girard, Charles............M.D., '56· Jan. 29, 1895.
Gleason, Aaron R...........M.D., '64· Mar. 4, 1904, Keene, N. H.
Goff, George Paul..........LL.B., '74; A. M., '80· Dec., 1896.
Gonzaga, Isaias, P..;......LL.B., '07· Sept. 21, 1908, Cebu, P. I.
Gooch, Dr. Philip C........A.M., '49·
Gough, Henry..............A.B., '18·
Gough, Stephen H..........A. M., '31·
Gouley, Louis G............A.B., '66; A.M., '71· Oct. 17, 1879, New
                              York City.
Gow, Edwin R..............LL.B., '96· Feb. 29, 1908, Wash., D. C.
Gow, James R..............LL.B., '93·
Green, Benjamin E.........A.B., '38· May 13, 1907, Dalton, Ga.
Green, John Matthew.......M.D., '75· Oct., 1881, Key West, Fla.
Green, Richardson.........A.B., '33·
Green, William G...........M.D , '68·
Green, William R..........A.B., '33·
Greenwood, Walter S.......LL.B., '11· Feb. 8, 1912, Phoenix, Ariz.
Griffin, Dennis Peter......LL.B., '99; LL.M., '00. Boston, Mass.
Griffiss, Edward J.........A.B., '74· July 4, 1904, Baltimore, Md
Griffiss, John I...........A.B., '76· Feb. 19, 1894, Washington, D. C.
Grymes, James W..........M.D., '53· 1862.
Guidry, Onesimus..........A.B., '36·
Gwynn, William...........LL.D., '31·
Gwynn, Dr. William H.......A.B., '55; A.M., '57· Prince George Co., Md.

Hainner, Geo. W............LL.M., '87. May, 1908.
Hall, Henry S...............M.D., '71· Hyattsville, Md. ·
Hallahan, John William.....A.B., '99; A.M., '00· July 2, 1910, Cape
                         May, N. J.
Hamilton, John B..........LL.D., '89·
Hamilton, John C. C........A.B., '51· July, 1862. Washington, D. C.
Hamilton, Patrick H........A.B., '35· Dec. 24, 1898, Elgin, Ill.
Hamlet, Wm...............M.D., '69·
Hammett, C. M.............M.D., '56· Nov. 22, 1898, Washington, D. C.
Hammond, William A......A.B., '68; A.M., '71· Sept., 1892, Ellicott
                         City, Md.
Hamner, George W.........LL.M., '87· May, 1908, Washington, D. C.
Hampson, Thomas..........LL.B., '82· April 22, 1888.
Hanley, Bernard T.........LL.B., '73· 1882.
Hanna, John F.............A.M., '70· Oct. 31, 1885, Washington, D. C.
Hannegan, Edward A.......LL.B., '90· June 12, 1891, Fort Monroe, Va.
Harding, W. R.............A.B., '36·
Harper, Robert W..........A.B., '52· Killed at Chickamauga.
Hartigan, James F.........M.D., '68· Jan. 31, 1894, Trieste, Austria.
Harvey, A. Thomas.........A.B., '76· Oct. 6, 1882, Washington, D. C.
Harvey, George E..........M.D., '84·
Harvey, Levin Allen........M.D., '75· Washington, D. C.
Hastings, Edward..........A.B., '36. Scholastic, S.J., Sept. 19, 1840,
                         Georgetown Col., Georgetown, D. C.
Haswell, John H...........LL.B., '73·
Hawes, John B.......... ...M.D., '86· Aug. 20, 1907, Denver, Col.
Hawkes, Dr. Wm. H........A.M., '90· Mar. 13, 1904.
Hayden, Joseph E.... .....LL.B., '76· 1902, Washington, D. C.
Hays, W. W................M.D., '61· July 3, 1901, Obisco, Cal.
Hayward, William H.......M.D., '69· 1896, California.
Hazard, Daniel C...........M.D., '71·
Hazen, David H............M.D., '73· Nov. 7, 1906, Washington, D. C.
Healy, Hugh C.............A.B., '49· Sept. 23, 1852.
Healy, Rt. Rev. James A.....A.B., '49; A.M., '51; D.D. '74· Aug. 5, 1900,
                         Portland, Me.
Healy, Rev. Patrick F., S.J...A.B., '50· Jan. 10, 1910, Georgetown, D. C.
Heard, John M.............A.B., '42; A.M., '47· 1895, Wash., D. C.
Hechtman, Henry J.........LL.B., '73· Jan. 17, 1912, Durango, Colo.
Heimler, Rev. Alphonsus,
    O.S.B. .................A.M., '60·
Helmer, Burton K..........LL.B., '91· 1905, Washington, D. C.
Henry, Charles T...........LL.B., '92; LL.M., '93· Dec. 16, 1908,
                         Colonial Beach, Va.
Herbert, J. Wells...........M.D., '59. Oct. 21, 1903.
Herran, Hon. Thomas......A.B., '63; A.M., '68; LL.D., '99· Aug. 10,
                         1904, Liberty, N. Y.
Hickcox, John Howard, Jr...LL.B., '79.

Hickling, Daniel Percy......Phar.B., '71; Phar.D., '72; M.D., '84. 1906, Washington, D. C.

Hill, Joshua.................LL.B., '93· 1883, Madison, Ga.

Hill, Major Nicholas S.......A.B., '58; A.M., '60· May 18, 1912, East Orange, N. J.

Hill, Raymond J.............A.B., '60· California.

Hill, Dr. Wm. Costilo........M.D., '97· Sept. 3, 1900, Huntsville, Ala.

Hill, William I..............A.B., '57; A.M., '60·

Hillen, Solomon.............A.B., '27·

Hindmarsh, Walter B.......LL.B., '96; LL.M., '97· July 22, 1910, Washington, D. C.

Hirschman, Norris.........LL.M., '05·

Hirst, William L...........A.B., '63· Mar. 19, 1880, Chicago, Ill.

Hoban, James F.............A.B., '60· Washington, D. C.

Holliday, John Edwin.......LL.B., '10; LL.M., '11· July 3, 1911, Washington, D. C.

Hollingsworth, John S.......A.B., '73· Jan. 14, 1895.

Holztman, Ernest...........LL.B., '93; LL.M., '94· Washington, D. C.

Hood, Col. Arthur..........A.B., '77· Feb. 24, 1901, Cuthbert, Ga.

Houston, Samuel...........M.D., '68· Nov. 17, 1907.

Howard, Flodoardo.........Phar.B., '71; Fhar.D., '72· Jan., 1888, Rockville, Md.

Howard, Joseph T..........M.D., '59· Jan. 30, 1910, Washington, D. C.

Howard, Robert............M.D., '67; A.M., '70; LL.B., '74· Dec. 1, 1869, St. Paul, Minn.

Howe, Franklin Theodore....M.D., '67; A.M., '89· July 28, 1908, Washington, D. C.

Howle, Peter C.............A.B., '45· Nov. 24, 1865.

Hoyt, Charles A............A.B., '57; A.M., '60· April 18, 1903, Pasadena, Cal.

Hullihen, Alfred F.........A.B., '55· . 1883.

Hunt, Presley C............M.D., '91· Dec. 15, 1910, Baltimore, Md.

Huntoon, Andrew J.........M.D., '67·

Huselton, Wm. S...........M.D., '65· Jan. 1· 1910. Pittsburgh, Pa.

Hyatt, P. F................M.D., '65· Mar., 1904.

Iglehart, James Alexis......A.B., '45· May 1, 1908, Davidsonville, Md.

Ironside, Geo. E............LL.D., '22· May 7, 1827.

Jackson, Albert L..........M.D., '89· Oct. 16, 1899, Herkimer, N. Y.

Jackson, W. C..............LL.B., '98· 1904, Florida.

James, Judge Charles P.....LL.D., '70·

Jenkins, Louis Wm.........A.B., '22; A.M., '31· Sept. 20, 1840, Baltimore, Md.

Jenkins, T. Robert.........A.B., '40·

Jenkins, Theodore.........A.B., '26·

Jewell, J. Gray............M.D., '55· Sept. 17, 1894.

Johnson, Dallas.............M.D., '68·
Johnson, Frank G..........M.D., '91· April 16, 1906, Kensington, Md.
Johnson, Jeremiah.........LL.B., '85; LL.M., '86.
Johnson, John Lewis........LL.B., '04· April 8, 1910, Wash., D. C.
Johnson, Walter A..........A.B., '91· Dec. 16, 1899, Americus, Ga.
Johnson, Wm. Carey........LL.B., '99; LL.M., '00· Washington, D. C.
Jones, Benj. C.............M.D., '68· May, 1898, Poplar Bluffs, Mo.
Jones, Charles S............LL.B., '91; LL.M., '92.
Jones, Sen. Chas. W.......LL.D., '82· Oct. 11, 1897, Dearborn, Mich.
Jones, E. S.....'..........M.D., '72·
Jones, Edwin C............LL.B., '95; LL.M., '96· April 7, 1908, Long
                            Beach, Cal.
Jones, Elcon...............A.M., '32· 1865, Washington, D. C.
Jones, Elwyn Thornton.....LL.B., '03· Washington, D. C.
Jordan, Edward L..........LL.B., '96· Jan. 8, 1907, Washington, D. C.
Jordan, James Hammer.....M.D., '56·
Jourdan, Arthur J..........A.B., '52· 1853, New Orleans, La.
Jouy, Joseph...............M.D., '69. Jan. 5, 1901.
Joyce, J. Williamson.......M.D., '73· Dec. 16, 1890.
Judd, Sylvester D..........M.S., '97; Ph.D., '98· 1905, Baltimore, Md.

Kalussowski, H. Corwin......M.D., '52·
Kane, Dennis D.............LL.B., '75.
Keables, T. A..............M.D., '72· Mar. 2, 1902.
Keene, P. T................M.D., '70·
Kellogg, Daniel M...:......LL.B., '93; LL.M., '94· 1900, Anacostia,
                            D. C.
Kelly, Rev. Charles F., S.J...D.D., '89. 1906, Philadelphia, Pa.
Kelly, Wm. E...............LL.B., '97· Dec. 18, 1899, Philadelphia, Pa.
Kelso, Paul................LL.B., '97·
Kengla, Bernard A.........LL.B., '87· Feb. 18, 1891, Wash., D. C.
Kengla, Louis A............B.S., '82; A.B., '83; M.D., '86· 1904, San
                            Francisco, Cal.
Kenna, Edward B..........A.B., '99· Mar. 22, 1912, Charlestown,
                            W. Va.
Kennedy, Beverly C........A.B., '58· Mar. 19, 1894, New Orleans, La.
Kennedy, Rev. Daniel B.....A.B., '62· Mar. 8, 1911, Baltimore, Md.
Kennedy, Rev. Duncan A., S.J.A.B., '34· Sept. 4, 1855, Eastport, Me.
Kennedy, Frank P..........LL.B., '97· April 4, 1911, Baltimore, Md.
Kennedy, George S.........A.B., '34· Scholastic, S.J., Nov. 9, 1837,
                            New York.
Kennedy, John A..........A.B., '40·
Kennedy, Judge Thos. H.....A.B., '32· Nov. 20, 1884, New Orleans, La.
Kennedy, Wm. E...........A.M., '32· July 10, 1888, New Orleans, La.
Kennon, J. C. W..........M.D., '57·
Kenny, Chas. Borromeo......A.B., '58; LL.D., '10· April, 1912, Pitts-
                            burgh, Pa.

Kenny, Lawrence..........A.B., '60· 1886·

Kernan, Senator Francis....LL.D., '80· Sept. 8, 1892, Utica, N. Y.

Kernan, Leslie Warnick.....A.B., '86· 1903, Utica, N. Y.

Kernan, Wm. J.............A.B., '80· Dec. 8, 1900, Utica, N. Y.

Ketcham, Orlando E........M.D., '71· July 30, 1890, Wash., D. C.

Kett, Michael C............M.D., '04· Aug. 6, 1909, Glenwood Springs, Colo.

Kidwell, John W...........A.B., '60; A.M , '66· Washington, D. C.

Keys, Frank R..:...........LL.B., '90; LL.M., '91· Jan. 4, 1911, Washington, D. C.

Kieckoefer, Frank J........A.B., '68; LL.B , '87; LL.M., '88; A.M., '89· Jan. 1, 1912, New York.

Kiggins, F. M.............LL.B., '85; LL.M., 86. Oct. 26, 1908, Washington, D. C.

King, Edwin F.......... ...A.B., '51; A.M., '55· Washington, D. C.

King, John F..............A.B., '52· Mar. 25, 1873, Washington, D. C.

King, Thos. B.............A.B., '52; A.M., '60· 1868, Charleston, S. C.

Kirby, Maurice Brown.......A.B., '98· Mar. 27, 1911, New York City.

Kirkpatrick, John L.........A.B., '43· Georgia.

Kleinschmidt, Chas. H. A....M.D. '62; Ph.D., 89. May 20, 1905, Washington, D. C.

Knighton, Nicholas ........A.B., '45·

Knowlan, Dominic F........A.B., '90· July, 1899.

Lafferty, Daniel L..........A.B., '64· 1866.

Lafferty, Francis F. S.......A.B., '65· 1868.

LaGrange, Ernest H........LL.B., '88; LL.M., '89·

Lamar, Lucius Q. C........LL.B., '95· Dec. 31, 1910, Dallas, Tex.

Lancaster, F. M...........A.B., '51; A.M., '57; M.D., '57·

Lancaster, Col. Francis A...A.B., '57· May 3, 1863, killed at Chancellorsville.

Landry, L. Valery..........A.B., '48· 1850.

Lang, Charles J............M.D., '87· April 9, 1900, Washington, D. C.

Lang, Henry J.............A.B., '40·

Laphen, James S...........A.B., '37· Alexandria, Va.

LaRoche, Dr. C. Percy de....A.B., '53; A.M., '61· Mar. 12, 1907, Rome, Italy.

Lathrop, John P...........LL.B., '74·

Lawler, Francis J..........A.B., '85· May, 1890, Prairie du Chien, Wis.

Lawler, Thos. C...........A.B., '79· April 17, 1908, Dubuque, Iowa.

Lawrence, James B........M.D., '73·

Lawton, John M...........LL.B., '86; LL.M., '87·

Leach, Hamilton E......... M.D., '72· May 19, 1893, Washington, D. C.

Leahy, Michael J..........LL.B., '06· Aug. 12, 1909, Wash., D. C.

Leckie, Richard............LL.B., '92· 1895, Richmond, Va.

LeCompte, S. B............M.D., '68·

Lee, Arthur...............A.B., '67· April 12, 1899, St. Louis, Mo.

Lee, Chapman..............M.D., '66·

Legendre, Adolphus.........A.B., '25·
Lenmann, Fredk. A.........LL.B., '75·
Lennon, Joseph Arthur.......A.M., '03; LL.B., '07· May 24, 1911, Bos-
              ton, Mass.
Lett, Frederick R...........A.B., '86· Sept. 14, 1900, New York.
Levey, A. L.................M.D., '94.
Lewis, Fielding.. ..........LL.B., '89; LL.M., '90· Nov. 12, 1908, Mc-
              Alester, Okla.
Lewis, James P.............M.D., '78· Dec. 22, 1901, Wash., D. C. ·
Lewis, Wm. H..............A.B., '40· Tennessee.
Lilly, Rev. Samuel M., S.J...A.B., '42· Nov. 25, 1854, Baltimore, Md.·
Little, John J..............M.D., '71· Washington, D. C.
Littlewood, James B........M.D., '68· Feb. 7, 1906.
Locke, Herbert M..........LL.B., '94; LL.M., '95· Washington, D. C.
Long, Wm.................M.D., '87· May 14, 1909.
Longstreth, John Cooke.....A.B., '47; A.M., '51· Dec. 29, 1891, Phila-
              delphia, Pa.
Longuemare, Eugene........A.B., '54·
Loomis, L. C...............M.D., '63· Oct. 17, 1905.
Loomis, Silas L............M.D., '57· June 22, 1896.
Loughborough, Alex. H.....A.B., '55; A.M., '58; LL.D., '89· Jan. 29,
              1897, San Francisco, Cal.
Lovelace, Robert...........A.B., '59·
Lowe, E. Louis.............LL.D., '53· Ex-Governor of Maryland.
Lowe, Enoch M............·A.B., '52. June 11, 1879, Alexandria, ·Va.
Luckett, Oliver A..........A.B., '39· Mar. 30, 1900.
Luckey, Nelson E..........LL.B., '94; LL.M., '95·
Lyden, Michael J...........LL.B., '95; LL.M., '96· Aug. 2, 1901.
Lynch, Edward A..........A.B., '22; A.M., '31· Frederick, Md.
Lynch, Rev. James.........A.M., '28· 1828, Mt. St. Mary's College,
              Emmitsburg, Md.
Lynch, John G.............A.B., '24·
Lynch, Rev. Joseph Thomas..A.B., '02· May 8, 1908, Northampton, Mass.
Lynch, Patrick Michael.....M.D., '01· Springfield, Mass.
Lynch, William D..........A.B., '86· 1888.
Lynch, Cap. W. F., U. S. N.. A.M., '44· Oct. 17, 1865. Baltimore, Md.
Lyon, William B..........M.D., '67·

McAllister, Richard, Jr.....LL.B., '73·
McAuley, Rev. John, S.J.....A.B., '55.· Dec. 2, 1885, Worcester, Mass.·
McBlair, J. Hollins, Jr......M.D., '69· Dec. 13, 1899.
McBride, Parks R..........LL.B., '94; LL.M., '95· Mar. 17, 1897.
McCabe, John..............A.B., '49. Providence, R. I.
McCahill, Edwin...........A.B., '65; A.M., '67· Oct. 23, 1878, New
              Brunswick, N. J.
McCarthy, John J..........LL.B., '99; LL.M., '00· Atlanta, Ga.
McCauley, Joseph A........M.D., '72·
McCloskey, Very Rev. Geo...D.D., '89· Aug. 3, 1890.

McCloskey, Very Rev. John...D.D., '75· Dec. 24, 1880.
McCloskey, Joseph J.........LL.B., '85·
McComas, Hon. Louis E.....LL.D., '02· 1907, Washington, D. C.
McConnell, James C.........M.D., '68· July 25, 1904.
McCormick, Charles.........M.D., '61· July, 1868.
McCoy, George.............M.D., '57· Oct. 8, 1880.
McCreedy, Dr. Jeremiah .....A.B., '24; A.M., '32·
McCullough, Henry.........A.B., '63· 1873.
McDermott, John A.........A.B., '84· 1907, Washington, D. C.
McDonough, James A........A.B., '63· Aug. 15, 1907, Boston, Mass.
McElhone, John J..........A.M., '83· 1890.
McElmell, Rear Ad. Jackson,
    U. S. N.................A.M., '72· May 31, 1908, Philadelphia, Pa.
McElroy, James P..........A.B., '64· 1866.
McFaul, John B.............A.B., '87· Dec. 23, 1890, New York City.
McGahan, Charles F.........B.S., '81· Feb. 15, 1910, Aiken, S. C.
McGovern, Edward M........A.B., '52; A.M., '64· Sept. 19, 1897, Lan-
    caster, Pa.
McHenry, Philip J., Jr......A.B., '87; A.M., '91; LL.B., '96·
McIntire, Hugh Henry.......M.D., '68· Aug. 13, 1906, Barnard, Vt.
McIntyre, T. C..............M.D., '54· 1862
McLaughlin, D. J............A.B., '88· June, 1905, San Francisco, Cal.
McLaughlin, James F........A.B., '60; A.M., '62; LL.D., '89· 1903, New
    York City.
McLaughlin, William L......A.B., '82; A.M., '84; LL.B., '84· Deadwood,
    S. D.
McLeod, James M...........A.B., '57; A.M., '60· Killed by Indians
    Feb. 11, 1867, Texas.
McLeod, Wilfred M.........M.D., '76· Feb. 11, 1897.
McManus, Francis Patrick...A.B., '80· April 17, 1885, Baltimore, Md.
McNeirny, Michael J.........LL.B., '77· Jan. 26, 1911, Boston, Mass.
McNulty, Frederick J.......M.D., '60· June 14, 1897, Boston, Mass.
McSherry, James............A B., '33·
McSherry, William D.......A.B., '42· Scholastic, S.J., Oct. 16, 1845,
    Martinsburg, W. Va.
McVary, Stephen A.........M.D., '80·
Mabrey, Richard L.........LL.B., '96·
Macdonald, Martin A.......LL.B., '93; LL.M., '94·
Mackall, James McV........A.B., '70; A.M., '74; M.D., '74. June 25,
    1909, Washington, D. C.
Mackey, Beckford..........LL.B., '83· 1911, Mexico.
Mackin, Very Rev. Dean   A.B., '71; A.M., '89· Feb. 15, 1905, Rock
    Thos. V. G.....;..........   Island, Iowa.
Macshane, Col. James.......A.M., '58· Halifax, Nova Scotia.
Madan, Philip A.............A.B., '58· Cuba.
Madigan, James C..........A.M., '50· Oct. 16, 1879, Houlton, Me.
Magale, Joseph F..........A.B., '91· Magnolia, Ark.
Maginnis, Charles B........A.B., '62· July 6, 1867.

Magruder, Caleb C.........A.M., '34·
Maguire, Dominic....:......A.B., '52; A.M., '58.
Major, Daniel G............A.M., '59. Feb. 24, 1889, St. Vincent's
                              Hospital, New York.
Major, John J............A.B., '64; A.M., '72· Mar. 31, 1889, St.
                              Vincent's Hospital, New York.
Malcolm, Granville.........M.D., '67· April 23, 1911, Denver, Colo.
Mallory, Hon. Stephen R....A.B., '69; A.M. '71; LL.D., '04· Dec. 23,
                              1907, while U. S. Senator from
                              Florida, Pensacola, Fla.
Mann, Harry E.............A.M., '89· May 4, 1910, Baltimore, Md. .
Marbury, Wm..............A.B., '43· Dec. 18, 1879, Georgetown, D. C.
Markriter, John J..........M.D., '82· July 13, 1891, Washington, D. C.
Marshall, John P...........A.B., '59·
Marshall, T. W M..........LL.D., '72· Dec. 14, 1877, Surrey, Eng.
Martin, James O......... ...A.B., '59.
Martin, Hon. John M.......A.M., '91; LL.D., '94.
Martyn, Francis G.........LL.B., '90; LL.M., '91· Washington, D. C.
Mason, E..................A.B., '23·
Mason, John E....:......M.D., '68·
Mattingly, Francis Carroll...LL.B., '97; LL.M., '98. Mar. 5, 1908,
                              Washington, D. C.
Maury, Matthew F....... . A.M., '45· Jan. 31, 1873, Lexington, Va.
Mauss, Richard G....... ..M.D., '72. April 30, 1891.
Mayo, George Upshur.. ...A.M., '89· Feb. 3, 1896.
Mellen, Edward L..........B.S., '81·
Melville, Admiral George
   Wallace, U. S. N....: ....LL.D., '99· Mar. 17, 1912, Philadelphia, Pa.
Menke, John R.......... :..M.D., '80· Sept. 30, 1882.
Mercier, Hon. Honore......LL.D., '89 Oct. 30, 1894, Montreal, Can.
Merrick, Richard T.........LL.D., '73· June 23, 1885, Chicago, Ill.
Merrick, Col. Wm. D........A.M., '31· U. S. Sen. from Maryland, 1870.
Merrick, Hon. William M. .LL.D., '75· Feb. 4, 1889.
Meyerhardt, Louis.........LL.B., '86·
Middleton, Johnson, V.D....M.D., '55· Jan. 29, 1907. ·
Millard, Dr. Edward V.. ...A.B, '32· 1882, Grand Coteau, La.
Miller, John S........ .. ..M.D., '65· Mar. 1, 1908, Redlands, Cal.
Miller, Samuel F.... ......LL.D., '72·
Minnick, W. H. H...........M.D., '73. Aug. 24, 1904, Wash., D. C.-
Mitchell, Wm. M...........M.D., '70· June 15, 1908, Ferndale, Cal.
Montgomery, Hon. Zachariah.LL.D., '89·
Mooney, Paul ....:.....A.B., '21.
Moore, Charles T...:......LL.B., '83· 1910, Virginia.
Moore, J. B..............M.D., '71· Oct 1908, Washington, D. C.
Moore, J. Hall............ M.D., '54. Dec. 28, 1906' Richmond, Va.
Morales, Aug. Jose... ......LL.D., '59·
Moran, Rev. Dennis C.......A.B., '62 July 23, 1889, Adams, Mass.
Morgan, Ethelbert C........Ph.D., '89· May 5, 1891, Washington, D. C.

Morgan, James E..........A.B., '06· Neola, Iowa.
Morgan, J. Felix..........M.D., '58· Leonardtown, Md.
Morgan, James Lamotte......A.B., '78· Jan. 30, 1904, New York.
Morris, Hon. Martin F......LL.D., '77· Associate Justice, Ct. of Appeals, Sept. 12, 1909, Wash., D. C.
Morris, P. Pemberton........A.B., '36; A.M., '40· 1888, Phila., Pa.
Mudd, Jeremiah............A.M., '24·
Mullaly, James F. S.........A.B., '73· 1887. Spokane Falls, Wash.
Mulligan, Rev. John A.......A.B. '50; A.M., '52· Dec. 16, 1861, Falls Village, Conn.
Murphy, Patrick J..........M.D., '73; A.M., '73· Oct. 3, 1891, Washington, D. C.
Murray, Neal T.............A.B., '73; LL.B., '76· 1898, Wash., D. C.
Muruaga, Hon. Emilio de.....LL.D., '89· Minister from Spain in 1889.

Nally, Charles F............M.D., '68· Mar. 4, 1876, Wash., D. C.
Nally, Denis...............A.B., '27·
Neale, Rev. James Pye.......A.B., '59· Mar. 20, 1895, Philadelphia, Pa.
Neel, Hon. Wm. J...........LL.B., '87; LL.M., '88· Mar. 24, 1908, Cartersville, Ga.
Nelson, James Ed..........M.D., '95· Washington, D. C.
Netherland, Thos. H........LL.B., '95· 1903, Alexandria, Va.
Neuhaus, Paul Immanuel...LL.B., '83; LL.M., '84· Washington, D. C.
Nevins, John C.............A.B., '46· Alexandria, Va.
Newman, Henry M.........M.D., '76· Nov. 11, 1910, Washington, D. C.
Newton, Louis E...........M.D., '68· Feb. 3, 1899.
Nichols, Joshua............A.B., '39·
Nicodemus, Bvt. Maj. Wm.
 Jos. Leonard, U. S. A.....A.M., '65; M.D., '67. Jan. 6, 1879.
Nolan, Joseph A...........A.M., '66· 1898, Pennsylvania.
Normile, Judge James C.....A.M., '67· 1892.   •
Nowlin, Homer Edgar......M.D., '96· Feb. 8, 1910, Washington, D. C.

O'Brien, Hon. Denis........LL.D., '93· May 18, 1909, Watertown, N. Y. Min to Paraguay and Uraguay.
O'Brien, Joseph P...........A.B., '80; LL.B., '82; A.M., '89· 1904, Adirondacks, N. Y.
O'Bryan, John Duross.......A.B., '62; A.M., '64· Mar. 1, 1904, Paris, France.
O'Byrne, Dominic A.........A.B., '51· Feb. 17, 1896, Savannah, Ga.
O'Connell, Jeremiah D.....LL.B., '80; LL.M., '81·
O'Connor, Charles E........A.B., '78· 1899, California.
O'Connor, F. J.............M.D., '77. Washington, D. C.
O'Connor, Patrick J........LL.B., '80· Dec. 9, 1908. Savannah, Ga.
O'Doherty, George..........LL.B., '84; LL.M., '85·
O'Donnell, Daniel J.........A.B., '89; LL.B., '92· Mar. 3, 1893, Scranton, Pa.

Offutt, George W...........M.D., '74· Sept. 13, 1878, Wash., D. C.
O'Flynn, Cornelius John.....A.B., '58· Nov. 19, 1911, Detroit, Mich.
O'Keefe, Rev. Charles M.....D.D., '89· Sept. 28, 1892.
O'Leary, Charles W........M.D., '72·
O'Neill, Francis J..........LL.B., '88; LL.M., '89· England.
O'Neill, Ignatius P..........A B., '80; A.M., '89· Aug. 8, 1898, Sum-
                                    merville, S. C.
O'Neill, James F...........A.B., '83; A.M., '89·
O'Neill, John H............A.B., '41· Dec., 1890, Chicago, Ill.
Ongley, A. Hugh...........LL.B., '97· 1898.
Oppenheimer, Bernard.......A.B., '72· Feb. 26, 1882, Baltimore, Md. :
O'Reilly, J.................A.B., '36·
O'Reilly, John Boyle.......LL.D., '89· Aug. 10, 1890, Hull, Mass.
O'Sullivan, Rev. Florence T.,
    S.J. ....................A.B., '43· April 2, 1907, Santa Clara, Cal.
O'Toole, Rev. Lawrence J...A.B., '72· West Newton, Mass.

Page, R. A.................M.D., '71· 1898.
Parkinson, Clinton.........M.D., '69·
Parsons, Isaac.............A.B., '61·
Paschal, Hon. George W.....LL.D., '75· Feb. 16, 1878, Wash., D. C.
Patterson, John Scott:......M.D., '70·
Patterson, Rev. Richard J...A B., '63· Dec. 31, 1900, Clinton, Mass.
Payne, Howard T...........M.D., '70· Washington, D. C.
Payne, Col. James G.......LL.D., '85· Dec. 28, 1909, Wash., D. C.
Peabody, James H.........,.M.D., '60· Sept. 11, 1906, Denver, Colo.
Pearson, Joseph W.........LL.B., '97; LL.M., '98·
Perkins, Edward Dyer......M.D., '95· Aug. 24, 1906, Wash., D. C.
Perry, Walter S............A.B., '74· Baltimore, Md.
Phillips, Bennett...........LL.B., '89·
Pise, Rev. Chas. Constantine.A.M., '30· May 26, 1866, Brooklyn, N. Y.
Pixzini, Juan A............A.B., '65; A.M., '82· Nov., 1891, Rich-
                                    mond, Va.
Pope, Francis..............LL B., '90; LL.M., '91·
Porter, Henry R............M.D., '72· Mar. 3, 1903, Agra, India.
Porter, Horace T...........M.D., '70· Aug. 14, 1879.
Forter, J. H...............M.D., '61· Feb. 5, 1908.
Posey, G. Gordon...........A.B., '71· April 29, 1891, Silver City, N. M.
Pospispel, Joseph...........M.D., '94· June 7, 1908, Washington, D. C.
Potbury, Edwin, Jr.........M.D., '00· Feb. 18, 1901, Washington, D C.
Power, Edmund Murray.....M.D., '00·
Power, James D'Alton......LL.B., '80; LL.M., '81· April 12, 1901,
                                    Manila, P. I.
Power, Very Rev. John.....D.D., '33· April 14, 1849, New York.
Power, Very Rev. John J...A.B., '51; D.D., '74· Jan 27, 1902, Worces-
                                    ter, Mass.
Power, Dr. Maurice A.......A.M., '31·
Powers, William,...........LL.D., '22·

Pratz, Frederick C.........LL.B., '91; LL.M., '92. Nov. 3, 1910, Washington, D. C.

Prendergast, Very Rev. F. J..D.D., '89· Oct. 1, 1899.

Prentiss, Charles E.........M.D., '68· Mar. 19, 1908.

Preston, Thomas............A.B., '37·

Preston, Rt. Rev. Mgr. Thos. S. D.D., '89· Nov. 4, 1891, New York City.

Pryal, Andrew D., Jr.......LL.B., '88· June 2, 1892, Wash., D. C.

Puebla, Luis de............A.B., '68; A.M., '69· July 24, 1893, Coatzacoalcos, Mexico.

Purcell, Rev. John B.......A.B., '64· Mar. 24, 1873, Boston, Mass.

Putman, Wm. D............. M.D., '68· Sept. 16, 1884.

Queen, Charles R...........M.D., '55·

Radcliffe, Samuel J.........M.D., '52; A.M., '66· July 9, 1903, Washington, D. C.

Raines, Benjamin R........M.D., '67·

Rand, Charles F...:........M.D., '73· Oct. 13, 1908, Washington, D. C.

Ransom, Thomas R.........A.B., '85· Nov. 14, 1896, Northampton County, N. C.

Rawlings, Carroll M........M.D., '84· 1894.

Ray, Hon. Robert.... .......A.B., '54; A.M., '59· Oct. 25, 1899, Monroe, La.

Read, Wm. G...............LL.D., '42.

Reid, Louis Henry....... ...M.D., '70· June 25, 1908, Atlanta, Ga.

Reily, Edward S............A.B., '64; A.M., '76; LL.B , '72· 1882. Conewago, Pa.

Reilly, Wm. B.............:...LL.B., '92; LL.M., '93· Washington, D. C.

Rice, Joseph A.............A.B., '63; A.M , '64· Oct., 1901, Alexandria, Va.

Richards, F. P........... ..M.D., '63·

Richardson, John Robert. ...LL.B., '96· Monroe, La.

Richardson, Wm. A.'........LL.D., '81· Judge, Monroe, La.

Ridelle, Philip.............M.D , '79, 1896. Woodstock, Va.

Riehl, Charles F............I.L.B., '93· 1894.

Riley, Ambrose Joseph.'....A.M., '98· St. Louis, Mo.

Riley, John C.... ........A.B., '48; A.M., '51· Feb. 22, 1879, Washington, D C.

Rindge, Joseph B.........:...A.B., '40· Oct. 1, 1901, San Francisco, Cal.

Ritchie, Joshua A..........A.B., '35; A.M., '40· 1887.

Ritchie, Louis W.............M.D , '63· Sept. 9, 1901.

Robertson, J. Caldwell. .....A.B., '75; A.M., '77· Columbia, S. C.

Robinson, Samuel A..:.:....A B , '58· Dec., 1894.

Robinson, Thomas Somerset.M.D., '59· 1905.

Rochford, Richard..........A.B., '47· Feb. 15, 1909, Galway, Ireland.

Roebuck, Jarvis H..........**A.B., '20·**

Rogers, Joseph Sebastian....Ph.B., '92; LL.B., '94· Aug. 20, 1898, Hyattsville, Md.

Rogers, Wm. Elwin.........M.D., '04.   Nov. 22, 1908, Wash., D. C.

Rosecranz, Gen. Wm., S.,   LL.D., '89· Mar. 11, 1898, near Los An-
  U. S. A.................. geles, Cal.

Ross, John W..............LL.D., '85· Washington, D. C.

Ross, Wm. H...............M.D., '69· Nov. 20, 1900.

Rosse, Irving C.............A.M., '89· May 3, 1901.

Rost, Alphonse.............A.B., '60· Killed in Civil War.

Rudd, Frank...............A.B., '61; A.M., '68· Oct. 1, 1911, New
                            York City.

St. Clair, F. O.............M.D., '69; A.M., '89· April 7, 1908, Wash-
                            ington, D. C.

Sakuri, Elchi...............D.D.S., '07· Japan.

Salter, Geo. W.............LL.B., '72· Aug., 1912, Washington, D. C.

Salter, Geo. W.............LL.B., '79· May, 1880.

Saxton, Francis G..........LL.B., '73· 1900.

Scaggs, James F...........LL.B., '84; LL.M., '85· Dec. 19, 1907,
                            Washington, D. C.

Schade, Herman R.........LL.B., '99· Washington, D. C.

Scharf, J. Thomas..........A.M., '81; LL.D., '85· 1898.

Scheib, Prof. Edward E.....A.B., '71· 1900, Louisiana.

Schley, Rear Ad. Winfield
  Scott, U. S. N............LL.D., '99· Oct. 2, 1911, New York City.

Schoolfield, Charles S......A.B., '78. May 26, 1885, Baltimore, Md. ·

Searcy, Reuben Martin.....M.D., '92·

Semmes, Rev. Alexander J..A.B., '50; A.M., '52· Sept., 1898, New
                            Orleans, La.

Semmes, Alphonso T.......A.B., '50; A.M., '53· Jan. 5, 1895, Canton,
                            Miss.

Semmes, Benedict J........A.B., '53; A.M., '55· May 29, 1879, Canton,
                            Miss.

Semmes, P. Warfield........A.B., '60· Feb. 16, 1906, Memphis, Tenn.

Semmes, Thos. J...........A.B., '42; A.M., '45; LL.D., '80· June 23,
                            1899, New Orleans, La.

Sharp, DeHaven............M.D., '04· Feb. 4, 1906, Washington, D. C.

Shaw, Clarence.............LL.B., '99; LL.M., '00·

Shea, John Gilmary.........LL.D., '89· Feb. 23, 1892, Elizabeth, N. J.

Shekell, Ben R.............A.B., '59· Washington, D. C.

Sheridan, Denis............A.B., '71· Cumberland, Md.

Sherman, Henry T..........Mus.Doc, '89· Sept. 29, 1896.

Sherrett, Wm. L...........LL.B., '88; LL.M., '89· Dec. 9, 1890, De-
                            Land, Fla.

Shipley, Charles E.........LL.B., '04· June 1, 1904, Washington, D. C.

Shoulters, George H........M.D., '83· Dec. 14, 1906.

Shyne, Michael R...........M.D., '55·

Sigur, Lawrence S..........A.B., '37· ....

Slattery, Daniel J..........LL.B., '02· April 3, 1910.

Sloan, J. G................M.D., '69· Nov. 2, 1897.

Sloan, James H............A.B., '81· Oct. 23, 1884, Baltimore, Md.

Smith, Dexter A............M.D., '84· Dec. 16, 1910, Chicago, Ill.

Smith, Edmund L...........A.B., '49·

Smith, Fred Leof....,......A.B., '54; A.M., '58· April 10, 1898, Reading, Pa.

Smith, John E.....:.........M.D., '67· Jan. 22, 1907, New York City.

Smith, Joseph A............M.D., '55·

Smith, Joseph Edward.......M.D., '00· Aug. 14, 1909, Bardstown, Ky.

Smith, Lloyd...............M.D., '70· , York, Pa.

Smith, Peter Xavier........A.B., '82; A.M., '84; LL.B., '84 Feb. 3, 1896, Norfolk, Va

Smith, Philip...............A.B., '18·

Smith, Wm. F...............A.B., '78; LL.B., '80·

Smith, Wm. M...............A.B., '53; A.M '57· May 4, 1892, Atlantic City, N. J.

Sonnenschmidt, C. W.......M.D., '67· Feb., 1908, Washington, D. C.

Sothoron, James J..........M.D., '65· Sept. 27, 1897, Washington, D. C.

Spellissy, James M.........A.B., '55; A.M., '56· June, 1875, New York City.

Squier, Algernon Marble.....M.D., '67·

Stack, Maurice J...........M.D., '76· Oct. 17, 1909, Wash., D. C.

Stafford, Rev. Denis J.......D.D., '90· Jan. 3, 1908, Washington, D. C.·

Stafford, James Raymond....LL.B., '98·

Stafford, John J............M.D., '85; A.M., '86· Mar. 17, 1902.

Stang, Rt. Rev. Wm........D.D., '89· Late Bishop of Fall River, Mass. Feb. 2, 1907, died in Minnesota.

Starr, Joseph A............M.D., '02· 1903, Washington, D. C.

Stead, Mark Aloysius........A.M., '98· St. Louis, Mo.

Stearns, S. S...............M.D., '68· June, 1911, Washington, D. C.·

Steinmertz, William R.......M.D., '65· Jan. 26, 1908, Walbrook, Md.

Stier, Henry Clay, Jr........LL.B., '98; LL.M., '00·

Stockstill, Francis W........LL.B., '83·

Stone, Charles..............A.B., '59· 1867, New Orleans, La.

Stone, George H............M.D., '68· Feb. 19, 1899, Savannah, Ga.

Stonestreet, Rev. Chas. H., A.B., '33· Pres. of G. U., July· 3, 1885, S.J. .... Holy Cross College, Worcester, Mass.

Stonestreet, Nicholas........A.B., '36; A.M., '40· 1889.

Stout, Alexander M.........M.D., '80· Chicago, Ill.

Stout, Stanley S............LL.B., '74·

Strass, Henry..............A.B., '26·

Stratton, John T...........M.D., '73· Jan. 31, 1911.

Strawbridge, Henry.........A.B., '37·

Stringfield, Francis M......M.D., '70· Sept. 12, 1903, Chicago, Ill.

Strong, Michael R..........A.B., '60; A.M., '62·

Sullivan, George N.........LL.B., '74· Nov. 1, 1909, Washington, D. C.

Sullivan, Rev. James F......A.B., '52· Nov. 15, 1871, Quincy, Mass.

Sullivan, John Joseph.......A.B., '98· Aug., 1898, Washington, D. C.

Sullivan, Patrick Thomas....M.D., '95· July 6, 1910, McKees Rocks, Pa.

Sullivan, Thomas J.........LL.B., '85; LL.M., '86· May 4, 1908, Washington, D. C.

Sylvester, George...........M.D., '64·

Taggart, Hugh T. Fairgreave.LL.B., '02; LL.M., '03. Oct. 2, 1911, Washington, D. C.

Talbot, Maj. J. Theodore,
U. S. A....................A.M., '47· April 22, 1862.

Tarkington, J. A...........M.D., '70· May 1, 1902.

Tauzin, Emil M.............A.B., '55· Louisiana.

Taylor, Judge John Lewis...LL.D., '28· Sup. Court, Jan. 29, 1829, Raleigh, N. C.

Taylor, Leroy M.............M.D., '60· Sept. 27, 1905.

Taylor, J. Archibald........M.D., '85· 1898, Washington, D. C.

Taylor, Thomas.............M.D., '82· Jan. 22, 1910, Washington, D. C.

Teeling, Very Rev. John.....D.D., '54· Dec. 12, 1870, Dubuque, Iowa.

Thatcher, John.............M.D., '68

Thompson, John C.........A.B., '42· April 17, 1895, Baltimore, Md.

Thompson, Dr. John H......A.M., '65· Rome, Italy.

Thurn, George A...........M.D., '70·

Tierney, Matthew D........LL.B., '88; LL.M., '89· Hyattsville, Md.

Tierney, Michael V.........LL.B., '86; LL.M., '87· Sept. 12, 1906, Washington, D C.

Tilden, Wm. C..............M.D., '67·

Tinley, John A.............LL.B., '97·

Toner, Dr. Joseph M........A.M., '67;. Ph.D., '89· July 30, 1896, Cresson, Pa.

Tonry, Prof. William P.......Ph.D., '75· Oct. 3, 1905, Baltimore, Md.

Torrey, Turner.............M.D., '73· Dec. 3, 1895, Washington, D. C.

Toumay, Francis...........LL.B., '82· 1896, Asheville, N. C.

Tower, Fredk. W...........LL.B., '90; LL.M., '91·

Tracy, Rev. James..........A.B., '59. July, 1866, Boston, Mass.

Trautman, B...............M.D., '74· Philadelphia, Pa.

Tree, Charles M............M.D., '67· Dec. 3, 1881.

Trott, Thomas H...........M.D., '67· April 23, 1896.

Tucker, Maurice...........M.D., '62·

Tuomy, Rev. John..........LL.D., '21·

Turner, John F.............LL.B., '05· Nov. 9, 1907.

Turner, S. S...............M.D., '63· Dec. 11, 1904.

Turpin, Henry W..........M.D., '64·

Underwood, Robert L.......LL.B., '99· Washington, D. C.

Van Arnum, John W.......M.D., '67· Nov. 9, 1884, Washington, D. C.

Van Bibber, Dr. Claude.....A.B., '74· July 11, 1910, Baltimore, Md.

Vandenhoff, George.........A.M., '58· 1883, New York.

Vanel, Andrew .V...........A.B., '39·

Van Gieson, Henry C.......M.D., '64. Mar. 7, 1905, Omaha, Neb.
Vest, Hon. George Graham...LL.D., '00·
Voorhees, Charles S.........A.B., '73. Dec. 26, 1909, Spokane, Wash.

Wagner, R. B...............M.D., '70·
Walker, William A......... A.B., '60· New Orleans, La.
Walker, Gen. Wm. Stephen..A.B., '41· June 5, 1898, Atlanta, Ga.
Wall, Very Rev. Stephen, V.G.D.D., '89· Aug. 21, 1894.
Wallace, M. T...............M.D., '73·
Walsh, John K..............M.D., '65· Jan. 4, 1894.
Walsh, Redmond D.........A.B., '78· June, 1911, California.
Walter, John, Jr............M.D., '68· Nov. 17, 1906.
Ward, William L............ M.D., '71· April 12, 1909.
Wardell, Eugene McC.......LL.B., '93; LL.M., '94· Washington, D. C.
Ware, Edward H...........·..M.D., '65· Pacific Coast.
Warman, Philip C..........LL.B., '80· Nov. 25, 1908, Wash.;̣ D. C.
Warren, Charles............M.D., '68·
Waters, Elkhanah N..,......LL.B., '76· Oct. 26, 1908, Frederick, Md.
Waters, Thos. B............LL.B., '91·
Watkins, John C...........M.D., '65· 1895, Buffalo, N. Y.
Watkins, Richard James.... A.B., '97; LL.B., '99; LL.M., '00· Dec. 5,
        1911, Washington, D. C.
Watterson, George W.......A.B., '32; A.M., '43; LL.D., '59·
Watterson, Rt. Rev. John A .D.D., '78· Bishop of Columbus, Ohio,
        April 17, 1899, Columbus, Ohio.
Weber, Casper C........ ..LL.B., '90; LL.M., '91· April, 1893, De-
        troit, Mich.
Weber, Julius Henry, U. S. A.LL.B., '99· Jan. 30, 1908, Imperial, Cal.
Wellman, George M.........M D., '68· Jan. 13, 1902.
Wendell, Robert Paine......M D., '92· Aberdeen, Miss.
Werle, Charles M...........LL.B., '96·
Wheeler, Gen. Jos., U. S. A...LL.D., '99· Jan., 1906, New York City.
Whelan, Benjamin L........A.M., '57·
Whitefoot, R. M............M.D., '66· July 25, 1906, Bozeman, Mont.
Whiting, Wm. H. C., U. S. A..A.B., '40; A.M., '50· Confederate Gen.,
        Mar. 10, 1865.
Whitley, W. H..............M.D., '66; A.M., '85· Paterson, N. J.
Wiggin, A. W...............M.D., '65· 1887.
Wikoff, William............A.B., '27·
Wilcox, John H...........,...Mus.Doc., '64· Boston, Mass.
Wilcox, William J...........A.B., '76; A.M., '89· 1895.
Wildman, Joseph C.........LL.B., '73·
Wilkerson, Oliver D........,LL.B., '95; LL.M., '96· 1908.
Willett, Archibald M.......LL.B., '95· Oct. 19, 1905.
Willett, J. Edward..........M.D., '55· Jan. 21, 1887.
Williams, Dr. R. E..........M.D., '70· Dec. 30, 1902, San Francisco,
        Cal.

Williams, William F. .... A.B., '63· Sept. 9, 1892, Washington, D. C.
Williams, W. Mosby .... LL.B., '90; LL.M., '91· Oct. 1, 1909, Washington, D. C.
Willige, J. Louis .... LL.B., '90· Washington, D. C.
Wills, William Xavier .... A.B., '51; A.M., '59· June 25, 1865, Charles County, Md.
Wilson, Augustus .... A.B., '60· Sept., 1903.
Wilson, Eliel Soper .... A.B., '46; A.M., '48· Sept., 1860, Anne Arundel County, Md.
Wilson, Henry Peter .... A.B., '91· Nov. 29, 1897, Los Angeles, Cal.
Wilson, Hon. Jeremiah M. ... LL.D., '83· 1903.
Wilson, John E. .... A.B., '45; A.M., '47· 1909, Wakefield, Va.
Wilson, Lawrence .... M.D., '70·
Wimberly, Warren W. ...... M.D., '92· April 27, 1908.
Winter, John T. .... M.D., '70· June 22, 1902, Wash., D. C.
Winthrop, Col. Wm., U. S. A. . LL.D., '96· April 8, 1899, Wash., D. C.
Wise, James A. .... A.B., '58. Feb. 23, 1875, Austin, Tex.
Wise, Thomas W. .... M.D., '66· Feb. 17, 1891, Wash., D. C.
Wolf, Dr. J. S. .... M.D., '67· Dec. 7, 1898.
Wolhanpter, William E. ..... M.D., '90· Jan. 21, 1896.
Woodbury, Edward C. .... M.D., '63· Jan. 15, 1905.
Woodbury, H. E. .... M.D., '63· Jan. 15, 1905. Wash., D. C.
Woodley, Rev. Robt. D., S.J. . A.B., '25· Oct. 25, 1857, St. Thomas, Md.
Woodward, Thos. Pursell .... LL.B., '89· Jan. 26, 1911, Wash., D. C.
Wootton, Edward .... A.B., '58· April 1, 1910, Poolesville, Md.
Wright, A. Clarke .... A.B., '82; A.M., '84; LL.B., '84· Mar. 10, 1908, Savannah, Ga.
Wynne, Capt. Robert F. ..... LL.B., '97· 1912, Washington, D. C.

Yeatman, Samuel M. .... LL.B., '83; A.M., '89. Dec. 13, 1905, Washington, D. C.
Yoshida, C. .... D.D.S., '02· Japan.
Young, Noble .... A.M., '76· 1883, Sacketts Harbor, N. Y.
Young, Parke G. .... M.D., '72· July 20, 1906, Washington, D. C.
Yrarrazabal, Manuel .... A.B., '52· Feb. 14, 1896, New York City.

Zane, Edmund P. .... A.B., '55; A.M., '60· May 7, 1893, San Francisco, Cal.
Zappone, A. .... M.D., '60· Washington, D. C.
Zegarra, Felix Cypriano ..... A.B., '64; A.M., '65; LL.D., '77· April 4, 1897, Lima, Peru.

Geographical Register.

ALABAMA.

Andalusia.
Jones, R. H.
Ashville.
Herring, J. L.
Attalla.
Hainner, E. D.
Hammer, E. D.
Bayou La Batre.
Shea, E. M.

Birmingham.
Altman, J. W.
Bingham, G. W.
Calhoun, C. A.
Craven, C. A.
Denegre, C. M.
Denton, J. S.
Johnston, R. D., Jr
Joliat, L F.
Lamkin. G.
Lowe, F. M.
Pugh, J. C.
Senn, C. A
Smith, E. D.
Stern, S B.
Watts, R. B.
Woodson, L. G.

Brewton.
Smith, G. W. L.
Calvert.
McRae, I. C.
Clayton.
Wright, J. D.
Demopolis,
Morango.
Harrison, W. C.
Epes.
Hilman, J. G.
Eufaula.
Speight, J. J.
Fort Payne.
Isbell, J. B.
Huntsville.
McDonald, J. C.
Milligan, L. P.

Jasper.
Bankhead, J H. Jr.
Bankhead, W. B.

Mobile.
Allen, E. P.
Dreaper, E. B.
Hodgson, T.
Lyons, H. H.
Prince, S. R.
Regan, R. B.
Touart, T. J.
Townsend, C. G.

ALABAMA.

Montgomery.
Carey, J. M.
Kirtland, M.
New Decatur.
Blackwell, S.
Pell City.
Greene, J. G.
Selma.
Reese, H. T.

---

*Donegan, J. H.
*Lindsay, D. R
*Walthall, W. J.

ALASKA.

Juneau.
Brown, E H.
Jennings, R. W.
Seward.
Finnegan, J. J.
Valvez.
Hubbard, O. P.

ARIZONA.

Bisbee.
Flora, W. K.
Clifton.
Hampton, J. R.
Nogales.
French, G. K.
Phoenix.
O'Neill, E. J. B.
Prescott.
Yount, C. E.
Tempe.
Ayer, F. C.
Tueson.
Ives, E. S.

ARKANSAS.

Camp Verde.
Pearman, J. M.
Douglas.
Romadka, C. A.
Fayetteville.
Atkins, J. W. G.
Ham, H. H.
Hot Springs.
Bouic, W. G.
Garnett, A. S.
Little Rock.
Gracie, A. C.
Gray, J. A.
Hargrove, K. A.
Hyatt, W. A.
Quinn, J. G.

ARKANSAS.

Lonoke.
Walls, C. A.
Magnolia.
Kelson, F. A.
Upton, E. A.
Prescott.
Wilmeth, J. F.
Rob Roy.
Gracie, J. P.
Rogers.
Garrot, F. H.
Wye.
Allen J.

---

*Carroll. L J.
*Dunn, L. B.

CALIFORNIA.

Alturas.
Adams, J. W.
Angel Island.
Glover, M. W.
Berkeley.
Crossfield. C. B.
Kidwell, E.
O'Neill, T. J. L.
Burlingame.
Grant, J. A.
Campo.
Boyd, C. B.
Fresno.
Jackson, G. E.
Koch, A. A.
Grapeland.
Keene, W. P.
Lodi.
Breitenbucher, E. E.
Lompoc.
Fox, P.
Long Beach.
Scanlan, A. C.
Los Angeles.
Alexander, C. W.
Conaty, T. J.
Dowling, P. V.
Downing, G. E.
Eddy, R. T.
Keys, M. B
Helm, G. W.
Hughes. A. J.
Jenal, F. P
Montgomery, F. S.
Rex, T. A.
Scott, T. E.
Wilson, C.

CALIFORNIA.

Los Gatos.
Hicks, L. R.
Reiley, H. A.

Marysville.
Weightman, R. H.

Napa City.
Brown, J. R.

Oakland.
Ayer, D. E.
Ayer, R. B.
Clark, L. A.
Clark, M J.
Montgomery, J. P.

Ontario.
Taylor, F. M.

Pueblo.
Heller, P. H.

San Diego.
Davis, W. J.
Smart, R.

San Francisco.
Arnold, J. D.
Barney, J. W.
Coleman, J. V.
Cox, H C.
Curtis, M.
Daniels, R. P.
Downing, M. A.
Driscoll, T. A.
Flanagan, L. J.
Fleharty, W. W.
Flood, P. H.
Golden, W P.
Heizman, C. L.
Houston, C. J.
Jackson, W. A.
Lavin, J. P.
Lennon, L. C.
Lennon, M. B.
McClosky, W C.
McDevitt, W. M.
Martin, F. R.
Martin, W. S.
Moynihan, D. L.
Murphy, D. C.
O'Connell, Daniel
O'Neill, J. B.
Parks, C. J.
Power, J. N.
Shipman, J. B. C.
Tobin, C. P.
Tobin, E. J.
Tobin, J. S., Jr.
Troy, R P.
Wallace, H. S.
Watts, Frederick, Jr.

San Jose.
Murphy, Martin
Regli, J. A. S.

San Mateo.
Parrott, John, Jr.

San Rafael.
Byrnes, C. W.

Santa Clara.
O'Keefe, L. E A.

---

*Marstelleo, M. H.
*Rice, N. E.

COLORADO.

Aspen.
Bradshaw, Moses
Dunn, C. A.

Colorado Springs.
McKay, A. F.
Wallace, J. T.

Denver.
Clark, E N.
Connolly, J. E.
Cudlipp, M. A.
Daly, W. F.
Eggleston, J. D.
Finerty, W. N.
Ford, B. J
Gove, Frank E.
Green, W. M.
Gwynn, R. N.
Holcombe, E. P.
Lacy, E. B.
Lyman, W. F.
McGovern, T. F.
Mullen, C. V
Pickens, A. H.
Shoemaker, F.
Tralles, G. E
Trowbridge, G. E.
Walsh, J. J.
Williams, Serman

Durango.
Smith, L. E.

Edgewater.
Carroll, A. L.

Glenwood Springs.
Speer, A. M.

La Junta.
Finney, Frank

Montrose.
Staggers, J. W.

Manzanola.
Russell, E. O.

Trinidad.
Abrahams, H. B.

CONNECTICUT.

Bridgeport.
Bray, W J.
Fallon, F. B
McElroy, J. A.

Hartford.
Armstrong, W. P.
Davis, J M. K.
Smith, T. S.
Kingsley, J. M.
Lawler, J. H.
Spellacy, T. J.
Welch, T F.

Jewett City.
Hennon, J. F.

Manchester.
Gorman, J. F.

Meriden.
Cahill, J. H

New Britain.
Conlon, C. F.
Phelan, W. J.

New Haven.
Minor, P. E.

Norwalk.
Allen, Edward

CONNECTICUT.

Norwich.
Cassidy, C. W.
Duggan, J. R.
McLaughlin, J. A.
McNamara, J. G.
Smith, A. P.

Rockville.
Flaherty, J. E.
Kelly, L. J.

Sandy Hook.
Walsh, W. S.

South Manchester.
Foley, J. F.

South Norwalk.
Pardee, M D.

Stamford.
Munson, L. W.
Reynard, W. A.

Thomaston.
Green, J J.

Torrington.
Chapin, H. B.

Waterbury.
'Brennan, J E.
Cassidy, J. H.
Cassidy, L. T.
Coyle, W. E.
Dawson, A. D.
Devine, T. F.
Gaffney, J. L.
Grady, J. A.
Guilfoile, J. C.
Hayes, T. F.
Kennedy, W. C.
Lawler, W. K.
O'Brien, E. M.
O'Neill, J. J.
Walsh, E. F.
Watts, J. F.

Wethersfield.
Woodhouse, D. R.

*O'Leary, W. J.
*Turner, L. J.
*Brown, C. F.
*Henry, W. J.

DELAWARE.

Clayton.
Cobb, J. S.

Smyrna.
Stockly, C. D.

Wilmington.
Brennan, J. S.
Curley, C. F.
Maguire, J. A.

*Brapley, J. T.

DISTRICT OF COLUMBIA.

Anacostia.
Allen, A. R.
Mundell, J. J.
Roberts, C. F.
Roberts, E. B.
Watson, J. A.

Brookland.
Brooks, J. H.

DISTRICT OF COLUMBIA.

Cleveland Park.
Hodge, H. B.

Takoma Park.
Adams, J. L., Jr.
Cottrell, S., Jr.
Kroll, W. A.

Washington.
Abbott, J. F.
Abel, Joseph
Adams, J. R.
Adams, R. D.
Adams, S. S.
Adams, W. W.
Addison, F. G., Jr.
Adkins, J. C.
Adler, Leon
Aikin, W. E.
Alexander, A. A.
Alleger, W. W.
Allen, H. C.
Allen, J. B.
Anderson, G. M.
Anderson, H. L.
Anderson, J. W.
Anderson, L. S.
Anderson, R. T.
Andrews, B. W.
Andrews, M. V.
Andrews, W. A.
Andrews, W. R.
Andrews, W. T.
Ansart, L. L.
Appleman, F. S.
Archer, J. B., Jr.
Armstrong, W. J.
Arnold, E. F.
Arth, C. W.
Ashford, Mahlon
Atkins, P N.
Atkinson H. L. B.
Atkinson, W. H.
Augenstein, M. M.
Babcock, H. J., Jr.
Babcock, L. A.
Babendreier, L. M.
Bacon, W. J., Jr.
Baden, J. H.
Baden, W. H.
Bailey, L. A.
Baker, A. B.
Baker, D. W.
Baker, F. B.
Baker, Frank
Baker, G. L.
Baker, H. A.
Baker, J. N.
Baker, S. S.
Baker, W. N.
Balzer, H. J.
Bandel, G. E.
Bangs, R. E.
Barber, H. A. L.
Barber, H. W.
Barber, J. H. M.
Barnard, Clarence
Barnard, R. P.
Barnhart, W. P.
Barr, H. W.
Barrett, P. M.
Barton, W. M.
Bayly, C. B.
Bayne, J. B.

DISTRICT OF COLUMBIA.

Washington, *Cont'd.*
Beale, J. F.
Beall, B. M.
Becker, G. H.
Becker, Joseph
Behrend, Adajah
Behrend, E. B.
Behrend, R. B.
Belew, R. P.
Bell, D. W.
Beller, F. F.
Benham, W. R.
Benjamin, C. F.
Bergin, F. J.
Bernhard, E. J.
Berry, W. R.
Birckhead, Edward
Birckhead, O. W.
Birgfeld, W. E.
Birkby, W. T.
Biscoe, F. L.
Bishop, A. G.
Black, P. S.
Blackburn, J. W., Jr.
Blackistone, F. D.
Blackistone, J. C.
Blaine, R. G.
Blake, O. B.
Blanchard, E. C.
Blanford, E. M.
Bliss, G. R.
Block, E. H.
Block, L. A.
Bloomer, G. B.
Bobst, A. E.
Boe, E. J.
Bogan, J. A.
Bogue, A. P.
Bomberger, Lincoln
Bond, G. J.
Booth, E. H.
Borchardt, Herbert
Borden, F. W.
Borger, B. L.
Borger, G. L.
Bowie, G. C.
Bowles, B. A.
Bowles, N. S.
Boyd, Howard
Boyd, W. H.
Boykin, L. E.
Boyle, F. A.
Braden, F. W.
Bradenbaugh, C. C.
Bradfield, J. D.
Bradley, J. F.
Bradshaw, Aaron
Bradshaw, T. G.
Brady, E. D. F.
Brady, Edmund
Bragaw, G. D.
Brand, J. S.
Brashears, J. W., Jr.
Brashears, S., Jr.
Breckenridge, S. D.
Breese, E. C.
Brennan, F. J.
Brennan, J. C.
Brennan, P. H.
Bresnahan, F. J.
Brez, S. C.
Brice, C. H.
Brickenstein, J. H.

DISTRICT OF COLUMBIA.

Washington, *Cont'd.*
Bride, W. W.
Briggs, E. B.
Brisboe, Arthur
Brock, F. B.
Bronson, C. E.
Brooke, J. C.
Brosnan, J. J.
Brown, B. C.
Brown, C. J.
Brown, C. O.
Brown, C. O.
Brown, E. C.
Brown, H. S.
Brown, O. P. M.
Brown, S. K.
Brown, W. N.
Brown, W. E.
Browning, W. L.
Brumbaugh, G. M.
Brummett, R. B.
Bryan, H. L.
Brylawski, Fulton
Buckley, J. J.
Burbank, Caryl
Burdine, E. F.
Burger, J. C. S.
Burger, L. C. E.
Burke, T. W.
Burns, J. W.
Burton, H. R.
Busick, A. F.
Butler, J. A.
Butler, J. H.
Butler, Ulysses
Bryne, J. F.
Byrne, J. J.
Byrnes, J. C.
Byrns, W. F.
Coflin, C. B.
Cahill, M. H.
Callaghan, D. O'C.
Callan G. C.
Calliflower, C. E., Jr.
Calliflower, J. E.
Campbell, C. B.
Campbell, J. P.
Cannon, W. D.
Cantwell, E. J.
Cantwell, Thomas
Carman, L. D.
Carmody, J. D.
Carr, W. J.
Carroll, T. A.
Carroll, W. C.
Carter, J. B.
Carusi, C. F.
Carusi, T. A.
Cary, Frederick
Cary, W. G.
Casey, D. E.
Cassin, J. L.
Catlin, B. R.
Chamberlin, F. T.
Chamberlin, J. M.
Charles, Garfield
Chew, P. W.
Chewning, A. C.
Chick, H. S.
Choate, Rufus
Church, J. B.
Clabaugh, H. M.
Clapp, Woodbridge

DISTRICT OF COLUMBIA.	DISTRICT OF COLUMBIA.	DISTRICT OF COLUMBIA.
Washington, *Cont'd.*	Washington, *Cont'd.*	Washington, *Cont'd.*
Clark, E. B.	Decker, A. J.	Esher, A. D.
Clark, T. R.	Degges, A. R.	Eslin, J. F.
Clarke, H. H.	DeLacy, W. H.	Estabrook, L. M.
Cleary, F. J.	Delaiplaine, P. H.	Estabrook, W. T.
Clements, J. E.	DeLashmutt, D. A.	Etchison, H. M.
Clevenger, O. B.	Demerritt, J. H.	Evans, P. W.
Cobb, N. H.	Dennis, W. H.	Evans, W. W.
Cohen, Morris	Devine, James	Evans, Warwick
Cohnan, E. J.	Devlin, A. J.	Fague, J. R.
Colbert, M. J.	Dickey, R. B.	Fairbanks, L. C.
Cole, J. T.	Digges, J. H.	Fallon, J. T.
Coleman, W. E.	Diggs, C. F.	Fay, J. B., Jr.
Colfer, J. T.	Dillon, J. R.	Fegan, Hugh, Jr.
Colliere, G. R.	Dismer, L. C.	Felten, A. L.
Collins, W. H.	Dixon, W. S.	Felter, Herman
Colúmbus, W. F.	Dodge, Clarence	Fergell, J. A.
Coneby, W. H.	Dodge, J. E.	Ferguson, A. H.
Conner, W. W.	Doing, C. H.	Ferris, N. S
Connolly, A. A.	Dolan, H. F.	Ferry, J. T.
Connolly, J B.	Dolan, P. V	Fields, F. H.
Connor, G. A.	Dolmadge, M. M.	Finch, G. A.
Conradis, Charles	Donaldson, R. G.	Finn, W. T.
Constas, J. N.	Donaldson, R. N.	Finney, H. W.
Cook, J. P.	Donlon, A. J.	Fisher, Charles
Cookerow, M. W.	Donnelly, H. J.	Fisher, C G.
Copp, Z. H.	Donnelly, R. J.	Fitman, T. H.
Coppinger, C. W. B.	Donnelly, W. J.	Fitzgerald, E. A.
Coppinger, J. G. B.	Donohoe, C F.	Ftzgerald, Morris,
Corbin, W. E.	Donovan, E P.	Fitzgerald, T. R.
Corcoran, H. E.	Donovan, T. J.	Fitz-Gibbon, J. E.
Corcoran, J. A.	Dooley, F. X.	Flanagan, J. J.
Costello, J. F.	Donch, W. A.	Flannery, J. S.
Costigan, I. J. J.	Dorsey, R. J. C.	Flannery, M. M.
Cotterill, C. E.	Downey, R J.	Flather, A C.
Coughlin, J. T.	Downing, R. F.	Flaherty, R. B.
Cowles, A. E.	Downs, N C	Flynn, J. A.
Cox, C. R.	Downs, N L	Flynn, J. B.
Cox, E. M.	Doyle, M. M.	Foley, J. D
Craig, A. E.	Doyle, W. T S.	Foote, J A
Craighill, G. D.	Dudley, J. G.	Forbes, D. R.
Cramer, Dick	Duehring, F. E.	Forney, E O
Crane, W. L.	Duff, E. H.	Forrest, Bladen
Craven, T. J.	Duffey, H. C.	Fort, J. C.
Crawford, J. C.	Duffy, C. H.	Fortune, T. L.
Crawford, W. A.	Duffy, J. T.	Forwood, W. H.
Crawford, W. G.	Dufour, C. R	Foster, D. S.
Cromelin, P. B.	Dufour, Everett	Foster, W. C.
Crook, Harrison	Dugan, C. L.	Fowler, W. E.
Crosson, H. J.	Dumont, Francis	Fox, E. K.
Crowe, J. W.	Duncan, J. J. K.	Franc, H. L.
Cruikshank, T. A.	Dunne, W. G.	Frank, M. E.
Cuddy, S. A.	Dunnigan, J. P.	French, E. R.
Cummisky, E. F.	Dunnington, C. C.	French, E. S.
Curriden, S. W.	Durfee, R. B.	Frey, C. E.
Curry, Daniel	Duryee, J. B.	Frye, G. R.
Curtin, R. A.	Duvall, E S, Jr.	Fuchs, W. R.
Daiker, F. H.	Duvall, W. S.	Fuhrman, W. J.
Daish, J. B.	Duvall, W. T. S.	Fulton, C. M.
Daly, J. T.	Earl, Charles	Furbershaw, T. L.
Danforth, R F.	Easby-Smith, J. S.	Furbershaw, W. S.
Daniels, R. D.	Easterday, G. J.	Gaddis, E. T.
Darby, J. J.	Easterling, H. V.	Galiher, S. S.
Darlington, J. J.	Eckstein, Otto G.	Gallagher, P J.
Darr, C. W.	Edwards, R. L.	Gallatin, D. B.
Davenport, H. B.	Edwards, W. W.	Gannon, J. A.
David, Levi	Eliot, J L.	Gantt, D. J.
Davidson, E. R.	Eliot, T. J.	Garabedian, A. L.
Davis, B. N.	Elliott, S. H.	Gardiner, W. G.
Davis, D. G.	Ellis, D. C.	Gardner, F. D.
Davis, J. H	Ellsworth, G. D.	Garrison, F. H.
Davis, W. J.	Emery, W. H.	Gates, C. J.
Davison, J. W.	Emmons, C. M.	Geis, H. E.

DISTRICT OF COLUMBIA,	DISTRICT OF COLUMBIA.	DISTRICT OF COLUMBIA.
Washington, *Cont'd.*	Washington, *Cont'd*	Washington, *Cont'd.*
Geneste, L. F.	Hartnett, F. J.	Houghton, A. M.
Gengler, A. C.	Hartsfield, A. M.	Houston, H. I.
George, J. M.	Harvey, H. E.	Howard, A. C.
Gerald, H. P.	Harvey, T. M.	Howard, A. L.
Gettinger, W. M.	Harveycutter, Austin	Howard, J. C.
Gibbs, A. C.	Hasbrouck, E. M.	Howard, L. O.
Gibbs, F. R	Hassan, D. T.	Howard, S. W.
Gibson, F. P.	Hayden, Reynolds	Howell, J. H.
Gilchrist, W. S.	Hayes, Edward	Howell, S. P.
Gill, J. E.	Hazen, W. P. C.	Hudson, W. E.
Gillan, E. F.	Healy, C. B.	Hughes, C. L.
Given, Ralph	Healy, E. C.	Hughes, C. E.
Glennan, C. P.	Healy, T. F.	Hughes, W. J.
Glennan, J. W.	Hearst, W. T.	Hunt, G. M.
Gloetzner, Anton	Hedrick, C. J.	Hunter, E. C.
Gloetzner, A. A.	Hedrick, J. T.	Hurney, T. J.
Gloetzner, H. F.	Heffernan, B. J.	Hutchinson, E. A.
Glueck, Bernard	Hegarty, H. A.	Huyck, T. B.
Goddard, W. H	Heldeman, Ivan	Hynson, N. T.
Goldsborough, J. A.	Heiskell, R. A.	Irwin, J. W.
Golladay, J. E.	Heitmuller, H. A.	Israeli, Baruch
Goodman, W. R., Jr.	Heller, J. M.	Jackson, W. S.
Gould, A. M.	Helmick, W. J.	Jaffe, S. S.
Govern, Frank	Helmus, John	James, C. C
Gower, H. R.	Helton, A. S.	Jamison, A. B
Graff, C. J. F.	Hemler, W. F.	Jenkins, Charles
Graham, W. H.	Henderson, J. M.	Jenner, N. R.
Grant, Thomas	Hendler, C. T.	Jennings, J. W.
Green, A. J.	Hendrick, D. S.	Jewett, N. J.
Green, B. R.	Henry, T. S	Jirdinston, W. C.
Green, F. K.	Hermesch, H. R.	Johnson, B. R.
Green, J. B.	Heron, A P.	Johnson, Hayden
Green, L. H.	Herron, W. F.	Johnson, J D.
Greene, Wallace	Hickey, A. I	Johnson, J. T.
Gregg, W. S.	Hickey, H. K.	Johnson, L. B. T.
Griffin, W. Y.	Hickling, D. P.	Johnson, L. A.
Griffith, E. C.	Hicks, J. A.	Johnson, P. B. A.
Griffith, J. E.	Hildreth, A. L.	Johnson, P. E.
Griffith, M. J.	Hill, E. M.	Johnson, S. C.
Grogan, S. S.	Hill, H. F.	Johnson, T. W.
Gross, A. G.	Hilton, E. J.	Johnson, W. A.
Gunnell, F. M.	Hilton, J. F.	Johnston, L. J.
Gwynn, W. C.	Hillyer, C. S.	Jones, B. S
Haas, C. D.	Hillyer, C. R.	Jones, C. M.
Hahn, H. W.	Hinton, J. R.	Jones, F. A.
Hall, H. T.	Hipkins, ... A.	Jones, G. M.
Hall, J. D.	Hird, J. D.	Jones, J. S.
Hallam, P L.	Hitchcock, T. D.	Jones. J. K.
Haltigan, P. J.	Hiltz, W. H.	Jordan, Llewellyn
Hamby, L. L.	Hodge, E. R.	Journey, C. W.
Hamill, J. H.	Hodges, H. W.	Joyce, J. I.
Hamilton, G. E.	Hodges, W. S.	Judd, T. M
Hamilton, J. J.	Hof, C. R.	Julihn, M. L
Hamilton, R. A.	Hoffar, N. S.	Junghans, J. H.
Hammett, C. M.	Hogan, F. J.	Kage, H. W.
Haney, L. T.	Holden, R. T.	Kalbfus, S. T.
Hanger, H. H.	Holder, W. B.	Kane, J. J
Hanger, McCarthy	Holland, G. W.	Kappler, C. J.
Harbin, G. F., Jr.	Holland, T. S.	Kaveney, J. J.
Hardie, J. C.	Hollander, H. H.	Keane, M. A.
Hardy, C S.	Holliger, F. S.	Keane, M. J.
Harlow, L. P.	Holt, J. H.	Kearney, George
Harmon, J. O.	Hoover, G. P	Kearney, R. F.
Harper. B. E.	Hoover, W. D.	Keegin, W. C.
Harr, W. R.	Hopewell, E N.	Keelly, W. E.
Harrington, E. P.	Hopkins, A. F.	Kelleher, G. E.
Harrison, Walton	Horgan, William	Kelly, D. J.
Harrison, W. A.	Horigan, J. B.	Kelly, J. F.
Hart, J. T.	Horigan, W. D.	Kelly, J. J.
Hart, Ringgold	Horn, Elihu	Kelly, W. F.
Hart, T. J.	Horton, W. E.	Kendall, W. C.
Hartnett, D. J.	Hough, W. H.	Kennedy, H. F.

DISTRICT OF COLUMBIA.

Washington, *Cont'd.*

Kent, O. B.
Kerr, Denis
Kettler, M A.
Kidwell, T. W.
Kilgour, R. M.
Kilkenny, F. J.
Kilroy, J. T.
Kimball, C. O.
Kimball, E S
King, A. S.
King, C. C.
King, C. F.
King, G. S.
King, J. L G
Kinyoun, J. J.
Kirby, Thomas, Jr.
Kitch, J. B
Kirby, W. P.
Kitchin, E. M.
Kleinschmidt, H C.
Klinger, D. B.
Klopfer, Norman
Klopfer, W. H.
Knight H. S
Knode, T. E.
Kober, G. M.
Kolipinski, Louis
Kratz, J. A., Jr.
Krichelt, F. W.
Kuhn, J. O'R., Jr.
Kuhn, J. A.
Lacey, A. B.
Lainhart, J. W., Jr.
Lamar, G. C.
Lamar, W. H., Jr.
Lamb, D. S.
Lambert, T. A.
Lambert, W. J.
Lancaster, C. C.
Lancaster, C. S.
Landers, Eugene
Lang, J. R.
Lansdale, A. L.
Lanston, Aubrey
Larkin, P. E.
Leahy, D. F.
Leary, F. P.
Leckie, A. E. L.
Lecomte, R. M.
Lee, F. D.
Lee, Henry
Lenahan, W. D.
Leonard, J. D.
Leonard, R. B.
Lesh, P. E.
Lever, A. F.
Lewis, J. E.
Lewis, W. H.
Lieberman, C. D.
Lieuallen, Grant
Lingamfelter, N. S.
Linton, Howard
Linton, W. C.
Little, A. B.
Lochboehler, G J.
Logan, E. A.
Loughran, J. M
Loughran, L D.
Loughran, P. H.
Lowe, Louis
Lowe, T. F.
Lowe, V. L.

DISTRICT OF COLUMBIA.

Washington, *Cont'd*

Lozane, C. I.
Luce, C. R.
Luthy, J. H.
Lyon, Frank
Lyon, R. B.
Lyon, Simon
McArdle, T. E.
McCarthy, C. A.
McCarthy, J. C.
McCarthy, J. J.
McCoy, J. S.
McCormick, M. A.
McDonnell, E. De L.
McFarland, W. R.
McFarlan, W. S.
McGill, J. N.
McGlue, G. P.
McGuire, J. C.
McIntyre, A. J.
McKaig, J. F.
McKee, E. J.
McKee, Frederick
McKenna, D. P. J.
McKenna, R. T.
McKeon, F. H.
McKernan N. M.
McLachlen, J. M.
McMahon, J. J.
McMahon, J. J.
McMahon, R. W.
McNally, Valentine
McNamara, R. E.
McNeal, M. J.
McNeir, C. S.
McNish, A. M.
McQuillan, Francis
Machen, F. S.
Mackley, A. R.
Macnamee, A. M.
Madigan, J. J.
Madigan, J. P.
Madigan, P. S.
Madison, B. F.
Magee, M. D'A.
Magie, E. R.
Magruder, C. C.
Magruder, G. L.
Magruder, R. A. C.
Maguire, F. S.
Maguire, J. T.
Mahony, W. F.
Mallan, T. F.
Malone, H. D.
Mangan, M. F.
Mangan, W. J.
Manghum, H. B.
Manghum, Mason
Manning, J. N.
Manogue, W. H.
Marbury, C. C.
Marks, L. C.
Marmion, W. V.
Marr, S. S.
Marsden, F. T.
Marshall, Cloud
Marshall, P. J.
Martin, R. H.
Marye, T. T.
Masterson, D. S.
Matthews, William
Mattingly, C. M.
Mattingly, J. C.

DISTRICT OF COLUMBIA.

Washington, *Cont'.*

Mattingly, L. H.
Mattingly, R. E.
Maurer, R. A.
Mawhinney, R. J.
Maxey, C. T.
Mead, Theodore
Melling, George
Merritt, A. D.
Meritt, E. B.
Merrill, H. C.
Mess, H. F.
Metzger, Percy
Meyer, Robert
Meyers, W. F.
Milburn, J. R.
Milburn, J. W.
Miller, C. C.
Miller, C. H.
Miller, J. E.
Miller, J. H.
Miller, W. G.
Millot. Eugene
Millrick, D. A.
Miner, F. H.
Mitchell, G. D.
Mitchell, P. V.
Mock, J. J.
Mohun, Barry
Molloy, John
Montgomery, C. P.
Mooney, H. F.
Moran, C. V.
Moran, J. F.
Moran, J. R.
Morgan, J. D.
Morgan, J. V.
Morrill, Chester
Morris, Ballard
More, A. P.
Moser, J. M.
Moulton, I. B.
Mudd, S. E., Jr.
Mueller, C. C.
Mulcahy, D. D.
Mulhall, F. J.
Mullaly, J. F.
Mulligan, T. E.
Muncaster, Alex.
Muncaster, S. B.
Murdock, E. F.
Murphey, J. J.
Murphy, C. J.
Murphy, E. V., Jr.
Murphy, H. L.
Murphy, J. A.
Murphy, J. W.
Murray, L. O.
Murray, O. H.
Nash, J. A.
Neale, A. W.
Neale, R. A.
Neill, C. P.
Neill, T. E.
Neilson, F. K.
Nelson, C. F.
Neubeck, F. L.
Nevins, J. D.
Newman, C. R.
Newman, E. S.
Newton, J. T.
Nichols, J. L.

DISTRICT OF COLUMBIA.

Washington, *Cont'd.*

Nordlinger, I. W.
Nye, E. B.
Obenchain, C. A.
Ober, G. C.
O'Brien, J. L.
O'Brien, M. C.
O'Brien, T. W.
O'Connor, C. E.
O'Connor, J. I.
O'Connor, Michael
O'Dea, P. H.
O'Donoghue, D. W.
O'Donoghue, J. A.
Offutt, Armand
O'Hanlon, Michael
Oller, G. E.
Olmstead, E. B.
Opisso, A. M.
O'Reilly, Thomas
Orleman, C. S.
O'Shea, J. A.
Osterman, O. H.
Ottenburg, Louis
Ourdan, V. L.
Owens, S. L.
Owens, W. D.
Pace, L. D.
Packard, H. M.
Painter, J. I.
Paladini, F. S.
Palmer, A. C.
Palmer, Dennis
Palmer, J. A. C.
Palmer, T. S.
Parke, C. LeR.
Parker, B. H.
Parsons, L. L.
Patterson, H. S.
Patterson, T. H.
Pattison, A. S.
Payne, J. S.
Payne, L. A.
Pearce, W. R.
Peck, H. E.
Peck, W. D.
Pelzman, F. M.
Pendleton, F. C.
Pennington, P. K.
Pennybacker, I. S.
Pennybacker, J. E.
Perkins, L. L.
Perry, D. B.
Perry, F. C.
Perry, F. S.
Perry, R. R.
Perry, R. R.
Petteys. C. V.
Pettis, H. S.
Peyser, J. L.
Pickett, T. J.
Pierce, H. F.
Pimper, H. K.
Pitts, G. B.
Polk, J. K.
Pollock, G. F.
Posey, O. J.
Postley, C. E.
Potbury, J. E..
Poulton, W. E.
Poulton, W. E.
Powell, W. F.
Powers, J. S.

DISTRICT OF COLUMBIA.

Washington, *Cont'd*

Price, R. E.
Pugh, J. L., Jr.
Purman, L. C.
Quay, J. B.
Quicksall, W. F.
Quigley, E. T.
Quinlan, E. S.
Quinn, H. L.
Quinn, J. A.
Quinter, H. R.
Quinter, R. De S.
Raby, St. G. R.
Rainey, F. H.
Ralston, J. H.
Rankin, J. M.
Rauterberg, L. B.
Rea, G. W.
Ready, M. J.
Redmond, E. J.
Redrow, W. L.
Reeside, F. P.
Reeve, J. N.
Reeves, I. S. K.
Reeves, J. R. T.
Reeves, W. P.
Reid, G. C.
Reilly, J. F.
Reisinger, E. W.
Repetti, F. F.
Repetti, F. F., Jr.
Repetti, J. J.
Rhoads, W. L.
Rice, F. J.
Rich, W. J.
Richards, Alfred
Richmond, C. W.
Richmond, E. E.
Richmond, J. A.
Richmond, Paul
Ridgely, H. S.
Ridgway, F. H.
Riley, B. C.
Riley, H. B.
Riley, J. F.
Riordon, J. A.
Roach, C. E.
Roach, F. de S.
Roach, W. N., Jr.
Roane, S. B.
Robbins, T. A.
Robinson, Thomas
Rodgers, C. H.
Rogers, F. J.
Rogers, J. C.
Romaine, F. W.
Rosenberg, M. D.
Rosenthal, S. H.
Roth, J. A.
Rothschild, David
Rover, L. A.
Rowland, H. B.
Roys, Chase
Ruffin, Thomas
Rupli, J. T.
Russell, A. M.
Russell, Bert
Ryan, P. J.
Sacks, John
St. Clair, F. A.
Salomon, Joseph
Sanders, C. H.
Sanders, Scott

DISTRICT OF COLUMBIA.

Washington, *Cont'd.*

Sands, F. P. B.
Sanger, Monie
Saul, J. A.
Saunders, J. N.
Sawtelle, H. W.
Scanlon, Edward
Schick, J. P.
Schildroth, H. T.
Schlosser, F. B.
Schmaltz, O. J.
Schmidt, O. P.
Schneider, E. C.
Schneider, F. T.
Schreiber, H. R.
Schreiner, Edmund
Schubert, B. F.
Schulteis, H. J.
Schwartz, E. M.
Scott, T. W.
Semmes, A. H.
Sessford, C. E.
Sessford, J. S.
Sewell, E. D.
Shaw, K. A.
Shea, T. J.
Shechan, J. D.
Sheehy, F. P.
Sheehy, J. C.
Sheehy, V. A.
Sheibley. S B.
Shekell, A. B
Shelse, R. C.
Shepard, Seth
Sheriff, A R
Shervill. E. B.
Sherwod, C. R.
Shinn, G. C.
Shoemaker, L. P.
Sholes, W. H.
Short, W. O.
Shugrue, Patrick
Sibley, G. J.
Sillers, Albert
Sillers, R. F
Simmons, Leo
Simonton, J. P.
Simonton, V. de P
Sinclair, A. L.
Sisler, W. J. L.
Sizer, Adrian
Slaughter, W. D.
Slinder, M. E.
Smith, A. T.
Smith, C. A.
Smith, C. P
Smith, H. M.
Smith, J. E.
Smith, J. F.
Smith, J S.
Smith, R. E. L.
Smith, T. C.
Smith, Walter
Snow, R. W.
Snyder, H. C.
Sohon, Frederick
Sohon, H. W.
Solback, L. W.
Soper, J. S.
Sour. Louis
Southerland, J. J.
Spear, J. M.
Speiden, C. E.

DISTRICT OF COLUMBIA.	DISTRICT OF COLUMBIA.	DISTRICT OF COLUMBIA.
Washington, *Cont'd.*	**Washington,** *Cont'd*	**Washington,** *Cont'd.*
Spiess, L. A.	Townsend, J. G.	White, R. R.
Stack, J. C.	Trembly, R. H.	White, W. H.
Stackhouse, G. M.	Tschiffely, S. A.	Whitehead, J. C.
Stafford, W. P.	Turton, W. E.	Whiteley, R. P.
Staley, C. M.	Tyler, F. S.	Wilcox, A. D.
Stallings, T B.	Ucker, C. S.	Wilcox, J. A.
Stearman, Mark	Vale, F. P.	Wilkinson, A. D.
Stearns, J. S.	Van Den Chatten,	Wilkinson, W. H.
Stebbing, E. J.	Baron	Willey, H. P.
Stein, J B.	Van Dyne, Fred'k	Williams, G. F.
Stein, Robert	Van Nest, R. H.	Williams, J. G.
Stephan, Anton	Van Sant, Frank	Williams, J. R.
Stephens, T. A	Van Vranken, Fred'k	Willis, S D.
Stephenson, J. G.	Varnell, M. K.	Willis, T. C.
Sterling, H M.	Vaughan, D. C.	Willson, A. B.
Stetson, C. W.	Vaughan, M. V.	Willson, Prentiss
Stevens, E. E.	Verbrycke, J. R., Jr.	Wilmeth, G. M.
Stevenson, Charles	Verrill, C. H.	Wilson, Andrew
Stewart, W. W.	Vierbuchen, Julius	Wilson, C. R.
Stitt, F. S.	Vierbuchen, R. J.	Wilson, E. L.
Stockbridge, V. D.	Vincent, T. N.	Wilson, H. O.
Stockman, F. J.	Wagner, G. H.	Wilson, J. C.
Stohlman, Frederick	Wahly, W. H.	Wilson, Nelson
Stonebraker, S E.	Walker, Francis	Wilson, T. J.
Stoutenbergh, J. A.	Walker, L. A., Jr.	Wimsatt, W. K.
Strasburger, Milton	Walker, R. E.	Windle, C T.
Streater, Wallace	Walker, R. H.	Wissner, F. J.
Street, D. B.	Walker, R. E.	Witman, E R.
Street, G. A.	Walker, W. G.	Woerner, O. E.
Street, H R.	Walker, W. H.	Wolf, Alexander
Strickland, R. T.	Wall, J. S.	Wolfe, J. M.
Sudler, O. R.	Wall, M. J.	Wollard, P D.
Sullivan, F. P.	Wallace, E. L.	Wood, A. E.
Sullivan, G. E.	Walsh, E J.	Wood, E. C.
Sullivan, J. D.	Walsh, Francis	Wood, G. W.
Sullivan, M. W.	Walshe, P. J.	Wood, L. C.
Sullivan, T J.	Walter, W. F.	Wood, W. C.
Sullivan, T. V.	Wanamaker, W. H.	Woodward, H. E.
Sullivan, W. C.	Wand, A. J.	Woodward, W. C.
Sullivan, W D.	Ward, F. M	Woolf, O. P.
Summey, B. W.	Ward, G A.	Worthington, A. S.
Swingle, E A.	Warder, J. F.	Wright, H. F.
Sylvester, J. H.	Warner, R. A.	Wright, H T.
Taggart, G. R	Warren, Bates	Wright. W. L.
Taggart, R. J.	Warren, J. L.	Wynn, F. S.
Talbott, E. M.	Warriner, W F.	Yeatman, R. H.
Tastet, J. M.	Wasser, H R.	Young, R. A.
Taylor, A. S.	Watkins, S. E.	Yturbide, A. de
Taylor, G. W.	Watkins, V. E.	Zabel, J. H.
Taylor, W. C.	Watson. M. M.	Zepp, Jesse
Teicher, J. G.	Watson, Robert	Zimmerman, H. J.
Teller, S. J.	Weaver, A. S.	Zimmerman, Mervin
Tennent, E. H.	Webster, B. T.	Zinkhan, A. M.
Tepper, B. L.	Weikert, C. B.	———
Tepper, J L.	Weinstein, D. D.	*Brennan. M. F.
Thian, P. E.	Welch, C. B.	*Brown, T. H.
Thomaides, G. T.	Welch, T J.	*Cull, A. H.
Thomas, C. F.	Welch, Williams	*Davis, G. M
Thomas, E. H.	Weller, J. I.	*De Knight. E. W.
Thomas, E. W.	Wells, B. W.	*Ruth, C. H.
Thomas, J. B	Wells, W. A.	
Thomas, J. E.	West, V. E.	
Thomas, R. W.	Wetmore, J A.	**FLORIDA.**
Thomas, Roy	Weyrich, J. R	
Thomas, W. B.	Wheeler, A. M., Jr.	**Cattarangus.**
Thompson, E. St. C.	Wheeler, M. D.	Heberle. J. J.
Thompson, Smith, Jr.	White, C. A.	**Fernandina.**
Tindall, William	White, C. J.	Carleton, R. P.
Tobin, R. F.	White, E. D.	**Gainesville.**
Toner, J. E.	White, F. P.	Waldo. G. S.
Toomey, J. A.	White, G H.	
Torrey E. G.	White, J. R.	

FLORIDA.

Jacksonville.
Acker, A. E.
Cockrell, Alston
Loretto.
Nolan, T. J.
Marianna.
Carter, Paul
Pensacola.
Jones, J. B.
Leary, R. J.
Starke.
Pace, C. F.

*Stanton, L. J.

GEORGIA.

Atlanta.
Ahlgren, W. B.
Atherton. L T.
Cabanis, E. G.
Hull, M. McH.
Jones, W. P.
McLarin, H. M.
Neely, E. A.
Payne, J. C
Spalding, Hughes
Augusta.
Eve, O. R.
Konigsberg, M. H
Cartersville.
Stansell, W. K.
Covington.
Edwards, W. A.
Elberton.
Allison, G. W.
Griffin.
Vaughan, W. J.
Macon.
Morgan, Cecil
Monroe.
Walker, C. M.
Quitman.
King, J. T.
Rome.
Hamilton. Harper
Maddox, G. E.
Whipple. U. V.
Savannah.
Cohen, G. M.

*Cook, A. B
*Pierce, W. P
*Pierce, W. P.
*Wikle, Douglas

IDAHO.

Boise City.
Booth, C. M.
Coeur d'Alene.
McFarland, W. B.
Hailey.
Goodwin, W. D.
Ilo.
Maple, A. H.

IDAHO.

Kellogg.
Millott, A. F.
Mackay.
Higgins, A. J.
Moscow.
Morgan, W. M.
Nezperce.
Henry, Wesley
Twin Falls.
Smith, H. F.
Wallace.
Pfirman, Franklin
Quigley, F. L.

ILLINOIS.

Aurora.
DeRiemer, A H.
Freeman, J. E.
Bloomington.
McDonnell, J. J.
Carmi.
Clark, H. C.
Carrollton.
Dunsworth, M. J.
Carthage.
Culkin, W. P.
Chicago.
Aspern, H. T.
Banfield, C. P.
Barry, J. D.
Bennett, W. A.
Brady, J. T.
Bremner, V. A.
Bridges, W. S.
Brosseau, L A.
Callahan, J. E
Callander, W. F
Corcoran, Vincent
Cullen, L. J.
Daly, J H.
Dunne, J. P
Duvall, W. H.
English, J. J
Fitzgerald, G. W.
Fogle, J. L.
Fowler. A. L.
Fuller, W M
Garvy, W. J.
Geringer, E J.
Gorman, G. E
Grau, P. A.
Hayden, D R.
Hilliard, P. R.
Hopkins, F. A.
Hopkins. L. M.
Igoe, M. L
Lantry. T P
McBride. C. R
McDowell. J E.
McNulty, J. D.
Merrick, R. T.
Niblack, W. C.
O'Donnell. P H.
O'Neill. W F
Parsons, John
Quinlan, G. A.
Ryan, J H.
Sears, F. H

ILLINOIS.

Chicago, *Continued.*
Sherman, T. E.
Test, F. C.
Walters, H. A.
Wilson, J. S.
Woods, C. F.
Wright, A. W.
Carlinville.
David, F. E.
Danville.
Gilmore, W. T.
Jewell, W. R., Jr.
Kiningham, R. B.
Williamson, J. A.
Evanston.
Burchmore, J. S.
Farmersville.
McCarron, J. F.
Galena.
Ryan, J. McN.
Geneseo.
Ferry, L A.
Joliet.
Lennon, M. F.
Mahoney, J. J.
Marshall.
Graham, H. C.
Phillips, R. L.
Mattoon.
Smith, P. W.
Morrison.
Bradley, H. A.
Neoga.
Ragan, G. T.
Paris.
Hemphill, J. C.
Pittsfield.
Wassell, H E.
Quincy.
Smith, L. D
Peoria.
Conigisky, J. P.
Peru.
Dillon, Patrick
Richmond.
Ward, S. R.
Salem.
Teller, E D
Savanna.
Brearton. J L.
Springfield.
Nelms. W. H
Tuscola.
Phillips, F E.
Roberts, T. W.
Urbana.
Williamson, F. E.
Virgen.
Neely, W. C
Waukegan.
Warren, H B.

ILLINOIS.

White Heath.
Cline, R. R.
Wilmette.
Prescott, C. C.
Yorkville.
Van Emon, W. C.

---

*Hoard, F. DeV.
*Fouts, F. A.
*Porter, J. W.
*Roman, Richard
*Woodward, R. E.

INDIANA.

Anderson.
Willson, S. C.
Bergan.
Beegan, J. F.
Connersville.
Barrows, F. I.
Corydon.
Cook, W. E
Douglass, W. B.
Sims, Grant
Tracewell, R. N.
Covington.
Baker, J. E.
Dunkirk.
Borden, J. A.
Elkhart.
Murphy, Daniel
Sawyer, G. R.
Fort Wayne.
Carroll, J. C.
Lewis, G. W.
Frankfort.
Brown, C. F.
Indianapolis.
Baumgardner, Ray
Beckman, J. J.
Hodges, E F
Keach, LeRoy
McSheehy. Thomas
Posey, R. B.
Ragan, J. J.
Kingsbury.
Webster, Ben
Knox.
Pentecost, W. C.
Lafayette.
Ball, W. J.
Logansport.
Se Legue, C. A.
Smith. P. D.
Muncie.
McClellan, F. F.
O'Neill, J. J.
Newcastle.
Rich, T. C.
North Vernon.
Norris, R. W.
Peru.
Helm, C. J.

INDIANA.

Petersburg.
Green, V. R.
Poland.
Chamberlain, W. L.
Richmond.
Jessup, Wilfred
Rolling Prairie.
Dudeck, Joseph
Rome City.
Pulskamp, Bernard
Terre Haute.
Crawford, C. A.
Sudbrink, J. T.
Vincennes.
LaPlante, J. B. E.
Washington.
Hoffman, J. O.
Woodburn.
Betts, A. P.

---

*Davis, J. N.
*Demoss, W. R.
*Kuehn, O. F.
*Lovett, J. W.
*McCoy, W. I.
*Skinner, G. A.

IOWA.

Anamosa.
Sheean, J. A.
Cantril.
Grinstead, J. R.
Cedar Rapids.
Miles, M. J.
Chariton.
Horrigan, J. J.
Clinton.
Langan. R. C.
Wolfe, J. L.
Davenport.
Donegan, M. F.
McCarthy, D. J
Des Moines.
Hanawalt, G. P.
Parsons, H. K.
Dubuque.
Cooney, M. D.
McCabe, H. F.
Fairfield.
Myers, A. F.
Fayette.
Dorman, J. E.
Fort Dodge.
Condon, W. F.
Garner.
Sincox, G. R.
Grand Junction.
Harker, C. O.
Leon.
Sharp, E. H.

IOWA.

Lohrville.
Fisher, W. J.
Malcolm.
Tyler, G. W.
Oelwein.
Lee, O. W.
Pocahontas.
Atkinson, C. D.
Sheldon.
Wellman, G. T.
Spencer.
Lawler, J. C.

---

*Sparks, A. R.

KANSAS.

Atchison.
Ingalls, Ellsworth
Ingalls, Ralph
Coffeyville.
Wells, W. H.
Council Bluffs.
Pirtle, W. J.
Council Grove.
Smart, A. H.
Emporia.
Williams H. H.
Fort Riley.
Boiseau, L. T.
Fort Scott.
McQuaid, G. J.
Girard.
Phillips, L. H.
Hoyt.
Pettijohn, J. W.
Iola.
Dresbach, H. V.
Junction City.
Cramer, H. W.
Kansas City.
White, T. J.
Larned.
Athey, T. F.
Manhattan.
Thompson, G. F.
Mulvane.
Davis, C. S.
Newton.
Norton, J. M.
Olathe.
Nelligan, J. J.
Osage City.
Randall, T. G.
Lakin.
Nelson, T. C.
Leavenworth.
Kimmel, G. P.
Seneca.
Hayes, Noah

KANSAS.

Topeka.
Kinksley, H. A.
Mills, C. A.
Turner, Emmett
Wellington.
Collins, R. L.
Westmoreland.
Hart, H. L.

*Dallas, E. J.
*Green, J. C.

KENTUCKY.

Covington.
Richmond, J. A.
Danville.
Kincaid, D. H.
Flat Lick.
Farley, F. P.
Frankfort.
Clay, W. R.
Hardinsburg.
Mercer, Claude
Harean.
Kelly, Frank
Louisville.
Boldrick, S. J.
Burke, F. H.
Cooper, J. S.
Rudd, T. S.
Watson, J. M.
Marysville.
Collins, J. M.
Maysville.
Browning, A. G.
Paintsville.
Stewart, J. F.
Pikesville.
Langley, J. W.
Prestonsburg.
Ferguson, S. C.
St. Matthews.
Monohan, E. S.
Somerset.
Clothier, A. J.
Springfield.
Hardin, Palmer
Vanceburg.
Pugh, R. W.
Willard.
Hackworth, G. H.

*Davis, J. G.
*Haines, W. S.
*Mason, H. L.
*Wainscott, George
*Waters, Francis

LOUISIANA.

Baton Rouge.
Barrow, W. M.
Jackson.
Gleeson, J. K.

LOUISIANA.

Jeanerette.
Bourgeois, S. J.
Lake Charles.
Fournet, G. A.
New Orleans.
Atkinson, L. C.
Briant, L. P.
Byrnes, W. H.
Clark, T R.
Devlin, D. J.
Dimitry, C. P.
Fairfax, J. W.
Fitch, W. S.
Flynn, T. D.
Gelpi, M. J.
Grima, Alfred
Hopkins, Ralph
Kathman, J. A.
Laplace, A. J.
Montgomery, J. W.
Rost, Emile
Smith, J. A.
Solis, Frederic
Stagg, J. A.
Taylor, W. I.
Tighe, J M.
Tremoulet, J. S
Waguespack, W. J.
Plaquemine.
Grace, A. L.
St. Martinsville.
Martin, J. J.
Shreveport.
Fisher, H. C.
Thibodeaux.
Badeaux, T A.
Beary, J. V. H.

*Becnel, Alphonse
>Braud, P. S.
*Buard, L A.
*Delacroix, J. D.
*Delacroix, P. D.
*Des Londe, Edward
*Landry, Anatole
*Landry, P R
*Lapretre, J. B. A.
*Lastrappes. Ludger
*Laumont, H. B.
*Ray, C. B.
*Swayze, S. C.
*Thomas. E. J.
*Waite, G. W C.
*Williamson, H. C.

MAINE.

*Haven, C. L
Auburn.
Murphy. E. J.
Oakes. R S.
Augusta.
Cony, R A., Jr.
Maher, B. F.
Bangor.
O'Connell. R. T.
Triplett, C. E.
Baring.
Trott, F. P.

MAINE.

Fort Kent.
Madean, A. J.
Houlton.
Clark, R. E.
Madigan, A. W.
Madigan, J. B.
Merritt, F. C.
Pierce, J. M.
Shaw, Herschel
Lewiston.
McCarthy, A. E.
Roy, R. G.
Limington.
Moody, L. J.
Orono.
Alexander, G. W.
Pittsfield.
Lancaster, F. H.
Portland.
Conley, M. S.
Connelan, J. A.
Connolly, T. S.
Donahue, C. L.
Fox, J. C.
Harvey, R. E.
Mulloney, D. C.
Noyes, G. F.
Reynolds, E. C.
Stockman, C. W.
Rockland.
Hill, J. C.
Standish.
Higgins, R. H.

MARYLAND.

Aquasco.
Bowen, H. M.
Baldwin.
Totten, Howe
Baltimore.
Addison, Joseph
Andrews, O T.
Boggs, W. J.
Boone, E. D.
Boyd, J. A.
Brady, G M.
Brent, Henry
Brown, F. E.
Carr, W S.
Cuddy, M. F.
Donegan, P. J.
Dougherty, L. J.
Doyle, F. J.
Gately, M. J.
George, I. S.
Green. R. J.
Greenfield, W. E.
Grimes, W. H.
Grogan, T. J.
Grogay, P. J
Haydon, W. T.
Homer, C. C.
Jones, G. W.
Kelly, C B
Kelly, C. N.
Kelly, J. V.
Kelly, P. A.

MARYLAND.

Baltimore, *Cont'd.*
Kennedy R. J.
Linn, S. F.
Longshaw, L. M.
Lyons, T. H.
O'Donovan, Charles
Phillips, E. L.
Pike, A. H.
Pugh, H. L
Townsend, S D.
Wade, J. D
Walters, Henry
Wells, J. B.
Wessel, J. F.
White, J. W.

Beltsville.
Doing, R. B.

Berwyn.
Baukhages, F. E., Jr
Tarbert, F. P.

Bethesda.
Loughborough, L. H
Morgan, D P.
Shoemaker, A. E.

Boyds.
Norris, R S.

Brandywine.
Robinson, A. T., Jr.

Brentwood.
Van Horn, R L

Charlotte Hall.
Southoron, L. J.

Chevy Chase.
Bernstein, I. I.
Baradshaw, Leonard
Brown, W. H J.
Callaghan, W. J.
Conrad, T. K.
Harper, J. E.
Kram, J. C.
Newton, Philip
Ridgeway. A. B
Ridgway. R. A
Shealy, R P.
Wedderburn G C
Yancey, G E

Chillum.
Ray. J. E , Jr.

Collington.
Hardisty, J T.

Cumberland.
McDonald, T B.

Darnestown.
Nourse, C H.

Dawsonville.
Nourse, U. D.

Denton.
Fullerton, R. P.

Doncaster.
Smith, Benjamin

Emmitsburg.
Bradley, B. J.
Jourdan, C H.
Lagarde, Ernest
Thompson, M. J.
Tierney, J. J.

MARYLAND.

Forest Hill.
Warren, C. S.

Frederick.
Koontz, Clarke
Posey, Fabian
Rager, W. H.
Smith, E. J.
Smith, J F.
Smith, W. M.
Walsh, T. J.

Friendship H'ghts.
Dunn, C. C
Sullivan, S. E.

Gaithersburg.
Owen, C W.
Thompson, A. C.

Germantown.
Waters, E. H.

Gessie.
Wellenreiter, O F.

Golden Hill.
Applegarth, W. F.

Hagerstown.
Humrichouse, H H.
Myers, S. H.

Havre de Grace.
Stephens, Jeremiah
Wells, G M

Hyattsville.
Dyer, J T . Jr.
Fuller. E A.

Ilchester.
Creecy, D B.

Jerusalem.
Walsh. R S L.

Kensington.
Bradley, J N.
Dalton. A. S
Rice. C E
Rowdybush, C R

Kloppers Station.
Caulfield, John

La Plata.
Cooksey. F. C.
Diggs, J T
Mudd, W G

Leonardtown.
Abell. E. B
Camalier, B H.
Camalier. F. A
Combs, R C.
Wallis, S B

Linden P. O.
Birgfeld. F A.

McDonough Sta.
Lyles, D. C.

Mechanicsville.
Morgan. Z. R.

Mitchellville.
Dufour. J. F. R.

Mount Rainier
Harmon. M. C.
Heron, B. F. L.
Sweeney, H. J.

MARYLAND.

Myersville.
Willis, J. H.

Prince George Co.
Blanford, J. H.

Riverdale.
Brady, E. J.
Burlingame, Harry
Warren, C. E.

Rockville.
Henderson, J. A.
Waters, B. F.

Rosaryville.
Clagett, H. W.

Seat Pleasant.
Johnson, J. A.

Silver Spring.
Shannon, A. C.
Whitney, C. F.

Stevenson.
Sloan, R. N.

Takoma Park.
Connolly, B. M.

Tennallytown.
Hawken, S. McC.

Upper Marlboro.
Hill, F. S.
Hill, R. S
Magruder, M. H.

Urbanna.
Brien, L. T.

Waldorf.
Mudd, W. A.

Washington Grov
Patterson, J. C. C.

Westminster.
Shriver, J. N

Woodstock.
Earls, Mitchell
Knight, J. S.

Woodwardville.
Anderson, S. H.

*Borroughs, Dent
*Brent, W. M
*Bryan, R H
*Conway, W. O.
*Hodges, B. F
*Horsey, C. C L.
*Mullan, H. E.
*Naylor, V. D.
*Nicholson, J. T
*Reid. John
*Reynolds, W. E.
*Rice, J. W.
*Ruff, J A
*Shaw, C. O
*Spalding, S E.
*Ward, E. J
*White, E. H.

MASSACHUSETT

Adams.
Burdick, M. H.

Ashmont.
Murphy, W. A.

MASSACHUSETTS.

Athol.
Casey, J T.

Atlantic.
Sweeney, M T

Auburn.
Stone, F. N.

Beverly.
Coleman, D C.

Boston.
Bossidy, J. C.
Brickley, B. A.
Buie, W. A
Connelly, M. F.
Connolly, A. L
Coulthurst, J. A.
Cunniff, M. M.
Cunniff, P S.
Curran, R J
Douglas, J. J.
Duffy, A. F.
Fegan, E. J.
Fitzpatrick, W. H.
Gapen, Nelson
Gaynor, H. A.
Grayson, W. W.
Horgan, J I.
James, Howard
Lloyd, G H
McCarthy, C C
McKenna, H. C.
McLaughlin, F. J.
McLaughlin, J. D.
McLaughlin, J. I.
McManus, Joseph
McNamara, W. F.
McQuaid, W P.
Martell, C J
Michener, A S.
Monarch, J. L.
Murphy, J. R.
O'Connell, J J.
Ogden, W. G.
O'Hara, J J.
O'Leary, T. S.
Phelan, F. M.
Powers, E. P.
Rooney, C. D.
Scanlan, M. J
Slattery, F E.
Smith P M.
Sproules, J A.
Sullivan T F.
Todd, W. G
Wiecker, Otho

Brockton.
McCarthy, J L.
Martin, J W.
Paine, A. E.

Brooklin.
Breck, Samuel

Cambridge.
Chisholm, J. L. B.
Quinn, E. L.
Thompson, J. S.

Charlestown.
Barry, J. A.
McMahon, J. W.

Chelsea.
Furlong, F. M.

MASSACHUSETTS.

Chicopee Falls.
Shea, M. I.

Clinton.
Kenney, J. E
McNamara, M. J.
O'Brien, J. H.

Concord.
Flavin, P. T.

Dennisport.
Wixon, I. F

Dorchester.
Bowen, J M
Duff, V S
Grace, P. J.
McSorley, C D.
Macdonald, A. A.

Everett.
Hart, J H.

Fall River.
Cuttle, L. X.
Davis, E. A
Murphy, D A.
Solomon, C. A.

Fitchburg.
Brown, W. A
Flynn, C. T.

Gardner.
Goggin, G. F.

Gloucester.
Conant, Thomas
Longan, J M

Greenfield.
Donohue, F. W.

Haverhill.
Kerrigan, G E
Sargent, L. L

Holliston.
Quinlan, R J

Holyoke.
Cavanaugh, T. E.

Housatonic.
Noonan, P J.

Hyde Park.
Burns, J. P.

Lawrence.
DeCourcy, C A.
Keleher, M J
Mahony, D. W.
Shaw, F L

Lenox.
Mackey, W. T.

Long Meadow.
Reedy, F. H.

Lowell.
Callahan, C. J
Hagan, C. J.
Kenney, J. P
Loughran, J. E.
Mahoney, M. P.
Moloney, B. J.
Watson, Robert

Lynn.
Donovan, G. T.
Donovan, M. R.

MASSACHUSETTS.

Malden.
Gallagher, N. A.
Holland, W. J.
Reddy, A. C.

Mansfield.
Sherman, W. I

Medford.
Sage, M W

Medway.
Spence, G B.

Melrose.
Clark, J S
Lucey, D J.

Milford.
Smith, C. J.

Monson.
Fuller, G E.
Leahy, W. E.

Nahant.
Connolly, J W.

Natick.
McGlone, A. V.

Needham.
Kingsbury, A. D.

Needham Heights.
Shine, H. L

New Bedford.
Desmond, S W
Desmond, W. P
Rogers, F L

Newburyport.
Binley, W. S.

Newton.
Curran, J J.
Ramsdell, G. P.

Newton Highlands.
Owings, W. R

North Adams.
Boland, J B
Lally, J J
O'Hara, F J.
O'Hearn, W A.
Quinn, J H.
Sullivan, E. R.

North Andover.
Morrill, C P.

North Weymouth.
Sweeney, M. J

Pittsfield.
Burke, F. H
Cassidy, F. W
Connor, J. E.
Dougherty, F. P.
Fallon, James
Reynolds, G. E.

Quincy.
Fitzpatrick, C E.
O'Hara, J. J

Roxbury.
Corbett, J. W. H.
Fitzgerald, T. J.

St. Lawrence.
Schaake, F. W.

12

MASSACHUSETTS.

Salem.
Elwell, C. B.
Feenan, A. M.
Somerville.
Brennan, J J.
Murphy, C. A.
South Boston.
Duffy, B F.
Fallon, J. D.
McNamara, F. B.
Slattery, J. R.
Timmins, P. J.
Southbridge.
Styll, H. H.
Springfield.
Beaven, T. B.
Carroll, M. J.
McKechnie, W. G.
Mahoney, E. J.
Maloney, J. M.
Mulcare, J. H.
Vineyard Haven.
Mead, F. W.
Walden.
Fitzpatrick, F. P.
Waltham.
Doud, E. F.
Griffin, J. J.
Ware.
Deery, J. P.
Watertown.
Gallagher, J. M.
Waverly.
Adams, E. H.
Webster.
Casey, J. J.
West Fitchburg.
Hanrahan, J. V.
West Newton.
Healy, G. L.
Weymouth.
Martell, L. A.
Winthrop.
Boehs, C. J.
Woburn.
Moore, J. E.
Worcester.
Belisle, G. E.
Butler, B. W.
Butler, F. J.
Carney, P. J.
Lynch, W. F.
McGauley, W. G.
McLoughlin, P J.
McLoughlin, W. I.
Marble, J. O.
Rogers, J. W.
Wright, J. H.

*Breen, James
*Caldwell, G. H.
*Conley, Francis
*Sheridan, D. R.
*Turner, O. C.
*Wood, G. F.

MICHIGAN.

Battle Creek.
Brown, J. C.
Burton Harbor.
Hall, F. L.
Detroit.
Alexander, J. C.
Bell, Charles
Brown, P. J.
Brownson, H. F.
Burke, F. B.
Du Charme, A. J.
Dwyer, W. A.
Grove, S. D.
Hutchings, F. W.
Nolker, J. J.
Norton, F. P.
Palms, C. L.
Palms, F. A.
Tracey, L. L.
Wollenberg, R. A. C.
Erie.
Gilday, A. L.
Fenton.
Larzelere, C. LaV.
Grand Rapids.
Murray, J. D.
Murray, L. J.
Kalamazoo.
Luby, E. S.
Minica.
Spencer, L. M.
Pontiac.
Mitchell, C. P.
Moroney, E. B.
Rockland.
Jeffs, Benjamin
Saginaw.
Camp, E W.
Scholz, W. J.
Schoolcraft.
Smith, H. S.
Ypsilanti.
Hatch, W. B.

*Palmer, Oscar

MINNESOTA.

Ashby.
Paulson, P. C.
Bemidji.
Arnold, F. S
McCann, T. A.
Duluth.
Alexander, F. C.
Greene, W. E.
Maginnis, C. H.
Sullivan, F. W.
Fergus Falls.
Eriksson, Leonard
Glenwood.
Ronning, H. T.
Le Sueur.
Williamson, G. M.

MINNESOTA.

Mankato.
Hall, J. E.
Bowen, Ivan
Hartley, Wilbur
Minneapolis.
Butler, P. J.
Carson, F. D.
Donnelly, Charles
Dyer, J. F.
Horgan, J. C.
Martinson, J. E.
Sweeney, J. A.
Thian, L. R.
Montevideo.
Smith, L A.
Red Wing.
Jones, A. W.
Rochester.
McGrath, B. F.
St. Paul.
Drill, L. L.
Fitzpatrick, T. C.
Johnson, E. M.
Lawler, D. W.
Lethert, C. A.
McAuliffe, M. J.
McTarnaghan, Arthur
Monaghan, M. M.
Winona.
Murphy, C. J.

*Cummings, G. W.

MISSISSIPPI.

Biloxi.
Smith, B F.
Columbus.
Youngblood, R. K.
Crawford.
Ervine, A. J., Jr.
Hattiesburg.
Watkins, Elton
Indianola.
Sims, E. K.
Jackson.
Whelan, T. A.
Neely.
Fain, J C.
Starkville.
Harrison, W. B.
Tutwyler.
Harrison. W. H.
Woodville.
Coon, J. B.

*Johnson, Joseph

MISSOURI.

Aurora.
Minor, L. J.
Ava.
Mitchell, C. W.
Carthage.
Wise, O. A.

MISSOURI.

Edina.
McCullough, F. H.
Joplin.
Calvin, C. W.
James, G. C.
Murphy, J. M.
Kansas City.
Donaldson, G. R.
Duncan, J. M.
Finney, W. B.
Follens, A. J.
Hill, E. F.
Kennedy, J. M.
Latshaw, H. J.
Latshaw, R. S.
McCardle, Battle
Miller, Jozach
Mitchell, W. A.
Reilly, J. A.
Ryan, W. D., Jr.
Stevens, F. L.
Thompson, J. H., Jr.
Wimsatt, W. T.
Kinloch.
Walsh, J. S., Jr.
Marble Hill.
Drun, J. W.
Nevada.
Dulin, E. A.
St. Joseph.
Allen, T. B.
Slattery, P. A.
St. Louis.
Barrington, R. L.
Bates, J. S.
Bevington, M. R.
Broderick, J. K.
Chew, J. P.
Desloge, G. T.
Dickson, M. T.
Dillon, Paul
Farish, J. H.
Ganahl, A. E.
Gauss, J. J.
Hargis, S. O.
Jones, W. J.
Keith, R. L.
Leahy, J. S.
Mohrmann, H. J.
Newsom, Herbert
Peters, J. W.
Pierce, T. M., Jr.
Risque, F. W.
Roche, C. H.
Rogers, T. M.
Schlafly, J. J.
Starek, Emil
Willson, H. A.
Slator.
Gwinn, C. A.
South West City.
Hall, W. D.
Springfield.
Johnson, W. H.

*Bradley, T. H.
*Hoote, L. C.
*Clarke, J. C. B.
*Murray, Thomas

MONTANA.

Billings.
Reilly, E. F. J.
Swank, W. R.
Butte.
Lavelle, T. E.
Dillon.
Pease, H. F.
Vlymen, J. R.
Forsyth.
Horkan, G. A.
Galata.
Thorne, W. W.
Great Falls.
Adams, F. J.
Crowley, R. E.
La Bossiere, E. A.
Helena.
Donnelly, J. P.
Lantz, Ira
Power, C. B.
Power, J. M.
Kalispell.
Mackall, B. McV.
Swanberg, A. V.
Miles City.
Allee, J. G.
Roundup.
O'Neil, D. J.
St. Ignatius.
Lusk, A. K.

NEBRASKA.

Alliance.
Walters, H. F.
Ashland.
Wiggenhorn, E. C.
Manley.
Higgins, W. L. D.
Omaha.
Bennewitz, J. A.
Brogan, F. A.
Burnam, H. E.
Butler, Henry
Coad, W. J.
Erskine, H. L.
Fallon, J. P.
Gurnett, J. M.
Hamilton, C. W.
Herring, C. E.
Jamieson, Thomas
Loos, J. G.
Lynch, Thomas
Merrow, D. W.
Pierce, A. S.
Spethman, E. F.
Plattsmouth.
Gering, Matthew
Shelton.
Lucas, Charles

NEVADA.

Carson City.
Norcross, F. H.
Elko.
Carroll, V. L.

NEVADA.

Goldfield.
Dunn, F. T.
Seitz, C. J.
Reno.
Bartlett, G. A.
Burton, C. F.
Woodburn, Wm., Jr.
Tonopah.
Corcoran, R. P.

NORTH CAROLINA.

Albemarle.
Bivins, J. D.
Chapel Hill.
Bocock, J. B.
Charlotte.
Sprinkle, T. H.
Martin, J. H.
Fayetteville.
Breece, A. B.
Fort Caswell.
Springer, R. W.
Greensboro.
Douglas, R. D.
Douglas, R. M.
Greenville.
Flanagan, R. C.
Hamptonville.
Reavis, Wade
Hickory.
Yount, M. H.
Jarvisburg.
Newbern, J. M.
Leaksville.
Osborne, H. G.
Lexington.
Sink, H. O.
Newberne.
McCarthy, W. T.
Newton.
Sigmon, J. C.
Salisbury.
Horah, J. H.
Warrentown.
Green, B. G.
Washington.
Grimes, J. D.
Weldon.
Green, G. C.
Winston-Salem.
Manley, Clement
Pell, G. P.

NEW HAMPSHIRE.

Dover.
O'Doherty, J. D.
Enfield.
Finning, T. J.
Greenville.
Doonan, G. W.

NEW HAMPSHIRE.

Littleton.
Donovan, J M.
Manchester.
Forscuth, C. S.
McDonald, R. F.
Nashua.
Mulvanity, A F.
New Hampshire.
Moulton. C. L
Somersworth.
Conley, M J.

*Norcross, G. J.
*Snow, W. S.
*Sullivan. J K.
*Wilder, A. M.

NEW JERSEY.

Atlantic City.
Flett, J. H.
Bayonne.
Cogan, W. J.
Belford.
Budlong, Orsemus
Bordentown.
Mahan, C J.
Camden.
Gallagher, T. D. J.
Elizabeth.
Halpin, J. A.
Lamason, O. B
Schleimer, David
Englewood.
Murphy, Richard
Fanwood.
Brick, G. J.
Hackensack.
Jackson, J. J.
Jersey City.
Carnes, E I
Collins. L M
Crowley. L. F.
Gagien, T. R.
Gottbrath, N. J.
Hampton, G R
McDermott, T. J.
Meyer, A. J
O'Regan, John
Long Branch.
McCue, T. E.
Merchantville.
Cunningham, F. A.
Morristown.
Owen, F. W.
Newark.
Kerns, F. J.
Korn, L L.
Passaic.
Schott, G. J VanV.
Patterson.
Connors, G R.
Philipsberg.
Hart, H L.

NEW JERSEY.

Plainfield.
Linke, F. O.
Lowrie, H. H.
Rafferty, W. V.
Princeton.
O'Connor, J. T.
Roselle.
Pierson, H. C.
Somerville.
McConnell, F. S.
Trenton.
Cody, J. K. L.
Wayman, E H.
West Hoboken.
McCauley, F. H
Williamstown.
McClure, James

*Conover, J. C.
*Whilley, W. H

NEW MEXICO.

Albuquerque.
Burg, J B
Dykes, J W.
Kauffman, H B.
McGowan, D. F.
Moran, J J.
Neis, C. J.
Fort Sumner.
Edwards, K. W.
Mesilla.
Reynolds, W C.
Roswell.
Gibson, T. W.
Santa Fe.
Harroun, W S.
McCullough, H E
Solignac, G L

*Collier, C. N
*Hubbell, S T.

NEW YORK.

Albany.
Crummey, E J.
Grapt, J H
Hawley, C. S.
Lyon, J F
McEnriy, W. P.
Power, J. H.
Stuart, J M.
Stuart, T. A
Tracy, J F.
Ward, S B.
Albion.
Thompson, F M
Amsterdam.
Murnigham, R J.
Angelica.
Kanaley, F. T
Antwerp.
Maloney, R. L.

NEW YORK.

Ballston.
Sweetman, J T.
Binghamton.
O'Neil, A. M.
Brockport.
Dailey, Vincent
Brooklyn.
Armstrong, S. E
Brent, George
Byrne, E L.
Byrne, W. L.
Carlin, J. F.
Carr, E Q
Clary, T. J.
Drew, H. C.
Elliott, J B.
Fitzgerald, T. J.
Hine, O C.
Houghton, P. F.
Jullien, C S.
Lehman, Hugo
McCoy, E. A.
McGirr, J. B.
Murray, D. B
Perskin, Israel
Prendergast, J. M.
Potts, L J.
Short, F. J
Taylor, J. A.
Walsh, J. H.
Walsh, Thomas
Weinberger, Louis
Weed, C. A
Welsh, J. J.
Buffalo.
Carroll, S W.
Clayson, H.
Eagan, S. B.
Fitts, H. F.
Ginther; C. F
Healy, C. L.
Miller, E. L.
Schaus, J. P
Simon, Gerhard
Smith, H T
Spratt, M. C
Taylor, J. W.
Burke.
Patterson, George
Cambridge.
Harris, E. F.
Corona.
Klein, A. E.
Courtland.
Farrell, F. C.
Dundee.
Malony, J. M
Ellenville.
Cox, F. B.
Elmira.
Byrne, W C.
Cain, W. S.
Connelly, D J
Deneen. John
O'Connor, C. B.
Wickham, E B.
Fort Wood.
Adair, G. F

NEW YORK.

Fulton.
Pendergast, R. J.
Hempstead.
O'Hara, W. L.
'Vlymen, H. T.
Highland Falls.
O'Neill, W. M.
Hornell.
Maguire, C. F., Jr.
Hudson.
McDonald, M. Q.
Macdonald, M Q.
Independence.
Crandall, S. B.
Jamaica.
Curry, F. L.
Linnehan, G. A.
McLoughlin, Edward
Jamestown.
Rask, H. G.
Robbins, A. J.
Kingston.
Flynn, D J.
Lima.
Guinan, J P
Keating, J. J.
Long Island City.
Brown, L J.
Kelly, J. B.
Madison Barracks.
Rutherford, R G., Jr
Mechanicsville.
Flanagan, J L
Monticello.
Purcell, R. E.
Mt. Vernon.
Seitz, J. W.
New Rochelle.
Mohun, P. V.
Palen, C. de S
New York City.
Agar, J. G.
Aimone, V. A.
Albertson, W. F.
Allen, William
Anguelo, Charles
Arnold, T. J.
Ashley, W F.
Austin, W. F.
Backes, E. H.
Barrett, J. M
Barrie, George
Bell, Henry
Best, J V.
Blake, T. C.
Brady, J S
Brown, H. H
Brownell. H B.
Byrne, W. M.
Carlin, F. A.
Carlin, F. T.
Carlin, H. V.
Cashman, J. S.
Cavanaugh. R. B.
Christiancy, G A. C.
Clapp, H. M.
Clark. J. F.

NEW YORK.

New York, *Cont'd.*
Clarke, W. S.
Cockran, W. B.
Cohen, Nathan
Cole, P. L.
Collier, R. J.
Collins, J. F.
Comerford, P. P.
Conboy, Martin
Corbin, E. L.
Cortelyou, G. B.
Cruse, G E
Dammann, Milton
Darby, S E
Dawley, W. J.
Des Garennes, J. F. P.
Des Garennes, J. P.
Dessez, T H.
Devereux, F. L.
Devine, John
Diamond, W. C.
Dilkes, J. A.
Loud, D. P.
Doyle, J H.
Drown, J H.
Duross, C. E.
Duross, J E.
Dyer, D. M.
Dyer, R. N.
Earle, H. M.
Easton, E. D.
Edmonds, D. S.
Edmonston, P P.
Ewing, J K M.
Ewing, Thomas, Jr.
Fink, E. X.
Fitzgerald, J. S.
Fox, W. T.
Fox, W. T.
Freeman, J. E.
Freeman, J. H.
French, L. E.
Frey, J. L.
Gavan, J. W.
Geoghan, W. F. X.
Govern, C. J
Govern, Hugh, Jr.
Griffin, J H.
Groden, P. F.
Haggerty, L. C.
Hale, William
Hamersley, L. R.
Hanigan, H A.
Harris. C. N.
Hays, M. A.
Hefferman, J. F.
Hicks. F C.
Holt, G. A.
Horsey, O, Jr.
Hoyt, A. G.
Huff, T. S
Illman, Harold
Jennings, E J.
Kernan, N E
Kernan. W. N
Keyes, E. L., Jr
Killeen. Thomas
Kinkston, A. T. Y.
Kirby, J. J.
Knight, H. E.
Knight, W. E.
Lannon. J. D.
Larcombe, J. A.
Lauve, L L
Lecouteulx, Louis

NEW YORK.

New York, *Cont'd.*
Lordan, J. J.
Lynch, A. V.
Lynch, J D.
McAnerney, F. B.
McCloskey, F. R.
McCole, T. A.
McCullough, C. E.
McDonough, F.. X.
McDonough, J. S.
McElhone, J. F.
McGill, G. L.
McGrath, J B.
McKenna, B. C.
McLaughlin, H. E.
McNamara, S.
McNeir, George
McQuirk, John
MacElhinney, J. A.
Mackaye, H. S.
MacMahon, P. W. A.
MacMahon, Thos, Jr.
Macnulty, A. C.
Madeira, F P.
Major, Henry
Malabre, A L.
Malone, E. H.
Maloney, W. R. P.
Morgan, D. O.
Mullaly, G. LeG.
Mullan, F. D.
Murchison, K. S.
Murphy, J. A.
Murphy, W. J.
Murray, G. F.
Murray, T. J
Nast, C M.
Nichols, H. J.
Nolan, J M
Noonan, L. T.
Oblinger, E. V.
O'Brien, E. C.
O'Brien, E D.
O'Brien, J. F.
O'Brien, J. P
O'Brien, John
O'Brien, M. M., Jr.
O'Day, C. F.
Ogden, H. G.
O'Gorman, J. A.
O'Gorman, M. J.
O'Leary, J. G.
Oxnard, G C.
Pallen, C B.
Payn, A. S.
Peck, C W.
Pitts, W. S
Pool, S C.
Porter, H C
Quinn, John
Rague, C W. S.
Raney, R J.
Rice, W. R.
Ring, John
Rogers, Hamilton
Roosa, F. M.
Rorke, A. I.
Rosell, C A.
Sands, W. F.
Sefton, Edwin
Seger, W. T.
Shipman, A. J.
Short, W. H
Sims Charles
Skerrett, R G.

NEW YORK.

New York, Cont'd.
Smith, F. E.
Spiller, James
Stewart, F. J.
Stuart, D. D. V.
Thomas, A. A.
Thorn, C. E.
Tierney, M. J.
Toohey, Frank
Tracy, F. M.
Trenholm, Frank
Trenholm, W. de S.
Valentine, C. F.
Van Casteel. Gerald
Van Duzer, Clarence
Wagner, W. H.
Walker, J. B.
Walker, J. B. F.
Walker, J. S.
Walker, W. H.
Walsh, H. C.
Walsh, J. J.
Washburn, A. H.
Wheatley, J. W,
Wheeleck, G. L.
White, L. C.
Williams. C. F.
Woods, Joseph
Woodward, R. D.
Wright, Arthur
Yeatman, C. R.

Newburgh.
Hanretty, L M., Jr.

Nyack.
Thompkins, R S.
Woertendyke, H. P

Olean.
Hunt, B L.

Palatine Bridge.
Flume, A. G.

Plattsburg.
Clark, J. A.
Looby, P. W.

Poughkeepsie.
Wheaton, I. S.

Rochester.
Davis, R. H.
Donoghue, J K.
Duffy. J P. B.
Gorham, N. B.
Reilly, J. V.
Rich, J. S.

Rye.
O'Day, D. E.

Sag Harbor.
Kiernan, C. A.

Sandy Hill.
Howe, T. G

Schenectady.
Powell, F. H.

Syracuse.
Cahill, W. A.
McClusky, W. J.
Roche, P. A.

Troy.
Fitzgerald, Edmd. ,Jr.
Fitzgerald, W. E.
Murphy, Edward 2d
Murphy, J. J.
Webster, C. S.

NEW YORK.

Utica.
Brennan, L W.
Buckley, J. T.
Kernan, T. P.
Kernan, W. J.
Lynch, James

Wampsville.
Parkhurst, L. A.

Watertown.
Major, J. A.

West Brooklyn.
McCann, D. F., Jr.

Yonkers.
Flynn, C. B.
O'Brien, D. F.
Walsh, W. A.

*Bower, S. W.
*Dartt, J. F.
*Munger, M. J.
*Smith, E. R.
*Stephens, J. J.
*Stone, A. G.
*Stone, W. C
*Thompson, G. S.
*Turner, H. V.
*West, B. H.
*Wheaton, Henry

NORTH DAKOTA.

Dickinson.
Cain, J P.

Grafton.
Dougherty, J. F.

McHenry County.
Clements, E. E.

Minot.
McCannel, A. J.

OHIO.

Akron.
Duffy, Joseph

Ashtabula.
Alicoate, J. W.

Batavia.
Wasner, W. H.

Bellaire.
Hunt, L. J.
O'Leary, W. J.

Cadiz.
Wassen, R. B.

Camden.
Murray, P. E.

Canton.
Johat, A. L. F.
Lynch, J. K.
O'Hara, J. F.

Celina.
Howick, Thomas

Cincinnati.
Lincoln, J. L.
Mitchell, R. C.
Mulvihill, J. A.
Owen, J. W.

OHIO.

Chillicothe.
Poland, J. A.
Poland, N. A.
Dickinson, D., Jr.
Faulkner, J. B.
Slough, Martin
Storer, Bellamy,

Cleaves.
Hayes, S. H.

Cleveland.
Calkins, T. J.
Davis, Edward
Drum, J. C.
Fitzgerald, J. F. L.
Flick, C. P.
Gentsch, Charles
Hudson, A. J.
Ironside, C. N.
Leahy, M. D.
Pritchard, H. D.
Strong, Shepard
Westenhaver, D. C.
Wing, G. C.

Columbus.
Corbett, E. P.
Fisher, H. C.
O'Connell, R. F.
Price, J. G.
Quigley, Frank

Corning.
Miller, James

Dayton.
Baker, R. T.
Brenner, C. F.
Ferneding, T. A.
Finke, A. J.
Focke, B. M.
Hughes, A. L.
McDonald, A. C.

Dundee.
Benfer, J. P.

Eau Claire.
Etty, R. A.

Galion.
Schuler, H. R.

Hamilton.
Pater, A. J.
Reed, C. C.
Snider, M. F.

Kenton.
Crow, P. M.
Digan, J. C.

Lancaster.
Beck, H. K.

Lorain.
Kolbe, L. A.

Middleport.
Bryan, P. S.

Mowrystown.
Galliett, H. H.

Napoleon.
Donovan, D D.

Newark.
Kennedy, W. J.

New Philadelphia.
Gentsch, D. C.

OHIO.

St. Paris.
Nixon, C. R.
Sebring.
Jones, R. J.
Shawnee.
Benson, C. J.
Springfield.
Malone, J. B.
Seward, W. B.
Stockport.
McDermott, F. B.
Toledo.
Carr, J. McA.
Dollaway, L. M.
Effler, E. R.
Hall, A. A.
Sullivan, J. D.
Upper Sandusky.
Hare, W. C.
Van Wert.
Hines, J. A.
Wapakoneta.
Nichols, E. L.
West Elkton.
Dougherty, D. N.
Wilmington.
Denver, M. R.
Woodville.
Emch, G. H.
Youngstown.
Connor, W. P.
Rudge, W. H.
Willo, J. A.

---

*Ashfield, J. M.
*Binckley, J. M.
*Cleverdon, J. S.
*Edwards, R. H.
*Green, J. H.
*Hill, G. W.
*Howell, B. R.
*Jones, W. E.
*Karch, C. M.
*Kennedy, James
*Murphy, T. J.
*O'Neill, J. H.
*Rieckelmann, John
*Smith, Lucius
*Swayne, N. H., Jr.
*Tibbals, W. T.

OKLAHOMA.

Anadasko.
Blackmon, H. C.
Coweta.
Cook, J. C.
Guthrie.
Bierer, A. G. C.
Hopeton.
Linney, R. Z.
Muskogee.
Block, T. L.
Dial, J. A.

OKLAHOMA.

Miami.
Durant, H. B.
Martin, Villard
Powell, J. L.
Vance, H. M.
Wait, C. B.
Wait, S. S.
White, C. H.
White, W. N.
Oklahoma City.
Bolen, H. L.
Bragg, C. G.
Keaton, J. R.
Kuhn, J. F.
Lee, A. J.
Loeffler, Louis
Montgomery, Denny
Paddock, L. M.
Tibbitts, O. O.
Weiss, T. F.
Otoe.
Stanion, R. P.
Shawnee.
Maxey, J. H.
Stelzner, R. H.
Spencer.
Taylor, C. B.
Stillwater.
Crocker, J. H.
Stillwell.
Woodruff, W. A.
Tahlequah.
Paschal, George
Tulsa.
Bryant, F. W.
Hyams, W. W.
Wrightman, C. J.
Wagoner.
Gallagher, L. J.
Gallaher, E. McH.
Kirby, E. L.
Wilburton.
Haycock, I. C.

OREGON.

Bay City.
Geneste, E. A.
Keamath Falls.
Carnahan, J. H.
North Yamhill.
Burton, Linnoir
Portland.
Beckman, J. J.
Carter, C. T.
Irvin, John
Johnson, E. A.
Kinsell, Tyson
Lusk, H. S.
Maguire, R. F.
Moon, J. B.
Moulton. C. E.
O'Rourke, L. W.
Pargon, A. J.
Rondeau, F. P.
Smith, W. H.
Staley, W. F.
Story, L. E.

OREGON.

Salem.
Krebs, Conrad
Zinkhan, P. H.

PENNSYLVANIA.

Altoona.
Bangert, R. F.
Bloomsbury.
Bittenbender, J. A.
Braddock.
O'Halloran, T. M.
Canton.
Burk, J. W.
Carbondale.
Boland, J. E.
Murrin, J. S.
Carlisle.
Wiener, David
Chambersburg.
Maclay, J. P.
Scheller, T. K.
Chicora.
Litzinger, L. P.
Clearfield.
Brockbank, S. T.
O'Laughlin, J. P.
Connelsville.
Duggan, John, Jr.
Covington.
Waters, D. C.
Devon.
Gallagher, J. A.
Donally Mills.
Fosselman, J. J.
Easton.
Timmins, T. J.
Ebensburg.
Sharbaugh, F. C.
Erie.
Barrett, G. T.
Cornell, M. C.
Cranch, Edward
English, C. H.
Fitzmaurice, J. E.
Milloy, A. M.
Neff, A. R.
Eschol.
Baker, J. G.
Everson.
Byrne, A. L.
Germantown.
Berry, A. E.
Greensburg.
Head, M. W.
Head, P. J.
Harrisburg.
Clark, J. N.
Heckschersville.
O'Donnell, E. P.
Hummelston.
Nye, L. F.

PENNSYLVANIA.

Jeanette.
Reidt, U H.
Jessup.
Reddington, C. T.
Johnstown.
Martin, J. J.
Martin, F. P., Jr
Oil City.
Geary, D. J.
Lancaster.
Eckenrode, J. W , Jr.
Ergood, C. E.
Garvey, T Q.
Regar, R. S.
Lebanon.
Wolfe,W. L.
Lockhaven.
Gross, F. C.
Miners Mills.
Mayock, P. P.
Minnooka.
Kane, F. A., Jr.
Kane, J. F.
Nanticoke.
Corgan, C. E
Shea, C A
New Castle.
Smith, J. S. W.
Oil City.
Joynt, M E.
Quinn, F. A.
Old Forge.
Marcy, W. L.
Philadelphia.
Arnold, J D.
Baby, R F.
Bolan, H. A.
Byrne, F. J
Chambers, J. P.
Cooney, J. J.
Curran, J. D. J.
Daily, L. J.
Devereux, A. J. A.
Devereux, Ashton
Dilkes, C. E.
Dohan, J M.
Dougherty, P. J.
Dunn, J. T. F.
Francis, C. De La R.
Gallen, W. J.
Halstead, Thomas
Harley, R. J.
Heintzelman, J A.,Jr.
Hirst, A. A.
Kean, T. J.
Keating, J. P.
Kelly, H I.
Koebel, W. J.
Laplace, Ernest
Levy, Michael
McAleer, J. H
McAleer, William, J:.
McAleer, J L
McGrath, W. V., Jr
Mitchell, H. F.
Monaghan, H. L
O'Donnell, W. A.
O'Leary, C R.

PENNSYLVANIA.

Philadelphia, Cont'd.
O'Malley, Austin
O'Malley, Joseph
Ristine, J. C.
Russell, G. M.
Schladt, H. A.
Spellisy, J. M
Stritmatter, T P.
Tete, L. F.
Tillman, L M.
Twibill, A H.
Wade, E. J
Wales, O G
Ward, F. X
Welch, B T.
Wilcox, J M.
Phoenixville.
Armstrong, J. D.
Pittsburgh.
Bernstein, Hyman
Brand, C. M.
Broe, W. B
Collins, J. H.
Day, E W.
Duffy, C. A.
Evert, H C.
Foy, F. M
Gulentz, Charles
Haag, J D
Hayes, S Q.
Kane, C J.
Lamb, W. J. C
Laughlin, J. E.
McLaughlin, J. W.
McMeal. B C.
Mann, G M
Mohn, E J.
Moran, J L.
Moran, T J
Munhall, H N
Pritchard, H T.
Schoyer, G. S
Smith, F. T.
Talmadge, Theodore
Thomas, J. T
Vilsack, C. G
Wilson, T. B
Pittston.
Fitzpatrick, J. P.
Pottsville.
Gallagher, A. J.
Haag, H. O.
Whitehouse, J. S.
Scranton.
Bell, J.F.
Fitzpatrick, W. J.
Gerrity, H. J.
Gillespie, J B
Golden, P E.
Jones, J R
Kilcullen, P. E.
Martin, J T
Philbin, E. T
Walsh, M. J.
Webb, D A.
Zychowicz, J. F.
Shamokin.
Koch, Joseph
Timmes, J. W.
Sharon.
Boyle, T. M.

PENNSYLVANIA.

Shenandoah.
Ferguson. D J.
Monaghan, J P.
South Bethlehem.
Coyle, D. J.
Swarthmore.
Osterman, A. H.
Tamaqua.
Kelly. J J.
Towanda.
Griffin, J C
Tullytown.
Erwin, Frank, Jr.
Warren.
Stone, R W.
Washington.
Cashman, T F.
Darrah, J R.
Srowls A. D
West Philadelphia.
Cook, R. M
Whitehaven.
Marstellar, A. C.
Wilkesbarre.
Mayock, T J.
Morris. J. L
Mulligan, James
Warfield, R. S.
Wilkinsburg.
Wymard, N. L
Williamsport.
Reynolds, W. B.
Shaw, C. E

———

*Brown, J. C.
*Daily, B. E
*Healy, J M
*Jones, Edward
*Lynch, P. H
*Mueller, J. M.
*Rodrique, A.
*Shomo, H. L.

RHODE ISLAND.

Berkely.
Devlin, H. M
Bristol.
Leahy, E. L.
Cranston.
Barry, W. F.
Manion.
Dooley, J. E
Newport.
Burke, J C
Moriarty, D J.
Pardee, E. W.
Sullivan. J, A.
Pawtucket.
Barry, W. E.
Costello, M. F.
Daniels, J. W.
Fitzgerald, J J.
Higgins, J H
McMahon, R. J
Nolan, L F.
Perrier, C. E

RHODE ISLAND.

Providence.
Brennan, J. P.
Bromson, Solomon
Casey, S. J.
Connolly, J. E.
Croghan, F. E.
Cullen, T. F.
Curran, J. L.
Downing, A. H.
Fanning, W M.
Feeley, W G.
Flynn, J. A
Flynn, W. S
Gorman, C. E.
Hussey, J. P.
Joslin, P E.
McCanna, G F
McDonnell. T. F
McDonough, F P.
McElroy, B. W
McGowan, L A
Mulhearni, C. E
Mulhearn, F R.
Mulvey, W. A
Murphy, L T.
Murphy. M. J.
Nee, F J
O'Donnell. David
O'Neill, J H
Rattigan, M. A.
Smithers, J. T.

Warren.
Conway, J J.
O'Brien, M. J.

West Barrington.
Stanton, W. J.

SOUTH CAROLINA.

Anderson.
Pearman, S D.

Bishopville.
Tatum, T. H.

Charleston.
Cogswell, J E
Farrow, Patillo
Northrop, George
Stuart, B R.

Columbia.
Legare, G. S.
Blease. C L.
Lipscomb, M. B.

Darlington.
Parrott, P B.

Edgefield.
Scott, O H. P.

Greenville.
Watson, R F.

Lowndesville.
Latimer, E. F.

Newbury.
Blease. H. H

Orangeburg.
Brantley, A A.
Brantley, T F.
Ziegler, E. M.

Ridgeway.
Thomas, C. T.

SOUTH CAROLINA.

Spartanburg.
Gantt, R J.

Troy.
Latham, S B

Union.
Butler, A. J.

Varnville.
Peeples, A McB

---

*Choice, William
*Cleveland, J F.

SOUTH DAKOTA.

Waterboro.
Black, R R

Aberdeen.
Crane, G. W.

Canton.
Hummer. H. R.

Deadwood.
Wingard, E. V.

Forest City.
Hassler, A. M.

Hoover.
Yoder, F W

Lemmon.
McCall, R. S

Pierre.
Blount, J. W.

Pine Ridge.
Ross, R H.

Sturgis.
Brooks, J. D

Rapid City.
Denue, A. R

Sioux Falls.
Freeman, A. M.
Westfall, H M

White River.
Manson, C. F.

Yankton.
Roane, James

TENNESSEE.

Cedar Hill.
Washington, J. E

Chattanooga.
Wolfe, H L, Jr.
Moross, W. P. D

Columbia.
Whittharne, W. C

Cookeville.
Morgan, D. H.

Dayton.
Gannaway, T. D

Grand Junction.
Smyth, J. J.

Greensville.
Neas, W. H.

Johnson City.
Crouch, R. W.

TENNESSEE.

Knoxville.
Von Rosen, F. G.
Pless, W A
Luttrell, W. McM.

Lebanon.
Adams, A A.

Lewisburg.
Bullock, E. C.

Memphis.
Barton, McK., Jr.
Dillard, J E
Sullivan, W. L.

Morristown.
Halley, J. H.

Mulberry.
Boone, N. F.

Nashville.
Alford, J. R.
Copeman, W H
Holmes, W. C
Jennings, D E.
Rhodes, Eugene
Ryan, J A
Settle, T. G.
Smith, E. J
Smith, T. W.
Zepf, L R

Pulaski.
Ballentine, J. G

Rutledge.
Booth, J F.

Vale.
Bilbrey, J H

*Brown, Orlando
*Hall, J H
*Marshall, George
*Roberston, S A.

TEXAS.

Austin.
Logan, A. T
Orleman, L H, Jr
Pye, J B
Von Rosenberg, F C.

Beaumont.
Cooper. S. B
Pelton, C R

Cleburne.
O'Dell, W. M.

Dallas.
Hughes, Ellis
Randle. E T.
Scay, H L
Shepard. Seth, Jr.

Del Rio.
Foster, J. J

Fort Sam Houston.
Mortimer, C G

Fort Worth.
Marple, R. W.

Galveston.
Lobit, Joseph, Jr.
Wilson, D. J.

Greenville.
Kennedy, C. T.

TEXAS.

Hidalgo.
Chalmers, Nills
Houston.
Bruhl, C. E.
Bute, J. H.
Colgin, E. B.
Hamilton, E. J.
Millard, W. J.
Nelson, C. W.
Knox City.
Culver, I. J.
Marlin.
Bounds, E. W.
Rockwell.
Jones, Thomas
San Antonio.
Barnes, R. L.
Barnitz, H. D.
Campbell, D. G.
San Benito.
McDonald, J. E.
Smithville.
Hickman, G. W. V.
Temple.
Sullivan, J. H.
Weatherford.
Spangler, W. A.

*Neale, Francis
*Paschal, George

UTAH.

Centerville.
Whitaker, W. E.
Ephraim.
Rasmussen, Clyde
Ogden.
Gery, Joseph
Salt Lake City.
Beck, J. A.
Cheney, A. W.
Flood, T. A.
Ford, W. F.
Gibson, T. C.
Hilton. W. A.
Light, G. A.
Morgan, N. G.
Whelan. J. A.

Sunnyside.
McDermid, C. E

VERMONT.

Lowell.
Sheehan, D. J.
Newport.
Farrell, C. H.
Rutland.
Harman, W. P.
Waterville.
Hodgins, C. L.
Wells River.
Bailey, F. J.

*Harvey, W. F.

VIRGINIA.

Arcola.
Hutchinson, C. P.
Alexandria.
Ashton, J. T.
Beach, S. E.
Crump, C. E.
Delaney, M. D.
Fickling, T. H.
Fisher, S. P.
Gorman, E. A.
Mackey, Crandall
Moore, S. B.
Normoyle, J. D.
Pettey, R. M.
Ramage, J. C.
Simpson, F. C.
Wirt, R. W., Jr.

Arlington.
Johnston. R. W.
Wills, J. W.
Ballston.
Douglass, W. W.
Burke.
Watt, Alexander
Calvin Run.
Brown, F I.
Carysbrook.
Snider, C. V.
Casanova.
Cowhig, J. J.
Charlottesville.
Dunn, W. G.
Cheriton.
Henning, R. M.
Clarendon.
Collins, W. G.
Finney, R. G.
Gardner. R. B.
Sutton, R. N.
Clifton.
Sanford, J. L.
Clifton Forge.
Payne, W. G.
Covington.
Hooper, L. M.
Culpepper.
Fennell, R. B.
Royston, J. P.
Stearns, C. P.
East Falls Church.
Albrecht, J. A.
Fellows, H. A.
Fairfax.
Farr, R. R.
Farr, W. M.
Richardson, F. B.
Ritchie, A. C.
Fairfax Ct. House.
McCandlish, F. S.
Fairfax Station.
Swetman, F. H.

VIRGINIA.

Falls Church.
Birge, H. C.
Hodgson, R. M.
Howard, J. T. D.
Fifes.
Ford, Horace
Fort Myer.
Wibirt, W. C.
Front Royal.
Moore, E. F.
Glencarlyn.
Seaton, C. H.
Harrisonburg.
Morrison, J. W.
Herndon.
Hutchinson, E. B.
King George.
Clarke, D. E.
Lewinsville.
Money, J. T.
Lincoln.
Hughes, H. C.
Lorton.
Holt, R. O.
Louisa County.
Morris, J. P.
Luray.
Miller, C. A.
Lynchburg.
Marshall, Hunter, Jr.
McGaheysville.
Yancey, C. L.
Manassas.
Brand, E. A.
Meredith, E. C., Jr.
Ruffner, C. E.
Markham.
Carter, G. W., Jr.
Marshall, C. A.
Norfolk.
Barry, C. M.
Doran, C. M. C.
Johnston, Robert
Macnair, A. W.
Scott, E. B.
Smith, A. J.
Smith, E. R.
Smith, E. V.
Vandeventer, Braden
Wertenbacker, C. I.
Williams, A. R.
Occoquan.
Starkweather, C. L.
Petersburg.
Harrison, F. R.
Portsmouth.
Ballard, T. V.
Prospect Hill.
Barbee, R, A.
Quicksbury.
Henkel, S. D.
Rediviva.
Browning, G. L.

VIRGINIA.

Richmond.
Brady, J. P.
Davison, F. D.
Dooley, J. H.
Garnett, L. C.
Sitterding, W. H.
Taylor, C. B.
Waggaman, S. J., Jr.
Watsky, Jacob
Roanes.
Seawell, C. W.
Saluda.
McCandlish, H. S.
Snow Creek.
Davis, B. A.
Sterling.
Shreve, Benjamin
Swetnam.
Swetnam, C. R. K.
Tanners Creek.
Powell, W. A.
The Plains.
Owens, Winter,
Timberville.
Lohr, V. J.
Warrenton.
Semmes, F. J.

*Archer, J W.
*Butcher, C. T.
*Graham, J. W.
*Harrison, J. C.
*McGary, P. J.
*Montgomery, G. C.
*Osburn, Alexander
*Rudd, J. S.
*Woodley, T. A.

WASHINGTON.

Colville.
Wentz, H. T.
Fort Flagler.
Smart, W. M.
Manette.
Anderson, J. W.
North Yakima.
Mullins, G. H.
Proesser.
Green, A. de Y.
St. John.
McIntyre, Douglas
Seattle.
Allain, L. B.
Blewett, R. L.
Brown, W. S.
Carter, E. V.
Cauthorne, R. G.
Donworth, George
Ennis, C. H.
Field, E. R.
Flueck, E. H.
Hall, R. C.
Hardin, T. B., Jr.
Heaton, H. J.
Hood, Edward
Hopkins, W. A.

WASHINGTON.

Seattle, *Continued.*
Ittig, Henry
Murphy, J. A.
Murphy, J. T.
Reagan, F. C.
Underwood, F. R.
Todd, H. C.
Watson, J. T.
Wayland, C. L.
Wheeler, L. H.
Spokane.
Dillard, J. P.
Elston, A. G.
McChesney, C. E.
Morton, J. F.
Neely, J. R.
Robertson, F. C.
Schade, Frederick
Takoma.
Garnett, R. S.
McMullen, F. P.
Whitney, J. W.
Vancouver.
Tempes, F. W.

*Powell; B. F.

WEST VIRGINIA.

Aurora.
Latham, B. F.
Benwood.
McGarrell, A. P.
Charleston.
Horan, J. S.
Clarksburg.
Goff, Nathan
Morgan, Haze
Earnshaw.
Earnshaw, F. L.
Elkins.
King, M. H.
Rabbett, J. A.
Fairmont.
Abbaticchio, R. J.
Fayetteville.
Osenton, C. W.
Grafton.
Jennings, J. K.
Horton.
Crittenden, T. B.
Huntington.
Davis, H. N.
Holt, J. H.
Sharitz, B. C.
Stephens, F. W.
Via, L. R.
Workman, A. C.
Martinsburg.
Karicofe, W. H. A.
Parkersburg.
Durkin, M. J.
Gaynor, H. E.
Kenney, A. E.

WEST VIRGINIA.

Philippi.
Casteel, F. A.
Gall, J. C.
Point Pleasant.
Whitten, J. L.
St. Mary's.
Barron, C. L.
Wheeling.
Coniff, J. J.
Cummins, J. W.
O'Leary, J. J.
Reilly, C. J.
Russell, H. M.

*Hullihen, M. S.
*Koonce, C. J.

WISCONSIN.

Baraboo.
McNaught, Arch
Black River Falls.
Cole, H. D.
Brillian.
Werner, G. P.
Cadott.
Watson, F. E., Jr.
Chippewa Falls.
Le Boeuf, P. G.
Darlington.
Osborn, H. S.
Eau Claire.
Singleton, J. W.
Fond du Lac.
Crosley, J. F.
Downs, T. C.
Fort Ward.
Hood, J. H. P.
Janesville.
Cammerer, A. B.
Vlymen, W. J.
Kenosha.
Shearer, N. L.
La Crosse.
Bosshard, Otto
Campbell, L. J.
Lancaster.
Calvert, C. W.
Lodi.
Simons, H. N.
Madison.
Brabant, L. J.
Drew, Walter
Frederick, A. E.
Jamison, Alexander
Milwaukee.
Bach, E. J.
Boden, F. X.
Carpenter, M. H.
Devine, H. J.
Dutcher, G. C.
Eline, F. M.
Fitzsimmons, J. I.
Hennessy, J. F.

WISCONSIN.

Milwaukee, *Cont'd.*
Hennessy, V. B.
Johnston, J. A
Kane, H V
Kopmeier, N. J.
Nemmers, E. P.
Reilly, H. F.,
Rix, C B.
Romadka, F. J
Shenners, M J
Somers, P J.
Tighe, Alvin
Tobin, J H.

New London.
Jennings, R. S.

New Richmond.
Dear, W T

Racine.
Hubacek, F R.
Miller, W. W.
Naylor, L W.

St. Lawrence.
LaBoule, J. F.

Superior.
Bruder. A J.

Warsaw.
Brawley, W. C

Waupun.
Johnston, J. M.

Winter.
Pilon, J A

*Cashell, Jóseph
*Eldridge, W. A.

WYOMING.

Casper.
Shipp, E R

Cheyenne.
Coughlin, J. V.
Lane, C. E.

Lander.
Dillon, John

HAWAII.

Honolulu.
Breckons, R W.
Durney, C. P.
Long, C. A.
Long, E. A. C.
Mills, Ellis

Mt. View.
Cannario, L V

*Schellberg, L E

PHILIPPINES.

Bagino.
Faris, Asterio

Balanga.
Tuason. Pedro

Cebu.
Cuenco, J M

PHILIPPINES.

Manilla.
Algue, Jose
Bastion, J.E.
Bourne, C P.
Branagan, F. A.
Campbell, Richard
Crossfield, A. S.
De Yeaza, Y M. I.
Falconer, B. L
Flores, Placido
Kemp, J. F.
Lacson, R J
Newberne, R. L. E.
Olesen, Robert
Ross, Tenney

Mindanao.
Baker, F. C.

Paco.
Reyes Rio

Santa Cruz.
Legaspi, Villaflor

Son Jose.
Jaranilla, Delfin

Tarlac.
Ramos, Joaquin

PORTO RICO.

Cayey.
Garcia, B F.

Coamo.
Rivera, R R

Humacao.
Herrero, Juan

San German.
Porrata, N R
Riverva, Pascual

San Juan.
Ashford, B K
Fernandez. Benigno
Nussa, R. L

Morovis.
Rivera-Pagan, P..M.

Ponce.
Fornaris, Ferdinand

CANADA.

ALBERTA.
Landry, J C.

BRIT. COLUMBIA.

Vancouver.
Dunton, J. F.

MANITOBA.

Winnipeg.
Gillen, C F.

NEW BRUNSWICK.

Moncton.
Cullinen, A A.

*Paby M. W
*Crozier, St. G B

NEWFOUNDLAND.
Macdonald, C. J.

NOVA SCOTIA.

Halifax.
Donohue, A. R.

Lourdes.
Macdonald, M. R.

Port Hawkesburg.
Macdonald, Howard

*Barton, F. R.

ONTARIO.

Hamilton.
Tureaud, Benjamin

QUEBEC.

Montreal.
Ashford, F. A.

Quebec.
Chauveau, C A.

St. Hyacinthe.
Dessaulles, Casimir

SASKATCHEWAN.

Regina.
Wadden, J. J

MEXICO.

Guadalajara.
Remus, R. E.

Mexico City.
McManus, Joseph

Morelos.
Davila, A O.

Yucatan.
Casares, E. E.

*Ryder, T. J.
*Escobar, J.

CENTRAL AMERICA.

NICARAGUA.
Brisbane, H. P.

PANAMA.

Canal Zone.
Blackburn, S. E.
Drennan, L. M
Jacobson, B L.
McCormick, J. J.
Markey, J. F.
Sinclair J. McD.
Stirewalt, J. P.

*Sanders, W. A.

SOUTH AMERICA.

ARGENTINA.

Buenos Ayres.
Elia, Ezechiel de

CHILI.

Punta Arenas.
Latham, C L

PERU.

Arequipa.
Nunez, M. I.

URUGUAY.

Zunigan, M. G. de

WEST INDIES.

CUBA.

Havana.
Jorrin, S. L
Landa, G. M.
Penichet, J. M.
Ross, J. R.
Santa Clara.
Del Pica, Sergio

*Dominguez, Virgil

JAMAICA.

Delany, F. X.

*Bowen, Thomas

AUSTRIA.

Reichenberg.
Burg, J. P.
Vienna.
Winter, F. E.

DENMARK.

Copenhagen.
Egan, G. M.
Egan, M. F.

ENGLAND.

Hull.
Haskell, Louis
London.
Thornton, R. H.

*Aplin, Alfred
*Ashmore, N. S. S.
*Davies. Gomer
*Duke, D. W.
*Cooper, Moses
*Gouldston, J. C.
*Mansell, E. R
*Roberts, William

FRANCE.

Dragicsevics, A O.

GERMANY.

Bergedorferstr.
Stebens, H. L.
Berlin.
Hayes, H. L .

*Mayer, R. D.

IRELAND.

*Malone. John
*Wall, Michael .

ITALY.

Nice.
Keyes, F. C.

POLAND.

Hernitz, Stanislaus

RUSSIA.

Wladimer.
Sebiakin-Ross, W.

SPAIN

*Lavalle, D. J A de

CHINA.

Hongkong.
Dessez, P T.
Hough, J. S.
Shanghai.
Curtis, G. F.
Ransom. S. A

JAPAN.

Nagasaki.
Nishio, Shohaku

PERSIA.

Teheran.
Russell, C. W.